EC LEGAL SYSTEMS
AN INTRODUCTORY GUIDE

MAURICE SHERIDAN
LL.M. (Cantab)
Barrister of the Middle Temple

JAMES CAMERON
LL.M. (Cantab)
Barrister of the Inner Temple

Consultant Editor
John Toulmin QC, M.A. (Cantab) LL.M. (Michigan)
Bencher of the Middle Temple
Vice President of the CCBE

Published with the assistance of members of the CCBE

Butterworths
London   Dublin   Edinburgh   Brussels

1992

United Kingdom	Butterworth & Co (Publishers) Ltd 88 Kingsway, LONDON WC2B 6AB 4 Hill Street, EDINBURGH EH2 3JZ
Australia	Butterworths, SYDNEY, MELBOURNE, BRISBANE, ADELAIDE, PERTH, CANBERRA and HOBART
Belgium	Butterworth & Co (Publishers) 48 Rue de Namur/Namurstraat 1000 BRUSSELS
Canada	Butterworths, TORONTO and VANCOUVER
Ireland	Butterworth (Ireland) Ltd, DUBLIN
Malaysia	Malayan Law Journal Sdn Bhd, KUALA LUMPER
New Zealand	Butterworths of New Zealand Ltd, WELLINGTON and AUCKLAND
Puerto Rico	Equity de Puerto Rico Inc, HATO REY
Singapore	Malayan Law Journal Pte Ltd, SINGAPORE
USA	Butterworths Legal Publishers, ST PAUL, Minnesota, SEATTLE, Washington, BOSTON, Massachusetts, ORFORD, New Hampshire, AUSTIN, Texas and D & S Publishers, CLEARWATER, Florida

---

Editors
Sandra Dutczak LL.B.
Helen Britton B.A.

Editorial Assistant
Maria D'Souza

© Butterworth & Co (Publishers) Ltd, 1992   P O 3736
ISBN 0 406 02738

Printed in Great Britain by Ashford Colour Press Ltd, Gosport, Hampshire

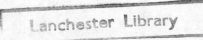

MAURICE SHERIDAN
LL.M. (Cantab)
Barrister of the Middle Temple

JAMES CAMERON
LL.M. (Cantab)
Barrister of the Inner Temple

Consultant Editor
John Toulmin QC, M.A. (Cantab) LL.M. (Michigan)
Bencher of the Middle Temple
Vice President of the CCBE

Belgium : De Bandt, van Hecke & Lagae
Denmark : Koch-Nielsen & Grønborg
England and Wales : Maurice Sheridan and James Cameron
France : Danet Copper-Royer Burg
Germany : Melchers Schubert Petersen Stocker Sturies
Greece : Bahas, Gramatidis & Associates
Ireland : Mary Finlay Geoghegan SC
Italy : Manca Amenta Biolato Corrao & C
Luxembourg : Schiltz et Delaporte
The Netherlands : De Brauw Blackstone Westbroek
Portugal : Coelho Ribeiro Associados
Scotland : Matthew G. Clarke QC
Spain : Bufete Mullerat & Roca

Published with the assistance of members of the CCBE

FOREWORD

The European Community's 1992 programme, due to be completed by 1st January 1993, is aimed at establishing within the 12 Member States an internal market within which the free movement of goods, persons, services and capital is ensured. Increasingly, numbers of individuals and companies are coming into contact with the legal systems in the Member States as a result of a variety of activities. These are not confined to the increasing amount of business activity which is taking place across national borders but include property transactions, matrimonial law and even criminal law and personal injury law. Yet most lawyers know very little even about the legal systems of their immediate neighbours. We shall need increasingly to have a basic understanding of the legal systems in the 12 Member States. This applies not only to lawyers both inside and outside the European Community but also to individuals. Anything that can be done to clarify and demystify the law must be for the public benefit.

This book is an introductory guide to the legal systems of the Member States not only for the lawyer, but also for the non-lawyer. It has the added benefit that for the first time it will enable comparisons to be made between the forms of procedure in the different legal systems within the EC since the same topics are dealt with for each country in an accessible and easily understandable manner. It will surprise many that these different legal systems have so much in common.

Many of the authors of the individual chapters are drawn from the delegations of the CCBE. The CCBE (the Council of the Bars and Law Societies of the European Community) with its offices in Brussels, consists of national delegations representing the legal professions in each of the 12 Member States together with observer delegations from Austria, Cyprus, Czechoslovakia, Finland, Norway, Sweden and Switzerland. Its tasks are to represent the legal profession before the EC institutions and the European Court of Human Rights, to constitute a forum within which the Bars and Law Societies may consult and work together and where possible find solutions designed to co-ordinate and harmonise the practice of the legal profession, and to represent the Bars and Law Societies of the EC in their dealings with other organisations in the legal professions and third parties. The CCBE through its constituent Bars and Law Societies promotes at EC level measures which are of practical benefit both to members of the legal profession and the public which they serve.

This book is of similar intent. It has been a considerable challenge for each contributor to cover so much ground in a comprehensible way in a very limited space. The challenge has been well met. The members and former members of the delegations to the CCBE and the other individual contributors are pleased to have given assistance to this project which I am sure will be of practical benefit to all lawyers and others who need to have an insight into the legal systems of the Member States of the European Community.

John Toulmin QC
Vice-President CCBE
3 Gray's Inn Place
London WC1R 5EA

PREFACE

The idea for this book emerged in a classic form - a conversation with our publisher! A discussion about developments in our respective practices at the Bar revealed the need for an introduction to the legal systems of the Member States of the European Communities. Although European Community law has brought the legal systems of the Member States together, they still remain separate legal systems, each with their own arms to the European legal body. Their separateness is often as important as their connections.

Most law firms conduct transborder legal business involving other European countries. We see this book as the equivalent, for lawyers, to learning a language to facilitate successful business in Europe. Knowing the central structures and concepts furthers understanding and respect and is good for business. In compiling this work we have undergone an enjoyable educational course in the legal systems of the Member States. The overriding impression we have gained from that course is that we have more in common than in conflict. We obviously owe a great debt to the great legal harmonisers of the past, the Romans!

Recent developments in European Community law make parts of this book essential for successful legal practice in Europe : one example being the Rome Convention on Contractual Obligations. Commercial lawyers grappling with the selection of remedies for transnational contractual disputes will be required to analyse the remedies available in the contracting states. We hope the first step will be to reach up and pull this book off the shelf.

Similarly, under the agreement establishing the European Economic Area, European Community law will extend into the EFTA countries. As a result, some 19 legal systems will thereby be connected. With further similar agreements with the countries of Central and Eastern Europe, the number of countries so connected might ultimately rise to 22, 25, or more. It is for this reason that we have decided to continue the enterprise started by reference to the Member States of the European Communitites to those of the EFTA countries. We hope therefore to have a companion introduction to the legal systems of the EFTA countries published in the near future.

We are deeply indebted to all our co-authors, and to our consultant editor John Toulmin QC, for his support and contribution. The book is as much theirs as ours. A particular thanks is extended to Volker Heinz, for his continued helpful advice and assistance. We wish, too, to acknowledge the great assistance of Sven Deinman, Amanda Green, Anne Hockaday, Kate Jenkins, Carole Leconte, Jonathan Nash, Ailsa Wall and Clare Walker.

We trust that the book will prove interesting and useful.

Maurice Sheridan
James Cameron
3 Gray's Inn Place, Gray's Inn, London

CONTENTS

TABLE OF LEGISLATION

Hague Convention on the Service Abroad of Judicial and Extrajudicial Documents in Civil or Commercial Matters (15 November 1965)	Denmark - 18 France - 25 Germany - 25 Neth - 19 Portugal - 18 Spain - 30, 54
Hague Convention on the Taking of Evidence Abroad in Civil and Commercial Matters (18 March 1970)	Belgium - 26 France 25 Germany - 31 Ireland - 21 Italy - 29 Lux - 23 Neth - 21 Portugal - 20 Scotland - 21
Hague Convention relating to Civil Procedure (17 July 1905)	Denmark - 20 Neth - 20
Hague Convention relating to Civil Procedure (1 March 1954) art 17	Belgium - 25 Denmark - 20 Germany - 27 Italy - 29 Lux - 21 Neth - 19
"Lugano Convention" (the Convention on Jurisdiction and the Enforcement of Judgments in Civil and Commercial matters) (7 February 1989)	E&W - 9, 63 Italy - 55 Neth - 39
New York Convention on the Recognition and Enforcement of Foriegn Arbitral Awards (10 June 1958)	Italy - 9 Spain - 58
Nordic Convention	Denmark - 44
Treaty establishing the European Coal and Steel Community ("ECSC")	Lux - 1
Treaty of 31 March 1965 establishing the Benelux Court of Justice	Lux - 9
Treaty on European Union (Maastricht Treaty)	Spain - 3
Universal Declaration on Human Rights	Spain - 7 Portugal - 5
Vienna Convention on Consular Relations 1963	Belgium - 11
Vienna Convention on Diplomatic Relations 1961	Belgium - 11 France - 25 Greece - 15 Spain - 10

LEGISLATION OF THE MEMBER STATES

BELGIUM

DENMARK

ENGLAND AND WALES, SCOTLAND

FRANCE

Code of Civil Procedure ("ZPO") (*Cont*)

s 148	22
ss 148 et seq	22, 25
s 157 II	33
ss 166 et seq	25
s 166 I	25
ss 166-207	25
ss 166-213 a	25
s 176	25
s 181	25
s 180	25
s 193	25
s 194	25
s 198	25
s 202 II	25
s 203	25
ss 208-213a	26
s 209	2
s 211	19, 25
ss 214 et seq	26
s 217	19
s 223	22
s 223 III	19
s 223(2)	51
s 233	22
ss 239 et seq	21, 24
ss 246 et seq	22, 25
s 253	19, 21, 24
s 253 I	24
s 253 II	21
s 253 IV	24, 25
s 256	47
s 260	21, 25
s 261	22, 24
s 262	22
s 263	22
ss 265 et seq	21, 22
s 267	22, 25
s 269 IV	27
s 269	19
s 270 III	24, 29
s 272	28
s 272 II	19
s 273	29
s 273 II	19, 28
s 273 IV 1	19, 28
s 275	19, 26
s 275 II	19
s 276	19, 26
s 276 I	19, 29, 30
s 278	31, 32
s 278 I	19
s 282	3, 29, 30
s 285 I	33
s 286	28, 31, 32
s 287	45, 46
s 293	3, 29, 30
s 294	19, 28
s 296	27, 29, 30
s 300	27
s 300 I	19
s 302	19, 27
s 307	26, 27
s 308 II	34
s 310	19, 26, 34

IRELAND

ITALY

LUXEMBOURG

THE NETHERLANDS

PORTUGAL

TABLE OF CASES

BELGIUM

Carl Bevernage
De Bandt, van Hecke, Lagae, Brussels

CONTENTS

CHAPTER 1 : SOURCES OF LAW

The *Belgian Constitution* was adopted in 1831 when Belgium gained its independence from the Kingdom of the Netherlands. It was strongly influenced by the principles of the French revolution and was one of the first "liberal" constitutions of continental Europe.

Belgium was originally conceived as a unitary decentralised state. *Unitary v federal* This structure remained fundamentally intact until 1970. Growing *system* conflicts between the Dutch-speaking Flemings, living in the northern part of the country, and the French-speaking Walloons, living in the southern part, then made the move to a federal structure inevitable. Although this conflict was for most of its history maintained more as a debate over language, it was never merely that. On the one hand lay an historical dominance by the French-speaking group in the political, economic and social life of the country, while on the other there was the numerical majority of the Flemings demanding influence commensurate with this.

Reform of the Belgian state to a federal state took place by virtue *Communitaris-* of three major constitutional reforms (in 1970, 1980, and 1988). *ation v* The country is now subdivided into three Communities : the *regionalisation* Flemish, the French and the German-speaking Communities (*Constitution, arts 3ter, 59bis and 59ter*), and three Regions - the Flemish Region, the Walloon Region and the Region of Brussels-Capital (*Constitution, art 107quater*). The division of the country into four language regions (the Dutch-speaking, the French-speaking, the German-speaking region and the bilingual region : (*Constitution, art 3bis*) serves to define the territorial scope of the Acts of the Communities and Regions (with competence ratione loci of decrees and ordinances).

The move towards "communitarisation", to grant each Community control over matters such as education and cultural affairs, was mainly a response to a long-standing demand of the Flemish movement directed at attaining genuine recognition for and development of their own language and culture. The move towards "regionalisation" on the other hand sought to address the wishes of the Walloon people who wanted economic decentralisation, with control over government investment decisions and expenditure exercised at regional level. They argued that a central government increasingly dominated by the Flemish would result in favouring Flanders so far as allocating economic benefits was concerned.

If one refers to the basic distinction between two models of federalism - integrative federalism and devolutionary federalism, it will already be clear that Belgium can be considered as an example of "devolutionary federalism" : a constitutional order that redistributes the powers of a previously unitary state among subsequent component entities. These entities acquire an autonomous status within their own field of responsibilities.

A distinguishing feature of the federal state is the existence of two distinct legal orders, that of the federal level and that of the federated level, each with its own systems of laws and its own legislative assembly and executive body. In Belgium, the Communities and Regions have distinct legal personality from the national (federal) state and have their own legislative and executive organs.

Distribution of powers

In a federal state, the distribution of powers between the central and regional authorities is effected by a constitution with a fair degree of rigidity, so that its basic terms are "entrenched", that is, they cannot be amended at the sole discretion of the centre or of any region or combination of regions. In Belgium, the powers of the Communities and the Regions are entrenched either in the *Constitution* itself, or in so-called Community legislation, which must be passed by a special majority vote.

Communities and Regions exercise their powers by enacting decrees which have the same legal standing as decrees of the national Parliament. The Region of Brussels-Capital enacts "*ordinances*" which differ very little from the "decrees" of the other Regions and Communities. Unlike decrees, ordinances are subject to a limited judicial review by the judiciary as well as, in certain cases, limited administrative control by the national authorities "to protect Brussels' international role and its function as the capital". The special notion of "ordinances" can be explained by reference to the political discussion which took place between the Flemish and the Walloon on whether the Region of Brussels-Capital should be given equal status with the Walloon and Flemish Regions as a Region in its own right.

The powers of the Communities and Regions are limited to those expressly enumerated in the *Constitution* or in legislation adopted by special majority implementing constitutional provisions. The central government, which is still perceived as the ordinary holder of sovereignty, remains competent in all matters that are not explicitly entrusted to the Communities and the Regions, and hence holds "residual powers".

The expressly enumerated powers of the Communities and Regions are very broad. The Communities have responsibility for cultural affairs, education, personal matters, international co-operation in such matters and the use of languages in administrative matters and relations between employers and employees. The Regions have exclusive or partial competence in respect of land use and planning, environmental matters, housing, water policy, economic policy, energy policy, subordinate authorities, employment policy, public works and transport policy. In Belgium, the federal, respectively Community or Regional, level in which legislative powers are vested is in principle where the executive power lies, too.

The exclusive nature of the powers allocated both ratione materiae and ratione loci has been confirmed several times by the Constitutional Court (the "Court of Arbitration"). This principle of exclusivity was meant to give each component entity the power to determine its own policy on certain matters with no other authority being able to interfere there.

Should the policy of one authority conflict with that of another where neither acts ultra vires, the Court of Arbitration will apply the proportionality rule : no authority may take such radical measures in administering a policy entrusted to it without a minimum of good cause if in doing so another authority is seriously obstructed in the effective prosecution of its own policy.

The Belgian federal practice of essentially interwoven spheres of action for the federal, community and regional authorities made it necessary to develop several techniques for co-operation, the joint exercise of powers and joint institutions, as examples of an evolution towards some form of co-operative federalism.

The principal written documents containing the law applied in Belgium are :

Principal written documents

- the *Constitution;*
- the *Special Majority Law of 8 August 1980 on institutional reforms,* as amended by the *Law of 9 August 1988;*
- the *Law of 31 December 1983 on the institutional reforms of the German-speaking Community;*
- the *Special Majority Law of 6 January 1989 on the Court of Arbitration;*
- the *Special Majority Law of 12 January 1989 on the Brussels institutions;*
- the *Special Majority Law of 16 January 1989 concerning the financing of the Communities and Regions;*
- the *Laws on the Council of State,* co-ordinated by the *Royal Decree of 12 January 1973;*
- the *Law of 29 March 1962 on zoning and urban planning;* the *Laws on language use in administrative matters,* co-ordinated by the *Royal Decree of 18 July 1966;*
- the *Law of 14 July 1976 on public contracts in works, supplies and services;* the *Code on Belgian nationality* (the *Law of June 28, 1984);*
- the *Civil Code* (1804);
- the *Judicial Code* (1967);
- the *Commercial Code* (1872);
- the *Criminal Code* (1867);
- the *Code of Criminal Procedure* (1878);
- the *Income Tax Code* (1964);
- the *V.A.T. Code* (1968).

Application of national law to foreigners	There is no difference in the way national civil law is applied to foreigners as compared with nationals. The absence of any discrimination between foreigners and nationals applies only in respect of civil rights and not to political, economic or social rights nor in respect of the right of access to national territory.

As far as social and economic rights are concerned, as with the right of access to national territory, EC foreigners benefit from the particular rules of EC law.

Pursuant to *Article 196 of the Law on commercial companies*, any legal person having its real and effective seat abroad is recognised in Belgium and is permitted to enjoy civil rights there.

Monist v dualist system

Pursuant to *Article 68 of the Belgian Constitution*, international treaties are incorporated into the Belgian legal system when ratified by the Belgian Parliament.

The question whether international law can be applied directly by the courts and civil rights be enforceable does not admit of a simple answer. Some treaties are considered sufficiently accurate to be applied directly; others are too vague and only generate obligations on the state.

Application of EC law

The EC Treaties were incorporated into the Belgian legal system when ratified by the Belgian Parliament. Some articles of the EEC Treaty have direct effect and can be invoked directly before the national courts. No further implementation measures are necessary to that effect.

Regulations

In Belgium, as in any other EC Member State, regulations are directly applicable independent of any implementing measure into national law (*EEC Treaty, art 189*). The European Court of Justice confirmed that "the direct application of a regulation means that its entry into force and its application in favour of or against those subject to it are independent of any measure of reception into national law" (*Case 34/73 F.lli Variola SpA v Amministrazione Italiana delle Finanze* [1973] ECR 981 at 990).

Directives

In Belgium, directives are implemented into Belgian law in the same way as for any other legislative act. After the expiry of the prescribed implementation period, provisions of directives may have direct effect. The Belgian State Council, which is the highest administrative court, had already decided in 1968 that a directive could have such direct effect (*Corveleyn c. Etat Belge*, J.T., 1969, p694).

National courts and EC Law

The Belgian Court of Cassation ("*Cour de Cassation*"/"*Hof van Cassatie*") held on 27 May 1971 that "when there is a conflict between internal Belgian law and a Treaty rule of international law which has direct effect, the latter should prevail; this precedence flows from the nature of international law; this is all the more so if there is a conflict between a Belgian law and

Community legislation" (*Fromagerie Le Ski*, J.T., 1971, p471).
Since this judgment of the Court of Cassation, Belgian courts
adopt the principles of Community law unequivocally.

Under Belgian law, foreign law is treated as a question of law and
not as a question of fact. As a result, it does not have to be
established nor translated by the parties. If necessary, the judge
is obliged to carry out his own research as to the content of any
foreign law which he considers applicable in the proceedings.

*Citation of
foreign law in
national
proceedings*

There is no legal presumption that foreign law is the same as
national law. Some authors, however, are of the view that Belgian
law will apply when the content of a foreign law is very difficult to
establish (for instance, the law of some developing countries).

In Belgium there are no annotated texts of the *Constitution*.
Commentaries can be found in textbooks.

*Annotated texts
of the
Constitution*

CHAPTER 2 : FUNDAMENTAL RIGHTS

The basic principles guaranteeing justice are to be found in several articles of the *Constitution*, but most of all, in *Articles 5 and 6 of the European Convention on Human Rights* which are directly applicable before the Belgian courts.

Constitutional provisions guaranteeing justice

As far as the *Belgian Constitution* is concerned, the following Articles may be referred to :

Under *Article 94 of the Constitution* no tribunal court of arbitration may be set up save by law. No extraordinary commissions or courts may be set up at all. This Article should be looked at in conjunction with *Article 8 of the Constitution* which prescribes that no person may be withdrawn from the judge assigned to him by the law, save with his consent.

The courts

The independence of the Judiciary from other governmental functions, especially from the Executive, is guaranteed by several constitutional provisions. Judicial authority is exercised by courts and tribunals (*Constitution, art 30*). Judges are appointed for life and retire at an age determined by law, receiving a pension laid down by law. No judge may be deprived of his office or suspended save by a specific judgment (*Constitution, art 100*); their salaries are fixed by law (*Constitution, art 102*) and no judge may accept a salaried post from the government unless he exercises it without remuneration and is not involved in certain activities declared by law to be incompatible with his office (*Constitution, art 103*).

Independence of the Judiciary

The principle of publicity is guaranteed by *Articles 96 and 97 of the Constitution*. Hearings in courts and tribunals are held in public unless such publicity would be prejudicial to good order and morality. In such a case, the court shall give a specific decision to this effect in an official ruling. In matters regarding political or press misdemeanours, a session in camera can only be ordered on a unanimous decision of the court (*Constitution, art 96*). By virtue of this principle, *Article 757 of the Judicial Code* requires that pleadings, the reports of judges and judgments be made public. This rule does not apply in criminal cases to the gathering of evidence during the investigation of the case, ie to the witness hearings, any expert investigation or interrogation of the parties.

The principle of publicity

According to *Article 97 of the Constitution* every judgment shall be reasoned and given in open court. According to existing case law from the Court of Cassation and the Council of State, decisions of administrative courts must also be reasoned, even if

Judgments

the law does not expressly lay this down as an obligation; the obligation to provide reasons results from the very nature of judicial power (Cass., October 29, 1975, *Pasicrisie*, 1958, I, 215).

Juries

Juries are empanelled to deal with all criminal matters and with political or press misdemeanours (*Constitution, art 98*).

Protection of the rights of foreign nationals

As a general rule, any foreigner who is on Belgian territory enjoys the same protection granted to nationals and their property, save in exceptional cases laid down by law (*Constitution, art 128*).

Interpretation of the Constitution by national courts

According to *Article 107 of the Constitution*, royal decrees, ministerial, provincial or municipal decrees and other regulations or administrative acts are applied by the courts only insofar as they are compatible with the *Constitution*, statute law, and provisions of international treaties which have direct effect.

Time limits for challenging laws

If challenged in timely fashion, that is, within 60 days after their publication, royal decrees, ministerial decrees, regulations or administrative acts may be annulled by the Council of State if the government or administration has acted ultra vires, ie if it has exceeded its powers, abused its powers, or if it did not comply with certain substantial formalities or prescribed formalities. According to existing case law, the courts are not entitled to rule on the constitutionality of the laws enacted by the national legislature, the Community legislatures, or Regional legislatures.

While legislative authority has ceased to be unitary and national, Community and Regional legal rules all have the force of law within their different areas of competence. Hence it was no longer possible to consider the legislature as the sole arbiter on the constitutionality of the statutes enacted by it.

Court of Arbitration

The Court of Arbitration was therefore established in the 1980 constitutional review (*Constitution, art 107ter* and the implementing *Law of 28 June 1983*) as a specialised judicial body responsible for ensuring that none of the legislative bodies overstepped the limits of their specific competences. According to one of its own judgments, the Court of Arbitration may be considered as "a constitutional court of limited jurisdiction" (Court of Arbitration, *Judgment No 32, 29 January 1987*). The power to review on grounds of constitutionality was restricted to dealing with the rules allocating powers between the state, the Communities and the Regions. Moreover, the right to institute annulment proceedings was reserved solely to the national Cabinet of Ministers and to the Executive of a Community or a Region.

The 1988 constitutional revision and the *Special Majority Law of 6 January 1989 on the Court of Arbitration* considerably widened the jurisdiction of the court. The right to institute proceedings for annulment before the court, hitherto reserved solely to governmental authorities, was extended to any natural person or private law corporate body. Most important, however, is the extension of the courts' powers of judicial review to ensure that legislation complies with three exhaustively enumerated fundamental rights : the principles of equality; of non-discrimination (*Constitution, arts 6 and 6bis*); and freedom of education (*Constitution, art 17*).

Annulment proceedings must be brought within six months (60 days in case of a law, decree or ordinance ratifying an international treaty) of the date of publication of the law, decree or ordinance in the Official Gazette (the *"Moniteur belge"*), regardless of whether that law, decree or ordinance has already entered into force or acquired binding effect or otherwise. *Annulment proceedings*

An application may be made to the court to order the suspension of all or part of a law, decree or ordinance against which proceedings for annulment are pending. This will be granted when the immediate application of the contested law, decree or ordinance might cause serious loss which could not easily be compensated.

Like the annulment judgments of the Council of State in the case of administrative acts, annulment judgments delivered by the Court of Arbitration operate erga omnes and ex tunc.

Article 26 of the Special Law of 6 January 1989 empowers the Court of Arbitration to give preliminary rulings on questions regarding the infringement by a law, decree or ordinance of a rule of competence laid down in or enacted under the *Constitution*, or of *Articles 6, 6bis and 17 of the Constitution*. The referring court and all other judicial tribunals called on to give a ruling in respect of the same matter are bound by the ruling given by the Court of Arbitration as to the way they should resolve the dispute which gave rise to the reference being made. *Preliminary rulings*

When the court required to give a preliminary ruling declares that a law, decree or ordinance violates the constitutional rules of competence or *Articles 6, 6bis and 17 of the Constitution*, a new six month period begins to run within which the governmental authorities may bring annulment proceedings before the court in order to remove completely that legal rule from the legal order.

The assistance, however, of an attorney at law before this court is not obligatory. All attorneys at law, including apprentices (*"avocats-stagiaire"*), may appear before the Court of Arbitration. *Appearance before the Court of Arbitration*

Proceedings before the Court of Arbitration take on average : *Length of proceedings*

(i) two months for preliminary proceedings and applications for suspension;
(ii) ten months for proceedings on a referral for a preliminary ruling;
(iii) eleven months for annulment proceedings.

CHAPTER 3 : JURISDICTION OF THE COURTS

The rule that the person of the King is inviolable, provided for in *Article 63 of the Constitution*, is absolute. The King is exempt from any civil or criminal proceedings. Ministers and secretaries of state are subject to specific rules derogating from the common law rules with respect to their liability, in order to safeguard their freedom to act. This relates mainly to their civil and criminal liability. *Scope of civil proceedings*

Only civil claims for acts not arising out of criminal offences and committed outside the exercise of their function, and for criminal offences which are not committed in the exercise of their function and which are prosecuted when a member of the government no longer remains in office, fall under the common law rules and can be brought before the ordinary courts.

In general, no judgments can be enforced against public authorities. Public assets cannot be seized. There is a draft bill pending before Parliament, and already passed by one of the chambers, under which such immunity from seizure would only apply to goods necessary for the provision of public services. Belgian law has adopted a restrictive interpretation in respect of a foreign state's immunity from jurisdiction. Immunity can be invoked only with respect to truly sovereign actions. *State immunity*

Recently, however, the Council of State was given the power to condemn public authorities to pay a civil fine where they fail to execute an annulment of judgment of of the Council of State.

Belgium has ratified the *Vienna Convention* of 18 April 1961 and of 24 April 1963 on the status of diplomatic and consular agents.

The assumption of jurisdiction by the domestic courts must be specifically provided for in the *Code of Civil Procedure* or in the *Code of Criminal Procedure*. *Jurisdiction*

In civil and commercial matters the jurisdiction of the Belgian courts is provided for in *Articles 622ff of the Code of Civil Procedure*. Bilateral and multilateral treaties may provide otherwise for the assumption of jurisdiction by domestic courts.

Article 635 of the Judicial Code sets out 11 grounds on which Belgian courts may assume jurisdiction in respect of foreigners. These include cases relating to real estate located in Belgium, the inheritance of a foreigner who is domiciled in Belgium, bankruptcy proceedings, contracts to be performed in Belgium, etc. In other cases, a plaintiff domiciled in Belgium may sue a defendant domiciled abroad before the Belgian courts, only if the defendant would have the same right against the plaintiff before the courts in his own country.

In the *Code of Criminal Procedure* the Belgian courts may assume jurisdiction either because the accused is a Belgian national (if the offence was committed abroad) or because the offence was committed in Belgium.

Universal jurisdiction

Belgian criminal courts have universal jurisdiction over the following offences :

- attempts on the state's security;
- counterfeiting (and other related offences);
- offences against a Belgian national if the act in question is punishable in the country where it was committed with at least a possible penalty of five years in jail.

Domicile

The domicile of an individual is the place where he is registered in the file of the local authority ("*Registre de la commune*") (*Code of Civil Procedure, art 36*).

The seat of legal persons is located at the place where they have their central administration (*Civil Code, art 197*).

CHAPTER 4 : ADMINISTRATION OF JUSTICE

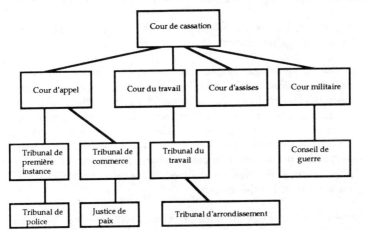

The judicial system is for the most part that laid down by the *Law of 10 October 1967* which enacted the *Judicial Code*. Within the judicial system, there are four tiers of ordinary courts :

    (1)   Justice of the Peace Courts - Police Courts;

    (2)   Courts of First Instance, Labour Courts, Commercial Courts and District Courts;

    (3)   Courts of Appeal, Labour Courts of Appeal and Courts of Assizes; and

    (4)   The Court of Cassation.

It is important to remember the distinction between Justice of the Peace Courts (*"Justice de Paix"*/*"Vredergerecht"*) which only hear civil matters, and the Police Courts (*"Tribunal de Police"*/*"Politierechtbank"*) which only hear criminal matters. The Justice of the Peace Courts and the Police Courts are the lowest courts in the Belgian court hierarchy.

Justice of the Peace Courts/Police Courts

There are over 200 Justice of the Peace Courts, one for every judicial canton. A canton is the smallest geographical subdivision of the country for organisational purposes in the court system. It usually comprises several governmental municipalities. In larger cities, the courts are joined with a separate Police Court. In small cantons, a Justice of the Peace Court serves a double function, being both a Justice of the Peace Court and a Police Court.

The Justice of the Peace Court has original jurisdiction to hear civil and commercial cases (but never labour cases) involving claims of up to BF 50.000 except where otherwise specifically provided for by law or when the parties have agreed to submit to arbitration (where this is allowed (*Judicial Code, art 590*)).

Regardless of the amounts involved, a Justice of the Peace Court has exclusive jurisdiction over a variety of specific cases, the most important of which are disputes concerning residential and agricultural leases, the joint ownership of real estate and alimony (*Judicial Code, art 591*).

Appeals against the decisions of the Justice of Peace Courts are brought before the Court of First Instance or the Commercial Court, depending on the subject matter and the parties involved.

Appeals against decisions of the Police Courts are brought before the Court of First Instance.

Judicial districts In the Belgian legal system the country is subdivided into 26 judicial districts. Each judicial district comprises several judicial cantons. In each of the 26 judicial districts there are three separate courts : a Court of First Instance, a Labour Court and a Commercial Court, each with different jurisdiction as regards subject matter or persons. Apart from these three courts there is also a District Court, composed of the Presidents of the three other courts, which deals with questions of the proper allocation of jurisdiction within the district.

Courts of First Instance The Courts of First Instance are composed of three divisions - civil, criminal and juvenile - and may have several Chambers. In general, a single judge may hear any case. The presence of a three-judge panel is required only in special cases, such as for an appeal against the decision of the Police Courts or an appeal against the decision of Justices of the Peace at the request of one of the parties.

The Courts of First Instance are headed by a President (*"le président"*/*"de voorzitter"*). He is responsible for the organisation of the court. He assigns judges to the various Chambers at the beginning of each judicial year, which starts on 1st September. He also allocates cases among the various Chambers. Apart from his organisational function, the President has jurisdiction to deal with summary proceedings.

The Courts of First Instance have a general original jurisdiction over all civil and criminal cases (*Judicial Code, art 568-571*), except where otherwise provided for by law; and an appellate jurisdiction over decisions of the Justice of the Peace Courts in cases involving more than BF 15.000, and over decisions of the Police Courts.

Labour Courts In each judicial district, there is also a Labour Court (*"Tribunal de Travail"*/*"Arbeidsrechtbank"*), with at least two Chambers. Each Chamber is presided over by a professional judge of that court, assisted by lay judges representing employers' associations, or associations of blue collar and white collar workers.

The jurisdiction of the Labour Court encompasses labour disputes and security matters (*Judicial Code, art 578-583*). The President of the Labour Court has jurisdiction over summary proceedings. Appeals against decisions of the Labour Court are heard by the Labour Court of Appeal.

Finally, there is in each judicial district also a Commercial Court ("*Tribunal de Commerce*"/"*Rechtbank van Koophandel*") which is presided over by a professional judge assisted by two lay judges in commercial matters who are usually businessmen. The Commercial Courts hear commercial disputes between businessmen or against a businessman, where the value at stake exceeds BF 50.000. They also have jurisdiction over corporate matters and bankruptcy or related proceedings (*Judicial Code, arts 573-578*). The President of the Commercial Court also has jurisdiction over summary proceedings as well as dealing with unfair trade practices. Appeals against decisions of the Commercial Courts are heard by the Court of Appeal. *Commercial Courts*

The District Court ("*Tribunal d'Arrondissement*" / "*Arrondissementsrechtbank*") is a special court composed of the Presidents of the Court of First Instance, the Labour Court and the Commercial Court for the district. It serves as arbiter over jurisdictional disputes among these three courts when either a judge or any such court of its own motion or the litigants themselves challenge the assumption of jurisdiction by or venue of any court (*Judicial Code, arts 631-644*). No appeal against its decisions is possible. *District Courts*

Belgium has five Courts of Appeal; five Labour Courts of Appeal; and nine Courts of Assizes, one per province. *Courts of Appeal*

There are five Courts of Appeal ("*Cour d'Appel*"/"*Hof van Beroep*"), located in Antwerp, Brussels, Ghent, Liège and Mons, each consisting of a civil, a criminal and a juvenile division. Some Chambers of the courts are composed of three justices, others of only one. Only specific cases, such as appeals against decisions of the juvenile section of the Court of First instance, can be distributed to a Chamber composed of one justice. The Courts of Appeal have appellate jurisdiction over the decisions of the Courts of First Instance and of the Commercial Courts (*Judicial Code, arts 602-606*). They also have jurisdiction over appeals from decisions in tax administration matters.

There are five Labour Courts of Appeal ("*Cour du Travail*"/"*Arbeidshof*") which hear appeals from the decisions of the Labour Courts (*Judicial Code, art 607*). Their composition is the same as that of the Labour Courts, ie the chambers are presided over by a professional justice of the court, assisted by two lay judges. *Labour Courts of Appeal*

The nine Courts of Assizes ("*Cour d'Assises*"/"*Hof van Assisen*"), one in each province of the country, are distinct from all other courts in that they are not permanent, but assemble only for certain periods of session as determined by the President of the Court of Appeal. The bench is composed of a Presiding Justice, who is a member of the Court of Appeal, and two associate judges who are members of the Court of First Instance. The Court of Assizes sits with a jury of 12 lay members. Felonies punishable with imprisonment of more than five years, as well as political and *Courts of Assizes* press delicts, are tried before the Court of Assizes. Convictions by the Court of Assizes may be appealed only to the Court of Cassation.

Court of Cassation The Court of Cassation ("*Cour de Cassation*"/"*Hof van Cassatie*") is located in Brussels and consists of three different divisions : civil and commercial, criminal and labour. Each Chamber is composed of a French-speaking and a Dutch-speaking panel, each of five justices.

Appeals As a general rule, first instance decisions of a lower court can be appealed to the court of the next level, which rehears the case de novo, both as to the facts and the legal issues.

The Court of Cassation reviews decisions only when all other possibilities of appeal or opposition have been exhausted. The court merely reviews whether the lower court has correctly applied the law. It does not reconsider the facts as determined in the earlier proceedings nor judge the case on its merits (*Judicial Code, art 608*). For that reason, the Court of Cassation is not really to be regarded as an instance of appeal but rather as a partial (legal) review.

If the Court of Cassation decides that a lower court did not apply the law properly it quashes that decision, lays down a declaration of principles that should be applied in the case and refers the case back to another court of the same level as the court whose decision was quashed. This court is not bound by the decision of the Court of Cassation, unless there are two decisions of the Court of Cassation on the same legal issue in the same case.

There are two main types of appellate procedures (*Judicial Code, art 21*) :

(a) The ordinary appellate procedures of appeal ("*Appel*"/"*Beroep*") and opposition ("*Opposition*"/"*Verzet*"). As a rule ordinary appellate remedies are available to the parties in all cases without prior leave by a court. An appeal normally acts as a stay on enforcement of the judgment appealed (*Judicial Code, art 1397*).

(b) The extraordinary appellate procedures are the petition for cassation ("*Pourvoi en Cassation*"/"*Voorziening in Cassatie*"), the third party opposition ("*Tierce opposition*"/"*Derdenverzet*"), the request that a decision be withdrawn ("*Requête civile*"/"*Rekwest civiel*") and the action for damages against judges ("*Prise partie*"/"*Verhaal op de rechter*"). These extraordinary appellate procedures are only permitted under specific conditions provided for by law. They do not result in a stay of enforcement of the judgment under appeal save where otherwise provided for by law.

As a general rule, once a notice of appeal has been served enforcement of the judgment under appeal is no longer possible.

However, except in certain family law matters (divorce, nullity of marriage, adoption), the court may decide that its judgment may be immediately enforceable notwithstanding any appeal.

Belgium has ratified the *European Convention on the Protection of Human Rights and Fundamental Freedoms*, by the *Law of 13 March 1955*. It also recognises the jurisdiction of the European Commission of Human Rights to accept individual applications under *Article 25 of the Convention*, as well as the jurisdiction of the European Court of Human Rights, under *Article 46 of the Convention*. Therefore, Belgium must abide by the decisions of this court. The provisions of the *European Convention on Human Rights* are directly applicable to the extent that these are self-sufficient, ie are formulated in a sufficiently clear and legally complete manner so as to enable a court to determine whether the provision requires the state either to refrain from a certain action, or to carry out some action, and whether this provision creates rights and obligations which can be invoked by private citizens against the state. If these conditions are fulfilled with respect to a certain provision of the *Convention*, all national courts have to apply this provision of the *Convention*.

European Commission and Court of Human Rights

According to *Article 177 of the EEC Treaty*, where a question on the interpretation of the EEC Treaty or on the validity and interpretation of derived EEC legislation is raised before a national court, that court can refer the question to the European Court of Justice for a preliminary ruling if it considers that a decision on the question is necessary to enable it to give judgment.

References under Article 177 of the EEC Treaty

There is an obligation to refer the matter to the Court of Justice if the question is raised before a court against whose judgment there is no further appeal. In Belgium these courts are : the Court of Cassation ("*Cour de Cassation*"/"*Hof van Cassatie*"), the State Council ("*Conseil d'Etat*"/"*Raad van State*") and the Court of Arbitration ("*Cour d'Arbitrage*"/"*Arbitragehof*").

Questions are referred to the European Court of Justice by way of an interlocutory judgment. The national courts have not laid down any requirements which should be met before an *Article 177* reference should be made.

According to the case law of the European Court of Justice, there is, however, no obligation on a court against whose judgment there is no further appeal to refer a question to the Court of Justice if :

(a)   the question raised is not relevant to the resolution of the proceedings; or

(b)   the same question has already been the subject of a preliminary ruling of the Court of Justice; or

(c)   the correct application of Community law is evident leaving no room for any reasonable doubt (the acte clair doctrine) (Case 283/81 *Srl CILFIT and Lanifico di Gavardo SpA v Ministry of Health* [1982] ECR 3415, [1983] 1 CMLR 472).

The Benelux Court of Justice   Belgium, the Netherlands and Luxembourg signed a Treaty on 3 February 1958 organising an Economic Union between their three countries called the Benelux. The Benelux led to several uniform laws, which are applicable throughout the three countries, such as the *Uniform Benelux Law on Trademarks* of 19 March 1962 and the *Law on Industrial Designs* of 25 October 1966. *Article 6 of the Treaty of 31 March 1965* provides for a judicial interpretation procedure over questions of Benelux law. This procedure is optional for lower courts, but mandatory for the Supreme Courts of the three countries.

CHAPTER 5 : STRUCTURE OF THE LEGAL PROFESSION

There is a single profession and hence no division into solicitors *Structure*
and barristers.

All lawyers ("*advocaat*" - "*avocat*" - "*Rechtsanwalt*") duly admitted
as members of a local Order of Lawyers ("*Orde van advocaten*" -
"*Ordre des avocats*") by the Council of the Bar ("*raad van de
Orde*" - "*conseil de l'Ordre*") may exercise their profession in all
respects, except for a few special rules on rights of audience and
representation in court, as set out below.

There is as such no monopoly over the provision of legal services. *Provision of legal*
However, the drawing up or authentication of certain documents *services*
or deeds (pertaining to the transfer of immovable property,
mortgages, one type of will, matrimonial contracts), the
certification of signatures, and public sale by auction of
immovable goods, is reserved to notaries public ("*notaris*" -
"*notaire*" - "*Notar*") who are public officials, appointed by Royal
Decree (by the Minister of Justice).

Representation in court is also restricted to qualified lawyers, with
the few exceptions outlined below.

Professions such as accountants often provide legal advice as an
auxiliary activity, as do consumer organisations, in areas related
to their main practice or activities.

Tax advisers who seek to be officially recognised as autonomous
liberal professionals provide services ranging from the filing of tax
returns, handling complaints at the administrative level to giving
advice on tax law and regulations and tax planning.

Patent attorneys, who are not very numerous, generally restrict
their services to patent searches and registrations.

All lawyers who are members of the Bar (local Order) may appear *Advocates*
in courts throughout the country and within the EC under the *1977
Lawyers' Services Directive*[1].

Stagiaires may not appear before the Council of State, which
hears questions of administrative law.

Representation before the Supreme Court ("*Hof van Cassatie*" -
"*Cour de Cassation*") in litigation other than criminal proceedings
is reserved to sixteen qualifying lawyers, designated for life, by the

---

1.   Council Directive (EEC) 77/249 (OJ L78 26.3.77 p17).

Minister of Justice out of a list of candidates who have successfully completed five years ad hoc training organised by the Order of the lawyers and admitted to practise before the Court of Cassation and by this Court. The list is drawn up by the Court of Cassation.

Lawyers who are members of the Bar may not hold themselves out as "specialists" in any given field but they may communicate to the local Bar and their clients their area of preferred practice.

In practice, many lawyers are known or generally recognised as "specialists", eg in maritime, criminal, administrative, family, tax, labour, construction, company, EC law, etc.

Rights of audience Every citizen has the right to represent themselves before the courts. However, in criminal proceedings the courts will - through the Head of the Bar ("*stafhouder*" - "*bâtonnier*") - assign a lawyer to a defendant who has not sought or who is unwilling to seek professional assistance.

In the Labour Courts, union representatives and representatives of Mutual Health Societies may represent their members in claims pertaining to job security, salary conditions, disability, professional disease indemnities, etc.

Before the commercial courts, companies may be represented by a director.

Legal practices Lawyers are free to collaborate and form partnerships under all statutory forms other than as private company ("*naamloze vennootschap*" - "*société anonyme*"), or any other share capital company.

Any such collaboration or partnership must be notified to and approved by the local Bar Council.

There are a few restrictions on *stagiaires* doing this.

Partnerships may "employ" associates and *stagiaires* in any form other than a subordinate capacity (employee status).

Lawyers and partnerships may collaborate and even form partnerships with lawyers or with partnerships belonging to other Bar districts both in Belgium and abroad.

In Brussels, to be followed by other districts in Belgium, foreign lawyers or law firms seeking to collaborate or form a partnership with local lawyers or law firms must register their local residents on a so-called B list.

Lawyers with a Belgian degree while hired by foreign lawyers or law firms cannot register with a local Bar.

Branch offices The Brussels Bar (expressly) and the other Belgian Bars allow branch offices to be set up abroad, without any restriction other than required by the rule of reason. Thus far, no branch offices have been allowed in other Belgian districts. The Brussels Bar allows a single branch office to be set up within the Brussels district.

Under the *Judicial Code*, which is the organisational body for the profession of lawyers, members of the Bar must determine "moderately" what fees to charge to clients, in line with the "dignity of the profession" (*art 459*).   *Fees*

Contingent fees or "no win, no fee" arrangements are forbidden.

The National Bar Council has issued a recommendation containing a set of guidelines for computing fees for court related services in a broad range of areas. The local Bars may have varying schemes. These guidelines are available at the offices of the local Bars and many lawyers refer to them in discussing fees with clients or in their final invoice.

Disputes over fees are settled either by arbitration organised by the local Bar Councils or by the courts if a dispute does not go to arbitration. Before giving their verdict, the courts will almost always seek the opinion of the local Bar Council which will hear the plaintiff and the lawyer whose fees are disputed.

Fees will be subject to VAT as of 1 January 1993 at a temporary rate of 12% and subsequently to the rate uniformly applicable in the EC.

Fees are generally calculated with regard to the "importance" of the case or opinion, the actual work done, the reputation, skills and experience of the lawyer, the financial situation of the client, etc. Hourly rates are more and more used as an overriding reference.

Fees of the winning side cannot be recovered from the losing side, except for a nominal amount not exceeding +/- BF 25,000 (first instance and any appeal taken together).

Pro bono arrangements exist for all clients earning less than a given amount, irrespective of nationality. This assistance is provided by *stagiaires* under the supervision of the local Bar Council.

The local Head of the Bar and the Bar Councils by law have jurisdiction in disciplinary matters regarding members of the profession.   *Professional conduct*

Complaints are generally lodged by clients, sometimes by an opponent, in a letter to the Head of the Bar who will question the parties involved and, if necessary, initiate disciplinary proceedings after a full investigation by a member of the Bar Council before the Bar Council.

The Head of the Bar may decide after the investigation that the complaint is unfounded or that no formal proceedings are warranted and may issue a variety of "warnings".

The Bar Council may suspend and even disbar a lawyer who may appeal this decision to an Appellate Level Disciplinary Tribunal presided over by the President of the Courts of Appeal, assisted by lawyers designated by the Bar Councils of the entire district of the Court of Appeals.

The local Bar Councils have contracted on behalf of their members professional liability insurance limited to BF 15 million per mistake.

The Brussels Bar carries insolvency insurance as well.

Practice by foreign lawyers

Duly licensed EC lawyers may appear in Belgian courts under the *1977 Lawyers' Services Directive*.

Pending the introduction of a draft directive on the freedom of establishment prepared by the CCBE (Council of the Law Societies and Bars of the European Community) EC lawyers may only establish and practise (before the courts on a regular basis) under their home title.

Non-EC lawyers who wish to practise from an office in Belgium must obtain a professional card (*"beroepskaart"* - *"carte professionnelle"*) from the Ministry of Middle Classes ("Ministère des classes moyennes"/"Ministereie van Middenstand") (this ministry deals with small businesses of up to 50 people). They may not practise Belgian law, and must use their home title.

In-house counsel have no rights to practise as independent lawyers.

As set out above, foreign lawyers and law firms, whether established in Belgium or not, may collaborate with local lawyers and, under certain conditions, form partnerships.

Instruction of lawyers

Any citizen or client can instruct a lawyer.

Litigants may represent themselves in court, except in criminal proceedings as explained above.

Directory of legal services

The local Bar Councils publish a directory every year with all the names and addresses of individual members and partnerships as well as a list of "preferred areas of practice" as notified by the lawyers themselves.

The directories can be obtained by writing to or calling the local Bar secretariat which is generally located in the main court building of the district.

The courts are listed in the telephone directory under "Ministry of Justice" ("*Ministerie van Justitie*" - "*Ministère de la justice*").

In most international directories one will find an extensive list of Belgian and foreign lawyers practising in the main Belgian districts.

CHAPTER 6 : CIVIL PROCEDURE

The basic allocation of competences between courts is set out in Chapter 4. *Division of competences*

The capacity to sue and to be sued is governed by the rules of civil law (for natural persons), of company law (for companies) and of administrative law (for public legal entities). In principle, all natural persons who have reached the age of majority, and all legal persons, ie those organisations which have the status of a legal entity under the law, such as corporations, non-profit organisations, the Belgian state and its subdivisions and certain state organisations, may sue or be sued in court proceedings. *Parties to proceedings : locus standi*

Natural persons reach the age of majority ("*majorité*"/"*meerderjarigheid*") at the age of 21 (*Civil Code, art 388*). Until that age, a minor ("*mineur*"/"*minderjarige*") is represented in court by the person who has the legal right to administer the goods of that minor. Where both parents are alive and married, each parent has full capacity to administer the goods of their minor children (*Civil Code, art 389*). When both parents are deceased custody over minors, which encompasses the right to administer the goods of children and to represent them in court, is entrusted to a guardian ("*tuteur*"/"*voogd*") (*Civil Code, arts 405-419*). *Minors*

A person who is in a permanent state of insanity, may be declared incompetent ("*interdit*"/"*onbekwaamverklaard*"). The rules on minors and guardianship apply to incompetent persons who must be represented in court by their guardian (*Civil Code, arts 489-512*). *Insanity*

Natural persons or companies can no longer act as plaintiff or defendant as from the date when they are adjudicated bankrupt or insolvent, but must be represented by the receiver of the estate in bankruptcy (*Commercial Code, art 452*). *Bankruptcy*

A company must act in court through its legal representatives called its organs ("*organes*"/"*organen*"), as provided for by law. Thus, the most common type of company, the "*société anonyme*"/"*naamloze vennootschap*", is represented in court by its Board of Directors ("*Conseil d'Administration*"/"*Raad van Bestuur*") (*Company Law, art 54*) which, in practice, will instruct counsel. As from the date of a winding-up order ("*dissolution*"/"*ontbinding*") commercial companies are deemed to exist for the purposes of their liquidation. Companies in *Companies* liquidation are represented in all legal proceedings by their liquidators, who are normally appointed by the shareholders in general meeting.

A branch in Belgium of a foreign company is not a legal entity separate from the foreign company and therefore cannot act as such (*Commercial Court of Brussels, 26 November 1973, J.T. 156 (1974)*).

Labour unions

Labour unions can, although they actually lack specific status as a legal entity under Belgian law, bring certain legal actions in respect of collective labour affairs (*Law of 5 December 1968 on Collective Labour Agreements, art 4*).

Striking out parties

If a party has been sued in a case, and it appears that the case has nothing to do with it, the court may order that this party be dismissed from the case.

Similar claims

Plaintiffs with similar but separate claims against a defendant(s) will often bring separate actions before the same court, and then ask the court to handle all these similar claims at the same hearing, though without the various claims being judicially joined.

Joint action against a single defendant

Several individual plaintiffs can also begin an action jointly against a single defendant by serving one writ of summons, or ask the court that several actions commenced separately be combined, provided that all claims are so closely related that, for the sake of the due process of law, it is advisable that they be handled by the same court and determined in one judgment. These claims are then considered to be connected ("*connexité*"/"*samenhang*") (*Judicial Code, art 30*).

Third party intervention

The basic principle is that the parties, not the court, decide which parties must be sued. Forced intervention of a given party cannot be ordered by the court of its own motion. This rule applies even in a case of indivisible claims ("*indivisibilité*"/"*onsplistbaarheid*").

Hence, when two claims are so closely related that they should be decided together in a single judgment because the enforcement of two differing judgments might otherwise be materially impossible, a court is not authorised to order of its own motion that a third party must be brought into the proceedings in respect of one of the two claims, even when the judgment to be handed down is likely to prejudice the rights of that third party. Any party to the proceedings is free to compel a third party to intervene, and any third party may intervene voluntarily to protect its interest. If it does not intervene, and a judgment given does prejudice its rights, it may file a third party opposition ("*tierce opposition*"/"*derdenverzet*") action by suing all parties to the original proceedings before the same judge. The original judgment can be set aside, not only as regards the third party, but also with respect to the original defendant and plaintiff.

If, for example, a successor or assignee of a deceased or the receiver of an estate in bankruptcy of a party will not resume an action voluntarily, he can be summoned at the request of another party to intervene in the proceedings and resume the action. If he does not intervene, judgment in default will be given.

If a party to an action wishes to bring in a third party who may be liable to guarantee it for all or part of the claim of another party, it can compel that third party to intervene in the proceedings by serving a writ of summons.

A third party can intervene in any pending proceedings up until the presentation of arguments has ended, either on his own initiative, or he can be forced to intervene on the application of one of the parties to the case.

In cases of voluntary intervention, the third party wishing to intervene must file a request with the court where the case is pending, asking to be admitted to the proceedings, and indicating its interest in intervening and the legal arguments supporting its intervention (*Judicial Code, art 813*).

Intervention may not, however, prejudice the rights of any intervening party with respect to any orders already given in the proceedings. The court may order that certain discovery measures be carried out again, such as, for example, an examination by an expert appointed by the court, who will then have to repeat his/her examination in the presence of the intervening party. The intervention may not delay the handling of the original claim, and, if it would, the original plaintiff may ask the court to render a judgment on the original claim first and to defer the claim on the intervenor to a later hearing for judgment (*Judicial Code, art 814*).

Finally, intervention may not take place for the first time at the appellate level when an order is sought against any party (*Judicial Code, art 812 (2)*).

Class actions in principle are not permitted in Belgium. Although *Class actions* in certain cases a person with the right on which a claim is based may be represented by another in a court action, such representation is limited to that one plaintiff, and cannot be extended to an entire class of plaintiffs in a single action.

Pursuant to *Article 11 of the Judicial Code,* a court can address *Evidence abroad* even of its own motion, a rogatory commission to another court in Belgium or abroad in respect of any judicial enquiry. In the absence of a particular treaty dealing with the case, the efficacy of this measure depends on the law of the state to which the rogatory commission is addressed.

Belgian courts are obliged to carry out a rogatory commission sent from abroad, if the rogatory commission is authorised by the Ministry of Justice (*Judicial Code, art 843*).

Belgium has signed the *Hague Convention on Civil Law Procedure* of 1 March 1954 (brought into effect in Belgium by the *Law of 28 March 1958*, Mon. belge, May 11, 1958) and other related bilateral treaties. Belgium has not signed, however, the *Hague Convention on the Gathering of Evidence Abroad*.

CHAPTER 7 : CRIMINAL PROCEDURE

Criminal offences are divided into different classes, depending on *Offences* the penalty laid down by the *Penal Code* or in a specific statute :

    (a)   police offences ("*contravention*") : criminal offences punishable by imprisonment not exceeding seven days and/or a fine of BF 25;

    (b)   offences ("*délits*") : criminal offences punishable by imprisonment from seven days to five years and/or with a fine exceeding BF 25;

    (c)   crimes : criminal offences punishable by imprisonment exceeding five years.

Jurisdiction over these different offences lies with different *Jurisdiction* courts :

    (a)   Police Courts ("*Tribunal de police*") have jurisdiction over police offences, offences committed under extenuating circumstances and other certain specific offences;

    (b)   Criminal Chambers of the Court of First Instance ("*Tribunal correctionnel*") have jurisdiction over offences and certain crimes committed under extenuating circumstances;

    (c)   Courts of Assizes ("*Cour d'Assises*") have jurisdiction with respect to crimes (and political and press offences).

Proceedings before the Police Court and before the Criminal Chambers of the Court of First Instance are identical. In these courts there are no jury trials. In proceedings before the Court of Assizes, a lay jury does take part in (part of) the decision, in accordance with specific rules.

Some criminal offences are tried by specific courts depending upon the person of the accused. In general, criminal offences committed by a juvenile offender will be tried by the Juvenile Courts ("*Tribunal de jeunesse*"), criminal offences committed by persons during military service will be tried by the military courts ("*le conseil de guerre*" and "*la cour militaire*").

Public and private
prosecutions

Prosecutions are in principle carried out by the state (ie the Public Prosecutor). If the state does not prosecute, the victim of an offence can either

(a)   bring a damages claims before the investigating judge, who must carry out an investigation, which might lead the state to prosecute;

(b)   under certain circumstances, serve a summons upon the offender to appear before the Police Court or the Criminal Chamber of the Court of First Instance. These circumstances are, inter alia, that no writ of summons has been served by the Public Prosecutor; that there has been no decision from the investigating court to send the case to the court which will judge the merits of the case; and that the offence is a police offence or offence falling under the jurisdiction of the Police Court or Criminal Chamber of the Court of First Instance.

Commencement of
prosecution

The prosecution is commenced by

(a)   the *"réquisitoire à fin d'informer"* (a claim by the Public Prosecutor's Office requesting that an investigation be carried out by the investigating judge);

(b)   the Public Prosecutor summonsing the accused to appear before the court having jurisdiction to judge the merits of the case;

(c)   the *"réquisitoire de disqualification et de renvoi devant une jurisdiction inférieure"* (a claim by the Public Prosecutor to downgrade a crime or offence because of extenuating circumstances in order to have the matter judged by the Criminal Chamber of the Court of First Instance, or the Police Court instead of by the Court of Assizes and the Criminal Chamber of the Court of First Instance respectively);

(d)   the victim summonsing the accused person to be brought before the court having jurisdiction to judge the merits of the case;

(e)   bringing a claim for damages by the victim of criminal activity before the investigating judge.

The decision whether to prosecute is taken by the Public Prosecutor's Office, which will take into consideration the chances of success. In some cases, a prosecution is mandatory, inter alia, where ordered by the Attorney General Public (*"Procureur Général"*) or by the Court of Appeal.

The only alternative to prosecution is to file the matter without prosecution.

Prior to bringing the prosecution proceedings before a court, the Public Prosecution Officers will carry out a preliminary information procedure to investigate the case and to gather evidence.

When the preliminary information procedure is concluded the Public Prosecutor's Office ("*Procureur du Roi*") will either :

(a) decide that the matter is to be closed without any further proceedings being taken;

(b) serve a writ of summons on the accused person in order to bring the case before the court empowered to judge the merits of the case; or

(c) inform the investigating judge ("*juge d'instruction*").

During the preliminary information stage, an accused is not specifically entitled to be informed of the offence of which he is accused. In some cases, a copy of any official affidavits of any interrogations of the accused person must be sent to the accused person.

In principle, the investigation is secret and non-adversarial. According to *Article 5 of the European Convention on Human Rights*, on being arrested, an accused is entitled to be informed as soon as possible of the offence of which he is accused.

If an accused person is formally arrested, the arrest order will mention the facts on the basis of which the person was arrested. *Arrest* When a warrant of arrest is issued (ie at the latest, 24 hours after arrest) the arrested person is entitled to have a copy of all examination reports ("*procès-verbaux d'audition*") carried out since his arrest. The criminal file can be consulted by the person arrested and his/her legal counsel 24 hours before the hearing of the Chamber of the Council which has to decide whether to maintain the arrest.

If an accused is not formally arrested, neither the accused nor his/her legal counsel may have access to his file pending the investigation, until 48 hours before the hearing of the Chamber of the Council which has to decide whether to send the case to court.

A person can be detained on the basis of a decision of the Public *Time limits on* Prosecutor in order to be put "at the disposal of the judge". This *detention* detention may not exceed 24 hours. Within these 24 hours the person detained must either be heard by the investigating judge or, if a person is for some reason not "at the disposal of the judge", he must be notified of a warrant issued by the investigating judge to bring that person before him ("*mandat d'amener*"). In such a case, this warrant permits the person to be detained for another 24 hours. This warrant must mention the grounds for detention, including the offence alleged against this person.

After questioning the detained person, the investigating judge can issue an arrest warrant ("*mandat d'arrêt*") within 24 hours of the person being brought before him. In such a case, this warrant allows the person to be detained for another 24 hours. This warrant must mention the grounds for his detention, including the offence alleged against him.

The warrant of arrest is valid for five days, during which the detained person must appear before the "*Chambre du Conseil*" (investigating court) which must decide within the same time whether to maintain his detention. The decision to maintain it is valid for one month, during which time the *Chambre du Conseil* must again decide, after having heard the detained person, whether to maintain detention further. There is no maximum length of time set for any overall detention.

Bail

An accused is not entitled to bail, but the investigating judge can (but is not obliged to) decide, on his own initiative or at the request of the Public Prosecutor or of the accused, to release the accused on certain conditions and for a maximum period of three months. One of the conditions may be payment of bail, the amount of which is set by the investigating judge. There is no financial limit on the amount of bail that can be set. The judge will take such a decision if, for example, he has serious suspicions that money or valuables resulting from the offence have been hidden or transferred to another state. The accused person can apply to the investigating judge or, once the decision has been taken, to the *Chambre du Conseil* to modify any such conditions imposed upon him.

The preparatory investigation

The preparatory investigation which is carried out by the investigating judge is mandatory for all crimes and political and press offences and facultative in the case of other offences.

The investigating judge is in most cases in charge of the preparatory investigation :

(a)   upon a formal and prior request of the Public Prosecutor's Office;

(b)   where the victim has made a formal complaint and brought a claim for damages before the investigating judge ("*constitution de partie civile*");

(c)   in case in "flagrante delicto".

At the close of the preparatory investigation, the investigating judge will transmit his report to the Public Prosecutor's Office for the latter to formulate the charges. Subsequently, the investigating judge will report to the investigating court ("*la jurisdiction d'instruction*"), which is, for most offences, the Chamber of Council ("*Chambre du Conseil*") of the courts.

The investigating court will in most cases decide either

(a)   to file the matter without taking further proceedings;

(b)   to remit the matter to the court having jurisdiction to judge the merits of the case;

(c)   to transmit the case to the General Public Prosecutor if the acts committed amount to crimes;

(d)   to suspend the case until more detailed information is available;

(e)   to send the matter to the Public Prosecutor if the investigating court has no jurisdiction to deal with it.

The court having jurisdiction to judge the merits of the case will in most cases come to the case after : *Judgment on the merits of the case*

(a)   the Public Prosecutor's Office has served a writ of summons;

(b)   the investigating court has decided to send the matter to the court having jurisdiction to judge the merits of the case.

During the proceedings before the court which will deal with the merits of the case, the accused is informed of the offence with which he is charged by the introductory summons which must contain an accurate description of the facts and an indication of the Penal Code or specific statute provisions which are thereby alleged to have been breached.

Except for the formal conditions related to the writ of summons, such as signature etc, there are no specific legal requirements as to the form the information relating to the offence and given to the accused person must take. The accused cannot challenge the form of the information; he/she could, however, challenge the accuracy of the information if this information did not allow the accused adequately to prepare his/her defence. *Information relating to the offence*

Evidence for the prosecution is collected during the preliminary information and the investigation stages, by means of interviews, visits to the place where the offence is alleged to have been committed, witness testimony, review of documents, expert research, film, etc. *Evidence*

All evidence which has been obtained legally and in compliance with the general principles governing a fair trial can be put before the court.

An accused is deemed to be innocent until proven guilty. This means that the burden of proof rests on the prosecution. The defence could theoretically simply adopt a passive attitude, but in practice generally co-operate in the gathering of evidence. The court will evaluate at its discretion the evidence before it. Requests to call any additional witness or for any additional expert evidence which can be filed by any party will be decided upon by the court and will only be allowed if the requests are relevant to the court's search for the truth.

Appeals against decisions of the investigating court

Decisions of the investigating court deciding whether to send the case to court for trial or to dismiss it ("*règlement de procédure*") may be appealed by the Public Prosecutor as well as by the victim if the decision of the investigating court might prejudice proceedings.

The accused can only lodge such an appeal on the basis that the investigating court lacked jurisdiction, and provided he challenged jurisdiction before the investigating court. This appeal, called "*opposition*", is filed by a declaration at the Clerk's Office of the investigating court within 24 hours of the decision in question as far as the Public Prosecution is concerned, and within 24 hours of notification of the decision as far as the victim is concerned, being 24 hours as from the moment when he could have had knowledge of that decision. The appeal is heard by the "*Chambre des mises en accusation*" (Chamber of Indictment) which is part of the Court of Appeal.

The Public Prosecutor's Office and the accused are entitled to challenge any decision of the investigating court to maintain the "*détention préventive*" (detention on remand) by lodging an appeal with the Chamber of Indictment, within 24 hours of the decision for the Public Prosecutor, and within 24 hours of notification of the decision for the accused.

Plea-bargaining

Belgian criminal law does not provide for any plea-bargaining, as such, and a defendant must prepare his defence as he will. The prosecuting authorities may not bargain with a defendant once a prosecution is underway in any event.

Juries

Only the Court of Assizes is a jury court. It consists of three professional judges and a jury of 12 effective members. Jurors are chosen from a list of jury members, which will be drawn up on a case-by-case basis. Jurors must comply with certain aptitude rules and cannot be subject to any incompatibilities laid down by law.

However, jury trials remain the exception, with trials before a professional court being the rule. In these courts each trial judge will express his view as to the merits of the case. The parties are excluded.

The list is notified to the accused at least 48 hours prior to the first hearing of the Court of Assizes. At this hearing, the "*jury de jugement*" (the judgment jury) is formed by drawing lots. The accused and the prosecution are entitled to challenge an identical number of jurors, depending upon the number of substitute jurors ("*jurés suppléants*") available. The accused and the prosecution cannot make public their grounds for challenging a juror. The jury is then formed by 12 non-challenged jurors.

Conduct of the trial

The accused person as well as the victim can be assisted by a counsel, who must be an "avocat" (lawyer) admitted to the Bar.

In practice, the presentation of argument in a criminal trial is as follows:

(a)   examination of the accused person by the President of the court;

(b)   examination of any prosecution witnesses, the victim and the accused, examination of any experts;

(c)   oral pleadings by the victim;

(d)   oral summary of the facts and charge by the prosecution officer;

(e)   oral pleadings by the defence as to guilt, level of penalty and as to any civil damages claim;

(f)   consideration by the judge ("*délibéré*") and then judgment.

In contrast to the preliminary information and investigation stages, which are inquisitorial in nature, trial before the court is adversarial. The burden of proof rests on the prosecution (and the victim where a civil claim is made in the criminal proceedings); the court will in principle assess in its own discretion the probative value of any evidence.

The court plays an active role in the fact-finding. It can apply techniques of proof, such as examination of the parties, calling expert evidence, and visiting the place where the offence is alleged to have been committed. It can, however, only call as witnesses persons whom one of the parties has requested be examined. The court will assess any need to call a witness requested by a party.

Hearings in camera

Hearings are, in principle, in public. According to *Article 96 of the Constitution*, the court is entitled to decide to hear the case in camera on the grounds of *"ordre public"*, national security, in the interests of juveniles or for the protection of privacy or in the interests of the decision-making process.

Judgment

The judgment itself is given in public.

Verdict

The verdict is given solely by any jury, excluding the three professional judges. If the accused is found guilty, the jury and the judges decide the penalty. The judges decide, without the jury, any civil damages claim.

The President of the Court of Assizes will remind the jurors of their function and put to them the issues they must decide. These questions cannot be complex, nor can they deal with legal points. The jurors retire to a separate room which they can only leave once their deliberations are over. Communication with the outside world is prohibited.

Their decision which may be by majority is presented as unanimous except when guilt is decided by a simple majority (seven to five), in which case this must be mentioned. If the votes are equally divided, the accused is acquitted.

If the accused person is found guilty by a simple majority of the jury, the accused will only actually be finally found guilty if the court (the President and the two judges) decide by a majority that the accused is guilty.

Once a prosecution is dismissed, an accused person cannot be prosecuted in respect of the same facts.

If, however, it appears from the proceedings that other acts, not mentioned in the initial charge, may have been committed by the accused, the President of the court will order a new investigation to be carried out by the investigating judge.

A verdict must be unanimous if the decision, on appeal by one of the parties with respect to the prosecution charge, aggravates the situation of the accused person. In all other cases, judgment may be rendered by majority decision of the justices.

Alternative offences

A person can be found guilty of an alternative offence to that with which he has been charged, provided this alternative offence is within the facts in respect of which the accused was prosecuted and provided the accused person has been offered the chance to present his/her defence to this. The accused can only be held guilty in respect of facts other than those mentioned in the summons or in the decision of the investigating court to send the case for trial, if the accused has accepted, during the proceedings, to defend himself/herself against these new facts.

Sentencing

The accused has only one opportunity, ie his/her oral pleadings, to deal with the question of guilt, mitigation, penalty and civil damages. Any assessment of the defendant's character (when relevant) is not subject to any specific rules.

The sanction-reducing grounds influence the severity of the sanction. All sanction-reducing or sanction-excluding grounds have to be provided for by statute.

The most important sanction-excluding grounds are (for specific offences) :

- family relationship;
- declaration by the author of the facts prior to the prosecution;
- providing information to the authorities of the planned facts;
- indemnification.

The most important grounds here are (for specific offences) : provocation; young age in general; failure in any attempted assault.

Other matters include the fact that little prejudice resulted from the offence; that it was carried out on the spur of the moment; the attitude of the victim; age; a difficult material situation; the past of the convicted person; and regret.

The court can, in its discretion, take previous convictions into account.

In the Court of Assizes, if the verdict is guilty, the parties, except the victim, are entitled to present oral arguments as to what the appropriate penalty should be. The defence can only present arguments on the sanction requested by the Public Prosecutor; the existence of any facts or legal argument on the basis of which no sanction could be applied; and as to any extenuating circumstances.

Decision is by a majority of the three judges and the jury. The Court of Assizes is bound by the jury's view on any extenuating circumstances.

Juveniles are generally sentenced by separate juvenile courts ("tribunal de la jeunesse") which have jurisdiction over juveniles under 18 at the time the offence was committed.

Penalties which can be imposed

No penalty can be imposed if not explicitly provided for by law. Penal sanctions are provided for by the *Penal Code* and by specific legislation. *Article 7 of the Penal Code* contains a list of the most important penalties; this list is not exhaustive. According to *Article 7*, the following sanctions can be applied :

- for crimes : the death penalty (not applied); forced labour; imprisonment;
- for crimes and offences : deprivation of certain civil or political rights;
- for offences and police offences : imprisonment;
- for crimes, offences and police offences : a fine; specific confiscation.

Specific provisions provide for other penalties, such as publication of the judgment; prohibition on operating a specific business; and deprivation of one's right to drive a car.

Appeals

If the decision of the Police Court or of the Criminal Chamber of the Court of First Instance is given in the defendant's absence, the latter is entitled to have recourse to the "opposition" procedure and the case then comes back before the same court. The opposition must be lodged within 15 days of notification of the default judgment.

If the decision of the Police Court or of the Criminal Chamber of the Court of First Instance is given in the presence of the defendant, the latter can lodge an appeal against this decision within 15 days. The appeal will come before the higher court, respectively the Criminal Chamber of the Court of First Instance for appeals against decisions of the Police Court, and the Court of

Appeal for appeals against decisions of the Criminal Chamber of the Court of First Instance. Only one appeal is possible.

The only remedy against the decision on appeal consists of the *"pourvoi en cassation"* before the *Cour de Cassation* (Supreme Court). The decisions of the Court of Assizes can only be challenged by introducing a *"pourvoi en cassation"*.

Extradition

The *Statute of 15 March 1874* as well as various international treaties govern extradition from Belgium.

The following requirements must be complied with for the Belgian state to reply positively to a request for extradition made by another state :

(a) The request will only be accepted if the international treaty to which the Belgian state and the requesting state are parties provides for reciprocal extradition.

(b) The *1874 Statute* and the applicable treaty must explicitly set out whether the alleged acts are such that extradition may be granted in respect of them. In addition, these acts must be punishable according to the domestic criminal law of the requesting state. Extradition for political offences is excluded.

(c) Belgian nationals cannot be the subject of an extradition order. A person requested must be over 18 years.

CHAPTER 8 : REMEDIES

Damages can be recovered only in the judicial courts. Belgian law provides for two main bases for compensation for damage : for breach of contract; or breach of tortious obligations pursuant to *Article 1382 of the Civil Code*, which states that every act which causes injury to another obligates the one by whose fault the injury occurred to provide redress. Both claims require a breach, a causal connection and damage which can be legally compensated for. *Damages*

The primary differences between damages for breach of contract and damages for breach of tortious obligations are as follows :

(a)   As a rule, in contract cases, damages are available only for foreseeable injury. The concept of "foreseeable" is, however, broadly interpreted.

(b)   It is only in cases of breach of tortious obligations and of the contractual obligations of merchants that there is any joint and several liability.

As a rule, the plaintiff can only obtain relief in respect of an already existing dispute and the plaintiff's interest in bringing the claim must still exist when the claim is actually brought. Proceedings may also be commenced if brought to prevent impairment of a seriously threatened right (*Judicial Code, arts 17 and 18*). *Right to bring proceedings*

There is no fixed amount for compensation for personal injuries if a plaintiff is temporarily disabled, as the level of damages is based on the professional income lost by the person injured. An indemnity, the amount of which varies between the courts, is also awarded for any mental distress suffered while injured. *Personal injury - quantum of damages*

In the case of permanent injury, there are various methods used to assess the level of damages. The first is the capitalisation of the loss of income based on the age of the injured person. A second method is to award a pension based on an assessment of the injured person's loss of income. When those methods are not appropriate due to the peculiarities of the case, the court will assess the quantum of the damage "ex aequo et bono".

In fatal accident cases, heirs can recover the compensation due to the deceased for any period of temporary disability as well as compensation for their own loss.

Mental distress	Damages are available for mental distress in various circumstances including physical suffering, loss of a parent, and mental suffering. The assessment of such damages is made "ex aequo et bono".

Loss of reputation Damages are available for loss of reputation. Generally though, a victim will only be awarded a "symbolic france" - 1 BF - as compensation, if loss of reputation had no economic repercussions.

Restitution *Article 1376 of the Civil Code* states that one who by mistake or knowingly receives what is not due to him is obliged to return it to the one from whom he has received it unduly. Under *Article 1377 of the Civil Code*, a person who mistakenly believes himself to be a debtor and who pays a debt, has a right to recover that sum unless the creditor has destroyed his title.

Enrichment without cause There is a concept of enrichment without "cause". The following conditions must be met to invoke this remedy : that one person is enriched and another impoverished; that the enrichment is due to no other cause (cannot originate in any contractual relationship, a tort or under any particular law); and that the enrichment and the impoverishment are causally linked.

Avoidance of agreements A court may declare void any agreement entered into by mistake, deceit or fraud. Inadequacy ("*lésion*") nullifies only certain contracts with respect to certain persons. These contracts include the sale of an immovable if the price is too low by more than seven-twelfths (*Civil Code, art 1874*); partitions for inadequacy of more than one quarter (*Civil Code, art 887*); employment contracts if by more than one half (*Law of 20 July 1955, art 6*); or partnership agreements if one of the partners does not participate in the benefits or in the losses of the partnership (*Civil Code, art 1855*).

Simple imbalance may also allow one to invalidate all types of agreements concluded by minors.

Penalty clauses Penalty clauses are acceptable as long as they can be considered as compensation. However, in some agreements they are prohibited or regulated. If a court considers that the penalty does not really reflect the level of damage suffered, it will be declared contrary to public policy and void.

Specific performance The court can order specific performance if this is practically possible and does not constitute an abuse of right. The court may issue an injunction ordering a defendant to perform its obligations as well as to issue a prohibitory injunction. Both types of injunctions are usually backed by the sanction of a civil fine.

Frustration Frustration ("*cas fortuit*" or "*force majeure*") is defined as an obstacle as a result of which performance of that obligation has become impossible. The degree to which something is impossible to perform must be reasonably understood and considered with regard to the obligation that has to be performed.

For an event to amount to frustration it cannot have been foreseeable. This second condition is also to be understood in the context of the obligation to perform. The court will examine whether or not the parties could reasonably have agreed who would bear that risk.

Monetary judgments carry a right to interest at a legal rate fixed by Royal Decree. Currently, this rate is 8% per year. *Interest*

Where an ordinary winding-up of a company is sought, an administrator is appointed to carry out the winding-up (*Law of Companies, arts 178ff*). In this case the courts are not invloved. *Winding-up*

Bankruptcy is another basis on which one may seek a winding-up of a company. The *Commercial Code* provides for bankruptcy as follows : *Bankruptcy*
- merchants (non-merchant companies cannot be declared bankrupt);
- who have ceased paying their debts;
- and whose credit has been imperilled.

Merchants in such a situation must declare this state of affairs within three days of it arising to the Commercial Court. The Commercial Court is empowered to declare a merchant bankrupt of its own motion or at the request of the Public Prosecutor's Office. Finally, creditors, too, may commence bankruptcy proceedings either ex parte or inter partes.

Once bankruptcy has been officially declared, the bankrupt is deprived of his right to deal with or dispose of his assets. The court appoints one or more receivers who will take possession of these assets. The court will appoint from its members a referee-judge who will act in a supervisory function.

CHAPTER 9 : MATRIMONIAL DISPUTES

According to *Article 213 of the Civil Code*, spouses owe one another the duties of fidelity, aid and assistance.

Jurisdiction of the courts

Moreover, *Article 203* of the same Code states that parents have are obliged to nourish, raise and educate their children.

During the marriage, a spouse can be compelled by the other to perform his/her obligations. Such claims are filed with the Justice of the Peace who must first attempt to reconcile the parties. The Justice of the Peace is allowed to order temporary measures. He may, for instance, give custody of the children to one spouse, or order one spouse to pay certain sums as alimony to the other, etc.

The Justice of the Peace has only this limited jurisdiction in divorce and his measures remain effective only until one or both spouses file for divorce before the Court of First Instance.

During the proceedings before the Court of First Instance, any decisions on custody, access, alimony and domicile of the spouses are taken provisionally by the President of the Court of First Instance. A final decision on those issues is taken by the Court of First Instance in its judgment granting the divorce.

Except before the Justice of the Peace, questions of custody, access, visiting rights or alimony remain subsidiary to the divorce suit itself.

The various stages of typical "divorce for cause" proceedings are as follows :

Proceedings

The first stage is filing a written application by the plaintiff before the President of the Court of First Instance or his deputy.

The President addresses any relevant matters to the plaintiff and directs him to appear before him at a future hearing.

The other spouse is given notice to appear at the second hearing. At this hearing, held in chambers, the President attempts to reconcile the spouses. If he cannot convince the plaintiff to withdraw his/her application, the judge will attempt to obtain the agreement of both spouses on any provisional measures on access, custody, alimony and visiting rights, which will remain effective during the divorce proceedings.

The President then sends the case to the Court of First Instance for a hearing "in chambers".

For a period of six months (which can be reduced to two months when the cause of divorce is indisputable or undisputed and which does not apply when the cause of divorce is separation for at least five years) the plaintiff cannot sue the defendant to appear before the Court of First Instance at an ordinary public hearing.

After this period, the plaintiff can sue the defendant.

At this stage, the hearings and the proceedings are broadly similar to ordinary proceedings before this court. Some forms of evidence, for instance the hearing of witnesses, are of course more used than other means of proof of the cause alleged.

The proceedings end with a judgment granting or refusing divorce. The judgment will only be effective when it becomes definitive (if no appeal is filed within one month after the decision is notified to the defendant by the bailiff) and if it is registered in the communal register on civil status.

If the judgment is not registered within two months from the date when it became final, it lapses and the whole proceedings have to be resumed.

As mentioned above, the President of the Court of First Instance tries, at the second private hearing where both spouses are present, to obtain their agreement on any provisional measures on access, custody, etc.

If no agreement is reached, any spouse may serve a writ of summons upon the other to appear in a summary procedure before the President of the Court of First Instance (in a public hearing).

The President will order provisional measures on custody of and any visiting rights over the children, access to the former domicile or any alimony to be paid, etc. Those measures remain effective until the judgment granting the divorce is registered (or until judgment refusing divorce).

When a divorce is sought with the mutual consent of both spouses, the procedure is quite different. This type of divorce is only available after two years of marriage and when both spouses are at least 23 years old. In the first stage, spouses who seek to divorce by mutual consent have to agree to a preliminary contract covering custody, visiting rights over any children, division of matrimonial property, possible alimony to be paid by one spouse to the other and the alimony to be paid for the children. Both spouses then file an application before the President of the Court of First Instance or his deputy. After a first hearing two subsequent hearings are set, each at least six months apart. At each hearing, both spouses have to confirm that they still wish to divorce in accordance with the terms of their preliminary agreement. If the legal conditions for divorce are fulfilled, the court grants the divorce and its decision has to be registered within two months in the communal register on civil status.

Finally, it is worth noting that the Public Prosecutor attends most of the hearings in divorce proceedings and is asked to give his opinion about the case. This opinion is particularly important on matters of custody of and access to the children.

As set out above, urgent applications in relation to custody, access or orders ousting one of the parties from the matrimonial home are filed with the Justice of the Peace whilst any marriage subsists and provided no divorce suit has been filed with the court. *Urgent applications*

According to *Article 223 of the Civil Code*, measures can be taken by the Justice of the Peace if one the spouses seriously fails in his/her duties or if the understanding between the spouses is disturbed. In practice, the Justice of the Peace has the discretionary power to determine whether those conditons are fulfilled.

The basic grounds for divorce or separation are : *Grounds for divorce/judicial separation*

(i)   adultery, a breach of the duty of fidelity, which has to be proved beyond any doubt;

(ii)   excesses, brutality or serious insult, which are failures of all other duties of the marriage; excesses or brutality are self explanatory; serious insult is any act which affects the honour or respect of the other spouse, for instance, an unjustified refusal to have a child, slander or libel, recurrent drunkenness, the unjustified abandon of the matrimonial home, etc. Idleness, prodigality, bad housekeeping, etc, are not considered grounds for divorce;

(iii)   five years' separation if the breakdown between the spouses is irremediable or when it is the consequence of a serious mental disturbance of one spouse; even in a divorce for longstanding separation the party seeking divorce will be considered at fault.

The spouse declared to have been at fault can be ordered to pay the other such allowances compensating the alimony which is discontinued at the breakup of marriage. *Matrimonial property*

How any matrimonial property is shared is not to be linked with any issue of the cause of the divorce or any question of fault of the parties.

The rules on dividing the matrimonial property are settled in accordance with any marriage contract or settlement entered into by the spouses before the marriage.

If there is no marriage contract, the division of the property is governed by the general law, the "*régime légal*".

In the "*régime légal*", all goods and income acquired or debts made by the spouses or by one of them after the marriage are held in common except, amongst others : goods inherited or received by one spouse from his/her family, tools and other professional instruments, personal effects such as clothes, intellectual property rights, rights to various allowances, compensation for personal injury, etc.

The choice between division in kind or simple cash division depends on the characteristics of the property.

When a divorce has been registered, the matrimonial property is shared between the spouse with retroactive effect as from the date the petition for divorce was filed.

CHAPTER 10 : PROPERTY TRANSACTIONS

A sale is a bilateral contract whereby one party transfers to another party property in an asset in return for a price to be paid by the latter. This agreement is formed by there being a correlation of one party's offer with another party's acceptance of that offer. In principle, the transfer of the property occurs at the time the contract is concluded where the property sold exists and has been sufficiently precisely identified. However, the transfer of the property, or of the risks in relation to the property sold, or the payment of the price may be set for a later time.

The agreement of sale is governed by the common law of *Agreement of sale* contracts and also by the special rules in *Articles 1582 to 1701 of the Civil Code*. Some kinds of sales are also subject to more specific Belgian or international regulation, such as the sale of new motor vehicles, military effects, places of habitation to be built or being built, the international sale of movable corporeal objects, hire purchase, the sale of stocks or securities, the sale of businesses (*"fonds de commerce"*/*"handelszaak"*), the sale of animals and so forth. In the commercial domain, sales, in particular, international sales, may be governed by legal custom as in force from time to time (for example, the *"incoterms"*).

The seller's principal obligation is to deliver an asset true to the asset agreed to be sold, and the purchaser's obligation is to pay the price agreed. In principle, the seller assures the purchaser complete possession of the asset and guarantees that the asset sold is not affected by any defect. In the event that one of the parties does not perform his obligations, the other party is entitled to ask the courts to cancel the contract or may cancel it himself if the contract so provides.

An agreement of sale does not have to be in any particular form and it may be oral. However, some regulations require use of a written agreement in order for the sale to be enforceable vis-à-vis third parties, or require compliance with specific formalities such as authorising somebody to complete an act, for example, in the case of the sale of goods belonging to a minor, or to request that a sale be carried out by way of a court order (in order to guarantee the price).

Although a sales agreement is a formal contract in itself, a written document may be necessary to establish the evidence that the contract exists and as to its contents. *Article 1341 of the Civil Code* provides that a written text or written evidence is necessary in the case of a sale relating to goods the value of which exceeds BF 15,000. However, this does not apply in commercial matters.

Enforceability against third parties

In addition, certain kinds of sales must comply with specific formalities in order to be enforceable vis-à-vis third parties. Generally, such formalities are required when the owner's right is subject to some requirement like registration, deposit, or publicity (eg where the good sold is a trademark, a patent, a registered share or a building) or when the asset sold is a third party debt. In the first case, the formality required for the sale to be enforceable vis-à-vis third parties generally consists in notification of the transfer to the authorities responsible for registration, deposit or publicity. In the second case, in principle, it is necessary to notify by writ (*"signification"*/*"betekening"*), the fact of transfer to the third party concerned (the debtor of the transferred debt) or to ensure that he recognises this by notarial deed or judgment.

Real estate

The principles mentioned above apply to sales of real estate. Such sales also call for the steps outlined below.

Private sales agreement

In order to complete a real estate transaction, the first step is to conclude a sales agreement in which the parties agree on the property to be sold and the price.

Although such an agreement between the parties is not subject to any specific formalities (a verbal agreement being valid but difficult to prove), there will usually be a signed written agreement (*"compromis de vente"*/*"verkoopcompromis"*) containing the terms and conditions of purchase. Save where both parties are merchants, such an agreement is to be signed in as many original copies as there are parties (*Civil Code, art 1325*).

A real estate agreement must be entered in the records of the mortgage registry (*"Registres du Bureau de Conservation des Hypotheques"*/*"Register van het kantoor van bewaring der hypotheken"*) to be enforceable vis-à-vis third parties (*Law of 16 December 1851*). An entry can only be made when the agreement has been authenticated by a notary public and when the agreement has been registered (*Registration Tax Code, art 29;* see, however, *Article 173 of the Registration Tax Code* authorising the entry of a notarial deed in the records of the mortgage registry prior to its registration if such an entry is requested by the notary within four days after the date when the deed has been executed).

The notary public

The notary public is responsible for carrying out all these formalities, and must verify the identity of the parties, their legal capacity, the mortgage registers as to ownership, whether any other mortgages apply in respect of that property, if there have been any seizures, and whether taxes are still due from the seller. He must request from the relevant authorities an extract from the land survey (*"relevé cadastral"*/*"kadastraal uittreksel"*) to be attached to the notarial deed.

The notary's fees are determined on the basis of a percentage, established by law, of the sale price, depending on the level of this price, plus his/her charges.

According to the *Registration Tax Code*, any agreement (even **Registration** private or oral) transferring the ownership of real estate located in Belgium has to be registered within four months from the date of the agreement being signed. Registration corroborates, in fact, the entry of the agreement in the records of the receiver of registration taxes. This registration is subject to a registration tax of (usually) 12.5% of the purchase price.

Furthermore, all notarial deeds must be registered by the notary within, in principle, 10 days after the deed has been executed. Usually, such registration is effected after the agreement has been authenticated by a notary public.

As stated above, the sale of land triggers the levy of a registration **VAT** tax of 12.5%. On the other hand, if a building is new (within the meaning of the *Value Added Tax (VAT) Code*) and the seller has paid VAT on its construction or acquisition, or if the building is still to be set up, the sale can be subject to VAT at 17%.

As mentioned above, the formality of an entry in the records of the mortgage registry (*"transcription"* / *"overschrijving"*) is required to make the sale enforceable vis-à-vis third parties. It consists in the literal reproduction of the notarial deed of purchase in the appropriate mortgage registry record.

The notary public authenticating the purchase deed is required to submit the deed for entry in the records within a period of two (or three) months after the date the deed was executed. This formality is, in principle, subject to the prior payment of a mortgage registrar's fees and stamp duty.

CHAPTER 11 : RECOGNITION AND ENFORCEMENT OF FOREIGN JUDGMENTS

When there is no specific treaty on this matter between Belgium *General rules* and the state where the foreign judgment was given, the Belgian courts may authorise enforcement of this judgment according to *Article 570 of the Judicial Code*. The following conditions must be met :

- that the judgment does not offend Belgian public policy;
- that the judgment is final according to the law of the state in which it was given;
- that the rights of the defendant have been respected;
- that the jurisdiction of the foreign courts was not based solely on the nationality of the plaintiff; and
- that a certified authentic copy of the judgment is provided.

Belgian courts may also re-examine the merits of the case albeit that such re-examination is rather exceptional.

Belgium has implemented a number of treaties on the *The Brussels* recognition and enforcement of foreign judgments including the *Convention* *Brussels Convention on Jurisdiction and the Enforcement of Judgments in Civil and Commercial Matters* signed in Brussels on 27 September 1968.

Apart from the rules on recognition and enforcement in Belgium *Registration of* there is no specific procedure for registration of foreign *foreign decisions* judgments. Foreign decisions cannot be registered.

Recognition of a foreign judgment will be refused when the *Refusing* judgment is contrary to public policy, ie contrary to a law or a *recognition* principle which relates to the basis of the state or to the essential basis of its economic or moral order.

Within the scope of the *1968 Brussels Convention*, the basis for refusing to recognise a foreign judgment on the grounds of public policy only operates as an exception. The mere fact that the foreign judgment does not contain any developed recitals is not sufficient to justify refusing recognition.

The mere fact that there is some difference between the law which would have been applied by a Belgian court and the law actually applied in the decision it is sought to have recognised is not sufficient to justify non-recognition.

Examples where recognition will not be granted are most common in the area of family law. Fraud, breach of a principle of international law or the fact that the foreign judgment contradicts a decision of a Belgian court on the same matter between the same parties can also be invoked as a basis for refusing to grant recognition.

Appeals

Appeals against registration of a foreign judgment must be lodged before the Court of Appeal within one month after the decision given at first instance has been served.

BIBLIOGRAPHY

Cambier, C., *Droit Judiciaire Civil*, Larcier, Brussels, 1974

Fettwies, A., *Manuel de Procédure Civile*, 1985

Moureau, S., en Lagasse, J.P., *La Cour d'Arbitrage, Jurisdiction Constitutionelle* (The Arbitration Court; Constitutional Jurisdiction) Larcier, Brussels, 1984

Rigeaux, F., *La nature du contrôle de la Cour de Cassation*, Bruylant, Brussels, 1966

Rouard, P., *Traité élémentaire de droit judiciaire privé*, Bruylant, Brussels, 1979

Constitutional Law

Delpérée, F., *Droit constitutionnel, Tome I - Les données constitutionnelles*, Larcier, Brussels, 1987 (2nd edn); *Tome II - Le Système constitutionnel - Livre Ier. Les pouvoirs*, Larcier, Brussels, 1986; *Livre II. Les fonctions*, Larcier, Brussels, 1988.

Mast, A., Dujardin, J., *Overzicht van het Belgisch grondwettelijk recht*, Story-Scientia, Brussels, 1987, (9th edn)

Velu, J., *Droit public, Tome premier - Le statut des gouvernants (I)*, Bruylant, Brussels, 1986

Administrative Law

Dembour, J., *Droit administratif*, (3rd edn), M. Nijhoff, La Haye, 1978

Flamme, M.A., *Droit administratif* (4 tomes), Bruxelles, Presses universitaires de Bruxelles, 1988, 1989, 1981 and 1982

Mast, A., Alen, A., Dujardin, J., *Précis de droit administratif belge*, Story-Scientia, Brussels, 1989

Sources of Law

Bossuyt, M.J., *The Direct Applicability of International Instruments on Human Rights (with special reference to Belgian and U.S. Law)*

L'effet direct en droit belge des traités internationaux en général et des instruments internationaux relatifs aux droits de l'homme en particulier, Ed. Bruylant, 1981, 55 and 79.

Velu, J., *Les effets directs des instruments internationaux en matière de droits de l'homme*

DENMARK

Christian Emmeluth
Michael Rekling
Koch-Nielsen & Grønborg
Copenhagen and London

CONTENTS

CHAPTER 1 : SOURCES OF LAW

Denmark has a unitary structure of government. Laws are enacted by the Danish Parliament ("*Folketing*") which has 179 members. Even though the *Constitution* provides that the municipalities ("*Kommuner*") are self-governing, these bodies do not have any legislative competence. *Unitary v federal system*

The principal source of law is the *Danish Constitution of 1953* ("*Grundloven*"). All other codes passed by the Parliament must be in accordance with the *Constitution*. The other most important sources of law are the *Codes of Procedure* ("*Retsplejeloven*"), the *Penal Code* ("*Straffeloven*"), the *Bankruptcy Code* ("*Konkursloven*"), the *Purchase and Sales Code* ("*Købeloven*"), the *Code on Agreements* ("*Aftaleloven*"), various *Tax Laws* ("*Skattelove*"), and the *Family and Inheritance Law* ("*Familie-og Arveret*"). *Principal sources of law*

National law can be relied on by foreigners and is applied equally to foreigners as to nationals. *Application of national law to foreigners*

The Danish legal system is a dualist system requiring international law to be incorporated into Danish law before it may be applied by the courts. *Monist v dualist system*

The EC Treaties were incorporated into Danish law by various laws. EC directives are implemented by Acts passed by the Danish Parliament. Where Community law is applicable directly from the original texts, these do not need to be ratified by Parliament. The courts fully accept, adopt and implement the principles of Community law. *Application of EC law*

Foreign law will generally only be applied by the Danish courts if it is invoked by one of the parties. There is no legal presumption that foreign law is the same as national law. Foreign law questions are treated as questions of law. The courts often have a problem in obtaining clear and precise evidence on the status of a foreign law. That law may be proved by an expert witness or by a statement from a party competent to give evidence on a specific law. The foreign law will often have to be translated into Danish. *Proving foreign law*

The *European Convention on Human Rights* has not been incorporated into Danish law and national courts cannot apply case law deriving from the *Convention* directly in the cases before them. *European Convention on Human Rights*

**Principles of
interpretation**

Danish courts apply a literal, as well as a purposive interpretation of Danish Acts of Parliament, seeking to reconcile the purpose of the legislation with the literal meaning of the words in the statute. Previous decisions of Danish courts have the effect of precedents, and the decisions of higher courts will usually bind lower courts, unless a case is clearly distinguishable.

**Interpretation of
the Constitution**

There are no authorised annotated texts of the *Constitution*.

CHAPTER 2 : FUNDAMENTAL RIGHTS

The *Danish Constitution* contains a list of fundamental rights *Basic freedoms* which are protected under the *Constitution*. According to *Article 71* personal freedom is inviolable. No Danish citizen can be detained on account of political or religious belief or because of origin. A person may only be detained as a result of some action on the part of that person which renders him liable to detention.

Anybody detained shall, within 24 hours, be brought before a judge who shall decide whether the individual can be released. A judge must make a final decision within three days. An appeal may be made against this decision.

According to *Article 72* the personal dwelling of an individual is *Personal property* inviolable. A court warrant is required for any search, seizure or investigation of letters and other papers and before any telephone-tapping may be undertaken.

Private ownership is protected under *Article 73*. Nobody can be *Private* required to dispose of his property unless it is required for the *ownership* benefit of the public. In such a case, it can only be compulsorily acquired according to law and if full compensation is paid.

Free enterprise is protected under *Article 74*. Limitations can only *Free enterprise* be imposed if required for the public good.

Freedom of speech is protected under *Article 77*. Censorship and *Freedom of* other restrictions cannot be introduced. The protection of *speech* freedom of speech does not prevent a claim for slander or libel or the making of a court order to restrain an unlawful publication.

Under *Article 78* citizens of Denmark have a right to associate for *Right of* any lawful purpose. The *Constitution* does not contain a definition *association and* of the term "lawful purpose". *assembly*

Article 79 gives Danish citizens the right to assemble without prior permission. This right does not prevent the police from requiring a prior notification of such an assembly.

The Courts of Appeal ("*Østre og Vestre Landsret*") and the *Judicial review of* Supreme Court ("*Højesteret*") are considered by legal authors to *government* be competent to rule on the legality/illegality of a law in *action* proceedings under an administrative action. The courts have so far never set aside any Danish law as being a violation of the constitutional rights contained in the *Danish Constitution*. Any citizen has a right to challenge any government action affecting him.

Constitutional Court   There is no separate Constitutional Court in Denmark.

CHAPTER 3 : JURISDICTION OF THE COURTS

Litigation should be initiated against an individual in the court in the area in which he is a resident (*Code of Legal Procedure : abbr. rpl, s 235*).
Actions against an individual

Cases concerning rights over land and property should be brought where that property is located (*rpl, s 241*).
Land or property actions

Cases concerning contractual obligations may be brought before the court in the area where the contract is to be performed (*rpl, s 242*). An action in tort may be brought in the court in the area where the accident took place (*rpl, s 243*). A consumer may sue a manufacturer in the court in the area where the consumer has his/her residence (*rpl, s 244*).
Actions in contract and tort

Litigation should be initiated against sole traders and partnerships in the court in the area where their business is conducted (*rpl, s 237*).
Actions against sole traders or partnerships

Companies, associations, private institutions and other legal entities should be sued in the court in the area in which they have their registered or main office. If the location of such an office cannot be determined, litigation may be initiated in the area where a board member is resident (*rpl, s 238*).
Actions against companies etc.

Litigation should be initiated against foreign individuals, companies, associations, private institutions or other associations in the court for the area in which the chattel or other goods of the defendant in question is located, provided that *Sections 237, 238.2, 241, 242, 243 and 245* do not apply (*rpl, s 246*). Cases involving the seizure of a ship must be brought before the court which granted the seizure.
Actions against foreigners

Danish citizens who are living abroad without having a permanent residence in Denmark and who are not subject to the jurisdiction of their country of residence (eg diplomats) should be sued in Copenhagen (*rpl, s 236*).
Actions against Danish citizens living abroad

Municipalities should be sued in the area where their headquarters are located (*rpl, s 239*). The State of Denmark should be sued in the municipality in which the particular branch of the government has its office (*rpl, s 240*).
Actions against public authorities

The parties may agree where the case shall be brought (*rpl, s 245*).

Grounds for challenging jurisdiction

The jurisdiction of a Danish court may be challenged on the grounds that there is a more appropriate forum, or that the parties had previously agreed upon arbitration or that the parties themselves had agreed upon another forum.

Universal jurisdiction

There is no rule of universal jurisdiction in Denmark for serious crimes except for the highjacking of aircraft and the criminal offences stipulated in *Section 8 of the Danish Penal Code*.

State immunity

There are no restrictions on bringing actions against the state or organs of the state acting in a purely commercial capacity.

CHAPTER 4 : ADMINISTRATION OF JUSTICE

The following diagram sets out the hierarchy of the courts in the Danish Legal system :   *Structure of the court system*

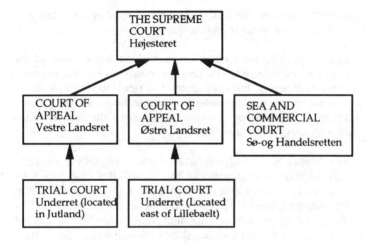

Litigation must be initiated at Trial Court level, unless otherwise provided in the *Code of Legal Procedure* (*rpl, s 224*). The Trial Court may, upon the request of one of the parties, transfer a case to the Court of Appeal for a trial at first instance (*rpl, s 226*) if :

- the outcome of the case is of significant general importance; the case is of extreme importance for one party; the matter is against a public authority or an institution; or, the case involves questions concerning EC law or foreign law; or

- the Court of Appeal certifies that it would be most advantageous for the case to be heard at the same time as a case already pending before the Court of Appeal;

- the claim exceeds an economic value of over DKK 500,000, in which case it must be referred to the Court of Appeal if one of the parties so requires. Such cases may be brought directly before the Court of Appeal;

- the matter involves a question of employment law and requires specialist knowledge, in which case it will be referred to the Sea and Commercial Court in Copenhagen (*rpl, s 226.3*). This court otherwise deals with maritime and commercial cases where the defendant resides in Greater Copenhagen.

Matrimonial matters cannot be brought before the Court of Appeal at first instance (*rpl, s 226.2*).

Rights of appeal

For the right of appeal see Chapter 6, post.

References under Article 177 of the EEC Treaty

A reference to the European Court of Justice (ECJ) under *Article 177 of the EEC Treaty* may be obtained by one of the parties to legal proceedings by making an application to the national court in question for the court to make a reference to the ECJ. The parties' application for a reference can be filed at any time during the legal proceedings, but is usually made when the parties first plead before the court.

In accordance with the *EEC Treaty* the Danish courts can also make a reference on their own initiative.

The party applying for a reference must draft the wording of the question to be referred. The national court makes the decision whether to accede to the application. If a reference is to be made, the precise wording of the reference is negotiated by the parties, and if they cannot agree, the court will make a decision as to the precise wording of the question.

In its reference to the ECJ, the national court will set out the facts, the claims and the arguments of the parties. If a case has been started in a Trial Court and has then been appealed to the Court of Appeal, the Court of Appeal is considered under *Article 177(3)*, as the court against whose judgment there is no further appeal, even though in some exceptional cases which have been started in a Trial Court leave can be obtained to take an appeal to the Supreme Court.

The Supreme Court is always regarded as a court against whose judgment there is no further appeal.

A decision of a first instance court, whose final judgment can be appealed (the Trial Court or the Court of Appeal in first instance), to make a reference or not can be appealed to the higher court (the Court of Appeal or the Supreme Court).

Apart from the requirements of the *EEC Treaty*, the Danish national courts have not laid down any specific requirements to be met before an *Article 177* reference can be made.

CHAPTER 5 : STRUCTURE OF THE LEGAL PROFESSION

The Danish legal profession is a one tier professional body. The *Structure* UK distinction between barristers and solicitors does not exist nor does the civil law distinction between advocates and notaries. The professional title of a Danish lawyer is *"advokat"*. Other professional groups, such as accountants, and banks, do provide legal advice, but lawyers (*advokater*) have the sole right to represent a party before the courts (*rpl, s 131*).

There is no special group of lawyers who specialise in appearing before the courts, but lawyers may notify the court that they are willing to undertake trial work on legal aid.

All lawyers admitted to the Danish bar have the right to represent *Professional* clients before the lower courts. A Danish lawyer is admitted to the *rights of audience* bar after having worked as a trainee for three years with a fully qualified lawyer. When admitted to the bar the lawyer is entitled to appear before the Trial Courts (*rpl, s 132*).

A lawyer will be admitted to the Courts of Appeal if he/she passes a special test (*rpl, s 133*). The test consists of arguing two cases before the Courts of Appeal which then decide whether the lawyer has passed the test and is competent to appear before the Court of Appeal (*rpl, s 133*).

Having been admitted to the Courts of Appeal for five years, a lawyer may apply to the Supreme Court for admission. Admission is usually granted if the lawyer has during the five year period argued cases before the Courts of Appeal on a regular basis and is of good standing (*rpl, s 134*).

Lawyers may conduct their business as sole practitioners, as *Legal practices* partners in a partnership or they may incorporate their practices (*rpl, s 124*). Danish lawyers are not entitled to enter into business relationships with foreign lawyers. They are, therefore, not permitted to enter into partnerships with foreign lawyers or employ or be employed by them. There are no territorial restrictions on partnership practice within Denmark.

There is no restriction on the number of branch offices which a *Branch offices* Danish lawyer may set up within Denmark or within the European Community.

The Danish Bar Association has published recommended scales *Fees* of fees for certain services. These fees apply in litigation, matters involving preliminary remedies, collection of debts, administration of estates of deceased persons, and bankrupt estates, the conveyancing of land, transfer of businesses and the administration of individuals' assets.

These fee scales are publicly available and a lawyer is only entitled to derogate from them if it is deemed appropriate, ie in a case of particular difficulty.

In other matters there are no guidelines, but under the *Code of Legal Procedure* a lawyer may not charge a higher remuneration for his work than can be considered reasonable (*rpl, s 126.2*).

A client who finds that a lawyer has charged an unreasonably high fee may complain to a special body within the Bar Association ("*Kredsbestyrelsen*"). The dispute is decided by this body. An appeal may be made to another body of members of the Bar Association ("*Advokatnævnet*") (*rpl, s 146*).

These bodies decide the matter. If the parties still find the decision unacceptable the matter may be brought before the Courts of Appeal (*rpl, s 147*).

All fees carry a value added tax presently at the rate of 25%.

Professional conduct

The *Code of Legal Procedure* requires every lawyer to be a member of the Danish Bar Association (*rpl, s 143*). Complaints concerning the conduct of a lawyer are submitted to the *Advokatnævnet* (*rpl, s 147.b*). If the *Advokatnævnet* finds that a lawyer has violated his duties according to the law or is in breach of any regulations issued under the law, the lawyer may be given a warning or ordered to pay a fine of up to DKK 200,000. If a lawyer has violated his duties as a lawyer in such a way that there is reason to believe that he will not conduct his business in a reasonable manner in the future the *Advokatnævnet* may withdraw his authorisation to practise as a lawyer. Such a withdrawal can be made for a period of between six months and five years or indefinitely until further notice.

Any decisions taken by *Advokatnævnet* in disciplinary proceedings can be taken by the lawyer on appeal to the Courts of Appeal (*rpl, s 147.d*).

Foreign clients have the right to use this complaints procedure.

Professional indemnity insurance is compulsory. Lawyers must take out insurance for a minimum of DKK 993,000. The amount is adjusted annually in accordance with a special index.

Practice by foreign lawyers

According to *Regulation No 94 of 15 March 1979*, as subsequently amended, lawyers who are established in another EC Member State can provide services in Denmark and appear before Danish courts together with a Danish lawyer. The Regulation lists which foreign lawyers are competent to act in Denmark.

Business conducted by the foreign lawyers shall comply with *Articles 3 and 4 of Council Directive (EEC) 77/249*[1].

The Danish authorities and courts can demand proof that a foreign lawyer has the right to act as a lawyer in his home country. A foreign lawyer can only appear before a Danish court together with a Danish lawyer who is entitled to appear before that particular court.

Lawyers from other parts of the world are not at present entitled to practise in Denmark. Foreign lawyers are not at present permitted to establish offices in Denmark.

Instructing lawyers

Clients are able to instruct a lawyer directly to provide legal services. In criminal matters the court may instruct a lawyer to provide certain services, and lawyers may notify the court that they are willing to undertake legal aid work.

Directory of legal services

The Danish Bar Association has published a directory of the services provided by the individual firms in Denmark. The directory carries the title "*Advokatfirmaer i Danmark*".

1.　　Council Directive (EEC) 77/249 (OJ L78 26.3.77 p17).

CHAPTER 6 : CIVIL PROCEDURE

Court proceedings are started when a writ of summons including a complaint ("*stævning*") is filed with the competent court. The writ of summons is served on the defendant, together with a form explaining to the defendant the necessary steps he must take if he wishes to defend himself.

Structure of court proceedings

Next, the court gives notice to the parties to attend a preliminary meeting at the court, usually about two weeks after service of the summons. At this meeting the defendant must submit any documents on which he will base his defence. If the case is pending before the Courts of Appeal, the defendant must file an answer ("*svarskrift*") to the complaint, at the latest, at the first meeting.

In a case pending before the Courts of Appeal the plaintiff will also file a reply ("*replik*") and the defendant a rejoinder ("*duplik*").

The court will thereafter hear the case including any witnesses and give its judgment.

Unless otherwise provided for in the *Code of Legal Procedure*, all civil matters are heard in the first instance by the Trial Court which has jurisdiction over the defendant.

The Trial Court may upon application of one of the parties transfer a matter to the Courts of Appeal on the grounds set out in Chapter 4.

Division of competences

Specific provisions require that the following matters must always be brought before the Courts of Appeal :
- appeals against decisions rendered under the *Social Security Act* by the Social Appeal Board;
- decisions rendered by the Patent Appeal Board, the Monopoly Appeals Board, Customs Appeal Board, the VAT Appeal Board and the Tax Court. Certain matters concerning the registration of ships, and the legal title over land and property must be brought before the Courts of Appeal in the first instance.

If the parties have agreed that a dispute shall be settled by arbitration, such an agreement will usually be upheld by the ordinary courts. Any writ of summons filed by a plaintiff in such a matter will be dismissed by the court if disputed by the defendant.

Arbitration

Detailed provisions setting out the competence of the courts are contained in *Chapter 21 of the Code of Legal Procedure.*

Parties to the proceedings

The *Code of Legal Procedure* does not explicitly list which parties are able to bring proceedings, but stipulates that the issue must be determined according to the specific law in question (*rpl, s 255*). The decision whether individuals, companies, partnerships, associations of trade unions or collective interest groups may bring proceedings is thus decided on a case-to-case basis. Generally, individuals, companies registered with the Commercial and Companies Agency (equivalent to the UK Companies Registry), and partnerships may be a party to a law suit. As to the ability of an association to act as a party to legal proceedings, the courts have taken the view that in general an association cannot be party to legal proceedings if the association consists of an unknown number of members and has a very loose structure. If there are no specific individuals or institutions which can act on its behalf such an association cannot be a party to legal proceedings.

Government actions

The government has entered into an agreement with one law firm in Denmark to act on its behalf in legal matters. This firm initiates and defends any actions on behalf of the government.

Joinder of claims

A plaintiff may make several claims against a defendant, if :
- all the claims are subject to the general jurisdiction of the Danish courts; or
- the court in question has jurisdiction in respect of one of the claims; or
- the court is competent to deal with one of the claims and all claims can be dealt with under the same procedural rules (*rpl, s 249*).

Counterclaims

A defendant may make a counterclaim, provided such a claim can be dealt with under the same procedural rules as the plaintiff's claim. The counterclaim can only be heard at the same time as the claim if the counterclaim is subject to Danish jurisdiction or the claim is based on the same events as the plaintiff's claim.

Joinder of parties

Several parties may sue as plaintiffs or be sued as defendants in one action (*rpl, s 250*) if :
- all the claims are subject to the jurisdiction of the Danish courts; or
- the court before which the actions are brought has jurisdiction in respect of one of the claims; or
- the court has competence to deal with one of the claims; or
- all claims can be dealt with under the same procedural rules and none of the parties objects to the joining of the actions; or
- the claims have such a connection that they should be dealt with in single proceedings even though objections are raised by one of the parties (*rpl, s 252.2*).

Further, any parties to an action may raise a claim against a third party in the same action, if :
- the third party is subject to Danish jurisdiction; and
- the claim can be dealt with according to the same procedural rules as the original claims; and
- none of the other parties or the third party objects or the claim has such a connection with one of the other claims that it should be dealt with with that action disregarding any objections that have been made.

Third party proceedings

If objections are made to different claims or counterclaims (including third party proceedings) being heard together and are upheld by the court, the court will deal with the claims separately or transfer a claim to the court having jurisdiction in that particular case (*rpl, s 252.3*).

A court may, upon the application of an original party the the proceedings, dismiss a claim against a third party if the claim should have been brought into the action at an earlier stage (*rpl, s 252.5*).

A third party may become a party to existing legal proceedings (*rpl, s 251*) by submitting a writ of summons to the court if :
- the third party's claim is subject to Danish jurisdiction; and
- the claim can be dealt with according to the same procedural rules as the existing claims; and
- the third party is making a claim which depends on the outcome of the original action or the third party's claim has such a connection with the original claim that the claim should be dealt with in the same proceedings.

Such joinder must not cause unreasonable disadvantage to the original parties. If the court would not have been competent to deal with the matter if an independent action had been brought, the court may refer the claim to a court having such jurisdiction. The court may upon application from the original parties dismiss a claim by a third party if such a claim should have been made at an earlier stage.

A third party with a valid legal interest in the outcome of the matter may intervene in the proceedings to support one of the parties (*rpl, s 252*). A public agency has the same right. An application to intervene should be submitted in writing to the court or, with the court's permission, be made orally at a (preliminary) hearing. The court determines in what manner the intervening party is entitled to participate in the matter. An intervening party may be awarded costs.

A court may stay the litigation if it finds such a course to be reasonable. It will normally do so in order to await the outcome of other court or administrative proceedings which may influence the proceedings in question. The court shall notify all parties concerning the stay which is, thus, a matter for the discretion of the court (*rpl, s 345*).

Stay of proceedings

Class or representative actions

Only in very limited circumstances may a class or representative action be brought. Where a public agency has negotiated with an ad hoc group or association, the courts have accepted that such an association may be a party to court proceedings. However, if the class or association consists of an indefinable and uncertain number of persons without any bye-laws or economic liability for its members, the court will usually not accept such an entity as a class entitled to appear as a party to a case.

Limitation of actions

The general limitation period is twenty years and is laid down by statute. However, a limitation period of five years is provided for the most common claims under *Act No. 274 of 22 December 1908* (*"Lov om Forældelse"*). The two limitation periods run simultaneously and a claim needs only to be barred under one Act to be rendered ineffective. The most important claims under the *1908 Act* are : claims based on a dispute concerning the sale and purchase of goods and chattels which cannot be considered as fixtures and fittings to property; the leasing of property and chattels; the transportation of goods and persons; personal services; certain taxes on real property; claims for payment of interest; pensions; alimony and similar regular payments which are not a repayment of a principal or of a loan; taxes and other public dues; claims for damages for a tortious act and claims for repayment of unjust enrichment.

The five year limitation period does not apply if the claim is recognised by the debtor in writing, or is part of a settlement or is in a settlement of a court judgment which has determined the claim.

The five year statute of limitation runs from the time the cause of action arose and can only be halted by starting a legal action. A reminder to the debtor, however, is sufficient to stop the twenty year period of limitation from running.

In the case of a claim for debt where the creditor is not aware of the true facts and does not know where the debtor resides, the statute of limitation runs from the time when the creditor should have been in a position to make his claim.

Starting an action

The *Code of Legal Procedure* lays down the requirements as to the contents of the writ of summons (*rpl, s 348*).

Writ of summons

The writ of summons shall contain the following information :

- the name and address of the plaintiff and defendant;
- a postal address to which any notices to the plaintiff can be forwarded;
- the name of the court at which the writ is filed;
- the plaintiff's claim;
- a short statement of the factual grounds on which the claim is based; and
- a list of documents and any other evidence which the plaintiff intends to rely on.

The writ of summons must be submitted in one original version with three copies together with one copy of all documents. The writ of summons and the copies must be in A4 format.

Proceedings before various complaints tribunals are started by submitting a written complaint concerning the decision taken by a lower ranking public authority. No special documents or forms are required.

For the purpose of the running of time limits/limitation periods the various actions/proceedings are deemed to have been started when the complaint or writ of summons has been filed with the competent court.

A minimum fee of DKK 500 shall be paid. When the claim exceeds DKK 6,000 an additional fee of 1% of the amount in excess of DKK 6,000 is payable. At the time the case is heard by the court an additional fee of one fifth of the fee originally paid becomes due. A fee of DKK 250-500 is usually payable at the time when any complaints are lodged before the the Tribunal.

The Code of Legal Procedure stipulates three different ways in which service of proceedings can be effected. The relevant documents may be forwarded to the person in question requesting written confirmation of receipt (*rpl, s 155*); or they may be forwarded by registered mail so that the postal service can give evidence of delivery; or the documents may be served by a process server from the court. Service is deemed effective on the date the recipient acknowledges receipt of the document or, if the receipt is not dated, the date of the postmark when the receipt is returned. *Service of proceedings*

The general rule is that documents must be formally served (*rpl, s 157*). However, if personal service is not possible service may be acceptable if effected at the residence of the person in question, or where the person works, or where he conducts his personal business. Where such service appears impossible and it is not possible to serve the party to the proceeding abroad, notice may be served by publishing it in the Legal Gazette ("*Statstidende*") (*rpl, s 158*).

Companies, partnerships and associations must be served at the place where the company, institution, association or partnership has its head office or where one of the members of the board has his residence.

Service of proceedings on parties outside Denmark may be carried out by one of the following methods : *Service of proceedings outside the jurisdiction*
- documents may be forwarded to the Danish Ministry of Justice, who will see that the documents are served according to the rules of the foreign jurisdiction;
- the documents may be forwarded to the Danish Embassy or the Danish Consulate in the country in question and may be served through these entities;

- service may take place by ordinary mail;
- service may be made according to the *Hague Convention of 15 November 1965* concerning service of notices abroad in matters concerning civil or commercial questions;
- notification concerning the enforcement of a foreign judgment under the *Brussels Convention on Jurisdiction and Enforcement of Judgments in Civil and Commercial Matters 1968* shall be made in accordance with the rules described above concerning service of Danish legal documents (*Section 6 of Act No 325 of 4 June 1986 on the Brussels Convention*).

Execution of judgments

The bailiff decides the time and place for execution and must notify the party applying for execution (*rpl, s 491*). The debtor is also to be notified (*rpl, s 493*). An appeal from the bailiff's decision must be made within one month after the decision by the bailiff was given. Execution can be levied even if an appeal against the bailiff's decision is pending.

Judgment in default

If the proceedings have been duly served, and the defendant does not appear before the court in accordance with the notice accompanying service, the judge will enter a judgment in default on the plaintiff's claim provided that the claim is supported by the factual description in the writ and by the other information submitted to the court (*rpl, s 354.3*). If the information is unclear or the claim can be seen to be incorrect in a significant respect, the court will dismiss the claim.

Security for costs

A claim for security for costs can only be made if the plaintiff is a non-resident. Such an application must be made on the first day the parties appear before the court (*rpl, s 323*).

Summary judgment

The concept of summary judgment does not exist as such in Danish legal procedure.

Striking out a claim

The parties are free to withdraw a claim at any time. The court also has a general discretion to decide that the preparation or the actual hearing shall be limited to a part of the claim or, if the matter concerns several claims or issues, to one of these (*rpl, s 253*). The Act does not stipulate on what grounds such a decision must be made.

A court may, further, come to a decision on a part of the claim or one of several claims.

Execution of interim judgments

Separate decisions on counterclaims or claims against which counterclaims have been raised can only be executed if it is explicitly stated in the decision that they may be executed with or against security. An appeal against the court's decision concerning execution of any interim decision can only be made in any appeal against the final decision in the case, unless the decision can be executed or the decision concerns an issue of formality or the superior court has permitted the decision to be brought before the superior court. These provisions may apply where issues under the statute of limitation or on questions involving EC matters are involved.

The court may at any time request the parties to submit information which may lead to the case being dismissed or the case being transferred to another court (*rpl, s 337*). If a court decides to dismiss a case because of the information submitted at its request, an appeal may be made to a superior court.

A plaintiff is required to list in the writ of summons and complaint the documents and other evidence that he intends to rely on in support of his claim (*rpl, s 348*). Similar requirements apply to any defence in answer (*rpl, ss 348-351*). These requirements apply to all civil cases. In matters pending before a Trial Court, the defendant may give his answer orally. *Discovery of documents*

Chapter 29 of the Act sets out under what conditions a party is required to disclose documents. The court can, at the request of one of the parties, order the other party to disclose documents which are in his possession (*rpl, s 298*). If a party does not disclose such documents the court may draw conclusions adverse to that party and find that the factual situation is as claimed by the party requiring the documents to be disclosed. A party cannot be required to disclose documents if it cannot be compelled to appear as a witness. *Disclosure of documents*

Documents which may support an opponent's case may thus have to be disclosed. The documents are disclosed to the other party and the court. Generally, a lawyer is not required to disclose the documents received from a client which are privileged. However, the court may direct the lawyer to disclose such documents unless the lawyer can be excused as a witness (*rpl, s 299*).

Discussions/documents passing between opposing sides are not privileged. Statements, recommendations or proposals made during without prejudice negotiations cannot be made public in support of a claim, but there is no procedure actually preventing a *Evidence*

party from mentioning the fact that such negotiations have taken place.

The gathering of evidence is in principle to be carried out by the parties and not by the court, but the court may request a party to disclose specific documents, experts' reports or other evidence. The documentary evidence and the oral evidence of witnesses is presented before the Trial Court and the Courts of Appeal during the hearing of the case (*rpl, s 340*). In the case of the Supreme Court, the evidence is usually presented in writing, and the hearing of any witnesses is carried out before a Trial Court, which then submits a written statement of the outcome of the hearing to the Supreme Court (*rpl, s 340.3*). The Supreme Court may in exceptional circumstances hear oral evidence itself.

A party is required to notify the other side about the evidence he intends to present to the court one week before the case is to be heard (*rpl, s 340.2*).

Prior to this date a party will have had the opportunity to request the other side to disclose evidence, as mentioned above. In such circumstances the court can at the request of the other party require the production of such documents or draw inferences against the party in default.

Admissibility of evidence

The Code of Legal Procedure contains provisions concerning challenges to the admissibility of any evidence before trial (*rpl, s 341*). The court is entitled to refuse to admit evidence which is of no importance or relevance to the case.

Hearsay evidence

There are no rules governing hearsay evidence.

Collection of evidence abroad

On the application of one of the parties evidence may be taken abroad. The court can require the party applying for the evidence to be taken to give security for the costs of the hearing. The application shall be made in accordance with the applicable Conventions (*rpl, s 342*). The *Hague Conventions of 1905 and 1954* on the collection of evidence abroad are part of national law.

Witnesses

As a general rule, anyone may be called or be compelled to appear as a witness before the courts (*rpl, s 168*). The *Code of Legal Procedure* contains several exceptions to the general rule :

-    Civil servants may not, without permission from their particular agency, appear as a witness and give evidence about the agency's activities (*rpl, s 169*).
-    Members of the Danish Parliament must obtain permission from the President of the Parliament and the particular Minister in question (*rpl, s 169*).

If the government agency or the President of the Parliament refuses to give such permission the court can request the particular agency or the chairman to explain the reasons for their refusal. If the court decides that the evidence is important to the case the individual can be required to appear as a witness.

However, this rule does not apply if the refusal is based on reasons concerning national security or relations with other countries.

Priests of the State Church and recognised religious societies may refuse to disclose documents or appear as witnesses on grounds of privilege (*rpl, s 170*). However, doctors and lawyers, except for defence counsel, may be required by the court to appear if the evidence is of significant importance for the outcome of the case.

Members of the family of a party are not normally required to appear as witnesses in a case involving another member of the family. However, the court may direct a member of a family to appear as a witness if the evidence is important to the outcome of the case, and the case is of sufficient importance to justify a requirement that the family member should give evidence (*rpl, s 171*).

A third party may refuse to appear as a witness on the grounds stipulated above. The court shall explain to a witness the grounds on which he/she may be exempted from giving evidence.

Witnesses are summoned in writing to appear before the court. The summons shall contain the following information :
- the identity of the witness;
- the purpose of the summons;
- the court where the proceedings are taking place;
- the time of the proceedings;
- information about the notice which the witness must be given; and
- information about the consequences of failing to appear (*rpl, s 175*).

A party may be privileged from appearing as a witness if he would be subject to the risk of criminal prosecution or loss of welfare, if his family would risk criminal prosecution or loss of welfare or the witness would inflict on himself or his family substantial damage (*rpl, s 171*).

The court may require a party to answer specific questions if his evidence is important to the outcome of the case and the court is justified in compelling him to answer. However, such an order cannot be made if the witness would risk criminal prosecution or loss of welfare (*rpl, s 171.3*).

If a witness does not appear, the witness may be fined and may be arrested and brought to court by the police, and may also be required to pay any costs which result from their failing to appear. The fine may be a daily amount for up to a period of six months, or until the person appears before the court (*rpl, s 178*).

Appointment of expert assessors

In civil cases a party may apply to the court for it to appoint an expert assessor. Generally, an assessor does not need any particular qualifications, but must be of good standing. However, expert assessors are available in certain specialised cases and, if particular skills are required, only experts qualified in the particular field should be appointed (*rpl, s 199.2*). Each party may recommend a particular expert assessor, but the court is not bound by such recommendations. The court is required before appointing an expert assessor to give the parties an opportunity to submit any objections which they may have towards the person the court is considering appointing. If the objections are upheld by the court there is no right of appeal. However, if the court does not uphold the objection and confirms the appointment, an appeal may be made.

Experts' reports

As a general rule, a party is required to inform the other party of any evidence it will rely on at trial seven days before the trial. An expert's report obtained by one of the parties will not be considered on its own as compelling evidence by a court because the other party will not have had the opportunity to submit questions to the expert.

Final review before trial

Under *rpl, s 355*, a court may summon the parties to a special meeting to review the case before the actual court proceedings start. Any documents which a party intends to present to the court in evidence shall be submitted to the court and to the opposing parties at least one week before this meeting. The purpose of the meeting is to clarify the parties' understanding of the facts and the legal issues and to establish whether there are certain factual or legal questions which are not disputed, and which facts the parties intend to prove. The parties are required to inform the court how such evidence will be given

These meetings will usually take place in cases before the Trial Courts and the Courts of Appeal. The court has a discretion as to whether to call such a meeting and the court may call such a meeting on its own initiative if one has not already been requested by the parties.

Representation

A party is entitled to appear before the court on his own or be represented by his lawyer (*rpl, s 259*). Lawyers in Denmark have a monopoly on the right to act as agents on behalf of clients. A party is not required to engage a lawyer unless so directed by the court (*rpl, s 259.2*). Corporations do not usually represent themselves.

Before the various tribunals, anybody may represent a claimant.

The presentation of evidence, and the arguments are made orally before the court (*rpl, s 365*). This applies to all courts. In hearings before Tribunals the presentation of arguments may be by written pleadings or oral arguments or a mixture of both.

There is no time limit for oral argument.

The course of the hearing

The course of a normal hearing is as follows : the plaintiff outlines the facts of the case, and the plaintiff's and the defendant's witnesses are heard. The plaintiff then presents his legal argument and the defendant presents his legal argument. The plaintiff has a right of reply, and the defendant has the final say (*rpl, s 365.2*).

Examination and cross-examination of witnesses

The rules provide that a witness shall be questioned in such a manner that clear and true answers to the questions are obtained. The witness shall to the greatest possible extent be entitled to answer the questions without being interrupted. The court decides whether the witness is entitled to use any notes or other documents which the witness has brought into court (*rpl, s 184*). The court may intervene if the questioning is conducted in an improper manner, and the court may ask questions itself if the court finds such a step to be necessary. The judge may not only ask the witness questions, but may also visit the locus in quo. However, the court will not of its own initiative call for new evidence.

The judgment must set out the party's claim, a review of the facts, *Judgment*
the arguments presented by the parties, and, if required, any
statements made by the parties and their witnesses and those
factual and legal circumstances which the court finds important
in determining the matter (*rpl, s 366a*). The *Code of Legal
Procedure* does not contain any time limit within which a
judgment must be given except in criminal cases where a
judgment must be given, at the latest, within a week after the
conclusion of the hearing of the matter. Dissenting opinions can
be given.

Orders for costs may be made by the ordinary courts, but not by a *Costs*
tribunal. The general rule is that costs are awarded by the court
(*rpl, s 311*). The losing party is normally required to compensate
the successful party for any costs incurred at the trial, unless the
court finds that there are exceptional reasons to deviate from this
rule. This may be the case if the successful party is to blame for
certain acts carried out during or before trial. The losing party will
not be asked to pay any costs which cannot be considered as
necessary expenditure in the conduct of the litigation. The court
determines in its own discretion what expenses are necessary.
The court fixes a lump sum to be paid by way of costs. A party's
legal representative may be responsible for costs incurred by the
other side, if the legal representative has acted in a negligent
manner in the conduct of the case (*rpl, s 321*). It is difficult to say
what percentage in practice of a party's costs is recovered under
an order for costs.

The costs which are awarded normally include lawyers' fees and
the general costs of preparing the case.

A party may make a payment in part or in full satisfaction of a *Payment before*
claim. The effect of such a payment depends on the time when *trial*
such a payment is made. If the payment is made at an early stage
of the proceedings this will be taken into account by the court
when determining the question of costs. However, if the payment
is made after the case has been heard by the court, such a step
will have no effect on the award of costs.

Cases brought before the Trial Courts are usually heard within six *Length of*
months, whereas cases pending before the Courts of Appeal may *proceedings*
be heard after a period of 18 to 24 months. An appeal to the
Supreme Court takes on average one year. There is no real
difference in this respect between cases relating to contractual
disputes, commercial actions or personal injury.

Decisions of a Trial Court may be appealed to the Courts of *Appeals*
Appeal. Decisions of the Courts of Appeal may only be before the
Supreme Court appealed with leave of the Ministry of Justice.
Cases heard by the Courts of Appeal as a court of first instance
may be appealed to the Supreme Court as of right. The average
length of time between a judgment at first instance and appeal is
one to two years although cases can be heard more quickly if the

matter is urgent. The time for bringing an appeal is set out in the following table :

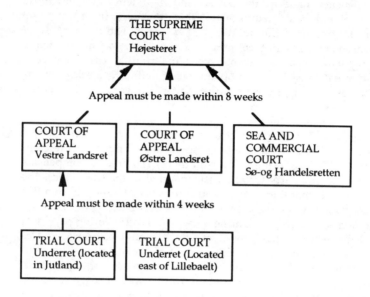

Legal aid

According to regulations in the *Code of Legal Procedure, Chapter 31*, a party can obtain free legal aid in the form of free legal assistance in connection with litigation. It can be granted upon the application of a party if this party :

- has essential reasons to litigate; and
- cannot without suffering substantial hardship afford to pay the costs of the case.

In order to fulfil the latter condition the applicant must come within certain income limits which are specified in a notice from the Ministry of Justice and which are adjusted annually on the basis of a price index. Applications for free legal assistance at first instance are considered by the State County.

For appeals, applications for free legal assistance are considered by the Ministry of Justice. However, free legal assistance only applies to civil cases and not to criminal cases.

A grant of free legal assistance means that the party concerned will not be required to pay to the state the court fee, that he will have an "*advokat*" assigned whose fee will be paid by the state and that he is exempt from any requirement to pay the other party's costs. The opposing party must pay costs as if his opponent were not granted free legal assistance, but in these cases costs must be paid to the state. Where a party is granted legal aid and is able to pay the costs of the case, at the end of the case the court can require it to repay to the state the costs of the free assistance.

It should be emphasised that sums paid as free legal assistance only include those costs that are not covered by a legal assistance insurance or any other kind of insurance.

There is a parallel system of public legal aid to the system of free legal assistance. Lawyers who are appointed by the state to appear for parties receiving free legal assistance in connection with litigation provide public legal aid except for the conduct of the case to persons whose economic conditions fall within those required to obtain free legal assistance.

Public legal aid covers counselling and making a few preliminary inquiries, helping with applications for free legal assistance, the drawing up of simple wills etc. There are a number of subjects not covered by public legal aid and, in general, it is not available for commercial matters.

There are several institutions dealing with legal aid which fall into two groups, the lawyers' advice services (under the legal advice service of the Danish Bar Association), and the private legal aid institutions. The lawyers' advice services offer an anonymous oral consultation for which in principle everyone is eligible irrespective of their financial circumstances. The consultation only covers a short - often introductory - oral opinion on simple matters. This consultation between the client and the lawyer may lead to the reference to another lawyer on a regular fee basis, but in such cases it may be possible to make use of the system of public legal aid carried out by lawyers or the system of free legal assistance. These lawyers do not receive payment from anyone - not even from the state - for their work with the lawyers' advice services.

In the private legal aid institutions the matter will regularly be more extensively dealt with. However, in the private legal aid institutions assistance is also free; for instance, law students give legal advice in these private legal aid institutions.

Finally it should be noted that legal expenses insurance is often a part of the ordinary family insurance which is taken out by Danish families.

CHAPTER 7 : CRIMINAL PROCEDURE

The majority of all criminal cases are instituted in a Trial Court - *Structure of court* depending on the character of the case, either with one legally *proceedings* qualified judge to try the case, or with one judge and two lay assessors. In more serious cases both the prosecution and the defence are free to appeal against the decision of the Trial Court to the Court of Appeal. In the Court of Appeal the case is tried either by three legally qualified judges or by three legally qualified judges and three lay judges. The decision of the Court of Appeal is usually final.

The public prosecution authority consists of three elements within *Prosecution* the Ministry of Justice : the Chief Constable, the Public Prosecutor and the Chief Public Prosecutor. The head of the Prosecution Service is the Chief Public Prosecutor who, in addition to being the head of the Prosecution, conducts criminal cases in the Supreme Court. Below him the Chief Public Prosecutor has a number of regional Public Prosecutors who head the Prosecution Service in their regions. In each region there are a number of police districts which are managed by a Chief Constable, who is both the head of the police in the district and of the local Prosecution Service. In criminal cases in the Trial Court the Chief Constable usually appears for the Prosecution. The regional Public Prosecutors appear for the Prosecution Service in the Court of Appeal either in cases appealed from the Trial Courts or in cases instituted in the Court of Appeal as the court of first instance.

Ordinarily all prosecutions are carried out by the state. However, *Private* in certain circumstances it is possible to bring private *prosecutions* prosecutions. This right is little used - probably less than once a year in the whole of Denmark. Defamation is regarded as a civil wrong not a criminal wrong and such cases are brought by individuals under the rules of the civil administration of justice.

There are different procedures for different classes of offences. *Offences* The least serious criminal cases, ie cases in which the sentence is a fine or simple detention (up to six months in a local prison) are prosecuted by the Chief Constable and the case is tried by a single judge sitting alone.

More serious criminal cases are prosecuted by the Public Prosecutor, and these cases are tried in the Trial Court by one judge and two lay assessors, who are ordinary citizens without legal qualifications. The judge and the two lay assessors have one vote each and participate equally in deciding the case.

The most serious cases, ie cases carrying a sentence of imprisonment for four years or more, are tried in the Court of Appeal as a court of first instance with a jury. The jurors alone decide the question of guilt. Their verdict of guilty, however, can be overruled by the judges. The result in such cases is that the accused is acquitted. The decision of the jurors to acquit the accused cannot be overruled by the judges. The three judges together with the twelve jurors fix the sentence. In these cases the decision of the Court of Appeal is final on the question of guilt or innocence which cannot be the subject of an appeal. However, the decision of the Court of Appeal in these cases on the question of sentence can be appealed to the Supreme Court.

Commencement of proceedings

A prosecution is commenced by a complaint to the police from the aggrieved person. The police will investigate the complaint. The police reject the complaint if they find that no criminal offence has taken place. If it is thought, however, that the prosecution stands a reasonable chance of success the police can - depending on the character of the case - decide either to prefer a charge itself or to recommend to the regional Public Prosecutor or the Chief Public Prosecutor that they prefer a charge. At all levels at which prosecutions can be initiated, a decision not to prefer a charge can be taken by the aggrieved person to the next level in the public prosecution authority. Thus, the regional Public Prosecutor's decision not to prefer a charge can be appealed to the Chief Public Prosecutor. Ultimately the Ministry of Justice makes the final decision whether or not to proceed with a prosecution.

In the most serious cases the defendant can be taken into custody while the case is being investiged and will remain in custody until the case is presented to a court. The decision to take the defendant into custody is taken by a judge and it is normally only done for special reasons, ie if there is a risk that the defendant will escape.

Information relating to the offence

Before the police interrogate a defendant he must be informed of the charge and that he is not obliged to speak. The defendant has a right to acquaint himself with the version of his evidence in the police report before answering any charge.

When and if an indictment has been prepared this must be served on him.

Pleas

At the beginning of the case the defendant is asked if he admits his guilt to the charge set out in the indictment. The defendant may plead guilty to less serious charges than set out in the indictment, for instance, violence of a less serious character than that charged.

The defendant is allowed to withdraw a confession during the hearing of the case.

Plea-bargaining

It is not possible for the defendant to negotiate with the prosecution in an attempt to to persuade the prosecution to accept a plea of guilty to a lesser charge on condition that the prosecution does not proceed with a more serious charge. However, the prosecution can at any stage of the case withdraw more serious charges and frequently does so after the accused has pleaded guilty to a number of charges or to charges of lesser offences which are nevertheless acceptable to the prosecution. In complex and serious cases it often happens that after questioning the defendant and assembling the evidence, but before the hearing itself, the prosecution elects not to proceed on some of the charges and concentrates on the counts on which it is most likely to obtain conviction.

As mentioned above a jury must participate in the more serious *Juries* cases.

Jurors are selected in the same way for both lay assessors and jurors. A committee set up by the local council compiles a so-called Jurors' Book comprising the persons who are considered qualified to act as jurors and lay assessors. Persons connected with the legal system, for instance lawyers and employees of the central administration, are not eligible to be entered on the lists. There are also other groups of persons who can ask to be excused. The jurors' books comprise a relatively large number of persons. The lists of lay assessors and lists of jurors (hereafter called the panels) are chosen by lot from among the persons listed in the Jurors' Books.

The task of acting as a juror or a lay assessor is a civic duty and cannot be refused. The persons on the panels are listed at random. When lay assessors or jurors are needed they are picked out from the panels in the order in which they are listed. The panels are valid for four years. Jurors and lay assessors cannot participate in a case in which they have a substantial interest in the outcome or have a close relationship with any of the parties involved. Both the prosecution and the defendant each have a right to challenge two jurors, or in cases of political violations four jurors. There is no similar right of challenge in the case of lay assessors.

In the Trial Court the defence can be conducted by any lawyer. *Conduct of the* Only those lawyers who have obtained the right to do so by *trial* proving their skills may plead before the Court of Appeal.

A criminal case is started by reading out the indictment, and the defendant is asked if he pleads guilty or not guilty. Then evidence is adduced first by counsel for the prosecution and then by counsel for the defendant. The court can at any time decide that particular evidence should be produced.

Oral submissions on behalf of the prosecution and defence are made when the evidence has been presented and are essential to the outcome of the case. If the defendant so requests he may comment on the case at the end.

Hearings in publiclin camera	Court hearings are usually held in public. However, in criminal cases in which the accused is under 18 years old the court can decide that the hearing shall be in camera. Whether the hearing is in open court or closed session the sentence itself must be pronounced in open court.

In special circumstances the court will also hear cases in closed session. It is possible in appropriate cases for the court to prohibit any publication of the proceedings or of the defendant's name.

Verdict

In cases tried by jury the question of guilt is decided by a statutory majority, ie at least 8 of the 12 jurors must vote for conviction. The questions to the jury must always be phrased so that the jurors can answer yes or no.

The jurors only have to answer the question of guilty or not guilty, plus additional questions, if any, concerning any aggravating circumstances or which may affect any remission of sentence.

In cases with lay assessors the judge participates equally with the two lay assessors in the trial of the case. Each of them has one vote. In these cases the case is discussed by the lay assessors and the judge in order to reach a decision. It is possible to find the defendant guilty of a count less serious than that charged provided that the defendant has had the opportunity to defend himself also against that charge.

In the Court of Appeal each of the three lay assessors and the three judges has one vote.

Sentencing

In cases with a jury both counsel for the prosecution and counsel for the defendant will, after a verdict of guilty, be allowed to make submissions as to what the appropriate sentence is. The judges and the jurors participate in the decision fixing sentence. Each of the twelve jurors has one vote whereas the three judges have four votes each so that the number of votes is equally distributed between the jurors and the judges. The sentence is decided by a simple majority, and where an equal number of votes are cast the sentence passed will be the one most favourable to the accused.

In cases with lay judges the sentence is decided at the same time as the question of conviction.

Persons who at the time of the crime were of unsound mind or suffering from diminished responsibility are not punished. In such cases the court will order a medical report. The medical report is not binding upon the court although the court will consider it with great care.

When fixing sentence the court must consider the gravity of the offence, information about the criminal's personal circumstances including his personal and social condition, his condition before and after the crime and his motives for the crime.

In *Article 84 of the Danish Criminal Code* there is a list of a number of grounds which serve to reduce the normal punishment. For example, if the criminal was under 18 or if the crime was executed in the heat of the moment, whether the accused was provoked by an unlawful assault or by insulting words. *Mitigating circumstances*

The *Danish Criminal Code* sets out the elements of each crime and the maximum sentence that can be passed for each. The maximum sentence is rarely given by the court. The court will have some regard to sentences given in comparable cases.

A defendant can be sentenced to imprisonment, simple detention, community service or a fine.

The age of criminal responsibility is 15, ie persons under 15 cannot be convicted of a crime. *Age of criminal responsibility*

For persons between 15 and 18 there are certain offences which carry lesser sentences than for persons over 18. Further, the age of the defendant is a relevant consideration in passing sentence, and those under 18 often receive lighter sentences than those who are older.

Simple detention involves the loss of liberty for up to six months. The sentence is served in local county jails and not in regional prisons. *Imprisonment*

Imprisonment can be for life or for a specified period, between a minimum of one month and a maximum of 16 years. A prison sentence can be unconditional or conditional. If a sentence is conditional the sentence is only made effective if the defendant within a certain period, which is normally two years, commits another criminal offence. Conditional imprisonment can be imposed without fixing the length of the sentence. A conditional sentence is often imposed on the first occasion on which a person commits an offence for which he is liable to a sentence of imprisonment.

The sentence of community service is used as an alternative to unconditional imprisonment. This sanction is normally used for offences which would have resulted in an immediate sentence of imprisonment of less than one year. The sentence of community service is only possible when the defendant agrees to accept this punishment. *Community service*

The period allowed for an appeal against decisions from the Trial Court and the Court of Appeal is 14 days, usually counted from the time sentence was imposed. Appeals to the Supreme Court by way of a second appeal require the special permission of the Ministry of Justice, and the application must normally be submitted within 14 days after judgment was given. *Appeals*

In exceptional situations an appeal may be heard even though it was lodged out of time.

The prosecution's appeal is made by giving notice of the appeal to the defendant, the defendant's appeal by submitting a written application of appeal to the Public Prosecutor or the Court of Appeal.

When an appeal has been argued before the court it is set down for judgment. The judgment is delivered as soon as the court has decided the question of guilt. The judgment is often delivered on the same day as the case has been heard or very soon thereafter.

Extradition

Denmark has entered into agreements with a number of states regarding extradition. In addition, various conventions regarding the enforcement of judgments have been concluded.

Time limits

A person arrested by the police must within 24 hours either be presented before a judge or set free.

The judge will decide whether an arrested person is to be taken into custody or set free. If the judge is not in a position to make a final decision he may remand a defendant three times for a maximum of 72 hours. At the end of this period he must decide whether the person should be taken into custody or released.

Detention pending trial

A defendant can be remanded in custody for any offence where he is liable to a sentence of imprisonment for 18 months or more and it is necessary for the defendant to be remanded because there is a real possibility that he would interfere with the investigation of the case, tamper with the evidence, seek to interfere with the evidence or otherwise come within statutory conditions that make him liable to be remanded in custody.

It is also possible to take a person into custody when it is strongly suspected that he has committed a serious crime for which he is liable to be sentenced to a term of imprisonment for 6 years or more, and the gravity of the offence indicates that the accused should not be released pending trial.

Further, a defendant can be remanded in custody where he is suspected of committing a crime of violence for which he is liable to be unconditionally sentenced to imprisonment for at least 60 days and the considerations of the administration of justice indicate that the accused should not be released pending trial.

A person may not be remanded in custody for more than four weeks at a time, but a period of four weeks can be prolonged by the addition of another four weeks.

A person may not be remanded in custody where the outcome of the case is expected to result in punishment in the form of a fine or simple detention or if the loss of liberty would be out of proportion to the disturbance custody would cause to the life of the accused, to the importance of the case and to the expected legal consequence if he is found guilty.

The *Code of Legal Procedure* provides that in situations where **Bail** custody pending trial is permitted so-called custody substitutes can be used instead. Bail is mentioned among these substitutes.

These substitutes can only be used if custody would have been permitted in the case in question, and if the accused agrees to the use of the substitutes. In practice bail is very rarely used.

CHAPTER 8 : REMEDIES

To obtain damages in tort, a plaintiff must be able to prove *Damages* negligence on the part of the defendant, actual causation and damage. The defendant may argue that the plaintiff did not take the necessary steps to mitigate his loss.

Damages in contract may be claimed if a contract is terminated without cause and an economic loss is suffered. Such damages may only be recovered in the ordinary courts. The concept of a jury in civil cases is unknown in Danish law. The award of damages is thus always the task of a judge.

Act No 599 of August 9 1986 (as subsequently amended) on damages (*"Erstatnings-ansvarsloven"*) sets out the basis for assessing damages. The Act stipulates how various claims are to be assessed if a defendant is held responsible for the personal injury suffered, and deals with the following type of claims :
- loss of wages,
- pain and suffering,
- injuries of a permanent nature,
- loss of support,
- damages to a spouse or co-habitant,
- loss of a provider for children.

The Act further lays down provisions concerning interest on damages and the effect of any insurance coverage, and sets fixed amounts of compensation for pain and suffering, and permanent injury and introduces a cap on the damages to be paid for the loss of capacity to work and for damages to a spouse or co-habitant.

The following amounts are payable :
- for pain and suffering DKK 160 for each day on which the injured has to stay in bed and DKK 60 per day until he has completely recovered;
- the maximum damages to be paid for permanent injury is DKK 2,565,000;
- for loss of income the maximum damages is DKK 449,000 per annum;
- damages to be paid to a spouse or co-habitant amounts to 30% of the damages which the deceased would have been entitled to;
- damages payable to children are equivalent to the child support which a child would have been entitled to under the matrimonial laws.

The amounts stipulated above are increased each year according to an index.

Damages may be claimed for a negligent violation of an individual's freedom, peace, honour or person under *Act No 599 of 9 August 1986*, as subsequently amended. Damages awarded by the courts would by international standards be considered as rather low.

Damages for breach of a contractual obligation will only be awarded if an economic loss can be proved by the plaintiff.

Setting aside contracts

Under *Section 36 of the Danish Act on Agreements*, a court may set aside an agreement in full or in part if it would be unreasonable or contrary to reasonable behaviour to enforce the contract. This applies to consumers as well as to commercial transactions. In deciding whether the agreement should be set aside in full or in part, the court is required to take into consideration the circumstances prevailing at the time when the agreement was signed and any subsequent events.

Penalty clauses

It is possible to seek an award of an agreed sum. However, it is possible to avoid paying a sum contractually agreed as representing an estimate of damages on the grounds that the sum is a penalty, if the case falls within the scope of *Section 36 of the Danish Act on Agreements*.

Specific performance

An order for specific performance of an obligation can be obtained if it is possible to have the specific performance carried out by the bailiff of the court.

Interest

Under *Act No 583 of 1 September 1986* ("*Renteloven*") interest is payable on a claim from the date the writ of summons was filed with the court. However, the Act provides that interest shall be paid from a due date if that date has been stipulated in the agreement between the parties. In the absence of a stipulated due date interest is payable a month after a claim for payment has been made where it was expressly stated in the claim that interest would be claimed according to the Act if payment were not made in time. The interest rate is that fixed by the National Bank plus 5%.

Winding-up of a company

A winding-up order will be granted if a company is insolvent when the order is filed with the Probate Court. A company is deemed insolvent under the *Bankruptcy Act* ("*Konkursloven*") if it cannot pay its creditors when their claims become due.

Arbitration

If the parties have agreed that any dispute between them shall be settled by arbitration the Danish courts will usually accept such an arbitration clause and dismiss any actions brought in the ordinary courts. A court is under a duty to try to obtain a settlement in the first instance after the matter has been heard (*rpl, s 268*). This may be attempted at an earlier stage in the proceedings.

CHAPTER 9 : MATRIMONIAL DISPUTES

Proceedings for divorce, custody and access are instituted at the Trial Court closest to the defendant's home. There are no specially assigned judges or specific courts dealing exclusively with family law cases. Lay judges do not hear family cases. *Jurisdiction*

Divorce cases and cases relating to custody and access can be agreed by the parties. If the parties are able to deal with these issues by consent, the case will not have to be tried by the courts, but the terms of the agreement must be approved by the State County. *Consensual proceedings*

Before divorce or separation can be granted by consent the couple must agree not only that they wish to be divorced or separated but also about the custody of the children (if any), contributions to support the other spouse, division of pension rights, which of them will take over the matrimonial home, and finally, whether one shall have a share of the other party's separate estate.

If the couple cannot reach agreement the case is heard by the court. The case must be instituted at the venue of the defendant, ie the party wanting separation or divorce must institute proceedings at the venue of the other spouse. Often the pleadings before the hearing are rather short as one party often has a clear legal claim for separation or divorce. The specific regulations for the conduct proceedings are set out in *Chapter 42 of the Code of Legal Procedure*. *Contested proceedings*

Cases of custody and access are more complicated. The essential question is what will be best for the child. This is a legal standard to be judged by the courts. In order to make the finding, the parents are questioned during the hearing.

Section 26 of the Act of Majority stipulates that if a child is more than 12 years old the child must be asked his/her view unless such a discussion would be harmful to the child or the decision is clear cut.

Custody and access

If a child is less than 12 years old the judge will decide whether and under what circumstances the child's view should be sought. For instance, the judge can decide that the opinion of the child should be obtained in the absence of the parents. Thereafter the court will decide which of the parents should be granted custody.

The authorities are anxious, if it is at all possible, to maintain the child's link with both parents and will give a right of access to the parent who is not granted custody. The right of access is granted following an application to the State County. However, if it is in the best interests of the child, the State County can refuse to grant a right of access.

It is important to note that the parents can make an agreement to the effect that the custody is transferred to one of them, but such an agreement must be approved by the State County.

As long as the parents are married they have joint custody of the children of the marriage. On separation or divorce it must be decided which of the parents shall be given custody unless this has been settled previously (*Act of Majority, s 11*).

If the parents agree, joint custody can continue after separation or divorce. This must be approved by the State County, and will be approved unless the agreement conflicts with what is best for the child.

If the parents cannot agree or the State County does not approve their agreement the question of custody is decided judicially. In such cases custody will be given to only one of the parents.

While a question of custody is pending a final decision, the court can decide to whom custody shall be given provisionally (*Act of Majority, s 18*). A provisional decision can be altered later.

Decisions relating to custody and access can be enforced by compulsory fine or by intermediate enforcement (*Administration of Justice Act, s 536*). The party wanting to enforce the custody or access decision can request assistance from the court. If necessary the court can obtain the assistance of the police to ensure that the decision is carried out.

Property issues   As far as rented property used as a joint residence is concerned, a spouse who pays rent has the right to dispose of this joint residence.

If both spouses are registered as owners or tenants of the joint residence both spouses can seek to recover possession with the assistance of the court. In these matters the law does not distinguish between married couples and co-habiting couples. During the marriage, one spouse cannot sell or mortgage the family house if it is jointly owned (*Marriage Act, s 18*). When the marriage comes to an end, the spouse who owns the matrimonial home is entitled to sole possession of it.

A spouse can always ask for an order for separation instead of divorce. The grounds for divorce mentioned below also apply to separation.

Divorce can be sued for in the following situations :

Under *Section 33 of the Marriage Act* in cases of adultery the other spouse can sue for a divorce, except where the adultery has been accepted or condoned or the spouse has otherwise

abandoned the right to sue for divorce. The right is normally considered abandoned if he/she continues to cohabit after having known about the adultery.

Further, proceedings must be instituted within six months from the time when the wronged spouse knew about the adultery.

A spouse also has a right to sue for a divorce if the other spouse has been maliciously violent to the former spouse or the children (*Marriage Act, s 34*). Proceedings must be instituted within one year from the time the spouse knew about the act and always within three years of when it happened.

The spouse also has a right to sue for a divorce if the other spouse commits bigamy (*Marriage Act, s 35*).

If the couple have lived apart for more than two years due to incompatibility this is also a ground for divorce (*Marriage Act, s 32*).

Finally, divorce can be obtained if the couple after six months of separation agree upon divorce. If they do not agree to divorce one of them can sue for a divorce after one year's separation (*Marriage Act, s 31*).

A spouse who cannot continue to cohabit can sue for a separation order (*Marriage Act, s29*). It is not necessary to give any specific reason for this, but the court demands that married life is actually terminated.

If the couple resume married life a separation order will lapse (*Marriage Act, s 30*).

In a marriage the regimes of joint property, separate property or a combination thereof apply.

Joint property is held in common, and when the estate comes to be divided it is divided on the basis of the principles set out below. Separate property is not included in the division, but is taken out in advance by the party to whom it belongs.

If not otherwise arranged, the couple will share joint property when they are married. By the terms of the marriage contract or by agreement during marriage it can be agreed that a part of or the whole of the assets shall be the separate property of one of the spouses.

Separate property can also be agreed in the event of divorce. Thus, it can be agreed that in the event of divorce or separation a division of assets shall be made as if separate property had been agreed for that part of the assets comprised in that arrangement. However, if there is a subsequent division of the assets due to the death of one of the spouses, division shall be made as if a complete joint property regime had existed during the marriage.

The division shall be made qualitatively as well as quantitatively. As regards the qualitative division the main rule is that the spouse who appears to be the owning spouse has the right to take out the asset in question.

As concerns quantitative division, this is made by a division of the assets to determine which assets and liabilities belong to each of the spouses. Half of the positive net property is then transferred to the other spouse.

In addition to these rules on division under *Section 56 of the Marriage Act*, one of the spouses may be granted a part of the separate property of the other spouse where the first spouse would be placed at an excessive economic disadvantage compared to the other spouse.

Further, the question of marital support by way of periodic payments must be determined. This is normally fixed by the State County and is based on the difference in incomes of the spouses. Unless there are special circumstances periodic payments will not be ordered for a period of more than ten years.

CHAPTER 10 : PROPERTY TRANSACTIONS

A conveyance is usually a two-step transaction. An estate agent will draft the initial document, which is binding upon the parties. This document is designated in Danish as "*slutseddel*" which may be translated as the bill of sale. It will be based on a standard form.

The document will set out the price, the date of transfer, the amount to be paid in cash, which is deposited with the agent and the seller's bank, and the amount to be paid by way of mortgage. Further, it will refer to any easements on the property. The purchaser may seek legal advice at this initial stage, but it is normal to obtain legal advice after the initial document has been signed and to ask the lawyer to prepare the deed of conveyance ("*skøde*"). This is the second stage of the conveyance.

Lawyers are authorised to draft deeds of conveyance, whereas real estate agents are specifically prohibited from doing the conveyancing.

The deed of conveyance is the document which sets out the final conditions for transfer. Usually there will only be minor alterations compared to the initial document. When the deed has been signed by both parties, it will be filed with the local municipality for registration for tax purposes and afterwards with the land registry, which is a department of the local Trial Court. Usually it takes from three to six weeks to have a deed registered.

When the deed has been registered and it is confirmed that no mortgages except the ones taken out by the purchaser himself or taken over as part of the sale are registered on the property, the lawyer will instruct the bank and the broker involved to release the purchase sum to the seller. Further, a completion statement will be made setting out expenses which may have been paid by the seller in advance and which the purchaser should refund, or vice versa.

CHAPTER 11 : RECOGNITION AND ENFORCEMENT OF FOREIGN JUDGMENTS

Under the *Code of Legal Procedure* the Minister of Justice can issue regulations concerning the recognition of foreign judgments.

The *1968 Brussels Convention* has been implemented in Denmark. A Convention made in 1977 between the Nordic countries concerning the recognition and execution of judgments in civil matters has also been signed and ratified. Further, a Convention was entered into with Germany in 1938 concerning the recognition of decisions rendered by German courts. This is still in force.

Relevant Conventions

Judgments rendered by a court in another EC country can be executed in Denmark by a Danish bailiff under *Act No 325 of 4 June 1986 ("Lov om EF-Domskonventioner m.v.")*. A request for execution is submitted to the bailiff in the municipality where the defendant has his residence. Together with the request for execution the following documents must be submitted :

Enforcement

- a transcript of the judgment certified by the court in question;
- evidence that the judgment can be executed in the country where it was made and that this has been served on the defendant;
- in the case of a default judgment, proof that a writ of summons and/or a similar document was properly served on the defaulting party.

The bailiff can demand a certified translation in Danish of the above-mentioned documents. If the party requesting enforcement has his permanent residence outside Denmark a person resident in Denmark must be nominated in the application as the person to whom any communications concerning the matter can be forwarded.

The bailiff decides whether to grant permission to enforce the judgment. The bailiff can only refuse to execute the decision on the grounds mentioned in *Articles 27-28 of the Convention* and *Article 2, subsection 2 of the Protocol* attached to it.

There is a similar procedure under the *Nordic Convention*.

Public policy   A Danish court will only refuse to recognise a foreign judgment on the ground that it is contrary to public policy if the foreign law on which it is based is contrary to Danish legal principles. A court will not set aside a foreign judgment on its own motion but only if the argument is raised by one of the parties. Only very few decisions have been made on this ground. The concept has been applied where a foreign government has within its own territory nationalised property or expropriated goods without giving due compensation. In these cases no compensation was ordered by the Danish courts and the Danish courts refused to recognise the nationalisation.

BIBLIOGRAPHY

Jacobsen, Lotte, *Danish Legal Bibliography*, the Royal Library, 1989

Møller, Jens/Spang-Hanssen, Aage/Pontoppidan, Niels/ Tronning, Christian, *Legal Formulary*, DJØF Publishing, 1989

Von Eyben, W.E./Gulmann, Claus/Nørgaard, Jørgen, *Karnov*, Karnov, 1992

Von Eyben, W.E./Vinding Kruse, A., *Preamble of the law of property, the Civil Law*, (26th edn), G.E.C. Gad, 1987

ENGLAND AND WALES

Maurice Sheridan
Barrister, 3 Gray's Inn Place
James Cameron
Barrister, 3 Gray's Inn Place

CONTENTS

CHAPTER 1 : SOURCES OF LAW

The United Kingdom has a unitary legislative system. There is
one legislature for the whole of the United Kingdom, but three
separate legal jurisdictions : England and Wales, Scotland and
Northern Ireland.

*Unitary v federal
system*

The United Kingdom does not have a written constitution. The
sources of law are what Parliament lays down in Acts of
Parliament and in subordinate legislation as interpreted by the
courts, and court decisions on areas where Parliament has not
acted - common law strictu sensu.

There is in practice little fundamental difference between
nationals and foreigners insofar as national law which can be
relied on and applied is concerned, although non-citizens are
subject to restrictions on being able to vote in elections and to
stand for Parliament. Directly effective rights under EC law are
available to all EC citizens to the extent to which they are entitled
to rely on the same. Non-EC citizens are, in principle, subject to
applicable laws without such distinction.

*Application of
national laws to
foreigners*

The United Kingdom is, in international law terms, a dualist
system. This requires international treaties to be incorporated
into UK law by an Act of Parliament (see *J. H. Rayner (Mincing
Lane) Ltd v Department of Trade and Industry [International Tin
Council Case]*[1]). This rule does not, however, apply to treaties
concerning the conduct or cession of war.

*Monist v dualist
system*

Rules of customary international law are regarded as part of
English law and are to be applied insofar as they are not
inconsistent with an Act of Parliament or any previous judicial
decisions of courts of final authority which are not based on
redundant principles of international law (see the *International
Tin Council Case*, above).

There is a presumption of interpretation that in incorporating an
international treaty the United Kingdom intends to fulfil its
international obligations, and the courts have referred to the text
of the relevant treaty itself to resolve ambiguities or to deal with a
matter which is obscure (see *Quazi v Quazi*[2]). However, where

*International
treaties*

---

1.   *J. H. Rayner (Mincing Lane) Ltd v Department of Trade and
        Industry [International Tin Council Case]* [1990] 2 AC 418 at 500,
        [1989] 3 All ER 523, HL.
2.   *Quazi v Quazi* [1980] AC 744, [1979] 3 All ER 897, HL.

the words of an Act of Parliament are clear and unambiguous, they must be given effect even if the decision results in a breach of international law (see *Salomon v Commissioners of Customs & Excise*[3]).

Incorporation and application of EC law	The Treaties of the European Communities and European Community law were incorporated into the law in England and Wales by the *European Communities Act 1972*.

The courts of England and Wales apply European Community law in the light of and reflecting the spirit of the Treaties, Community secondary legislation and the decisions of the European Court of Justice, and will construe UK legislation so far as is possible in conformity with the purpose of EC legislation (see *Litster v Forth Dry Dock & Engineering Co Ltd*[4]).

The courts have not, in general, demonstrated any reticence in applying Community law and increasingly interpret it so as to give a purposive construction to national law applicable in a Community context (see *Litster v Forth Dry Dock & Engineering Co Ltd*[5]). However, the House of Lords has stated in the case of *Duke v G.E.C. Reliance Ltd*[6] that Community law does not enable or constrain the courts to distort the meaning of a British statute in order to enforce against an individual a Community directive which has no direct effect between individuals (see further *Webb v EMO Air Cargo (UK) Ltd*[7]).

Proof of foreign law

Foreign law is treated as a question of fact to be determined by the courts on the evidence adduced before them. There is generally said to be a presumption that foreign law is the same as English law in that a party asserting that a foreign law applies in the proceedings has the of burden of proving that that foreign law differs from English law.

Generally, foreign law will be proved by calling an expert witness who must give his evidence on oath. The evidence may, with the leave of the court, be given on affidavit (see *RSC Ord 38, r 2(1)*), although the court may order that those who made the affidavits should be available for cross-examination (see *RSC Ord 38, r 2(2)*).

Where an English court has determined a point of foreign law in a previous case, that may normally be relied upon in a later case on the point (see *Civil Evidence Act 1972 s4(2)* and *RSC Ord 38, r 7*).

---

3. *Salomon v Commissioners of Customs & Excise* [1967] 2 QB 116 at 143 per Diplock LJ, [1966] 3 All ER 871, CA.

4. *Litster v Forth Dry Dock & Engineering Co Ltd* [1990] 1 AC 546 at 559 per Lord Oliver, [1989] 1 All ER 1134 at 1140.

5. *Litster v Forth Dry Dock & Engineering Co Ltd* [1990] 1 AC 546 at 558 per Lord Templeman, [1989] 1 All ER 1134; and also *Woolwich Equitable Building Society v Inland Revenue Commissioners*, Independent, 13.8.92, HL, in a non-Community context.

6. *Duke v G.E.C. Reliance Ltd* [1988] AC 618, [1988] 1 All ER 626, HL.

7. *Webb v EMO Air Cargo (UK) Ltd* [1992] 1 CMLR 793, [1992] 2 All ER 43, CA.

Proceedings of the courts must be in English (see *Re Trepca* *Language of* *Mines Ltd*[8]). Affidavits presented to a court must also be in *proceedings* English, and the evidence of an expert witness should also be in English (if necessary given through an interpreter).

The *European Convention on the Protection of Human Rights* *European* *and Fundamental Freedoms* is not part of English domestic law *Convention on* (or of Scotland or Northern Ireland). National courts are not *Human Rights* empowered to enforce directly the provisions of the *Convention* or the case law of the European Court of Human Rights (see *R v Home Secretary, ex p Brind*[9]), save to the extent that these have been adopted by the European Court of Justice as part of applicable European Community law (see further *Society for the Protection of Unborn Children Ireland Ltd (S.P.U.C.) v Grogan*[10]).

However, in construing domestic legislation the courts will presume that Parliament intended to legislate in conformity with the *Convention*, and not in conflict with it (see *R v Home Secretary, ex p Brind*[11]).

Where the words of English statutes are plain and unambiguous *Statutory* they must be applied in their ordinary and natural meaning (see *interpretation* *ACT Construction Ltd v Customs and Excise Comrs*[12]) taking into account their subject matter and object and the context in which they are being used (see *NWL Ltd v Woods*[13]).

Where words are ambiguous, the courts look to the statute as a whole, then to other legislation, then to contemporaneous circumstances and finally attempt to establish from its wording what mischief the statute was directed to rectify, what was the remedy chosen and why (see Halsbury's Statutes Vol 44, para 858). However, the interpretation of an ambiguity should not lead to unreasonableness (see *Bromilow & Edwards Ltd v IRC*[14]), great harshness or injustice (see *F v F*[15]).

There is a presumption that consolidating statutes are not intended to alter the existing law (see *Edwards (Inspector of Taxes) v Clinch*[16]).

8.   *Re Trepca Mines Ltd* [1960] 3 All ER 304, [1960] 1 WLR 1273, CA.
9.   *R v Secretary of State for the Home Department, ex p Brind* [1991] 1 AC 696, [1991] 1 All ER 720, HL.
10.   Case C-159/90 *Society for the Protection of Unborn Children Ireland Ltd (S.P.U.C.) v Grogan* [1991] 3 CMLR 849; and see further, Case C-62/90 *Re Private Imports of Medicines; EC Commission v Germany* [1992] 2 CMLR 549.
11.   *R v Home Secretary, ex p Brind* [1991] 1 AC 696 at pages 747-8 per Lord Bridge.
12.   *ACT Construction Ltd v Customs and Excise Comrs* [1982] 1 All ER 84, HL.
13.   *NWL Ltd v Woods* [1979] 3 All ER 614, [1979] 1 WLR 1294, HL.
14.   *Bromilow & Edwards Ltd v IRC* [1970] 1 All ER 174, [1970] 1 WLR 128, CA.
15.   *F v F* [1971] P 1.
16.   *Edwards (Inspector of Taxes) v Clinch* [1981] Ch 1.

The courts may not refer to the Parliamentary debates on a draft statute (see *Fothergill v Monarch Airlines Ltd* [17]), but may refer to a White Paper (which precedes a statute being introduced into the Houses of Parliament) in construing resulting legislation[18], although it has been suggested that this is only done in rare cases to enable the courts to carry out Parliament's intention[19]. However, the courts do not take such a restrictive view of extra-statutory material when construing legislation in the light of Community law (see *R v London Boroughs Transport Committee, ex p Freight Transport Association Ltd*[20]).

Save in the face of clear and unambiguous wording the courts will not interpret a statute to deprive a subject of his constitutional rights (see, for example, *Raymond v Honey*[21] — right to have unimpeded access to the courts), or to interfere with established private rights, eg that property is not intended to be taken away without a legal right to compensation (see *Re De Keyser's Royal Hotel Ltd, De Keyser's Royal Hotel Ltd v R*, affirmed, *sub nom A-G v De Keyser's Royal Hotel*[22]).

Statutes providing for criminal sanctions, and fiscal and revenue statutes should be construed strictly and go no further than their clear meaning (see *R v Cuthbertson*[23]).

Unless the wording is clear and unambiguous, no retrospective effect will be given to any statute (see *Harrison v Hammersmith and Fulham London Borough Council*[24]).

Effect of legislation on the Crown

Unless the contrary is stated or by necessary implication the Crown is not bound by the provisions of a statute, the Crown, here, meaning government ministers, and those charged with carrying on executive government (see *AG v Hancock*[25]); although, unless expressly excluded the Crown may take the benefit of a statute (see *Crown Proceedings Act 1947, s31(1)*).

Ratio decidendi

Only the principles applied as necessary grounds for a decision are regarded as the "*ratio decidendi*" of the case and form a binding precedent (see *Close v Steel Co of Wales Ltd*[26]; and Halsbury's Statutes Vol 26, para 573). Other statements in a

---

17. *Fothergill v Monarch Airlines Ltd* [1981] AC 251 at 281 per Lord Diplock.
18. *Duke v Reliance* [1988] 1 All ER 626, [1988] 2 WLR 359.
19. See Bennion, *Statutory Interpretation*, 1992, p455.
20. *R v London Boroughs Transport Committee, ex p Freight Transport Association Ltd* [1992] 1 CMLR 5.
21. *Raymond v Honey* [1983] 1 AC 1, [1982] 1 All ER 756, HL.
22. *Re De Keyser's Royal Hotel Ltd, De Keyser's Royal Hotel Ltd v R* [1919] 2 Ch 197, CA, affirmed, *sub nom A-G v De Keyser's Royal Hotel* [1920] AC 508, HL.
23. *R v Cuthbertson* [1981] AC 470 at 481, per Lord Diplock, [1980] 2 All ER 410, HL.
24. *Harrison v Hammersmith and Fulham London Borough Council* [1981] 2 All ER 588, [1981] 1 WLR 650, CA.
25. *AG v Hancock* [1940] 1 KB 427 at 431, [1940] 1 All ER 32.
26. *Close v Steel Co of Wales Ltd* [1962] AC 367, [1961] 2 All ER 953 HL.

judgment not within the scope of the *ratio decidendi*, but which lay down a rule of law, are called *"dicta"*. They are not binding on another court but are regarded as of persuasive value.

The House of Lords is the highest appeal court for the United Kingdom. Its decisions are binding on all courts inferior to it. Its decisions are (unless there are exceptional circumstances) binding upon itself (see *Practice Statement (Judicial Precedent) 1966*[27]).

Precedent : a) House of Lords

The decisions of the Court of Appeal on questions of law bind Divisional Courts and Courts of First Instance, and generally also bind the Court of Appeal until overruled by the House of Lords except that :

b) Court of Appeal

-     the Court of Appeal may decide which of two of its own conflicting decisions it will follow;
-     it is bound to refuse to follow its own decision if it is inconsistent with a decision of the House of Lords even though not expressly overruled by the House of Lords;
-     it is not bound to follow its own decision if that decision was given *"per incuriam"* (ie in ignorance of one of its own or of a House of Lords' decision, or of the terms of a statute or rule having statutory force) (see *Young v Bristol Aeroplane Co Ltd*[28]).

One court of first instance is generally not regarded as bound by the decisions of another court of first instance. However, a judge at first instance will follow a previous decision of another such judge unless the latter judge is sure that the first decision was wrong (see *Huddersfield Police Authority v Watson*[29]).

c) Courts of first instance

Since there is no written constitution for the United Kingdom, there are no authorised texts or commentaries.

Authorised texts or commentaries

---

27.   *Practice Statement (Judicial Precedent)* [1966] 3 All ER 77, [1966] 1 WLR 1234, HL.
28.   *Young v Bristol Aeroplane Co Ltd* [1944] KB 718, [1944] 2 All ER 293, affirmed at [1946] AC 163, [1946] 1 All ER 98, by the House of Lords.
29.   *Huddersfield Police Authority v Watson* [1947] KB 842, [1947] All ER 193, DC.

CHAPTER 2 : FUNDAMENTAL RIGHTS

Although there is no written constitution for England and Wales there are a number of rights which have been developed both by statute and by the courts administering the common law. Technically, Parliament has the power to abolish these rights but this is regarded as no more than a theoretical possibility.

The rights are :

- right to life - *28 Edw 3 c 3* (Liberty of Subjects) (1354). The death penalty has been abolished save for treason and a few other limited cases - *Murder (Abolition of the Death Penalty) Act 1965, s 1(1)*;
- right to personal liberty and freedom from wrongful detention - *Magna Carta of Edward I* (1297), c 29;
- right to freedom of expression - see the *Bill of Rights (1688), s 1;*
- right to vote in a secret ballot;
- right to have unimpeded access to the courts - *Magna Carta of Edward I (1297), c 29; Raymond v Honey*[1];
- right to legal representation in the interests of justice, and to confidential legal advice
- right to be judged by a person of independence;
- "*audi alteram partem*" - a right to have a reasonable opportunity to present one's case;
- right that one's property not be expropriated without a legal right to compensation (as a legal presumption) - *Re De Keyser's Royal Hotel Ltd, De Keyser's Royal Hotel Ltd v R* , affirmed *sub nom A-G v De Keyser's Royal Hotel Ltd*[2]);
- right to peaceful enjoyment of one's property;
- no taxation other than in accordance with an Act of Parliament - *Bowles v Bank of England*[3];
- freedom of conscience, which includes freedom of thought, opinion and religion and the right to practise one's chosen religion;
- right of public assembly for the religious worship of any religion, protected by the law from disturbance - *Places of Religious Worship Act 1812, s 12;*
- right of lawful assembly;

---

1.   *Raymond v Honey* [1983] 1 AC 1, [1982] 1 All ER 756, HL.
2.   *Re De Keyser's Royal Hotel Ltd, De Keyser's Royal Hotel Ltd v R* [1919] 2 Ch 197, CA, affirmed *sub nom A-G v De Keyser's Royal Hotel Ltd* [1920] AC 508, HL.
3.   *Bowles v Bank of England* [1913] 1 Ch 57.

-   right not to be punished for an act that did not constitute a crime at the time it was committed (as a presumption) *Waddington v Miah*[4].

Constitutional courts   There are no special courts which deal with the protection of such rights or other constitutional questions. These questions may arise in any court.

Judicial review   A Division of the High Court called the Divisional Court staffed by judges with particular knowledge of administrative law deals with questions of the judicial review of administrative action by the government and other public bodies.

---

4.   *Waddington v Miah* [1974] 2 All ER 377, [1974] 1 WLR 683, HL.

CHAPTER 3 : JURISDICTION OF THE COURTS

A defendant always has the right to challenge the jurisdiction of a particular court. An English court has a discretion under *Order 11 of the Rules of the Supreme Court* to determine whether the English court or the foreign court is the appropriate court (*"forum conveniens"*) in any case. The test which the court applies is whether the interests of justice are best served by proceedings in England or abroad (see *Spiliada Maritime Corpn v Cansulex Ltd*[1]). *Right to challenge jurisdiction*

However, the court has no discretion to stay proceedings on the ground of *forum non conveniens* or *lis alibi pendens* if the proceedings fall within the scope of the *Brussels Convention on Civil Jurisdiction and Enforcement of Judgements in Civil and Commercial Matters 1968,* incorporated into English law by the *Civil Jurisdiction and Judgments Act 1982* (see *S & W Berisford Plc v New Hampshire Insurance Co*[2]). The *Convention* applies only where there is a conflict between the jurisdictions of the contracting parties. The *Convention on jurisdiction and the enforcement of judgments in civil and commercial matters* (the *"Lugano Convention"*) entered into force in the United Kingdom on 1 May 1992. *The Brussels Convention*

There is a rule of universal jurisdiction in English law for certain serious crimes which are international in character such as piracy - extending to hijacking and the trafficking of narcotics - and crimes against humanity. *Universal jurisdiction*

The *State Immunity Act 1978* restricts state immunity to acts of a governmental nature and excludes acts of a commercial nature (see, too, *Trendtex Trading Corpn v Central Bank of Nigeria*[3]). *State immunity*

Prior to the *1968 Brussels Convention* coming into force in English law, a person born legitimate acquired the domicile of his father, or the domicile of his mother if born illegitimate. This domicile of origin may be changed by operation of law, by marriage and by choice. *Domicile - individuals*

---

1.   *Spiliada Maritime Corpn v Cansulex Ltd* [1987] AC 460, [1986] 3 All ER 843, HL.
2.   *S & W Berisford Plc v New Hampshire Insurance Co* [1990] 2 QB 631.
3.   *Trendtex Trading Corpn v Central Bank of Nigeria* [1977] QB 529, [1977] 1 All ER 881, CA.

A person may acquire a domicile of choice by settling in another jurisdiction. However, if a domicile of choice is abandoned and a fresh domicile of choice is not acquired, the domicile of origin revives (*Udny v Udny*[4]).

Since the *Domicile and Matrimonial Proceedings Act 1973*, the domicile of a woman married after the Act came into force is, instead of being the same as a husband's by virtue of marriage, ascertained by reference to the same factors as in the case of any other individual capable of having an independent domicile.

Under the *Civil Jurisdiction and Judgments Act 1982* an individual is domiciled in the United Kingdom if and only if (a) he is resident in the United Kingdom; and (b) the nature and circumstances of his residence indicate that he has a substantial connection with the United Kingdom (*Civil Jurisdiction and Judgments Act, s 41*). The same test applies mutatis mutandis in determining in which part of the United Kingdom a person is domiciled. As a general rule, United Kingdom domicile involves three levels at the same time, namely, whether in the United Kingdom, a specific part of the United Kingdom and a specific place in the United Kingdom.

- Corporations

Section 42 of the 1982 Act provides detailed rules to determine the seat of corporations and associations which is treated as their domicile. There are two criteria for the domicile of companies or associations in the United Kingdom and it is sufficient if either one or the other is established : that the company or association was incorporated or formed under the law of a part of the United Kingdom and has its registered office or other official address in the United Kingdom; and that its essential management and control is exercised in the United Kingdom. If a company has its registered office in England but its central management and control is in Scotland, it will be domiciled in both jurisdictions.

Prior to the *Brussels Convention*, and thereafter in respect of non-Convention parties, registration or incorporation of a corporation would be sufficient to determine the domicile of a corporation.

---

4.   *Udny v Udny* (1869) LR I Sc and Div 441, HL.

CHAPTER 4 : ADMINISTRATION OF JUSTICE

The organisation of the English judicial system makes a *The court system*
distinction between "the High Court", "inferior courts" and "quasi-
judicial" bodies, such as tribunals.

The main courts are outlined below :

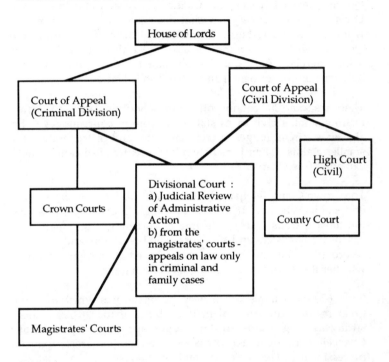

House of Lords

Court of Appeal
(Criminal Division)

Court of Appeal
(Civil Division)

High Court
(Civil)

Crown Courts

Divisional Court :
a) Judicial Review
of Administrative
Action
b) from the
magistrates' courts -
appeals on law only
in criminal and
family cases

County Court

Magistrates' Courts

The Privy Council is the last court of appeal from certain *Privy Council*
Commonwealth countries and Dependent Territories, and for
certain bodies within the United Kingdom such as the General
Medical Council, and the General Dental Council.

The House of Lords is the highest court in the court hierarchy. It *House of Lords*
hears a small number of cases a year (perhaps 40 or 50) of
particular legal importance. It is staffed by the Lord Chancellor,
and ten Lords of Appeal in Ordinary who are members of the
Upper House of the legislature.

Cases are heard by a panel of at least three Law Lords and usually
by a Bench of five. Each Law Lord is entitled to express his own
opinion in the form of what is called a speech.

When the House of Lords hears appeals from Scotland there is a convention that at least one Scottish law lord will sit on an appeal.

Court of Appeal   The Court of Appeal is for most cases the court of final appeal. It has 28 Lord Justices presided over by the Master of the Rolls. Cases are normally heard by three judges and a majority is sufficient for a decision. The Criminal Division of the Court of Appeal sits as a specialised section of the Court of Appeal dealing only with criminal matters. The cases are generally heard by a Lord Justice and two judges from the Queen's Bench Division. There is normally only one judgment of this court, although each judge may give a separate judgment.

The High Court   The High Court of Justice is made up of three Divisions, the Queen's Bench Division, the Chancery Division and the Family Division. The Chancery Division deals primarily with company work, trusts and estates and intellectual property. Within the Queen's Bench Division there is also a specialist Admiralty Court, a Commercial Court and the Divisional Court, which reviews decisions of governmental and other public bodies.

County courts   There are some 300 county courts throughout England and Wales hearing smaller civil cases staffed by county court judges (who also sit as circuit judges in criminal cases) and district judges for smaller claims. Their jurisdiction has recently been considerably extended (see Chapter 6).

Crown Court   The Crown Court, set up by the *Courts Act 1971*, has an exclusively criminal jurisdiction. It is staffed by High Court judges (who try the most serious cases), full-time circuit judges and part-time practising barristers and solicitors called recorders and assistant recorders. A jury of 12 lay persons selected at random determine whether the defendant is found guilty or not guilty.

Magistrates' courts   Some 620 magistrates' courts hear the small cases which form the great majority of criminal matters. Most of the 26,000 justices sitting as magistrates are lay judges appointed by the Lord Chancellor. In the larger towns and metropolitan areas, some 60 professional judges sit as stipendiary magistrates. Magistrates are assisted on matters of law by a legally qualified clerk.

Magistrates' courts hear less serious criminal cases where trial by jury is either not elected or is not available. They also have significant jurisdiction in civil matters relating to domestic issues such as maintenance payments to deserted wives and children, adoption proceedings concerning care of children and disputes. There is some overlap with other jurisdictions, in particular with the county court, in these matters. Magistrates also have jurisdiction with regard to disputes arising out of statutory debt collection (ie income tax, national insurance and social security contributions, and property tax payments).

A special court presided over by a High Court judge with *Restrictive* specialist members called the Restrictive Practices Court, has *Practices Court* been created to deal with litigation under the *Restrictive Trade Practices Act 1976* and the *Fair Trading Act 1973*.

There are also some 60 different tribunals mostly hearing *Tribunals* disputes that are "administrative" in nature. The range of subject matters includes immigration law, social security, industrial relations/unfair dismissal and sexual and racial discrimination.

The Criminal Injuries Compensation Board, composed of lawyers *Criminal Injuries* who are expert in the field of personal injury work, adjudicates on *Compensation* claims made by victims claiming compensation from the state for *Board* crimes of violence committed against them.

In civil cases, a right of appeal lies to the Court of Appeal from all *Civil appeals* three Divisions of the High Court and from the county court. The appellate jurisdiction for civil cases originating from domestic disputes in the magistrates' courts is exercised by the Family Division's Divisional Court consisting of two High Court judges from the Family Division. Appeals from the Divisional Court also lie to the Court of Appeal.

Exceptionally, it is possible under *Sections 12 and 13 of the Administration of Justice Act 1969* to bring an appeal directly from the High Court to the House of Lords. "Leap-frog" appeals require : the consent of the parties; a certificate from the judge stating that the case involves a point of law of general public importance concerning either (a) the construction of a statute, or (b) a matter fully considered by the Court of Appeal in a previous case; and leave from the House of Lords.

Except for interlocutory judgments and proceedings concerning an application for leave to bring proceedings for judicial review, an appeal from judgments of the High Court to the Court of Appeal lies as of right. Leave must be obtained for all appeals from the county court to the Court of Appeal in litigation involving less than half the maximum amount for which county courts have jurisdiction.

Leave must be obtained for appeals from the Court of Appeal to the House of Lords to which appeal normally lies only on points of law of general public importance. If an application for leave to appeal to the House of Lords is refused by the Court of Appeal it can be renewed before the House of Lords.

In civil matters the appeal is heard on the basis of transcripts of the proceedings at the trial. However, under *Ord 59, r 10 of the Rules of the Supreme Court* ("RSC"), the Court of Appeal has the power exceptionally to receive fresh evidence on questions of fact in an appeal.

The Court of Appeal can make any order that would have been available to the trial court. However, it will not substitute its judgment for the trial court judge's ruling unless the trial court judge can be shown to have made his decision under a mistake of law, under a misapprehension as to the facts, or on the grounds that the judge has taken into account irrelevant matters or failed to exercise properly a discretion vested in him.

Criminal appeals A criminal appeal can be brought against conviction and/or sentence. In criminal cases defendants may either appeal from decisions of magistrates to the Crown Court or, on a point of law only, by way of written case stated, to the Divisional Court. The Crown Court when hearing cases on appeal from magistrates sits with one judge who presides and two lay magistrates, but without a jury. These appeals are as of right. The court has power on a rehearing to increase the sentence but only within the magistrates' original powers.

Appeals from the Crown Court to the Court of Appeal's Criminal Division require leave unless the appeal is brought on a point of law only. If it is refused by the single judge, who makes his decision after reading the papers, an application for leave can be renewed before the full court of three judges. As in civil matters, leave has to be sought either from the Court of Appeal or from the House of Lords to bring an appeal before the House of Lords.

Appeal against The prosecution's right to appeal against an acquittal is extremely
acquittal limited. An appeal lies to the Divisional Court from an acquittal by magistrates resulting from an error of law. If such an appeal is successful the case can be sent back to the magistrates' court with a direction to convict or to reconsider the matter in the light of the Divisional Court's ruling.

Appeal against Under the terms of the *Criminal Justice Act 1988* the Attorney
lenient sentence General, acting for the Crown, with leave from the Court of Appeal, has the power to bring an appeal against sentences which appear to be much too lenient.

The Court of Appeal normally decides appeals on the basis of transcripts of the trial and submissions made on behalf of each party to the case. The Court of Appeal has power, in exceptional circumstances, to receive fresh evidence under *Section 23 of the Criminal Appeal Act 1968*. The Crown Court, when hearing appeals from the magistrates' court, re-hears all the evidence.

Powers of Court of The Court of Appeal can allow an appeal against conviction on
Appeal the grounds that the verdict is unsafe or unsatisfactory, or, if fresh evidence is admitted, it can order a retrial. However, if it considers that in fact no substantial miscarriage of justice occurred it may uphold the conviction and sentence despite the error. It will not do so if there has been a breach of a fundamental right of a defendant (see *Criminal Appeal Act 1968, ss 2 and 7*).

The Court of Appeal has the power to reduce sentences on the grounds that they are significantly too severe. It also has power in the case of frivolous appeals to order that time already spent in custody pending appeal will not count towards the sentence of imprisonment.

RSC Order 114 allows the court to make an order for a reference to the European Court of Justice either on the application by either party or of the court's own motion and may be made at any stage during the proceedings. If a party wishes to make an application for a reference before the hearing the application must be made by motion (*RSC Ord 114, r 2(2)*).

Reference for preliminary ruling to the European Court of Justice

The effect of an order for a reference is to stay proceedings unless ordered otherwise by the court. The order for the reference contains the question on which the preliminary ruling is brought, in a schedule. Together with the schedule the order is transmitted to the European Court of Justice by the Senior Master of the Queen's Bench Division.

Under *RSC Ord 114, r 6* and *Ord 19, r 11 of the County Court Rules*, an order for a reference is made as a final decision from which appeal lies without leave to the Court of Appeal. Notice of appeal against an order for a reference must be served within 14 days and consequently the order is not transmitted to the European Court of Justice until this time limit has expired. In contrast, an appeal against a refusal to make a reference requires leave to be obtained, as a refusal to grant an order for a reference constitutes only an interlocutory judgment and not a final judgment.

The decision on European law must be "necessary" to enable the court to give judgment before it can be referred under *Article 177*. Lord Denning laid down guidelines in the case of *Bulmer v Bollinger*[1] on what amounts to "necessary".

- the point must be conclusive, ie it must be necessary in order for the English court to give judgment;
- if substantially the same legal point has already been determined by the European Court of Justice and/or the point of Community law is so clear and free from doubt that the English court need not seek help in interpreting the Treaty, a reference is not necessary;
- the facts must be decided first;
- other relevant factors which might include the time it took to get a ruling and whether any injustice might result from the continuation of the stay, expense, and the wishes of the parties.

These indications are valuable as guidelines, but they are not strict rules. The first guideline is the critical one.

---

1.   *H.P. Bulmer Ltd v J. Bollinger SA* [1974] Ch 401, [1974] 2 CMLR 91, [1974] 3 All ER 1226, CA.

References to the
European Court of
Human Rights

The courts of England and Wales have no jurisdiction to refer cases to other supra-national courts. References to the European Court of Human Rights are governed by the conditions for bringing a case before the Commission of Human Rights under the *Convention.* Essentially, these require that all local legal remedies for seeking relief against an aggrieving act by the state or one of its organs have been exhausted.

CHAPTER 5 : STRUCTURE OF THE LEGAL PROFESSION

The legal profession in England and Wales comprises two distinct branches of solicitors and barristers.

Structure of the profession

The first point of contact for any member of the public seeking legal services will normally be a solicitor. The advice of a barrister may usually only be obtained by reference from a solicitor. Exceptionally barristers may now receive instructions in England and Wales directly from lawyers from other jurisdictions and from certain other professions without them having to instruct a solicitor first.

Solicitors

There are about 70,000 solicitors of whom about 49,000 are in private practice and the rest employed as solicitors in industry. Solicitors' firms generally deal with a wide range of matters including conveyancing of property, litigation, general business advice, commercial work, company mergers and acquisitions.

Barristers are a referral profession receiving instructions through solicitors or foreign lawyers and some other professions. Solicitors normally have the exclusive right to instruct barristers in cases before the English courts.

Barristers

There are just over 7,000 independent practising barristers of whom about 10% are senior barristers, or Queen's Counsel. They tend to be specialists, and will give advice on questions of law in their particular specialist field and draft pleadings and other documents required in litigation, but they are also advocates, entitled as of right to appear before all courts within the jurisdiction, as well as before the European Court of Justice and the Court of First Instance.

Rights of audience - barristers

Legal executives qualify as legal advisers by passing examinations of the Institute of Legal Executives. They undertake some areas of solicitors' work and are employed to assist within a solicitors' firm.

Legal executives

Finally, tax advisers, accountants and patent agents give legal advice to clients within their specialised field. These professions are not regarded as part of the legal profession but there is no monopoly on the giving of legal advice for lawyers or other professionals.

Tax advisers, accountants and patent agents

Solicitors have for many years had rights of audience in the magistrates' courts, which deal with minor civil and criminal matters, and the county court, dealing with smaller civil claims.

Rights of audience - solicitors

They may also represent their clients before tribunals which deal with matters such as employment rights and immigration. They do the detailed preparatory work on the cases in the higher civil and criminal courts.

Recently, the *Courts and Legal Services Act 1990* has given the Law Society the right to apply to a new judicial advisory committee to extend their rights of audience in the Crown Court (criminal cases) and the High Court (civil cases). Applications for extension of rights of audience have been made but no decision has yet been taken.

It should be noted that members of the public (but not corporate bodies) may, if they wish, appear without legal representation as "litigants in person" in all courts and tribunals.

Organisation - Solicitors

Solicitors may either practise as "sole practitioners", or in a partnership. In addition to the equity partners, who receive a share of the profits, a firm will often include salaried partners and assistant solicitors. Although there are a small number of firms with over 100 partners the vast majority of firms have under 10 solicitors.

There is no statutory limit on the number of solicitors who may join together in one partnership, nor any territorial restrictions on the practice of a partnership. *Section 89 of the Courts and Legal Services Act 1990* paved the way for the creation of multinational partnerships, ie partnerships consisting of solicitors and foreign lawyers. Under detailed provisions which came into effect on 1 January 1992 the Law Society regulates multinational partnerships to ensure that the clients of such a practice receive broadly the same protection as if they had instructed a firm of solicitors. Solicitors are also free to employ other lawyers both within and outside the jurisdiction.

Barristers

Barristers in private practice are self-employed. Barristers will combine together in chambers for the purpose of sharing administrative support services, but since they do not share fees, they are not members of a partnership. Each will receive payment directly from those instructing him for each piece of work which he undertakes, and barristers in the same chambers may appear in court on opposite sides of a case. Barristers may also combine together for a particular case where it is necessary that the team should consist of more than one barrister. It will frequently consist of a Queen's Counsel and a junior barrister but in complex matters the team may be significantly larger. Under the Bar rules a barrister in chambers may not employ another barrister.

Branch offices

There is no restriction on the number of branch offices which a firm of solicitors may set up either within the United Kingdom or within a European Community Member State. Barristers' chambers may also have offices in more than one location although this is less common.

Solicitors generally charge their clients on the basis of the amount of time spent, the hourly rate varying according to the seniority of the lawyer concerned. Additional charges for "care and attention" may then be added to the time cost, together with disbursements incurred and VAT which is at present 17.5%.

Fees are not generally publicised, but Standard 1.1 of the Law Society written standards states that, on taking instructions, the solicitor should give his client the best information he can about the cost of the matter. Under the *Solicitors' Remuneration Order 1972, SI 1972/1139*, a solicitor's charges must be "fair and reasonable", having regard to factors such as the complexity or difficulty of the matter; the skill, labour and specialist knowledge involved; the nature and value of any property involved and the time expended.

Any dispute as to fees charged may be referred by a dissatisfied client to the Law Society. The Council of the Society has the power to reduce the bill if it thinks it appropriate to do so. In a matter involving the *Solicitors' Act 1974* the client has the right to call for the taxation of his bill, and the fees charged will then be assessed in the discretion of an independent taxing officer (see *RSC Ord 62, rr 15, 17*).

A similar system operates for barristers, who will charge a fee dependent on the work done and their seniority. The fee negotiation will normally take place through the barrister's clerk although matters of difficulty can be discussed with the barrister directly. A barrister will bill his instructing solicitor, or other professional, who then passes on the cost to the client.

Members of the Bar are subject to the *Code of Conduct of the Bar of England and Wales*, whilst solicitors are subject to the *Law Society's Professional Conduct Rules for Solicitors*. Both Codes incorporate the CCBE Code of Conduct for cross-border activities involving lawyers. These rules on discipline are to protect clients and guarantee certain minimum standards. The *Solicitors' Accounts Rules* ensure that solicitors do not misuse their clients' money. Barristers in England and Wales do not hold clients' money although they may in overseas offices.

Complaints about the work of solicitors or barristers may be made by any aggrieved client to the Law Society or the Bar Council respectively. This includes complaints relating to work carried out outside the jurisdiction. Each of these bodies has investigative powers and the disciplinary tribunals may impose penalties for misconduct ranging from a reprimand to substantial fines or prohibition from further professional practice. *Section 35 of the Solicitors Act 1974* also gives the Law Society the power to intervene in a solicitor's practice where it is necessary in order to safeguard clients' interests.

Foreign lawyers are free to set up branch offices in England and Wales. They may advise on any law (including English law) if they are competent to do so. They may not call themselves by the professional title of solicitor or barrister. They may not instruct barristers in court without the intervention of a solicitor. This may be subject to the exception that EC lawyers may be able to do so if they come within the provisions of the 1977 *Lawyers' Services Directive*[1]. Further, they may not execute official documents for the transfer of land or prove wills. They may also perform services from offices outside the United Kingdom under the *Lawyers' Services Directive*. Both the Bar and the Law Society have made regulations implementing the *Professional Diplomas Directive*[2]. In each case the regulations deal with applications to become full members of the Bar or Law Society from lawyers qualified outside the Community as well as those subject to the Directive.

The Law Society and the Bar Council decide in each individual case which subjects need be taken to make up the deficit in knowledge of English law. A foreign lawyer may be exempted from all or part of the text if he or she has relevant knowledge and experience which qualifies for exemption.

---

1.   Council Directive (EEC) 77/249 (OJ L78 26.3.77 p17).
2.   Council Directive (EEC) 89/48 (OJ L19 24.1.89 p16).

CHAPTER 6 : CIVIL PROCEDURE

The main guides to the rules of civil procedure are, for the High Court, the "Supreme Court Practice" (known as the "White Book") and for the county court, the "County Court Practice" (known as the "Green Book"). Rules of procedure are indicated in the White Book by the terms "O" for "Order"[1] and "r" for "rule" of an Order of the Rules of the Supreme Court - "RSC". In the Green Book, the denomination is for Orders and rules of the County Court Rules - "CCR".

Rules of procedure

The principal civil court of first instance in terms of the gravity of the case is the High Court. The county court is a civil court of first instance where the less serious cases in terms of monetary value and complexity of law are dealt with.

Court structure

By the *High Court and County Courts Jurisdiction Order 1991, SI 1991/724*, actions for personal injury worth less than £50,000 are to be tried in the county courts, those above that limit in the High Court. Other claims, in general, of a value of less than £25,000 are to be tried in the county court, those of £50,000 or above in the High Court. Those in between will be tried in the High Court or county court according to criteria set out in *Regulation 7* to the SI, including the complexity of the factual elements of the case, of the legal issues, the remedies, the overall value of the sums in question and whether the case has an importance for others beyond the immediate parties.

Jurisdiction of the courts

There is also a small claims court which hears claims up to £1,000.

Any natural and legal person not suffering a legal disability may sue and be sued in the civil courts. Persons under a legal disability include :
- minors, under the age of 18;
- "patients", that is, persons who by reason of mental disorder within the meaning of the *Mental Health Act 1983* are incapable of managing and administering their own affairs.

These parties can only bring a claim by a next friend or guardian ad litem (see *RSC Ord 80, r 2*) who is empowered to take all measures for the benefit of the person in the proceedings in question.

Right of access to the courts

A party seeking to restrain interference with a public right, to stop a public nuisance or compel the performance of a public duty,

---

1.   The abbreviated form used in this book for "Order of the Rules of the Supreme Court" is "RSC Ord".

can only sue with the consent and in the name of the Attorney General in a "Relator" action (*Gouriet v Union of Post Office Workers*[2]).

RSC Order 15, r 12 permits proceedings to be taken by or against an identified group or class of persons who have the same interests in the proceedings. *RSC Order 15, r 13* permits a court to appoint one or more persons to represent a group of persons who cannot individually be ascertained in proceedings concerning the estate of a deceased person, proceedings involving property subject to a trust or the construction of a written document including a statute.

State immunity

The *State Immunity Act 1978* provides (subject to exceptions) for statutory immunity from process in the English courts for the sovereign or other head of a sovereign state acting in a public capacity and for the governments and other state entities of other states exercising sovereign authority.

The main exceptions to this immunity are : commercial transactions (*s 3(1)(a)*); contractual obligations to be performed in the United Kingdom (*s 3*); contracts of employment made or to be performed in the United Kingdom (*s 4*); personal injury or claims of damage to property caused by misconduct in the United Kingdom (*s 5*); where a state is a member of a corporate or incorporate entity set up in or controlled from the United Kingdom (*s 8*; and see *Maclaine Watson & Co Ltd v International Tin Council*[3]); or where the state has submitted to the jurisdiction of the courts (*s 2*, and *s 9* regarding arbitrations).

A certificate from the Secretary of State for Foreign Affairs is conclusive evidence that a country is a state, part of a federal state, or that a person is regarded as a head of state or of government (*s 21(a)*).

The courts will not adjudicate on the propriety of an act of the Crown concerning its relations with a foreign state in the exercise of sovereign power, nor on the propriety of an act of a recognised foreign state performed on the territory of that foreign state (see *Empresa Exportadora de Acuzar v Industria Azacurera Nacional SA*[4] and *Maclaine Watson & Co Ltd v International Tin Council*).

The *Diplomatic Privileges Act 1964* grants immunity to a foreign sovereign or head of state, members of his household and private servants (*s 20*).

The *International Organisations Acts of 1968 and 1981* empower the Crown to designate by Order in Council which international

2. *Gouriet v Union of Post Office Workers* [1978] AC 435, [1977] 3 All ER 70, HL.
3. *Maclaine Watson & Co Ltd v International Tin Council* [1989] Ch 253, CA.
4. *Empresa Exportadora de Acuzar v Industria Azacurera Nacional SA* [1983] 2 Lloyd's Rep 171.

organisations (and their staff) shall have immunity from proceedings in court.

Barristers and solicitors are immune from legal process for negligence in the conduct of litigation or in compromising an action without authority. *Lawyers' immunity*

Under *RSC Ord 15, r 1*, a plaintiff may combine in a single action more than one claim against the same defendant where the defendant is liable in the same capacity in the different causes of action. An application for leave to do so must be made ex parte, before issue of the writ, by affidavit stating the grounds of the application. *Joinder of causes of actions*

The main provisions respecting joinder of parties are to be found in *RSC Ord 15, r 4* - two or more parties may at the discretion of the court be joined as plaintiffs or defendants in an action arising out of the same transaction or series of transactions where there are common questions of law and fact to be tried. *Joinder of parties*

The court may on its own initiative, or on the application of an existing party to an action, order the joinder of any party whose presence is necessary for the court to determine the issues effectively or order the disjoinder of a party to an action where a party is improperly or unnecessarily made a party (*RSC Ord 15, r 6*).

Under *RSC Ord 15, r 13A*, in actions relating to the estate of a deceased person or to property under a trust, the court may, on its own motion or on application, order that notice of the action be served on any person who is not then a party but who will or may be affected by the judgment in the action.

The High Court may stay any proceedings before it on the grounds of *forum non conveniens* or for other lawful reason provided its action is not inconsistent with the *Brussels Convention on the Recognition and Enforcement of Foreign Judgments in Civil and Commercial Matters 1968* - see *The Civil Jurisdiction and Judgments Act 1982, s 49*. In addition, where the High Court grants leave for judicial review of an administrative action, any proceedings in a county court are stayed until determination of the proceedings in the High Court, or until the High Court determines (see *County Courts Act 1984, s 83*). *Stay of proceedings*

Where there is an agreement in a contract to submit a matter to arbitration, and one of the parties has taken no steps in the court proceedings, the court may make an order staying the court proceedings (*Arbitration Act 1950, s 4*).

Where the court orders a plaintiff company to give security for costs under the *Companies Act 1985, s 726(1)* it may stay all proceedings until security has been given.

Legal aid is provided for proceedings in court through a government-funded scheme under the *Legal Aid Act 1988*. The legal aid system is operated by the Legal Aid Board to provide *Legal aid* legal advice, assistance and representation to those who might otherwise not be able to obtain this by reason of their means (*Legal Aid Act 1988, s 1*). The *Civil Legal Aid (General) Regulations 1989, SI 1989/339*, set out the detailed rules. The legal aid limit for assistance is at present £6,800 of annual disposable income after various deductions have been made.

There is provision for legal aid to be awarded immediately in an emergency. Where the assisted party has been assessed as liable to make a contribution, the Legal Aid Board shall have a first charge for the recovery of sums that remain unpaid over any property recovered or preserved for that assisted person in the proceedings.

Limitation of actions

The principal provisions on limitation of actions are set out in the *Limitation Act 1980* :

- Actions founded on tort - six years from the date on which the cause of action accrued - *s 2*;
- Actions founded on simple contract - six years from the date on which the cause of action accrued - *s 5*;
- Actions in respect of personal injury for negligence, nuisance or breach of duty - three years from the date on which the cause of action accrued, or from the date of knowledge (if later) of the person injured - *s 11(4)(a) and (b)*; if the person injured dies before this period the cause of action survives for the benefit of the estate for three years from the date of death, or the personal representative's knowledge, whichever shall be the later - *s 11(5)(a) and (b)*;
- Actions in respect of claiming a contribution - if entitled to claim a contribution in respect of any damage from another person under the *Civil Liability (Contribution) Act 1978, s 1* - no action to recover shall be brought after two years from the date on which that right accrued - *s 10(1)*. The relevant date is the date on which a judgment or arbitration award was given - *s 10(3)*; or outside of these cases the date on which an agreement is made to make a payment (whether an admission is made regarding liability or not) - *s 10(4)*;
- Actions in respect of sums recoverable by virtue of a statute not within *Section 10* - six years from the date on which the cause of action accrued - *s 9*;
- Actions on a specialty (action on an obligation under seal) - 12 years from the date on which the cause of action accrued - *s 8*;
- Actions to recover land - in general, 12 years from the date on which the cause of action accrued to a person who takes the action or through whom the action is claimed - *s 15*;
- Actions to enforce judgments - six years from the date on which the judgment became enforceable - *s 24*;
- Action for libel or slander - with respect to causes of action arising from 30 December 1985 - three years from the date on which the cause of action accrued - *s 4A*.

Separate provisions apply to persons under disability.

In any action where the period of limitation is prescribed by the *Limitation Act 1980* and the action is based on the fraud of the defendant, or where any fact relevant to the plaintiff's right of action had been deliberately concealed from him by the defendant, or the action is for relief from the consequences of a mistake, the period of limitation does not begin to run until the plaintiff has discovered the fraud, concealment or mistake, or could with reasonable diligence have discovered it (*s 32*).

Effect of fraud on limitation

The court has a discretion not to apply the three year time limit of *Sections 11 and 12* in respect of fatal accidents and personal injuries in special circumstances where it would be equitable not to do so (*s 33*).

Service of proceedings is governed, in general, by *RSC Ords 10 and 65*. Normally personal service is not required. Under *RSC Ord 10, r 1* the writ must be served personally on the defendant or his agent, alternatively a copy may be served by ordinary first-class post at the defendant's last or last known address, or by personally posting it through the post box at such an address. Service is deemed to have been effected, in general, where the defendant acknowledges service or his solicitor acknowledges service with a statement that he is authorised to accept service on the defendant's behalf.

Service of proceedings

Service on a corporate entity other than a limited company is normally effected by personal service on one of a specified list of officers which include the President, treasurer or such similar officer (see *RSC Ord 10* and *Ord 65, r 3*).

Service on a limited company must comply with the rules set out in the *Companies Act 1985, s 725*. The writ must be sent by post to the registered office of the limited company.

There is also provision under the Rules of the Supreme Court to order substituted service where the court is satisfied that personal service is impossible.

Service out of the jurisdiction is permissible where the claim is one which falls within the provisions of the *Civil Jurisdiction and Judgments Act 1982* provided there are no other proceedings pending in the courts of another contracting party's territory or part of the United Kingdom and the defendant is domiciled in any part of the United Kingdom. The time limits within which the defendant must acknowledge service are 21 days if the defendant is within Scotland, Northern Ireland or the European territory of a contracting party, and 31 days if in the non-European territory of a contracting party; see also the Supreme Court Practice 1991, Vol 2, Part 3C, para 902.

Service out of jurisdiction

Outside cases falling within the *1968 Brussels Convention* or any other specific Act, leave of the court is required for service out of the jurisdiction (*RSC Ord 11, r 1*). The application for leave is made ex parte to the master in an affidavit which should set out that the plaintiff's claim is within the terms of the rule and that the plaintiff has a good arguable case. Any ambiguity is resolved in favour of the intended defendant.

Acknowledgment of service

The rules concerning acknowledgment of service are set out in *RSC Ord 12*. The acknowledgment of service must be completed by the defendant personally, or by a solicitor acting on the defendant's behalf, and by returning it to the office out of which the writ was issued either by hand or by post. In the case of a corporate defendant the address is that of the principal or registered office. The date of acknowledgment is the date when it is received at the relevant issuing office. The time for acknowledgment is, for actions served within the jurisdiction, 14 days from the date of service (including that day), and where service has been out of the jurisdiction, within the time period specified as appropriate.

Notice of intention to defend

Under *RSC Ord 12, r 8,* where a defendant wishes to dispute the jurisdiction of the court, notice of intention to defend should be given, and an application should be made by summons in the Queen's Bench Division or by summons or motion in the Chancery Division for an order to set aside or discharge the writ or service. In such cases, the acknowledgment does not act as an acknowledgment submitting to the jurisdiction of the court.

Failure to give notice

Where a writ has been properly served and proved by an affidavit of service and the time for acknowledging service has passed with no notice of an intention to defend, then, if the claim is for a sum of money determinable by an act of arithmetic (a liquidated claim) the plaintiff may proceed to enter judgment for such sum (*RSC Ord 13, r 1*). Where the claim is for damages that require to be assessed, judgment can be entered for damages to be assessed (*RSC Ord 13, r 2*). There is an exception for claims arising from a mortgage transaction (*RSC Ord 88*).

If service out of the jurisdiction has been made in accordance with the *Civil Jurisdiction and Judgments Act 1982* the plaintiff may not enter judgment without leave of the court. The plaintiff should apply ex parte to the court with an affidavit which states that the claim is one within the *1982 Act* which the court is able to hear and determine, that no other court has exclusive jurisdiction under the terms of *Schedules 1 or 4 to the Act*, and that service has been effected in accordance with *Schedules 1 or 4 to the Act* as required.

Applications to set judgment aside

Where the plaintiff is unable to effect service of the judgment he is required to apply to the court ex parte to have the judgment set aside or to apply for directions (*RSC Ord 13, r 7(3)*).

The court has a discretion to set aside or vary any judgment entered under this Order if it thinks fit (*RSC Ord 13, r 9*). Generally the application should be supported by an affidavit showing that there is a defence on the merits that should go to trial. Where the judgment is irregular, the defendant is entitled to have it set aside subject to the court's power under *RSC Ord 13, r 9* to correct any irregularity (see the Supreme Court Practice 1991, para 13/9/6).

RSC Order 14 governs applications in the High Court for summary judgment which is available in all actions begun by writ except an action for libel, slander, malicious prosecution or false imprisonment; an Admiralty action in rem; or an action for specific performance under *RSC Ord 86 and Ord 14, r 1*. The hearing will normally be before a master or district judge in chambers. The defendant must have given notice of intention to defend. The statement of claim must have been served on the defendant. The application should be made by summons supported by an affidavit verifying the facts of the claim, or part of the claim to which the application relates, and stating that in the deponent's belief there is no defence to the claim, or that part, except as to the amount of damages. The affidavit in support may contain statements of information and belief (*RSC Ord 14, r 2(2)*).

Summary judgment

Unless the defendant satisfies the court that there is an issue or question in dispute which ought to be tried or that there is some other reason for there to be a trial, judgment will be entered for the plaintiff for the whole or part of the claim (*RSC Ord 14, r 3*). The court will grant the defendant unconditional leave to defend if it is of the view that there is an arguable defence. Where the court is uncertain whether or not there is an arguable defence, it may grant leave to defend on such terms as it thinks fit (*RSC Ord 14, r 4(3)*), which may include ordering the defendant to pay into court all or part of the sums claimed.

Unconditional leave to defend

On the application of a party at any stage of the proceedings, a court may determine any question of law or the construction of a document arising in the proceedings. An application is made by summons or motion to the master (see *RSC Ord 14A, rr 1(4) and 2*) or to the judge in the case of an injunction. The court may also act of its own motion under this provision if the parties have consented to such a hearing or have had an opportunity to be heard on the point and where it appears to the court that the matter does not require a full trial and where the determination by the court will finally resolve the proceedings either completely or in relation to a claim or issue in the proceedings (*RSC Ord 14A, r 1*). Affidavits in support must only contain information within the knowledge of the deponent (see *RSC Ord 41, r 51*).

Summary judgment on a question of law etc

An appeal against a decision under *RSC Ord 14* generally lies from the master (or district judge) to the judge as of right (*RSC Ord 58, rr 1 and 4*), but, save where the contrary is ordered, an appeal will not act as a stay of the proceedings (*RSC Ord 58, r 1(4)*). Appeals must be made promptly. The appeal is dealt with as a hearing de novo, and the judge has a discretion to admit new evidence (see *Evans v Bartlam*[5]).

Appeals against Summary Judgment Orders

---

5.   *Evans v Bartlam* [1937] AC 480.

An order from the judge refusing unconditional leave to defend may be appealed against without leave to the Court of Appeal (*Supreme Court Act 1981, s 18(2)(a)*). An order granting unconditional leave to defend, or dismissing the application for lack of jurisdiction, may be appealed against with the leave of the judge or of the Court of Appeal (see *Supreme Court Act 1981, s 18(1)(b)* and see *RSC Ord 59, r 1A(6)(aa)*).

If judgment is given under *RSC Ord 14A* for the plaintiff or the defendant the action will stand finally determined. An appeal will lie to the judge from the master or district judge as under *RSC Ord 14*, but an appeal from the judge to the Court of Appeal may only be made with leave.

Judgment in default of pleadings

Entering judgment in default of pleadings is available where there has been a default in service of a defence or a statement of claim.

Striking out part of the pleadings

Under *RSC Ord 18, r 19* an application to strike out pleadings should only be made in the clearest of cases. The application should always be made promptly, and generally before the close of pleadings.

By *RSC Ord 18, r 19(1)* the court may order a pleading or endorsement to be struck out or amended if :
- it discloses no reasonable cause of action or defence; or
- it is scandalous, frivolous or vexatious; or
- it may prejudice, embarrass or delay the fair trial of the action; or
- it is otherwise an abuse of the process of the court.

Abuse of process

The court also retains an inherent jurisdiction to stay all proceedings which are clearly an abuse of process or frivolous or vexatious (*RSC Ord 18, r 19*). Where an application is made under *RSC Ord 18, r 19(1)(a)* to strike out pleadings on the grounds that they disclose no reasonable cause of action, no evidence may be admitted (*RSC Ord 18, r 19(2)*). In other circumstances evidence may be admitted by affidavit. An appeal lies to the judge in chambers from the master and is treated as a rehearing (see *RSC Ord 58*), but an appeal to the Court of Appeal is only available with leave (see *RSC Ord 18, r 19* and the Supreme Court Practice 1991, para 18/19/6).

Striking out a claim

Under *RSC Ord 25, r 1(4)* the court will strike out a claim where there has been an "intentional and contumelious" default or inordinate and inexcusable delay in prosecuting the action. In the case of inordinate and inexcusable delay it must be shown that that delay will give rise to a substantial risk that it will not be possible to have a fair trial of the issues in the action or that it is such that it is likely to cause or to have caused serious prejudice to the defendants. For recent treatment of these principles see *Rath v C.S. Lawrence and Partners*[6].

---

6.   *Rath v C.S. Lawrence and Partners* [1991] 1 WLR 399, CA.

Under *RSC Ord 94, r 15*, the Attorney General may apply to the *Vexatious* Divisional Court of the High Court for an order preventing a *litigants* person who has habitually or persistently started vexatious legal proceedings from starting or continuing other legal proceedings without the leave of the High Court. Where a person has been declared a vexatious litigant, leave to allow that person to institute or continue proceedings should not be readily granted (see the Supreme Court Practice 1991, para 94/15/3 and *Ex parte Ewing*[7]).

Under *RSC Ord 23, r 1* the court may order the plaintiff to give *Security for costs* security for the defendant's costs where :

- the plaintiff is ordinarily resident out of the jurisdiction; or
- the plaintiff (not suing in a representative capacity) is only a nominal plaintiff, and there is reason to believe that he would not be able to pay any costs of the defendant if ordered to do so by the court; or
- the plaintiff's address is not stated on the writ or is misstated and that this is not due to a mistake or with an intention to deceive; or
- that the plaintiff has changed his address during the proceedings in order to evade the consequences of the litigation.

A limited company may be ordered to give security for costs if it appears to the court that it will be unable to pay a successful defendant's costs (*Companies Act 1985, s 726*).

Where a reference is made by an English court to the European *Reference to the* Court of Justice ("ECJ") under *Article 177 of the EEC Treaty* the *ECJ under Article* national proceedings shall, unless the court orders otherwise, be *177 of the EEC* stayed until the ECJ has given a preliminary ruling on the *Treaty* question referred (*RSC Ord 114, r 4*).

Under the *Brussels Convention 1968, art 45*, security cannot be required where a party is seeking to enforce a judgment under that Convention. It should be noted that there are also Conventions with various countries relating to security for costs (see the Supreme Court Practice 1991, para 23/1 - 3/17).

The courts have jurisdiction to make interlocutory orders under *Injunctions -* the *Supreme Court Act 1981, s 37* which provides : *General*

"37.   (1) The High Court may by order (whether interlocutory or final) grant an injunction or appoint a receiver in all cases in which it appears to the Court to be just and convenient to do so .

(2) Any such order may be made either unconditionally or on such terms and conditions as the Court thinks just."

Such orders will be made in accordance with *RSC Ord 29*.

---

7.   *Ex parte Ewing* [1991] 3 All ER 192, [1991] 1 WLR 388, CA.

For cases of extreme urgency there is always a judge available on call outside normal court hours to whom applications can be made.

-Mareva injunctions

Mareva injunctions (named after the 1975 case *Mareva Compania Naviera SA v International Bulkcarriers SA*[8]) may be granted where there are good grounds for believing that the plaintiff will succeed in his action, and there is a risk that the defendant has assets within the jurisdiction which may be removed or dissipated or otherwise dealt with so as to make them unavailable or untraceable when judgment has been given. There is a large and complex body of case law dealing with the grant and operation of Mareva injunctions (see the Supreme Court Practice, para 29/1/20*ff*).

In respect of an application for a Mareva injunction :
- There is a continuing obligation to make full and frank disclosure of all material facts.
- The plaintiff should set out his case against the defendant, state the grounds for believing that the defendant has assets against which the order can operate, and that there are grounds for believing that they will be removed or dissipated or otherwise rendered inaccessible to the court in satisfaction of any final judgment against the defendant.
- The plaintiff will have to give an undertaking in damages, backed in appropriate cases by some form of security, in the event that the plaintiff is ultimately unsuccessful in the action. This will include an indemnity against any costs that any third parties may suffer in complying with the order.
- A Mareva takes effect with regard to all assets covered as soon as it is pronounced, and is normally stated to be for a short period of time after which there will be an opportunity for the defendant to apply to the court to discharge the order.
- All with knowledge of the terms of a Mareva applicable to them are under an obligation to do all that they can to preserve such assets, failing which they run the risk of being in contempt of court.

The court may in certain circumstances grant a Mareva covering specific assets abroad (see *Derby & Co Ltd v Weldon*[9]), subject to the proviso that the order shall not affect third parties unless, and to the extent, it is enforced by the courts of the state in which the assets are located (see *Babanaft International Co S.A. v Bassatne and another*[10]).

---

8.   *Mareva Compania Naviera SA v International Bulkcarriers SA* [1980] 1 All ER 213n, [1975] 2 Lloyd's Rep 509, CA.
9.   *Derby & Co Ltd v Weldon (Nos 3 and 4)* [1990] Ch 65, sub nom *Derby & Co Ltd v Weldon (No 2)* [1989] 1 All ER 1002, CA.
10. *Babanaft International Co S.A. v Bassatne and another* [1990] 1 Ch 13, [1989] 1 All ER 433.

The courts may also in certain circumstances grant a pre-judgment worldwide Mareva in support of proceedings abroad,

even though there is no substantive relief sought in the United Kingdom, provided the application for relief can properly be served on the defendant under the Rules of the Supreme Court (*Republic of Haiti v Duvalier*[11]).

Marevas may be granted under the terms of *Article 24 of the 1968 Brussels Convention* even though the courts of another Member State have jurisdiction in respect of the substance of the matter.

The courts retain an inherent jurisdiction to make orders for the preservation and detention of the subject matter of a cause of action and of documents and articles connected with it. These orders authorise a plaintiff to enter the defendant's premises "forthwith", although if entry is refused no force should be used (see *Anton Piller KG v Manufacturing Process Ltd*[12]); and "forthwith" means after a reasonable opportunity has been allowed to the defendant to obtain legal advice (*Bhimji v Chatwani*[13]) and to take away such items as are relevant to the cause of action. The application is made ex parte to the judge in chambers with an affidavit in support, and takes effect as an in personam order only over persons and in relation to premises subject to the jurisdiction of the courts, although this can include an order in respect of premises outside the jurisdiction (*Cook Industries Incorporate v Galliher*[14]). The plaintiff must, inter alia, (a) give a cross-undertaking in damages, (b) undertake to serve the order by a solicitor, (c) serve copies of the evidence with copies of the copiable exhibits, and (d) save in special cases, warn the defendant of his right to take legal advice. *-Anton Pillar Orders*

The purpose of interim injunctions is to preserve the status quo prior to the determination of the rights of the parties at trial. *-Interim injunctions*

The courts will only grant a mandatory injunction as an exceptional form of relief (see *Morris v Redland Bricks Ltd*[15]). *-Mandatory injunctions*

Where the grant or refusal of the injunction will effectively resolve the issue between the parties, the plaintiff must show a prima facie case of a wrong by the defendant and that the plaintiff would be entitled to an injunction at trial, and that the balance of convenience favoured the grant of the interlocutory injunction (see *NWL Ltd v Woods*[16] and *Cayne v Global Natural Resources Plc*[17]). *Grant/refusal of an injunction*

11.   *Republic of Haiti v Duvalier* [1990] 1 QB 202, [1989] 1 All ER 456, CA.
12.   *Anton Piller KG v Manufacturing Process Ltd* [1976] Ch 55, [1976] 1 All ER 779, CA.
13.   *Bhimji v Chatwani,* [1991] 1 All ER 705, [1991] 1 WLR 989.
14.   *Cook Industries Incorporate v Galliher* [1979] Ch 439, [1978] 3 All ER 945.
15.   *Morris v Redland Bricks Ltd* [1970] AC 652, [1969] 2 All ER 576, HL.
16.   *NWL Ltd v Woods* [1979] 3 All ER 614, [1979] 1 WLR 1294, HL.
17.   *Cayne v Global Natural Resources Plc* [1984] 1 All ER 225, CA.

In other cases the main principles to be applied were set out in the House of Lords case of *American Cyanamid Co v Ethicon Ltd*[18] per Lord Diplock :

- the plaintiff must establish a good arguable claim to the rights he seeks to protect;
- it is enough to show a serious case to be tried;
- if the plaintiff passes these tests the court must assess whether to grant the interim injunction on the test of a balance of convenience.

On the balance of convenience the court looks to the following points :

- If damages will be sufficient remedy, an injunction ought not be granted.
- Damages will not be sufficient if the wrong is irreparable, outside the scope of economic compensation, or difficult to assess.
- Would more harm be caused by granting than by refusing the injunction? In general, it is usually taken as better not to risk damaging an established activity.

The hearing will be by motion in the Chancery Division where the hearing will be in open court, or in the Queen's Bench Division in closed session.

Breach of an injunction is dealt with as a contempt of court.

Interim payments   Interim payments may be applied for under *RSC Ord 29, rr 9ff* on account of any damages, debt or other sum (though not costs) which the defendant may be held liable to pay where the claim is for damages for personal injuries (see *RSC Ord 29, r 11*). Orders for interim payment may be made in certain circumstances only.

An order for interim payment shall not, unless the defendant consents or the court otherwise directs, be disclosed to the court before trial on liability and assessment of damages (*RSC Ord 29, r 15*).

Directions   The Directions Stage is the last stage of the proceedings before trial (*RSC Ord 25*). At this stage the court has a duty to consider all relevant matters, including ordering an exchange of witness statements, the admissibility of hearsay evidence under the *Civil Evidence Act 1968, Part I*, any amendments to the writ or pleadings that may be required, the estimate of time required for the trial, and whether the case is one that should be transferred to the county court (*County Courts Act 1984, s 40*).

In cases of actions for personal injury, there is (except in Admiralty cases and cases involving allegations of medical negligence) in relation to the discovery of documents, expert evidence, witnesses, etc, a system of automatic directions under *RSC Ord 25, r 8*.

---

18.   *American Cyanamid Co v Ethicon Ltd* [1975] AC 396, [1975] 1 All ER 504, HL.

Natural persons are normally competent to give evidence and *Witnesses* may be compelled to do so by subpoena when their evidence is relevant to the issues at trial. Failure to comply with a subpoena amounts to a contempt of court, for which a person may be fined or imprisoned.

In general, witnesses are required to swear an oath to tell the truth (see the *Oaths Act 1978*) and, to give their evidence in open court (*RSC Ord 38, r 1*).

The Sovereign and other heads of sovereign states cannot be *- Heads of* compelled to appear as a witness. In certain circumstances, *state/diplomats* diplomats and members of international organisations are partially or totally immune from having to appear as witnesses.

Following the *Evidence (Amendment) Act 1853, s 1* and the *- Spouses* *Evidence Further Amendment Act 1869* spouses of a party to civil proceedings are competent and compellable. A former spouse may be be compellable to give evidence of events that happened during the marriage.

Children may give sworn evidence if they have sufficient *- Children* appreciation of the solemnity of the occasion, and of the added responsibility to tell the truth which is involved in taking an oath. They may now also give unsworn evidence by reason of the *Children Act 1989, s 96(3)*.

Bankers have a limited immunity under the *Bankers Books* *- Bankers* *Evidence Act 1879, s 6* which provides that a banker or officer of a bank shall not in any legal proceedings to which the bank is not a party be compelled to produce a banker's book which could be proved under that Act, or to appear as a witness to prove the contents save by order of a judge.

Certain makers of statements under the *Civil Evidence Act 1968* *Witnesses not* need not be called as witnesses at trial. By *RSC Order 38, r 25* the *required to be* circumstances are where : *called*
- the person is dead;
- the person is beyond the seas (which for these purposes includes the Channel Islands and the Isle of Man);
- the person is unfit by reason of bodily or mental condition;
- despite the exercise of reasonable diligence, the person has not been able to be identified or found;
- the person is not reasonably to be expected to have any recollection of matters relevant to the accuracy or otherwise of the statement in question.

By the *Civil Evidence Act 1972, s 3(1)* where a person is called to *Expert evidence* give evidence in any civil proceedings, his opinion on any relevant matter on which he is qualified to give expert evidence shall be admissible in evidence. However, the evidence on which the expert bases the expert opinion must be proved by admissible evidence. The weight that any tribunal of fact gives to the expert evidence presented before it is a matter for the tribunal.

Expert witnesses   An expert witness must be properly qualified in the subject on which he/she intends to give evidence. It is for the judge to assess this.

Expert witnesses are competent and compellable (see *Harmony Shipping Co SA v Saudi Europe Line Ltd*[19]).

Under *RSC Ord 38, r 36* no party may adduce expert evidence at trial save with leave of the court or where all parties agree, or where evidence is to be given by affidavit unless that party has first applied to the court for relevant directions for the giving of such evidence and complied with those directions of the court or the evidence is given in accordance with the automatic directions for the giving of expert evidence under *RSC Ord 25, r 8(1)(b)* in the case of personal injury actions. This rule does not apply to patent actions which follow a special procedure under *RSC Ord 104, r 13*.

Appeals : House of Lords   Individuals may appear in person or by counsel before the House of Lords. Companies must be represented by counsel. The rules relating to written submissions prior to the hearing are set out under Directions as to Procedure and Standing Orders Applicable to Civil Appeals (July 1988 Edition). Parties must set out a succinct statement of the issues they consider arise in the appeal. Where the House of Lords will be invited to depart from one of its previous decisions this should be set out explicitly.

Court of Appeal   In the Court of Appeal the oral procedure is similar to the House of Lords. Except where appeals are heard as a matter of urgency, or where the respondent relies solely on the judgment of the court below (in which case counsel for the respondent should lodge a letter to that effect), the parties must put in a formal document setting out briefly the legal grounds relied on in the appeal and a skeleton argument setting out a summary of the arguments which will be put before the court. The appellants must also submit a chronology of relevant events.

Course of proceedings in the High Court   The procedure in the High Court is governed by *RSC Ord 35, r 7*. Unless the burden of proof lies on the defendant, it is the plaintiff, normally through his counsel, who opens the case before the court, explaining the plaintiff's case, the arguments the court will have to determine and the factual issues. The plaintiff will then call any witnesses to support the case. After each witness has been examined-in-chief by the plaintiff, the defendant is able to cross-examine the witness. After the defendant has finished the cross-examination, the plaintiff may re-examine on matters that

---

19.   *Harmony Shipping Co SA v Saudi Europe Line Ltd* [1979] 3 All ER 177, [1979] 1 WLR 1380, CA.

have been dealt with in the cross-examination. When the defendant calls evidence he will be able to open his case, call his witnesses, and the process of examination and cross examination of witnesses will be repeated. After the defendant's witnesses have been called, the defendant will be able to sum up his case. The plaintiff is then able to reply to the issues that the defendant has dealt with during the presentation of his case and sum up his case. Where the defendant does not call any evidence the plaintiff makes the closing speech before the defendant. The same procedure is followed in the county court as in the High Court.

The evidence to be given by witnesses must in general be given orally in English and be subject to cross-examination in open court (*RSC Ord 38, r 1*). The judge is at liberty to ask a witness questions to clarify points that are left obscure or which have not been dealt with in examination, but must not "descend into the arena" (see *Yuill v Yuill*[20]). The court may recall a witness, but may not call a witness if the parties object (see *Coulson v Disborough*[21]; and Halsbury's Statutes, Vol 37, para 510). The judge's role is therefore wholly different to that of the examining judge in civil law countries.

The judge may inspect anything or any place within or outside the jurisdiction if it assists him in deciding any question arising in the proceedings (*RSC Ord 35, r 8* and *Tito v Waddell*[22]).

Judgments in hearings in chambers (closed court) are normally *Judgment* given in chambers and are not reported unless a matter of general legal importance is raised. Judgments given after open hearings can be reported. The judgments will include reasons. In cases at first instance they are often given at the conclusion of the hearing. On appeal the court will more frequently reserve its judgment, particularly when considering new points of law. Dissenting judgments can be given.

Costs are dealt with under *RSC Ord 62*. Under the *Supreme Court* *Costs* *Act 1981, s 51*, subject to any rule to the contrary, the costs of and incidental to all civil proceedings in the High Court or the Court of Appeal shall be at the discretion of the court. This is a discretion that the court must exercise judicially - see *Aiden Shipping Co Ltd v Interbulk Ltd*[23] per Lord Goff of Chieveley - "in accordance with reason and justice". This will allow the court, in an appropriate case, to award costs against a successful party.

The main rule for awarding costs is that costs will be awarded against the losing party, such amount to be that allowed on taxation (often stated to be "taxed if not agreed") save where the court considers that the costs should be paid on an indemnity

20.   *Yuill v Yuill* [1945] P 15, [1945] 1 All ER 183, CA.
21.   *Coulson v Disborough* [1894] 2 QB 316, CA.
22.   *Tito v Waddell* [1975] 3 All ER 997, [1975] 1 WLR 1303.
23.   *Aiden Shipping Co Ltd v Interbulk Ltd, The Vimeira* [1986] AC 965, [1986] 2 All ER 409, HL.

basis. Costs are taxed by a taxing master or taxing officer against a tariff of what was a reasonable cost for what was reasonably incurred in the proceedings, any doubts are to be resolved in favour of the paying party (see *RSC Ord 62, r 12*). In practice, where an order for costs is made the successful party is entitled to recover the substantial part of its costs including lawyers' fees.

Costs in interlocutory proceedings are usually ordered to be "costs in cause" so that the ultimate loser will pay all the other side's costs incurred at all stages of the proceedings. However, a party may be ordered to pay the other side's costs of a particular hearing regardless of the final outcome of the action (normally termed "costs in any event").

Payments into court

On acceptance of a payment into court of a sum in settlement of a party's claim, a plaintiff is entitled to such costs as he shall have incurred up to the time of giving notice of acceptance. If a payment into court is not accepted and the plaintiff recovers more than the sum paid into court then the usual rules as to costs apply. Where the plaintiff fails to recover more than the sum which the defendant has offered by way of the sum paid into court, then the plaintiff is entitled to his costs up to the date of the payment in, but the defendant will recover his costs as from the date of payment in.

Length of proceedings

From when the writ is issued until judgment at first instance is given the time taken is approximately 12 months unless expedited in the case of proceedings for judicial review; 6 months for an action in the county court; and between 5 and 18 months for an action in the High Court. Appeal proceedings take from between 9 to 12 months to be heard.

CHAPTER 7 : CRIMINAL PROCEDURE

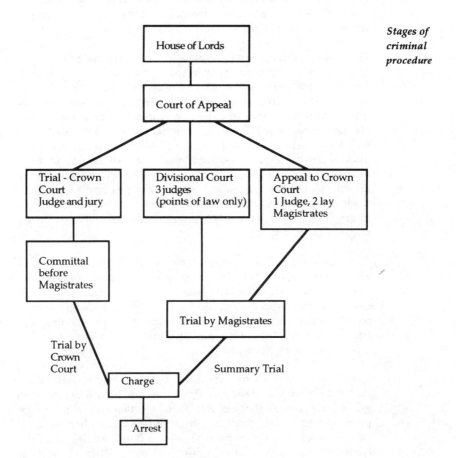

Stages of criminal procedure

Offences are categorised by the way they can be tried. There are three types of offences : indictable offences triable only before the Crown Court sitting with one judge and a jury, summary offences that can be tried summarily before a magistrates' court, and offences that can be tried either way.

Categories of offences

Formal charges are usually brought by the police[1]. The prosecution of these charges is taken over by the Crown Prosecution Service, which was set up under the *Prosecution of Offences Act 1985*, and which has power to decide whether proceedings should be continued and, if so, what charges should be brought (the *Prosecution of Offences Act, s 23*).

Charges

---

1. In fact, these can be brought also by Customs, the Serious Fraud Office, Local Authorities, or private persons.

*Private
prosecutions*

The 1985 legislation left the power of individuals and public bodies to bring a prosecution intact. Various statutes still require the consent either of the Attorney General or of the Director of Public Prosecutions in order for a prosecution to proceed.

The task of the police is to investigate crimes and to charge suspected criminals. The Crown Prosecution Service has the task of prosecuting suspected criminals. If the offence is not a serious one and the suspect admits it the police may caution the offender rather than bring charges.

*Powers of
Detention*

The powers of the police to arrest a suspect and detain him or her without a warrant are now contained in the *Police and Criminal Evidence Act 1984*. *Section 42* of the Act provides that after 24 hours of detention a senior police officer has to review whether the grounds for continued detention without a warrant still exist. He can order a maximum of another 12 hours of detention without a warrant. After a maximum of 36 hours the suspect has to be brought before a magistrates' court and there has to be a hearing (*s 43*). The magistrate may issue a warrant authorising another 60 hours of detention without charges being brought if the investigation concerns a serious arrestable offence. If after 96 hours no charges have been brought, the suspect has to be released (*ss 42 and 43*).

Bail

A person who has been detained by the police may at any time after arrest apply for bail. This must be granted under the criteria of the *Bail Act 1976* unless the police have reasonable grounds for detaining the suspect (a) to secure or preserve evidence relating to the offence, or (b) to obtain such evidence by questioning him (subject to *s 42* above). He may also apply for bail at any time after he has been charged.

Most applications for bail are made before a magistrates' court. Both the Crown Court and the High Court also have jurisdiction to grant bail. Under the *Bail Act 1976*, *s 4* there is a statutory presumption in favour of granting bail to those charged with criminal offences. Consequently, the onus of proving that the conditions for a refusal to grant bail are fulfilled is on the prosecution. If a previous application has been refused further bail applications in the magistrates' court are only likely to succeed if there has been a change in circumstances. Applications for bail are treated as matters of urgency by the courts and are heard promptly.

Bail may be granted unconditionally or conditionally. Where the accused is released on unconditional bail, the sole obligation he is under is to appear in court when required to do so. If the court believes it to be necessary to ensure the defendant's appearance in court or thinks it expedient to take precautionary measures so as to prevent the accused from committing other offences or obstructing the course of justice, it may impose conditions, eg it may ask a third party to stand surety in a sum of money which will be forfeited if the defendant fails to comply with bail conditions;

he may be ordered to reside in a particular place or not to be in contact with persons who may be witnesses in the case or to report to police stations at regular intervals. The present conditions for bail are under review.

The collection of evidence against a person suspected of having committed an offence forms part of the criminal investigation usually carried out by the police. Under the *Police and Criminal Evidence Act 1984,* the investigation and interrogation of suspects and their identification at identification parades is closely regulated. *Evidence*

Under *Section 58* of that Act a person when held in custody at a police station may request access to a solicitor at any time. The detention, treatment and interrogation of suspects at police stations is governed by a code of practice (*Code of Practice for the Detention of, Treatment and Questioning of Person by Police Officers (Code C)*) issued by the Home Secretary under powers conferred on him by the *Police and Criminal Evidence Act.* A breach of the provisions laid down in the Code can be taken into account by the court if this appears to be relevant to any question arising in the proceedings (*Police and Criminal Evidence Act, s 67(1)*).

When a defendant is tried for indictable offences, the bill of indictment has to fulfil certain formal requirements to be valid. Every indictment must name the offence or offences with which the defendant is charged and set out the particulars necessary to give reasonable information as to the nature of each offence, which must be set out as a different charge or count. *Bill of indictment*

Where the defendant appears before a magistrate to answer charges for a summary offence, he is asked whether he pleads guilty or not guilty after the substance of the information against him has been put to him by the magistrate's clerk. He is not normally given the prosecution statements in advance of the trial. *Summary trial*

If the defendant is charged with an offence triable either way, ie by magistrates or by a jury at the Crown Court, he must be told, prior to any hearing of his case in the magistrates' court, of the right to opt for trial at the higher level. *Offence triable either by magistrates or by a jury at the Crown Court*

If a defendant is charged with an offence only triable on indictment, or if he elects Crown Court trial in respect of an offence triable either way, he has to appear first before a magistrate for committal for trial by jury. It is the magistrates' duty to determine on each charge whether there is sufficient evidence to commit the accused for trial by jury. Under the *Magistrates' Courts Act 1980* the defendant may call some or all of the prosecution witnesses for examination or cross-examination during this preliminary hearing. Frequently the defence wait until trial before cross-examining prosecution witnesses. Most committals, however, are dealt with on papers only. It has been suggested that committals should be abolished entirely.

**Witness
statements**

Prior to the committal proceedings, the defence must be supplied with copies of the evidence which the prosecution intends to call. The prosecution may serve notice of additional evidence at a later stage provided the defence is not prejudiced. Evidence that emerges in the course of the inquiry but that the prosecution does not intend to rely on during the trial must be disclosed to the defence subject to the exceptions in the Attorney General's Guidelines (and see *R v Judith Ward*[2]). Failure to disclose evidence or witnesses' names may result in the conviction being quashed on appeal for a breach of the rules of natural justice (*R v Leyland Justices, ex p Hawthorn*[3]).

Pleas

The defendant may plead guilty to a lesser charge. The prosecution must decide whether such a plea is acceptable to dispose of the case or whether they wish to proceed on the more serious charge. If the prosecution accepts a plea of not guilty by a defendant, that concludes the case on that particular charge. A conviction on a guilty plea can be quashed if the appellant can show that he was pressured into pleading guilty. During the trial, a plea can be changed at any time before sentence from not guilty to guilty. A plea of guilty will normally be regarded by the court as a mitigating factor when it comes to sentencing.

In criminal cases in the Crown Court where the defendant pleads not guilty the issue of the guilt or innocence of the defendant is decided by the jury deliberating alone in secret. If the judge is of the view that there is no case to answer he can direct a not guilty verdict. The subsequent sentence is a matter for the judge alone.

Juries

Under the *Juries Act 1974* juries are chosen at random from the electoral register. A person is qualified to sit on a jury if he is between eighteen and seventy, is included on the electoral register and has been a resident in the United Kingdom for at least five years since the age of 13. There are certain categories of persons who cannot or who do not have to sit on juries.

A jury of 12 jurors is chosen at random from a larger panel who are summoned to appear before the Crown Court on the day of the trial. Before the swearing in of each juror the defence can challenge a juror on the grounds that he/she knows the defendant or one of the witnesses or is ineligible or disqualified. The prosecution have an unfettered right to challenge jurors. Prima facie evidence of a juror's unsuitability must be available when challenging the juror.

2.   *R v Judith Ward* (1992) The Times 8.6.92.
3.   *R v Leyland Justices, ex p Hawthorn* [1979] QB 283, [1979] 1 All ER 209, DC.

The sequence of events is similar but not identical in Crown Courts and magistrates' courts. The prosecution normally begins with an opening speech outlining the charges and the substance of the evidence which will be called to support them. The witnesses are then called to give their evidence in person to support the prosecution's case unless their evidence is accepted, in which case it can be read. Defence counsel may cross-examine any of the witnesses called by the prosecution to challenge any evidence that they have given or to bring out points favourable to the defence. Factual assertions that the defence do not wish to challenge may be formally admitted. If counsel for the defence objects to any evidence as inadmissible, the prosecuting counsel will generally be told of this before trial. In his opening speech counsel for the prosecution will not present this evidence and a preliminary trial may take place in the absence of the jury at the end of which the judge will decide whether or not the evidence is admissible.

Course of proceedings before the magistrates' court and the Crown Court

Before defence counsel presents the case for the defence, the judge has a discretion, on a submission to that effect by the defence, to direct the jury to acquit the accused on the grounds that the evidence adduced by the prosecution did not disclose a case to answer. The jury has a discretion at any stage of the proceedings after the close of the prosecution's case to bring in a verdict of not guilty. After the prosecution case is concluded the defence has a right, if it is going to call witnesses other than the defendant, to address the jury, setting out the defence case (a right not often exercised) after which any defence witnesses are called by the defence and cross-examined by the prosecution. Where there is more than one defendant the co-defendant's counsel is entitled to cross-examine witnesses called by another defendant.

With the exception of alibi and expert evidence, the defence is under no obligation to reveal its evidence to the prosecution prior to trial. When giving evidence in his own defence, the accused is not protected against giving self-incriminating answers to questions. Other witnesses are protected from giving answers which may incriminate themselves. Where the defendant has chosen not to have legal representation, he is entitled to call witnesses and cross-examine them himself. After the parties have presented their cases, counsel deliver their closing speeches. In the magistrates' court the prosecution does not have the right to make a final speech.

In the Crown Court, before asking the jury to retire to a separate room and reach a verdict, the judge sums up the case. He directs the jury on the law and summarises the evidence. The judge's task is to present the evidence to the jury in such a way that they will understand the issues of fact which they have to decide. He must do this fairly, summing up the case put by both prosecution and defence. He must make it clear that it is for the jury to decide the issues of fact and that if he has expressed an opinion with which they disagree they must disregard his opinion.

Summing up and direction of the jury

Hearings in public or in camera

Subject to minor statutory restrictions, the strict rule has always been that trials should be held in public. All evidence should be adduced orally. The court should only grant leave to hold hearings in camera in exceptional circumstances. There are statutory restrictions on the right to report criminal proceedings to protect official secrets, juveniles, and rape victims against undue and harmful publicity. Under the *Contempt of Court Act 1981* there is a general duty to refrain from reporting criminal proceedings if there is a substantial risk of prejudice to the course of justice.

Verdict

After the judge's summing up, the jury retire to reach their verdict. If the jury require further assistance in reaching a verdict, they may send a note to the judge who will assist them by giving further directions in open court on the evidence which has already been given. It is too late in the trial for fresh evidence to be called at this stage.

Although the judge directs the jury at the end of his summing up to reach a unanimous verdict, juries have been allowed to return majority verdicts of 11-1 or 10-2 since the coming into force of the *Juries Act 1974* but only after they have tried to reach a unanimous verdict for at least two hours and ten minutes. A jury may acquit a defendant on some counts in the indictment but convict on others. Under the *Criminal Law Act, s 6(3),* juries may acquit the defendant on one charge but return a verdict of guilty on a lesser offence which is a less serious alternative to the one charged.

Except for ambiguous or inconsistent verdicts or for a verdict which the jury has no power to return, the judge has no power to reject a jury's verdict.

Sentencing

If the defendant has pleaded guilty or the jury has found the defendant guilty on one or more counts in the indictment, the judge has the duty of sentencing the defendant. He can either sentence at the end of the trial or adjourn the proceedings to allow reports on the convicted person to be prepared by a probation officer and, if appropriate, medical reports to be prepared.

After a plea or finding of guilt in the magistrates' court, the magistrates may similarly adjourn the case for reports. They may also conclude that their sentencing powers are inadequate to deal with the defendant and may commit him to the Crown Court to be sentenced (see the *Magistrates Court Act 1980, s 88*).

Mitigation of sentence

Before either the magistrates or the judge can pass a sentence they will hear a presentation of the facts of the offence by the prosecution (where there has been a plea of guilty), evidence of previous convictions and the offender's circumstances by a police officer, and any reports on the offender. Frequently, probation officers submit social inquiry reports to the court which contain detailed information on the offender's personal background and upbringing as well as the circumstances that may have led him to commit the offence. Before the judge or magistrates can make an order for the offender's detention in a mental hospital under *Section 37 of the Mental Health Act 1983*, medical and psychiatric reports will also have to be compiled to comply with the statutory requirements.

Once the judge (or magistrates) has read the reports, defence counsel presents the case in mitigation, calls any character witnesses and puts in any evidence in support, eg that a job is available, or a testimonial in favour of the accused. Mitigating circumstances can arise either from the facts of the offence, or from the offender's personal background.

Most offences are statutory offences. Parliament provides a maximum penalty although rarely a minimum sentence (except, for example, in the case of disqualification for offences of drunken driving). A conviction for murder carries a mandatory sentence of life imprisonment although the offender may subsequently be released on licence. *Section 20(1) of the Powers of the Criminal Courts Act 1973* specifically provides that first-time offenders may not be sentenced to a term of imprisonment unless there is no other way of dealing with them appropriately. Further restrictions on sentencing to terms of imprisonment are contained in the *Criminal Justice Act 1991* which comes into force in October 1992. *Sentencing rules and guidelines*

General guidelines on sentencing policy are issued from time to time by the Magistrates Association for magistrates' courts. In addition, there are a number of guideline cases decided by the Court of Appeal in relation to particular types of offence, eg drug offences, rape and social security fraud. These cases set out what the Court of Appeal (normally presided over the Lord Chief Justice as the senior criminal judge) regards as the appropriate range of sentence for cases of different levels of seriousness.

The maximum sentence that magistrates may impose is six months' imprisonment on a single charge or 12 months' imprisonment overall or, as a general rule, a fine of £2,000. Higher fines are available in some cases, for example : fines of up to £20,000 for offences under the *Environmental Protection Act 1990*.

The range of sentences for adults includes sentences of imprisonment which may be wholly or partially suspended[4]. If the sentence is partially suspended the offender must serve a part of the sentence while the balance is held in suspense and will not be activated unless the person commits another offence punishable with imprisonment. In appropriate cases, the court *Range of sentences - custodial*

---

4.   New rules on sentencing are contained in the Criminal Justice Act 1991, which comes into force in October 1992.

may make a hospital order under the *Mental Health Act 1983, ss 37-43*, committing an offender to hospital to undergo psychiatric treatment or to be detained without limit of time in order to protect the public.

- non-custodial

As an alternative to or in addition to a sentence for a term of imprisonment the court may impose a fine on this offender. An order can be made that an offender complete a certain number of hours service to the community. The court may also order an offender to pay compensation or restitution to the victim (see *Powers of Criminal Courts Act 1973 ss 34, 35* (as amended)). If there has been a formal application to the court for compensation by the victim, the victim retains the right to take proceedings in the civil courts. As a further alternative, the court can give a conditional or unconditional discharge.

If the offender has reached the age of 17 he may be placed on probation by the court. A probation order requires the offender for the period stated in it to report regularly to a probation officer under whose supervision he is then placed. Failure to comply with a probation order may result in the offender being brought back to court and sentenced for the offence for which he was placed on probation. He may also be fined up to £400 for breach of probation.

Young offenders

Offenders and juveniles under the age of 21 may not be sent to prison. Instead, if the court finds that there is no alternative to custody they can be sentenced to (i) detention in a young offenders institution, or exceptionally (ii) detention under *Section 53 of the Children and Young Persons Act 1933* for an extended period.

Appeals against sentence

A person convicted in a magistrates' court may appeal to the Crown Court against conviction or sentence. A circuit judge or recorder (part-time judge) sitting with two lay magistrates will then re-hear the case. Appeals on points of law by way of case stated lie to the High Court. This procedure is available both to the prosecution and the defence, whereas an appeal to the Crown Court is not available in the event of an acquittal in the magistrates' court.

Appeal from the Crown Court lies to the Court of Appeal with leave of the Court of Appeal either against conviction or against sentence. Leave to appeal is not required if the trial judge in the Crown Court issues a certificate that the case is fit for appeal, or if the part taken is purely one of law.

A further appeal lies to the House of Lords on points of law of general public importance, but only if either the Court of Appeal or the House of Lords grant leave.

Extradition

Under the *Extradition Act 1989, s 5* a person may be extradited if extradition procedures between the state requesting extradition and the UK are available and if the extradition request is made in respect of a crime covered by extradition. Under *s 2(2)*, extradition crimes are defined as crimes which would carry a sentence of at least 12 months' imprisonment if they had been committed in the United Kingdom and which are punishable under the laws of the state requesting extradition.

Where no extradition arrangements exist under a treaty between the United Kingdom and the foreign state, *Section 22 of the Extradition Act* allows the making of an Order in Council which can give the same effect to certain international Conventions specified in the Act as an extradition treaty would have between the United Kingdom and the foreign state that is party to the Convention. This applies only, however, to the offences which are relevant to the Convention in question.

CHAPTER 8 : REMEDIES

The following is a brief outline of remedies in civil cases :

Damages are awarded pursuant to common law and statute and are available in many areas of law (contract, tort, judicial review, breach of statutory duty, company law etc). Their purpose is to compensate for damage suffered. The plaintiff must show loss or damage caused by the wrong, otherwise only "nominal" damages are recoverable. In limited circumstances, the court may award "aggravated damages" (to compensate the plaintiff) or "exemplary damages" (to punish the defendant).
Damages

In most cases, it is the task of the judge to assess the quantum of damages to be awarded. A judge may, exceptionally, call in an assessor (*Supreme Court Act 1981, s 70; RSC Ord 33, r 6*), or may refer the assessment to a Supreme Court Master (*RSC Ord 37, r 1*) or special referee (*RSC Ord 37, r 4(1)*). This is only done in exceptional circumstances. An application for trial by jury can be made in the following types of action : libel, slander, false imprisonment, malicious prosecution and, in exceptional cases, personal injury (see *Supreme Court Act 1981, s 69; RSC Ord 33, r 5* and the note thereto). This will be refused where the complexity of the case renders it unsuitable for trial by jury.

In personal injury cases, damages awarded take account of pain and suffering, loss of earning capacity and special medical needs. Most injuries have a more or less established value for pain, suffering and loss of amenity and judges will be guided by the main text on awards in previous cases (see Kemp and Kemp, The Quantum of Damages).
Personal injury cases

As a general rule, damages are not available for mental distress which has no medical basis. Damages have been awarded where the purpose of a contract was to afford peace of mind to the innocent party (*Biss v Lambeth, Southwark and Lewisham Area Health Authority*[1]). In tort, damages have been awarded for nervous shock suffered as the result of witnessing an accident (see *McLoughlin v O'Brian*[2]).
Mental distress

Where the plaintiff has suffered a loss of reputation, by reason of words which have been spoken or written, his remedy lies in an action for the tort of defamation. In recent years, juries have made very substantial awards. Such awards have been much
Loss of reputation

---

1.   *Biss v Lambeth, Southwark and Lewisham Area Health Authority* [1978] 2 ALL ER 125, [1978] 1 WLR 382, CA; and see further the "holiday" case - *Jarvis v Swans Tours Ltd* [1973] QB 273, [1973] 1 All ER 71, CA.
2.   *McLoughlin v O'Brian* [1983] 1 AC 410.

criticised. There is no recovery in contract for loss of reputation caused by a breach of contract, except in cases of breach of a contract designed to give a person an opportunity to enhance his reputation, in which case damages may be recoverable for that loss of opportunity.

Contract and tort compared

Although there are principles common to the assessment of damages in both contract and tort, it is important to distinguish between the two. Damages for breach of contract aim to put the plaintiff in the position that he would have been had the contract been performed, whereas damages in tort aim to restore the plaintiff to the "status quo ante" the tort : accordingly damages for loss of a bargain are recoverable only in contract. Further differences are as follows :

Liquidated damages

- Liquidated damages (a sum fixed by the parties prior to the breach) may be available in contract but not in tort, where damages are unliquidated. The sum fixed by parties to a contract by way of liquidated or fixed damages can be challenged in the courts on the grounds that it is not a genuine attempt to estimate the true loss but amounts to a penalty and is therefore unenforceable.

Exemplary damages

- Exemplary damages are not awarded in contract but only in tort. They are available only in very limited circumstances : see *Rookes v Barnard*[3] : Lord Devlin at 1220, 1226 sets out three categories : (i) cases of oppressive, arbitrary or unconstitutional action by servants of the government, (ii) where the defendant's conduct was calculated by him to make a profit for himself which may well exceed the compensation payable to the plaintiff, (iii) statute, eg *Copyright, Designs and Patents Act 1988, s 97(2)*.

Contributory negligence

- Contributory negligence by a plaintiff reduces damages in an action in tort (*Law Reform (Contributory Negligence) Act 1945*), whereas in an action framed in contract damages are reduced only where the breach of contract is an act or omission which would also even in the absence of any contract have given rise to liability in tort (see *Forsikringsaktieselskapet Vesta v Butcher*[4]).

Similarity in damages between tort and contract

Damages in tort and contract are similar in the following ways :
- The "duty" on the plaintiff to mitigate his loss;
- Damages for loss already suffered and for all prospective losses flowing from a single cause of action must be recovered in one action;
- Agreements to exclude liability or remedies in contract and in tort are now regulated by *Part I of the Unfair Contract Terms Act 1977*.

---

3.   *Rookes v Barnard* [1964] AC 1129.
4.   *Forsikringsaktieselskapet Vesta v Butcher* [1988] 3 WLR 565, CA; affd on other grounds [1989] AC 852, [1989] 1 All ER 402, HL.

Damages for pure economic loss are recoverable in contract. *Economic loss*
Accordingly, loss of profit (or loss of use) is recoverable
("expectation interest") together with any expenses incurred by
the plaintiff due to the breach of contract. Expenses incurred by
the plaintiff in performance prior to the breach ("reliance
interest") can be recovered as an alternative where the plaintiff
cannot rely on loss of profits as a basis to recover damages (see
Anglia Television Ltd v Reed[5]).

In 1964, the House of Lords allowed a claim for pure economic *Negligent mis-*
loss against an adviser who had made negligent *statement*
misrepresentations to the plaintiff. The plaintiff, in reliance on the
advice, incurred expenditure, and suffered a purely economic
loss. There was no contractual relationship but damages in tort
were awarded because the court concluded there had been a
"special relationship" between the parties (see *Hedley Byrne &
Co Ltd v Heller & Partners Ltd*[6]; see also *Caparo Industries Plc v
Dickman*[7]). However, as a general rule, in the absence of physical
damage, loss of profits are not actionable. Loss is recoverable
only if it arises out of physical damage and there is foreseeability
of this, proximity between the plaintiff and defendant and no
policy objections (*Leigh & Sillavan Ltd v Aliakmon Shipping Co
Ltd*[8]; *Murphy v Brentwood District Council*[9]; *Department of the
Environment v T. Bates and sons Ltd*[10]).

Where property is damaged, damages are generally assessed on *Damage to*
the basis of a diminution in value, and, where misappropriated, *property*
on the basis of the market value. Loss of profit from or loss of use
of property is also recoverable, as are expenses incurred by
reason of the breach.

Restitution is a remedy which seeks to return value or property in *Restitution*
circumstances where it is no longer right that the transferee retain
it at the expense of the transferor. A claim can be either
proprietary (the plaintiff "follows" his property or money into the
hands of recipients and is entitled to recover it) or personal (the
recipient is obliged to pay a sum of money to the plaintiff).
Restitution commonly arises out of contracts which for one reason
or another are ineffective, or where a trustee or fiduciary has
enriched himself at the expense of the beneficiary in breach of
his fiduciary position.

---

5.   *Anglia Television Ltd v Reed* [1972] 1 QB 60, [1971] 3 All ER 690,
        CA.
6.   *Hedley Byrne & Co Ltd v Heller & Partners Ltd* [1964] AC 465,
        [1963] 2 All ER 575, HL.
7.   *Caparo Industries Plc v Dickman* [1990] 2 AC 605, [1990] 1 All ER
        568, HL.
8.   *Leigh & Sillavan Ltd v Aliakmon Shipping Co Ltd* [1986] AC
        785, [1986] 2 All ER 145, HL.
9.   *Murphy v Brentwood District Council* [1990] 2 All ER 908, HL,
        [1990] 3 WLR 414.
10.   *Department of the Environment v T. Bates and sons Ltd* [1990] 2
        All ER 943, [1990] 3 WLR 457, HL.

The underlying policy of restitution is that a person should not be enriched at the expense of another as this is unjust. The principle of unjust enrichment is the unifying thread of restitution but is not yet a distinct cause of action.

Specific performance

The remedy of specific performance of a contract is an order of the court which compels a defendant to do what he promised to do. This remedy will be granted at the court's discretion as an alternative to, or in addition to, damages only where it is both appropriate and practicable (see the *Supreme Court Act 1981, s 49*).

It is not appropriate to grant specific performance in cases where damages would be an adequate remedy (see *Tito v Waddell (No 2)*[11]). Damages are not regarded as adequate (a) to compensate purchasers of land; (b) in a number of cases where there is an inherent difficulty in quantifying damages; and (c) under a contract to deliver "specific or ascertained" goods (*Sale of Goods Act 1979, s 52*).

In general, specific performance is not appropriate to remedy breaches of contracts of employment (see *Johnson v Shrewsbury & Birmingham Rly Co*[12]. Nor is it appropriate to enforce a contract when to do so would involve the court in constant supervision of the performance ordered (see *Ryan v Mutual Tontine Westminster Chambers Association*[13]).

An order for specific delivery of goods wrongfully detained is available in an appropriate case against a defendant in possession or control of those goods, pursuant to the *Torts (Interference with Goods) Act 1977, s 3(2) (a)*. This remedy is available at the discretion of the court and is usually coupled with an order for payment of any consequential damages. Specific delivery will not usually be granted in respect of ordinary articles of commerce.

Frustrated performance

Where, without fault of either party, performance of a contract has become physically or commercially impossible or will require something radically different by reason of a change in circumstances after the contract was concluded, the contract is said to have been "frustrated" (see the *Law Reform (Frustrated Contracts) Act 1943*). The following have been held to be frustrating events : change in the law rendering performance illegal; outbreak of war; where the physical subject matter of the contract has perished or has been requisitioned by the government; frustration of the common venture (*Jackson v Union*

---

11.   *Tito v Waddell (No 2)* [1977] Ch 106, [1977] 3 All ER 129.
12.   *Johnson v Shrewsbury & Birmingham Rly Co* (1853) 3 De GM & G 914.
13.   *Ryan v Mutual Tontine Westminster Chambers Association* [1893] 1 Ch 116.

Marine Insurance Co Ltd[14]); cancellation of an event; incapacity or death of a person obliged to perform a contract. However, financial loss or inconvenience to a party in performing a contract does not suffice to frustrate the contract. Clearly, the remedy of specific performance is not available in such cases.

Parties to a contract may agree that, in the event of a breach, the party in breach shall pay to the other an agreed liquidated, or fixed, sum of money. Where such a liquidated sum is in essence a genuine pre-estimate of damages, such sum will be recoverable. A penalty clause being one which does not set such a pre-estimate and which provides that an arbitrary sum of money will be paid on breach may not be relied upon (see *Dunlop Pneumatic Tyre Co Ltd v New Garage and Motor Co Ltd*[15]). *Penalty clauses*

Interest is available on monetary judgments pursuant to the *Supreme Court Act 1981, s 35A* but only if specifically claimed. The power to award interest is discretionary. Interest is awarded as of right in cases of personal injury or wrongful death (see *Supreme Court Act 1981, s 35A(2).*) The parties to a contract may agree that interest is to be payable under the contract which may then be claimed as of right. *Interest on money judgments*

Under *Supreme Court Act 1981, s 35A* the maximum period for which interest may be awarded is the period between the date when the cause of action arose and the date of judgment. In general, simple rather than compound interest is awarded (see the *Supreme Court Act 1981, s 35A*). While the rate at which interest is awarded is normally discretionary it is the practice of the Commercial and Admiralty courts to award interest at a rate representing the bank base rate plus 1%.

A declaration of the rights of a party without any reference to their enforcement may be given in a public law claim or in a private law claim. The declaration claimed must be of some tangible benefit to the plaintiff and may not be simply the answer to a hypothetical question. The court will not exercise its discretion to make a declaration where an adequate alternative remedy is available or where it would be inequitable to do so. Declarations that directly or indirectly affect the Crown may be made on the same principles as those that affect a subject (see the *Crown Proceedings Act 1947, s 21* and generally). *Declaration of rights*

The rules governing the winding-up of companies are found in *Part IV - VII of the Insolvency Act 1986* and *Part 4 of the Insolvency Rules 1986 (SI 1986/1925)* and the *Insolvency Regulations 1986 (SI 1986 /1994) as amended (Parts VIII to XI of the Act govern the bankruptcies of individuals).* A winding-up can be voluntary (on the occurrence of an event stipulated in the *Winding-up of companies*

14. *Jackson v Union Marine Insurance Co Ltd* (1874) LR 10 CP 125, [1874-80] All ER Rep 317.
15. *Dunlop Pneumatic Tyre Co Ltd v New Garage and Motor Co Ltd* [1915] AC 79, 86-88, [1914-15] All ER Rep 739, HL.

constitution of the company or by resolution of the members (*s 84*) or compulsory (by order of the court - *s 122 (1)*). Jurisdiction lies with the High Court and, if share capital is below a certain level, also in the county court (*s 117*). It can be used as a remedy by a variety of parties : by a creditor of the company to apply pressure; by an aggrieved minority shareholder; by the members of a successful company who wish to dissolve the company and realise their assets; by the Secretary of State on the grounds of public interest (*ss 124 and 124A*); or more indirectly, by a person (who has locus to petition) who is a party to, or anticipates, litigation with the company, as a means to trigger the operation of *ss 126 and 130* and frustrate that litigation.

The court may make a winding-up order in the circumstances listed in *s 122(1)* if :

(a)   the company has by special resolution resolved that the company be wound up by the court;

(b)   being a public company which was registered as such on its original incorporation, the company has not been issued with a certificate under *Section 117 of the Companies Act* (public company share capital requirements) and more than a year has expired since it was so registered;

(c)   it is an old public company, within the meaning of the *Companies Consolidation (Consequential Provisions) Act 1985*;

(d)   the numbers of members is reduced below two;

(e)   the company is unable to pay its debts (defined in *s 123*);

(f)   the court is of the opinion that it is just and equitable that the company should be wound up.

The last ground gives the court a discretionary catch-all power but is available to petitioning members only as a last resort (*s 125(2)*). The "just and equitable" ground has been held to cover circumstances where the company was formed for a fraudulent purpose, where the whole purpose of the company has gone, where the company is in effect a quasi partnership and the partnership has broken down or there is a deadlock in management, or where the majority of members have operated a fraud on the minority, see *In Re Westbourne Galleries*[16].

Administration of companies   The *Insolvency Act 1986* also introduced a new procedure as an alternative to winding-up, known as "administration" (see *Part II* of the Act). Administration is an order of the court placing the affairs of the company in the sole control of an administrator who must be a qualified insolvency practitioner. The jurisdiction of the High Court and county court is the same as for winding-up (*s 117 IA of the 1986 Act and s 744 of the Companies Act 1985*). The court

---

16.   *In Re Westbourne Galleries* [1973] AC 360, [1972] 2 All ER 492, HL.

will only make an order if satisfied that one of the purposes listed in *s 8(3)* exists :-

    (a)   the survival of the company, and the whole or any part of its undertaking, as a going concern;

    (b)   the approval of a voluntary arrangement under Part I;

    (c)   the sanctioning under *Section 425 of the Companies Act* of a compromise or arrangement between the company and any such persons as are mentioned in that section; and

    (d)   a more advantageous realisation of the company's assets than would be effected on a winding-up.

The company, the directors or a creditor or creditors can apply for an administration order (*s 9*). From the making of the application, the company is protected from winding-up and from litigation, and security over the company's property cannot be enforced (save with leave of the court or administrator); this protection continues throughout the administration (*ss 10 and 11*). The aim is to give the company a chance to work itself out of its difficulty. It is still too early to judge the success of administrations, but it is proving popular to date.

Where a secured creditor of a company fears that the company is in financial difficulty, rather than await a general administration or winding-up, the creditor may wish to protect its own security interests by appointing a receiver of the property (or administrative receiver who must be a qualified insolvency practitioner, defined by *Section 29(2)* as a receiver and manager of the whole or substantially the whole of the company's property). The appointment of an administrative receiver blocks any application for an administration order (*s 9*). But an administration order overrides a mere receiver and he must vacate his office if required to do so by the administrator (*s 11(2)*). *Receivers*

Both the High Court and county court have jurisdiction to appoint a receiver "in all cases in which it seems just and equitable to do so" (*Supreme Court Act 1981, s 37(1); County Court Act 1984, s 38*). The court will appoint a receiver at the instance of a chargee if the security is in jeopardy or the charger has failed to comply with the security agreement. Applications for a court-appointed receiver by contributors of the company have succeeded where directors were neglecting their duties or there was deadlock in management (see *Stanfield v Gibbon*[17]; *Trade Auxiliary Co v Vickers*[18]; *Featherstone v Cooke*[19]).

Administrative law remedies are available pursuant to *RSC Ord 53* which sets out the procedures for all remedies by way of judicial review of governmental action or administrative action by other public bodies. The prerogative orders of mandamus, prohibition and certiorari may be made as well as the remedies of declarations, injunctions and awards of damages. The various *Administrative law remedies*

---

17.   *Stanfield v Gibbon* [1925] WN 11.
18.   *Trade Auxiliary Co v Vickers* (1873) LR 16 Eq 303.
19.   *Featherstone v Cooke* (1873) LR 16 Eq 298.

forms of relief may be joined in one application either alternatively or in addition to one another but only if the forms of relief claimed arise out of, or relate to, the same matter. All the above forms of relief may be granted at the court's discretion only. The claim may also include a claim for damages. An injunction may be granted on an application for judicial review against a public body or a government minister.

Prerogative orders defined

Prohibition is an order restraining an inferior court or tribunal or a public authority from acting outside its jurisdiction. Certiorari is an order which brings up to the High Court to be quashed a decision of an inferior court or tribunal or of a public authority.

Mandamus is an order requiring an inferior court or tribunal or a person or body of persons charged with a public duty to carry out its judicial or other public duty.

Judicial review

The remedy of judicial review lies against persons or bodies with judicial or quasi-judicial functions and bodies exercising administrative powers with a "public" dimension (see *Ridge v Baldwin*[20]). An interlocutory injunction has been held to be available against a government minister on an application for judicial review, to restrain that minister from enforcing provisions of statute and regulations made thereunder on the ground that the statute and regulations complained of were in conflict with the laws of the European Community (see *R v Secretary of State for Transport, ex p Factortame Ltd*[21]).

Before an application for judicial review can be made the applicant must be granted leave to apply. An applicant for judicial review must have "sufficient interest in the matter to which the application relates" (*Supreme Court Act 1981, s 32(3)* and *RSC Ord 53, r 3(7)*).

In cases where the applicant has no direct personal interest in the application, it is for the court to decide whether the applicant has the required standing. The court approaches the question having regard to all the circumstances of the case but taking into particular account the relationship between the applicant and the matter to which the application relates (see *R v Inland Revenue Commissioners, ex p National Federation of Self Employed and Small Businesses Ltd*[22]). The grant of leave to apply does not preclude further consideration of the applicant's standing at the hearing itself (see *R v Inland Revenue Commissions (supra)* at p630).

Compensation

A criminal court may make a compensation order against a person convicted of an offence instead of or in addition to dealing with him in any other way. Where such an order is made,

---

20.   *Ridge v Baldwin* [1964] AC 40, [1963] 2 All E R 66.
21.   *R v Secretary of State for Transport, ex p Factortame Ltd* [1990] 2 AC 85, [1989] 2 All ER 692, HL.
22.   *R v Inland Revenue Commissioners, ex p National Federation of Self Employed and Small Businesses Ltd* [1982] AC 617, 659 [1981] 2 All ER 93, HL.

damages awarded in a subsequent civil action for the same injury loss or damage must be assessed without regard to the order; but the plaintiff in that civil action may only recover a sum equal to the aggregate of :

(a)   any amount by which the civil damages exceed the compensation.

(b)   a sum equal to any portion of the compensation which he fails to recover.

Any person who satisfies the Criminal Injuries Compensation Board that he has sustained a qualifying injury or that he is a dependant of a person who died after sustaining a qualifying injury will be entitled to an award of compensation (see the *Criminal Justice Act 1988, ss 108-117*[23]).

Written agreements to arbitrate are governed by the *Arbitration Acts* (see the *Arbitration Act 1950, s 32* and the *Arbitration Act 1975, s 7*). If court proceedings are brought by a party to an arbitration agreement in respect of any matter agreed to be referred, the court may, in the case of a domestic arbitration, or must, in the case of a non-domestic arbitration, stay those proceedings on the application of a party served in those proceedings who has taken no further steps in those proceedings (see the *Arbitration Act 1950, s 4(1)* and the *Arbitration Act 1975, s 1(1)*. Such stays are granted to give effect to the arbitration agreement and the court is not precluded from making orders ancillary to the arbitration (see *Zalinoff v Hammond*[24]).

Arbitration

An arbitrator may make an award providing for the payment of money by one party to the other and/or a declaration as to the parties' respective rights or the right of one party to be indemnified by the other. Arbitrators usually also have the power to award specific performance (see the *Arbitration Act 1950, s 15*).

---

23.   This put the previous scheme of compensation for victims of crimes of violence on a statutory basis.

24.   *Zalinoff v Hammond* [1898] 2 Ch 92 at 95.

CHAPTER 9 : MATRIMONIAL DISPUTES

The *Children Act 1989* establishes a concurrent jurisdiction which covers the High Court, county court and magistrates' court. This enables cases involving children to be heard at an appropriate level or transferred to be heard with other related proceedings such as divorce and division of property. The *Children (Allocation of Proceedings) Order 1991, (SI 1991/1677)* provides for the reorganisation of the court structure and facilitates transfer of cases between courts. *Jurisdiction of the courts*

Magistrates sitting in Family Proceedings Courts may hear applications under *Section 8 of the Children Act 1989* relating to the care of children (see below) and other private family proceedings outside divorce. *Magistrates' courts*

The county courts' jurisdiction is divided into four categories : *County courts*
-     Non-divorce county courts which can grant injunctions in cases of domestic violence and order a party to leave the matrimonial home and to refrain from molesting the aggrieved party;
-     Divorce county courts which can issue private law family proceedings. However, all contested matters will be transferred to Family Hearing Centres;
-     Family Hearing Centres, which have full jurisdiction in private law family proceedings; and
-     Care Centres which have full jurisdiction over private and public law matters. This includes cases, where the parent and family are unable to provide adequate care, to commit the child to the care of the local authority.

The *Family Proceedings (Allocation to Judiciary) Directions 1991* allocates work between judges in the county court.

The High Court, Family Division has full jurisdiction to hear all cases involving children including private wardship proceedings. *High Court, Family Division*

A divorce petition may not be presented within one year of marriage (*Matrimonial Causes Act 1973, s 3(1)*). There is only one ground for divorce in England and Wales namely that the marriage has irretrievably broken down (*Matrimonial Causes Act 1973, s 1(1)*). However, the court must be satisfied that one or more of the facts in *Section 1(2) of the Matrimonial Causes Act 1973* has occurred before it can find that the marriage has irretrievably broken down. *Presentation of divorce petition*

Grounds for *divorce*	These facts are :

- that the respondent has committed adultery and the petitioner finds it intolerable to live with the respondent;
- that the respondent has behaved in such a way that the petitioner cannot reasonably be expected to live with the respondent;
- that the respondent has deserted the petitioner for a continuous period of at least two years immediately preceding the presentation of the petition;
- that the parties have lived apart for a continuous period of two years immediately preceding the presentation of the petition and the respondent consents to a decree being granted; and
- that the parties have lived apart for a continuous period of at least five years immediately preceding presentation of the petition.

Judicial
separation

A petition for judicial separation may be presented to the court on the ground that any of the facts in *Section 1(2) of the Matrimonial Causes Act 1973* exists. The court does not have to determine whether the marriage has irretrievably broken down but only has to be satisfied that one of those facts exists. Unlike divorce, there is no time bar on presenting a petition for judicial separation.

Children

The philosophy behind the *Children Act 1989* is contained in four basic principles :

- The Welfare Principle - *Section 1(1)* states that the court should have regard to the child's welfare as the paramount consideration when determining any question relating to the child's upbringing or the administration of the child's property. The court is guided as to the application of this principle by the checklist in *s 1(3)*;
- Avoidance of Delay - the court must have regard to the principle that delay is likely to prejudice the child's welfare, *s 1(2)*;
- The Principle of Non-Intervention - *Section 1(5)* of the Act precludes the making of any Order unless the court is satisfied that to make an order is better for the child than making no order at all. Therefore, if the parties are in agreement, the court will generally make no order.
- Parental Responsibility - this concept largely replaces that of custody. *Section 3(1)* states that "parental responsibility means all the rights, duties, powers, responsibilities and authority which by law a parent of a child has in relation to the child and his property". *Section 2* governs who automatically has parental responsibility and who may obtain it. Married parents have parental responsibility; if the parents are unmarried, parental responsibility is vested solely in the mother; however, the father may acquire it by court order or by agreement (*s 4*).

Section 8 of the Act empowers the court to make, vary or discharge a whole new range of orders. These replace custody, care and control and access.

-     Contact Order - this "requires the person with whom a child lives or is to live to allow the child to visit or stay with a person named in the order". Contact orders may also provide for telephone calls and letters;
-     Residence Order - this states with whom a child shall live. A residence order may be made in favour of more than one person and can state the amount of time a child should spend with each person;
-     Specific Issue Order - this provides for settling any particular dispute regarding a child's upbringing - for example, removing a child from the jurisdiction, or a dispute over schooling; and
-     Prohibited Steps Order - this prevents anyone taking steps "which could be taken by a parent in meeting his parental responsibility".

The rules governing divorce proceedings in the county court are the *Family Proceedings Rules 1991, (SI 1991/1247)*. Every divorce suit is commenced by petition which must state what relief the petitioner seeks. This, together with the marriage certificate and a statement as to arrangements for children (form M4), must be filed with the court. This statement should contain information such as schooling and health, and proposals for residence and contact after the decree. The petition is served upon the respondent (and any co-respondent) and the respondent must acknowledge service, stating whether he/she intends to defend the divorce suit and whether he/she agrees with the arrangements for the children. The respondent may file an answer and cross-petition. If a suit is undefended it should enter the special procedure list (*Family Proceedings Rules 1991, r 2.36*).

The district judge gives directions setting a date for the preliminary ruling of decree nisi to be pronounced in open court if satisfied that the petitioner has sufficiently proved the contents of the petition.

If the parties do not agree about arrangements affecting the children, the district judge may give directions to arrange a conciliation appointment for the parties; he may request a court welfare officer to report to the court; and he may consider any relevant evidence. If necessary, the district judge will transfer the matter to the appropriate court for a full hearing. An application for the decree to be made absolute may be made six weeks after decree nisi. The judge may make the decree absolute if he is satisfied that there are no outstanding matters, as set out in the *Family Proceedings Rules 1991, r 2.49*, and is satisfied with the arrangements for the children. The marriage is dissolved on decree absolute and both parties are free to remarry should they so wish.

Section 8
Applications

Applications under the *Children Act 1989* are governed in the magistrates' court by the *Family Proceedings Courts (Children Act 1989) Rules 1991, (SI 1991/1395)* and in the county court by the *Family Proceedings Rules 1991, (SI 1991/1247)*. If there are on-going proceedings (such as divorce), all proceedings should be consolidated and any Section 8 application made to the court where the existing proceedings are in progress. An application should be made on the prescribed form, one application for each child, except in divorce proceedings. Unless the court directs otherwise, service is on 21 days' notice (see *Schedule 2 to the Family Proceedings Courts (Children Act 1989) Rules 1991* and *Appendix 3 to the Family Proceedings Rules 1991*). The respondent should answer within 14 days. The court has a duty under the Act to minimise delay. At the first appointment, consideration will be given as to time-tabling, and the next review/hearing date should be fixed. Parties must file evidence in the form of statements if so directed by the court (*Children Act 1989, s 7*). In contested applications, the court may request a court welfare officer to prepare a report, and this must be filed at least five days before the hearing. Often the court will make an interim order until the full hearing. It should be noted that no order in relation to children is ever final.

Ancillary relief

In ancillary relief matters, the court has a wide discretion as to what orders it can make, each case being considered on its merits. See statutory guidelines under *Section 25 of the Matrimonial Causes Act 1973*.

The children's welfare is the first consideration but it is not the overriding or paramount consideration (*Suter v Suter*[1]).

Section 25(2) directs the court to have regard to specific matters, including income and resources, earning capacity, financial needs and responsibilities, the standard of living enjoyed by the family before the breakdown of the marriage, the age of the parties, the duration of the marriage and the contributions made by each party whether financial or in caring for the family, (*Wachtel v Wachtel*[2]).

Section 25A obliges the court to consider whether it would be just and reasonable to achieve a final clean break between spouses on divorce, if financial resources should be divided once and for all and each party be financially self-sufficient. Clearly, this is not totally possible if children are involved (*Dipper v Dipper*[3]).

1.   *Suter v Suter and Jones* [1987] Fam 111, [1987] 2 All ER 336, CA.
2.   *Wachtel v Wachtel* [1973] Fam 72, [1973] 1 All ER 829, CA.
3.   *Dipper v Dipper* [1981] Fam 31, [1980] 2 All ER 722, CA.

CHAPTER 10 : PROPERTY TRANSACTIONS

These are normally carried out by solicitors and licensed conveyancers although an individual may do his own conveyancing .

The following steps normally take place : a property will be offered for sale at an asking price either privately or more usually through an estate agent. The purchaser will make an offer usually on the basis of a survey of the property by a surveyor. The offer is not binding in law - it commits neither party to the sale. This is so even when the offer has been accepted by the vendor. At this stage a refundable deposit of 10% of the purchase price will be paid . The purchaser must then make enquiries and searches to ensure that the vendor can pass good title and that there are no plans, such as for developments or road widening schemes, or other local government plans in prospect that would devalue the property.

On receiving the replies to the local searches, amendments may be made to the draft contract or further questions put to the vendor or lessor's solicitor on any relevant matter.

Thereafter, the draft contract will be drawn up, engrossed and signed. It is exchanged with the vendor by post or telephone. At that point insurance will be required to cover the full amount of the purchase price of the property.

After contracts are exchanged a draft conveyance, or transfer of title, is prepared and a date for completion is fixed. The documents will be signed executing the conveyance together with details of the mortgage, insurance and the agreed price to be paid on completion.

On completion the keys are exchanged and the property is vacated for immediate possession.

CHAPTER 11 : RECOGNITION AND ENFORCEMENT OF FOREIGN JUDGMENTS

The relevant procedural rules are set out in the *Rules of the* *Relevant rules*
Supreme Court Order 71.

In addition to the *Brussels Convention,* discussed below, England *Reciprocal*
and Wales have two reciprocal enforcement treaties in force : *enforcement*
- *Foreign Judgments (Reciprocal Enforcement) Act 1933* *treaties*
(for a list of the countries to which this Act applies see
the Supreme Court Practice 1991, paras 71/1/5 and 6).
- *Administration of Justice Act 1920* (for a list of the
countries to which this Act applies see the Supreme
Court Practice 1991, para 71/1/2).

Enforcement under both Acts is by registration. The rules *Enforcement by*
governing such registration are broadly similar to those governing *registration*
the recognition and enforcement of judgments from *Brussels*
Convention countries. The *Brussels Convention* was
implemented in the United Kingdom by the *Civil Jurisdiction and*
Judgments Act 1982 (the "*CJJA*").

Applications for the registration of a judgment must be made ex *Brussels*
parte (*RSC Ord 71, r 27*) to the High Court under *CJJA, s4*, which *Convention 1968*
lays down :
- (*s 3*) that a judgment registered under *Section 4* shall
have the same force and effect for the purposes of
enforcement as if it had been originally given by the
registering court; and
- (*s 2*) that the reasonable costs of registration of the
judgment under *Section 4* are recoverable as if they
were sums ordinarily recoverable under the judgment.

The *Lugano Convention* was ratified by the United Kingdom on 5
February 1992 and entered into force on 1 May 1992.

An application to register a judgment under the *Administration of* *1920 Act*
Justice Act 1920 or under the *Foreign Judgments (Reciprocal*
Enforcement) Act 1933 is made ex parte (*RSC Ord 71, r 2(1)*) to the
High Court in the first instance, but the court may direct that a
summons must be issued.

- *Section 9(3)(a)* directs that once a judgment is
registered it shall be of the same force and effect for
the purposes of enforcement as if it had been
originally given by the registering court.

- *Section 9(3)(c)* directs that the reasonable costs of and incidental to the registration of a judgment are recoverable as if they were sums ordinarily recoverable under the judgment.

By *Section 9(1) of the 1920 Act*, an application to register must be commenced within 12 months of the date of the judgment (although the court has a discretion to extend that period).

The judgment must have been given in civil proceedings and be for the payment of a sum of money only (*s 12*); *Section 9(2) of the 1920 Act* and the Supreme Court Practice 1991, para 71/1/2 set out the circumstances when a judgment will not be registered, and those grounds include the absence of jurisdiction of the original court (*s 9(2)(a)*), which can therefore be investigated.

The court otherwise has a discretion to register a judgment if it thinks it "just and convenient" to do so (*s 9(1)*).

1933 Act

Section 2(2) of the Foreign Judgments (Reciprocal Enforcement) Act 1933 directs that once a judgment is registered it shall be of the same force and effect for the purposes of enforcement as if it had been originally given by the registering court. Under *Section 2(6)* the reasonable costs of and incidental to the registration of a judgment are recoverable as if they were sums ordinarily recoverable under the judgment.

The application to register the judgment must be commenced within six years of the date when the judgment was sought to be enforced (*s 2 of the 1933 Act*).

A judgment is deemed to be final and conclusive for the purposes of registration under this Act even if an appeal is pending or it is still subject to appeal (*s1(3)*). However, in those circumstances the court has a discretionary power to set aside registration or adjourn the application to set aside the registration for sufficient time to have the appeal disposed of (*s 5(1) of the 1933 Act*).

The jurisdiction of the court in which judgment was given can be contested before the court asked to register it. *Section 4(2) and (3) of the 1933 Act* and the Supeme Court Practice 1991, para 71/9/1 set out the circumstances when the court in which judgment was given will be deemed to have had or not to have had jurisdiction.

Applications under CJJA 1982

An application under *Section 4 of the CJJA* must be supported by an affidavit in proper form (*RSC Ord 71, r 28 (1)*).

The affidavit must be accompanied by the documents required under *Articles 46 and 47 of the Brussels Convention*.

For the purposes of the other documents required by *Articles 46 and 47*, s 11(1)(b) makes clear that the original or a copy shall in England and Wales be evidence, and in Scotland be sufficient evidence, of any matter to which the document relates.

If the judgment is not in English, a translation into English, certified by a notary public or a person qualified for the purpose in one of the Contracting States or authenticated by affidavit, must also be exhibited to the affidavit (*RSC Ord 71, r 28(1)(a)(iv)*).

An application under the *1920 Act* and the *1933 Act* must be supported by an affidavit in proper form (*RSC Ord 71, r 3(b) and (c)*). The affidavit must exhibit the judgment or a verified or certified or otherwise duly authenticated copy thereof, and where the judgment is not in English, an English translation certified by a notary public or authenticated by affidavit (*RSC Ord 71, r 3(1)(a)*).

Applications under the 1920 and 1933 Acts

An application to register under the *1933 Act* must be accompanied by such other evidence of the enforceability by execution of the judgment in the court which originally gave it, and of the law of the country under which interest has become due under the judgment, as is required by the Order in Council which extends the Act to that country (*RSC Ord 71, r 3(3)*).

The amount for which judgment was given should not be converted into sterling in the affidavit supporting the application. The applicable exchange rate is that prevailing at the time of payment. The judgment will be registered in the foreign currency or its sterling equivalent at the time of payment.

An address within the jurisdiction of the United Kingdom court at which the person applying for registration under the *CJJA* or the *1920 or 1933 Acts* can be served must be given in the supporting affidavit (*RSC Ord 71, r 28(1)(c) and r 3(1)(b)* respectively).

Address for registration

Notice that a judgment has been registered under either the *CJJA* or either the *1920 Act* or the *1933 Act* must, by *RSC Ord 71, r 32 and r 7* respectively, be served on the person against whom the judgment was obtained, either by delivering such notice to him personally or by sending it to his last known address. The notice must state not only full particulars of the judgment and the name and address of the person who applied to have it registered but also the existence of a right to appeal and the time limits set by the court for doing so (*RSC Ord 71, rr 32(3) and 7(3)*).

Service of notice of registration

English courts have consistently refused to recognise or enforce judgments obtained by fraud.

Refusal to recognise foreign judgments

In addition, in *Israel Discount Bank of New York v Hadjipateras*[1] the Court of Appeal said that an English court would be justified in refusing to enforce an American judgment where that judgment was based on an agreement obtained by undue influence, a ground which entitles a party to have a contract set aside under English law.

---

1. *Israel Discount Bank of New York v Hadjipateras* [1983] 3 All ER 129, [1984] 1 WLR 137, CA.

By *RSC Ord 71, r 33(1)* appeals against either the order for registration, or the refusal to order registration, under the *CJJA* must be made to a judge by summons. By *RSC Ord 71, r 9,* an application to set aside registration of a judgment under either Act must also be made by summons.

RSC Order 71, rule 33(2) sets out the time limits for appeal under the *CJJA*. If the appeal is against the registration, the summons must be served within one month of the date on which the notice of registration was served pursuant to *RSC Ord 71, r 32* (as explained above). If the appeal is against a refusal to order registration, service must be effected within one month of the date on which registration was refused.

If the party against whom the judgment was obtained is domiciled outside the jurisdiction, and an application is made within two months of service of the notice of registration, the court may extend the period during which an appeal may be made against the order for registration under the *CJJA (RSC Ord 71, r 33(3))*.

BIBLIOGRAPHY

The following is a short selection of the many textbooks and practitioners books available on the law of England and Wales.

Comprehensive guides to English Law

Halsbury's Laws of England , (4th edn), Butterworths

Halsbury's Statutes of England and Wales, (4th edn), Butterworths

As to the Rules of Civil Procedure :

The County Court Practice, 1992 (The Green Book), Butterworths

The Supreme Court Practice, 1991 (The White Book), General Editor Sir Jack I. H. Jacob, Sweet & Maxwell

For an English Treatise on EC Law

Vaughan : Law of the European Communities, (Looseleaf), General Editor David Vaughan QC, Butterworths

Chapters 1- 3

Bennion, F.A.R., *Bennion : Statutory Interpretation*, (2nd edn), Butterworths, 1992

Dicey and Morris : Conflict of Laws, (11th edn), 1987 with 1991 supplement, General Editor L. A. Collins, Sweet & Maxwell

Pollard, D., and Hughes, D.J., *Pollard & Hughes : Constitutional and Administrative Law, Text and Materials*, Butterworths, 1992

Chapters 4 - 5

James, P.S., *James : Introduction to English Law*, (12th edn), Butterworths, 1989

Chapter 6 - Civil Procedure

Howard, M.N., Crane, P., & Hochberg, D.A., *Phipson on Evidence*, (14th edn), Sweet & Maxwell, 1990

Tapper, C., *Cross on Evidence*, (7th edn), Butterworths, 1990

The Supreme Court Practice, *The County Court Practice* (above)

Chapter 7 - Criminal Procedure

Archbold : Criminal Pleading, Evidence and Practice, General Editor P.J. Richardson, Sweet & Maxwell, 1992

Criminal Practice (2nd edn), Editor in Chief Peter Murphy, Blackstones, 1992

Smith, J.C. and Hogan, B., *Smith & Hogan : Criminal Law*, (7th edn), Butterworths, 1990

Stone's Justices' Manual 1992, (125th edn), Edited by John Richman, and A.T. Draycott, Butterworths, 1992

Tapper, C., *Cross on Evidence*, (7th edn), Butterworths, 1990

Chapter 8 - Remedies

Bernstein, R., *Handbook of Arbitration Practice*, (2nd edn), Sweet & Maxwell, 1992

Boyle and Sykes, *Gore-Browne on Companies*, (Looseleaf), (44th edn), Jordans & Sons Ltd

Cheshire, Fifoot and Furmston's Law of Contract, (12th edn), Butterworths, 1991

Chitty on Contracts, (26 edn), General Editor A. G. Guest, Sweet & Maxwell, 1989

Clerk and Lindsell on Torts, (16th edn), 1989 with 1991 supplements, General Editor R.W.M. Dias, Sweet & Maxwell

Evans, J.M., *de Smith's Judicial Review of Administrative Action*, (4th edn), Sweet & Maxwell, 1980

Goff, R., & Jones, G., *Law of Restitution*, (3rd edn), Sweet & Maxwell, 1986

Jones, G. & Goodhart, W., *Jones and Goodhart : Specific Performance*, Butterworths, 1986

Kemp, D.A. McI, *Kemp & Kemp : The Quantum of Damages* (Looseleaf), Sweet & Maxwell, 1992

McGregor, H., *McGregor on Damages*, (15 edn), Sweet & Maxwell, 1988

Mustill, M. J. & Boyd, S. C., *Mustill and Boyd : Commercial Arbitration*, (2nd edn), Butterworths, 1989
Palmer's Company Law (Looseleaf), (25th edn), Editor G. K. Morse, Sweet & Maxwell, 1992

Salmond and Heuston on the Law of Torts, (19th edn), Sweet & Maxwell, 1987

Spry, I. C. F., *The Principle of Equitable Remedies*, (4th edn), Sweet & Maxwell, 1990

Wade, H.W.R., *Administrative Law*, (6th edn) Oxford University Press, 1988

Chapter 9 Matrimonial Disputes

Jackson and Davies, Matrimonial Finance and Taxation, (5th edn), Butterworths, 1992

Rayden & Jackson on Divorce and Family Matters , (16th edn), with supplement, Butterworths, 1991

Chapter 10 Property Transactions

Burn, E.H., *Cheshire & Burn : Modern Law of Real Property*, (14th edn), Butterworths, 1988

Chapter 11 Recognition and Enforcement of Foreign Judgments

O'Malley, S. & Layton, A., *European Civil Practice*, Sweet & Maxwell, 1989

FRANCE

Bâtonnier Guy Danet
Danet Copper-Royer Burg, Paris

Béatrice Weiss-Gout
Avocat at the Cour d'Appel, Paris

CONTENTS

CHAPTER 1 : SOURCES OF LAW

As France is not a federation, there is one national law applied throughout France, with one minor exception - in Alsace-Lorraine a few ancient rules of German law continue to be applied in very special cases.

Unitary v federal system

The rules of law are principally those contained in the following documents :
- the *Constitution of the Vth Republic,*
- the Codes, which set out by special subject matter the consolidated laws which were originally enacted by way of legislation or regulation. In particular, these are : the *Civil Code*, the *Code of Civil Procedure*, the *Criminal Code*, the *Code of Criminal Procedure*, the *Commercial Code*, the *Labour Code*, the *General Tax Code*; and highly specialised codes, such as the *City Planning Code*.

Pursuant to *Article 11 of the Civil Code* :
"The foreigner in France shall enjoy the same civil rights as are or will be granted to French nationals in the country to which the foreigner belongs."

Application of national laws to foreigners

However, in the area of private rights, the interpretation of *Article 11 of the Civil Code* given by the *"Cour de Cassation"* (Supreme Court) has resulted in a nearly identical treatment of foreigners and nationals, irrespective of any question of reciprocity. This applies in general both to individuals and to corporate entities.

Moreover, the extension of the concept of fundamental rights has led to the acknowledgment that public freedoms also apply broadly to foreigners. Nevertheless, discrimination does exist in the right to exercise a profession. There is a very long list of professions to which access is denied to foreigners.

France has a dualist system of law which requires that international treaties be ratified by Parliament before they can be incorporated into substantive national law and implemented.

Dualist system

As soon as they are passed into national law, duly ratified treaties or international agreements carry a higher authority than other laws, provided that each agreement or treaty is applied by the respective other parties.

These principles are inscribed in *Title VI of the Constitution of 4 October 1958 (Articles 52 to 55).*

Application of EC law	Community treaties are incorporated into the French legal system on the same principles as other international treaties, ie, they must be ratified by Parliament. Where Community law is applicable directly from the original texts, no ratification of that law is required.
Proof of foreign law	A foreign law can be applied by the French courts if the French conflicts-of-laws rules designate it as applicable to the dispute. There is no presumption that it is identical to French law. It is treated as a question of law, not of fact. Its existence is proved by producing the text in the foreign language, together with a French translation attested by a qualified translator, and normally accompanied by an affidavit by an authorised person, who will normally be a duly qualified foreign lawyer.
Human rights	The *European Convention on Human Rights* was ratified by Parliament, and then published, and entered into force by a Decree dated 3 May 1974. The text of the Convention is therefore applied directly by the national courts, which take the jurisprudence of the European Court of Human Rights into account.
Principles of interpretation of Conventions	The principles governing the interpretation of Conventions are set forth in *Articles 1156 to 1164 of the Civil Code.*

The essential principle is set forth in *Article 1156* :
> "In Conventions, one must look for the common intention of the contracting parties rather than focus on the literal meaning of the words."

Otherwise the principle to be applied is that of literal interpretation. Case law is regarded as one of the sources of law, and therefore valuable as a reference, but decisions of higher courts have no binding effect on lower courts.

Interpretation of the Constitution	There is no official annotated text of the Constitution or of the different Codes that can be regarded as authoritative. However, the rulings handed down by the *"Conseil Constituionnel"* (Constitutional Council), especially in the last few years, are increasingly regarded as authoritative as constitutional disputes are its reserved province.

CHAPTER 2 : FUNDAMENTAL RIGHTS

The main constitutional provisions guaranteeing justice for the citizens are :
-   the *preamble of the Constitution of 4 October 1958,* which expressly refers to the *Declaration of the Rights of Man of 1789;*
-   *Article 66* of the same *Constitution,* according to which: "No one may be arbitrarily detained. The judicial authority, which is the keeper of individual liberty, ensures that this principle is observed in any laws."

The conformity of individual laws to the *Constitution* falls within the exclusive competence of the *"Conseil Constitutionnel"* (Constitutional Council) whose composition and powers are set out in *Title VII of the Constitution.* *The Conseil Constitutionnel*

The *Conseil Constitutionnel* is composed of nine members whose term of office is nine years and may not be renewed. Three of its members are appointed by the President of the Republic, three by the President of the National Assembly, three by the President of the Senate.

All "organic laws" must be submitted to the *Conseil Constitutionnel* prior to their promulgation. *"Organic laws"*

Other laws may, pursuant to *Article 61 of the Constitution,* be referred to the *Conseil Constitutionnel* before their promulgation either by the President of the Republic, or by the Prime Minister, or by the President of the National Assembly, or by the President of the Senate, or, lastly, by 60 deputies or 60 senators. *Other laws*

There is no appeal against the decisions of the *Conseil Constitutionnel.*

Should a law be declared unconstitutional by the *Conseil Constitutionnel,* it may neither be promulgated nor implemented, even if passed by both legislative assemblies.

Administrative regulations alleged to be invalid can be challenged in one of two ways : *Administrative regulations*
-   Any individual may plead before the civil or criminal courts that the action against them is based on an illegal administrative instrument and is, therefore, itself illegal.
-   Any individual with a real interest may also file proceedings for nullity of the regulation or administrative act before the administrative courts.

Citizens may not plead that a regulation or administrative act is unconstitutional unless they have a real interest.

However, there are constitutional provisions guaranteeing that fundamental human rights must be respected in treaties, in international Conventions and in French law including subordinate regulations.

Conseil
Constitutionnel -
procedure

The *Conseil Constitutionnel* must rule on questions before it within a period of one month. This period may be reduced to eight days at the government's request. The rules of procedure provide that lawyers cannot appear before the *Conseil Constitutionnel*.

CHAPTER 3 : JURISDICTION OF THE COURTS

A defendant may always challenge the jurisdiction of the court before which he is brought provided he does so prior to any defence on the merits of the case. The court itself may also declare that it has no jurisdiction to deal with a case. *Challenging jurisdiction*

The absence of jurisdiction may be argued "*ratione materiae*" or "*ratione loci*", ie it can be argued either that the case is expressly reserved by law for another court (for example, a "*Tribunal de Grande Instance*" (Court of General Jurisdiction) in civil matters, and the Commercial Court in business matters), or that the case should be referred to a court in another place.

There is no national court in France; the organisation of the judicial system expressly requires that jurisdiction assumed by the appropriate court for the case, be based either on its location or on the nature of the case. For example, in a case dealing with an alleged felony, only the "*Cour d'Assises*" has jurisdiction, and the accused must be tried by the *Cour d'Assises* of the place where the felony is alleged to have been committed. *Jurisdiction of courts in France*

There is no limitation on bringing actions against the state or its organs when they act in a strictly commercial capacity. However, it is virtually impossible to obtain enforcement of a judgment against the state, since the state's property may not be seized. *Action against the state*

Under *Article 42 of the New Code of Civil Procedure* the court with territorial jurisdiction is, unless otherwise specified, that of the place where the defendant lives. Under *Article 43* of the same Code, the place where the defendant lives is understood to be : *Jurisdiction dependent on defendant*

- in the case of an individual, the place where the defendant has his domicile, or failing this, his ordinary residence;
- in the case of a company, the place where the defendant is established.

For individuals "domicile" is defined in *Article 102 of the Civil Code* as the place where the individual has his principal establishment. *Domicile*

The case law makes it clear that domicile is a question of fact, and that it is essential to prove that the individual intends to have his principal establishment in a given place.

For companies, the principle is that its head office is the place where the company resides; however, case law has consistently held that one can issue a summons against a company at one of the company's other offices, provided that that office is directly concerned in the dispute.

CHAPTER 4 : ADMINISTRATION OF JUSTICE

The court system is set out in diagrammatic form as follows : *The court system*

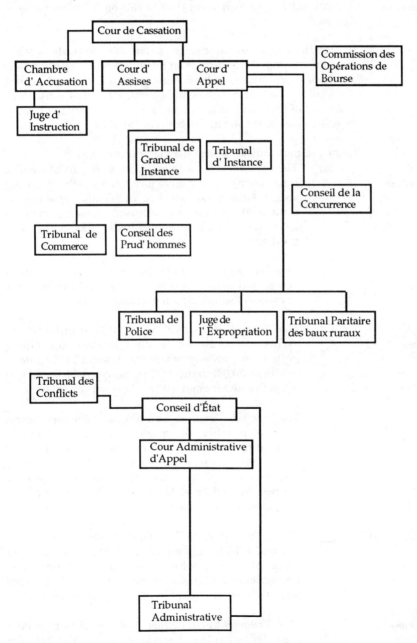

One of the main characteristics of the French system of justice is the separation of jurisdiction between the administrative courts which deal with disputes involving the administration of the state, such as, the "*Tribunal Administratif*" and the "*Conseil d'État*", and the courts of "ordinary" jurisdiction.

If there is any conflict of jurisdiction between the administrative courts, and the ordinary judicial courts, it is referred to the Court of Disputes, which has exclusive jurisdiction in such matters.

Administrative courts

Administrative courts are competent to rule on "administrative disputes".

In certain cases, including, in particular, appeals against regulatory or individual decrees on the grounds of abuse of power and appeals on the grounds of abuse of power directed against the regulatory acts of ministers, the *Conseil d'État* has jurisdiction as a court of first and last resort, and the dispute does not have to be referred to an administrative court at any time.

In the ordinary judicial system the major courts are :

Tribunal de Grande Instance

(a) The "*Tribunal de Grande Instance*" (Court of General Jurisdiction) has exclusive jurisdiction in the following areas : status of individuals, civil litigation, ante-nuptial settlements, estates of deceased persons, disputes over nationality, patents and trademarks, and certain tax disputes.

The *Tribunal de Grande Instance* is also a court of general jurisdiction, ie it is competent to hear any case not within the jurisdiction of another court.

Tribunal d'Instance

(b) The "*Tribunal d'Instance*" (Court of First Instance) has exclusive jurisdiction in civil matters concerning persons or property where the amount in dispute is less than 30,000 francs. It is the court of last resort when the amount in dispute is less than 13,000 francs.

The *Tribunal d'Instance* also has exclusive jurisdiction over a number of matters, including actions concerning contributions for the maintenance of dependants, actions relating to rental of residential premises, as well as a great many matters precisely defined in *Articles R.321-3 to 321-23 of the Code de l'Organisation Judiciaire*.

Criminal decisions

Within the *Tribunal de Grande Instance* and the *Tribunal d'Instance* there are divisions specialising in criminal cases, which are called "*Chambres Correctionnelles*" in the *Tribunal de Grande Instance* and "*Tribunal de Police*" in the *Tribunal d'Instance*.

The criminal justice system

The "*Tribunal Correctionnel*" has jurisdiction to hear cases defined in law as misdemeanours. The *Tribunal de Police* has jurisdiction over breaches of police regulations ("*contraventions*").

(c)   Felonies are judged by the "*Cour d'Assises*," which is a division of the "*Cour d'Appel*" (Court of Appeal) composed of three magistrates and a lay jury of nine.

The criminal justice system also includes the investigative divisions, which are, at the first level, the "*Juge d'Instruction*" (Examining Magistrate), and at the second level, the "*Chambre d'Accusation*" which reports to the *Cour d'Appel*.

(d)   The Commercial Court has jurisdiction under *Article 631 of the Commercial Code* over :   *Commercial Court*
(i)   disputes relating to the commitments and transactions of traders, merchants and bankers,
(ii)   disputes between partners in a commercial company,
(iii)   disputes of a commercial nature between any persons.

(e)   The "*Conseil des Prud'hommes*" (Conciliation Board) is competent to determine disputes that may arise in connection with an employment contract.   *Conseil des Prud'hommes*

(f)   The "*Conseil de la Concurrence*" (Competition Board), created by *Ordinance No 86-1243 of 1 December 1986*, has competence in the area of unfair trading practices, restrictive practices and monopolies. The Competition Board also advises the government on certain aspects of competition policy.   *Conseil de la Concurrence*

(g)   The "*Commission des Opérations de Bourse*" (Stock Exchange Transactions Commission), created by *Ordinance No 67-833 of 28 September 1967*, is in charge of overseeing the protection of savings invested in securities or any other investments connected with public offerings, information for investors, and the proper functioning of markets in which stocks or listed financial instruments or negotiable futures are traded. The Commission has the power to order the cessation of illegal practices and to levy fines.   *Commision des Opérations de Bourse*

(h)   The "*Juge de l'Expropriation*" is the judge that, in the event of a compulsory purchase of property, sets the amount of the compensation to be paid to the property owner.   *Juge de l'Expropriation*

(i)   The "*Tribunal Paritaire des Baux Ruraux*" (Joint Board of Rural Leases) rules on disputes relating to rural leases.   *Tribunal Paritaire des Baux Ruraux*

Within all these civil courts there is a division, which consists of a single judge, called "*Formation de Référé*" (Courts of Summary Proceedings).

In urgent cases or when an obligation cannot be seriously disputed, the *Tribunal d'Instance* gives a provisional decision within a very short time that can even be in a few hours in cases of extreme urgency. This decision is immediately enforceable even though an appeal may be pending.

Geographical areas of court jurisdiction

The districts within the jurisdiction of the various courts do not correspond to political districts or to geographic regions. However, each *Département* includes at least one *Tribunal de Grande Instance*, one Commercial Court, one *Conseil des Prud'hommes* and several *Cours d'Instance*.

Appeals

A matter is referred to the *Cour d'Appel* by means of a "declaration of appeal" filed with the clerk of the *Cour d'Appel* by an *"avoué"* entitled to practise at that court.

Appeal to the *Cour d'Appel* is by way of a re-hearing of the entire dispute, in the same manner as before the (lower) court. *Article 561 of the New Code of Civil Procedure* specifies that :
"The appeal remits the decision for judgment to the *Cour d'Appel* in order to obtain a new ruling of fact and law."

New evidence on appeal

Under *Article 563* of the same Code "in support of an appeal on claims submitted to the first judge, the parties may invoke new grounds, introduce new documents or offer new evidence."

New claims on appeal

Article 566 authorises the parties to add to their existing claims any additional claims which are accessory, subsidiary or consequential.

On the other hand, under *Article 564* of the same Code, "the parties may not submit new claims to the court, except in order to oppose a demand for compensation, plead for the rejection of opposing claims or for the adjudication of matters arising out of the intervention of a third party, to give evidence of an unexpected event or to explain an existing fact, or the occurrence or disclosure of a fact."

Cour de Cassation

The recourse to the *Cour de Cassation* is in the form of a "*pourvoi en cassation*" (lodging of an appeal) by an attorney entitled to plead before the Supreme Court. A *pourvoi en cassation* may be lodged only against judgments of courts of last resort.

The *Cour de Cassation* only gives opinions on matters of law. Either it rejects the appeal, terminating the action, or it allows the appeal, annuls the decision that gave rise to it, and refers the case back to a court of the same level as the referring court but in a different territorial area.

Stay of execution on appeal

In criminal cases an appeal always results in a stay of execution. In civil or commercial cases, the appeal results in a stay of execution of the judgment given by the court of first instance unless that judgment is accompanied by an order for provisional enforcement.

Provisional enforcement takes immediate effect in certain cases, for instance, where temporary measures are ordered in divorce proceedings, orders issued by the *Juge des Référés*, etc. When provisional enforcement is not to take immediate effect the *Tribunal d'Instance* may nevertheless order it, stating its reasons.

Provisional enforcement

On appeal, any provisional enforcement due to take immediate effect may be suspended by the Presiding Judge of the *Cour d'Appel* at the request of the appellant but only in the cases specified in *Article 524 of the New Code of Civil Procedure*, ie if the provisional enforcement is prohibited by law or if it might lead to consequences which are manifestly excessive and unreasonable.

If the measure of provisional enforcement requested by the plaintiff is not granted by the *Tribunal d'Instance*, and the defendant lodges an appeal, pursuant to *Article 525 of the New Code of Civil Procedure*, the plaintiff is entitled to ask for measures of provisional enforcement from the Presiding Judge of the *Cour d'Appel* exercising a summary jurisdiction, but only in cases of urgency.

If a party wishes to ask for a dispute to be referred to the European Court of Justice in Luxembourg in the form of a question formulated by the court, it must proceed in the same way as with any other legal or factual issue. However, the plaintiff must formulate the question he wishes to ask although it is for the court to decide finally on the question to be remitted and to remit it to the European Court of Justice.

Article 177 EEC Treaty References

The court against whose decision there is no appeal within the meaning of *Article 177 of the EEC Treaty* is the *Cour d'Appel* or, when the amount at stake in the dispute is less than 13,000 francs, the Court of First Instance.

The jurisprudence of international courts other than the court at Luxembourg may be invoked before the national courts in the same way as national case law, with no binding effect. The jurisprudence most often cited is that of the European Court of Human Rights.

Judgments in other international courts

CHAPTER 5 : STRUCTURE OF THE LEGAL PROFESSION

From 1 January 1992, the exercise of legal activities in France (including the giving of legal advice and the preparation of documents) is reserved solely to persons who can show that they have both a university degree in law establishing their competence and professional indemnity insurance.

An "*avocat*" may exercise his profession only if he is a member of a Bar. The Council of that Bar must previously have satisfied itself that the *avocat* fulfills the conditions of competence and good standing required by law. He or she is qualified to give legal advice, prepare documents and plead anywhere within the jurisdiction of that Bar, and has a monopoly on representation before the *Tribunal de Grande Instance* for the area in which his Bar is established. The *avocat* has a monopoly on rights of audience before all civil law courts. Amongst the *avocats* are a special body which has exclusive rights of audience before the *Conseil d'Etat* and the *Cour de Cassation*. *Avocats*

"*Conseils Juridiques*" were legal professionals, regulated since 1971, who gave legal opinions and drew up documents. However, they did not have rights of audience except before courts where the *avocats* did not have a monopoly. They could not represent parties before the *Tribunal de Grande Instance*. *Conseils Juridiques*

From 1 January 1992, a new profession of *avocat* has been created, combining *avocats* and *conseils juridiques*. All *conseils juridiques* previously registered as such or exempted from registration requirements have become members of the new profession of *avocat*, whether they are French nationals, come from other EC countries or even non-EC countries. *The new profession*

"*Notaries*" are officials exercising a public office, nominated by the Minister of Justice, residing in Chambers established in each *Département*. They are qualified to certify all original deeds, contracts and documents, and to ensure their retention as official documents. They have a monopoly in dealing with transactions in respect of real property, which must be evidenced by authenticated deeds. They can also give legal advice. *Notaries*

The "*avoué d'appel*" are appointed by the Ministry of Justice to practise from Chambers in a particular *Département*. They have a monopoly over preparing written pleadings to be filed before the *Cour d'Appel* to which they are attached; they have no right to plead in court. *Avoué d'Appel*

Commissaires priseurs	The *"commissaires priseurs"* are appointed by the Ministry of Justice. They have the exclusive right to carry out official auction sales of furniture and personal objects. They are also qualified to value personal property items.
Other professions	There are also related professions, such as patent attorneys, who specialise in trademarks and patents. On the other hand, accountants, chartered accountants and auditors are not part of the legal profession. They come under the jurisdiction of the Ministry of Finance, not of the Ministry of Justice.
Rights of audience in the courts	In theory any individual may prepare his own defence and represent himself in court. However, before the *Tribunal de Grande Instance* and *Cour d'Appel* he must be represented for the written procedure by an *avocat* or an *avoué* and receive the assistance of an *avocat* for the oral argument.
Organisation and specialisation	There is no specialised Bar. Every *avocat* must be registered with the Bar established in the area of a particular *Tribunal de Grande Instance*. Each Bar is led by a *"Bâtonnier"* elected for two years by all members of that Bar and controlled by a *"Conseil de l'Ordre"* whose members are also elected (for three years). The *Conseil de l'Ordre* is responsible for the entire management, administration and discipline of the Bar.
Directories of avocats	At present no specialisations are recognised within the profession of *avocat*, but in certain Bars, the directory of *avocats* may contain a reference to the *avocat's* professional activity. In addition, on the initiative of the *"Syndicats d'Avocats"*, private law directories are multiplying. The Paris Bar also has a private directory mentioning specialisations, which is only available to other *avocats*. In all these directories the nomination of a specialisation rests with the *avocat*.
Practice - prior to 31.12.91	Until 31 December 1991, an *avocat* was able to practise alone; in co-operation with another *avocat* pursuant to a specific contract submitted to the *Conseil de l'Ordre* of his Bar; or in an association, in the company of other *avocats*, with whom the *avocat* shares the operating expenses of the firm but not income; or

- in partnership with other *avocats* who share income and expenses on the basis of a fixed agreed percentage contained in a partnership contract submitted to the local Bar; or
- in a group known as a *"Société Civile Professionelle"*, which constitutes a genuine autonomous structure within which each *avocat* owns shares that entitle him to a portion of the profits.

From 1.1.92	From 1 January 1992, a member of the new profession of *avocat*, whether a French national or foreign national, may be the employee of another *avocat*.

There are now also *"Sociétés d'Exercice Libéral"*, ie commercial companies with a purely civil purpose, and joint ventures.

Whatever the form of practice, the liability of an *avocat* is always unlimited.

An *avocat* may also, with the authorisation of both respective Bars, open a second office in a different area from that in which he is registered. He may organise a European Economic Interest Group (EEIG) with European colleagues, which will result, in fact, in a limited form of multinational partnership. On the other hand, inter-professional partnerships with persons who are not *avocats* are not at present permitted.

There is no limit to the number of employees or partners who can be engaged.

Since 1 January 1992 the establishment of foreign lawyers in France is governed directly by the fact that the exercise of the profession of *avocat* is exclusively related to qualification as *avocat* in France and membership of a French Bar. For the countries of the Community, qualification is regulated by the Directive on the mutual recognition of diplomas[1]. Flexible provisions have since 1985 permitted lawyers registered in an EC country to become full members of a French Bar by taking a simple examination. As regards non-EC countries, the *Law of 31 December 1990* requires prospective candidates to pass an examination which will probably be more complex and whose content will be determined shortly.

Foreign lawyers

Foreign lawyers in the new profession of avocat

There are liberal transitional provisions enabling those foreign lawyers established in France before 31 December 1990 to become automatically members of the new profession. Those foreign lawyers who contravene the law will be liable to criminal prosecution. Under the *1977 Lawyers' Services Directive*[2] lawyers from other Member States of the EC are able to provide occasional services (including giving legal advice and appearing in the French courts) provided they do not establish offices in France.

There is a schedule of fees for procedural steps taken before the *Tribunal de Grande Instance* and the *Cour d'Appel*. According to the law, an *avocat's* fees must result from a freely negotiated agreement between the *avocat* and his client; they are to be based on the time spent, the difficulty of the case, the result obtained, the reputation of the *avocat* and any other factors specific to the case.

Lawyers' fees

Negotiation of fees

No recommended fee schedules exist. These would be considered unlawful by the "*Conseil de la Concurrence*" (Competition Council).

---

1.   Council Directive (EEC) 89/48 (OJ L19 24.1.89 p16).
2.   Council Directive (EEC) 77/249 (OJ L78 26.3.77 p17).

The *avocat* must inform his client in advance of the financial terms of his services. *Pacta quota litis* ("no-win-no-fee") agreements are prohibited. However, to reward success it is possible to agree with the client a specific fee payable if a successful result is obtained.

Review of fees

If the client requests it, the *avocat* must at the conclusion of the work deliver a detailed statement of his expenses and fees. Under French law an *avocat* is authorised to pursue recovery through the courts if necessary. If a difficulty arises over the level or amount of the fees, it must be submitted to the *Bâtonnier*, who will ask a member of the *Conseil de l'Ordre* to try to reach a settlement between the parties, and, failing this, to prepare a detailed report. The *Bâtonnier* then issues a ruling which is enforceable immediately, unless an appeal is lodged within one month. This appeal is heard by a Magistrate of the *Tribunal de Grande Instance*, and then if necessary by the *Cour d'Appel*.

VAT

An *avocat's* fees are subject to VAT at the present rate of 18.6%. In legal aid cases, a fee is prohibited; the *avocat* is entitled only to a lump sum indemnity the level of which is set by Decree. The indemnity is at present subject to VAT at 5.5%.

Discipline of lawyers

Avocats are regulated exclusively under the jurisdiction of the *Conseil de l'Ordre*, acting under the supervision of the *Cour d'Appel*. On the complaint of a client or colleague, proceedings may be started directly, either on the initiative of the state's *Procureur General*, before the *Cour d'Appel*, or on the initiative of the *Bâtonnier*, even if no complaint has been filed by a client.

Complaints against avocats

Any complaint must be sent to the *Bâtonnier*. The disciplinary proceedings are governed by the Bar's internal rules and result in a decision of the *Conseil de l'Ordre*, which may be referred to the *Cour d'Appel*, either at the request of the *avocat* penalised or of the state's *Procureur General*. Any client, even one of foreign nationality, may file a complaint.

In addition, the professional competence of any *avocat* may be challenged in front of the *Tribunal de Grande Instance*.

Insurance

Insurance is compulsory, and is carried out by the relevant Bar. Each Bar takes out two insurance policies for each *avocat*, one guaranteeing the professional liability risks, the other guaranteeing repayment to the client of any client's money that he may have entrusted to his *avocat*. These amounts must be

CARPA

deposited in a special account whose sole holder is the *Bâtonnier* and which the *avocat* may operate only by delegation of the *Bâtonnier*. In effect, each Bar creates under the control of the *Conseil de l'Ordre* a CARPA ("*Caisse de Règlements Pécuniaires de la Profession d'Avocat*" (Advocates' Professional Fund)) in which all monies handled by the *avocats* must be deposited.

CHAPTER 6 : CIVIL PROCEDURE

Detailed procedure varies from one court to another. However, using the *Tribunal de Grande Instance* as a model, the procedure in general can be described briefly as follows :

The course of proceedings

- The plaintiff serves an instrument called an *"assignation"* (complaint) through a *huissier* (process server).

Service

- The plaintiff must file this complaint with the court within four months, under penalty of nullity.

Complaint

- The clerk of the court assigns the case to a chamber or division of the court.

- In parallel, the defendant has fifteen days within which to appoint an *avocat* who must, during the next fifteen days, enter an appearance before the court by filing a document called a *"constitution"*.

Notice to defend

It should be noted that this fifteen-day period is a formality, and in practice the *avocat* for the defendant can always be appointed before the date for the oral hearing of the case is set down.

- Once the case has been assigned to a chamber, the *avocats* are informed by a notice which fixes a first date on which one of the three judges on the bench will review any procedural difficulties that might arise in the case.

- If the single judge feels that the case is relatively complex, he chooses a procedure called *"Mise en État"* (joinder of issue) (see *Articles 763 to 781 of the New Code of Civil Procedure*).

Mise en État

- In this procedure a judge called the *"Juge de la Mise en État"* is appointed for the purpose of following the file with particular attention.

He summons the parties at regular intervals and makes orders, for example to disclose documents, file pleadings, etc. He is also competent to deal with requests for provisional measures, expert reports, provisional judgment, etc.

"Circuit Court"

- If the case seems relatively simple or is not likely to require a long procedural stage, it stays in what is called *"le Circuit Court"* (*art 761*).

- One or two subsequent hearings are called in order to verify that each party has complied with the required procedure, and in particular that it has set out its case in writing.

Before the end of the first hearing, the plaintiff must, in principle, have served on the defendant the documents on which he intends to base his claim.

Service of written pleadings

By the second hearing the defendant must have filed his written response to the plaintiff's claim setting out his general arguments, and have served on the plaintiff the documents that he intends to introduce in the proceedings.

Close of written procedure

- Whether the procedure is the long procedure or the short procedure, there comes a stage when the judge, on a date he has fixed in advance, closes the written procedure (*art 782 ff*).

After that date, no new documents and no new written pleadings may be exchanged.

Oral hearing

- Shortly after the "closing" date, the case is presented orally by the *avocats* for the parties, without the parties having to be present.

Judgment

In general, judgment is given four to eight weeks later.

Intervening parties

The rules on parties intervening in an action are contained in *Articles 325 to 338 of the New Code of Civil Procedure* :

- Pursuant to these articles, intervention is permitted only if there is a sufficient connection with the claims of the initial parties.
- Intervention may be voluntary or compulsory.

Voluntary intervention

A voluntary intervention may be as a principal party or as an accessory. Intervention is as a principal party when it leads to a judgment of a claim filed by the intervening party. It is as an accessory if it limits itself to supporting the claims of either of the original parties to the suit.

Compulsory intervention

Compulsory intervention may happen where one seeks a judgment against the party compelled to intervene, or simply in order that the judgment be declared to apply to it as well as to the principal parties.

A voluntary intervention takes place before the *Tribunal de Grande Instance* through the appointment before the court of an *avocat* and filing documents substantiating the reasons for, and purposes of, the intervention.

Compulsory intervention follows on the same conditions as the original suit, ie by filing a writ of summons.

Office of the Parquet

Certain proceedings must be instituted at the office of the "*Parquet*" (the public assessor), particularly in family matters (adoption, etc.).

Joinder and severence of actions

Under *Article 367 of the New Code of Civil Procedure* the judge may, at the request of the parties or on his own initiative, order the joinder of several actions pending before him if there is such a link between the actions that it is in the interest of justice that they be examined or heard together.

He also has the power in the interests of justice to order separate trials of parts of the same action.

Article 368 specifies that these decisions relate to the administration of justice, which means that they come within the discretionary power of the judge and may not be appealed.

The adjournment or suspension of an action because of proceedings pending before other courts is governed by *Articles 378 to 380-1 of the New Code of Civil Procedure.* The most common reason for adjourning a civil action is that criminal proceedings are pending.

Competing jurisdictions - criminal/ civil

Article 4 of the Code of Criminal Procedure provides that if civil jurisdiction is exercised separately from the criminal proceedings, judgment in the civil action must be deferred until the criminal proceedings have been finally concluded.

The parties may, if there is a link between two suits brought before two different courts, make the plea of "*connexité*" provided for in *Article 101 of the New Code of Civil Procedure.* In this case, either judge may ask the other to defer to his jurisdiction, or may refer the matter to the other court.

Connexité

If the courts in question are not on the same level, the successful plea of *connexité* can only result in the case being referred to the higher court.

It is not possible to initiate a "class or representative action" in France.

Class actions

There are two obstacles to obtaining advisory opinions : first, the adage "no individual may plead through a state official"; second, *Article 5 of the Civil Code* which stipulates : "Judges are not allowed to give general opinions on the cases referred to them."

Advisory Opinions

The provision of legal aid was first instituted by the Decree of 1 September 1972, which has since been modified on many occasions.

Legal aid

At present, those who may benefit from comprehensive legal aid, ie for the assistance of *avocats, huissiers,* etc. are individuals whose average monthly income during the previous calendar year, excluding family allowances, was less than 3,645 francs. An individual is entitled to partial legal aid, ie the partial reimbursement of fees and expenses, if he can show that his average income is less than 5,250 francs. The limits are extended by 390 francs for each family dependant of the individual concerned.

Who may benefit

When persons who meet the income conditions wish to initiate legal proceedings, they must make a request for legal aid to the *Tribunal de Grande Instance.*

Procedure for obtaining legal aid

This request is examined by the legal aid bureau made up of magistrates and officials.

If the person who is granted legal aid has obtained the assistance in advance of an *avocat* who accepts legal aid work, the legal aid office ratifies that choice.

Appointment by Bâtonnier

Otherwise, the legal aid office asks the *Bâtonnier* to appoint an *avocat* who, except on grounds of conscience, does not have the right to refuse his appointment.

Avocats' fees

Avocats do not receive fees for this work. They are only indemnified for their expenses. For instance, an *avocat* receives a lump sum of 2,250 francs for a divorce, regardless of the difficulty and length of the proceedings.

Supervision by the Legal Aid Board

The legal aid agency has no right to oversee the manner in which the *avocat* discharges his duties, as the relationship between him and his client is governed by the ordinary rules of the *avocat's* profession. However, in practice, the legal aid office often asks the *avocat* how the case is progressing if the *avocat* has not reported within a reasonable time that the case has been completed.

Limitation on bringing proceedings

The rules regarding time limits in proceedings are contained in *Articles 2219 to 2281 of the Civil Code.*

They are as follows :

General rules

(a) A party may not waive the statute of limitations in advance, but it is possible to waive a limitation period already underway.

(b) The statute of limitations is not applicable to cases that have nothing to do with commerce.

(c) In principle, the statute of limitations is 30 years, except in cases expressly set out by law.

Exceptions

(d) However, there are many exceptions. The limitation period is ten years for actions relating to contractual liability. Actions for payment of wages, alimony, rents and generally those that relate to anything payable in annual or shorter periodic instalments have a five year limitation period. In insurance matters, the limitation period is two years; in transport, one year; in the area of nullity of corporate actions, three years, and so on.

Interruption of time limits

Time periods are interrupted by a summons to the court, even in summary proceedings, or an order or attachment served on the person entitled to invoke the statute.

Case law has consistently held that the statute of limitations does not run against a person who is unable to act because of an obstacle arising either under the law or from the contract or from force majeure.

Commencement of court proceedings

Before the *Tribunal de Grande Instance, Tribunal d'Instance* and the Commercial Court, the plaintiff must cause the *huissier* to serve a summons on the other party which is then filed with the court.

Before the *Conseil des Prud'hommes*, the *Conseil des Opérations de Bourse,* and the *Conseil de la Concurrence*, the plaintiff must submit and file a document with the court, which in turn sends the summons to the defendant.

Generally

The initiative in starting proceedings always rests with the plaintiff and no prior formality is imposed on him; moreover, since justice is free, he has nothing to pay to the court.

When a *huissier* is charged with delivering the initial notice, he may serve it on the individual, or on the legal representative of a corporation.

Methods of service

Service is also valid if it is made on a person who agrees to accept personal service or if it is filed at the *"Mairie "* (Town Hall) of the defendant's domicile.

If it is filed at the *Mairie*, the *huissier* informs the defendant by letter by registered letter that the summons has been deposited at the *Mairie*.

When the court decides to summon the defendant, it does so by registered letter with return receipt requested.

Special rules relating to service abroad are contained in *Articles 683 to 689 of the New Code of Civil Procedure.*

When a foreign party has elected domicile in France, service is validly effected at this domicile.

Service on foreign nationals

Any process that must be served abroad on a party itself is filed with the *Procureur de la République* who forwards copies of the summons to the Ministry of Justice, which transmits it to the country concerned.

On the same day as delivery is effected to the *Procureur*, or at the latest on the next working day, the *huissier* sends the addressee a certified true copy of the document being served by registered letter with return receipt requested.

At the hearing, the judge must verify that the addressee received the document in due time.

These rules apply only where there is no other rule applicable under an international treaty.

The *Brussels Convention on Jurisdiction and Enforcement of Judgments in Civil and Commercial Matters 1968* has been incorporated into national law through ratification and publication and is directly applicable.

The Brussels Convention

Pursuant to *Article 643 of the New Code of Civil Procedure*, when a complaint is filed before a court whose seat is in metropolitan France, a two month extension is granted to persons residing abroad for appearance, appeal, objections, review and lodging of an appeal to the *Cour de Cassation*.

Extension of time

The two month extension, pursuant to the *Order of December 1986*, does not apply in the case of appeals to the *Conseil de la Concurrence* or to the *Cour d'Appel* in rulings in competition matters.

Shortened procedures

There are certain shortened procedures available in particular circumstances which are outlined below :

Failure to follow procedure

(a)   *Failure by a Party to follow Procedure*
The consequences of a failure to appear are governed by *Articles 467 ff of the New Code of Civil Procedure.*

Failure to appear

When the defendant does not appear, judgment is given "by default". If the summons was not delivered in person and the judgment is a final judgment the defendant may file a formal objection to this decision once informed of it. After a successful objection, the case is returned to the same court.

Judgment

If the summons was properly served on the defendant, or the judgment is not a final judgment, the judgment is "*réputé contradictoire*" (deemed to have been given after hearing both sides). In this case, the only avenue open to the defendant is to appeal.

A judgment given by default or *réputé contradictoire* is invalid if not served on the other party within six months of its date of issue.

Service abroad

A judgment by default or *réputé contradictoire* given against a party residing abroad must expressly indicate which steps were taken in order to serve the summons on the defendant.

If, after appearing, a party fails to carry out the required legal procedure the judge will give his ruling after giving both sides an opportunity to be heard.

Summary judgment on the merits

(b)   *Summary Judgment on the Merits*
The procedure by which a case can be decided by summary procedure where the court decides that one party has no arguable case on the merits, is not available in France. However, a party may ask the court to rule that an action has become purposeless, eg where the amount claimed has been paid. In these circumstances the court will only rule on the question of costs.

Striking out part or all of party's pleadings of a claim/defence

(c)   *Striking Out Part or All of a Party's Pleadings of a Claim/Defence*
This procedure, by which parts of a claim can be decided by summary procedure where the court decides that a part of one party's claim or defence has no merits and must be summarily dismissed, is not available in France.

The "*caution judicatum solve*" no longer exists in French procedure. At present, therefore, initiation of proceedings is not subject to any financial conditions, whether proceedings are filed by a national or a foreigner.

Security for costs

In respect of the written procedure there are specific rules which apply to each of the different courts.

Conduct of the written procedure

The most elaborate procedure is that before the *Tribunal de Grande Instance*, under which the judge intervenes on many occasions, particularly within the framework of the "*Mise en État*", during which the *Juge de la Mise en État* examines the case from the procedural point of view. The *Juge de la Mise en État* only exists in the *Tribunal de Grande Instance*.

The judge's task is to see to the proper ordering of the procedure and that the time limits for exchanges of documents and written proceedings have been complied with. He fixes the time periods at each stage of the case.

Duties of the Juge de la Mise en État

He may ask the *avocats* to reply to grounds other than those set out in the written case, and require them to set out such explanations of fact or law as he considers necessary to resolve the dispute. He may also ask the parties to involve other parties whose presence he deems necessary to be able to resolve the dispute.

Pursuant to *Article 771 of the New Code of Civil Procedure*, the *Juge de la Mise en Etat* is also competent to grant provisional measures, and protective measures, and to order any investigative step which seems to him to be necessary. He may even, at the request of one of the parties, award a provisional sum to a creditor or an amount of costs to be paid before trial.

The *Juge de la Mise en État* makes orders either by formal order or, in the case of "administrative house-keeping" measures, by a simple entry in the dossier. Save in exceptional circumstances the orders may only be appealed at the same time as a judgment on the merits.

Appeals from orders o the Juge de la Mise en État

The judge can also make orders which cannot be appealed. For example, if one of the *avocats* has not carried out the required procedure within the stipulated time, he then pronounces the closure of the investigative phase. This decision cannot be appealed.

There is a comparable institution, the "*Juge-Rapporteur*" (Reporting Judge) in the case of the *Tribunal de Commerce* and the *Conseil des Prud'hommes*.

The rules on evidence in judicial proceedings are contained in *Articles 132 to 332 of the New Code of Civil Procedure*.

Evidence

Production of documents	The rules relating specifically to documents to be used in the proceedings are contained in *Articles 132 to 142 of the New Code of Civil Procedure*.

A party which refers to a document is required to disclose it to every other party to the action.

If documents are not disclosed voluntarily, the judge may be asked informally to require their disclosure; if necessary, the judge fixes the time and any terms on which disclosure must be made, under penalty of a fine for failing to comply with the order for disclosure. |
| *Reference to a document at trial* | If, during proceedings, a party wants to refer to a deed to which it was not a party, or to introduce a document in the possession of a third party, it may ask the judge to whom the case was referred to order delivery or disclosure of the deed or document. There is no special form for this request.

Whether or not to accede to the request is a matter within the judge's discretionary power. In cases of difficulty, or if some legitimate objection is raised, the judge who ordered delivery or disclosure may, on the application of the other party, reverse or modify his decision. |
| *Confidentiality of documents* | An *avocat* is bound by the absolute rule of professional secrecy not to obey a court order to disclose a document in his possession. In principle, letters exchanged by *avocats* are confidential (even to their clients), especially when they concern negotiations aimed at reaching a settlement. However, confidentiality may be waived by the *Bâtonnier* with jurisdiction over the *avocats* appearing at a particular court after an informal procedure involving the *avocats* for both sides, particularly when the exchange of correspondence ends in a genuine agreement. |
| *Documents - Inadmissibility*

Failure to disclose in time

Forged documents | A party may cause a document to be removed from the proceedings where it was not disclosed in time and because the party did not have the necessary time to examine the document and give instructions on it to his *avocat*. In cases where there are allegations of forgery, there is a special procedure called the "*procédure d'incident de faux*" (plea of forgery), which must be introduced before the substantive hearing (*Articles 285 and 286*) in order to determine whether or not a document is genuine and therefore admissible. Once introduced before the court it is for the court to decide whether or not to rule on this as a preliminary issue in a separate judgment or to add the issue to those to be decided at trial. |
| *Criminal complaints for perjury* | A party may always file a criminal complaint for perjury or that public or private documents have been forged. In such a case if the judge considers that the document in question is essential to resolve the dispute, he must adjourn the case until after the criminal proceedings have been determined. |

Articles 733 to 735 of the New Code of Civil Procedure govern the rules relating to letters rogatory requesting evidence to be taken in a foreign state. These articles follow the provisions of the *Hague Convention*. Under these articles, the judge may, at the request of the parties, or even on his own initiative, cause the investigative measures he deems necessary to be taken in a foreign state by issuing letters rogatory addressed either to the judicial authorities within the foreign state, or to the French diplomatic or consular authorities. Otherwise, the rules relating to the taking of evidence abroad are identical to the rules relating to the taking of evidence in France.

Evidence taken abroad

The rules on witness evidence are contained in *Articles 199 to 231*. Evidence can be presented either by written affidavits or orally before the judge. Affidavits are subject to certain formal rules set out in *Article 202*. In particular, the affidavit must indicate that its author is aware that it will be used in a court of law.

Witnesses

Affidavits

When an investigation is ordered, either by the judge on his own initiative, or at the request of the parties, the witnesses named are required to give evidence unless they have a legitimate reason not to do so. Parents or direct relatives or the spouse of one of the parties may refuse to testify. Pursuant to the *Vienna Convention* published by decree of 29 March 1971, those with diplomatic immunity cannot be required to give evidence.

Oral evidence

The witnesses are heard by the judge in the presence of the parties, if they so wish, and of their *avocats* . The judge asks the questions. Pursuant to *Article 214*, the parties may neither interrupt nor question the witnesses, nor seek to influence them, nor address them directly under penalty of exclusion from the hearing.

Oral hearing of witnesses

After he has examined a witness the judge may ask further questions submitted to him by the parties. If an investigative enquiry is requested by one of the parties, both that party and the opposing party must indicate the facts they want to prove and the names of the witnesses to be subpoenaed. However, it is the judge who, in his decision ordering the investigation, rules on which facts must be proved as well as which witnesses will be required to give evidence.

There are no special rules governing the introduction of expert evidence obtained directly by one party. However, *Articles 232 to 284 of the New Code of Civil Procedure* govern the investigative measures executed by a technical expert appointed by the court as an assessor (*"technician"*). Judges tend to rely more and more on such experts for expert technical opinions on matters of fact. The judge defines the technical expert's duties precisely. The expert's duties must be carried out under conditions that respect the essential principles of a fair trial, including hearing both sides in the proceedings.

Expert evidence

The technical assessor

Pursuant to *Article 246*, it should be emphasised that while the judge is not bound by the findings or conclusions of the technical expert, in most cases he adopts them as his own.

Preparations before trial

Since properly speaking there is no "trial" in the French procedure, but only an oral hearing of submissions in which the *avocats* develop the points made in their written pleadings and comment on any documents, there are no "final preparations".

At a given point the judge will consider that all arguments have been exchanged in writing and that the case is ready for oral submissions. He closes the written procedure and from then on no new argument or new document may be introduced in the proceedings.

Oral argument

The persons qualified to plead before the courts vary depending on the court.

Only an *avocat* (and the party) may plead before the *Tribunal de Grande Instance*.

Before the *Tribunal d'Instance*, the *Tribunal de Commerce* and the *Conseil des Prud'hommes*, the party may be represented by an agent possessing a specific power of attorney for that particular hearing.

Irrespective of the court, during the oral argument, the party or its representative will refer to the arguments developed in the written proceedings, and, at the end of their argument, deliver a file containing the documents on which it relies to establish its case (*New Code of Civil Procedure, arts 430 to 446*).

In certain courts, such as the Paris Commercial Court, the "record of the pleadings", ie the file containing the documents, is delivered to the judge before the hearing, which then takes place very informally, as the judge, who will already have read the file, asks questions of the parties or their representatives.

The judge's powers

Under *Articles 179 to 183 of the New Code of Civil Procedure* the judge always has the power to investigate and make findings of fact, in particular on those in dispute and to visit the *locus in quo*.

Judgment

There is no specific time period within which a judgment must be given. In practice, there is an average period of six weeks between the oral hearing and judgment.

Judgment is given in public, except for hearings held in private, eg in divorce or affiliation proceedings.

The judgment must give the reasons on which the decision is based, but the judge rarely reads them out when announcing his decision.

When the court's decision is made by more than one judge, its deliberations may not be disclosed (*art 448*). There are no dissenting opinions.

Costs

The costs of the proceedings are divided into recoverable and non-recoverable costs.

The principle is that recoverable costs, also called "legal costs", *Recoverable costs*
are borne by the loser. These include the part of the other side's
avocat's fee which is allowed by the schedule of fees.

Irrecoverable costs are costs that are not automatically borne by *Irrecoverable*
the loser. These are the costs of the suit, including any balance of *costs*
the *avocat's* fees, the parties' travel expenses, or any other costs
incurred incidental to the suit.

Article 700 of the New Code of Civil Procedure provides that :
   "When the judge considers it unreasonable to require a
   party to bear the whole of the costs incurred by it that are
   normally non-recoverable, he may order the other party
   to pay an amount determined by him."

It should be emphasised that courts which order the unsuccessful
party to pay any irrecoverable costs award amounts that are much
lower than the successful party's actual costs.

In practice, since the principle is that an *avocat's* fees are agreed
freely between the *avocat* and his client, the balance of the fees is
never reimbursed to the successful party and the loser is never
ordered to pay them.

The defendant may ask the court to rule that the plaintiff's action *Purposeless*
has become purposeless, for example, because the amount *actions*
requested has been paid. If payment has been made out of court,
the court rules only on recoverable and non-recoverable costs
and damages, and interest, if any.

The average length of time taken for court proceedings is nine to *Length of*
twelve months of which six weeks is the time between the oral *proceedings*
procedure and judgment.

An appeal to the *Cour d'Appel* may be made on questions as to *Appeals*
the law and facts submitted to the court of first resort.

The Commercial Court, the *Conseil des Prud'hommes* and the
Tribunal d'Instance are courts of last resort when the amount in
dispute is lower than 13,000 francs.

In those cases the only appeal possible is to the *Cour de
Cassation*.

The *Cour d'Appel* is divided into specialised chambers to hear
cases that come before it. The average length of time taken for
proceedings before the *Cour d'Appel* is one year.

CHAPTER 7 : CRIMINAL PROCEDURE

The French criminal procedure system differs from the Anglo-Saxon system by being inquisitorial in nature, leaving the judge in complete control of the investigation of a case. The form of the investigation depends on whether the case is relatively simple or complex. *Introduction*

Inquisitorial nature

If the case is relatively simple, on a simple police report or complaint by the "*Ministère Public*", ie the representative of the state, or by the victim, the case is immediately referred to the court for judgment, and the court itself investigates the case and collects the evidence on both sides *Simple procedure - Ministère Public*

If the case is complex, prior to any hearing, it is assigned to a single judge, the "*Juge d'Instruction*" (Examining Magistrate), who collects evidence from both sides and is free to decide which measures to take in his search for the truth up to the point that the case is remitted to the court for hearing. *Complex cases - Juge d'Instruction*

Which court is competent depends on the types of offences. *Jurisdiction of criminal courts*

If the offence is a "police violation", it is decided by the "*Tribunal de Police*" (Police Court), which consists of a single judge. *Tribunal de Police*

If the offence is a misdemeanour, it goes before the "*Tribunal Correctionnel*," a division of the *Tribunal de Grande Instance* which specialises in criminal cases. In most cases, the *Tribunal Correctionnel* is composed of several judges. *Tribunal Correctionnel*

Felonies are judged by a "*Cour d'Assises*" made up of three professional magistrates and a lay jury of nine. This is the only French judicial institution in which there is a jury. *Cour d'Assises*

The only appeal from the decision of the *Cour d'Assises* is a "*pourvoi en cassation*" (appeal to the *Cour de Cassation*). Appeals from decisions of the *Tribunal du Police* and the *Tribunal Correctionnel* are made to the *Cour d'Appel*. This court has a "*Chambre d'Accusation*" which reports to the *Cour d'Appel* in the same way as the *Juge d'Instruction* reports to the *Tribunal de Grande Instance*. Decisions of the *Juge d'Instruction*, especially on questions of temporary detention, may be appealed to the *Chambre d'Accusation*. *Appeals*

Offences are defined on the basis of the type and level of the penalty specified in the *Criminal Code*. *Classification of offences*

      "An offence for which the maximum penalty is a fine or a term of imprisonment not exceeding two months is a police violation. An offence for which the maximum penalty is imprisonment is a misdemeanour.

An offence for which the maximum penalty is *"affliction et infamente"* is a felony." (*Criminal Code, art 1*) These cover the most serious offences.

Police violations are subject to a maximum sentence of imprisonment for a period not exceeding two months and/or a fine not exceeding 10,000 francs.

The maximum penalties for misdemeanours are imprisonment for two to five years, unless the law provides for a longer period (as in drug cases, in particular). A fine ranging from 10,000 to 250,000 francs can be imposed as an additional penalty.

The maximum penalties for felony cases are imprisonment or criminal detention for from 5 to 20 years, or for life.

Offences are in fact divided into five categories. The fifth category, felony cases, is for the most serious violations which are heard by the *Cour d'Assises*, by three professional magistrates and nine lay jurors.

Other offences are judged by professional judges : by a single magistrate in cases before the *Tribunal de Police*, by a court of judges before the other courts and at the appeal stage.

Who may prosecute

Criminal prosecution may be initiated by :

(a) the *Ministère Public* who represents the state. This is carried out by public officials who act with the authority of the Minister of Justice. The *Ministère Public*, even if requested to do so by a victim, decides for himself whether to prosecute;

The victim

(b) a victim, who may be an individual or a company, and who may adopt one of two procedures. If the case is a simple one, the victim may summon the person it wishes to be prosecuted directly before the *Tribunal Correctionnel* or the *Tribunal de Police*. This procedure is not available before the *Cour d'Assises*. If the case is relatively complex, the victim may file a *"plainte avec constitution de partie civile"* (a complaint with a claim for damages) before a *Juge d'Instruction* who must then investigate the whole matter.

Constitution de partie civile

Commencement of prosecution

A criminal prosecution may be initiated either directly before the court, or before the *Juge d'Instruction*. When the prosecution is initiated directly before the court, the individual prosecuted is summoned before the court on a fixed date by a charge served by specialised *huissiers* called *"huissiers audienciers"* or, in the case of flagrant violation, is immediately arraigned before the court.

When an *"instruction"* is held, the *Ministère Public*, either of his own motion or after a complaint by the victim before the *Juge d'Instruction*, requests that an investigation be opened, specifying the offences involved and the legal authority on which the charges are based. If the *Juge d'Instruction* decides that there is a case to answer by an individual, he notifies that individual of the indictment. The accused is then able to see the file of evidence against him and can only then be heard in the presence of his *avocat*.

If the case is subject to an investigation the procedure is more complex. Before an investigation opens, the offences are generally the subject of a preliminary investigation conducted by officers of the judicial police under the authority of the *Ministère Public*. In the course of this enquiry, the officers of the judicial police may hear witnesses whose statements are transcribed into a report. When, for the purposes of the enquiry, the officer of the judicial police responsible wants to hold the person for questioning for more than 24 hours, he must bring that person before the Public Prosecutor, who may order him to be placed in "*garde de vue*" (police custody) for a period which may not exceed 48 hours.

During this time, the person held in police custody may not communicate with anyone outside. Custody is under the control of the *Ministère Public*.

After this period of police custody, an order for further temporary detention may be ordered. This order must be issued by a judge, generally the *Juge d'Instruction*.

At the end of the preliminary enquiry, either the *Ministère Public* files the matter with no further action, or drafts preliminary charges to be heard by the *Juge d'Instruction* or refers the suspected persons to the court by way of a direct indictment.

The investigation, regulated in detail by *Articles 79 to 190 of the Code of Criminal Procedure*, consists essentially of hearings of the accused or of any witnesses, of challenges, searches, seizures, expert reports and so forth.

The accused may consult the file with his *advocat* 48 hours before his interrogation.

During the investigation, the aggrieved party or the *Ministère Public* may challenge the decisions of the *Juge d'Instruction* by appealing to the *Chambre d'Accusation*.

Requests to nullify investigative acts may also be referred to the *Chambre d'Accusation*.

The rules of the *Chambre d'Accusation* are contained in *Articles 191 to 230 of the Code of Criminal Procedure*.

Where the case is simple and is called before the court by way of a simple citation or within the framework of a procedure in flagrante delicto, the investigation takes place at the trial hearing. Before the hearing, the file often simply consists of a police report. If the charge comes directly from the complainant, the file

Hearings - preliminary enquiries

The trial hearing

The file

includes the documents which the victim has attached to the charge. Should the hearing have been preceded by an investigation, the file consists of all the documents and evidence collected during the investigation, as well as the written notes that the various parties to the proceedings may have given to the judge.

Role of the court   Irrespective of whether or not an investigation has taken place, the hearing before the court follows in an almost identical manner. One of the magistrates sitting on the bench describes the essential elements of the details in the file. Any witnesses are then called for questioning, followed by the defendant. Only the court asks questions. The parties to the proceedings and their *avocats*, including the representative of the *Ministère Public*, can only suggest questions to the court. The court then hears the oral presentation beginning with the complainant, followed by the *Ministère Public* and then the defence. Counsel for the defence always has the last word in reply.

Cour d'Assises and Tribunal Correctionnel   The rules of evidence are governed by *Articles 323 ff of the Code of Criminal Procedure* for proceedings before the Cour d'Assises and by *Articles 427ff* for criminal proceedings before the *Tribunal Correctionnel*.

Confessions   Pursuant to *Article 428*, the court is free to evaluate a confession as with any other kind of evidence, meaning that even where faced with a confession the *Tribunal* or the *Cour d'Assises* may discharge or acquit.

Standard of proof before the Cour d'Assises   Before the *Cour d'Assises*, pursuant to *Article 353 of the Code of Criminal Procedure*,
> "the law does not require judges to provide any reasoning as to their decision; it does not lay down any rules which set out a required standard of proof; it prescribes that they must question themselves, in silence and meditation, and seek, in the sincerity of their conscience, what impression the evidence presented against the accused and the oral submissions presented in his defence have made on their reason. The law asks of them only this one question, which contains the full measure of their duties : do you have an inner conviction?"

Standard of proof in other courts   As regards the *Tribunal Correctionnel*, *Article 427* provides that
> "save where the law provides otherwise, proof of the commission of offences may be established by any kind of evidence, and the judge decides according to his inner conviction."

Judges may base their decision only on evidence submitted to them during the proceedings and argued by both sides in front of them.

The French criminal justice does not recognise any prior declaration of guilt. Therefore, a plea of guilty entails no legal consequences, since, it has no binding force on the court. Nor will one find any negotiations or bargaining between the *Ministère Public* and the defence. Such negotiation would serve no useful purpose as neither the *Tribunal* nor the *Cour d'Assises* is bound by the decisions or requests of the representative of the *Ministère Public* particularly with regard to the level of punishment sought.

Guilty pleas

Rules for selecting juries are governed by *Articles 254ff of the Code of Criminal Procedure*. Only citizens over 23 who can read and write, who enjoy full political, civil and family rights and are not within certain categories of legal incapacity or incompatibility to act as jurors listed in the *Code of Criminal Procedure* may act as jurors. Legal incapacities result mainly from criminal or disciplinary penalties, or from mental illness. The question of incompatibilities mainly relates to political or judicial considerations. A list of potential jurors is drawn up in each jurisdiction of the *Cour d'Assises*; it includes from 50 to 700 names which are chosen at random. Thirty days before a session of the *Cour d'Assises*, 45 names are chosen at random. On the day of the hearing, the President of the *Cour d'Assises* chooses the nine lay jurors at random. First the accused or his counsel, and then the *Ministère Public*, may challenge lay jurors. They are not allowed to indicate the reasons for their challenge. The accused may not challenge more than five jurors and the *Ministère Public* more than four.

Selection of juries in the Cour d'Assises

The general rule is that proceedings are held in public. However, before both the *Cour d'Assises* and the *Tribunal Correctionnel*, if the President feels that publicity is a threat to public order or morality, he may order that the case be heard in camera. In the *Cour d'Assises*, in a case involving sexual allegations, the victim has the right to demand that the trial be held in camera.

Conduct of the trial in public

Trials may not be filmed.

The verdict may be given on the day of the hearing or adjourned for further deliberations. The *Cour d'Assises* must give its decision immediately after the hearing. When magistrates rule as a body, their decision must be unanimous. In the *Cour d'Assises*, a guilty verdict must be supported by a minimum of eight votes from the nine jurors and three magistrates.

Verdict

The *Tribunal Correctionnel* and the *Cour d'Assises* have the power to reconsider the facts referred to them. However, before any reconsideration can take place, the defence counsel's submissions must have been heard.

Sentence is generally given on the day of the hearing, after a short adjournment. If judgment is adjourned to another day further evidence may be produced in the meantime. Any review of this

Sentence

new evidence must take place in the presence of both sides, and may lead to the proceedings being re-opened. New evidence may not be produced for the first time on appeal. When Magistrates rule as a body they must be unanimous.

The French system provides for mitigation and extenuating circumstances to be put forward as reasons why a sentence should be reduced.

Mitigating and aggravating circumstances

Article 65 of the Criminal Code provides that
"No felony or misdemeanour may be excused, or the evidence mitigated, except in cases or circumstances where the law declares that the conduct is excusable or permits the application of a less rigorous sentence."

Mitigating circumstances

The extenuating circumstances defined by the law leading to a reduction of sentence under the legal minimum are :
- the excuse of minority, from 13 to 18 years
- the excuse of provocation in cases of self-defence.

On the other hand, extenuating circumstances are facts the judge is free to evaluate and which may result in a lowering of the sentence within the limits laid down by law (eg reparation being made for the injury, active repentance, no previous convictions). These circumstances do not, however, permit the judge to give a sentence below the statutory minimum.

Aggravating circumstances

Recidivism is an aggravating circumstance. *Articles 56 ff of the Criminal Code* sets out the various classes of recidivism and the penalties which they may incur.

Sentence on more than one charge

When an individual is charged with several felonies or misdemeanours before the criminal courts, the principle is that penalties will not be consecutive. Pursuant to *Article 5 of the Criminal Code*,
"if the accused is convicted of several felonies or misdemeanours, he is sentenced only to the heaviest penalty. The same applies as regards imprisonment in the case of most of the most serious (5th class) police violations."

Criminal responsibility for minors

Special procedural presumptions apply in the case of minors. Under the age of 13, there is an irrefutable presumption that the person is outside criminal responsibility. From 13 to 18, there is a presumption that a person is not to be regarded as criminally responsible for his actions, but evidence may be produced to counter this.

With regard to sentencing after a guilty verdict, sentence must be mitigated to take account of age for minors aged 13 to 15, this is optional for minors aged 16 to 18.

Range of sentences

The main sentences are confinement with loss of civil rights, imprisonment or fines.

Sentences may be suspended with or without probation. Where a sentence is suspended, the convicted person must fulfil a number of obligations in order to escape imprisonment, for instance, agree to undergo treatment if he has breached the anti-drug laws.

There are other alternatives to imprisonment. These often consist of work for the general public or to assist certain administrations or associations. They may be imposed only with the convicted person's agreement.

Hearings before the *Cour d'Appel* follow the normal path, save that the order of the pleadings is reversed so that the appellant speaks first. Should the appellant be the defendant, his counsel retains a right of reply to the oral submissions made by the other parties.

All decisions of the *Tribunal Correctionnel* or *Tribunal de Police* may be appealed within ten days of sentence or of the service of notice of sentence where the person convicted did not actually attend the hearing. The notice of appeal takes the form of a simple declaration to the office of the clerk of the court. The 10-day period and the appeal procedure which follows cause execution of conviction and sentence imposed by the inferior court to be stated.

Appeals from the decisions of the *Cour d'Appel* and the judgments of the *Cour d'Assises* are not subject to the same appeal process. An appeal may be lodged before the *Cour d e Cassation* only on questions of law. The grounds on which this form of appeal is open, are set out in *Articles 591 ff* of the *Code of Criminal Procedure*, including breaches of the rights of the defence, failure to observe rules of procedure, and so forth.

An appeal to the *Cour de Cassation* the must be lodged at the office of the clerk of the court where the decision was given within five days either from the issue or service of the sentence.

The length of time an appeal takes before a higher court or the *Cour de Cassation* varies greatly; it is very short if the accused is detained in custody.

Where there is no applicable treaty, extradition is governed by the *Law of 10 March 1927*.

The main conditions for extradition are :
  (a)   foreign nationality,
  (b)   absence of a political motive for the prosecution,
  (c)   that the crime is punishable under the law of the requesting state with a maximum sentence of two years or more of imprisonment or period of corrective training, and
  (d)   that the offence must be punishable by a criminal or correctional penalty under French law.

Procedure

The extradition procedure is as follows :
- (a) the request must be sent to the French government by diplomatic channel,
- (b) it is transmitted by the Ministry of Foreign Affairs to the Ministry of Justice, which verifies that the request has been made regularly,
- (c) the foreigner appears before the *Chambre d'Accusation* in a public hearing.

At the end of the hearing, the *Chambre d'Accusation*, whose decision may not be appealed, gives a reasoned opinion on the extradition request. A favourable opinion will be given unless the legal requirements are not met or there is an obvious error in the procedure.

- (d) if the opinion is favourable for extradition, the President of the Republic is free to allow extradition or to refuse it.
- (e) if the opinion is unfavourable the President of the Republic cannot allow the extradition

European Convention on Extradition

It should be noted that, by a decree of 14 May 1986, the *European Convention on Extradition* of 13 December 1957 was incorporated into French law.

Other international Conventions have been signed with other countries, but these do not fundamentally modify the rules provided for by the *Law of 19 March 1957*.

Detention on bail before trial

Misdemeanours

Temporary detention is strictly regulated. Before a person is charged, the period of police custody under the *garde de vue* rules may not exceed 48 hours (24 hours, renewable once). If a person is charged with a misdemeanour, the temporary detention period may not exceed four months. However, it may be extended under the following conditions :
- (a) if the accused has never been convicted before, extension of the detention period may not exceed two months;
- (b) in other cases, the accused may not be detained for more than one year, except for an exceptional extension of four months by order of the *Juge d'Instruction* who must give reasons.

Felonies

There is no limit in felony cases, except that the *Juge d'Instruction* must bring the accused before him every four months; otherwise, the accused may ask the *Chambre d'Accusation* for his immediate release on which the *Chambre d'Accusation* must rule within 20 days, failing which the accused must be released automatically. Requests for release may be made at any time, either to the *Juge d'Instruction* or, if the investigation stage is closed, before the court with jurisdiction to hear the case including the *Cour d'Appel*.

As an alternative to temporary detention, the *Juge d'Instruction* **Bail**
may place the accused on bail. Bail may involve complying with a
number of obligations, including that of reporting to the police at
regular intervals, and/or posting a bail bond. The bail bond is
intended to serve as a surety guaranteeing the rights of the victim.
In principle, it must be in an amount which corresponds to a
provisional evaluation of the injury sustained by the victim and
the costs of the legal proceedings. In principle, there is no limit on
the amount of bail.

There is no automatic right for a defendant to be released from
custody simply because he offers to put up money for bail. The
decision still rests with the responsible judicial authorities.

CHAPTER 8 : REMEDIES

Damages and interest may be claimed as reparation for loss or *Damages* damage following a tort or a breach of contract or criminal offence. Damages and interest arising out of a breach of contract *Generally* or tort may be claimed before any civil court. Damages and interest arising out of a criminal offence may be claimed before a civil court or the *Tribunal Correctionnel*. There are no cases where damages are awarded by a lay jury.

In the *Cour d'Assises* - the only court which includes a jury - after the sentence is passed, a "civil hearing" is held involving only the professional magistrates who fix the level of damages.

The amount of damages is based solely on the damage sustained, *Quantum of* which must be direct, actual and certain. There is no fixed tariff *damages* based on the kind of physical injuries sustained by the victim. However, decisions are frequently published setting out the level of damages awarded for particular types of physical injury. These published decisions are used as a reference in subsequent cases by *avocats* and magistrates. The court also has regard in fixing the level of the award to the circumstances of the plaintiff, eg his age and the nature of his employment. Other forms of loss, for example, mental distress and loss of reputation give a right to damages even where there is no physical injury. The amount of damages is based on the extent of the loss sustained.

The courts frequently award damages to the families of the victims. The courts have power to award damages for purely economic loss. The amounts awarded for non-quantifiable loss are not limited by law but are very moderate in practice. The evaluation of the amount is always made "in concreto".

In contract cases the parties are free, within the framework of *Penalty clauses* their contract, to stipulate in advance the types of damage for which the injured party will be indemnified and the amount of damages. However, the court retains the power to override such an agreement. *Article 1152 of the Civil Code* provides that :
"However, the judge may, of his own motion, lower or increase the penalty that had been agreed if it is obviously excessive or derisory. Any stipulation to the contrary shall be deemed not to have been written."

Restitution may be granted whenever the court orders that a *Restitution* contract be declared a nullity. However, it should be emphasised that, pursuant to *Article 1142 of the Civil Code*, in the case of non-performance the court will decide the on questions of damage and interest where it does not order restitution.

Theory of unjust enrichment	The theory of unjust enrichment is part of French jurisprudence. Unjust enrichment, by definition, means the enrichment of one estate to the detriment of another estate. There must, therefore, be both an enrichment and a corresponding impoverishment. However, an action for unjust enrichment is alternative to other forms of action.
Specific performance	A claim for specific performance of an obligation or to prohibit the doing of something is entirely permissible.
	In particular, pursuant to *Article 1143 of the Civil Code*, a claim may be made that what was in fact constructed in contravention of an agreement should be ordered to be destroyed.
	In the case of non-performance, pursuant to *Article 1144*, a plaintiff may be authorised to have an obligation performed at the debtor's expense.
	Further, in order to compel a defendant to perform, the judge may attach to his order a daily fine which accumulates for as long as the debtor does not meet his obligation.
Impossibility of performance	Pursuant to *Article 1148 of the Civil Code*, there are no grounds for damages where either, because of force majeure or an accidental event, a party is prevented from carrying out an obligation undertaken, or where such an act was prohibited by law.
	Case law has defined force majeure and accidental events very precisely. A case of force majeure can be summarised as follows: - it must be an external, unforeseeable and unpreventable event.
	The argument that the amount stipulated in a contract is not properly speaking compensatory but is a penalty is not sufficient to justify non-payment.
	However, as already explained above, pursuant to *Article 1152 of the Civil Code*, agreed damages provided for in a contract may be reduced to the extent that the amount stipulated is clearly excessive.
The passing of property	Articles 1604 to 1624 of the Civil Code regulate the passing of property and goods agreed under a contract of sale. In the case of real property, delivery takes the form of a surrender of the keys and the title deeds. In the case of personal property, it is evidenced by physical delivery of the property, or even by evidence of an agreement made by the parties. In the case of intangible rights, delivery is made either by way of surrender of the documents of title or of the use of the right by the buyer with the seller's consent.
Interest	In contract cases, pursuant to *Article 1146*, interest is due only if the debtor was given formal notice to meet his obligation. In criminal cases, interest may run only after the judgment has determined the amount of the indemnity to be paid.

Interest on monetary penalties ordered by a court will be legal interest the rate of which is fixed officially each year. For a long time, the interest rate was 9.5%. At present, it is 10.36%. Further, under *Article 1154 of the Civil Code*, interest payable on a capital amount may also incur further interest if it has been due for at least one whole year and if the court so decides.

Individuals or companies may refer a matter to a judge only if there is a dispute between them, that is , if the claims of one party are opposed by the other party. The existence of the claim and the fact that it is opposed are the two pre-conditions for starting an action, and, therefore, for it to be admissible. *Declaratory judgments*

French procedure does not permit a party to obtain a judgment which simply declares what the law is. There is even a provision that prohibits a judge from issuing a judgment by way of a general regulatory provision (*Article 5 of the Civil Code*).

A company may be wound up by a court either at the request of its managers or of a creditor, or, lastly, if the court so decides, of its own motion. *Winding-up of companies*

The ground for opening proceedings resulting either in the liquidation of a company or its reconstruction is when the company suspends payment, which is defined as the company's inability to pay its debts with its available assets.

It is worth emphasising that there are cases where a court can appoint a judicial administrator unless the company can show that it is able to pay its debts, particularly where there is a dispute between partners or directors which prevents the company from being managed normally.

All public bodies responsible for providing services may be sued in damages for failing to discharge their responsibilities. The remedy must always be in the form of money. Normally the judge in the administrative court may not issue injunctions against such bodies compelling them to act. However, a judge may do so when the administration has committed an abuse of its powers. The reason why it is so difficult to obtain injunctive relief is that the public body's assets belong to the state and by law the assets of the state may not be seized. Such proceedings take place before the administrative courts. *Actions by or against public bodies*

The victim of an offence may always obtain civil reparation for the injury before the criminal courts. In such a case, the victim must constitute himself a "*partie civile*" either during the investigative phase, if there is one, or at the hearing. *Civil remedies in criminal proceedings*

It should, however, be noted that when the victim elects between obtaining a remedy through the civil or the criminal courts he may not go back on his election. A victim who has constituted himself a *partie civile* may nevertheless obtain an order for provisional damages before the "*Juge Civile des Référés*", whose decision will not constitute *res judicata*. *Juge Civile des Référés*

Alternative procedures for settling disputes

The validity of a clause in a contract providing that the parties will go to arbitration in the event of a dispute under the contract is binding on all parties who are traders. In judicial proceedings determined by the courts, where a dispute has already arisen, the parties may agree that that dispute be judged with no possibility of appeal.

Conciliation

There is a prior conciliation procedure before the Conciliation Board and also before the Court of First Instance. Experience shows that these procedures have now become mere formalities and that the percentage of settlements there is extremely low.

Finally, it should be noted that it is the judge's express duty in all proceedings to try to bring the parties to a settlement and that he may take the initiative in attempting to achieve this. A practice has developed in the Paris Court of Appeal whereby the judge may authorise a mediator to try to reconcile the parties.

If such mediation succeeds, the protocol of agreement resulting therefrom has the same effect as a court decision.

CHAPTER 9 : MATRIMONIAL DISPUTES

Divorce and ancillary matters related to it come within the exclusive competence of the *Cour de Grande Instance*. The Family Court judge or judges constitute a division of the *Cour de Grande Instance*. They have the power to intervene at all stages in the divorce proceedings.

Competence of the Cour de Grande Instance

It is the only court competent to make orders in ancillary proceedings relating to the provision of financial support for the spouse and child support, questions of custody, where the children will reside as well as visiting and staying rights of access.

Jurisdiction over ancillary questions relating to the custody of children, the child's residence, visiting rights and the right to provide lodging in cases other than divorce, is as follows:

Jurisdiction

    (a)   while the marriage subsists and outside divorce proceedings, they fall within the competence of the *"Juge des Tutelles"* (Guardianship judge).

    (b)   where ancillary to divorce proceedings, ancillary proceedings over natural children fall within the competence of the Family Court judge, except that a joint proposal may be received by the *Juge des Tutelles*.

The court with territorial jurisdiction is that :

Territorial jurisdiction

    (a)   of the place where the family resides;

    (b)   if the spouses have separate residences, that of the place where the spouse with whom any children who are minors reside;

    (c)   in other cases, that of the place where the spouse who did not initiate the proceedings resides.

In French law, the grounds for divorce are identical to those for judicial separation from bed and board.

Basic grounds for divorce

In addition to converting judicial separation into divorce, there are four grounds for divorce, which may be divided into "wanted" and "contested" divorces.

The various forms of divorce procedure are outlined below.

Divorce procedure

(a) *By joint request*

Joint request

    -    filing of a joint request for divorce,

    -    first personal appearance of the spouses before the Family Court judge,

    -    a delay of a minimum of three months and a maximum of nine months before any renewal of the request for divorce,

-   a second personal appearance of the spouses before the Family Court judge and the issuing of the judgment for divorce.

Proceedings by one party accepted by the other

(b) *Divorce initiated by one party and accepted by the other* - divorce for breach of conjugal rights - divorce on the grounds of fault

-   filing of a request for divorce,
-   summons to the conciliation hearing before the Family Court judge, who, where reconciliation fails, issues an order specifying the temporary measures to be applied while the proceedings continue,
-   notification and development of the divorce proceedings before the court, which gives the pronouncement of the divorce and its consequences.

Divorce by joint request

A divorce by joint request leaves the grounds of the divorce secret. It does not have to be officially reported or published. It is subject to a special procedure, during which the Family Court judge verifies the free, current and serious consent of the spouses to divorce and ratifies their agreement on the ancillary personal and property-related consequences of the divorce.

Divorce requested by one spouse and accepted by the other

This type of divorce is at the same time voluntary and contentious: it involves the intervention of the *Tribunal* after that of the Family Court judge. The divorce results from two consecutive and unilateral expressions of the spouses' wish to divorce. They agree the facts, thereby justifying the terms of the divorce. The consequences of the divorce are then determined by the court. They are consistent with a divorce pronounced against both sides equally.

Divorce for breach of conjugal rights

(c) *Divorce for breach of conjugal rights*. There are two separate grounds for divorce for breach of conjugal rights: separation, in fact, for more than six years, and a change in mental faculties.

The spouse who petitions for divorce must submit proof that grounds for divorce exists and must pledge to assume the consequences and the burden of the divorce.

The other spouse may oppose the petition by establishing that the divorce would have material and moral consequences of exceptional hardship for him or herself, given as justification for that argument his or her age and the length of time the marriage has continued, or for the children.

The consequences of the divorce are those for a divorce pronounced exclusively against a petitioner, with special consequences such as retention of the use of the husband's name, the subsistence of the duty to provide financial assistance among spouses, covering medical expenses where mental faculties have altered.

(d) *Divorce for fault.* The notion of fault is assessed by the court. It is defined as :

> "Conduct attributable to the other party constituting a grave or repeated violation of the duties and obligations of the marriage, making continuance of communal life intolerable."

The defendant may file a counterclaim for divorce for fault. The divorce is pronounced either exclusively against one side or against both sides equally (even in the absence of a counterclaim). Damages and interest may be obtained for material or moral damage caused by dissolution of the marriage or for the damage caused by the violation of the duties of the marriage.

Following a divorce or judicial separation, extinction of the spouses' rights depends essentially on what type of ante-nuptial settlement they had. Where they had not signed a contract before a notary prior to celebration of the marriage, the spouses are deemed to have been married under the legal regime of community of property limited to the property acquired after marriage, ie they retain full possession of their own personal property and property inherited before marriage, the only common items being the property or financial assets of the household. The marriage contract may provide for a broader sharing of property or, on the contrary, for a total separation of property ownership.

The division of community property is done before a notary. Where difficulties arise, either spouse may refer the matter to the courts.

Apart from division of property, one of the spouses (generally the wife), may have allocated to him/her, with the agreement of the other spouse or of the court, maintenance in the form of monetary support for the children of whom he/she has custody, or alimony for himself/herself during the proceedings.

Save in the case of divorce by reason of separation for more than six years, any alimony allocated to a spouse is then transformed on divorce into a compensatory payment of an entirely different kind. It consists of an amount of capital, definitively fixed and not susceptible to future revision, save in exceptional cases, the purpose of which is to compensate for the disparity in the situations in which the spouses then find themselves. The purpose of this capital is to provide, when invested, a form of income. Only if the debtor is not able to pay such capital is the capital sum transformed into an order for monthly periodic payments index linked to the cost of living to be paid for a period determined by the court.

The notary keeps the original of the deed of division of assets and delivers a copy to each of the parties. This document alone constitutes good title to property and is valid for all purposes.

Parental authority, child's residence, visiting rights, lodging outside divorce

The procedure for changes to a divorce settlement after divorce are as follows:

- referral to the Family Court judge by way of a request or summary proceedings,
- summoning the parties to the hearing,
- the judge rules informally on the respective requests.

The procedure during marriage where no application for divorce is pending :

- referral to the *Juge des Tutelles* by way of a request or simple declaration to the clerk of the court
- summoning the parties to the hearing and decision.

In dealing with natural children the procedure is the same as for proceedings for variations after divorce.

It is important to note that there is more than one method of appeal provided for against the decisions of the court in these proceedings.

An expert's report may be ordered at any stage during the proceedings if the judge thinks that he does not have sufficient information to rule on the problems concerning the children or the terms of the monetary settlements between the spouses.

Urgent measures may be taken either by the Family Court judge or by the "*Juge de la Mise in État*" when the case is already before the court.

On a request for urgent measures, the judge rules very rapidly, ie within a period of from ten days to three weeks.

CHAPTER 10 : PROPERTY TRANSACTIONS

The rules relating to transactions involving real property are very simple. The agreement between seller and buyer generally takes the form of a promise of sale registered to take place on a certain date and provides for a forfeit clause in favour of the seller in case the buyer withdraws from the sale. But the sale itself may only result from an authentic deed prepared by the notary and containing, in particular :

- the full identification of both parties,
- a precise description of the property being sold,
- the origin of ownership, indicating the previous owners for the previous 30 years,
- the price and terms of payment,
- the date of occupancy and the terms of delivery of the property (condition of the buildings, easements, city planning, etc.),
- any involvement of a financial organisation lending funds required for the purchase.

The notarised deed must then be registered, the duties be paid to the state, and the deed published at the Mortgage Registry of the *Département*, where a file on each property sets out all transactions concerning it (the system is a little different in Alsace-Lorraine, where a *"livre foncier"* inherited from German law exists).

CHAPTER 11 : RECOGNITION AND ENFORCEMENT OF FOREIGN JUDGMENTS

The *Brussels Convention on Jurisdiction and Enforcement of Judgments in Civil and Commercial Matters of 27 September 1968* was published in France on 17 January 1973 and became effective law on 1 February 1973. It is, therefore, an integral part of French law.

Outside the scope of the *Brussels Convention*, judgments entered in a foreign state may be enforced in French territory by way of an exequatur, which only the *Tribunal de Grande Instance* may grant; the *Ministére Public* is consulted. The judge who is asked to grant the *exequatur* is only concerned to ensure that the foreign judgment has been regularly obtained and may not concern himself with the substance of the dispute, which has already been resolved.

Unless otherwise provided for by treaty, the *exequatur* procedure is introduced by service of process. The plaintiff in the action must present the decision and all documents establishing that proceedings were fair if applicable. He must request that the lawful effects of the judgment, including those aspects that have not been made explicit in the judgment be enforced. The judge must verify of his own motion that the foreign decision satisfies the conditions for it to be declared enforceable in France. The judge may ask the parties for any explanation or documents to prove that the decision has been regularly made according to international law.

The international grounds of *Ordre Publique* which must be satisfied before an *exequatur* can be obtained are much narrower than national public policy. The areas concerned are mainly the protection of human rights, as defined, in particular, by *the European Convention on Human Rights*.

The procedure, which takes place before a single judge, may be very quick taking somewhere in the order of three to four months. The channels for appeal are identical to those for ordinary matters referred to the *Tribunal de Grande Instance*.

GERMANY

Volker G. Heinz
Rechtsanwalt und Notar, Berlin
Barrister-at-law, London
Melchers Schubert Petersen Stocker Sturies
Berlin, Frankfurt/Main, Heidelberg, Zwickau
(as of October 1992)

The author is indebted to Joachim Gulich, Thomas Jestädt, Endrik Lettau, Andreas Weitbrecht and Solms Wittig, his colleagues of Wilmer, Cutler & Pickering (Washington DC, London, Brussels), for their assistance in the preparation of these chapters.

CONTENTS

CHAPTER 1 : SOURCES OF LAW

The Federal Republic of Germany is a federal state (*Article 20(1)* *of the German Constitution* (*the Federal Constitution* — *"Grundgeset"* (*"GG"*). It consists of sixteen regions or *"Länder"*. The highest German court on constitutional matters, (the Federal Constitutional Court), has held that the *Länder* have limited sovereign powers of their own that are not derived from the powers of the Federation (*see Decisions of the Federal Constitutional Court (BVerfGE) 1, 34; 60, 207*).

Unitary v federal system

Articles 70 et seq. of the *Constitution* allocate legislative powers between the Federation and the *Länder*. The basic rule is that, save where a power is specifically allocated to the Federation, any given subject matter falls within the legislative competence of the *Länder*. *Articles 70, 71 and 73 GG* reserve certain areas exclusively to the Federation. Certain other areas are subject to the concurrent competence of both the Federation and the *Länder* eg in *Articles 72 and 74 GG*. As long and in so far as the Federation does not use its legislative powers in these areas, the *Länder* are empowered to pass laws. *Article 75* authorises the Federation to enact framework regulations in respect of some areas which, in principle, remain subject to the legislative powers of the *Länder*.

This allocation of legislative powers between the Federation and the *Länder* results in the following division of authority to act : all matters relating to foreign affairs including defence, immigration, currency, and customs matters as well as transport and telecommunications (railways, postal services, air traffic, money and minting, weights and measures) are subject to the exclusive authority of the Federation. Concurrent competence of the Federation and the *Länder* affects mainly the following areas : police powers, cultural issues, local government matters, agriculture, water and waterways regulations, but also civil and criminal law. The Federation's legislative power to set framework regulations extends to laws concerning the civil service and universities. *Article 31* provides that in any conflict between a federal law and the laws of a *"Land"* the former prevails; this rule applies not only to federal constitutional law, but to any kind of federal law, which will thus take precedence over even the constitutional law of individual *Länder*.

The principal sources of law are :

Principal codifications

- the Federal Constitution, ("GG");
- the Civil Code ("BGB");
- the Code of Civil Procedure ("ZPO");
- the Commercial Code ("HGB");

- *the Penal Code ("StGB");*
- *the Code of Criminal Procedure ("StPO");*
- *the Code of Administrative Proceedings ("VwVfG");*
- *the Code of Administrative Court Procedure ("VwGO");*
- *the Tax Code ("AO");*
- *the Income Tax Code ("EStG"); and*
- *the German Unification Treaty, together with its appendices of 31-8-1990.*

Application of national law to foreigners

Save where expressly provided to the contrary, foreigners can rely on German law in the same way and to the same extent as German nationals. This is true in all the principal areas of constitutional, civil, criminal, administrative, tax, and procedural law. There are a few instances where certain legal provisions apply only to German nationals : for instance, the *Constitution* confers certain constitutional rights and obligations, eg the right to vote and the obligation to serve in the armed forces, only on German nationals; under *Section 110 ZPO*, a foreign plaintiff may be requested to provide security for costs in civil proceedings; and under *Section 917(2) ZPO*, it is easier pre-trial to attach the assets of a foreign defendant than of a German defendant. In general, where the law applies specifically to foreigners, these provisions apply also to EC nationals. The laws on immigration, in particular the *"Ausländergesetz"* (Foreigners Act), apply to foreigners (including EC nationals) only.

Monist v dualist system

The *German Constitution* reflects a mixed dualist/monist approach. Under *Article 59(2) GG*, international treaties need to be incorporated into domestic law by a statute adopted by the Federal Parliament in order to become binding law in Germany. Once incorporated, treaties have the same force as federal laws. They take precedence over any form of federal law except the *Constitution*. Also, in theory, the incorporated treaties can be superseded by later federal law. The Federal Constitutional Court can review the constitutionality of statutes that incorporate international treaties into German law. *Article 25 GG* establishes that, even without being specifically incorporated into domestic law, the "general principles of public international law" are "part of federal law". They take precedence over all federal and *Länder* laws and are directly applicable in the Federal Republic. The general principles of public international law include, for example, the rules on sovereign immunity and the principle of *pacta sunt servanda. Article 26 GG* specifically provides that the prohibition against preparing and conducting a war of aggression is part of German constitutional law.

Application of EC law

The EC Treaties were incorporated into German law in accordance with *Article 59(2)* and *Article 24(1) GG. Article 24(1) GG* specifically provides that the Federation may, by a statute adopted by the Federal Parliament, transfer sovereign powers to supra-national institutions.

Pursuant to *Article 59(2) GG* Community law is directly binding within the Federal Republic without needing any further incorporating acts. Directives need to be implemented in accordance with Community law to create direct legal effects domestically. Decisions and Regulations of the EC institutions are directly applicable.

Therefore, all primary and secondary Community law, in principle, takes precedence over German domestic law, including the *Constitution*. However, in a decision of 29-5-1974, the Federal Constitutional Court held that, as long as the Communities do not guarantee a standard of protection for fundamental rights which corresponds to the protection of these rights under the *GG*, Community acts can be challenged before the court to the extent that they violate a fundamental right protected by the *GG*. (*Solange-Decision, BVerfGE 37, 280*). In its decision of October 1986, the Federal Constitutional Court stated that the standard of protection afforded by fundamental rights under Community law can be regarded as equivalent to the protection provided under German constitutional law (see the *Solange II-Decision, BVerfGE 73, 378*).

When a German court applies foreign law, it must apply that law as it is interpreted in its home country. German law treats questions of foreign law as questions of fact. If a court has to apply foreign law and does not know the answer to a specific question of foreign law, it must take evidence on that question : *Section 293 ZPO* (applicable both in civil court proceedings and administrative court proceedings). Evidence may be provided by written submission or by expert testimony. If documents in a foreign language are submitted, the court may, but need not, ask for a German translation (*ZPO, s 142(3)*). — *Application of foreign law in national proceedings*

The *European Convention on Human Rights* was incorporated into German federal law pursuant to *Article 59(2) GG*. German courts do not have direct jurisdiction to hear cases alleging breaches of the *Convention*. However, the courts do look to the *Convention*, and to the case law deriving from it, where applying general statutory clauses such as *bonos mores* or public policy to a given set of facts, with the result that a breach of the *Convention* would be regarded as a breach of *bonos mores* or of German public policy. — *Application of the European Convention on Human Rights*

There are several methods used for interpreting legal provisions, which may be applied simultaneously. The starting point is the wording of the legal provision - the "*Grammatische Auslegung*" or "grammatical interpretation". Then, a German lawyer would look to the legislative materials which led to the provision to be interpreted - the "*Historische Auslegung*" or "historical interpretation". Further, the position of the legal provision in question within the framework of the relevant Code or other body of laws of which it is part must be taken into account - the "*Systematische Auslegung*" or "systematic interpretation". Finally, German law interprets legal provisions by attempting to identify their purpose - the "*Teleologische Auslegung*" or "teleological interpretation". — *Principles of interpretation*

In general, decisions of the higher courts have no binding effect upon lower courts; the principle of *stare decisis* is not recognised under German law. However, there are some exceptions : decisions of the Federal Constitutional Court are binding upon all lower courts. (*Section 31(1) of the Federal Constitutional Court Act - Gesetz über das Bundesverfassungsgericht*). Also, where a higher court refers a matter back to a lower court for final decision (ie after a successful appeal), the lower court is bound by the decision of the higher court.

Authorised texts of the Constitution

There are no official annotated versions of the *Federal Constitution*. The most authoritative commentaries on the *G G* are : Maunz/Dürig/Herzog/Scholz, *Grundgesetzkommentar*, (7th edn, 1991 et seq); Leibholz/Rinck/Hesselberger, *Grundgesetz* (6th edn, 1989 et seq). For the wording of the *Constitution* and other statutes see the collections of statutes of "Schönfelder, Deutsche Gesetze" and "Sartorius I" (Beck-Verlag Munich).

For commentaries on other legal texts see the bibliography in Chapter 12.

CHAPTER 2 : FUNDAMENTAL RIGHTS

The fundamental rights protected by law are listed in *Articles 1 to 18 GG*. These fundamental rights directly bind the legislative, executive, and judicial powers (*GG, art 1(2)*). The fundamental rights listed in *Articles 1 to 18 GG* can be divided into rights safeguarding liberties and rights against discrimination.

Constitutional protection of fundamental rights

The first group includes the freedom to develop one's personality and the freedom from injury (*art 2*); the freedom of religion and confession (*art 4*); the freedom to express one's opinion and the freedom of the press (*art 5(1)*); protection of the family (*art 6*); the freedom of the educational systems (*art 7*); the freedom of association and assembly (*arts 8 and 9*); the freedom of economic and social coalitions (*art 9(3)*); the right to petition (*art 17*); the freedom of movement (*art 11*); the freedom of choice of profession and place of work (*art 12*); the inviolability of the privacy of postal services and tele-communications (*art 10*); the inviolability of the home (*art 13*); the protection of property and inheritance rights (*art 14*); the right of asylum (*art 16(2)*).

The second group of basic rights arises from the general ban on discrimination under *Article 3(1)* and the particular ban on discrimination based on sex (*art 3(2)*), parentage, race, language, homeland and origin, faith, religion or political opinions (*art 3(3)*).

Article 19(4) GG guarantees any person whose rights are violated by the public authorities a right of recourse to the courts. In addition to the catalogue of fundamental rights in *Articles 1 to 18*, the *GG* contains guarantees of certain judicial rights, such as the principle of *habeas corpus* in *Article 104*; the right to a fair trial in *Article 101(1)*, and to be heard in court in *Article 103(1)*; the exclusion of retroactive criminal liability (*art 103(2)*); and the prohibition against being punished for the same offence more than once (*art 103(3)*). Finally, the *GG* has abolished, and prohibits, capital punishment (*art 102*).

All courts are directly bound to observe the *Constitution* (*art 1(3)*). Violation of the *Constitution* can be alleged in any court proceedings. Any court may quash judicial or administrative acts on the basis that they violate the *Constitution*.

Interpretation by the courts

As far as legislative acts are concerned, a distinction must be drawn between pre-constitutional and post-constitutional law. If a court is of the opinion that pre-constitutional legislation (ie that enacted before the *GG* entered into force) violates the *Constitution*, it may disregard that legislation. In the case of post-constitutional legislation, the Federal Constitutional Court alone has the authority to declare such legislation unconstitutional: where such legislation is in issue, lower courts must therefore refer any questions regarding its compatibility with the *GG* to the Federal Constitutional Court. This procedure is called "*konkrete Normenkontrollklage*" or "specific constitutional review of legislation". A general constitutional complaint against legislation that is not tied to a concrete case, the so-called "*abstrakte Normenkontrollklage*" or "abstract constitutional review of legislation", can only be brought by the federal government, a government of a *Land*, or a third of the members of the federal Parliament.

Federal Constitutional Court

Any person claiming there has been a breach of his fundamental rights under *Articles 1 to 18 GG* or of his judicial or citizen rights under *Articles 20(4), 33, 38, 101, 103 and 104*, may institute a "*Verfassungsbeschwerde*" or "constitutional appeal" directly before the Federal Constitutional Court (*GG, art 93(1) No 4a*). However, the plaintiff must first exhaust all appeals before the lower courts before his constitutional complaint can be heard.

Legal representation

Any lawyer admitted in the Federal Republic of Germany, or a professor of law at any German university may appear before the Federal Constitutional Court. Representation by a lawyer or a professor is required only for the oral hearings before the court. Special rules apply with respect to representation of legislative bodies, the federal government and the *Länder* before this court.

Length of appeal proceedings

There are no statistics available on the average time taken for constitutional appeal proceedings to be heard. A considered estimate is that such proceedings take, as a rule, between one and two years.

CHAPTER 3 : JURISDICTION OF THE COURTS

There are several challenges possible to the assumption of jurisdiction by a German court :

   (i)   that the matter brought before the court does not belong within that court's branch of jurisdiction ("*richtiger Rechtsweg*");

   (ii)   that the matter does not fall within the court's international ("*internationale Zuständigkeit*") or local jurisdiction ("*örtliche Zuständigkeit*");

   (iii) that the court's subject matter jurisdiction ("*sachliche Zuständigkeit*") does not cover the matter brought before the court; or

   (iv) finally, the court's functional jurisdiction ("*funktionelle Zuständigkeit*") may be challenged.

German law does not recognise the *forum non conveniens* doctrine as a basis of challenge.

The German court system is divided into several different jurisdictions (the ordinary courts for civil and criminal matters, labour courts, administrative courts, tax courts, social courts, and constitutional courts). Each court in which proceedings are brought, must review whether or not they are validly within its jurisdiction or should be referred to another jurisdiction (see *Section 13 of the Constitutional Court Act, Section 40 of the Code of Administrative Court Procedure, Section 2 of the Labour Court Act, Section 52 of the Social Court Act, Section 33 of the Fiscal Court Act*). If a court is of the view that the action brought before it belongs to another jurisdiction, it must refer the matter to the courts of that jurisdiction (*Article 17a (2)(1) Constitution of Courts Act*).

Different jurisdictions of courts outlined

In cases in which international and local jurisdiction are at issue the question is whether the German courts have jurisdiction at all to hear a case, and if so before which local court in Germany a court action is to be brought. German statute law does not contain any provisions on how to determine a court's international jurisdiction. If no specific international treaties apply (such as the *1968 Brussels Convention on Jurisdiction and Enforcement of Foreign Judgments*), the question on international jurisdiction is determined by applying the statutory provisions on local jurisdiction: if a court has local jurisdiction to hear a certain matter brought before it, it is deemed to have international jurisdiction in respect of the same matter. In general, local jurisdiction depends on the domicile or corporate seat of the defendant, the centre of gravity of a commercial transaction, the place where a tort was committed, and so forth. In civil and criminal proceedings, the international and/or local jurisdiction

International civil jurisdiction

of the court can be challenged only until the first oral hearings take place (*Code of Civil Procedure, s 39; Code of Criminal Procedure, s 16*).

Subject matter jurisdiction

The rules on subject matter jurisdiction determine which court in the hierarchy of courts of the same jurisdiction may hear a specific matter. The ordinary court system is the only jurisdiction which has different courts of first instance: the *"Amtsgerichte"* (District Courts) and *"Landgerichte"* (Regional Courts). Subject matter jurisdiction in the ordinary court branch is allocated depending on the value of the matter in dispute (for civil proceedings) and on the seriousness of the offence (for criminal proceedings). The less serious cases are heard in the *Amtsgerichte* and the more serious cases in the *Landgerichte* .

Functional jurisdiction

Functional jurisdiction determines which specific senate, chamber, or individual judge within a specific court has jurisdiction to hear a specific matter.

International criminal jurisdiction

German substantive criminal law is universally applicable, regardless of the place where the crime in question was committed, in respect of genocide; crimes committed by using nuclear, explosive, or radiation energy; crimes against aviation and maritime traffic; crimes in furtherance of prostitution and trade in human beings; drug trafficking; distribution of pornographic literature displaying children or animals; the counterfeiting of banknotes and securities certificates; and fraud in subsidisation procedures. German criminal courts are competent to hear all cases based on crimes committed abroad where the defendant is domiciled or arrested in Germany (*Code of Criminal Procedure, ss 8 and 9*).

Sovereign immunity

The Federal Republic of Germany, the *Länder*, and any foreign states can be sued without limitation in respect of acts committed in a purely commercial capacity (*acta de iure gestionis*). The Federal Republic and the *Länder* can also be brought before a court in respect of all acts committed in their sovereign capacity to the extent these acts infringe upon the rights of an individual. Foreign states enjoy immunity from legal action when they act in their capacity as sovereign states (*acta de iure imperii*).

Domestic civil jurisdiction

In civil proceedings, the domicile of the defendant generally determines the jurisdiction of the court (*Code of Civil Procedure, s 12*). As far as corporations are concerned, the court in whose district a corporation is registered generally has jurisdiction in respect of all court proceedings brought against that corporation (*Code of Civil Procedure, s 17*). In addition to the courts of the domicile of a person or of the seat of a corporation having jurisdiction, other courts may have jurisdiction depending on the subject matter of the dispute. Tort actions may be brought in the court in whose district the tort was committed (*Code of Civil Procedure, s 32*). Contract claims may be brought before the court in whose district the main contractual duty was to be performed (*Code of Civil Procedure, s 29*). Claims relating to a branch of a corporation can be brought in the court where the branch is located (*Code of Civil Procedure, s 21*). If a defendant has no domicile or corporate seat in Germany he may be sued in any German court in the district of which he owns assets (*Code of Civil Procedure, s 23*). The *1968 Brussels Convention* supersedes most of the provisions on jurisdiction in the *Code of Civil Procedure* (especially *Section 23*) where the defendant is an EC Member State national.

In criminal proceedings, generally it is the court of the district where the crime or offence was committed that has jurisdiction (*Code of Criminal Procedure, s 7*). Alternatively, proceedings can be commenced before the court in whose district the defendant has his domicile or habitual abode (*Code of Criminal Procedure, s 8*).

Domestic criminal jurisdiction

CHAPTER 4 : ADMINISTRATION OF JUSTICE

Structure of the Court System

Branch of Jurisdiction	Ordianary Courts (Civil and Criminal matters)	Administrative Courts	Labour Courts	Social Courts	Revenue or Fiscal Court
Code of Procedure	ZPO[1a], StPO[1b]	VwGO[2]	ArbGG[3]	SGB[4] (Chapter X)	FGO[5]
First Instance	Amtsgericht (Council Court) or Landgericht (Regional Court)	Verwaltungs- gericht (Administrative Court)	Arbeitsgericht (Labour Court)	Sozialgericht (Social Court)	Finanzgericht (Tax Court)
General Appeal (Berufung)	Landgericht (Regional Court) or Oberlandes- gericht (Higher Regional Court) (known as "Kammer- gericht" in Berlin)	Oberverwaltungs-gericht (Higher Administrative Court) ("Verwaltungs- gerichtshof)"	Landesarbeits -gericht (Regional Labour Court)	Landessozial- gericht (Regional Social Court)	—
Appeal on Questions of Law (Revision)	Bundesgerichts-hof (Federal High Court)	Bundesverwal- tungsgericht (Federal Administrative Court)	Bundesarbeits -gericht (Federal Labour Court)	Bundessozial - gericht (Federal Social Court)	Bundesfinanz- hof (Federal Tax Court)
Constitutional Appeal (Verfassungs- beschwerde)		BUNDESVERFASSUNGSGERICHT (FEDERAL CONSTITUTIONAL COURT)			

Code of Civil Procedure
Code of Criminal Procedure
Administrative Court Act
Labour Court Act
Social Court
Tax Court Act

Subject matter jurisdiction of ordinary courts	As regards the ordinary courts, subject matter jurisdiction is assigned as follows :
Civil proceedings	In civil proceedings, the *Amtsgericht* can hear matters up to a value of DM 6,000 as a court of first instance. The court also has unlimited jurisdiction over family matters including cases involving parents and children; and over landlord and tenant disputes. In all other civil cases, the *Landgericht* is the court of first instance.

Criminal Procedure

In criminal proceedings, the *Amtsgericht* is competent in all matters where a punishment of three years' imprisonment or less can be imposed.

Other branch jurisdictions

In all other branch jurisdictions, the respective court of first instance indicated above is competent to hear all cases as a court of first instance.

General Appeals

All final judgments of the courts of first instance (except those of the tax courts) are subject to a general appeal *(Berufung)* to their respective courts of appeal. In some branches of jurisdiction, the availabilty of an appeal depends on whether the value or importance of the appeal to the appellant exceeds a certain threshold: in civil proceedings, an appeal is only available where the value of the matter to the appellant exceeds DM 1,200. In labour proceedings, the threshold is DM 800, an appeal can be permitted, however, where the court of first instance expressly decides to allow this.

On appeal, the respective court of appeal reviews the decision of the court of first instance both as to whether the facts underlying the decision have been assessed correctly and whether the law was applied accurately. The court of appeal can receive additional evidence.

Appeals on questions of law

Appeals on questions of law ("*Revision*") are, as a rule, permissible only where expressly allowed by the respective court of appeal. In civil matters, *Revision* is permissible automatically where the value of the matter to the appellant exceeds DM 60,000. In tax matters, *Revision* is permissible where the value at stake exceeds DM 1,000. A court of appeal must allow *Revision* in those cases where its decision deals with a question of law in a different way from that dealt with in a decision of another court of appeal.

In principle, appeals operate as an automatic stay of enforcement proceedings (see *Sections 704 of the Code of Civil Procedure; 449 of the Code of Criminal Procedure; and 168 of the Code of Administrative Court Procedure*). In civil proceedings a party may enforce a judgment that is subject to appeal where the judgment is for not more than DM 1,500. In labour matters, judgments are enforceable even where an appeal has been lodged. Where a judgment is enforceable notwithstanding an appeal, the appellant always has a remedy against enforcement if he can show that enforcement notwithstanding his appeal would cause him unacceptable damage.

All lower courts have the right to make preliminary references pursuant to *Article 177 of the EEC Treaty*, but only the highest courts in each branch of jurisdiction (ie *Bundesgerichtshof, Bundesverwaltungsgericht, Bundesarbeitsgericht, Bundesfinanzgerichtshof und Bundessozialgericht*) as well as the *Bundesverfassungsgericht* must submit a question to the European Court of Justice if they have doubts as to the interpretation or validity of a provision of Community law which must be resolved for the court to decide the case before it.

References under Article 177 of the EEC Treaty

There are no other courts to which references on questions of law may be made.

CHAPTER 5 : STRUCTURE OF THE LEGAL PROFESSION

Legal services are provided mainly by "*Rechtsanwälte*". The legal profession is not split into barristers/solicitors or avocats/avoués; a *Rechtsanwalt* can both advise a client out of court and represent the client in litigation. In addition to *Rechtsanwälte*, there are certain other legal practitioners who may provide legal advice in specific areas, eg trade union officials, pension consultants, freight auditors, sworn auctioneers, debt-collecting companies, and legal experts in a foreign law. Tax consultants may provide an even wider range of services: they may appear in proceedings before the tax courts and to some extent as defence counsel in criminal tax cases. Notaries are independent holders of a public office to notarise legal documents. Their main areas of practice are conveyancing, registered companies and probate. *Structure*

Within the legal profession there are no other specifically identifiable organised groups of lawyers specialising in forensic activities.

Each *Rechtsanwalt* must be admitted to a specific local *Amtsgericht* and *Landgericht*. After having practised for five years before his local *Amtsgericht* and *Landgericht*, the *Rechtsanwalt* can apply to be admitted to practise before the *Oberlandesgericht* (in some *Länder* in addition to his previous admission). *Local admission of Rechtsanwälte*

In civil proceedings, the parties may appear and represent themselves before the *Amtsgerichte*. Before the *Landgerichte* and *Oberlandesgerichte*, they must be represented by a *Rechtsanwälte* admitted to practise before the respective court. *Representation*

In criminal proceedings, every *Rechtsanwalt* admitted to any bar in Germany may represent a client before any German court. Representation by a *Rechtsanwalt* is compulsory where the defendant is accused of a crime which is punishable with at least one year's imprisonment.

Before the "*Verwaltungsgerichte*" (Administrative Court) and "*Oberverwaltungsgerichte*" (Higher Administrative Court) the parties need not be represented by a *Rechtsanwälte*. Representation is compulsory, however, before the "*Bundesverwaltungsgericht*" (Federal High Court).

Legal practices   Lawyers can form partnerships with other lawyers, tax consultants, auditors or notaries (although notaries and auditors may not form a partnership). They may employ other lawyers as employees or as independent consultants. Nationwide partnerships formed by lawyers admitted to different local courts and partnerships with lawyers in other EC Member States are widely regarded as permissible.

Branch offices   A German lawyer may not practise regularly from additional branch offices in Germany but he is allowed to enter into partnerships with lawyers admitted to practise before courts in other parts of the country (interlocal or national partnership).

Fees   In the absence of a specific written agreement to the contrary, lawyers' fees are set in accordance with the Federal Ordinance on Lawyers Fees - *BRAGO*. In civil matters, the *BRAGO* ties the amount of fees to the value of the matter in dispute and the stages of the proceedings (filing of the action, first hearing, taking of evidence, settlement) that have been gone through. In criminal cases the *BRAGO* lays down framework fees, the amount of which increases with the number of instances before the court proceedings have gone through. A lawyer must determine within the statutory framework the specific fee that is reasonable taking into account the importance of the matter, the scope and difficulty of his activities as a lawyer as well as the financial position of his client.

It is common practice among German law firms that specialise in providing commercial advice to charge fees at an hourly rate. Sometimes lawyers agree on a flat rate with their clients.

Both fees computed by applying the *BRAGO* and fees agreed separately between lawyer and client carry VAT presently at the rate of 14%.

Professional conduct   The rights and obligations of a *Rechtsanwalt* are determined in accordance with statute law (*Federal Ordinance on Lawyers, ss 45 et seq*) and applicable ethical standards. If a client considers his lawyer is guilty of unprofessional conduct he may complain to the local law society, the "*Rechtsanwaltskammer*". The Council of the Bar may reprimand a lawyer if he has been guilty of minor infringements of his obligations. Major infringements can be pursued before a disciplinary board. The disciplinary board can impose sanctions ranging from a simple warning to exclusion from the legal profession. A lawyer is obliged to take out professional indemnity insurance. Similar rules apply to all other specifically admitted legal practitioners.

Practice by foreign lawyers   Lawyers from other EC Member States may practise their domestic law and EC law in Germany. They may only appear and act before a court of the Federal Republic within relatively tight strictures. They may only appear and act before a court with the written, prior and revocable consent of a German lawyer admitted to appear before this court. Other foreign lawyers need special permission to practise their domestic law in Germany.

Any person may instruct a *Rechtsanwalt* directly. As for the obligation to be represented in court, see above. *Direct access*

The German Lawyers' Association publishes annually a list of all admitted lawyers. Federal German professional ethics are undergoing radical change at the moment. Nonetheless, lawyers are generally forbidden to advertise, in particular, to advertise their field of specialisation, unless expressly permitted. *Directory of legal services*

CHAPTER 6 : CIVIL PROCEDURE

In order to commence a civil action a plaintiff must file with the court a statement of claim, as set out in *Sections 253 II, 130 et seq* ZPO. The court will serve it upon the defendant. The Presiding Judge will either decide to hold an early first hearing, under *Section 275 ZPO*, or will order that written preliminary proceedings be submitted to the court (ZPO, ss 276, 272 II). If he decides to hold an early first hearing, he may set the defendant a time limit within which to answer the claim (ZPO, s 275 II). Where written preliminary proceedings are ordered, he will ask the defendant to state within a strict time limit of two weeks (ZPO, s 223 III), whether he intends to respond to the claim; at the same time he will ask the defendant to lodge his defence within a further time limit of at least another two weeks (ZPO, s 276 I). The court will then summon the parties to attend the main oral hearing; where the parties must be represented by *Rechtsanwälte* (ie by professional advocates), at least one week's notice must be given (ZPO, s 217).

The course of proceedings

Commencement of proceedings

Time limits

At the start of the main oral hearing the parties or their representatives will submit their applications for relief (ZPO, s 137). The court will then, on the basis of the parties' written pleadings and its own preliminary review, draw up its report on the present state of the dispute (ZPO, s 278 I). To the extent that any relevant facts remain contentious, the court will order that evidence be taken (as to admissible evidence see ZPO, ss 371-444). Where appropriate, the court will (before or during the oral hearing) advise the parties to amend or supplement their pleadings and applications for relief (ZPO, s 139). The parties must state truthfully all the relevant facts in the case (ZPO, s 138). Oral hearings are prepared by written pleadings ("*Schriftsätze*") which contain the facts and (where necessary) a presentation of evidence ("*Beweisangebote*"); the written pleadings may also contain points of law. However, there is no duty on the parties to plead applicable law, let alone to bring to the court's attention to the applicable law during the oral hearing.

Oral hearings

Written pleadings

As soon as the matter is ready for the court to give its decision (ZPO, s 300 I) the court will pronounce judgment either at the end of the hearing or at a later date to be announced (ZPO, s 310). The one month time limits for instituting first and second appeals (*Berufung* and *Revision*) starts to run when the court serves its judgment on the party wishing to appeal (ZPO, ss 516, 552).

Judgment

Apart from temporary injunctive relief, and apart from where the court advises the parties before the oral hearing, or issues directions, German civil procedure does not countenance anything like the English-style pre-trial interlocutory proceedings

Pre-trial interlocutory proceedings

The German idea is to hold a short trial under the court's guidance, prepared for by the written pleadings of the parties. A trial may consist of a number of short hearings at different dates.

Jurisdiction by locality

On the question of jurisdiction by locality (the allocation of cases to courts of different location belonging to the same jurisdictional branch), as a general rule, jurisdiction by locality depends on the defendant's residence (*ZPO, ss 12 et seq*); or on physical location in cases involving land (*ZPO, s 24*). The place of residence of the defendant also determines which local Labour Court will be competent in labour law disputes (*ss 46 II ArbGG (Labour Courts Act), s 13 ZPO*), which are conducted before Labour Courts as specialised civil courts.

Subject matter jurisdiction

Subject matter jurisdiction in civil proceedings (the first instance allocation of cases according to the case involved) depends on the amount in dispute and the object of the claim. District Courts ("*Amtsgerichte*") have subject matter jurisdiction in respect of actions involving pecuniary claims up to an amount in dispute of DM 6,000 (*ZPO, ss 2 et seq*); also over all rent disputes and filiation and family matters at first instance (*GVG (Constitution of Courts Act), ss 23, 23a, 23b*). All other civil disputes, including non-pecuniary rights are assigned to the Regional Courts ("*Landgerichte*"), regardless of the amount in dispute (*GVG, s 71*; particularly note *GVG, s 71 II No. 2*) which deals with breaches of their official duties by civil servants and public employees.

Jurisdiction on unification

Regardless of the amount in dispute, the County Courts ("*Kreisgerichte*") in the five new Federal *Länder* exercise first instance jurisdiction over all matters coming before the court (*Unification Treaty, s 8, in conjunction with Appendix I, Chapter III para III No 1 e*).

Labour Law

In labour law proceedings, the Labour Courts ("*Arbeitsgerichte*") exercise jurisdiction at first instance (*ArbGG, ss 2 et seq*).

Locus standi

As a general rule, all individuals and corporate bodies are able to take part in any court proceedings ("*Parteifähigkeit*": capacity to be a party to legal proceedings). The Mercantile Partnership ("*Offene Handelsgesellschaft*") and the Commandite Company ("*Kommanditgesellschaft*") may also be parties to court proceedings (*HGB (Commercial Code), ss 124, 161*). In disputes before the Labour Courts, trade unions and employers' associations have capacity to be a party to the proceedings. Non-Mercantile Partnerships ("*BGB-Gesellschaften*") and Unincorporated Associations/Societies ("*Nichtrechtsfähige Vereine*") can neither sue nor be sued as they lack this legal capacity.

Representation before the courts

Only those parties who really require legal protection may seek redress before the courts. Unless specifically permitted in any given case, no one may set himself up as agent of or trustee for the interests of the general public without himself being directly affected by the matter in dispute. Therefore, legal actions instituted by someone on behalf of someone else, including the general public (altruistic class actions) are not admissible (limitation on the "right to conduct court proceedings" - "*Prozeßführungsbefugnis*"). There are some exceptions, however, for example, in *Section 13 UWG (Unfair Competition Act)* for restraining injunctions under competition law; and in *Section 13 AGBG (General Business Terms Act)* for injunctions to prevent the continued use of general business terms containing certain unlawful clauses. Again, such actions ("corporate class actions" - "*Verbandsklagen*") can be brought by associations to promote commercial interests or by consumer protection associations, only if they themselves are legally affected.

Parties may be represented by lawyers in all court proceedings.

Representation of parties

Generally, both government representatives and companies owned by the government can sue and be sued in civil proceedings. However, members of the Federal or Regional governments and the Federal President are in a privileged position as far as the obligation to testify as witnesses is concerned (*ZPO, s 367*). Members of diplomatic missions and consulates are exempt from German jurisdiction (*GVG, ss 18, 19*).

Immunities

The *ZPO* contains rules on the joinder of claims ("objective claims accumulation" - "*objektive Klagehäufung*" (*ZPO, s 260*)) and on the joinder of parties ("subjective claim accumulation" - "*subjektive Klagehäufung*"(*ZPO, s 59*)).

Joinder of claims

Where the same plaintiff has several claims against the same defendant these may be dealt with in the same proceedings, even though they concern different disputes, if the court has jurisdiction to deal with all the claims and the same type of proceedings applies to all the claims (*ZPO, s 260*). However, the court may decide that several claims raised in one action should be dealt with in separate proceedings (*ZPO, s 145*).

Several persons may bring an action jointly or have an action be brought against them jointly, provided they are linked by a unity of interest in respect of the matter in dispute or they all owe the same duties in respect of the same factual and legal issues (*ZPO, ss 59, 60*).

As a general rule, individual proceedings have no legal effect on any other party (*ZPO, s 61*). The situation is different where the issues in dispute cannot but be uniformly decided for or against joint litigants (compulsory joinder of parties, *ZPO, s 6*), an important example of which would be the case of joint owners of property. Where there is a compulsory joinder of parties, the parties to be joined are notified of the pending court proceedings by the court serving the relevant pleadings upon them. They are represented in court by whichever of the joint parties actually appears in court.

A change of party may follow as a result of a statutory provision, (*ZPO, ss 75-77, 239 et seq and 265 et seq*). This may also follow as a result of an agreement between the relevant parties. Where

Changes of parties

parties change by force of statute, the new party must take over the legal dispute as he finds it. A change of parties by agreement, insofar as the new party merely accedes to the proceedings, is deemed to be a change of claim in analogy to *Sections 263, 267 ZPO.*

Where a new defendant enters the proceedings, the original defendant ceases to be a party to the proceedings only if he consents (*ZPO, s 269*); otherwise the court will dismiss the claim against him. The new defendant will become a party to the proceedings only if he consents, or if the court determines that the change of claim is relevant and appropriate (*ZPO, ss 263, 267*).

The same rules apply where there is a change of plaintiff .

Intervention proceedings

Anyone with a legal interest in a dispute may take part in the proceedings by intervening ("*Intervention*").

Main intervention proceedings ("*Hauptintervention*") may be brought by anyone claiming an item or a right with respect to which legal proceedings are pending between two other parties (*ZPO, s 64*). This is effected by the intervener bringing a new action against both parties, in which case their proceedings may be adjourned temporarily (*ZPO, s 65*).

Anyone with a legal interest in a party succeeding in its legal proceedings may join that party by way of subsidiary intervention ("*Nebenintervention*" ((*ZPO, s 66*)).

Conversely, where a litigant who believes that should there be an unfavourable outcome of a legal dispute in which he is involved he will be able to claim under a guarantee against a third party, or who fears that a third party may make a similar claim against him, he may bring that third party into the proceedings by way of interpleader (*ZPO, ss 72, 73*). As with the case of a joinder of parties, this will result in what is termed the intervention effect ("*Interventionswirkung*" (*ZPO, ss 74, 68*)), meaning that the third party must accept the findings made to date in the extant proceedings in any subsequent proceedings. The party intervening is entitled to offer the party supported by him his full procedural assistance including the right to file his own pleadings and the right to lodge an independent appeal (*ZPO, s 67*).

Adjournment

Proceedings may be adjourned for the reasons set out in *ss 148 et seq. and 246 et seq. ZPO.* An important example of where this happens is where proceedings are adjourned pending a prejudicial decision of another court (*s 148 ZPO*), ie from another specialist court; a superior court; the Federal Constitutional Court; or the European Court of Justice under the *Article 177 of the EEC Treaty* preliminary reference procedure.

Legal aid

The rules on access to legal aid ("*Prozeßkostenhilfe*") are contained in the various codes of procedure, usually by reference to *Sections 114 et seq ZPO*, (see *ss 11 a ArbGG* (*Labour Courts Act*); *14 FGG* (*Non-Contentious Jurisdiction Act*); *379a, 397a, 406g*

StPO, (Code of Criminal Procedure); 166 VwGO, (Code of Administrative Courts Procedure); 142 FGO, (Code of Fiscal Courts Procedure); 73a SGG (Social Courts Act); and 18, 129 et seq PatG (Patent Act)).

To obtain legal aid the following two conditions must be met :

-   A party in a lawsuit must be unable to meet the costs of the proceedings out of his income and, insofar as is reasonable, from his other assets, or can only do so in (a maximum of 48) instalments (the means test);
-   The intended claim or defence must have sufficient prospects of success and must not be motivated by malice (the merits test) *(ZPO, s 114)*.

The competent court of first instance *(ZPO, s 127 I)* will decide on the application for legal aid. The application must be accompanied by a statement substantiating the applicant's personal and financial situation, and be supported by documentary evidence *(ZPO, s 117 II)*; court forms have to be used.

Legal aid will be granted by the court for proceedings at one instance only. For any appeal a separate legal aid court order is required. The new application must be lodged with the court hearing the appeal. Legal aid is always granted at a higher instance where an opponent has lodged the appeal *(ZPO, s 119)*. Where legal aid is granted, the state treasury cannot claim the court costs from the legally aided party or, if instalments were granted, can only claim under such instalments *(ZPO, s 122 I No. 1)*. Where a party must be represented by a lawyer *(ZPO, s 78)*, a lawyer will be assigned to the legally aided party by the court. This lawyer will be able to claim remuneration in accordance with the (lower) rates set under *Sections 121 et seq of the BRAGO (Federal Lawyer Fees Code)* against the state treasury, but not against the party he has represented *(ZPO, s 122 I No. 3)*. However, if his party wins the case, he may claim his fees and necessary expenses from the defeated opponent at the full rate under the *BRAGO (ZPO, s 126)*.

Public funding for professional legal assistance outside court proceedings *("Beratungskostenhilfe")* may be claimed by needy persons *(BerHG - Legal Advice Assistance Act, s 1)*. It should be noted that it is fairly common to take out insurance against the risk of suing or being sued, in particular, in cases involving the civil and criminal legal consequences of traffic accidents, or in rent and labour disputes.

Time limits for claims

All claims under civil law are subject to limitations of time, or prescription *(BGB - German Civil Code, s 194)*. Prescription, whereby a party has a right to refuse performance, must be pleaded expressly if it is to serve as a valid defence *(BGB, s 222 I)*. According to *s 195 BGB* the general prescription period is 30 years. More important, however, are the shorter statutory prescription periods.

Examples include : unlawful acts (torts), *s 852 BGB*: three years; road traffic liability, *s 14 StVG* (Road Traffic Act): three years; vendor's guarantee, *s 477 BGB*: six months; work agreements, *s 638 BGB*: six months/one year/five years; and transactions of daily life, *s 196 BGB*: two years.

The running of time for the purposes of prescription may be suspended for certain periods (*BGB, ss 202 et seq*), for example, where the parties have subsequently agreed on a postponement of the payment or other obligations, or where the debtor is temporarily entitled to refuse performance. Once the reason for a suspension ends, the period for prescription will continue to run.

Prescription is generally interrupted by the plaintiff initiating court proceedings (service of a statement of claim, see below), or by an act acknowledging the claim, eg by part payment (*BGB, s 209*).

In very special circumstances the debtor may, under the general rule of good faith (*BGB, s 242*), be prevented from successfully relying on the rules of prescription. However, the courts are extremely reluctant to reject such a claim. A debtor may waive his right to assert prescription. Once the reason for an interruption ends, a new full period of prescription will commence.

Statement of claim   A plaintiff initiates an action by filing a statement of claim with the competent court and the court serving it on the defendant (*ZPO, ss 253, 261*). The statement of claim must by *Section 253 II ZPO* set out:

-       a proper designation of the parties and the competent court; the object and the reasons (facts) of the claim; and an application for the exact relief sought.

In addition, the statement of claim should contain details of the estimated value in dispute (in non-pecuniary proceedings), and a declaration as to whether there are any reasons why the case should not be transferred to a single judge in cases where the Regional Court, ordinarily sitting with three judges, has jurisdiction (*ZPO, s 348*).

Where the parties have to be represented by lawyers, the statement of claim must be signed by a lawyer admitted to act before the court in question (*ZPO, ss 253 IV, 130 No 6*) (see further below).

Service of   Prescription is interrupted by the court serving the statement of
statement of claim   claim (*BGB , ss 253 I, 261, 262 ZPO, 209* (or by the court-approved
and other   Reminder Order - "*Mahnbescheid*")). Where the plaintiff
documents   intended service to be effected within a specific period of time, or service to interrupt a prescription period, these intended effects will occur at the time the statement of claim (or the application for a Reminder Order) is filed with the court, provided he enables the court to effect service "soon" after filing (*ZPO, s 270 III*, or *ZPO, s 693 II* in the case of the Reminder Order). As a

general rule, service is effected only when, at the time the statement of claim is filed, the general proceedings fee (*"Prozeßgebühr"*) and the expenses for effecting service (*"Zustellungsgebühr"*), both jointly called the down-payment for court costs (*"Gerichtskostenvorschuß"*), are paid into court (*GKG - Court Fees Act, s 65 I 1*). Therefore, to enable the court to effect service "soon", in most cases the plaintiff will have had to have paid into court the above down-payment before the relevant time period expires.

In civil proceedings, the service of documents (eg pleadings, certified copies of party documents, certified copies of judgments) is governed by *Sections 166-213a ZPO*. These rules differentiate between service effected by a party (*ZPO, ss 166-207*), and service effected by the court (*ZPO, ss 208-213a*). Service is effected either through the court bailiff (*ZPO, s 166 I*); from lawyer to lawyer (*ZPO, s 198*); or through the Court Sergeant (*ZPO, s 211*). As a general rule, the court bailiffs and the other persons entitled to effect service use the postal services (*ZPO, ss 193, 194*). Service may be effected at any place at which the recipient is physically present (*ZPO, s 180*). Where he cannot be served in person, substituted service may be effected (*ZPO, ss 181 et seq*). Where the defendant's place of abode is not known, public service may be ordered (*ZPO, s 203*).

Upon service, the person effecting service will sign a certificate of service (*"Zustellungsurkunde"*).

During the court proceedings, pleadings must be served on a party's lawyer (*ZPO, s 176*). Where both parties are represented by lawyers, they will effect service from lawyer to lawyer directly with the receiving lawyer returning an acknowledgement of service (*"Empfangsbekenntnis"*) prepared by the lawyer serving the relevant documents.

Service abroad

Service abroad must be effected in accordance with the *Hague Service Convention of 15 November 1965* (Federal Law Gazette 1977 II p.1453). The national judicial authority sends a request for service to the central authority of the country concerned (*art 3*). The latter issues a certificate of service (*art 6*), which constitutes the required proof of service (*ZPO, s 202 II*). The certificate of service must show service on the recipient, the time and place of service, and the documents served. As a recognised public document, this certifcate will have very strong probative value (*ZPO, s 418*).

Proof of service

Where service was intended to initiate court proceedings and the addressee has failed to indicate his readiness to defend, the court will not continue the proceedings before there is proof that service was effected on the intended defendant (*ZPO, ss 166 et seq*). Where the court makes its decision in the absence of such proof the defendant, on his application, may be reinstated to his previous legal position (*"Wiedereinsetzung in den vorigen Stand"* (*ZPO, s 233*)). Thereafter, proceedings will be resumed as if the court's faulty decision had not been taken.

Judgment in default

Where the defendant, despite being served with a proper summons (ZPO, s 214 et seq) fails to appear in court or to plead before the court (ZPO, s 333), and where the facts pleaded by the plaintiff (deemed to be admitted by the defaulting defendant) justify the relief sought (ZPO, s 331 II), a judgment in default may be entered against the defendant on the plaintiff's application (ZPO, ss 331, 335). In written preliminary proceedings a judgment in default may be given where the defendant, after having been warned of the adverse consequences of his default (ZPO, s 335 I No 4), fails to state his readiness to defend within the time limit set by the court, s 276 ZPO (ZPO, s 331 III). Where the facts pleaded do not justify the relief sought, the court will deal with the plaintiff's application for a judgment in default in his favour ("echtes Versäumnisurteil") by giving a default judgment in the defendant's favour ("unechtes Versäumnisurteil") (ZPO, s 330) that is, it dismisses the plaintiff's claim.

As a general rule, proceedings on a Reminder Order ("gerichtliches Mahnverfahren" (ZPO, ss 688 et seq)) can be used for non-contentious pecuniary claims. Irrespective of the amount involved, the District Courts (Amtsgerichte) have exclusive jurisdiction (ZPO, s 689 I). Reminder Order proceedings may only be brought for money claims where payment of a specific amount in national currency is sought. The claim must not be subject to the creditor having to carry out any further obligations incumbent upon him. The creditor applies on a court form for a Reminder Order (ZPO, s 690) which is issued and served upon the debtor by the clerk of the court, provided the application fulfills certain minimum legal requirements. Two weeks after service of the Reminder Order the clerk, upon further application of the plaintiff, issues and serves an Enforcement Order (ZPO, ss 694 I, 699). This order forms the basis of all ensuing enforcement proceedings (ZPO, s 794 No 4). If the debtor files a protest note ("Widerspruch") against the Reminder Order or an objection ("Einspruch") against the Enforcement Order (under ZPO, s 700), the District Court will transfer the action to the competent court after which ordinary court proceedings will follow. In this latter case, the creditor may continue to enforce the Order at the risk of later losing his case and having to pay damages.

Accelerated proceedings

The ZPO offers a few types of accelerated proceedings where it is not necessary to go through the whole process of a contentious oral hearing. One example is provided by the facility to file written proceedings under Section 128 II ZPO and to have the case determined on this basis alone. They may be initiated only where both parties consent. Section 128 III ZPO deals with written proceedings ex officio where the amount involved is less than DM 1,200, and where one of the parties cannot reasonably be expected to appear before the court.

Small claim proceedings

Small claim proceedings have recently been introduced ("Bagatellverfahren" (ZPO, s 495 a)). These are conducted before the District Courts. Where an amount not exceeding DM 1,000 is in dispute the court may determine its own procedural rules.

Where the defendant accepts a claim in full or in part, the plaintiff may apply for a (part) judgment by consent (*ZPO, s 307*). The application can be already in the statement of claim itself. The defendant may still appeal against such a judgment even though he initially consented to it.

The court may decide an action by way of a conditional judgment (*ZPO, s 302*). Conditional judgments still allow certain objections, mostly set off, to be raised at a later date.

Conditional judgment

The English concept of summary judgment is unknown in German civil procedure. However, there are certain summary proceedings provided for, as to which, see below.

Summary judgment

Within very narrow limits, a claim may be dismissed where a party taking the legal action lacks a legitimate interest ("*Rechtsschutzbedürfnis*"). Since the courts are part of state authority, nobody may address the judiciary needlessly or dishonestly. Asserting a claim normally suffices to establish prima facie a legitimate interest. In exceptional cases it may be denied, in particular, where the plaintiff is able to achieve his goal more simply and more effectively than by way of a court judgment, for example, where the plaintiff has already obtained a Reminder Order and could simply apply for an Enforcement Order (see above). Or where a plaintiff intends to use the legal proceedings in order to attain objectives not worthy of legal protection, for example where a lawyer on behalf of a client association controlled by him applies for an injunction under competition law rules when ultimately he is only interested in generating a claim for his fees to be paid by his opponent. However, where a claim arises out of an illegal or morally objectionable relationship, the claim cannot be dismissed for this reason alone unless otherwise provided for in a statutory provision. An example of the latter would be that gambling debts are unenforceable.

Dismissal of claim lacking legitimate interest

Generally, the English concept of interlocutory proceedings is unknown in German civil proceedings (see the introduction). As a result, there are no rules on striking out an action before trial.

Interlocutory proceedings

The provision of security for costs in respect of court proceedings is governed by *Sections 108 et seq ZPO*. However, security for costs is of minor practical significance. The main application of this rule lies in proceeding with or avoiding enforcement of a judgment (*ZPO, ss 707, 709-713, 719-720a*).

Security for costs

Foreign plaintiffs must provide a security for costs (*ZPO, s 110*). Where *the Hague Convention* of 1 March 1954 concerning civil proceedings applies, nationals of the signatory states are exempt from having to provide security (*Hague Convention, art 17*). However, agreements between the parties as to the nature, amount and purpose of any security provided or to be provided are admissible without limitation. *Section 269 IV ZPO* deals with a special case: where a plaintiff, having previously withdrawn a legal action on the same issues, brings an action on the same issue again, the defendant is entitled to refuse to serve his defence until the plaintiff has reimbursed him for the costs of the previous proceedings.

Temporary injunctive relief

Temporary injunctive relief may be sought to secure the future execution over moveable and immovable assets by way of a temporary attachment order ("*Arrest*" (*ZPO, ss 916 et seq*)). Temporary injunctive relief may also be obtained to secure a claim or to uphold law and order by way of a temporary injunction ("*Einstweilige Verfügung*" (*ZPO, ss 935, 940*)). The court competent to grant final relief also has jurisdiction to grant temporary relief (*ZPO, s 937*). No rigid time limits are provided for in the *ZPO* for this. However, for an interim injunction to be granted there must always be some urgent situation that needs to be addressed (*ZPO, s 937 II, 940*). Therefore, where the applicant (in full knowledge of all relevant facts) at first remains idle and only much later applies for injunctive relief, the court will dismiss the application for want of the relevant urgency.

Both the claim and the specific reasons for the injunction sought have to be supported by prima facie evidence (*ZPO, ss 920 II, 936, 294*). Apart from all the regular means of proof, sworn affidavits will be admissible in evidence. The court will usually decide at the end of an oral hearing by way of a judgment; exceptionally it may decide without prior oral proceedings (*ZPO, ss 21, 937*). The court has a wide discretion as to the contents of any interim injunction sought. However, the court's decision must not grant effectively final satisfaction of the creditor's claim and thereby pre-empt any subsequent regular court proceedings (*ZPO, s 938*). Any injunction granted can only be temporary in nature and effect.

Unlike an attachment order (*ZPO, ss 925 II, 923, 934*), an injunction may be lifted against security being provided in exceptional circumstances only. Where an injunction is subsequently lifted because it was unjustified ab initio or as a result of a change in circumstances, the creditor is liable for all damages arising from the prior enforcement measures (*BGB, ss 945 ZPO, 249 et seq*).

Oral hearings

In preparing for the oral hearing, the court will issue directions. *Section 273 II ZPO* contains a non-exhaustive list of admissible directions. The parties will be informed by the court of any directions given (*ZPO, s 273 IV 1*).

Further, the court must ensure that the parties give a full account of the issues involved. To that end, the court must draw the parties' attention to any relevant issue still not fully addressed by them (*ZPO, s 139*).

The court may *ex officio* order the parties to attend an oral meeting in person. It may also order the parties to submit certain documents (*ZPO, ss 141, 142*). Further, the court may order that there be a judicial inspection or may commission an expert; but this does not necessarily require a party to offer any evidence

(*ZPO, s 144*). Even before the oral hearing starts, the court may make certain orders in respect of evidence and direct that they be implemented (*ZPO, s 358a*).

Infringement of a court's duties under *Section 273 ZPO* (the order for directions) cannot form the basis of an appeal because the judgment will not rest on such an infringement. However, on appeal a judgment given on the basis of inexcusable delay on the part of the appealing party (*ZPO, ss 282, 296, 528*) may have to be reversed because the court of lower instance did not use the order for directions (*ZPO, s 273*).

In ordinary civil proceedings, documentary evidence (*ZPO, ss 415 et seq*) is introduced by submitting the original document (*ZPO, s 420*). Simply to produce a copy or the like will not suffice during an oral hearing. *Documentary evidence*

In special proceedings restricted to documentary evidence only, in particular, in summary proceedings based on a bill of exchange or a promissory note, all contested facts justifying a claim, including claims for interest and other secondary claims, must be proved by presenting the original documents (*ZPO, ss 592 et seq, 593 II, 595 III*).

Apart from the general duty to provide truthful and comprehensive pleadings (*ZPO, s 138 I*), a party is under no obligation to produce a document favourable to his opponent: exceptionally, this obligation arises where the opponent has expressly pleaded a piece of evidence relating to a specific document, and where under substantive law he has a valid claim against the party in possession to hand over that document (*ZPO, ss 421, 422*). In civil law, the most important instances of the statutory duty to deliver up documentary evidence are contained in *Section 810 BGB (German Civil Code)*. According to this section, "a person who has a legal interest in examining a document in the possession of another may demand from the possessor permission to examine it, if the document was drawn up in his interest, or if the document records a legal relationship existing between himself and another, or if the document contains the negotiations of any legal transaction which were carried on between him and another person, or between one of them and a common intermediary".

Parties need never disclose their correspondence with their lawyers (legal professional privilege). A lawyer may only disclose such documents with his client's express consent. Where a claim for delivery up of documents is founded under substantive law (*ZPO, ss 421 et seq*) the party required to deliver has no right to refuse to do so. Where he refuses, the court may hold that a copy presented to the court is correct, or that the allegations of the party offering evidence to prove the contents of the document which has been withheld are proved to be correct (*ZPO, s 427*, the thwarting of evidence). *Legal professional privilege*

Discussions/documents passing between opposing sides must be brought to the client's attention. They may be brought to the court's attention, unless the parties expressly agree otherwise.

As a general rule, only documents referred to in a formally pleaded offer to provide evidence (*"Beweisangebot"*) need be introduced into the proceedings. Exceptions are possible, eg where, under special circumstances, the court decides to order ex officio that evidence be taken, in accordance with *Section 124 I ZPO.*

The decision as to whether and with respect to which allegations the court may order evidence to be taken is principally one for the parties (*"Parteibetrieb"*). They may by agreement restrict the scope of admissible evidence. On the other hand, the actual taking of evidence (ZPO, ss 355 et seq, a separate procedural section of the court proceedings) is largely determined by the court acting *ex officio* (*"Amtsbetrieb"*); here the parties may co-operate, but not interfere with the court's general guidance.

Discovery of documents

There are no proceedings for discovery of documents.

Rule of evidential immediacy

As a general principle, evidence must be taken before the trial court, reflecting the so-called "rule of evidential immediacy" (ZPO, s 355). This rule is subject to many exceptions as a result of the court's power to delegate evidence-taking functions to another judge so instructed or requested (ZPO, ss 361, 362). In this context, the most important right the parties have is to attend any evidence-taking procedures (the rule of party publicity - *"Parteiöffentlichkeit"*(ZPO, s 357 I)).

Disclosure of evidence before trial

The parties are under no duty to disclose evidence before trial. However, in order that the court may order evidence to be taken during the trial, the parties must submit, in their written pleadings, by way of which evidential method a contentious fact should be proven. As mentioned above, evidential immediacy means taking evidence before the trial court (ZPO, s 355 I 1). The rules on evidentiary proceedings held by the court of its own motion do not expressly mention any duty on the parties to co-operate. However, in the face of a refusal, certain sanctions may be imposed upon any defaulting party. For example, evidence presented after an inexcusable delay may be rejected in accordance with *Sections 282, 296 ZPO*; the same rule applies on appeal (ZPO, ss 527 et seq). Further, the thwarting of evidence may be held to be such as to prove the contested facts or to corroborate other evidence with respect to these facts; it may even lead to a reversal of the burden of proof.

The taking of evidence is regularly preceded by a court order for evidence to be submitted (ss 355, 358 et seq. ZPO). Neither the way in which the taking of evidence is conducted, nor the decisions ordering or rejecting the taking of evidence, are open to independent appeal proceedings, leaving aside the few exceptions of no practical importance (*ZPO, s 355 II*). However, a party complaining of faulty evidentiary proceedings may, where admissible, lodge an appeal against the judgment as a whole.

A party is free to make written representations as to the admissibility of any evidence offered by an opponent. However, the court will not decide this issue before trial.

There are no express rules governing hearsay evidence. Apart from cases involving statutory presumption or statutory rules relating to the burden of proof, the court is free to find as proven what it believes to be true (*ZPO, s 286*). In such matters, the court exercises an unfettered discretion.

Hearsay evidence

However, where one party offers a particular witness, the court may not refuse to hear that witness on the grounds that his alleged statements were already known by way of hearsay evidence: such a decision would be incompatible with the rule of evidential immediacy (*ZPO, s 355 I*).

Evidence is taken abroad in accordance with *Sections 368, 369 ZPO* and the *Hague Convention on the taking of evidence abroad in civil or commercial matters of 18 March 1970, HZPruBK* (Federal Legal Gazette 1977 II, p. 1472). As a result, domestically, the way in which this evidence was taken cannot be challenged so long as *Article 14 HZPruBK* was complied with. The results, however, are assessed exclusively in accordance with German law. A court order for evidence to be taken abroad is governed by the general rules on evidence. The Presiding Judge will send an appropriate request to the competent authority of the other signatory state (*ZPO, s 363 I*).

Evidence taken abroad

The rules on the giving of evidence by witnesses are contained in *Sections 373-401 ZPO*. A party to a lawsuit cannot be a witness (*ZPO, ss 445 et seq*). A judge who is called to give evidence as a witness is excluded from acting judicially in the same case (*ZPO, s 41 No 5*). Otherwise, capacity to testify as a witness is unrestricted. Even children and mentally ill persons can be heard as witnesses. However, the court will be very cautious in assessing their testimony and its probative value. Anyone subject to German jurisdiction is under a duty to appear before the court, to give evidence and, if necessary, to swear to the truth of his statements (*ZPO, ss 377 II No 3, 390, 391*). Where a witness does not comply with these rules, the court may order disciplinary measures to be taken against him. It may also order the witness to pay costs. A witness repeatedly failing to comply may be arrested and brought before the court (*ZPO, ss 380, 390*). The obligation to testify will not apply where a witness has a statutory right to refuse to give evidence either for personal reasons (eg he is linked to a party as a fiancé, is the present or former spouse, is a member of a class of certain relatives, a clergyman, or a member of a profession under a professional duty not to disclose confidences) (*ZPO, s 383*) or for material reasons (eg where the witness would cause a member of his inner family immediate pecuniary damage, or where he would have to incriminate himself (*ZPO, s 384*)).

Witnesses

False statements A culpably incorrect statement made before the court is punishable as a false statement or as perjury (*StGB, (German Criminal Code), s 153 et seq*). Witnesses are compensated for their expenses and loss of earnings (*ZSEG (Witness and Expert Compensation Act), ss 1, 2, 9*). Judges and civil servants need permission to give evidence relating to certain areas which are governed by the maxim of official secrecy.

Members of the Government and the Federal President's Office may be called as witnesses although questioning them follows special rules (*ZPO, ss 376 II, IV, 382*).

Expert witnesses Experts may be appointed by the court on the application of a party (*ZPO, ss 402, 403, 373*) or *ex officio* (*ZPO, s 144 I*). The court has an unfettered discretion in choosing one or more experts. Experts chosen by the court need not be admitted by the court. However, experts other than those publicly appointed and sworn should only exceptionally be selected (*ZPO, s 404 II*). The parties may agree on an expert who will then be appointed by the court (*ZPO, s 403 IV*). On the other hand, the parties may reject an expert appointed by the court (*ZPO, s 406 I*) for the same reasons for which they are entitled to challenge a judge (*ZPO, s 42*). Any additional privately commissioned expert reports are freely assessed by the court as part of the pleadings of the submitting party (*ZPO, s 286*). Privately commissioned expert reports may be substituted for any court-ordered expert reports only where the parties have so agreed.

A written expert opinion is admissible in evidence, following the same principles.

There are no provisions for the exchange/disclosure of expert reports before they may be used in court.

If so ordered by the court, an expert must explain his written opinion which the court has previously sent to the parties for comment. To this end the expert must attend the oral hearing (*ZPO, s 411*).

Pre-trial review The court is under no obligation to conduct any pre-trial review proceedings other than those mentioned above. However, where the plaintiff seeks payment of a fixed sum, it is advisable to go first through (unsuccessful) Reminder Order Proceedings (*ZPO, ss 688 et seq*, see above). This will deny the opponent the chance to pass to the plaintiff the burden of costs where the opponent in his defence answering the statement of claim immediately acknowledges the claim (*ZPO, s 93*).

Representation in court A party must be represented before Regional Courts and other Higher Courts (*ZPO, s 78*). Certain family matters conducted before special District Courts also require professional legal representation. In general proceedings before the District Court (*ZPO, s 79*), any person capable of suing or being sued in court may act as a party's authorised agent or assistant (*ZPO, s 90*).

Civil proceedings are governed by the maxim of oral argument *("Mündlichkeitsgrundsatz" (ZPO, s 128 I))*. A decision may be based only on what has been orally pleaded before the court. However, references to written pleadings are largely admissible *(ZPO, s 137 II, III)*. As to some exceptions, ie where a case may be conducted on purely written proceedings, see above. The ZPO does not contain any rigid time limits for oral arguments. However, the Presiding Judge may act against endless verbosity by first issuing a warning and then ordering the speaker to stop *(ZPO, ss 136 III, 157 II)*. *Oral hearings*

At the beginning of the oral hearing the parties will plead the relief they seek *(ZPO, s 137 I)*. The oral arguments of the parties, not following any fixed rules, must elucidate the issues in dispute both as to the facts and as to the law *(ZPO, s 137 II)*. The Presiding Judge may, even before the close of the oral hearing, ask the parties to summarise their views for the court. Each party must truthfully and completely answer their opponent's allegations *(ZPO, s 138 I, II)*. Evidence having been taken, the parties have to deal with the results and consequences of the evidence received *(ZPO, s 285 I)*.

The Presiding Judge will close the hearing as soon as the court is of the opinion that the matter has been exhaustively argued *(ZPO, s 136 IV)*. *Closure of hearing*

Witnesses are questioned individually and in the absence of other witnesses who are to be heard later *(ZPO, s 394 I)*. The witness shall be invited to give a comprehensive account of the matter *(ZPO, s 396 I)* . Questions from the Presiding Judge *(ZPO, s 396 II)*, and any other judges *(ZPO, s 396 III)*, are intended to render the account more precise where this is necessary. The parties may, either through the Presiding Judge or directly, with his consent, ask the witnesses further questions *(ZPO, s 397)*. Such consent must be given to the lawyers representing a party. *Course of oral hearing*

The Presiding Judge directs the hearing *(ZPO, s 136)*. He will draw the parties' attention to the need to make comprehensive statements. To this extent he will, where necessary, give the parties directions *(ZPO, s 138)*. The Full Court decides any complaints on the directing of the proceedings by the Presiding Judge *(ZPO, s 140)*, and may *ex officio* order certain evidence to be taken *(ZPO, ss 141 et seq)* including an inspection by the court *(ZPO, s 144 I)*. The Associate Judges may question the parties *(ZPO, s 139 III)* as well as any witnesses and experts *(ZPO, ss 396 III, 402)*.

Judgments are given in open Court *(GVG, ss 169, 173 I)* and the parties need not attend *(ZPO, s 312 I)*. The ruling is effected by reading out the operative part of the judgment *("Urteilstenor")*. Where appropriate, the court will read out the full judgment, alternatively it will merely give the essential contents of the judgment *(ZPO, s 311 I, II)*. However, the court is under no duty to do so. The judgment may be given on a day after the oral hearing, *Judgment* provided a date for this was set at the end of the oral hearing. The pronouncement of the judgment should not be postponed for more than three weeks (ZPO, s 310) unless there are important reasons to do so, in particular, where the matter is unusually difficult or extensive. In such cases the judgment may be given by the Presiding Judge alone and by simply referring to the operative part of the judgment, provided (as is usual) none of the parties is present in court (ZPO, s 311 IV).

The court decides by simple majority. The public pronouncement of dissenting opinions is not permitted. *Section 43 DRiG (German Judges Act)* imposes on all judges a duty to keep the judicial decision-making process secret. In the case of a decision of the Federal Constitutional Court dissenting votes may be given. Otherwise, a breach of this duty of confidentiality constitutes a crime.

Costs

The party ultimately losing a case, or the party unsuccessfully lodging an appeal, will have to pay all the costs of the proceedings for which he was procedurally responsible (ZPO, ss 91, 97).

Where a party is merely successful in part, the costs are, by way of a court order, either allocated proportionately, or the court will order each of the parties to bear its own costs (this includes splitting court costs). Where the parties settle their dispute, the duty to bear costs follows the terms of the settlement. Where there are no such terms, each of the parties will bear their own costs (again including splitting the court costs) (ZPO, s 98). The lawyer of a losing party is under no duty to reimburse his costs to his client. He may claim fees against his own party on the basis of the statutory fee table contained in the *BRAGO (Federal Lawyer Fees Code)*, unless he and his client have entered into a differing prior private fee agreement.

The successful party is entitled to have his costs reimbursed by the losing party, but only to the extent that the costs incurred were necessary for the proper conduct of his case (ZPO, s 91). Apart from any court costs, necessary costs comprise the fees and expenses of his lawyer (ZPO, s 91 II). They also include other costs for the proper conduct of the proceedings, eg a party's travel expenses, and, under certain circumstances, the costs of a privately-commissioned expert opinion. The basic decision on costs is taken by the court as part of its judgment (ZPO, s 308 II). The specific amounts to be reimbursed are determined by the clerk of the court's office ("*Urkundsbeamter der Geschäftsstelle*") following the written application by the party entitled to be reimbursed (taxation of costs proceedings (ZPO, ss 103 et seq)). A lawyer may neither agree upon nor ask for a contingency fee.

The losing party can only avoid the burden of costs where it has given no cause for the court proceedings to have been commenced, and has acknowledged the claim immediately upon service (ZPO, s 93). It must be noted that the non-performing debtor, in particular where he owes money and Reminder Order proceedings have been unsuccessfully conducted (*ZPO, ss 686 et seq*) will ordinarily have given the creditor good reason to have initiated court proceedings. In competition law proceedings, it will usually be necessary for a creditor, prior to bringing court proceedings, to have given the debtor an out-of-court warning.

English-style payment into court proceedings does not exist in German civil procedure. However, where the defendant fully or partly performs his obligations while court proceedings are still pending, the parties may declare the cause of action finally disposed of (*ZPO, s 91a*). The court will then decide on costs by way of a court order as it thinks fit, based on a summary examination of the merits of the claim. This may result in the defendant obtaining a more favourable decision on costs than had full litigation proceedings continued. *Payment into court*

According to figures for 1990, civil cases including two appeals lasted approximately four years on average. *Length of proceedings*

First instance proceedings (including written preliminary proceedings) lasted about eight months on average.

An appeal ("*Berufung*"), opening a new instance where all the factual and legal issues are examined again (*ZPO, s 525*) may be lodged against all decisions of the District Courts where the (real or court-determined) value of the *gravamen* amounts to more than DM 1,200 (*ZPO, ss 511, 511a*). The appeal will be heard by the Regional Court which has jurisdiction by virtue of locality. *Appeals*

Appeals can also be lodged against first instance judgments of the Regional Courts (*ZPO, s 511*). The Higher Regional Court ("*Oberlandesgericht*") having jurisdiction by locality will hear such appeals.

Appeal judgments of the Higher Regional Court may be challenged by lodging a further appeal ("*Revision*") to the Federal Court of Justice ("*Bundesgerichtshof*"). That court's further examination will be restricted to legal issues (*ZPO, ss 549, 550*). Such further appeals may only be lodged where the value of the *gravamen* amounts to more than DM 60,000, or where the Higher Regional Court has given leave to appeal (*ZPO, ss 545, 546*). Where such further appeal proceedings ended in a judgment, they took about 15.4 months on average in 1989.

Appeals (*Berufung*) can be lodged against first instance judgments of the Labour Courts. The Regional Labour Court ("*Landesarbeitsgericht*") will hear the appeal. A further appeal (*Revision*) may be heard by the Federal Labour Court ("*Bundesarbeitsgericht*").

CHAPTER 7 : CRIMINAL PROCEDURE

As soon as the Public Prosecutor's Office ("*Staatsanwaltschaft*") has sufficient factual information suggesting that a criminal offence has been committed, it will institute an inquiry (*Code of Criminal Procedure ("Strafprozeßordnung" -"StPO", ss 152 II, 160 I)*). If that inquiry shows that there is sufficient cause for an indictment to be issued, the *Staatsanwaltschaft* will issue a writ of indictment ("*Anklageschrift*") (*StPO, s 170 I*).

The basic structure of court proceedings

Before issuing the writ of indictment, it will hear any accused (*StPO, s 163a I*). If the offence for which there is sufficient supporting evidence is of a minor character, the Public Prosecutor's Office can also, in its discretion, bring proceedings to a close at this stage (*StPO, ss 153 et seq*). If the evidence linking certain persons to a criminal offence is insufficient, the Public Prosecutor's Office will end the inquiry (*StPO, s 170 II*).

Preliminary proceedings (Vorverfahren)

The competent court will decide on the admissibility of the indictment in accordance with *Section 199 StPO*. If, on the basis of the evidence submitted by the *Staatsanwaltschaft*, there are sufficient grounds that indicate the accused has committed the offence, the main proceedings ("*Hauptverfahren*") will be opened (*StPO, s 203*). Otherwise the court will issue an order ("*Beschluß*") refusing to open the main proceedings (*StPO, s 204*).

Interim proceedings (Zwischenver-faren)

The main proceedings are preceded by their judicial preparation (*StPO, ss 113 et seq*).

Main proceedings (Hauptver-fahren)

The steps in the ensuing main hearing are as follows:
- calling the case (*StPO, s 243 II 1*)
- securing attendance (*StPO, s 243 II 2*), inter alia proceeding against an accused or witnesses failing to appear (*StPO, ss 230 II, 51*)
- warning witnesses (*StPO, s 57*)
- inviting witnesses to leave the court room (*StPO, s 243 II 1*)
- questioning of the accused as to his personal information (*StPO, s 243 II 2*)
- reading the writ of indictment by the pulic prosecutor (*StPO, s 243 III*)
- informing the accused that he has the right to remain silent (*StPO, s 243 IV 1*)
- taking evidence from the accused concerning the matters on the indictment (*StPO, s 243 IV 2*)

- taking evidence (*StPO, s 244 I*)
  a) Witnesses (*StPO, ss 47 et seq*)
     (i) Obliged to appear (*StPO, s 51*)
     (ii) Obliged to testify (*StPO, ss 68 et seq*)
     (iii) Obliged to testify under oath (*StPO, s 59*)
  b) Evidence from experts (*StPO, ss 72 et seq*)
  c) Evidence by visual inspection (*StPO, ss 72 et seq. 249*)
  d) Documentary evidence (*StPO, ss 249-259*)
  e) Right to ask questions (*StPO, s 240 II*)
  f) Objecting to questions (*StPO, s 241 II*)

- final pleadings (*StPO, s 248 I 3*)
- granting the the last word to the accused or his lawyer (*StPO, s 258 II*)
- consultation in secret of the members of the court (*StPO, ss 260-264*)
- announcing of the verdict and any sentence including the reasoning for the decision (*StPO, ss 260 I, 268*)
- announcing of the court orders (*StPO, ss 268 a I 2, 268 b*)
- giving information on appeals (*StPO, s 35 a*)

Regardless of the offence, the procedure in all the courts is basically the same.

Appeals (Rechtsmittel)

Appeals are complicated. If the court of first instance is the District Court ("*Amtsgericht*"), there is a right to appeal (including a right to take new evidence - "*Berufung*") to the Regional Court ("*Landgericht*") (*StPO, s 312 and GVG, s 74 III*). The judgment of the Regional Court in turn can be appealed to the Higher Regional Court ("*Oberlandesgericht*"), the appeal being limited to issues of law ("*Revision*") (*StPO, s 333 and GVG, s 121*). An appeal limited to matters of law (*Revision*) is available against judgments of the Regional Courts or the Higher Regional Courts where these courts sit as courts of first instance. This appeal will be decided by the Federal Supreme Court ("*Bundesgerichtshof*") (*StPO, s 333 and GVG, s 135*).

Jurisdiction and composition of court

In most cases the court will be composed of both professional judges ("*Berufsrichter*") and lay judges ("*Schöffen*"). There is no separate decision on the factual issues to be determined by the lay judges.

The competence of the courts of first instance and the composition of the courts depends on the gravity of the offence.

The jurisdiction of the District Court (*Amtsgericht*) is limited to offences for which there is a maximum punishment of three years' imprisonment (*GVG, s 24 Nr. 1*). Either a professional judge will decide alone ("*Einzelrichter*" - *GVG, s 25*) or there will be a three-judge panel (*Schöffengericht*) composed of a professional judge and two lay judges (*GVG, ss 28 et seq*).

In the Regional Courts (*Landgericht*), decisions are given by Chambers ("*Kammern*"), consisting of three professional judges and two lay judges, called the "Great Criminal Chamber" ("*Große Strafkammer* or *Schwurgericht*") deciding serious crimes at first instance (*GVG, s 76 II*). They will also rule on appeals against judgments of the *Schöffengericht*. Appeals against judgments of the *Einzelrichter* will be heard by a "Small Criminal Chamber" ("*Kleine Strafkammer*") consisting of one professional judge and two lay judges.

The Criminal Panels ("*Strafsenate*") of the Higher Regional Courts (*Oberlandesgerichte*) will hear appeals sitting as panels of three professional judges. They will be composed of five professional judges when deciding cases at first instance (*GVG, s 122*).

Criminal Panels (Strafsenate)

The Criminal Panels (*Strafsenate*) of the Federal Supreme Court ("*Bundesgerichtshof*") are composed of five professional judges (*GVG, s 139*).

The Public Prosecutor's Office ("*Staatsanwaltschaft*") is competent to prosecute a case in the Criminal Courts (*StPO, ss 151, 152 I, 170 I*).

Prosecutions

There are a number of exceptions to this basic "monopoly" of the Public Prosecutor's Office. These exceptions, however, are limited.

In criminal tax cases, the tax authorities can apply to the court to impose fines ("*Strafbefehlsantrag*") (*StPO, ss 407 et seq*) without having to co-operate with the Public Prosecutor's Office.

For certain kinds of offences an injured party may seek an indictment without having to rely on the Public Prosecutor's Office to bring the case to court. Such offences include trespass, libel and slander, simple cases of assault and battery. The proceedings are very similar to normal proceedings, with the injured party taking the role of the Public Prosecutor's Office.

If the Public Prosecutor's Office prosecutes a case in which the injured party was authorised to seek an indictment on its own, the injured party may instead join the public proceedings ("*Nebenklage*" (*StPO, ss 395 et seq*)).

The proceedings are commenced by filing a writ of indictment (*Anklageschrift*) with the competent court (*StPO, s 170 I*). The power to indict is vested with the Public Prosecutor's Office. If the Public Prosecutor's Office closes the proceedings without issuing an indictment, an injured party can appeal against the decision to the courts.

Commencement of proceedings

In the case of certain minor offences, the Public Prosecutor's Office may choose to ask for a punishment order ("*Strafbefehl*") pursuant to *Sections 407 et seq StPO*. This is a kind of abbreviated

Punishment orders

procedure. If the punishment order is issued by the court, the accused can ask for a hearing at which stage the normal procedure will resume (at a main hearing, *"Hauptverhandlung"*).

Stopping of proceedings

The Public Prosecutor's Office must close the proceedings if, as a result of its inquiry, there is insufficient evidence on which to proceed with an indictment.

The Public Prosecutor's Office may halt the proceedings if :
- the guilt of the suspect is considered limited and if there is no public interest in a prosecution (*StPO, s 153*); or
- in the case of minor guilt, conditions and orders (*"Auflagen"* and *"Weisungen"*) are sufficient to accommodate the public interest in a prosecution (*StPO, s 153 a*); or
- the punishment expected would be insignificant compared to the punishment handed out against the suspect in another matter.

Information relating to the offence

Before issuing a writ of indictment, the suspect has the right to be heard (*StPO, s 163 a I*). The suspect can request that evidence be taken.

If the suspect is interrogated by the police, the facts of which he/she is accused must be communicated to him/her (*StPO, s 163 a IV*).

Once the Public Prosecutor's Office has completed its inquiry, counsel for the accused has an absolute right to inspect the entire files of the case. The writ of indictment (*Anklageschrift*) will be communicated to the accused before the court decides whether to open the main proceedings or not (*StPO, s 201*).

The court that has received the writ of indictment will come to its own conclusions as to whether the evidence warrants an indictment.

Evidence

The evidence in support of a writ of indictment is, in principle, collected by the police and the Public Prosecutor's Office. There are no formal requirements as to the kind of evidence that needs to be put before the court. The Public Prosecutor's Office must collect not only evidence tending to incriminate the suspect, it must also seek evidence which will exonerate him/her.

Normally, the right to inspect the files of the case is sufficient to inform the defence about the evidence collected, as the files will contain summaries of witness statements, on-site inspections, the findings of experts, and so on.

Pleas

There are no rigid rules as to how a defendant is to plead. The defendant need not make any plea at all. He can plead guilty to a lesser offence. A guilty plea alone, however, will not suffice for a conviction for the offence charged, even though, of course, it will be given a great deal of weight. Notwithstanding a guilty plea, the court will examine the evidence available in order to ascertain whether it tends to support the defendant's guilty plea.

As there are no rigid rules in respect of pleas, there are likewise no rigid rules for changing a plea. If the defendant admits his guilt during the course of the proceedings, such an admission will be given all due weight. If a guilty plea is changed to a plea of not guilty, the credibility of such a change of plea will be examined carefully.

Plea bargaining, in principle, contradicts the maxim that the Public Prosecutor's Office is under a legal duty to prosecute all offences that come to its attention. Nevertheless, the Federal Constitutional Court ("*Bundesverfassungsgericht*") has ruled that within certain limits such plea bargaining is permissible (*Bundesverfassungsgericht, NJW 1987, 2662*).

As explained above, there are no juries in German criminal law. *Juries* Lay judges sit together with professional judges on most panels. They have the same rights as professional judges and will decide upon the issues of both guilt and sentence.

These lay judges are not picked for a particular trial but sit regularly on their respective panels. Lay judges are chosen by the lay judge election committee ("*Schöffenwahlausschuß*") for a period of four years (*GVG, s 40*). Which lay judges will sit on which days is determined by drawing lots.

The improper composition of the court can be challenged. *Challenging the* Grounds for challenge are either irregularities in the procedure *court's* for electing and assigning lay judges or they will be based on the *composition* persona of a particular lay judge. For instance, a judge who is a relative of the accused will be excluded from sitting on the court dealing with that particular case. The same is true if a lay judge (or a professional judge) gives any reason for the accused to doubt his or her neutrality.

In the main hearing ("*Hauptverhandlung*") all lawyers admitted *Counsel* to a German court and all professors at German law schools may appear as counsel (*StPO, s 138 I*). Lawyers from other EC Member States may appear in accordance with s 4 *RADG* (*Lawyer Services Act* ; see Chapter 5).

The main hearing (*Hauptverhandlung*) begins with the reading of *Main hearing* the writ of indictment by an official of the Public Prosecutor's Office. The taking of evidence is directed by the Presiding Judge rather than by the prosecution and defence. There is no "prosecution evidence" or "defence evidence". Witnesses will be questioned by the Presiding Judge with both the Public Prosecutor's Office and the defence being given the opportunity to ask additional questions.

The court can order witnesses and experts to give evidence and order any other evidence to be produced. The members of the court, whether professional or lay judges, must all assess the evidence.

The defence may submit at any stage that the case should be stopped because the evidence is insufficient or on the grounds of a procedural defect.

Public hearings All hearings are open to the public. Sound or motion picture recordings, television and radio broadcasts of the hearings are prohibited (*GVG, s 169*).

Hearings in camera The court can exclude the public if the security of the state, public order or decency is in danger, or if a person under 16 years of age is giving evidence. The verdict and sentencing is always open to the public (*GVG, s 173*).

Verdict As indicated above, there is no formal procedural distinction between reaching the verdict and handing down the sentence. There are no formal rules of evidence. The court reaches its verdict on the basis of the evidence produced before it ("*Beweisaufnahme*"), and soley on its own assessment and according to its own conclusions.

Quorum The verdict need not be unanimous. However, a two-thirds majority of all judges (professional and lay judges) is necessary for any decision against the accused. This applies both to the question of guilt as to sentencing.

The defendant can be found guilty of an alternative offence to the one with which he was originally charged. The defendant, however, must be informed of this during the trial and must be given the opportunity to adjust his defence accordingly, for example, by calling for new evidence.

Sentencing The information required for sentencing is collected during the main hearing (*Hauptverhandlung*). At an early stage of the proceedings the Presiding Judge will question the defendant about the circumstances of his or her personal life and about his or her financial means. The Presiding Judge will also reveal the accused's criminal record, if any (*StPO, s 243*).

Any evidence can be submitted as to the defendant's character.

Mitigation can be allowed in respect of individual offences (for instance "less severe cases" - see *Sections 249 II, 177 II Criminal Code (Strafgesetzbuch - StGB)*). An offence which was merely attempted but not completed can - but need not - be punished less severely than if the same offence had been successful (*StGB, s 23 II*). The punishment for someone who aided and abetted someone else's criminal offence must be less severe.

Criminal responsibility can be reduced as a result of the mental state of the offender or other factors (*StGB, s 21*).

If separate offences are the subject of the same criminal proceeding, a "composite sentence" ("*Gesamtstrafe*") will be imposed (*StGB, s 54*). In doing this, the punishment for the most serious offence is increased. Previous offences will generally be a reason to increase an otherwise intended sentence.

There are no formal guidelines for sentencing. The range of punishment possible is laid down by law in the legal provisions setting out the individual offences ("*Straftatbestände*"). Inspite of the lack of formalised guidelines, nevertheless there is a fairly consistent approach followed by the courts.

Guidelines for sentencing

There are separate rules relating to juveniles in the Code of Juvenile Courts ("*Jugendgerichtsgesetz*"). The Code of Juvenile Courts applies to persons aged between 14 and 21 years of age. Persons less than 14 years of age at the time when the offence was committed are deemed to be not criminally responsible (*StGB, s 19*).

Juveniles

The criminal law provides basically for imprisonment (*StGB, ss 38, 29*) and for fines (*StGB, ss 40 et seq*). Usually the legal provision creating the offence will provide that imprisonment or a fine can be imposed. In addition, an offender may be prohibited from driving a vehicle for a certain period of time; the instruments and proceeds of the crime can be impounded and forfeited to the state. These orders, however, are not regarded as forms of criminal punishment.

Imprisonment, fines and other orders

There are a number of crimes for which imprisonment is mandatory (eg murder, manslaughter, robbery).

Mandatory imprisonment

Appeals must be lodged within one week after judgment with the registrar of the court whose judgment is being appealed (the *iudex a quo*) (*StPO, ss 314, 341*). In the case of an appeal which is based on a question of law (*Revision*), the reasons for the appeal must be stated in writing within one month after the period for the appeal to be lodged (*StPO, s 345*). Appeals generally will be decided within less than a year. Often the time required will be much shorter.

Appeals

The rules on extradition are contained in the *Act for International Legal Assistance in Criminal Matters* (*Gesetz über die internationale Rechtshilfe in Strafsachen (IRG)*). The *European Convention on Extradition* is also in force between a number of European states. There are also other treaties upon which extradition may be based.

Extradition

The decision to extradite lies with the Higher Regional Court (*Oberlandesgericht*) (*IRG, ss 12-14*).

The Police or the Public Prosecutor's Office may detain a suspect only until the end of the day following arrest (*GG, art 104 II 2*).

Time limits

An arrested suspect must be brought before a judge, at the latest, on the day following his arrest (*StPO, ss 128, 115*). If the suspect is ordered to be detained during the course of the investigative inquiry, he or she can at any time request a hearing to decide upon the continuance of his/her detention. If detention has lasted for more than six months, a special hearing will be held before the Higher Regional Court (*StPO, s 122*).

Bail

There is no absolute right to bail. However, an application for bail can be made at any time. There are no special requirements. There are no limits as to the amount of bail, the level of which is fixed in the court's discretion (*StPO, ss 116, 116a*).

CHAPTER 8 : REMEDIES

Claims for civil law damages require that there has been either an infringement of some contractual or quasi-contractual obligation or the wrongful infringement of an absolute right or object of legal protection. Two circumstances must always be present for claims to damages to succeed :
- there must be fault on the part of the party opposing the claim (except in special cases of strict liability); and
- there must be proof of actual damage.

Civil damages

Anyone who culpably does not fulfil or imperfectly fulfils his obligations under contract must put the other party in the same position as if the contract had been properly fulfilled. Therefore, damages have to be paid also for damage to property or finances. Non-material damage will not be compensated (*German Civil Code - "Bürgerliches Gesetzbuch" (BGB), s 253*).

The principle of the contractual right to damages

Anyone who culpably infringes any of the rights or objects mentioned in *Section 823 (1) BGB* must compensate for any damage arising out of this infringement. Pure financial damages will not be compensated. In cases of physical injury or damage to health money might be awarded in accordance with *Section 847 BGB*.

The principle of wrongful damages

Damages may also be obtained where there has been an infringement of official obligations by holders of public offices (*BGB, s 839, GG, art 34*) or by notaries (*BNotO - Federal Code on Notaries, s 19*). These claims have to be pursued before the civil law courts.

Infringement of official obligations

In addition, under German law various claims for damages may be raised under public law. These claims have to be pursued partly before administrative, partly before civil law courts.

Claims under public law

Claims for damages which cannot be quantified precisely may be estimated by the courts in accordance with *Section 287 of the German Code of Civil Procedure ("Zivilprozeßordnung" (ZPO))*. Claims for pain and suffering in accordance with *Sections 823(1), 847 BGB* in cases of wrongful injury to one's body, health or in cases of an infringement of a personal right are assessed by the court in its own discretion (*ZPO, s 287*). The level of damages in such cases must take into account the nature and duration of the infringement, and all other relevant facts and circumstances.

Unquantifiable damages

Damages for physical injury

In cases of physical injury, damages will cover the costs of treatment. The following factors will be taken into account when assessing the amount of money that can be recovered :

- the extent and seriousness of any psychological and physical disturbance;
- the personal financial situation of the injured party;
- the extent to which life has been impaired;
- the magnitude, duration and violence of pain, suffering or of any disfigurement;
- the time taken for in-patient treatment, time incapacitated from work;
- the degree of fault on the part of the defendant and any contributory negligence;

There are no binding guidelines regarding the extent to which money can be recovered in German law.

"Shock damages"

So-called "shock damages" may also be obtained. "Shock damages" under German law are damages for the injury suffered by someone as a result of the death or injury of someone else. In order to claim these damages sucessfully the following circumstances must be satisfied :

- the person injured is a close relative;
- the damage to health is clearly above the usual level of suffering by close persons for this kind of cases;
- the shock is understandable (*Reports of the Judgments of the Federal Supreme Court of Germany (BGHZ) 56, 163*).

Damages for violation of personal rights

The recovery for non-material damage where general individual rights have been infringed is subject to the following conditions :

- the personal right must be seriously infringed; and
- forbearance, reply or evocation of the damaging act is not enough of itself to amount to satisfaction. The circumstances of each individual case will be taken into account. The level of damages will be decided according to *Section 287 ZPO*.

Restitution

Restitution is a general principle of the German law on damages, ie restitution will always be granted by a court where possible. Restitution is also, in principle, granted in cases of unjust enrichment (*BGB, s 812*). Restitution will also be granted in property actions (*BGB, s 985*). The principle of restitution also applies to commercial contracts.

Specific performance

Specific performance of an obligation is recognised under German law and can, where possible, always be granted by the court. A claim for damages is always a secondary remedy and usually requires additional conditions to be fulfilled.

Principle of good faith

The German law of obligations is subject to the principle of good faith (*BGB, s 242*). This general clause limits the exercise of rights under the guise of social ethics. Moreover, illegal, immoral or profiteering transactions are null and void. General commercial terms may also be judicially examined on the basis of what is fair and reasonable according to *Sections 9 to 11 of the Standard Business Terms Act ("Gesetz über Allgemeine Geschäftsbedingungen" (AGBG))*. These rules follow from the principle of contractual fairness.

A contract which seeks an objectively-impossible performance is null and void ab initio (*BGB, s 306*). Where performance becomes impossible after the contract is concluded, and none of the parties involved is responsible for this, the parties' mutual obligations under the contract are rendered void (*BGB, ss 323, 275*). Where the creditor is responsible for the supervening impossibility, a debtor may maintain a claim to the consideration moving from him (*BGB, s 324*). *Performance impossible*

Where the debtor is responsible for the supervening impossibility of performance, the creditor may at his discretion withdraw from the contract or demand damages for non-fulfilment in accordance with *Section 325 BGB*.

It is, in general, not possible to avoid paying a sum which was contractually agreed as representing a pre-estimate of damages on the grounds that the sum thereby required to be paid is a penalty. However, where contained in general commercial contractual terms, the sum agreed upon is subject to the requirement that it does not exceed the level of damages that may be expected in the normal course of things to occur. Moreover, a party will always have an opportunity to prove that the actual damages are less than the penalty agreed upon (*AGBG, s 11 lit. 5*). Contractual penalty agreements, intended to secure fulfilment of a main commitment are allowed by the *BGB* (*BGB, ss 339 et seq*). In non-commercial transactions the court may reduce an unusually high penalty in accordance with *Section 343 BGB*. In commercial transactions *Sections 348, 351 HGB (Commercial Code)* will apply. *Agreed damages and penalties*

Whether a seller must deliver up goods to the purchaser depends on the terms of the specific contractual agreement. An obligation to deliver up should be specifically agreed upon at the time at which the contract is made. If there is no specific agreement to that effect, the circumstances of the case will determine the point. The fact that the seller is to be responsible for the transport costs is no proof that the agreement is one for delivery up (*BGB, s 269 (3)*). In this respect German law does not distinguish between fungible and non-fungible goods. *Delivery up of goods*

Interest is available on monetary judgments. According to *Sections 291, 288 (1) BGB*, monetary debts are subject to interest at a rate of 4% as from the time when the action was filed with the court. Higher interest rates may apply in specific circumstances. *Interest*

According to *Section 256 ZPO*, actions for a declaration may be brought under the following conditions: *Actions for a declaration*
- where the declaration of the (non-)existence of a legal relationship is sought;

- where the declaration of the falsity of a legal document is sought;
- where the party seeking the declaration has a timely legal interest in the proceedings. The plaintiff will not have the requisite legal interest if there is a simpler or more effective way available to achieve the same aim, eg if he can bring an action for performance (actions for a declaration are always subsidiary).

The action for a declaration is used particularly to have the obligation of the other party to indemnify declared in respect of future and consequential damage, in cases where damages are uncertain. The purpose of such an action for a declaration therefore is to interrupt the running of time under the statute of limitation.

Composition and bankruptcy petitions

Composition and bankruptcy petitions (*ss 2 VerglO - Composition Code, 102(1) KO - Bankruptcy Code*) may be brought when a debtor is no longer able to pay his debts. Inability to pay will be assumed if the debtor has stopped making payments (*KO, s 102(2)*). The managing board of a stock corporation must register as bankrupt when the company's assets no longer cover its debts (*Stock Corporation Act ("Aktiengesetz" - AktG), s 92(2)*). Where assets no longer cover debts bankruptcy proceedings can be commenced in the case of a limited liability stock company (*Limited Liability Corporation Act ("GmbH-Gesetz"), s 63(l)*). The court has immediately to appoint a provisional administrator on receipt of a petition for composition (*VerglO, s 11*). On receipt of a petition for bankruptcy it may appoint a sequestrator in accordance with *Section 106(1) KO*. In the case of both composition and bankruptcy a garnishee order may be imposed on the debtor (*VerglO, s 12 and KO, s 106*). If the composition or bankruptcy petition is granted, the court must appoint a composition receiver or an administrator in bankruptcy (*VerglO, ss 20(1), 38 et seq.; KO, ss 110, 117 et seq*).

Recourse to the administrative courts

According to *Article 19(4) of the Federal Constitution ("Grundgesetz" (GG))*, recourse to the administrative courts is open to anyone with a legitimate interest claiming that there has been some unlawful interference on the part of the public bodies. Administrative court proceedings are governed by the *Administrative Court Procedings Act ("Verwaltungs-gerichtsordnung" (VwGO))*. Administrative acts imposing an obligation on the addressee can be contested by an action to have this act set aside (*VwGO, s 42(1)*). Infringements by public bodies which occur not by way of an administrative act but due to some concrete action, can be contested by the so-called "general action for performance" (*VwGO, s 43(2)*).

If a particular administrative act is requested and refused, proceedings to have a public body issue this act is allowed under *Section 42(1) VwGO*. A purely factual administrative action can be sought with a general action for performance.

In general, proceedings must be brought against the Federation, the State (*Land*) or the public body which issued the contested act or failed to undertake the administrative act applied for (*VwGO, s 78(1)*). Preliminary legal protection may be granted by the courts in administrative disputes under *Sections 80, 123 VwGO*.

Administrative procedural law is a tool to ensure that a person will gain all due legal protection, and is not a tool of public body control. Therefore, a person bringing an action under the *Administrative Court Procedings Act (VwGO)* needs to have standing, that is, he needs to be able to assert that a public law measure is unlawful and therefore violates his subjective rights or legitimate interests (*VwGO, s 42(2)*).

Juridical persons are not automatically excluded from legal protection under administrative law. This is also true for their basic liberties, see *Section 19(3) GG*. However, legal recourse by one administrative body against another administrative body is limited, because the administration is seen as a unitary body.

In criminal proceedings, it is possible to bring a civil claim against the perpetrator whose actions have caused damage (*Code of Criminal Procedure ("Strafprozeßordnung," - StPO), ss 403 et seq*). A prerequisite for this is that litigation in respect of the civil right claim is not already pending before a civil law court. If a criminal law court finds that the victim has a civil claim against the perpetrator, a corresponding judgment has the same effect as a final civil judgment given by a civil law court. Where the criminal court finds that the victim has no civil law claim, the victim can bring his claim again before the civil law courts (*StPO, s 406(1), (3)*). *Civil claims in criminal proceedings*

As far as litigation in the civil courts is concerned, recourse to state courts may be limited or prohibited by an arbitration agreement (*ZPO, ss 1025 et seq*). If the parties to an arbitration agreement are not businessmen within the meaning of the *HGB (Commercial Code)*, the arbitration agreement must be concluded expressly and in writing (*ZPO, s 1027*). Arbitration agreements are null and void if one party has thereby gained for itself an unfair advantage vis-à-vis the other party (*ZPO, s 1025(2)*). A lawful arbitration award has the same legal effect as an unappealable court judgment (*ZPO, s 1040*). It can only be reversed by bringing special legal proceedings. The grounds on which an award can be reversed are listed exhaustively in *Section 1041 ZPO*. An arbitration award can only be executed if it has been declared enforceable (*ZPO, s 1042*). Under certain circumstances this can be done without having to hold oral proceedings (*ZPO, s 1042 a (1)*). After an arbitration award has been declared enforceable, an action to reverse it can only be brought on the grounds that there is a good basis for an action for restitution, in particular, that the award has been obtained by criminal means (*ZPO, ss 1043, 1041 (1) lit. 6, 580, 1-6*). In the case of labour disputes, *Sections 101 et seq of the Labour Courts Act ("Arbeitsgerichtsgesetz" (ArbGG))* contain special regulations on arbitration agreements and arbitration procedures. *Arbitration*

CHAPTER 9 : MATRIMONIAL DISPUTES

In divorce matters (*ZPO, s 606(1)*), other family matters (*ZPO, s 621(1)*), affiliation proceedings (*ZPO, s 640(1)*) and questions of incapacity (*ZPO, s 645 et seq*) the District Courts have first instance jurisdiction by virtue of subject matter (*Law on the Constitution of Courts ("Gerichtsverfassungsgesetz " - GVG), ss 23a, 23b*). Jurisdiction by locality is governed by the place of the residence of the spouses or the child or the party incapacitated. *Jurisdiction of the courts*

Divorce proceedings are started by filing a petition for divorce (*ZPO, ss 621(1), 622(3)*). Consequential petitions (eg those dealing with questions of subsistence after divorce, the custody of children, equalisation of the surplus and the like (*ZPO, s 621*) may be joined to the divorce petition in compound proceedings (*ZPO, s 623*). The marriage is dissolved when the final judgment granting the petition becomes effective in accordance with *Section 1564 BGB*. This judgment can be appealed and reversed (*ZPO, ss 511, 621d*). Divorce by agreement is governed by *Section 630 ZPO*. The proceedings are speedier. However, representation by lawyers and a judgment are still required. *Divorce proceedings*

Proceedings as to incapacity are begun by petition (*ZPO, s 645(2)*). This petition must be brought by the spouse, a relative, the legal representative entitled to custody of the person alleged to lack capacity or the Public Prosecutor's Office (*ZPO, s 646*). The court will investigate the facts *ex officio*. The party whose capacity is in question must be heard (*ZPO, s 654*). The decision will make that person a ward of the court. The person may appeal but only within a peremptory period of one month (*ZPO, ss 223(3), 664*). Interim legal protection as to incapacity proceedings provides for the possibility to have an order for provisional guardianship over the person whose capacity may be removed (*BGB, s 1906*). *Proceedings as to incapacity*

Proceedings for the custody of children in cases of divorce may be brought in compound proceedings (*BGB, s 1671; s ZPO, 623*), or on their own (*ZPO , s 621(1) (BGB, ss 1672, 1678 and 1696)*). *Custody proceedings*

The court may settle the question of custody of the children pending the outcome of the divorce proceedings (*BGB, s 1672*). The same is true for questions of access and a claim for the surrendering of children (*BGB, s 1631(3)*). These petitions may also be submitted in compound divorce proceedings (*ZPO, ss 606(1), 620 sentence 1, 620a et seq*).

Where a married couple is already living apart or intends to separate, but divorce proceedings have not yet begun, the matrimonial premises may be assigned to one party in *Matrimonial property* accordance with *Section 1361 b BGB* by the Family Court in order to avoid serious hardship to one of the parties.

Pending resolution of the divorce petition, the use of the matrimonial premises may also be settled provisionally in accordance with *Section 620(1) ZPO*. Assignment of the matrimonial premises to one only of the spouses and a prohibition on entering the dwelling on the other spouse is only appropriate in cases of severe hardship. The court may also order a party to desist from any ill-treatment, molestation or threatening behaviour.

Grounds for divorce

The sole reason recognised by law for divorce is the irretrievable breakdown of the marriage, and not, as under the former divorce law, guilt or fault of one of the parties (*BGB, ss 1565, 1566*). *Section 1566 BGB* lays down two irrebuttable presumptions. A marriage has irretrievably broken down if the spouses have lived apart for one year (*BGB, s 1567*) and both spouses apply for divorce or the party on whom the petition is served agrees to the divorce, or the spouses have lived apart for three years.

If the spouses have not yet been separated for one year, a divorce may only be granted if continuation of the marriage would amount to an intolerable hardship for the petitioning party for reasons related to the behaviour of the other spouse (*BGB, s 1565(2)*). In special cases, where maintaining a marriage is urgently necessary in the interest of common minor children, the divorce will not be granted (*BGB, s 1568*).

Distribution of matrimonial property on divorce

Distribution of the property of a divorced couple depends on the matrimonial property regime. Where the spouses have not agreed contractually on a matrimonial property regime, the law applies the rules of the so-called "community of surplus" ("*Zugewinngemeinschaft*" (*BGB, s 1363(1)*)). Despite its name, this is not a true community of property between spouses but a separation of property with an equal division of the surpluses of both spouses. Each spouse owns and administers independently his/her own property being liable only for debts incurred by himself/herself. Any additional property brought in during the period the regime lasts remains the property of the spouse who so brought it in or created it. After a marriage has been dissolved the spouse with the lower surplus is entitled to claim an equalisation against the other spouse supported by a claim for disclosure (*BGB, ss 1378(1), 1375, 1374*).

Section 1414 BGB provides for a matrimonial regime based on the continued "separation of property" ("*Gütertrennung*") between the spouses. In cases of divorce, there is no equalisation between the property of the husband and the wife. The spouses' relationship is financially like that of unmarried people.

"Community of property" ("*Gütergemeinschaft*") means there is joint ownership of all goods between husband and wife (*BGB, ss 1415, 1419*). The common property is liquidated by an equal partition of the surplus after any common property liabilities have been settled (*BGB, ss 1471, 1476*).

Where spouses cannot agree on a settlement regarding the matrimonial dwelling, the furniture and other household effects, the judge, on a petition, may settle these issues without regard to the principles mentioned above (*Regulation on Household Goods* ("*Hausratsverordnung*" (*HrVO*), s 1).

CHAPTER 10 : PROPERTY TRANSACTIONS

On the question of transfer of property, German law distinguishes strictly between the contractual agreement which provides the basis for the obligation to transfer - act of obligation (*"Verpflichtungs-geschäft"*) (eg purchase or gift), and the actual agreement to transfer the property - act of transfer (*"Verfügungs-geschäft"*). This dichotomy follows the principle of separation. Both transactions are independent of each other. The nullity of one agreement does not affect the validity of the other - the principle of abstraction.

The contractual agreement giving rise to the obligation is usually not subject to any formal requirements, as far as moveable goods are concerned. The obligation to transfer real property requires a notarial certification to be effective (*BGB, s 313(1)*). The agreement to transfer ownership is effected in accordance with *Section 929(1) BGB* in the case of moveable items, ie by agreement and handing over the good. Real property is transferred by an agreement declared before a notary or certified by him (the deed of conveyance, *s 925 BGB*), and by filing the new owner for entry in the land titles register (*BGB, s 873(1)*).

CHAPTER 11 : RECOGNITION AND ENFORCEMENT OF FOREIGN JUDGMENTS

In the absence of a particular international treaty, the recognition of foreign civil judgments is governed by *Section 328 ZPO*. The Federal Republic of Germany has ratified the *1968 Brussels Convention on Jurisdiction and Enforcement of Judgments in Civil and Commercial Matters ("Europäisches Gerichtsstands- und Vollstreckungsübereinkommen" (EuGVÜ))*. Judgments handed down in a country adhering to the treaty are recognised without special proceedings.

Recognition of foreign judgments

The enforcement of civil judgments of courts belonging to countries which are or are not parties to the *EuGVÜ* must be authorised by the German court of the place of enforcement (*ZPO, ss 722, 723*).

Enforcement of foreign judgments

Where the *EuGVÜ* is applicable, a simplified method of recognition applies. Upon a petition from a party duly authorised by title the Regional Court (*"Landgericht"*) in the district where the debtor resides orders a certificate of enforceability to be issued provided there are no reasons why the certificate should be refused (*EuGVÜ, ss 27, 28*). The decision is given without any oral proceedings. There is no obligation to be represented by legal counsel. The legality of the foreign decision is not questioned. Once an execution notice is issued, execution of the judgment is governed by the applicable law of the country where the notice was issued. Judgments which are obviously incompatible with the fundamental principles of German law will not be recognised (*EuGVÜ, s 27*). The crucial factor is whether the judgment is "in such serious conflict with the basic concept(s) of German law and the ideas of justice contained in it that we hold it to be intolerable". The criterion on which an examination is based is a fundamental violation of German law (Federal Supreme Court (*BGH*), *NJW 1990, 2203*.

An appeal can be brought against the decision of the Regional Court which grants or dismisses an application for enforcement.

Remedies under the EuGVÜ

The appeal is lodged at the Higher Regional Court (*"Oberlandesgericht"*), a further appeal against the decision of the *Oberlandesgericht* lying within one month to the Federal Supreme Court (*Implementing Law to the EuGVÜ ("Ausführungsgesetz"), ss 17 to 20*).

All regular domestic remedies as to limitation periods and restrictions on enforcement during the execution proceedings, and all regular domestic remedies are available.

The Regional Court having issued the enforcement notice can lift or amend it on petition if the underlying authority has been reversed or amended (*Ausführungsgesetz, s 30*).

Remedies in the case of judgments of non-treaty countries

Judgments under *Sections 722, 723 ZPO*, which declare judgments of non-treaty countries enforceable may be appealed against under *Sections 511, 545 ZPO*.

BIBLIOGRAPHY

Civil Law

Baumbach/Duden/Hopt, *Kommentar zum HGB* (28th edn), Beck, Munich, 1989

Baumbach/Hefermehl, *Wettbewerbsrecht* (16th edn), Beck, Munich, 1990

Baur, *Sachenrecht* (15th edn), Beck, Munich, 1989

Beck'sches Rechtsanwaltshandbuch (2nd edn), Beck, Munich, 1991

Larenz, *BGB*, Allgemeiner Teil, (7th edn) Beck, Munich, 1989

Larenz, *Schuldrecht* (13th/14th edn), Beck, Munich, 1986 et seq.

Münchner Kommentar, *Kommentar zum BGB* (2nd edn), Beck, Munich, 1985 et seq.

Palandt, *Kommentar zum BGB* (50th edn), Beck, Munich, 1991

Staudinger, *Kommentar zum BGB* (12th edn), Schweitzer, Berlin, 1980 et seq.

Civil Procedure

Baumbach/Lauterbach/Albers/ Hartmann, *ZPO* (49th edn), Beck, Munich, 1991

Thomas/Putzo, *ZPO* (16th edn), Beck, Munich, 1991

Criminal Law

Dreher/Tröndle, *Kommentar zum StGB* (45th edn), Beck, Munich, 1991

Jagusch/Hentschel, *Straßenverkehrsrecht* (31st edn), Beck, Munich, 1991

Jeschek, *Lehrbuch des Strafrechts* (4th edn), Springer, Berlin, 1988

Schönke/Schröder, *Kommentar zum StGB* (23rd edn), Beck, Munich, 1988

Criminal Procedure

Kleinknecht/Meyer, *Kommentar zur StPO* (39th edn), Beck, Munich, 1989

Löwe/Rosenberg, *Kommentar zur StPO* (24th edn), De Gruyter, Berlin, 1988 et seq.

Public Law

Erichsen/Martens, *Allgemeines Verwaltungsrecht* (8th edn), De Gruyter, Berlin, 1988

Maunz/Dürig, *Grundgesetz-Kommentar* (7th edn), Beck, Munich, 1991

Münch, *Besonderes Verwaltungsrecht* (8th edn), De Gruyter, Berlin, 1987

Stein, *Staatsrecht* (12th edn), Mohr, Tübingen, 1990

Administrative Procedure

Kopp, *VwGO* (8th edn), Beck, Munich, 1989

Kopp, *VwVfG* (5th edn), Beck, Munich, 1991

European Law

Bleckmann, *Europarecht* (4th edn), Heymann, Cologne, 1990

Grabitz, *Kommentar zum EWG-Vertrag* (2nd edn), Beck, Munich, 1990

Reference Book

Creifelds, *Rechtswörterbuch* (10th edn), Beck, Munich, 1990

GREECE

Yanos Gramatidis
Bahas, Gramatidis & Associates
London, Athens

CONTENTS

CHAPTER 1 : SOURCES OF LAW

Greece is a unitary state and therefore one legal system applies throughout the whole country. The rules of law are principally contained in the following documents : *the Constitution of 1975; the Civil Code; the Penal Code; the Code of Civil Procedure; the Code of Criminal Procedure; the Commercial Code; and the Code of Private Maritime Law.*

Unitary v federal system

Article 4 of the Civil Code provides : "Foreigners shall enjoy the same civil rights as are granted to Greek nationals". The interpretation of this article in the area of private law by the *Conseil d'État* assimilates treatment of all foreign, natural or legal persons.

Application of national laws to foreigners

Article 28 of the Greek Constitution provides that international treaties must be ratified and incorporated into substantive national law. Once duly ratified and published, they retain their supremacy over any contrary provisions of Greek law, provided that their applicability is based on reciprocity. International treaties do not, however, prevail over the *Greek Constitution.*

Monist v dualist system

The Treaties establishing the European Communities have been ratified by Parliament and thereafter incorporated into the Greek legal system. Where Community law is directly applicable, it does not need to be ratified in order to be applied directly by the courts.

Application of EC law

Greek courts would be reticent in applying Community law where they fear that this would offend the fundamental freedoms enshrined in the *Constitution* (see the *Velka* case, Conseil d'État 1991).

Foreign law will be applicable in a case to the extent that Greek conflict of laws rules apply it to the case in question. There is no presumption that it is the same as national law and it is treated as a question of law. It is proved by presenting the relevant text in the foreign language accompanied by a Greek translation and an affidavit attesting the veracity of the translation by an authorised person who will be, as a rule, a qualified foreign lawyer.

Proof of foreign law in national proceedings

The *European Convention on Human Rights* was ratified by the Greek Parliament and was subsequently incorporated into Greek law by *Law 2329/1953.* Its provisions are therefore directly applicable by national courts which may also take into account the case law of the European Court of Human Rights.

Application of the European Convention on Human Rights

Principles of interpretation

The prevailing principles of interpretation are mainly purposive. *Article 174 of the Civil Code* stipulates that in interpreting the will of the parties one must look for the real (common) intention of the parties without strictly adhering to the words as such. The guiding principles are good faith and usage (*Civil Code, art 200*). Previous decisions of the courts are taken seriously into account by lower courts although precedent is not strictly adhered to as such. However, if a jurisprudence constante in a certain matter is created, lower courts would tend to follow the decisions of higher courts on that matter.

The jurisprudence of other international courts, albeit not of binding effect, may also be invoked before national courts. Such courts are the European Court of Human Rights and the International Court of Justice.

Texts of the Constitution

There are no authorised annotated texts to the *Constitution*. Annotated texts on the Codes that are considered as authoritative are listed below :

- *Greek Civil Code* (1982) (in English) by C. Taliadoros;
- *Tax Data Code* vols. I-III (1980) by N. Papadopoulos (in English);
- *Greek Code of Private Maritime Law* by T. Karatzas and N. Reade (1982);
- *Introduction to Greek Law* (1980) edited by K.D. Kerameus and P.J. Kozyris is perhaps the most authoritative treatment on the subject;
- Some of the Codes (eg *Civil Code*) have been translated into English (see the Bibliography).

CHAPTER 2 : FUNDAMENTAL RIGHTS

The main constitutional provisions guaranteeing justice are : *Article 5* which provides that "Personal liberty is inviolate. No one may be prosecuted, arrested, imprisoned or otherwise detained save in accordance with the law; and *Article 8* which provides that : "No one may be arbitrarily deprived of his natural judge". Fundamental freedoms under Greek law are also guaranteed for foreigners (*Constitution, art 5*).

Constitutional protection of fundamental rights

Judicial review of the constitutionality of law is exercised by the *Conseil d'État* (*Constitution, art 95*). Individuals have no right of direct recourse to any Constitutional Court to protect their fundamental freedoms. All decrees of a regulatory character must be submitted to the *Conseil d'État* before being promulgated, thereby providing a check on constitutionality by prior review.

Judicial review of the constitutionality of law

Only lawyers who have handled a significant amount of cases of an administrative character may qualify to appear before the *Conseil d'État* by decision of their respective Bar.

Legal representation before the Constitutional Court

CHAPTER 3 : JURISDICTION OF THE COURTS

The assumption of jurisdiction by a court may always be *Forum* challenged before the court rules on the merits of the case. Lack of jurisdiction may be argued "*ratione materiae*" or "*ratione loci*", that is, on grounds of the subject-matter or because the case is reserved for another court by a provision of the law (e.g. within civil courts by territory, value or subject-matter).

Universal jurisdiction is envisaged for serious crimes such as *Universal* piracy, smuggling and counterfeiting, that is, for the socially *jurisdiction* universal crimes (*delicta gentium*). Only the competent courts of criminal jurisdiction as set out in the Code of Criminal Procedure can deal with these crimes.

In principle, there is no restriction on actions against the state or *State immunity* state organs when they act in a commercial capacity. However, it is practically impossible to enforce judgments against the state or foreign states as such, since state property is not subject to seizure.

Article 51 of the Civil Code defines the domicile of individuals as *Domicile and* the place where an individual has his principal and permanent *other factors* establishment. In this sense domicile must be proved as a fact *determining the* before a court of law. *courts' jurisdiction*

Article 64 of the Civil Code provides that "a legal person has its seat at the place where it has its central administration, unless otherwise provided for by its Memorandum of Association". *Article 126 of the Code of Civil Procedure* states that a summons must be delivered to the representative of the legal person in question in any court proceedings.

CHAPTER 4 : ADMINISTRATION OF JUSTICE

One of the predominant features of the Greek administration of justice system is the separation of the ordinary courts from the administrative courts the competence of which is the settlement of disputes involving the day-to-day administration of the state.

Administrative jurisdiction

The most important ordinary courts are the following :

Structure of the courts

- The Court of Justice of the Peace, which has exclusive competence to hear disputes concerning leases, real property, transport, contracts, attorneys' fees, associations and co-operatives. The dispute in question must not involve more than 300,000 drs.
- The single judge Court of First Instance has exclusive competence in civil matters concerning persons or property regardless of the value involved. The same court also has exclusive jurisdiction in actions for parental custody and on fixing levels of rent for residential premises.
- The multi-member Court of First Instance is competent to determine disputes that do not fall within the jurisdiction of either the Court of Justice of the Peace or the Court of First Instance.
- Within the Court of Justice of the Peace or the Court of First Instance there are divisions which specialise in criminal cases, called Petty Offences Courts and Misdemeanours Courts, respectively, and which deal with criminal acts characterised either as petty offences or misdemeanours by the Penal Code.
- Felonies are adjudicated by the Jury Court, except those falling within the jurisdiction of the five-member Court of Appeal.
- Examples of special tribunals are the Trade-marks Tribunal and the Competition Board.

An appeal is filed with the clerk of the Court of Appeal against the decisions of the Courts of First Instance. The Court of Appeal rehears the entire dispute *de novo*. New grounds may be invoked provided they are introduced into the proceedings by filing a new document. Such grounds must be based on fresh evidence (*Code of Civil Procedure, arts 520 and 522*).

Appeals

Recourse to the *Cour de Cassation* may be assimilated to the lodging of an appeal but the *Cour de Cassation* rules on matters of law only. A *"pourvoi en cassation"* is filed with the clerk of the *Cour de Cassation* by an attorney qualified to appear before it. However, a *pourvoi en cassation* may be exercised only against judgments of courts of last resort. The court either rejects the appeal or allows it, annuls the decision of the lower court and remits the case to a court of the same level for final determination (*Code of Civil Procedure, art 580*).

In civil cases, the appeal results in a stay of execution of the judgment handed down by the Court of First Instance, save where a judgment is declared provisionally enforceable. In criminal cases, an appeal always results in a complete stay of execution.

Administrative courts

The administrative courts are competent to adjudicate cases pertaining to "administrative disputes". In some cases, such as appeals against Ministerial regulatory acts, the *Conseil d'État* acts as a court of first and last resort.

References under Article 177 of the EEC Treaty

The parties may ask the court to refer a dispute to the European Court of Justice, provided that the interested party formulates the question. It is, however, for the court to decide which question to refer to the European Court of Justice. The court against whose decision there is no further appeal, within the meaning of *Article 177*, is the Court of Appeal.

CHAPTER 5 : STRUCTURE OF THE LEGAL PROFESSION

There is no separation of the legal profession into barristers and solicitors. A qualified lawyer may exercise his profession only if he is a member of one of the Bars in Greece. A lawyer who is qualified is able to offer legal advice, prepare documents and plead before the courts of the jurisdiction of the Bar in question. Only attorneys with special qualifications may appear before the *Conseil d'État* and the *Cour de Cassation* (*"Areios Pagos"*). *Structure*

Only those lawyers who have handled a significant amount of cases, be they civil, administrative, etc qualify to appear before the Court of Appeal, the *Cour de Cassation* or the *Conseil d'État*. The Council of the Bar must be satisfied that the lawyer meets the requirements of competence and good standing required by law before giving the lawyer the right to appear before these tribunals and to engage in all necessary actions provided by the *Codes of Civil and Criminal Procedure*. *Advocates*

In theory any individual may appear and defend himself before any court. However, before the Court of First Instance or the Court of Appeal the presence of an attorney is required for the written as well as the oral pleadings. *Rights of audience*

Generally lawyers practise alone. However, they do have the option of co-operating with another attorney or of practising in partnership. In the latter case a lawyer may share income and/or expenses with his colleagues. As from 1 January 1992 a qualified lawyer, whether a Greek or foreign national, can be employed by another lawyer. Foreign lawyers may establish themselves in Greece provided that they become members of a Greek Bar. Lawyers registered in a Member State of the European Community may become members of a Greek Bar by passing a similar examination. Finally, a lawyer may establish another office in a different area from that in which he is registered provided that such a course of action has been authorised by both Bars. *Legal practices*

Pursuant to the *Lawyers' Services Directive* [1] of March 1977, lawyers from other Member States are allowed to offer services (eg legal advice or appearing before the Greek courts) on condition that they do not establish offices in Greece. *Branch offices*

---

1.   Council Directive (EEC) 77/249 (OJ L78 26.3.77 p17).

Fees

A schedule of fees is contained in the *Code of Lawyers*. In principle, fees must be freely agreed between the client and the lawyer and depend on the time spent, the difficulty of the case and the result obtained. If a dispute arises regarding fees, the client may file a complaint with the Bar in question.

Professional conduct

Disciplinary measures come within the jurisdiction of the Bar in question and may be taken against a lawyer in cases where he has violated the provisions of the *Code of Lawyers*. A complaint may be filed by a client or by a colleague to the Bar of the lawyer in question and proceedings may be initiated directly against that lawyer. For major offences a lawyer may be referred to the Court of Appeal at the discretion of the Board of the Bar.

Professional indemnity insurance is not, at the moment, compulsory for lawyers in Greece.

Instructing lawyers

In principle, every client may instruct a lawyer directly to provide legal services or represent him before a court of law.

Directory of lawyers

Lawyers' directories are kept at the offices of the Bar in question.

CHAPTER 6 : CIVIL PROCEDURE

These follow the basic procedure set out below :
-    suit is filed with the clerk of the court;
-    service of a copy is effected on the defendant within 30 days;
-    the clerk assigns the case to a chamber or division of the court;
-    the defendant must file any defence before the first hearing;
-    once the case has been assigned to a chamber, the date of the hearing is set;
-    where cases are adjudicated by a single judge, the parties may be summoned at regular intervals for disclosure of any documents, the oral examination of witnesses, filing of pleadings etc;
-    the same judge may also order provisional measures (*Code of Civil Procedure, art 682*);
-    before the end of the first hearing the plaintiff must in principle have served on the defendant the documents on which he intends to rely;
-    the defendant must have filed his written response to the plaintiff's claim and have served on the plaintiff the documents that he intends to rely on in the proceedings before the first hearing;
-    shortly after this, the case will be argued orally; and
-    judgment is generally delivered within three months.

Civil court proceedings

Competence over cases is divided in accordance with the following rules :
-    territorial (eg Athens Court of First Instance);
-    by value;
-    by subject matter;
-    Tax Tribunals and Administrative Courts have separate jurisdictions.

Division of competences

Basically any party may bring proceedings in the competent court, provided that if so required he is represented by a qualified lawyer. The Public Prosecutor may also bring an action when the public interest is at stake, but only in cases prescribed by law (eg those involving violation of public order, or those in the interest of minors).

Parties to proceedings/ locus standi

Government acts are not immune from action before Greek courts if they were acts by the state acting in a commercial capacity. This is also the case even for foreign states acting

State immunity

commercially. Immunity from jurisdiction does not necessarily mean immunity from execution. The courts would also entertain cases where the foreign state has waived immunity.

Joinder of action

Under *Article 246 of the Code of Civil Procedure,* the court may *ex officio* or at the request of the parties order the joinder of actions pending before it, if such actions are subject to the same procedure and the progress of proceedings is thereby facilitated or accelerated.

Third party intervention

The rules governing when third parties may intervene are set out in *Articles 79 and 80 of the Code of Civil Procedure.* The most common intervention is where a third party has a substantial interest in the whole or a part of the subject matter of the proceedings then pending between other parties. Intervention is allowed both at the first instance and also before the appellate jurisdiction. Intervention is also allowed where a third party has a legal interest in the outcome of the case. Such intervention may be made at any time up to when final judgment is given.

Under *Article 87 of the Code of the Civil Procedure,* the defendant in a real property suit may summon anyone who possesses that property or who exercises a right on behalf of someone else in respect thereof.

Multi-party actions

Under *Article 76 of the Code of Civil Procedure* where : (a) the subject matter of the proceedings will finally determine an issue affecting more than the immediate parties; (b) the judgment to be issued covers all relevant parties; (c) all the parties could sue or be sued together; (d) there will be no contradictory decisions and (e) the actions of one party will benefit or harm the others, then the parties which participate in the trial or which have been summoned but do not attend are deemed to have been represented by those who did attend.

Legal aid

Legal aid is provided under *Articles 194 to 204 of the Code of Civil Procedure.* At present the beneficiaries may be those whose average monthly income is insufficient to cover their basic needs. An individual is entitled to partial legal aid if he can prove that his average income is below the national average.

Rules on limitation/ prescription

The general rule of prescription is 20 years (*Civil Code, art 249*).

A five-year time limit applies to a number of contractual claims (eg rent, salaries, debts, etc) (*Civil Code, art 250*). A five-year time limit applies in the case of torts, and, in any case, may not be longer than 20 years (*Civil Code, art 937*). Sale of property has a time limit of six months and immovables, two years. A two-year time limit applies in the case of fraud (*Civil Code, art 157*).

Service of proceedings

Service may be effected either on the individual or on the legal representative of the legal person in question. Service takes place either at the domicile of a natural person or at the seat of a legal person.

Where the proposed defendant is domiciled or has its seat abroad, service is effected through the Public Prosecutor who forwards the summons to the Ministry of Justice. The Ministry will transmit it to the respective jurisdictions (*Code of Civil Procedure, art 134*). However, the *1968 Brussels Convention on the Recognition and Enforcement of Foreign Judgments* is directly applicable in Greek law.

On the same day on which the documents are delivered to the Public Prosecutor, or at the latest on the next working day, the server must send the defendant a certified true copy of the document being served by registered letter with a return receipt enclosed.

If a defendant is domiciled in Greece the time limit for giving notice of intention to oppose registration of a foreign judgment is one month; if he is domiciled abroad, the time limit is two months (*Code of Civil Procedure, art 518*). In both cases the time limit starts from the date of service of the judgment. If service has not been effected, a three-year extension is granted commencing on the date on which the final judgment was published.

Article 271 of the Code of Civil Procedure provides that if a defendant fails to appear, the court examines *ex officio* whether the action and the summons were served correctly and within the prescribed time limits. If they have not been served correctly, the court orders that they be served again. After this, a court may enter judgment in default against the defendant. In such cases the plaintiff's claims are presumed to be true .

Default judgment

If the plaintiff fails to appear or to comply with any required procedure, the court may reject his action and so give a judgment in default against the plaintiff (*Code of Civil Procedure, art 272*).

There is no procedure in the Greek legal system whereby the courts may decide that a party has no arguable case on the merits or as a matter of law. However, a party may ask the court at trial to rule that an action is in fact groundless.

Summary judgment

Security for costs orders do not exist in Greece.

Security for costs

Specific provisions on this apply to each court. The most detailed procedure is set out for the multi-member Court of First Instance. In particular, the President will review the case from the procedural point of view and has the discretion to summon the litigants or their legal representatives to a first hearing to

Interim procedures

clarify any issues which remain unclear, to ask for documents to be produced by public authorities or by the litigants themselves (*Code of Civil Procedure, art 232*).

The President of this court may also ask the parties' legal representatives to explain any issues of fact or law he considers are necessary to resolve the dispute. He may also ask the parties to call upon other third parties whose presence might be conducive to a quick settlement of the dispute (*Code of Civil Procedure, art 236*). The President of the court may also order provisional measures where the case is pending before the same court. This judge may also make orders that cannot be appealed : for example, if a litigant is ordered to produce documents and he fails to do so without justification, the President may order costs and a pecuniary penalty to be imposed on that party.

Production of documents

The provisions on evidence in judicial proceedings are contained in *Articles 335 to 465 of the Code of Civil Procedure*. The provisions on the production of documents to be used in the proceedings are contained in *Articles 341 to 351 of the Code of Civil Procedure*.

A party may refuse to disclose documents on the grounds of privilege (eg professional privilege). Such privilege can be overridden in cases where the document discloses a crime.

In principle, a party who relies on a document must disclose it to any other party to the proceedings. If a party refuses to disclose a document, he may be ordered to do so by the court, which will set the time and terms for such disclosure. In case of non-compliance the order may be accompanied by a penalty or fine.

Evidence

Under *Article 341(7) of the Code of Civil Procedure*, the Judge Rapporteur plays a decisive role in all procedural matters regarding the gathering of evidence. An investigation will be ordered either by the judge *ex officio* or at the request of the parties. In particular, he conducts the evidential procedure, examines witnesses, rules on any objection to excluding or identifying them; and appoints or replaces interpreters, where they are necessary for the proceedings.

Litigants are entitled to be present during the evidentiary stage (*Code of Civil Procedure, art 343*) and will be summoned by the party who initiated the proceedings three days before the evidentiary procedure starts. If one of the litigants is domiciled abroad this time limit is 20 days. If, on the other hand, the person summoned does not appear before the court, the proceedings will continue notwithstanding his absence.

Where any evidence may be jeopardised by the passing of time (eg where a witness is ill) the court may order that the evidentiary procedure be carried out immediately (*Code of Civil Procedure, art 348, 349*).

Except in cases expressly provided for by law, the court evaluates the evidence freely and rules at its discretion (*Code of Civil Procedure, art 340*). The judgment must state the reasons why the court formed its particular decision.

In the *Code of Civil Procedure* there are no specific rules on when letters rogatory will be used. However, the judge may, at the request of the parties, order the examination of witnesses abroad by issuing letters rogatory addressed either to the judicial authority within the foreign state or to the Greek diplomatic or consular authorities (*Code of Civil Procedure, arts 341 and 650*).

Evidence abroad

The rules for all civil courts concerning witnesses and evidence are set out in *Articles 393 to 414 of the Code of Civil Procedure*. Evidence can be produced either in affidavit form or orally.

Witnesses

A witness must appear and testify as to the facts of which he is aware, unless he has a legitimate reason not to do so. Where a witness does not attend without good reason he may be ordered to pay any expenses involved.

Priests, lawyers, notaries, doctors, pharmacists, as well as parents, spouses and direct relatives may refuse to testify (*Code of Civil Procedure, art 401*). Diplomats enjoying diplomatic immunity are not required to testify under the *Vienna Convention on Diplomatic Relations of 1961*, which has been incorporated into Greek law.

Professional privilege

The following persons may not be called as witnesses : priests; persons lacking perception; persons unable to reason (*Code of Civil Procedure, art 399*).

The rules on expert evidence are contained in *Articles 368 to 392 of the Code of Civil Procedure*.

Expert evidence and reports

Under *Article 368* the court may appoint one or more experts, if it considers that special scientific or technical knowledge is required in the case. Experts may also be appointed at the request of one of the parties. The court appoints the experts and gives them the necessary instructions so that they can carry out their duties (*Code of Civil Procedure, arts 370 and 379*). Experts are obliged to carry out their duties conscientiously (*art 385*), but the court will evaluate any expert opinions as it considers appropriate in the case (*art 387*).

Strictly speaking there is no trial as such in the Greek legal system. There is an oral hearing on the written arguments of the parties, during which the lawyers will elaborate on them and comment on any documents submitted. There are no final preparations before a trial in this sense.

Final preparations before trial

Parties must be represented by lawyers before the Court of First Instance, the Multi-member Court of First Instance, the Court of Appeal, the *Cour de Cassation* and the *Conseil d'État*.

Conduct of proceedings

The lawyers will refer to and elaborate on the written pleadings previously submitted. When the oral arguments are completed, the lawyers deliver a dossier containing all the documents on which their case relies (*Code of Civil Procedure, arts 233 to 281*). This procedure applies to practically all courts, with a few exceptions. Witnesses may be questioned both by the court as well as by the representatives of the parties.

The judge may ask witnesses questions, call witnesses, order the production of evidence, and visit the *locus in quo* if he deems this is necessary to evaluate the evidence (*Code of Civil Procedure, arts 341 to 344, 348 to 351, 355 to 358*).

Judgment

There is no specific time limit within which judgment must be given. A judgment is delivered in public, except in a few cases (eg divorce proceedings). Every judgment must be especially and fully reasoned (*Constitution, art 93*). Where there is disagreement within the court, the majority opinion prevails. A dissenting opinion is included in the reasoning of the judgment, if the minority so wishes (*Code of Civil Procedure, art 302*).

Costs

The main principles are set out in *Articles 176 and 178 of the Code of Civil Procedure*. Under *Article 176*, the losing party pays all recoverable costs (also called "legal costs"). These include lawyers' fees as set out in the Code of Lawyers. However, *Article 177* provides that if the defendant's position did not justify a defence and he has admitted the claim the court may order that costs be borne by the plaintiff. *Article 178* provides that where both parties partially win and partially lose, the court divides costs between them depending on the extent to which the parties have succeeded.

All costs are not borne by the loser in every case. Under this rubric fall such costs as lawyers' fees over the specified Bar limits, court costs and any other costs merely incidental to the action, such as expert fees and other expenses for preparatory work.

Article 187 provides that "with the reservation of a contrary agreement between interested parties, the expenses of judicial settlement are equally divided between the litigants, and costs pertaining to the terminated trial are also equally divided between them".

Length of proceedings

The average length of time court proceedings may take is from six to 12 months or, in some cases, even 18 months (eg before the Multi-member Court of First Instance).

Appeals

An appeal before the Court of Appeal may be raised on both law and fact. There is no appeal against the decisions of the *Conseil d'État*.

In cases set out in the *Code of Civil Procedure* under the heading "Basic competence of the Justice of the Peace, of the Court of First Instance", etc where the value of the case is below a certain limit, no appeal is allowed. The average length of time for proceedings before the Court of Appeal is at least one year. It may take two to three years for a judgment to be handed down by the *Conseil d'État*.

CHAPTER 7 : CRIMINAL PROCEDURE

Greek criminal procedure is inquisitorial in nature. Hence, the judges play a decisive role in the investigation of the case.

The assumption of criminal jurisdiction by any court depends on the type of offence and is exercised by the following courts :
- Petty Offences courts;
- Misdemeanours courts;
- Minors courts;
- Felony courts;
- Courts of Appeal; and the
- *Cour de Cassation*.

Basic structure of court proceedings

Offences are divided into three categories, depending on the severity of the punishment. Petty offences are subject to a maximum sentence of imprisonment not exceeding one month or a fine; misdemeanours for which the penalties are imprisonment not exceeding five years or a fine; and felonies, which are subject to imprisonment ranging from five to 20 years, or death.

Offences

Where the offence is a petty offence, it is remitted to the Petty Offences court. In the case of misdemeanours, the Misdemeanour court has jurisdiction. Felonies are subject to the jurisdiction of Felony courts, which are composed of three magistrates and a lay jury of four.

Decisions handed down by the Felony Court are subject to appeal only to the *Cour de Cassation*. Appeals against the decisions of the Petty Offences court and the Misdemeanours court are made to the Court of Appeal. Hierarchically, the Examining Magistrate reports to the Chamber of Accusation. The Chamber of Accusation operates within the Misdemeanour Court, and reports to the Court of Appeal.

Criminal proceedings may be initiated by
- the District Attorney, who represents the state; or
- the victim, who may summon the person he wishes to be prosecuted or file a complaint with the Examining Magistrate (*Code of Criminal Procedure, arts 42 and 43*).

Prosecution

Where an investigation stage is to take place, the District Attorney, either of his own motion or after the filing of the complaint with the Examining Magistrate, will order an investigation. This order must set out the offences and the relevant provisions of the Penal Code that have been violated. If the Examining Magistrate decides that such offences have been committed, he notifies the indictment to the District Attorney. If the court is of the view that no offence has been committed, the case is remitted to the archives.

Before being charged with an offence, a person may be detained for 24 hours (in police custody) : such detention may not exceed 48 hours (*Code of Criminal Procedure, art 419*). After being charged, a person may not be detained prior to an initial hearing for a period exceeding three months in cases of misdemeanours and six months in cases of felonies (*Code of Criminal Procedure, art 287*). After the end of the investigation stage, detention may not exceed six months or one year in misdemeanour and felony cases respectively (*Code of Criminal Procedure, art 287*).

Laying an information

Before any investigation stage starts, a preliminary enquiry is conducted by the officers mentioned in *Articles 33 and 34 of the Code of Criminal Procedure*. These officers may hear witnesses whose statements will then be incorporated into their report. The officer in question may hold a person for questioning for a maximum of 24 hours. An accused must within this time then be brought before the Public Prosecutor who may order him to be placed in police custody for a period not exceeding 48 hours. After this time, an order of further temporary detention may be issued by the Examining Magistrate.

The preliminary enquiry stage ends by summoning the accused to the competent court or by drafting a preliminary charge which is then forwarded to the Examining Magistrate (*Code of Criminal Procedure, art 245*).

The accused may have access to the dossier thereby compiled with the assistance of his attorney 48 hours before any investigation starts. Any orders made by the Examining Magistrate in respect of any investigative acts may be challenged before the Chamber of Accusation (*Code of Criminal Procedure, arts 305 to 320*).

The investigative stage

The investigation stage is conducted in accordance with *Articles 246-250 of the Code of Criminal Procedure*. The investigation consists of hearings, searches, seizures and any relevant expert reports (*arts 251 to 269*).

Where there is a violation of police rules, eg exceeding the speed limit, the procedure is initiated by a police report or complaint. Subsequently, the case will be referred to the competent court for judgment (ie Petty Offences Court). This court *ex officio* investigates the case in question, collects evidence and eventually delivers its judgment.

If the offence is a serious one, the case is assigned to an Examining Magistrate who will collect the evidence and remit the case to the court for the hearing.

In simple cases or in cases *in flagrante delicto*, the investigation takes place at the hearing. The dossier, as a rule, includes a police report and all the documents which the complainantwishes to be included. If there has been a preliminary investigation the dossier will include all the documents collected during this and any other available evidence and other pertinent material.

Proceedings

The main principles on procedure are set out in *Articles 329 to 332 of the Code of Criminal Procedure.* These principles include the publicity principle (*art 329*); the closed doors principle for cases which may be prejudicial to public order (*art 330*); the principle of oral argument (*art 331*); and the impartiality principle (*art 332*).

The procedure is almost identical whether or not any investigation has been carried out. The Presiding Judge will allow questions to be put by all the parties present, ie the Public Prosecutor, the litigants, their lawyers, the witnesses and the experts (*Code of Criminal Procedure, art 333*).

The judge is not obliged to follow the legal rules on evidence, but must follow his own conviction, taking into account his conscience, looking at the facts, the credibility of witnesses and the weight of the remaining evidence (*Code of Criminal Procedure, art 477*). Confessions, too, are assessed on this test.

The rules for selecting the jury are set out in *Articles 377 to 400 of the Code of Criminal Procedure.* The jury is composed of persons who have their full civil and political rights and are over 30 years old and who are not prohibited from sitting on a jury (see *Articles 381, 382* on incapacity and on incompatibility respectively and *Article 380*). Legal incapacity applies to one who has been subject to penalties or who suffers from mental and physical illness. Legal incompatibility applies to certain government or civil service employees who are not allowed to participate by law.

Juries

A list of potential jurors is drawn up by the Misdemeanours Court or the Court of Appeal Chamber in each jurisdiction annually. Fifteen days prior to the court sitting, between 60 and 100 names are chosen at random. On the day of the hearing the President of the Mixed First Instance or Appeal Jury Court confirms that those so chosen are present. However, the procedure may be challenged in accordance with the provisions of *Article 399 of the Code of Criminal Procedure.*

The Code provides in which cases the judge must issue a judgment or make an order (*Code of Criminal Procedure, arts 138 and 139*). However, all judgments and orders must be reasoned and a guilty verdict must set out the relevant provision of the *Penal Code* or other penal law in force which has been violated. The verdict is given either on the day of the hearing or is adjourned for further deliberations. The Felony Court must reach a verdict with a minimum of six out of ten

Verdict

jurors and three magistrates. However, when the court convenes as a body, its decision is presented as unanimous.

Sentencing

Sentences are handed out as a rule on the same day as the hearing. If judgment is adjourned, further evidence as to guilt may be produced at the later hearing. This evidence is reviewed in the presence of both parties. Fresh evidence may not be submitted on appeal.

Mitigating factors may be taken into account, which include : (a) previous honest personal, family, professional and social life; (b) that the accused was motivated by poverty, serious threats, or was under duress from another person; (c) that he was motivated by anger or sudden grief caused by an act directed against him; (d) that he has repented and tried to ease the consequences of his act; and (e) the fact that for a long period of time after the crime was committed he has behaved decently (*Penal Code, art 84*). In addition, sentences may be reduced for certain reasons set out in *Article 85 of the Penal Code*, for example, where the crime was committed under provocation or in self-defence.

Sentences may also be suspended with or without probation.

Recidivism as such is an aggravating circumstance. *Articles 88 to 93 of the Penal Code* set out the penalties for various categories of recidivism.

Under *Article 94* any penalties imposed in respect of various felonies or misdemeanours should be concurrent. The punishment imposed in such cases is the heaviest envisaged for any one of the crimes, subject to a further possible increase, depending on the crimes in question.

Minors are those under the age of 17 (*Penal Code, art 121*) and are subject to corrective or penitentiary measures only. The main sentences which can be imposed on minors are imprisonment, confinement, detention and fines (*Penal Code, arts 51 and 57*).

Appeals

A hearing before the Court of Appeal proceeds in the same way as before any other criminal court. Appeals may be lodged either against the decisions of the Petty Offences court or of the Misdemeanours court within three and five days respectively. The notice of appeal takes the form of a declaration filed with the clerk of the court. Appeals against the judgments of the Court of Appeal must be lodged within five days before the *Cour de Cassation*, which determines questions of law only. The grounds for appeals to the *Cour de Cassation* are set out in *Article 510 of the Code of Criminal Procedure*. They include breaches of procedure as to publicity of the hearing, the wrong application or interpretation of a substantive penal provision and so forth.

The length of time between the hearing and judgment on appeal varies depending on the grade and work-load of the court.

In the absence of a specific treaty, the rules and procedure for the extradition of foreign nationals are set out in *Articles 437 to 456 of the Code of Criminal Procedure*.

Under *Article 437* extradition may be granted if the following conditions are met :

(a)   if the foreign national is accused of a crime punishable under both the laws of the requesting and the requested state and which carries a maximum sentence of at least two years or the death penalty; or

(b)   if the criminal requested has been found guilty by the courts of the requesting state and sentenced to a penalty of at least six months for a crime characterised both by the laws of the requested and the requesting state as a misdemeanour or felony; or

(c)   if the foreign national expressly consents to being surrendered to the requesting state.

The extradition procedure envisaged by *Article 443 of the Code of Criminal Procedure* includes the following stages :

-    the request is sent to the Greek government by diplomatic channels;
-    this is then transmitted by the Ministry of Foreign Affairs to the Ministry of Justice;
-    the Ministry of Justice verifies that the request is lawful;
-    the request is transmitted to the President of the Court of Appeal;
-    the foreign national appears before the Chamber of Accusation of the Court of Appeal within 24 hours following receipt of the documents specified in *Article 446*.

At the end of the hearing the Chamber of Accusation rules on the extradition request and delivers a reasoned opinion (*Article 450*). Generally the opinion is favourable if the above conditions are met, unless there has been some procedural error.

The *European Convention on Extradition of 1957* is part of Greek domestic law. Moreover, bilateral extradition treaties have been signed with various countries such as Great Britain, Italy, Spain, the United States and Germany.

A temporary release of an accused may be ordered at any stage of the investigation on the application of the accused (*Code of Criminal Procedure, art 293*). This temporary release is subject to several restrictions. Among these are :

-    regular appearance before a judicial or other authority;
-    not going to the *locus delicti*;
-    providing a statement as to where he will reside or of any change of residence; and
-    the deposit of a sum of money as bail.

Temporary release may be ordered either by the Examining Magistrate or the Chamber of Accusation or the court (*art 295*).

The amount and the form of bail are decided by taking into account the potential penalty which may be imposed and the financial and ethical situation of the accused (*art 297*). Bail surety is deposited with the clerk of the court.

CHAPTER 8 : REMEDIES

Damages for breach of contract or damages in tort may be recovered in a civil court. Damages are awarded on the basis that reparation should be made for any injury or loss suffered. Damages may also be claimed before any criminal court, but no interest may be included in any sum awarded here. Under Greek law, damages are not assessed by a jury. Even in cases heard before the Mixed Jury Court only the judges decide the amount of damages.

Damages

A person who has injured another person due to his own fault is liable to provide compensation (*Civil Code, art 914*).

There are no fixed awards for particular types of physical injury. In fixing the amount of compensation the court may take into account factors such as the age, profession and financial situation of the person injured.

Under *Articles 919, 920 and 921 of the Civil Code* damages may be awarded
- (a) where the injury was inflicted intentionally and if this contravenes the morals of society; or
- (b) where the loss is of professional reputation or career; or
- (c) where the honour of a woman has been affronted. In all cases the amount of compensation is based on the actual loss sustained.

The assessment of such loss lies within the discretion of the court. Compensation may also be granted in cases of mental distress. What constitutes mental distress is a matter of case law, so is always subject to judicial discretion.

There is a distinction between damages for breach of contractual obligations and damages for breach of tortious obligations. In the former, compensation may include not only the amount of damage sustained but also lost profits (*Civil Code, art 298*).

Under *Article 297 of the Civil Code*, the court may order *restitutio in integrum* instead of awarding damages, depending on the circumstances. This decision, however, may not harm the interests of any lender.

The *Civil Code* contains a special chapter on "Unjust Enrichment". Under *Article 904* "a person who is, without legal justification, enriched from the property of, or at the expense of another is bound to return the benefit received. This obligation arises, in particular, if a person has received a payment for a debt which was not owed, or if any transfer or performance was made on a premise which did not happen or which subsequently ceased to exist or which was illegal or immoral. The plaintiff's loss and the benefit to the defendant must result from the same transaction. The recipient is bound to return the thing directly received in exchange for such a thing (*Article 908 of the Civil Code*). The principle of unjust enrichment does not apply to commercial contracts.

A contract which contravenes a provision of the law or public morals is null and void (*Civil Code, arts 174 and 178*).

Claims for specific performance of a contractual obligation may be made and *Articles 320 to 324 of the Civil Code* provide for the time and place of performance.

In cases of non-performance, the debtor is bound to compensate the creditor, if non-performance arises through the fault of the debtor (*Civil Code, art 335*). Moreover, the creditor may ask for interest as well as for any other loss sustained (*Civil Code, art 345*). However, the debtor is absolved, if his non-performance is due to *force majeure* or to accidental events (*Civil Code, art 336*).

Article 345 of the Civil Code stipulates that in monetary debts, the creditor may, where payment is overdue, ask for interest at the rate provided for by the law or by contract. The general rule is that interest is recoverable if the debtor was given judicial or extra-judicial notice to meet his obligations (*Civil Code, art 340*). The interest rate (at present 36%) is fixed by law and is periodically amended to keep pace with the rate of inflation.

A declaratory judgment, in the sense that such a judgment simply states what the law is (ie does not settle a dispute) is unknown in the Greek procedural system.

Winding-up a company

An order to wind up a company either at the request of its management or its creditors may be granted by a court. If a company suspends its payments, proceedings may be started for the liquidation of the company. The appointment of a liquidator does not necessarily mean that the company is unable to pay its debts. It may be that disputes going on for a considerable period of time between partners or directors are an obstacle to the efficient day-to-day administration and management of the company so that a third party liquidator has to be called in to resolve the state of impasse within the company.

Actions against public bodies

All decisions emanating from public bodies may be quashed before the administrative courts. The grounds include abuse of power or breach of the substantive law provisions regulating relations between such bodies and citizens. While in theory an order may be sought requiring a public body to follow a certain course of action, in practice, the relief granted is pecuniary. Thus, injunctive relief may not be granted because the assets belonging to the public body are state assets and, therefore, cannot be seized. Legal persons (eg associations) are represented by their administrators and they, too, may bring proceedings before the administrative courts.

Civil remedies (eg injury to the person) are available in criminal proceedings provided that the victim submits his claim for reparation prior to the oral hearing (*Code of Criminal Procedure, art 68*).

Arbitration clauses are often included in contracts between merchants. However, judicial proceedings are always available and it is the parties who decide what course of action they wish to follow.

There is a conciliation procedure in Greece. This takes place before a Conciliation Board. There is also a settlement procedure for disputes pending before the Court of Justice of the Peace or the Court of First Instance (*Code of Civil Procedure, arts 208 to 214 and 293*).

CHAPTER 9 : MATRIMONIAL DISPUTES

Matrimonial disputes include proceedings for divorce, the annulment of a marriage, determination of whether a marriage exists or not, and regulation of relations between spouses during the subsistence of a marriage (*Code of Civil Procedure, art 592*).

The competent court for matrimonial disputes is the Multi-member Court of First Instance. Specialised family court judges operate as a Division of this court and may intervene at any stage of the divorce proceedings (eg by summoning witnesses, etc). Matters such as alimony and child support, parental authority, the place of residence of children, and visitation rights fall within the exclusive competence of this court.

Ancillary questions concerning the residence and custody of children, visitation rights and alimony in other cases fall within the competence of the Court of First Instance under the general competence of *Articles 16 and 17 of the Code of Civil Procedure.*

The court has jurisdiction on territorial criteria :
(a) for the place where the last residence in common of the spouses is situated (*art 39*);
(b) for the place where the spouse with whom any minor children reside, if the spouses have separate residences;
(c) for the place where the spouse who did not initiate the proceedings resides; or
(d) on the criterion of the nationality of one of the spouses, if one is a Greek citizen (*Code of Civil Procedure, art 612*).

In Greek law, divorce is granted by means of an irrevocable judicial decision (*Greek Civil Code, art 1438*).

Law 1329/1983 has brought significant changes in the area of family law, noticeably in divorce. Thus, the *Civil Code* establishes a new system combining two possible approaches. The first is the so-called "irretrievable breakdown of the bond of matrimony" (*Civil Code, art 1439*). This concept comprises all divorce grounds recognised under the previous system ie bigamy, adultery, desertion and attempts on the life of the spouse. Such grounds are transformed into rebuttable presumptions that the marriage has in fact suffered an irretrievable breakdown so that continuation of the marital relationship is intolerable for the plaintiff.

However, "irretrievable breakdown" does not necessarily imply fault on the part of either spouse. However, under the new system separation is not recognised by Greek family law.

The second approach is the so-called "consensual divorce", which is granted on the joint request of the spouses (*Civil Code, art 1441*).

Once filed, a divorce petition may be either opposed or unopposed. However, "consensual divorce" practically means that both spouses admit that their marriage has already suffered an "irretrievable breakdown". Thus the proceedings can go straight ahead, given that strong evidence is already available.

Article 1441 of the Civil Code provides that two requirements must be met before an application for divorce can be made : the marriage must have lasted at least one year before the petition is filed; and the consent of the spouses must be given twice in person or by a special power of attorney before the court. The second occasion must be at least six months after the first. If there are any minor children involved, the spouses must submit a written agreement to the court setting out details for the care of and personal contact with the children.

Divorce procedure

The procedure by joint petition is as follows :
- filing of the joint petition;
- first appearance of the spouses in person before the Family Court Judge;
- a minium delay of six months before the second appearance of the spouses;
- second personal appearance of the spouses in person before the Family Court; and
- issue of the divorce judgment which will regulate all personal and property matters.

Where minor children are involved, the procedure includes the following :
- submission of a written agreement between the spouses setting out the details concerning custody and communication between them is submitted to the Family Court;
- ratification of the agreement by the Family Court. The agreement remains valid until a final judgment settling parental care matters is issued by the Court.

Where irretrievable breakdown has occurred the procedure is as follows :
- filing of the claim by the plaintiff;
- filing of any counterclaim by the defendant;
- rebuttable presumptions (bigamy, adultery, desertion and attempt on the life of the spouse) are dealt with;
- a presumption is irrebuttable if separation is proved to have lasted at least four years without interruption.

Where a marriage is dissolved or annulled, the regime of joint *Matrimonial* ownership of property comes to an end. Each spouse may *property* request the court to distribute any profits and gains deriving from the property of the other spouse to which he or she has contributed. To this end, there is a rebuttable presumption that the requesting spouse is entitled to one-third of any profits and gains (*Civil Code, art 1400*). The claim to a distribution may be made only by one of the spouses and lapses after two years from when the marriage is dissolved or annulled (*Civil Code, art 1401*).

Urgent measures may be granted by the Family Court Judge in cases pending before the Court (*Code of Civil Procedure, art 684*). The Judge rules on such matters very quickly, ie within one to three weeks of such requests being made.

CHAPTER 10 : PROPERTY TRANSACTIONS

Immovable property is transferred by delivery of keys and the title deeds to property. However, intangible rights are transferred by the surrender of the documents pertaining to title or the use of the right by the buyer with the approval of the seller. The ownership in real property may be transferred by an agreement specifying the legal grounds underlying the transaction (*Civil Code, art 1033*). The agreement must be made before a notary public and be registered.

As a matter of practice, the agreement emanates from a notarial deed which contains the following :
-        the identity of the parties;
-        a detailed description of the property;
-        title;
-        the price and terms of payment;
-        the terms for delivery over of the property; and
-        any other issues relating to the transaction in question.

The notarial deed must be subsequently registered with the Transcription Registry for the area in which such property is situated (*Civil Code, art 1192*). These files record all transactions affecting each piece of property. This will normally be accompanied by physical signs evidencing the transfer of property, normally the delivery up of the title deeds and the keys to the property to the new owner.

CHAPTER 11 : RECOGNITION AND ENFORCEMENT OF FOREIGN JUDGMENTS

Foreign judgments and/or awards may be recognised and enforced either by being invested with a *res judicata* effect or rendered directly enforceable by means of an *exequatur* issued by the Greek courts. The *Brussels Convention on Jurisdiction and Enforcement of Judgments in Civil and Commercial Matters 1968* is part of Greek domestic law.

Article 323 of the Code of Civil Procedure sets out five requirements which must be met before a judgment of a foreign civil court can be recognised in Greece :

- the judgment must be *res judicata* according to the law of the place where it was issued;
- the court must have had international jurisdiction according to Greek law (this is determined in accordance with the rules regulating the assumption of jurisdiction by the Greek courts);
- the losing party must not have been deprived of his right to defend and in general to participate in the trial, save if this took place under a provision which applied also to the citizens of the state of the court which issued the judgment;
- the judgment must not be inconsistent with a judgment rendered by a Greek court on the same case between the same parties which is *res judicata*.
- the judgment must not be contrary to morality or public order.

Judgments on non-contentious proceedings are *ipso iure* enforceable on two conditions :

- that the judgment complies with the applicable substantive Greek law and is issued by a court having jurisdiction according to that applicable substantive law;
- that the judgment is not contrary to morality and public order (*Code of Civil Procedure, art 780*).

Under *Article 905 of the Code of Civil Procedure*, which deals with enforceable instruments, *exequatur* proceedings take place before the judge of the one-member Court of First Instance. The defendant is not required to be summoned or notified. For an *exequatur* to be issued, the instrument must be enforceable according to its law of origin and must not be contrary to morality or public order.

Greek courts tend to confine public policy considerations to family law issues. On the other hand, Greek courts are more lenient in applying a provision they would have refused had it arisen in a question regarding a choice of law before them.

Although a defendant is not required to be summoned or notified, as a matter of practice he usually is. However, the defendant may challenge only procedural and not substantive issues pertaining to the *exequatur*. Such issues may be raised against execution of the judgment *per se*.

BIBLIOGRAPHY

General Works

Papantoniou, N., *General Principles of Civil Law* (3rd edn), A.N. Sakkroulas (1983) (in Greek)

Constitutional Law

Manessis, A., *Constitutional Law* Vol I, A.N. Sakkoulas (1980) (in Greek)

Manessis, A., and Papadimitriou, G., *The Constitution of 1975* , A.N. Sakkroulas (1989) (in Greek)

Tahos, G., *Greek Administrative Law* , A.N. Sakkoulas (1991)

Law of Obligations

Georgiadis, A. and Stathopoulos, M. (ed.), *Civil Code : A Commentary on the Articles* Vol II to Vol IV (1979-1982) (in Greek), A.N. Sakkoulas

Iatrou, A., *An Outline of the Greek Civil Law* (in English), A.N. Sakkoulas (1986)

Kafkas, K. and Kafkas, D., *Law of Obligations (A Commentary on the Articles). Special Part* (6th edn) Vol I (1981), Vol II (1982) (in Greek), P. Sakkoulas Bros

Lawson, G.H., *A Common Lawyer Looks at the Civil Law* , Westport, Connecticut, (1977)

Schlesinger, R.B., *Comparative Law : Cases, Texts, Materials* (4th edn) New York, (1980)

Stathopoulos, M., *General Law of Obligations* Vol I (1979), Vol II (1983) (in Greek), A.N. Sakkoulas

Zepos, P., *Law of Obligations*, (2nd edn) Vol I : *General Part* (1955), Vol II : *Special Part*, (1965) (in Greek), A.N. Sakkoulas

Civil Procedure

Iatrou, A., *Civil and Criminal Proceedings in Greece* (in English), A.N. Sakkoulas (1981)

Kerameus, K., *Civil Procedure Law* Vol I (1983), Vol II (1978), Vol III (General Part) (1986) (in Greek), A.N. Sakkoulas

Klamaris, N. and Beis, K. *International Procedural Law* (1986) (in Greek), A.N. Sakkoulas

Rammos, G., *Manuals of Civil Procedure*, Vols I-IV (1978-1985) (in Greek), A.N. Sakkoulas

Criminal Procedure

Kontaxis, A., *Commentary on the Code of Criminal Procedure*, Vols A-B (in Greek), A.N. Sakkoulas (1989)

Vouyoukas, K. *Penal Procedural Law*, Thessaloniki, Vol I (1988) Vol II (1989) (in Greek), A.N. Sakkoulas

Family Law

Deliyannis, G., *Family Law*, Vol I (1986), Vol II (1987) (in Greek), A.N. Sakkoulas

Gazis, A., *The New Family Law. The Problems*, (in Greek), A.N. Sakkoulas (1985)

Conflict of Laws

Ehrenzweig, A., Fragistas, C. and Yiannopoulos, A. *American Greek Private International Law*, Parker, School (1957)

Evrigenis, D., *Private International Law*, (in Greek), A.N. Sakkoulas (1973)

Maridakis, G., *The Execution of Foreign Judgments*, (3rd edn) (in Greek), A.N. Sakkoulas (1970)

Other Works

Karatzas, T. and Reade, N., *Greek Code of Private Maritime Law*, Martinus Nijhoff (1982)

Kerameus, K.D., and Kozyris , P.J. (Ed) *Introduction to Greek Law* (is perhaps the most authoritative treatment on the subject), Kluwer-Sakkoulas (1980)

Papadopoulos, E. *Tax Data Code* Vols. I-III (in Greek), A.N. Sakkoulas (1980)

Taliadoros, C., *Greek Civil Code* (in English), A.N. Sakkoulas (1982)

IRELAND

Mary Finlay Geoghegan S.C.
with assistance from :
Mary Ellen Ring B.L.
Justin Dillon B.L.
Ann Monaghan, Solicitor

CONTENTS

CHAPTER 1 : SOURCES OF LAW

Under the *1937 Constitution* there is one national law. The system *Unitary system*
of government in Ireland is therefore unitary. The principal
written documents which set out the law are as follows :
- *the 1937 Constitution,*
- *the Acts of the "Oireachtas"* (Parliament),
- *Acts of the former Parliament of Britain and Ireland* which applied to Ireland in 1922 and have not been repealed,
- *Statutory Instruments or Regulations* made under powers conferred by Acts,
- *Treaties of the European Communities* and self-executing provisions thereof.

With certain limited exceptions (eg only Irish citizens may vote in *Application of* a General Election) Irish laws apply equally to Irish nationals and *national laws to* to foreign nationals. Certain provisions of the *Constitution* refer *foreign nationals* expressly to Irish citizens but they have been construed as being capable of applying to aliens in certain situations. There is no discrimination in the application of the law as against nationals of Member States of the European Communities, save that which is permitted under the Treaties (eg *Articles 36 and 55* on the grounds of public order, public safety and public health).

Article 29.6 of the Constitution provides that no international *Incorporation of* agreement shall be part of the domestic law of the state save as *international* may be determined by the *Oireachtas*. In general, provisions of *agreements in* public international law are incorporated into the domestic law by *domestic law* either :
- an Act giving effect to the specific measure of public international law, or
- a Regulation made under an enabling authority under existing legislation which empowers the government to give effect to such a measure of public international law.

Ireland therefore operates a dualist system as far as public international law is concerned.

The *Community Treaties* and EC law are expressly permitted to *EC law and* be incorporated into Irish law by *Article 29.4.3 of the Constitution. domestice law* They are incorporated by *the European Communities Act 1972.* Where required, for example by EC Directives, effect is given to Community law either by the enactment of legislation or by Regulation under the 1972 Act or some other enabling provision under existing legislation.

The Irish courts adopt and implement the principles of Community law unequivocally and have not demonstrated any reticence in implementing provisions of Community law in a given case. There has been no consideration yet of the issue of a possible conflict between the provisions of Community law and the provisions of the *1937 Constitution* relating to fundamental rights.

Proof of foreign law

Foreign law must be proved as a fact either by oral evidence or by evidence on affidavit. If the law is not in either English or Irish, the official languages under the *1937 Constitution*, it must be presented to the court in the form of a certified translation.

European Convention on Human Rights

The *European Convention on Human Rights* has not been incorporated into domestic law. The Courts may not apply the provisions of the *Convention*. The case law of the European Court of Human Rights may not be relied upon by individuals directly before the Irish courts.

Principles of interpretation of legislation

The essential canon for the interpretation of legislation is that all provisions of laws made after 1937 must be construed if possible in accordance with the *Constitution*. Provisions of a Statute are interpreted in the context of the whole enactment in question and each word, save where a word may have been specifically defined either in the enactment or by virtue of judicial precedent, is given its ordinary meaning.

In principle, all prior decisions of the Supreme Court must be followed. However, this is not a binding rule; but there will only be a departure from precedent for a compelling reason (*The State (Quinn) v Ryan*[1]). The decisions of higher courts are binding on lower courts.

Interpretation of the Constitution

There are no authorised annotated texts to the *Constitution* or of the legislation.

"*The Irish Constitution*" by JM Kelly is, however, regarded as an authoritative text.

---

1.   *The State (Quinn) v Ryan* [1965] IR 70.

CHAPTER 2 : FUNDAMENTAL RIGHTS

Five articles of the *Constitution* guarantee fundamental rights. *Constitutional*
These are :
protection of
- *Article 40* (Personal Rights, including the right to an *fundamental*
Order for Habeas Corpus);
rights
- *Article 41* (The Family);
- *Article 42* (Education);
- *Article 43* (Private Property); and
- *Article 44* (Religion).

Furthermore, the Supreme Court held in the case of *Ryan v
Attorney General*[1] that, in addition to the rights expressly stated
in the *Constitution*, there are other unenumerated rights
guaranteed by *Article 40 of the Constitution*. The following are
examples of rights not enumerated in the *Constitution* which the
courts have held to exist and to be guaranteed by *Article 40* :
- the right to life (*Conroy v Attorney General*[2]);
- freedom of expression (*The State (Lynch) v Cooney*[3]);
- freedom to travel (*The State (KM) v Minister for Foreign
Affairs*[4]);
- the right to have access to the courts (*Macauley v
Minister for Posts and Telegraphs*[5]);
- the right to legal aid for representation in criminal trials
(*The State (Healy) v Donoghue*[6]);
- the right to fair procedures (*In re Haughey*[7]);
- the right to privacy in Marital Affairs (*McGee v Attorney-
General*[8]).

The other method of protection is that *Article 15.4 of the
Constitution* expressly prohibits the making of laws repugnant to
the *Constitution* and provides that any such law is invalid to the
extent that it is repugnant. *Article 34.3.2* empowers the High Court
to adjudicate upon the validity of laws having regard to the
Constitution.

Article 34.3.2 of the Constitution also restricts raising any question *Raising of*
as to the constitutional validity of a law in any court other than the *constitutional*
High Court or the Supreme Court (on appeal). While there is, *questions before
the courts*

---

1. *Ryan v Attorney General* [1965] IR 294.
2. *Conroy v Attorney General* [1965] IR 411.
3. *The State (Lynch) v Cooney* [1983] IR 89.
4. *The State (KM) v Minister for Foreign Affairs* [1979] IR 73.
5. *Macauley v Minister for Posts and Telegraphs* [1966] IR 345.
6. *The State (Healy) v Donoghue* [1976] IR 345.
7. *In re Haughey* [1971] IR 217.
8. *McGee v Attorney-General* [1974] IR 284.

therefore, no separate court specifically designated as a Constitutional Court, issues relating to the constitutionality of a law may be raised only in the High Court or the Supreme Court.

Any individual may apply to the courts to protect his rights, whether these be derived from statute or under the *Constitution*.

Representation before courts where constitutional questions are raised

Barristers and solicitors have rights of audience before all courts. Natural persons may also represent themselves. The same time limits apply to causes of action in which a constitutional point is raised as to the same cause of action without a constitutional point. There is no time limit on seeking to declare invalid a law as repugnant to the *Constitution*. If a constitutional point is raised in judicial proceedings, judgment on the point may be obtained within a few months of the action commencing.

CHAPTER 3 : JURISDICTION OF THE COURTS

The District Court and the Circuit Court are vested with specific limited jurisdiction (see Chapters 4 and 6). No action may be brought in either court in respect of a matter which is in excess of their respective jurisdictions except with the written consent of the parties to unlimited jurisdiction and any action so brought may be challenged on this ground. A party may agree also prior to the commencement of proceedings, to forego that part of his claim which is in excess of the courts' jurisdiction. *Challenging jurisdiction*

The High Court has full original jurisdiction in civil and criminal matters. Certain scheduled crimes are tried by the Special Criminal Court. *Universal jurisdiction*

There are no special rules restricting the bringing of actions against the state or organs of the state when it is acting in a purely commercial capacity. *Actions against the state*

A person has a domicile of origin which he may change to a domicile of choice. A person under a disability (a minor or a mentally ill person) has a domicile of dependency, ie that of his father or mother. The essence of the concept of domicile in Irish law is to establish a long-term relationship between a person and a place/legal system. *Domicile*

A company is domiciled in Ireland if it has its seat in the state, ie if it is incorporated under the laws of the state or its central management or control is exercised in the state (*Jurisdiction of the Courts and Enforcement of Judgments - European Communities Act 1988, s 13(2) and Fifth Schedule*).

CHAPTER 4 : ADMINISTRATION OF JUSTICE

There are proposals to create a Court of Appeal. Consequently, *The court system*
what follows is subject to possible modification in the near future.

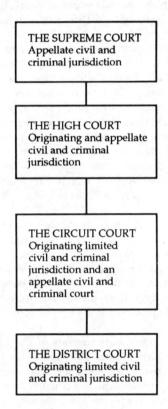

THE SUPREME COURT
Appellate civil and
criminal jurisdiction

THE HIGH COURT
Originating and appellate
civil and criminal
jurisdiction

THE CIRCUIT COURT
Originating limited
civil and criminal
jurisdiction and an
appellate civil and
criminal court

THE DISTRICT COURT
Originating limited civil
and criminal jurisdiction

The *Constitution* provides in *Article 34* that there shall be a Court
of Final Appeal called the Supreme Court and Courts of First
Instance which shall include the High Court and courts of local
and limited jurisdiction with a right to appeal as determined by
law. The courts currently operating under *Article 34 of the
Constitution* were established under the *Courts (Establishment
and Constitution) Act 1961* as amended and are as follows :

    (a)   District Courts : The state is divided into 23 District *District Courts*
            Court districts. The court consists of the President and
            no more than 39 judges. Claims of a value of up to
            IR £5,000 may be brought in this court. The District
            Court has no jurisdiction in respect of the tort of
            defamation, slander of title, malicious prosecution or
            false imprisonment. It exercises a summary criminal
            jurisdiction.

Circuit Courts

(b) Circuit Courts : The country is divided into seven Circuits and this court consists of a President and no more than 12 judges. Claims of up to IR £30,000 may be brought in this court. In land and probate matters the jurisdiction is restricted to IR £200 rateable value. In addition, the Circuit Court is empowered to hear certain matters without restriction on monetary value, eg Family law matters; and it may also hear, with the consent of the parties, cases where the subject matter of the dispute is in excess of its financial jurisdiction. Furthermore, a party may abandon that part of his claim which is in excess of the courts' jurisdiction. The Circuit Court also exercises criminal jurisdiction.

High Court

(c) The High Court consists of a President and no more than 16 judges. It has both a civil and criminal jurisdiction. Normally civil cases are heard by a judge sitting alone. Certain matters (eg defamation and assault) are tried by a judge sitting with a jury. It may also sit as a divisional court of three judges. It has an originating and appellate criminal jurisdiction. Serious criminal trials at first instance are heard by a High Court judge and jury. Appeals are heard by the Court of Criminal Appeal which comprises one Supreme Court and two High Court judges.

Article 34 of the Constitution vests full original jurisdiction in the High Court and empowers it to determine all matters and questions whether of law or fact, civil or criminal. In practice, where jurisdiction is assigned by statute to a specific court (eg below the financial limitations mentioned above) that court and not the High Court is the proper forum.

Supreme Court

(d) The Supreme Court consists of the Chief Justice and four ordinary judges. The President of the High Court is also ex-officio a member. The court may sit as a court of three and the full court is five. Subject to such regulations as may be prescribed by law, the Supreme Court has under *Article 34.4.1 of the Constitution*, appellate jurisdiction in respect of all decisions of the High Court and of such decisions of the other courts as may be prescribed by law.

The Supreme Court has a special jurisdiction under *Article 26.1 of the Constitution* to decide on the constitutionality of any Bill referred to it by the President.

Appeals from the District Court and Circuit Court

Decisions of the District Court may be appealed to the Circuit Court. Decisions of the Circuit Court may be appealed to the High Court. The appellate jurisdiction of the Supreme Court has already been referred to above. Appeals, save to the Supreme Court, are by way of re-hearing. In addition, a party may give notice that he wishes to appeal by way of case stated from the District Court to the High Court, ie to seek the view of the High Court on a point of law as applied to the facts of the case in question. The District and Circuit Courts may state a consultative case stated to the High and Supreme Courts respectively.

An appeal to the High Court or Supreme Court does not operate as an automatic stay on proceedings unless the court so orders (*Rules of the Superior Courts, Order 58, Rule 8 and Order 61, Rule 6*).

Stay of execution on appeal

It is a matter for the court either on the application of the parties or of its own motion to decide whether a reference to the European Court of Justice under *Article 177 of the EEC Treaty* should be made. Any court acting as a final court regards itself as bound to do so once the issues referred to in *Article 177* are present and require determination for the purpose of deciding the case before it. There are no domestic rules setting down pre-requisite conditions before a reference can be made.

References under Article 177 of the EEC Treaty

Judgments in other international courts have no binding effect.

Judgments in other international courts

CHAPTER 5 : STRUCTURE OF THE LEGAL PROFESSION

Members of the legal professions in Ireland are either barristers or solicitors. Other persons (eg tax advisers) can and do provide advice in relation to legal matters. There is no monopoly on the giving of legal advice, only on the provision of certain legal services.

While it is normally the barrister who appears before the Superior Courts, solicitors have had right of audience in any court since the *Courts Act 1971, s 17* came into force. In practice, solicitors rarely represent clients in the Higher Courts without a barrister.

Rights of audience

There are two levels of barristers. About 10% are appointed as Senior Counsel. The rest regardless of age or experience are known as Junior Counsel. Barristers work as independent practitioners. Each barrister works from the Law Library which is situated in the Four Courts, Inns Quay, Dublin 7. They do not have branch offices. They are sole practitioners who join together to pay their share of the administrative expenses of the Law Library but are not permitted to share their fees. Some also maintain chambers on a solitary basis.

Barristers

They do not have direct access to clients, save clients who are members of professional bodies approved by the Bar Council, and then only to give legal advice. Where litigation is contemplated the client must instruct a solicitor who in turn, if necessary, chooses a barrister.

Solicitors may be either sole practitioners or may form a partnership with, or be employed by, other solicitors. Solicitors may also be employed by companies as legal advisers. Solicitors' firms may and often do have a number of branch offices in a particular part of Ireland to provide services for local clients. The largest offices are nearly all situated in Dublin. Some firms have branches outside Ireland.

Solicitors

A client may always make an agreement on fees with the solicitor and, through the solicitor, with the barrister whom he instructs. Fees are subject to VAT, currently at 21%. If a client is dissatisfied with a fee that he has been charged he may make an application to the *Taxing Master*, a court official, who will determine the appropriate fee. There are scales for certain types of solicitors' work. Many firms of solicitors use hourly rates as a basis for charging. There are no fee scales for barristers' work.

Fees

Discipline of lawyers

The professional conduct of a barrister is regulated by the Bar Council which may administer disciplinary measures. A complaint about the quality of the legal services provided may be referred to the Bar Council which will investigate the matter wherever it occurs. Foreign clients may avail themselves of this procedure. Professional Indemnity Insurance is compulsory for barristers.

The Incorporated Law Society is the regulatory body for solicitors and also has a disciplinary procedure available to foreign clients. Insurance is not compulsory for solicitors but is encouraged and taken by a high proportion. A solicitors bill currently before the *Dail* proposes a compulsory scheme.

Practice by foreign lawyers

Lawyers from Member States of the European Communities may represent a client in a specific matter under the terms of Council Directive (EEC) 77/249[1]. Foreign lawyers may become full members of either the Irish Bar or the Irish Law Society upon qualification under Council Directive (EEC) 89/48[2]. They then have the same rights and duties as Irish barristers or Irish solicitors. These facilities do not extend to non-EC lawyers. Such non-EC lawyers must be qualified to practice in Ireland either directly by the relevant Irish professional body or indirectly by reason of any reciprocal arrangement for the recognition of legal qualifications. A foreign lawyer may give legal advice in Ireland since there is no monopoly for Irish lawyers on the giving of legal advice.

Instruction of lawyers

It is unlawful for a foreign lawyer to call himself a barrister or solicitor when he is not so qualified. A foreign lawyer may directly instruct a barrister or a solicitor for the purpose of obtaining a legal opinion. In litigation matters a foreign lawyer must have an Irish solicitor as his agent to represent the client on the court record. He can instruct a barrister through a solicitor acting as his agent.

Directories of legal services

The Bar Council publishes the Members Handbook that lists barristers who may indicate areas of specialisation. The Incorporated Law Society publishes the Law Directory which lists the names of solicitors. In addition many Irish lawyers are listed in international law directories.

---

1.   Council Directive (EEC) 77/249 (OJ L78 26.3.77 p17).
2.   Council Directive (EEC) 89/48 (OJ L19 24.1.89 p16).

CHAPTER 6 : CIVIL PROCEDURE

The rules and procedure of the supreme court and High Court are contained in the *Rules of the Superior Courts 1986 (SI 1986/15)*. The rules and procedure of the Circuit Court are governed by its *Rules of the Circuit Court 1950 (SI 1950/179*, as amended). The procedure before the District Court is governed by the *District Court Rules 1948*, as amended. *Applicable rules*

Essentially the structure of court proceedings in all three courts with originating jurisdiction is a preliminary written procedure followed by trial of the action. The procedure involves the service of the originating document and the exchange of written pleadings. These are the statement of claim by the plaintiff followed by the defence and the reply and (where the defence includes a counterclaim by the defendant) the defence to the counterclaim. These pleadings set out in summary form the facts on which each party relies together with the legal consequences resulting from those facts. They are in no sense written briefs such as are found in the civil law system. Further particulars of pleadings and documents may be sought by the opposing party. When this procedure is complete the action is set down for hearing and the trial of the action normally takes place by oral evidence. Some actions where facts are not contested are tried on the affidavit evidence of the parties. The procedure is similar to that in England and other common law systems but radically different from civil law procedures. *The course of proceedings*

A distinction must be made between the constitutionally guaranteed right of access to the courts and the *Rules of Court* specifying certain types of representation. Essentially, all natural and legal persons may bring proceedings before the courts. The *Rules of the Superior Courts* provide for representative actions and also the representation by a guardian or next friend in the case of minors and persons of unsound mind or who are incapable of managing their own affairs. *Parties to proceedings and locus standi*

Representative actions

All natural persons may appear personally or through legal representation. A legal person, ie a corporate entity, may only appear in court through a solicitor or solicitor and barrister.

Article 13.8.1 of the Constitution prohibits the bringing of proceedings against the President of Ireland. However, neither the state itself nor any other organ of the state has immunity since the decision of the Supreme Court in *Byrne v Ireland*[1]. *Proceedings against the government*

---

1.   *Byrne v Ireland* [1972] IR 241.

The government may and has been sued (*Boland v An Taoiseach*[2]). Normally the "*Taoiseach*" (the Irish Prime Minister) and Ministers of the government are named as defendants since the government as such is not a legal person. The state is sued as Ireland and the Attorney General. Civil proceedings on behalf of the state are brought in the name of the Attorney General.

The right to intervene

A defendant may join a person as a third party to proceedings in accordance with *Order 16 of the Superior Court Rules*. The courts have wide jurisdiction to add and dismiss parties from proceedings under *Order 15 of the Superior Court Rules*.

The right to intervene should be regarded as part of the constitutionally guaranteed right of access to the courts and therefore is available to any person making a claim to any part of the matter in dispute between the existing parties. *Order 61, Rule 1(13) of the Superior Court Rules* lays down a general procedure for persons seeking to intervene. There are also express rules relating to certain matters :
    (a)   in probate actions - *Order 12, Rule 14.*
    (b)   in actions for the recovery of land - *Order 12, Rule 18.*
    (c)   in admiralty actions - *Order 64, Rule 14.*
    (d)   in any matrimonial case - *Order 70, Rule 19.*

Notification of proceedings to non-parties

In certain types of proceedings, persons other than the defendant must be notified. For example, actions for the recovery of land must be served on all persons in possession of the property in question. In actions relating to a matrimonial home, the courts require that the defendant's spouse be served with notice of the proceedings. It is the normal practice that a person whom the plaintiff considers might be affected by proceedings but who is not joined as a defendant for the purpose of obtaining relief, should be served with notice of the proceedings. In judicial review proceedings, if an Order of a Tribunal is sought to be quashed, any other party to the proceedings before that tribunal is made a Notice Party.

Joinder and severence of actions

Order 18 of the Superior Court Rules provides for the joinder of actions. There are no express rules of court relating to the stay of proceedings because there are foreign proceedings pending. However, the Irish Superior Courts have a discretion to stay any proceedings in the interests of justice where proceedings are already pending in foreign jurisdiction. This jurisdiction is exercised upon the well-established principle of private international law (see Binchy, "*Irish Conflicts of Law*").

Class actions

Order 15, Rule 9 of the Superior Court Rules provides :
"Where there are numerous persons having the same interests in one cause or matter, one or more of such persons may sue or be sued or may be authorised by the court to defend in such cause or matter on behalf or for the benefit of all persons so interested".

---

2.   *Boland v An Taoiseach* [1974] IR 338.

There is a non-statutory civil legal aid scheme with very limited application. The Civil Legal Aid Board administers the scheme. There are a number of law centres throughout the country in which solicitors employed by the Legal Aid Board work. Persons who wish to apply for legal aid must go to a Legal Aid Centre and file an application to the Legal Aid Board for a certificate for legal aid. Legal aid is only available to persons with limited disposable income. The precise financial reckoning is complicated. The maximum disposable income is set currently at IR £6,200 per annum. In addition, there are allowances for spouses, children, mortgages, rent, tax paid, insurance and certain other items. Persons with gross incomes of more than IR £16,000 are not eligible. In many instances the maximum gross income would be in the order of IR £10,000 - IR £12,000. Legal aid is available for civil actions other than defamation, debt collection, disputes in relation to rights of land, arbitrations under the *Landlord and Tenant Acts*, licensing, conveyancing (except where connected with family matters) and election petitions. Financial contributions are sought from the persons granted legal aid. These range from IR £19 to IR £479 per case depending upon income.

Legal aid

Procedure for obtaining legal aid

Legal aid limits

Section 11 of the Statute of Limitations 1957 as amended by the *Statute of Limitation 1991* sets out the principal limitation periods.

Limitation on bringing proceedings

(a)   Six years from the date on which the cause of action accrued for :

Limitation period : 6 years

-    actions founded on the simple contract,
-    actions founded on quasi contract,
-    actions to enforce a recognizance,
-    actions to enforce an award where the arbitration agreement is not under seal or where the arbitration is under any Act other than the *Arbitration Act 1954,*
-    actions to recover any sum recoverable by statute (with certain exceptions),
-    tort other than that referred to in (b) below.

(b)   Three years from the date on which the cause of action accrued, or the date of knowledge (as defined) (if later), of the person injured :

Limitation period : 3 years

-    an action claiming damages for negligence, nuisance or breach of duty where the damages claimed by the plaintiff for the negligence, nuisance or breach of duty consist of or include damages in respect of personal injuries.

(c)   Three years from the date on which the cause of action accrued for :

-    an action claiming damages for slander.

(d)   An action for a contribution from a contributing wrongdoer may be brought either within the same period as the injured person is allowed by law for bringing an action against the contributor or within the period of two years after the liability of the claimant is ascertained or the injured person's damages are paid whichever is the greater (*Civil Liability Act 1961, s 31*).

Actions for a contribution from a wrongdoer

Limitation period : 12 years

(e) Twelve years from the date on which the cause of action accrued for :
- most actions relating to land,
- most actions relating to contracts under seal,
- an action on a judgment.

Actions against the estate of a deceased person

(f) Causes of action which survive and are maintainable against the estate of a deceased person must be commenced either within the relevant period under the *Statute of Limitations* or within the period of two years from the date of death whichever period first expires (*Civil Liability Act 1961, s 9*).

Fraud

Where an action is based on fraud or the right of action is concealed by fraud the limitation period does not begin to run until the plaintiff has discovered the fraud or could with reasonable diligence have discovered it (*Statute of Limitations 1957, s 71*).

Persons under disability

For persons under a disability, ie an infant or person of unsound mind, or certain convicted persons, the period of limitation, with certain exceptions, is six years from the date when the person ceased to be under a disability or died (*Statute of Limitations 1957, s 49* and *O'Brien v Keogh*[3]).

Court proceedings

In all courts, proceedings may only be commenced by filing documents either by the individual litigant in person or by solicitors. Companies must file proceedings through solicitors .

Originating documents before particular courts

The following are the originating documents for each of the courts:

District Court
Civil Process; Notice of Application or Notice of Motion for certain specified jurisdictions.

Circuit Court
Ordinary Civil Bill; all types of actions save where otherwise specified. *Equity Civil Bill;* essentially all types of actions in which equitable relief is sought. *Ejectment Civil Bill* to recover possession of land and Notices of Application and Notices of Motion for certain statutorily created jurisdictions.

High Court
Plenary Summons; all actions except otherwise specified. *Summary Summons;* types of action specified in Order 2. *Special Summons;* types of action specified in Order 3.

Petitions; many types of proceedings; *Companies Acts,* and other proceedings for which the *Petition* is specified under the *Superior Court Rules.*

---

3. *O'Brien v Keogh* [1972] IR 144.

Notice of Motion; certain newly created statutory causes of action such as under *Section 27 of the Local Government (Planning and Development) Act 1976* and judicial review.

Supreme Court
Notice of Appeal.

Proceedings are deemed to have been commenced as follows :

Commencement of proceedings

(a)   in the District Court, as in Circuit Court,
(b)   in the Circuit Court, upon the originating document being handed to a Summons Server for service or sent by post,
(c)   in the High Court, upon issue from the Central Office of the originating document,
(d)   in the Supreme Court, on service of the Notice of Appeal.

Originating documents are issued or filed in the following offices :

Filing of documents

(a)   District Court - the Office for the relevant District Court,
(b)   Circuit Court - the Office of the County Registrar for the appropriate circuit,
(c)   High Court - the Central Office of the High Court,
(d)   Supreme Court - the Supreme Court Office.

Thereafter, all other formal documents relating to the litigation are filed in the same office.

Fees are payable on the commencement of most types of actions. Family law proceedings are generally exempt from fees.

The rules as to service of originating documents in the Supreme Court and High Court are set out in *Order 9 of the Superior Court Rules.* Generally speaking, personal service is required save where a solicitor accepts service and undertakes in writing to enter an appearance on behalf of a client. There are particular rules for certain defendants in certain types of actions. *Section 379 of the Companies Act 1963* provides for service on companies by sending the originating document by post or by leaving it at the registered office of the company or, if the company has not given notice to the Registrar of Companies of its registered office, by registering the document at the Companies Registration Office. In the Circuit and District Courts service was formerly by Summons Server. Service by post is provided for in most instances where Summons Servers no longer exist. Where there is difficulty in effecting service there are provisions for substituted service in all courts.

Rules for service within Ireland

Separate rules now exist for service out of the jurisdiction. For cases within the *Brussels Convention* the relevant rules are set out in the *Rules of the Superior Courts (No 1) 1989.* For cases not within the Convention, an application must be made to the court for liberty to issue proceedings for service out of the jurisdiction. *Order 11 of the Superior Court Rules* sets out the types of action

Service out of jurisdiction - the 1968 Brussels Convention

and circumstances in which such leave will be granted. If the defendant is an Irish citizen, the originating document is served in accordance with the directions of the court. If the defendant is not an Irish citizen, then a Notice of the originating document is served in accordance with the order of the court. When giving leave, the court will specify the method by which service is to be effected and the time within which an appearance must be entered. The *Superior Court Rules* also apply both to the Circuit and District Courts.

Shortened procedures

Default of appearance or defence

There are provisions in the rules of each of the courts permitting judgment to be entered in default of either appearance or defence. *Order 13 of the Superior Courts Rules* governs judgments in default of appearance, and *Order 27*, judgments in default of defence. In actions for debts or liquidated amounts, judgment may be entered in the Central Office subject to certain provisos. In other types of actions application must be made by way of a Notice of Motion to the Court. Applications for judgment in default of defence are made by way of Notice of Motion to the Court. There are special provisions applying to persons under a disability.

Summary judgment

Uncontested cases

Contested cases

In the High Court, in all actions commenced by Summary Summons ie essentially for debt and the recovery of land, application may be made to the Master of the High Court for liberty to enter judgment. *Order 37 of the Superior Court Rules* sets out the detailed provisions. In uncontested cases the Master may give leave to enter final judgment. In contested cases he must transfer the matter to a High Court judge. The judge has a wide discretion whether to give leave to enter final judgment or to adjourn the matter to a plenary hearing. He may also give judgment for part of the claim and adjourn the balance of the claim to a plenary hearing. If there is more than one defendant, he may give judgment against one defendant and adjourn the action against the other defendant to a plenary hearing. He may adjourn the matter to a plenary hearing unconditionally or conditionally, for example on condition that a stipulated sum of money is lodged in court. Where the Master makes an order on an application for summary judgment there is a right of appeal to a High Court judge. There is a right of appeal from all the decisions of the High Court judge to the Supreme Court.

Circuit and District Courts

There are also *Rules in the Circuit and District Courts for Summary Judgment* which, whilst differing in detail, essentially give similar powers to the judge to decide upon the application summarily or to adjourn to a full hearing.

Grounds for striking out

No claim in law

The Superior Courts have three separate jurisdictions in relation to striking out claims :

(a)   Under the inherent jurisdiction of the court, jurisdiction to strike out a claim which upon undisputed facts must fail (*Barry v Buckley*[4]).

---

4.   *Barry v Buckle* [1981] IR 306.

(b)   Under *Order 19, Rule 28* which provides :
"The court may order any pleading to be struck out, on the ground that it discloses no reasonable cause of action or answer, and in any such case or in case of the action or defence being shown by the pleadings to be frivolous or vexatious, the court may order to be stayed or dismissed or judgment to be entered accordingly as may be just".

No cause of action; frivolous or vexatious actions

(c)   Under various specific rules of the *Superior Court Rules* to strike out a claim or defence in default of pleading or failure to comply with certain other preliminary procedural steps such as particulars, discovery, inspection, interrogatories. This jurisdiction is rarely used and normally the party in default will be given time to remedy the default. If, following such time, there is a particular significant failure to prosecute an action the court will exercise this jurisdiction.

Failure to comply with the Rules

Orders have been made by the Irish Superior Courts precluding habitual litigants from commencing actions without special leave of the court. These orders are made under the inherent jurisdiction of the court.

Habitual vexatious litigants

There are two separate jurisdictions:

Security for costs

(a)   *Section 390 of the Companies Act 1963* provides :
"Where a limited company is plaintiff in any action or other legal proceeding any judge having jurisdiction in the matter may, if it appears by credible testimony that there is reason to believe that the company will be unable to pay the costs of the defendant if successful in his defence, require sufficient security to be given for those costs and may stay all proceedings until the security is given".

Companies

(b)   *Order 29 of the Superior Court Rules* and *Order 13 of the Circuit Court Rules* contain provisions for the granting of security for costs essentially where plaintiffs are outside the jurisdiction. In order to obtain an order a defendant must show that he has a defence on the merits

Party outside Ireland

Both jurisdictions have been construed by the courts in the context of the constitutional right of access to the courts. If a plaintiff can show that its impecunious state flows from the alleged wrong of the defendant which is the subject matter of the proceedings, then security is unlikely to be ordered. Since the coming into force in Ireland of the *Brussels Convention*, the fact that the plaintiff is outside the jurisdiction is no longer alone a ground for obtaining security for costs if the cause of action is within the Convention. Applications for security are made on notice to the court after a demand in writing has been made to the party from whom it is sought.

Interlocutory relief

Applications for injunctions and other interlocutory relief are granted in cases of urgency. Where appropriate, they can be granted ex parte (without the other party being present or even being notified) although the party against whom the order is made has an early opportunity to have the injunction discharged. Under the *Constitution*, justice must be administered in open court save as prescribed by law. There are very limited statutory exceptions, and these are very strictly construed by the courts. Outside normal court hours applications for injunctions may of necessity be heard in a private hearing in the judge's chambers or home. Orders may not be obtained on the telephone. Injunctions will be granted prior to the issue of proceedings upon the undertaking of the applicant to issue a plenary summons. The Circuit Court has a jurisdiction to grant injunctions. The District Court does not have such a jurisdiction. The principles on which interlocutory relief is granted by the Irish courts is derived from Common Law. Broadly, they are that the person seeking interlocutory relief must establish (i) there is a fair issue to be tried between the parties; (ii) if he were to succeed at the full trial of the action that monetary compensation would not be an adequate remedy to compensate him for the damage which he would suffer by reason of the alleged continuing wrong in the intervening period; and (iii) that the balance of convenience between the parties favours the granting of the injunction. The current statements of these principles by the Supreme Court are to be found in *Campus Oil Ltd v Minister for Industry and Energy*[5] and *Westman Holdings Ltd v McCormack and Others*[6].

Direction as to further conduct of proceedings

The *Rules of Court* do not provide generally for a Summons for Directions when orders will be made for the subsequent conduct of the proceedings.

There are, however, specific provisions in petitions under the *Companies Act*, probate actions and certain other specified types of actions requiring a party to bring a Motion for Directions.

Appeals from directions

Appeals are available against such directions either where the directions are given by the Master of the High Court to the High Court, or, where given by the High Court, to the Supreme Court.

Discovery of documents etc

Order 31 of the Rules of the Superior Courts and *Order 29 of the Rules of the Circuit Court* provide for discovery and disclosure of documents.

Rules of Court

The obligation is to give discovery of all documents relevant to the issues in the proceedings and to disclose the existence of documents formerly in the possession of the party. This duty exists even when the documents assist the opponents case. Save where a special order is made by the court a lawyer is obliged to disclose the documents to his client. The existence of privileged documents must be disclosed to the opposing party, but their content need not be revealed.

---

5.   *Campus Oil Ltd v Minister for Industry and Energy* [1983] IR 42.
6.   *Westman Holdings Ltd v McCormack and Others* Supreme Court 1991 (unreported).

Privilege from production may be claimed upon grounds of legal professional privilege for all documents containing legal advice and other documents which came into being in contemplation of, or for the purpose of, the prosecution or defence of an action. Documents containing incriminating matters may not be disclosed and there are certain other limited types of privilege.

Confidentiality of documents

The extent to which the state may claim privilege for confidential documents is very limited. It must be something which goes to the security of the state. Where such a claim is disputed, a procedure has been developed by the courts whereby the documents must be produced to the judge and the judge rules on whether or not the state is entitled to claim privilege.

Claims of privilege by the state

"Without prejudice" documents passing between opposing sides in an attempt to compromise an action may not normally be used in evidence or brought to the attention of the court during a trial unless the party claiming the privilege waives this. Such documents passing between the legal representatives must normally be shown to their clients.

Documents "without prejudice"

The gathering of evidence is carried out by the parties and not by the court. The discovery of documents does not put those documents into evidence. The discovery procedure exists to assist the parties in the preparation of the trial. The party seeking to adduce the documents in evidence must prove the validity of the documents according to established rules of evidence. A party may not without special leave of the court put a document not discovered into evidence.

Evidence

Documents - admissibility

Parties may be forced to disclose evidence by means of the pre-trial rules of discovery and production. By these means a party, that has grounds for believing that the opposing party has documents which they ought to have disclosed, can obtain an order from the court before trial that such documents should be disclosed.

The admissibility of evidence is not normally challenged before the trial.

Generally, hearsay evidence (secondhand evidence of what a person has been told that someone has said to someone else) is not admissible at the trial of an action. It is normally admissible in affidavits in interlocutory applications.

Hearsay evidence

Ireland is not a party to *the Hague Convention on the collection of evidence abroad.*

Evidence taken abroad

Order 39, Rule 4 of the Superior Court Rules permits the court to make an order where it considers it necessary for the examination upon oath before the court or any other person on oath of any person either before the court or any other person at any place and may allow the deposition of such witnesses to be adduced in evidence on such terms as the court may direct.

This procedure is used to take evidence from willing witnesses or witnesses compellable by the Irish courts abroad.

Request to a foreign court

Under *Order 39, Rule 5* the court may order the issue of a request to a foreign court to examine a witness. This can only be done in relation to countries with which Ireland has ratified a relevant convention.

Witnesses

As a general rule, all persons are competent to give evidence, and may be compelled to attend to give evidence. The President of Ireland is probably not compellable. Persons of unsound mind or who by their youth or other cause are prevented from understanding questions put to them, are not competent witnesses. The spouse of a party to a civil action is competent to give evidence but not compellable to disclose communications made between them during their marriage. Representatives of foreign governments enjoying diplomatic immunity are not compellable witnesses.

Subpoenas

Witnesses may be compelled to give oral evidence by the service of a subpoena. In most instances subpoenas will be issued on the request of the parties from the Central Office. There are two types of subpoenas, a *subpoena ad testificandum* which commands a witness to attend and give evidence, and a *subpoena duces tecum* which commands a witness to attend and give evidence and to bring with him and produce certain documents specified in the subpoena.

Where witnesses are unable to come to court because they are abroad or are too ill to come, an order may be made for their evidence to be taken at some other place "on commission". The only difference from the normal procedure is that the evidence will be taken before a commissioner appointed by the court rather than the trial judge. In the most exceptional circumstances, where it is impossible for the evidence to be taken orally evidence on affidavit may be admitted. If it is disputed, it may be given less weight by the judge than evidence given orally since the evidence will not have been subject to cross-examination.

Leave of the court is required for the issue of a subpoena directing the production of documents in the custody of any officer of the state.

Expert evidence

Any party may call an expert to give evidence as a witness in proceedings. If the expertise is challenged, the court will only permit evidence to be given by the expert if it is satisfied that he is

genuinely an expert in the matters in respect of which he proposes giving evidence.

Only in admiralty matters may the judge appoint an assessor (*Order 64, Rule 43*).

There are no provisions for the mandatory exchange before trial of experts, reports or documents.

There are no rules providing for a final review by the court before trial.

Barristers and solicitors may appear in all courts. Natural persons may appear in person. Legal entities may only appear through lawyers.

The plaintiff will normally start the hearing. The only instance when this might not happen is where the claim is in effect admitted and the real issue arises on a counterclaim. Normally the plaintiff will make an opening submission, and then call evidence. Then the defendant will make an opening submission and call evidence and then the defendant will make a closing submission. The plaintiff normally has the right of final reply. In simple cases the defendant may dispense with the opening submission. In jury actions if the defendant does not call evidence, the plaintiff does not have the right of final reply.

The opening and closing submission and questioning of witnesses is done by opposing advocates. There are detailed rules relating to the direct examination of one's own witness, the cross-examination by opposing witnesses and the right of re-examination.

The judge will normally only ask a witness a question on any point he requires to be the clarified after the full direct examination and cross-examination of the witness. The judge does not call for evidence but decides the case on the evidence presented to him. Only in exceptional cases will a judge visit a locus in quo to see where the incident about which he is hearing evidence occurred He will normally rely on photographs and plans to supplement the evidence.

Normally there are no written submissions to the court setting out the legal arguments. At the end of the evidence the advocate makes detailed oral submissions in the course of which the judge or judges frequently ask questions to obtain clarification of the arguments that are being advanced. The Supreme Court in certain important and complicated actions may ask for written submissions. There is no time limit on oral argument.

Judgments are always given in open court except when the proceedings have been conducted in camera. There is no time within which judgments must be given, save on a reference by the President to the Supreme Court under *Article 26 of the Constitution* in which case the judgment must be given not later than 60 days after the date of the reference. In simple cases, judgments are normally given extempore immediately after the hearing has ended.

Dissenting judgments

Dissenting judgments may be given save on an appeal to the Supreme Court in an action which challenges the constitutionality of an *Act of the Oireachtas*.

Costs

The court is given a wide discretion on awarding costs. The general rule applying to the award of costs is that they follow the event, ie they depend on the result of the case. Normally no award of costs will be made at an interlocutory hearing. The costs will be reserved until the full trial of the action. There is no practice of ordering legal representatives to pay costs of another party but the courts have discretion to do so if the facts so warrant. There are no fixed charges. Costs are subject to taxation by the court unless they are agreed by the parties. They will not always amount to a full indemnity. Normally costs are on a party/party basis (which provides for less than a full recovery of costs) and are subject to assessment on taxation before a *Taxing Master* who will apply the relevant rules of court.

Recoverable costs

Payment into court

A sum of money may be lodged in court in full satisfaction of the opposing party's claim in accordance with *Order 22 of the Superior Court Rules*. In actions for debt or damages or in admiralty actions it may be made either with or without an admission of liability. In certain other actions such as libel, slander or where the defence raises questions of title to land, money may only be lodged if liability is admitted. It will often be lodged at the court at the same time as the defence is delivered but it can be lodged at any time.

Where money is lodged and the plaintiff at the trial of the action does not succeed in obtaining damages of more than the amount lodged then, unless the judge at the trial otherwise directs, the plaintiff is only entitled to his costs up to the date on which the money was lodged and the defendant is entitled to his costs against the plaintiff from that date other than in relation to the issues upon which the plaintiff may have succeeded. These two amounts must be set off against each other and if the balance remaining is in favour of the defendant then it must be paid out of the amount lodged in court before payment out to the plaintiff.

Length of proceedings

The length of the proceedings varies enormously depending upon the complexity of the case and the anxiety of the parties to expedite the case. The preliminary written procedures may last from approximately 3 to 12 months on average. From the date when the action is ready for trial and set down the following are average periods in the High Court :
- Contractual disputes - 1 to 3 months.
- Commercial/chancery actions - 3 to 9 months.
- Personal injury - 12 months.

Appeals

Appeals are in the form of full re-hearings on fact and law from the District Court to the Circuit Court and from the Circuit Court to the High Court. Appeals from the High Court to the Supreme Court are on points of law only; there is no re-hearing. The appeal is based on the transcript or note of the evidence given in the High Court.

The appeals from the District and Circuit Courts to the Circuit *Time* and High Courts vary in time depending upon the particular District and Circuit. The average is probably between 6 and 12 months. The average period from the High Court to the Supreme Court is probably 12 to 18 months. If a case for urgency is made out, the appeals may be taken within a shorter period.

CHAPTER 7 : CRIMINAL PROCEDURE

In Ireland the system of criminal justice is based on the accusatorial system and not the inquisitorial system. This means that the tasks of investigating a case and presenting the prosecution is entirely separate from judging the case. It is not part of the judge's task to conduct the type of investigation into the facts which the judge would undertake in the civil law system.

Introduction

The basic structure of court proceedings is as follows :
-    Service of Summons or arrest and charge.
-    Appearance by an accused person before a District Court (judge alone).
-    The provision of legal aid is considered.
-    If the offence alleged is a summary offence :
     (a)   a date for a hearing is fixed and the case proceeds by way of calling witnesses to give evidence on that date.
-    If the offence alleged is an indictable offence :
     (a)   the venue for the hearing of the charge is decided. In some instances this may be in the District Court. In other instances the case may/must go forward to the Circuit Criminal Court (judge and jury) or the Central Criminal Court (judge and jury) (eg murder can only be dealt with by the Central Criminal Court).
     (b)   Before going forward to a higher court the District Justice conducts a preliminary examination. An accused person will be served with copies of all prosecution witness statements and exhibits to be used in evidence at the trial of the action. The District Justice may dismiss the case at the conclusion of the preliminary examination if there is insufficient evidence to substantiate some or all of the offences alleged against the defendant. The District Justice may also direct the preferring of other charges against the accused following from the preliminary examination. Very often the preliminary examination is not contested and involves only a brief hearing.
The case proceeds to a Central or Circuit Criminal Court hearing before a judge and jury.

Structure of court proceedings

Preliminary examination

Special charges   -   In some special cases charges may be instituted in the Special Criminal Court, which is a three-judge court sitting without a jury. It is also possible to send cases from the District Court to the Special Criminal Court to be dealt with. The preliminary examination that is required in the District Court is also required for cases dealt with before the Special Criminal Court.

- A defendant who has been convicted by the District Court may appeal to the Circuit Court, which must conduct a full re-hearing of the case.

- A person convicted by the Circuit Criminal Court, the Central Criminal Court, or the Special Criminal Court may appeal to the Court of Criminal Appeal. This is a three-judge court, usually comprised of a Supreme Court judge and two High Court judges. In some instances, it is possible to appeal from the Court of Criminal Appeal to the Supreme Court or directly from the trial court to the Supreme Court.

Classification of offences

There are two types of offences; summary and indictable.

Summary offences

Summary offences are dealt with by District Justices (equivalent to Magistrates) alone.

Indictable offences

Indictable offences are dealt with by trial by judge and jury. In certain instances some indictable offences may be dealt with by a District Justice. There is a distinction between indictable offences which are felonies and those which are misdemeanours. In general the more serious offences are classed as felonies.

Under the provisions of the *Offences against the State Act 1939*, indictable offences under that Act and its schedules may be tried by a court sitting without a jury.

Who may prosecute?

Director of Public Prosecutions

The principal prosecutor for the state is the Director of Public Prosecutions. This role arises from the provisions of *Article 30.3 of the Constitution*. The office of the Director of Public Prosecutions was created by the *Prosecution of Offences Act 1974* and took over the prosecution of most criminal cases from the Attorney General. In some cases specified by law the Attorney General is still the prosecutor.

Private prosecutions

Private individuals or organisations may bring prosecutions as "common informers" only in the District Court.

Commencement of prosecution

There are a number of statutes which nominate specific bodies or government ministers who may prosecute offences under these statutes. The offences are, however, all of a summary nature.

Proceedings in court are commenced by way of summons or charge sheet. The collection of evidence for a prosecution is a matter for the "*Gardai*" (police) and, in matters dealt with summarily in the District Court, such evidence is not usually made known to the defence until the case is actually heard.

The burden of proof is at all times upon the prosecution. The court must be satisfied beyond a reasonable doubt on the evidence as to the proof of all the elements of a crime before a defendant can be convicted.

Burden of proof

In cases dealt with summarily there is no obligation on the prosecution to provide the defence with a note of any of the evidence to be called prior to the hearing. However, where there are reports of a forensic nature to be produced in court as part of the proofs of the case such reports should be made available to the defence in advance of the hearing.

Summary trial in the District Court

In cases triable on indictment which will go forward to the Circuit Criminal Court, Central Criminal Court or Special Criminal Court, the defence will be provided in the District Court with a book of evidence. The book of evidence is a compilation of the charges alleged against the defendant, the list of witnesses and their statements, a note of any statements made by the defendant, and the exhibits to be used in the case. Additional evidence which complies with the requirements of the *Criminal Procedure Act 1967* may be served upon the defendant at a later stage, but no evidence not included in the book of evidence or properly introduced as additional evidence may be relied upon by the prosecution at the hearing of the case.

The book of evidence

A defendant is entitled to apply to have the proceedings struck out either for lack of evidence or where the *Rules of Court* have not been complied with. This application may be made in the District Court. Where refused by a District Justice, or where there has been a procedural irregularity, such an application may be made to the High Court by way of judicial review proceedings.

Application to strike out the proceedings

Where a case is to be dealt with summarily in the District Court defendants are simply asked whether they plead guilty or not guilty to the offence charged. Where the offence alleged is an indictable offence which may be dealt with summarily with the consent of the defendant, the defendant must elect whether to be tried by the District Justice alone or by a Higher Court with a jury.

Pleas

District Court

Where a case has been sent for trial before a judge and jury the defendant pleads guilty or not guilty at the start of the trial and normally before the jury is sworn.

Trial by judge and jury

In some circumstances, a defendant may plead guilty to a lesser offence, eg guilty to manslaughter but not guilty of murder, guilty of careless driving but not guilty of dangerous driving, guilty of common assault but not guilty of assault occasioning actual bodily harm.

Pleas to lesser charges

A defendant is free to change his plea at any time. This extends to instances where in the District Court on the summary disposal of a matter a defendant pleaded guilty to the charges. On appeal to the Circuit Court where the case is a full re-hearing a defendant is free to plead not guilty to the same charges.

Change of plea

Plea bargaining	There is no formal plea bargaining system with the prosecuting authorities in Ireland.
Juries *Function of the jury*	In cases involving a jury the jury consists of 12 lay persons who hear the evidence. They are the sole judges of fact and bring in a verdict of guilty or not guilty on each of the charges against an accused after hearing the evidence at the trial and accepting the judge's direction on the law applicable to the case.
Eligibility of jurors	Juries in a particular court area are drawn at random from the list of registered voters in that area. This includes all persons over 18 years of age except for those who are ineligible.
Ineligible and disqualified persons	Under the *Juries Act 1976*, persons concerned with the administration of justice, members of the defence forces, the President of Ireland and certain persons such as those suffering from mental illness are ineligible to serve on juries. Other persons excusable from jury service include members of the Irish Parliament and persons over the age of 70 years.
	A person is disqualified from jury service if he has been convicted of an offence in any part of Ireland and has been sentenced to life imprisonment or if he has been convicted within the previous 10 years of an offence in any part of Ireland for which he has served a sentence of at least three months' imprisonment.
Challenges to jurors	Both prosecution and defence may challenge any number of jurors if either party can show cause as to why such persons should be so challenged. Both prosecution and defence may challenge up to seven jurors without having to show cause for such challenge.
Conduct of the trial *Representation*	Individual defendants are free to represent themselves at the hearing of the trial of an action both in the District Court and in the Higher Courts. The normal practice is to have a defendant represented by a solicitor and Junior Counsel (barrister) and in the cases of more serious offences by both Junior and Senior Counsel (barristers). The prosecution is similarly free to be represented by Junior and/or Senior Counsel.
Opening of the case	In all criminal trials the prosecution commences the proceedings. In jury trials, it is common practice for the prosecuting counsel to address the jury before calling all relevant witnesses for the prosecution's case.
No case to answer	In some cases, at the close of the prosecution's case, the defence may seek to have the case dismissed by the judge because, as a matter of law, there is no case to answer. If there are no legal submissions, or if such submissions are rejected the defence case begins. This may or may not involve calling the defendant and/or other witnesses to give evidence. If the defence does not offer any witnesses the prosecuting counsel is free to address the jury in closing. The defence counsel makes the final closing speech.

The role of the judge in jury actions is to adjudicate on matters of law and at all times to keep the proceedings within the rules of procedure and evidence. A judge is free to ask questions of witnesses but lengthy examinations of witnesses by a judge can lead on appeal to a retrial. The judge has no power to call witnesses.

Role of the judge during evidence

At the end of the evidence, the prosecution counsel will make a final speech to the jury summarising the evidence and seeking to persuade the jury that the defendant is guilty. The defence counsel will then make a speech bringing to the attention of the jury those matters that are favourable to the defendant, and pleading that the jury find the defendant not guilty. At the end of the speeches on behalf of the parties the judge will sum up the case to the jury summarising the evidence and setting out the law that the jury must apply. The jury are entitled to disregard any comment which the judge makes on the facts but must accept his directions on the law.

Final speeches and the judge's charge to the jury

All criminal cases must, in principle, be held in public. However, there are provisions for hearing cases in camera where the defendant is a juvenile or where the offence alleged is of a sexual nature. The only persons allowed in court in these instances are persons involved in the case and bona fide representatives of the press. In all cases bona fide representatives of the press are free to attend court.

Hearings in public

After the judge's summing up, referred to as the charge to the jury, the jury is directed to retire and consider its verdict. The jury must not communicate with persons outside the jury about the case once they have retired to their room. The jury is free to return to court to seek guidance from the trial judge but otherwise is not entitled to discuss the case with any other persons.

Consideration of verdict

Originally all verdicts had to be unanimous, but now there is a statutory provision that, where a jury is unable to agree after a minimum of two hours of consideration, a jury may be brought back to court and directed that a majority verdict will be accepted. The majority verdict is one of not less than ten persons. Where there is no prospect of a jury returning either a unanimous verdict or a majority verdict either for a conviction or for an acquittal on any charges before them, the jury is free to return to the court and a disagreement will be recorded. The jury will then be discharged. There may be a retrial of the case at a later date. Where the jury has failed to agree twice, the defendant will normally be discharged.

Majority verdict

There are some instances where a defendant may be found guilty by a jury of an alternative or lesser offence to that with which he has been charged. For example an indictment may only contain a charge of murder but a jury may come back with a finding of not guilty of murder but guilty of manslaughter.

Alternative verdicts

The trial judge takes no part in the decision or verdict of the jury. Any guidance that he is called upon to give to the jury must relate to questions of law and evidence already heard in the case and cannot involve fresh evidence.

Sentence

Welfare Reports

Upon conviction the judge may proceed directly to sentence the defendant or may defer sentencing to a later time. Before sentencing, the judge will call upon the prosecuting authorities to provide evidence as to the background of the defendant and any previous convictions recorded against him. The defendant will be given the opportunity to call witnesses in mitigation of any sentence and may seek to persuade the judge to ask the Probation Welfare Officers attached to the courts to provide a report on the family background and attitude of the defendant. courts will normally permit the defendant to call character witnesses prior to sentence being pronounced. The defendant may ask for other lesser offences to be taken into consideration when sentence is passed.

Sentencing guidelines

There are no sentencing manuals setting out the sentence which judges are bound to impose for specific crimes The court will be guided by pronouncements from the Court of Criminal Appeal and the Supreme Court laying down general guidelines on the appropriate range of sentences for particular offences. However, in each case a judge is free to exercise his or her own discretion based on the facts of the particular case unless specific guidelines are imposed by statute.

Young offenders

The sentencing of juveniles and young persons is subject to the provisions of the *Childrens Act 1908* as amended. Children over the age of 7 years are considered capable of committing crime. Between the ages of 7 and 14 years there is a presumption of "*doli*" (criminality) but such presumption may be rebutted by the defence. A child under the age of 15 years may be detained but may not be sentenced to a term of imprisonment. A young person between 15 and 17 years may in certain instances be imprisoned with adult offenders. The length of a child's or young person's detention and place of such detention is limited under statute.

Range of sentences

The main options in sentencing include imprisonment, fines or a combination of both. A suspended sentence of imprisonment, an order of community service, or probation are alternatives to imprisonment. The court may also order the offender to pay a fine, be given an absolute or conditional discharge or be bound over to be of good behaviour for a period in the future. In addition, the court may order the offender to pay the costs of the prosecution. The offence of murder carries a mandatory sentence of life imprisonment; this is the only offence which requires the court to send a convicted person to jail. Under the provisions of the Road Traffic Acts there are mandatory provisions disqualifying offenders from driving for a period of not less than 12 months where they have been convicted of driving while under the influence of alcohol or failing to give a sample of their blood and urine but there is no mandatory imposition of a jail sentence.

The maximum length of a sentence of detention to be imposed by a court is either regulated by the statutory provisions in respect of the offence charged or by the level of the court involved. A District Court may not impose any sentence in excess of 12 months or, where two or more offences are charged, a sentence in excess of 2 years. A jury court or the Special Criminal Court is only inhibited by the statutory maximum involved in the case.

In cases dealt with summarily in the District Court a person may appeal to the Circuit Court. This may involve a full re-hearing of the case. An accused person has 14 days from the date of conviction to lodge such an appeal, but in certain instances the time limit may be extended. A person who has been imprisoned following conviction in the District Court may be freed on bail pending the hearing of the appeal. The Circuit Court is bound by the jurisdiction of the District Court when imposing a sentence on an appeal. *Appeals*

Appeals to Circuit Court

A defendant who wishes to appeal from the Circuit Criminal Court, the Central Criminal Court or the Special Criminal Court may lodge an appeal to the Court of Criminal Appeal. The appellant must seek leave to appeal from the trial judge at the close of the trial or within three days thereafter. If leave to appeal is refused, the appeal takes the form of an appeal against the refusal of the trial judge to grant leave. The practice is that if the Court of Criminal Appeal grants leave it hears the appeal at the same time. *Appeals to the Court of Criminal Appeal*

An accused may appeal against both a conviction and sentence, or against conviction alone or against the severity of the sentence alone. The Court of Criminal Appeal may refuse the appeal, order a retrial of the charge or quash the conviction. The court may either reduce or increase a sentence which has been appealed.

The Court of Criminal Appeal may in certain circumstances certify that a decision of that court involves a point of law of exceptional public importance and direct that an appeal should be taken to the Supreme Court. In cases where a person is convicted by the Central Criminal Court appeals may go to the Court of Criminal Appeal or directly to the Supreme Court. *Appeals to the Supreme Court*

In most cases, courts dealing with appeals give judgment either on the date of the oral hearing or a very short time thereafter. Where the decision will include the release of a person in custody, courts normally order the immediate release of the defendant even when they give their reasons at a later date. *Time for judgment on appeal*

Extradition is governed by the *Extradition Act 1965*, as amended, which gives effect to the *European Convention on Extradition 1957*. A request for extradition must be communicated in writing by an accredited diplomatic representative or otherwise as provided by the relevant extradition provisions. It must be supported by evidence of conviction or sentence or a warrant of arrest, a statement and description of the offence, a statement of the foreign law and a description of the wanted person with any other relevant information as to his identity and nationality. This *Extradition*

Procedure in application for extradition

is served on the Minister for Justice. If he is satisfied that everything is in order, Minister for Justice directs a Justice of the District Court to issue a warrant for the arrest of the wanted person.

Urgent cases

In cases of urgency a District Justice may issue a provisional warrant without any Ministerial Order on the basis of information sworn by a member of the police. The information must state that a copy of the conviction or sentence, or of the foreign warrant, exists and it must give a description of the wanted person and the nature and time and place of the commission of the alleged offence.

Procedure before the District Court

When the wanted person is brought before the District Court on the authority of the warrant or provisional warrant the justice must satisfy himself or herself that the offence alleged is extraditable. This involves being satisfied that the alleged offence could be prosecuted under Irish law. Furthermore, the court must be satisfied that the person requested to be extradited is the person before the court. Once the District Justice is so satisfied he may then make the necessary order. However, the person to be extradited must be informed that he will not be surrendered to the requesting country without his consent until after 15 days and that he has a constitutional right to apply to the High Court for an Order of Habeus Corpus challenging the Order of the District Court.

Bars to extradition

There are a number of instances where extradition will not be granted, such as where the offence alleged is a political offence or one connected with a political offence; where it is one which is punishable by death in the requesting country; or where there is a prosecution pending in Ireland against the accused for the same offence.

Extradition may only be granted if the offence is punishable under the laws of the country requesting extradition by imprisonment for a maximum period of at least one year or where the wanted person has been convicted and sentenced in the requesting country and a sentence of imprisonment for at least four months has been imposed.

Time limits in criminal proceedings

Charging the defendant

A person who has been arrested must be brought before a court of law as soon as practicable. Where a person is arrested at night that person should be brought before a court of law to be charged on the following morning at the normal court sittings, or where such court sittings are not being held, before a special sitting of a court. If this cannot be done, that person should be granted bail pending a sitting of the courts.

Detention for questioning

A person may be detained for up to 48 hours under the *Offences Against the State Act 1939* and may be released without charge at the end of that period of detention.

Under the *Criminal Justice Act 1987* a person may be detained and questioned in relation to an offence for which he has been arrested for a period not in excess of 12 hours (or 20 hours where the accused person is permitted to sleep during the night). The detention and questioning must be related to the proper investigation of the crime.

A person charged with a summary offence cannot be charged later than six months from the date of the alleged offence. A person accused of committing an indictable offence is not subject to such a time limit.

Time limit in summary cases

A person to whom bail has been refused may not be remanded in custody for a period in excess of eight days unless he so consents.

Under the *Criminal Procedure Act 1967* there are time limits during which the book of evidence must be served on an accused. The court is empowered to extend those time limits only where the court feels no injustice will be done to the accused. In all cases a defendant is free to challenge the prosecution of a case in the higher courts on the grounds of undue delay on the part of the prosecuting authority.

Time limits for service

Detention on bail before trial is strictly regulated. There is no concept known to Irish law as the non-bailable offence. The question of whether a person is to be granted bail or not is one for the discretion of the courts. In some instances it may be a decision of the arresting *Gardai*, particularly when children are involved.

Bail

Generally

The application for bail is usually made to the District Court. It is usually made on the first appearance in court, and if refused, may be applied for again at a later stage. The most persuasive factor in a court's decision whether or not to grant bail is whether or not the *Gardai* opposes bail.

Application for bail

When fixing bail the court must look to the circumstances of the offence and to the circumstances of the accused. If bail is set at an excessively high amount this is, in effect, a denial of bail.

Bail may be refused where the court is of the opinion having heard evidence, that the accused person is unlikely to attend at the trial. The factors which the court can consider in reaching such a decision are whether the accused has failed on previous occasions to attend at court, the seriousness of the charge alleged, whether the defendant was caught red-handed and the nature of the evidence in support of the charge. The court will also consider whether there is a possibility that witnesses may be interfered with if bail is granted.

Refusal of bail

Where bail has been refused in the District Court or the amount fixed is excessive the defendant may apply to the High Court for bail or a reduction in the amount of money required to be offered as security for bail.

CHAPTER 8 : REMEDIES

Damages may be awarded by any court in an appropriate action. *Damages*
The principles upon which they are awarded are similar to those
in England and Wales. In addition, damages may be awarded for
breach of a constitutional right. There is no state immunity in
such cases.

Personal injury damages are assessed by a judge sitting without a
jury. Damages are awarded by a jury only in defamation and
assault cases.

In personal injuries cases damages are awarded to compensate *Personal injury*
for personal injuries. They include general damages for pain and *claims*
suffering to the date of trial and into the future and special
damages for actual financial loss or extra expenses already
incurred and for prospective financial loss in the future. There are
no fixed awards for different types of injury laid down by statute
but courts have regard to previous decisions in similar cases.

Damages for mental distress are available where this is a *Mental distress*
consequence of the act complained of. This must be
distinguished from grief or sorrow which is not assessed as a
separate head of damages. In fatal cases there is a statutory limit
of IR £7,500 for damages for mental distress resulting from death.

Damages are available for loss of reputation. The amount will be *Loss of reputation*
related to the monetary loss which has or is likely to be suffered.

Damages have been awarded by the High Court for pure *Economic loss*
economic loss.

The court would only consider the question of fairness or
reasonableness in relation to the validity of a contract where
required to do so by statute.

It is possible for the parties to agree to make an application "by *Awards by*
consent" (ie which the defendant will not oppose) for an award of *consent*
an agreed sum.

Specific performance, rescission and delivery up of goods are *Other remedies*
remedies which the court can order if it believes it to be just and
equitable to do so. There are well established principles as to the
circumstances in which both such orders will be made.

Under the *Courts Acts* interest may be awarded by the court *Interest*
currently at a rate of 8% and variable at the discretion of the

Minister for Justice (*Debtors (Ireland) Act 1840, s 23; Courts Act 1981, ss 19(1), 22*). The award of interest is a matter of discretion for the trial judge.

Declaratory relief Declaratory relief may be granted by the High Court or Supreme Court whether or not any consequential relief is or could be claimed (*Rules of the Superior Courts, Order 19, Rule 29*). However, the courts will not hear cases where there is no issue or dispute between the parties. They will declare existing rights but will not rule on future events unless there is a serious risk that they will occur, eg to restrain the threat of unlawful conduct by one party on the other.

Winding-up a company The law relating to the winding-up by Order of the Court is contained in the *Companies Act 1963, as amended by the Companies Act 1990* (which also applies to voluntary creditors and members' winding-up).

Grounds for winding-up a company The principal grounds on which a company may be wound up, by the courts are :
- that the company is unable to pay its debts,
- that it is just and equitable to wind up the company,
- where a member is being treated in an oppressive manner or where his interests are being disregarded,
- that the company itself has resolved that it be wound up by the court.

Related companies The *Companies Act 1990, s 141* also provides that, where two or more "related companies" are being wound up a court may order them to be wound up together as if they were one company.

Role of the liquidator When an order is made for the winding-up of a company a liquidator is appointed to supervise the sale of the assets and their distribution to the creditors according to an order of priority laid down by law.

Appointment of an examiner Under the *Companies (Amendment) Acts 1990* the company, its directors, a creditor (including a contingent or perspective creditor or an employee) or a member holding not less than one-tenth of the voting shares may petition the court for the appointment of an examiner. Any one or any combination of the foregoing may present such a petition. In the case of an insurance company or a bank, the petition may be presented only by the Minister for Industry and Commerce or the Central Bank respectively. The effect of the court appointing an examiner is to place the company under the protection of the court. His function is essentially that of rescuing the company rather than enforcing

Functions of the examiner any security or winding-up the company. The examiner conducts an examination of the affairs of the company and reports his results to the court within 21 days of his appointment or such longer period as the court may allow. Other duties may be conferred on him by the court. The essence of his report is that he should let the court know whether he thinks the company can survive as a going concern and if so what steps he thinks should be taken to ensure its survival.

Generally speaking, notwithstanding that an examiner has been appointed, the directors retain their powers. However, the court may vest all or any of the directors' powers exclusively in the examiner on his application, where the court considers it just and equitable to do so, having regard to any of the following considerations :

Role of directors where an examiner has been appointed

- The fact that the company's affairs are being conducted or likely to be conducted in a manner which is calculated or likely to prejudice the interests of the company or its creditors as a whole.
- The expediency of curtailing or regulating the directors' powers for the purpose of preserving the assets of the company or safeguarding the interests of the company or its creditors as a whole.
- A resolution by the company or its directors that such an order should be sought.
- Any other matters the court thinks relevant. Where such an order is made, the court may also order that the examiner is to have the same powers as a liquidator in a compulsory winding-up.

Where the court appoints an examiner, the company is deemed to be under the protection of the court from the date of the presentation of the petition for a period of three months. During this time :

Effect of the appointment of an examiner

- No voluntary or compulsory winding-up can be initiated;
- No receiver can be appointed or, if appointed less than three days before the presentation of the petition, can act as such;
- No attachment, execution, distress or sequestration can be enforced against the company's property or effects without the consent of the examiner;
- No secured creditor can take any steps to realise a security without the consent of the examiner;
- Goods of the company subject to Hire Purchase Agreements, retention of title clauses etc. may not be repossessed;
- No proceedings of any sort may be taken against a person liable for the company's debts, such as a guarantor, nor may any attachment, distress, sequestration or execution be put in force against his property in respect of the company's debts;
- No other proceedings in relation to the company may be commenced except with leave of the court, and the court may also start such proceedings on the application of the examiner.

Administrative law principles derive from the common law subject to the *1937 Constitution*. They are relatively similar to the principles in England and Wales with the important distinction that there is no state immunity. There are the additional grounds of violation of the right to fair procedures and violation of the constitutional rights of the individual citizen by public bodies and others making decisions concerning obligations under the Constitution.

Administrative law

Either party may apply after an appearance has been entered to the court to stay proceedings on the ground that there is an agreement to proceed to arbitration (*Arbitration Act 1980, s 5*).

Mediation and conciliation procedures only exist in Irish law in matrimonial matters. The purpose of a mediation and conciliation procedure is to see (i) if the parties could reconcile their differences and (ii) if not, to see on what terms the parties could agree to separate. This is not a "remedy" in the formal sense.

CHAPTER 9 : MATRIMONIAL DISPUTES

There is no divorce in Ireland. Issues relating to judicial *Generally* separation, custody and access rights are heard at first instance by the District Court, the Circuit Court or the High Court. The procedure is governed by the rules set out in *Order 70. Rule 19* deals with the rights of these parties to intervene.

The procedure is the same as for other civil cases except that the parties are called applicant and respondent. In cases of urgency the court may, on the basis of evidence on affidavit, make an order on an ex parte application which is for a limited time. At the expiry of that time, the party affected by the order may, if the other party seeks to renew the order, oppose renewal and have the order discharged.

The basic grounds for judicial separation are set out in the *Grounds for* *Judicial Separation and Family Law Reform Act 1989, s 2.1*. These *judicial* grounds are adultery; that the respondent has behaved in such a *separation* way that the applicant cannot reasonably be expected to live with the respondent; that the respondent has deserted the applicant for a continuous period of at least one year immediately preceding the date of the application; that the spouses have lived apart from one another for a continuous period of at least one year immediately preceding the date of the application and the respondent consents to a decree being granted; that the spouses have lived apart from one another for a continuous period of at least three years immediately preceding the date of the application; that the marriage has broken down to the extent that the court is satisfied in all the circumstances that a normal marital relationship has not existed between the spouses for a period of at least one year immediately preceding the date of the application.

Section 12 of the Married Women Status Act 1957 allows spouses *Disputes as to* to apply to the court to determine disputes between them as to *ownership of* the ownership of any property irrespective of whether there are *property* also judicial separation proceedings underway. If a spouse has made any direct financial contribution to the purchase of a house or has made any indirect contribution which assists the other spouse's payments for the house, that spouse will be entitled to a portion of the beneficial interest in the house in proportion to his/her contribution. However, under the *Judicial Separation and Family Law Reform Act 1989, s 20*, the court, having made an order for Judicial Separation, may make further orders relating, inter alia, to property assets and in so doing shall take into account a wide range of matters set out in that section including the spouses' contribution to the welfare of the family and, if just and equitable, the conduct of the other spouse.

CHAPTER 10 : PROPERTY TRANSACTIONS

Under Irish law an agreement for the sale and purchase of land must be evidenced by a note or memorandum in writing. No oral agreement at an earlier stage in the proceedings set out below is enforceable. The deposit described in step 5 is normally returnable if the transaction is not eventually completed. This depends on the terms in the agreement and the reason for non-completion.

The basic steps in a typical conveyancing transaction of the purchase and sale of property in Ireland are :

1. Location of title documents by vendor's solicitor.
2. Preparation of contracts for sale in duplicate.
3. The vendor's solicitor then forwards the contracts with a copy of the title to the purchaser's solicitor.
4. The purchaser's solicitor examines the contracts and negotiates any amendments. When satisfied with the same, he has the contract signed and executed by the purchaser and returns both copies to the vendor's solicitor.
5. The vendor's solicitor then has the contracts signed by the vendor and exchanges one part for a cheque for the deposit, which is normally 10% of the agreed price. The vendor's solicitor then produces the balance of the document title to the property to the purchaser's solicitor.
6. The purchaser's solicitor then investigates the title, raises his objections and requisitions on title within 14 days after delivery of the copy documents of title. At this stage, he will also, if possible, have prepared the draft deed for approval. These are all then sent to the vendor's solicitor. He must reply to the requisitions within 7 days after delivery of the same. The purchaser's solicitor may then issue rejoinders on title and these must be replied to by the vendor's solicitor and so on *toties quoties*. The vendor's solicitor, at the same time as replying to requisitions, will normally approve and amend, if necessary, the draft deed of assurance. The purchaser's solicitor then engrosses the deed of assurance and if the property is unregistered land he will also prepare a memorial which is used for registration purposes in the Registry of Deeds. The engrossed deed, approved draft and memorial are then sent to the vendor's solicitor for execution.
7. The vendor's solicitor then prepares all documents agreed to be handed over in both the contract and replies to requisitions for signing by the vendor.

8.   The vendor's solicitor furnishes an apportionment account with vouchers and arranges with the purchaser's solicitor a suitable closing appointment. He also sends along with the apportionment account any searches in his possession if the title is unregistered.

9   Closing then takes place at which time the balance of the purchase money is handed over by the purchaser's solicitor to the vendor's solicitor in exchange for the title documents, the deed of assurance, the keys and all other ancillary documents. The vendor's solicitor then advises his client to cancel any insurance on the property. The purchaser's solicitor then stamps the deed of assurance within 30 days of completion of the purchase. If the property is unregistered, he stamps the memorial also and sends it to the Registry of Deeds for registration.

10. If the property is registered land, after stamping the deed of assurance, he then lodges it with the other documents in the Land Registry to lead to registration of the purchaser's title.

CHAPTER 11 : RECOGNITION AND ENFORCEMENT OF FOREIGN JUDGMENTS

The *Brussels Convention on Jurisdiction and the Enforcement of Judgments in Civil and Commercial Matters 1968* has been given effect in Ireland by the *Jurisdiction of Courts and Enforcement of Foreign Judgments (European Communities) Act 1988*. Judgments awarded by countries other the Member States of the European Community are enforceable if rendered by a court of competent jurisdiction, if final and conclusive and for a fixed sum of money.

Judgments awarded by a court of an EC Member State are enforceable in accordance with the *Rules of Court* for implementing the provisions of the *1968 Convention* herewith. Other forms of judgments are enforced by way of a Special Summons.

It is open to the Irish courts to refuse to enforce a foreign judgment on the ground of public policy. Apart from the traditional common law principles of public policy this is also determined by reference to the *Constitution*.

BIBLIOGRAPHY

Binchy, William, *Binchy : Irish Conflicts of Law*, Butterworths (Ireland), Dublin, 1988

Byrne, Raymond and McCutcheon, Paul, *The Irish Legal System : Cases and Materials* (2nd edn), Butterworths, Dublin, 1989

Casey, J.P., *Constitutional Law in Ireland*, Sweet & Maxwell, London, 1987

Collins, Anthony M. and O'Reilly, James, *Civil Proceedings and the State in Ireland : Practitioner's Guide*, The Round Hall Press, 1990

Kelly, J.M., *The Irish Constitution* (2nd edn), Jurist Publishing, Dublin, 1984

Hogan, G.W. and Whyte, G., *Supplement to the 2nd Edition 1987* Jurist Publishing, Dublin, 1987

McMahon, Bryan M.E. and Binchy, William, *McMahon and Binchy : Irish Law of Torts* (2nd edn), Butterworths, Dublin, 1990

McMahon, Bryan M.E. and Murphy, Finbarr, *McMahon and Murphy : European Community Law in Ireland*, Butterworths, Dublin, 1989

Morgan, David Gwynn and Hogan, Gerald, *Administrative Law in Ireland* (2nd edn), Sweet and Maxwell, London, 1991

Ryan, Edward F. and Magee, Philip P., *The Irish Criminal Process*, Mercier, Dublin, 1983

Shatter, Alan Joseph, *Shatter's Family Law in the Republic of Ireland* (3rd edn), Wolfgang Press, Dublin, 1986

Wylie, J.C.W., *Irish Conveyancing Law*, Professional Books, Abingdon, 1978

ITALY

Gianni Manca
Antonio Corrao
Linda Longo
Manca Amenta Biolato Corrao & C
Rome, Edinburgh

CONTENTS

CHAPTER 1 : SOURCES OF LAW

The state is unitary in structure and divided into *"Regioni"* (Regions), *"Province"* (Provinces) and *"Comuni"* (Municipalities).

Unitary v federal system

The regions have elected assemblies which exercise a limited legislative competence over specific matters attributed to them under the *Constitution (art 117)*. This power must be exercised in accordance with the general principles of law of the state. Some *Regioni* have a special statute - *"Regioni a statuto speciale"* - and have as a result been granted broader legislative powers (under *Article 116 of the Constitution*) than other regions. Regional laws cannot conflict with the national interest or the interests of other regions. Any conflicts of jurisdiction between regions, or between the state and the regions are resolved by the Constitutional Court.

The main sources of law are :
- (a) statutes (constitutional and those of ordinary status); "ordinary" statutes are promulgated primarily by Parliament and, subordinately, by the regions within the limits of their respective competence; and
- (b) other acts having the force and value of law such as Law Decrees issued by the government and Decrees of the President of the Republic, although their legal effect is subject to special provisions.

Statutes, Law Decrees and Decrees of the President of the Republic

Statutes, Law Decrees and Decrees of the President of the Republic must be passed in accordance with the rules laid down in the *Constitution*.

The main areas in which the regions have legislative power, as laid down by *Article 117 of the Constitution*, are :
- Organisation of the offices and of the administrative bodies which depend on the regions,
- Council Districts,
- Urban and rural police,
- Fairs and markets,
- Public charity and health care,
- Education,
- Museums and local authority libraries,
- Town planning,
- Tourism and the hotel industry,
- Tramways and motorways of regional concern,
- Roads, aquaducts and public works of regional interest,
- Lake navigation and lake ports,
- Mineral waters and hot springs,
- Quarries and peat-bogs,

Areas of regional legislative power

- Hunting,
- Fishing in internal waters,
- Agriculture and forestry,
- Handicraft, and
- Other matters specifically assigned to the regions by Constitutional laws,

Conflicts between sources of law

Conflicts between sources of law are resolved on the basis of primacy of hierarchical status so that, for example, an ordinary statute cannot derogate from a constitutional law. As between ordinary statutes, Decree Laws and Decrees of the President of the Republic which have the same force the rule *lex posteriori derogat anteriori* applies.

Principal sources of law

The principal sources of law in Italy are : *the 1947 Constitution; the 1942 Civil Code; the 1932 Penal Code; the 1940 Code of Civil Procedure; the new Code of Criminal Procedure of 1988; and the 1942 Navigation Code.* The main revenue laws now in force were passed in 1973, and new laws governing the Administration of Justice were passed in 1971.

Application of national laws to foreigners

According to *Article 16 of the Provisions on the Law in General affixed to the Civil Code* non-nationals enjoy the same civil rights as nationals. *Article 16* also ensures that non-nationals and nationals should not be treated differently and, in general, foreigners in Italy are subject to Italian law without distinction. Some provisions dealing with police control do apply only to foreigners including EC citizens, such as those concerning the *"permesso di soggiorno"* (residence permit).

EC law

The *Italian Constitution* does not deal specifically with the incorporation and implementation of EC law in the Italian legal system. There are, however, general provisions in the *Constitution* on the incorporation of international law into the domestic legal system. *Article 10(1) of the Constitution* provides that "the Italian legal system shall conform with the generally recognised rules of international law", and *Article 11 of the Constitution* provides that Italy "consents, on a reciprocal basis with other nations, to such limitations on its sovereignty as are necessary for organisations promoting peace and justice among nations".

In its *Decision No 183/1973* the Constitutional Court held that by virtue of the Treaty of Rome Italy had limited its sovereignty in respect of regulations issued by the EC Council and the EC Commission. The automatic incorporation and implementation of EC law is therefore limited to these regulations only. Italy adopted and incorporated into Italian law the *1957 Treaty of Rome by Law No 1203 of 14 October 1957.*

Proof of foreign law

In the Italian legal system, a foreign law may be relied on in the same way as a domestic law whenever the former has been chosen by parties to govern a contract or when *"rinvio"* (*renvoi*) applies, as provided for by Italian law (*Article 17 of the Provisions on the Law in General* such as, for example, with questions of status and capacity of persons, and with family relations).

There is no legal presumption that foreign law is the same as national law. When *renvoi* is made to a foreign law, interpretation of the latter is treated as a question of law. The court seised of the issue must find out about that foreign law by such means as are available to it, with the assistance of the parties.

The *European Convention on Human Rights* was incorporated into the Italian legal system by *Law No 848 of 4 August 1955*, and, as a result, has the force of law of an ordinary statute and its provisions may be directly applied by the courts. As with all jurisprudence in Italy, case law on the *Convention* serves as a guide but does not bind any domestic court. *European Convention on Human Rights*

The main principles of interpretation are : *Interpretation of national law*
-    first, the literal interpretation whereby, in applying a law the court must if possible give it the meaning which is clear from a proper understanding of the words in question;
-    when a dispute cannot be resolved on the basis of a specific legal provision, the court will refer to provisions which apply to similar or analogous cases;
-    failing which, the court will apply the general principles of the Italian legal system.

Previous court decisions, even if issued by the Court of Cassation, the highest review body for cases within "ordinary" jurisdiction, only act as guidelines for other courts. There is no system of binding precedent and courts can, in theory, depart from consolidated case law.

There are no authorised annotated texts of the *Italian Constitution* and/or of the various Codes, and it cannot be said that there are any annotated texts which are regarded as the most authoritative. Any reputable text may have its own intrinsic value. *Texts of the Constitution*

CHAPTER 2 : FUNDAMENTAL RIGHTS

The principal constitutional articles guaranteeing justice are *Articles 24 to 28 of the Constitution.*

Constitutional protection of fundamental rights

Foreigners, individuals and companies enjoy the same civil rights as Italian citizens on the basis of reciprocity (*Article 10 of the Civil Code,* which refers back to *Article 10(2) of the Constitution*). A foreigner who is unable to exercise in his country the democratic liberties which are guaranteed by the Italian Constitution can claim political asylum in Italy in accordance with the provisions of Italian law. No foreigner can be extradited from Italy to face charges for political crimes.

The *droit de la défence* (the right of defence) is set out in the Constitution in these terms : "The right to a defence is an inviolable right" (*Constitution, art 24(2)*). This principle is generally understood as guaranteeing both protection of the rights of the individual as well as the right to the benefit of professional defence counsel in judicial proceedings. Therefore, in addition to the right to have the assistance of a lawyer during one's case, any party to the proceedings has the right that no decision will be given if there has been no opportunity to attend at trial, to be heard and to produce the evidence most appropriate to the defence.

Right of defence

A corollary to this principle, which applies to all proceedings, whether civil, criminal or administrative, is that a party must be validly summoned before the courts and given a reasonable time to prepare and pursue its defence.

Access to the courts is defined as follows : "Everyone is entitled to institute proceedings to protect his rights and his legitimate interests" (*Constitution, art 24(1)*). This principle guarantees not only that there is the widest right of access to the courts, both civil and administrative (these latter in respect specifically of interests which have allegedly been infringed by the Public Administration) but also guarantees, throughout the whole course of the proceedings, the right to effective and substantive protection by the courts. The principle can be limited only where it may conflict with other fundamental constitutional principles that may be deemed to override it in the specific circumstances of the particular case.

Access to the courts

Legal aid is guaranteed by *Article 24(3) of the Constitution* which says : "Those who are less well-off shall be granted the appropriate means through appropriate legislation to be able to bring actions in the courts and to defend themselves before any jurisdiction".

Legal aid

Article 24 of the Constitution sets out the principle that citizens shall be compensated for any damage suffered as a result of error by the courts : "The conditions and manner under and in which judicial error shall be compensated for in damages shall be laid down by law". A special law has recently been passed to this effect.

Principles of the forum and legality

Article 25 of the Constitution sets out the principles that there must be a pre-determined forum and the principle of legality. The rule that a court must already have been established is defined by the saying "No one may be removed from the competence of their natural pre-determined court established by law". This means that no judge can be appointed *ex post* to decide a specific case.

The principle of legality means that : "No one may be punished save in accordance with a law enacted before a punishable crime was committed". This principle is considered as embodying the three basic principles of criminal law namely that :
- all punishment must be laid down by law;
- criminal offences must have been defined and determined prior to the acts said to constitute such crimes; and
- no criminal law may be retroactive in effect unless the new law is more favourable to the accused.

Extradition

The first principle, the primacy of law, is intended to ensure that all penalties, particularly those that restrict personal liberty, will have been laid down by law, that is, by legislation passed by Parliament, which is regarded as the guarantor of individual personal liberties.

Under *Article 26 of the Constitution*, no citizen may be extradited save where specifically provided for under an international convention to which Italy is a party, and in any event a citizen may not be extradited for a political crime. Extradition can only be ordered by a judge and not by the administrative authorities.

Criminal responsibility

Article 27 of the Constitution sets out three further principles on criminal responsibility :
- criminal responsibility is personal in that no one can be held criminally responsible for an act of a third party;
- an accused is regarded as innocent until proven guilty, which means also that no one may be subjected to sanctions which apply on the supposition that a person is already guilty and which might anticipate any eventual punishment. However, it is accepted that this does not prevent detention on remand provided there is sufficient evidence which otherwise indicates guilt, and where custody is intended to prevent the defendant from escaping or destroying evidence or committing new crimes; and

- all punishment shall be in accordance with the principles of humanity and be directed at rehabilitating the person detained.

The Constitutional Court is the only court competent to rule on the constitutionality of any law issued by the state or by the regions.

Judicial review of the constitutionality of laws

Proceedings before the Constitutional Court are initiated by one of the following procedures :
- *Direct recourse* : the government of the Republic or of any region may apply directly to the Constitutional Court when they consider that a law issued by any region or by the state violates their own respective competences; or
- *Preliminary reference* : questions as to the constitutionality of a legal provision must be submitted to the Constitutional Court by a court in ordinary proceedings when one of the parties has specifically raised an objection that a legal provision is unconstitutional and the court considers that this constitutional issue must be decided as a preliminary question, and that this is essential for it to give its decision in the case. Individuals are not entitled to have their rights protected by the Constitutional Court by way of a direct action.

Therefore, whenever a question of constitutionality is raised by a party, the court must consider whether :
- it needs to resolve the constitutional point in order to be able to give its decision on the merits of the case; and whether
- the constitutional question is not "clearly without foundation", that is, whether it is reasonably foreseeable in its view that the Constitutional Court will, on the one hand, agree that the point is relevant for the decision in the case and, on the other, consider that the constitutional objection can be accepted and is well-founded.

If so, the court will then suspend the case before it and send it to the Constitutional Court, which initiates proceedings on the constitutional legality of the provision in question.

After a hearing it may reach one of the following decisions :
- a decision declaring the law to be unconstitutional (acceptance judgment - "*sentenza di accoglimento*");
- a decision declaring the question to be groundless ("*sentenza di rigetto*");
- a decision declaring the question without foundation because the provision in question is to be interpreted in the particular manner as stated by the court (interpretative judgment of rejection - "*sentenza interpretativa di rigetto*"); or

- a decision declaring the question to be well-founded on the basis of the interpretation which the court gives the provision in dispute (interpretative judgment of acceptance - "*sentenza interpretativa di accogli-mento*").

The latter two types of decisions are the result of the principle stated in numerous judgments of the court that the Constitutional Court may give the law brought before it under the procedure mentioned above an interpretation different from that given by the ordinary courts or by the petitioner. This therefore gives the Court a wide range of powers to deal with such issues.

The main purpose of the procedure outlined above is to give the ordinary court a limited competence to assess whether a law in the proceedings before them is constitutional, thus avoiding overloading the Constitutional Court with having to deal with questions of constitutionality which are clearly groundless, and to prevent parties from using the reference procedure simply as a means of delay, while reserving to the Constitutional Court the exclusive power to declare a law illegal on the grounds that it is unconstitutional.

Representation before the Constitutional Court

Only lawyers specifically qualified to act before the Court of Cassation may appear before the Constitutional Court.

Length of proceedings

The average time for proceedings to be heard before the Court is not less than one year.

CHAPTER 3 : JURISDICTION OF THE COURTS

Civil jurisdiction is exercised by the ordinary courts in accordance with the provisions of the *Italian Code of Civil Procedure.* *Civil jurisdiction of the courts*

The assumption of jurisdiction by the Italian civil courts cannot be challenged by the parties on the grounds that the jurisdiction of another state or of foreign arbitrators is more appropriate unless such a challenge is provided for under a specific international agreement (*Code of Civil Procedure, art* 2). The most important of such agreements which have been adopted by Italy are the multi-lateral Conventions such as the *New York Convention of 10 June 1958 on Arbitrations,* and the *Brussels Convention of 27 September 1968 on Jurisdiction and Enforcement of Judgments in Civil and Commercial Matters.* If there is no specific international convention on the point Italian courts are not prevented from assuming jurisdiction simply because there is another case pending before a foreign court concerning the same suit or a connected action (see *Article 3 of the Code of Civil Procedure*).

Italian courts will have jurisdiction over a foreigner in the following circumstances : *Jurisdiction over foreigners*
- when he/she is resident or domiciled in Italy or has appointed a representative in Italy or has accepted the jurisdiction of the Italian courts save where the claim concerns real property located abroad;
- where the claim concerns property in Italy, an inheritance of an Italian citizen, an inheritance originating in Italy, or obligations and commitments agreed to in Italy or to be performed in Italy;
- where the instant claim is connected with another claim which is itself pending before an Italian court or which refers to interlocutory measures to be implemented in Italy or which concerns matters which may be decided by an Italian court;
- when the courts of the state of the foreigner would be able to determine a similar claim if filed against an Italian citizen before the courts of that foreign state.

Criminal jurisdiction is exercised by the ordinary courts in conformity with the provisions of the *Italian Code of Criminal Procedure.* *Criminal jurisdiction*

The Italian courts are competent to assume jurisdiction when a crime has been committed in Italy. If a crime is committed outside Italy, the Italian courts will have jurisdiction only in a few cases and only under certain conditions, eg where a special request has been made to the state and/or authorisation granted to do so (political crimes, crimes against the Italian government, counterfeiting Italian money, etc).

Rule of universal jurisdiction

There is no rule of universal jurisdiction in Italian law. There is no special court competent to deal with serious crimes regardless of where they were committed. In principle, cases are dealt with by the court which has jurisdiction for the place in which the crime in question was committed.

State immunity

According to *Article 90 of the Italian Constitution*, the President of the Republic is not responsible for any actions carried out in his office, save for crimes of high treason and attacks against the Constitution.

Foreign states and their governmental authorities are immune from Italian jurisdiction only when they act in the exercise of their sovereignty, that is, to achieve the ends to which sovereignty is directed. However, where they act as private entities (for example, in commercial relationships) they will be subject to Italian jurisdiction under the same conditions as foreign citizens.

However, property of a foreign state can be seized and interlocutory measures enforced against a foreign state only on the basis of reciprocity and with prior authorisation from the Ministry of Justice (see *Law No 1263 of 15.7.26*).

Domicile and other factors determining the courts' jurisdiction

The Italian legal system envisages three situations here : domicile, habitual residence, and a person's place of abode - domicile being the principal place of one's business; residence being the place where one usually lives; the place of abode being the place where one is staying temporarily.

The jurisdiction of the civil courts is based primarily on where the defendant is. If the defendant is an individual, the plaintiff must look to the place where he/she is resident or has his/her domicile (but may chose which) : if the place of residence and of domicile are not known, the court competent is that of the place of abode. If the defendant is not resident or domiciled and/or with a place of abode in Italy or if these are not known, the court which will have jurisdiction is that of the place where the plaintiff is resident.

If the defendant is a corporation, the court competent is that of the place where the corporation has its seat or where it has a plant with a representative authorised to appear before the courts. The corporation's seat is considered to be the place where its registered Memorandum of Association is, but when this place is different from the real and effective place where the corporation carries out its principal activity, then the latter may be considered as the seat of the company (*Civil Code, arts 16 and 46*).

In the case of employment disputes, the court of the place where the office/plant in which the worker is employed will have jurisdiction.

Corporations and associations without legal status are considered to have their registered office in the place where they carry out their activities on a continuous basis.

When the claim concerns an obligation, jurisdiction may be assumed, at the plaintiff's choice, also by the court of the place where such an obligation arose or was to be performed.

The jurisdiction of the criminal courts depends on the place where the crime was committed. In the case of an attempted crime, the court of the place where the last act took place prior to the intended commission of the crime will have jurisdiction.

CHAPTER 4 : ADMINISTRATION OF JUSTICE[1]

The term *"giudice"* (judge) represents the authority with jurisdiction and power to determine a given dispute and indicates, in Italian law, a single (monocratic) judge as well as a court composed of three or more members. *Structure of the court system*

The judicial system is composed of three main jurisdictions : "ordinary" jurisdiction, itself divided into the civil and criminal branches; administrative jurisdiction; and fiscal jurisdiction. There is also the system based around the Constitutional Court.

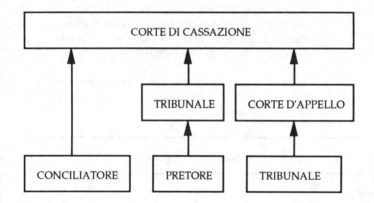

Ordinary jurisdiction

The civil courts are structured as follows, in ascending order of importance :
- the *"Giudice Conciliatore"*, who has competence only over civil matters involving sums of not more than Lit. 1,000,000. In particular, he has jurisdiction over disputes involving movables, the payment of sums of money in respect of real property, and landlord and tenant matters within the above monetary value limit;
- the *"Pretore"* (Praetor), a single judge with offices in the principal town for each district, has a general first instance competence over matters up to Lit. 5,000,000 and an exclusive first instance competence in respect of specific matters such as the recovery of possession

---

1.   Italy is in the process of enacting reforms which will introduce changes in the system of administration of justice and in the *Code of Civil Procedure*. The present survey is based on the legislation currently in force. As a result of the reforms, due to take effect as from 1993, the *conciliatore* will be replaced by the Justice of the Peace.

of real property, condemnation of new building works when there is a risk that they are unsafe or hazardous, certain summary proceedings, and actions concerning services in buildings in which ownership is held in common;

- the *"Tribunale"*, a court composed of three members, which has a general first instance competence over matters involving a value exceeding the *Pretore's* competence and an appellate jurisdiction with respect to the *Pretore's* decisions. As of 1 January 1992 the decisions of this court may also be given by a single examining judge;

- the *"Corte d'Appello"* (Court of Appeal), a court composed of several members, hearing appeals from the decisions of the Tribunale;

- the *"Corte di Cassazione"* (Court of Cassation), which may only examine and determine questions of law on appeal from an appellate decision and cannot amend the facts as already determined. It also has a special competence to determine conflicts between the various jurisdictions (ordinary, administrative and fiscal) indicating when one case falls within one or other jurisdiction, and conflicts of competence as between the various lower courts.

There is also a *"Tribunale per i Minorenni"* (juvenile court) which has competence over adoptions and the paternity of minors.

Criminal courts

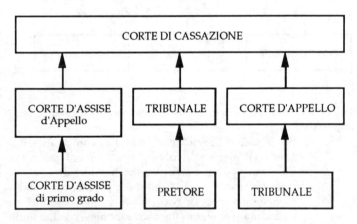

The criminal courts are structured as follows :
- the *"Corte d'Assise"* (Court of Assize at first instance), which is competent to judge the most serious crimes and, above all, premeditated homicide;
- the *"Pretore"*, who is competent to deal with cases where the penalty imposed may be imprisonment of up to four years, a pecuniary fine or both;

- the "*Tribunale*" (as criminal court), which has a general first instance competence over all crimes which do not fall within the competence of the Pretore or the Court of Assize at first instance;
- the "*Corte d'Appello*" (Court of Appeal), which exercises an appellate competence over the decisions of the Pretore, the Tribunale and the examining magistrate (*Code of Criminal Procedure, art 396*);
- the "*Corte d'Assise d'Appello*" (Court of Assize of Appeal), which has an appellate competence with respect to the decisions of the Court of Assize at first instance;
- the "*Corte di Cassazione*" (Court of Cassation), which determines principally questions of law, of competence and any conflicts of jurisdiction when recourse is made against the decisions of an appellate court.

There is also the "*Tribunale dei Minorenni*" (Juvenile Court), which exercises a general jurisdiction over crimes committed by minors.

These are structured on two main tiers :

Administrative courts

- the "*Tribunale Amministrativo Regionale*" or "*TAR*" (Regional Administrative Tribunal), which is a court of first instance; and
- the "*Consiglio di Stato*" (Council of State) which exercises appellate jurisdiction over the decisions of the Regional Administrative Tribunals.

The courts of the fiscal jurisdiction are called "*Commissioni*" and are structured in three tiers :

Fiscal Jurisdiction

- the "*Commissione Tributaria di primo grado*" (First Instance Commission);
- the "*Commissione Tributaria di secondo grado*" (Second Instance Commission); and
- the "*Commissione Tributaria Centrale*" (Central Commission).

Both the subject matter falling within this jurisdiction and the procedural rules for all the Commissioni are set out in and governed by a complex series of legislation which together form a special branch of law called "*diritto tributario*" which includes substantive as well as procedural law.

As appears from Chapter 2, questions concerning the constitutionality of legal provisions cannot be decided by the courts of the jurisdictions which have been outlined here but only by the Constitutional Court which has an exclusive competence in this field and operates within its own procedural rules. There is no right of direct recourse for private citizens to the Constitutional Court, but they may raise a question as to the constitutionality of a law in a case pending before a court of one of the jurisdictions indicated above, which in turn refers the matter to the Constitutional Court if it believes the question to be well-founded and necessary for it to determinate that case.

Effect of decisions of the Constitutional Court

The effect of a decision of the Constitutional Court is that, as from one day following the publication of its decision, a law which has been declared unconstitutional ceases to have any legal effect, not only in that case, but also in relation to pending cases as yet undecided. There is no appeal against the decisions of the Constitutional Court.

General points on appeals

The guiding principle of appeals in Italian procedural law is that the appellate court may only look at such points on which review is sought (*tantum devolutum quantum appellatum*).

An appeal to the higher courts such as to the *Corte di Cassazione*, which is called an appeal by way of recourse ("*ricorso*"), may only be made in respect of specific points of law, but not of fact.

First instance decisions, save for decisions in employment disputes, are not immediately enforceable by themselves unless specifically declared to be so in the body of that decision. Appellate decisions are always immediately enforceable. If recourse is made to the Court of Cassation, when the recourse is filed a party may ask for a stay ("*sospensione*") of the appellate decision, but this is very rarely granted.

References under Article 177 of the EEC Treaty

The procedure for making a reference to the European Court of Justice pursuant to *Article 177 of the EEC Treaty* is that provided for in the Treaty.

CHAPTER 5 : STRUCTURE OF THE LEGAL PROFESSION

The legal profession is a single unitary body which includes only *Structure* qualified lawyers to whom various titles are applied - *"procuratori"*, *"avvocati"*, *"avvocati cassazionisti"* - depending on the number of years they have been in practice, although special examinations can be taken to speed ascent up the title tree. Notaries, accountants, and others belong to separate professional associations.

Procuratori are graduates with law degrees who, having *Procuratori* completed a two year apprenticeship and passed the compulsory state examination, are allowed to represent clients in court within the district of a given Court of Appeal. There are 26 Courts of Appeal in Italy. After six years in practice, a *procuratore* becomes an *avvocato*, and is able to appear before courts throughout Italy, save before those reserved to *avvocati cassazionisti*, and are able to charge higher fees. *Avvocati cassazionisti* are lawyers who, after eight years as an *avvocato*, are allowed to appear before the Court of Cassation, the *"Consiglio di Stato"*, the Constitutional Court and other high special courts.

"Notai" - notaries - are public officers who have the exclusive *Notai* power to certify and authenticate contracts, the constitution of a company, and other unilateral acts such as gifts and wills. Some contracts, such as those for the transfer of real property, become valid vis-à-vis third parties only when certified and authenticated by a notary. Notaries form a professional group of their own.

"Commercialisti" - accountants - belong to a separate profession *Commercialisti* and undergo a training different from that for lawyers though their scope of practice includes many legal matters. They specialise in work associated with tax matters, balance sheets and book-keeping.

There are about 50,000 lawyers in Italy (7,000 in Rome, 4,400 in Milan), 5,200 *notai* and 15,000 *commercialisti*.

Procuratori, avvocati and *avvocati cassazionisti* are registered together as members of district professional bars, each one governed by a board called the *"Consiglio dell'Ordine"*. They cannot practice if they are not so registered. The *Consigli dell'Ordine*, of which there are 159, are organised and elected locally. However, national rules govern matters of ethics and fees and prohibit all forms of publicity. Disbarment is the ultimate sanction held by local bars over their members. At the head of this system is the "*Consiglio nazionale forense*" (the National Professional Bar), which acts as an advisory national Bar and also as an appeal tribunal against disciplinary decisions of the local Bars.

Advocates

As a matter of law, there is no distinction between lawyers who specialise in appearing before the courts and others who act more as advisory counsel. However, there is a *de facto* distinction in that some lawyers will do mostly court work, others will do none and others both. Another *de facto* distinction is that found between criminal lawyers, civil lawyers and administrative lawyers, but again quite a number of lawyers will practise in two or in all of these areas, especially in smaller towns.

There is no particular organisation of "litigation" lawyers. There is no such thing as a "specialised Bar" in a formal and official sense, all lawyers being members of the same common Bar, though criminal lawyers may group themselves in what is called the "*camera penale*".

Rights of audience

The *avvocati* have no right to represent clients before the courts unless they are registered also as *procuratori*. Then they have the right to defend cases throughout Italy, save before the Court of Cassation and the other higher special courts indicated above. The *avvocati cassazionisti* have the right to represent and defend clients before the Court of Cassation and the other superior courts indicated above but they can still be registered as a *procuratore* and an *avvocato* and retain the rights of audience that these lawyers have.

All lawyers have rights of audience before the lower court called the "*giudice conciliator*" and, in certain cases, before the court of the Pretore.

Legal practice

The legal profession in Italy is very fragmented. The majority of lawyers still practise in what are basically individual or family firms and larger firms sometimes suffer from a rapid turnover of members. This is mainly due to the resistance of Italians in general, and Italian lawyers in particular, to the idea of partnerships, where the *esprit de corps* of the firm has to prevail over the individual's ego and ambition. In many firms there is an assumption that sooner or later one or more partners will break away and set up their own firm, taking clients with them. However, with the increasing demand for larger-sized firms able to offer a wide range of legal expertise that the 1992 liberalisation of legal and other services is bringing, Italian lawyers will find themselves forced to group together in larger firms much against and in spite of their traditions.

There are roughly 50 "international" firms in Italy that deal with international legal transactions or local matters involving non-nationals. Their sizes range from a minimum of two or three partners with the same number of legal assistants and/or associates up to a maximum of 10 partners with about 20 legal assistants and/or associates. However, there is only one firm in Italy of this size and only about 15 have more than five partners. Some of these firms also have part-time associates, usually academics who provide specialist advice.

There are also a number of "specialist" firms practising exclusively in certain fields of law which usually comprise one experienced specialist lawyer, who will have two or three legal assistants. These firms sometimes work together with individual lawyers and/or with larger firms when their specialist skills are needed.

As stated above, there is no legal distinction between advocates and other lawyers. A partnership of lawyers cannot engage lawyers as employees because lawyers must be self-employed and responsibility in respect of work done lies always with the individual lawyer involved even when he/she is a member of a partnership. In legal matters a partnership cannot "sign" (not even in correspondence) with the name of the firm but each member must sign in his own name. Partnerships can be formed between lawyers in different parts of Italy and within the EC; however, EC partnerships will find there are certain technical and practical obstacles under national law. There are no territorial restrictions on the formation of partnerships other than restrictions to which each partner is subject commensurate with his qualifications and registration.

There are no restrictions on establishing and/or on the number of branch offices which may be set up within the state. The same can be said with regard to the Community, although the same technical and practical aspects referred to in the previous paragraph will apply. *Branch offices*

Fees are set in Italy on the basis of a "tariff" called the "*tariffa forense*" which is approved by the "*Consiglio nazionale forense*" and sanctioned by Ministerial Decree. The *tariffa* includes separate schedules of fees for in-court work and out-of-court work in the separate civil, criminal and administrative fields. The Professional Bars may be asked to give an opinion in respect of a specific bill whenever the tariff provides for a minimum and a maximum fee. But disputes as to fees are decided in the ordinary courts which will take into consideration the opinion, if any, of the Bar Association though it will not be bound by it. *Fees*

Among the "international" law firms, the practice is to apply a system of fees - especially for out-of-court assistance - calculated on a time basis, at a lesser rate for young graduates and associates, and at a higher one for the work of more senior lawyers, usually the partners of the firm. Some firms charge corporate and private clients different hourly rates and vary their charges according to the degree of technical difficulty or the risks and liability to which the firm is exposed in dealing with that work. These fees are not usually publicised by lawyers and, therefore, clients will not usually know in advance what fees will be charged.

A lawyer can charge higher fees to his client depending on the difficulty of the case and on the result, both economic and moral, of a successful conclusion to the case. A lawyer can agree with his client that, should they win, a supplementary fee ("*palmario*") will be paid, but a contingency fee basis (where the lawyer will receive no fee if the case is lost but a percentage of the sum recovered in the event of success), is prohibited.

Fees carry Value Added Tax at 19% and 2% for the Lawyers Pension Fund. However, VAT is not charged for services rendered to clients outside the EC.

Professional conduct

The professional conduct of lawyers is controlled by the Professional Bars which may take disciplinary action in the cases laid down by law and by the Bar's rules on ethics. Complaints must be filed with the Professional Bars. Anyone can use the complaint procedure.

It should be noted that professional insurance is not compulsory and is not very common.

CHAPTER 6 : CIVIL PROCEDURE[1]

The various steps in and tiers of court proceedings are laid down in the *"codice di procedura civile"* (the *Code of Civil Procedure (CCP)*) which was issued by *Royal Decree No 1443, 28 October 1940*. A very short outline of the main features is as follows :

The basic structure of court proceedings

There may be three judgments before a case is finally and irretrievably concluded. The first judgment is by a court of first instance which examines the case on the facts and the law. This decision, with the exception of decisions in employment matters, is only enforceable when the time for any appeal has passed without an appeal being filed, unless the court orders it to be immediately enforceable.

The second judgment is that given by a court of second instance (*"di secondo grado"*) which re-examines the same claim on the facts and on the law as a re-hearing where new claims are not admitted. The decision of a second instance court is always immediately enforceable. Against a second instance decision an appeal lies to the *"Corte di Cassazione"* (Court of Cassation) but only on points of law, never of fact. The notice of appeal must specifically indicate which legal rules are alleged to have been breached in the decision appealed.

When the *Corte di Cassazione* accepts that an appeal is well-founded, it cancels (in Italian *"cassa"*, hence *Cassazione*) *in toto* or *in parte* the decision of the appeal court and remits the case for a new examination of the facts to another court, at the same time laying down the principles with which the new judgment decision (*"giudizio di rinvio"*) must conform.

At first instance, and partly at second instance, the case goes through two distinct phases : the first (the *"fase istruttoria"*) which is carried out by the examining judge (*"giudice istruttore"*) who gathers the evidence submitted by the parties and takes any witness depositions; the second (*fase decisoria*) which follows on from the *fase istruttoria* is when the case is actually decided, which, in the case of the Tribunale is by all the members of the court by majority decision. The text of the decision is then written by the member of the court who acted as *giudice istruttore*. There is no jury in civil suits.

---

1.   Italy is in the process of enacting reforms which will introduce changes in the system of administration of justice and in the *Code of Civil Procedure*. The present survey is based on the legislation currently in force. As a result of the reforms, due to take effect as from 1993, the *conciliatore* will be replaced by the Justice of the Peace.

Civil law is enforced by the "*giudici ordinari*" which may be either a single judge or a pluri-member court (*CCP, art 1*).

The jurisdiction and competence of the court are settled at the beginning of the action, with reference to the claim, and cannot be changed later (*CCP, art 5*). The *Code of Civil Procedure* speaks in general terms of "*giudice*" which may refer to either a single judge or to a court, as the term *giudice* in Italian law is used as an abstract notion. First instance *giudici* are : the "*giudice conciliatore*", the *Pretore*, and the *Tribunale*. At second instance, the decisions of the *Pretore* and of the *Tribunale* are appealed respectively to the *Tribunale* and the *Corte d'Appello* (Court of Appeal). The decisions of the *giudice conciliatore* cannot be appealed to a second instance hearing, but can only be contested before the *Corte di Cassazione* on questions of law. The *Corte di Cassazione* has the primary duty to ensure the uniform and correct interpretation and application of all the legislation enacted in Italy (the duty of "*nomofilachia*"). Only the *Conciliatore* and the *Pretore* are single judge courts; all the other *giudici* are courts composed of three or more members (although in the fase istruttoria the Tribunale may act by a single examining judge).

Division of competences

Competence among first instance civil courts is allocated primarily on a territorial basis, by value and then by subject matter. The precise provisions are set out in the *Code of Civil Procedure*.

On the question of competence by subject matter, for example, for issues relating to employment disputes, social security, landlord and tenant and the recovery of real property, the *Pretura* is the principal court involved, while agricultural disputes go to the *Tribunale*. Enforcement of an arbitration award lies to the Pretore, whilst any dispute on such an award must go before the court which is competent for the value or subject matter involved in accordance with the ordinary rules on competence. It is important to note that employment disputes are dealt with by the Pretore under a special rapid procedure.

Tax questions are decided almost exclusively under the special tax jurisdiction of the fiscal Tribunals. Procedure before these *Commissioni* is governed by separate special rules.

Parties to proceedings

Proceedings may be initiated by individuals, companies, partnerships, associations of persons, trade unions, state enterprises and state agencies in accordance with the rules of civil and administrative law which set out the conditions under which a party may appear before the courts, how a party must be identified and by whom it may be represented. For example, the proper legal representative of a company is not the company lawyer but the person entitled to sign for the company and, therefore, to initiate or defend an action, whilst the lawyer who appears in court for the company is the *procuratore* (lawyer). Similarly, state agencies are represented by the minister in charge or some other official as the nominal party to the proceedings, whilst the legal representation will be taken by the "*Avvocatura dello Stato*" (State Advocates).

Anyone capable of exercising his/her rights freely has the capacity to be a party to legal proceedings. Those not capable of exercising their rights freely must be supported and assisted as provided for under the rules of civil law regarding minors or persons under mental disability.

The usual terminology to describe the party initiating a suit is the "*attore*" (plaintiff), while the party summoned is termed the "*convenuto*" (defendant). At second instance the party appealing is also called the "*appellante*", whilst the respondent is called the "*appellato*".

In a few cases (see *CCP, art 81*) a person with a particular interest of his own may set up a claim connected with the rights of another who fails to act; this is called "*sostituzione processuale*" (procedural substitution), an example of which would be a creditor who initiates an action in the place of a debtor against a third person who in turn owes money to the latter.

A basic distinction in Italian law is that drawn between rights (also called subjective rights - "*diritti sogettivi*") and interests (also called legitimate interests - "*interessi legittimi*"). As against government or state acts and actions, a private individual holds legitimate interests, but not rights. The difference is all-important since, whilst subjective rights may by protected in actions before the ordinary courts, legitimate interests may only be protected before the Administrative Tribunals. Whether one is dealing with a subjective right or a legitimate interest depends on various aspects of the particular case.

Subjective rights and interests

Where a court cannot give its judgment without a third party in the proceedings and where the decision would not be effective if it were not to have effect also as against this third person, the court will order that this third person be summoned by the interested party within a specified time (*litis consortio necessario*). This occurs usually in cases where real property rights are affected, rather than in actions for breach of obligations and contract.

Third party proceedings

In addition, any party with an interest in a case may voluntarily intervene either to support a party or to make an independent claim of his own. In a few exceptional civil cases, proceedings must be initiated by the "*Pubblico Ministero*" (Public Prosecutor), for example, to obtain a declaration of the presumed death of a person, whilst in other cases, the *Pubblico Ministero* is obliged to intervene in the proceedings for example, in cases concerning the status and capacity of persons, and in others he may intervene in proceedings when he recognises that there is a public interest to be protected. Each party to a case may also summon a third person by whom it wishes to be indemnified.

Dismissal of parties from proceedings

As a general rule a party may be dismissed from the proceedings only when the case is finally concluded.

When various cases on the same issue and facts are pending at the same time, the *Code of Civil Procedure* lays down the following rules :

- the fact that the same case or a connected case is pending abroad between the same parties does not prohibit Italian courts from assuming jurisdiction and therefore no question of suspending the action arises (*CCP*, *art 3*);
- when the same case is pending before two different Italian courts, the second court seised of the case must issue a decision declaring that there is a duplication of proceedings (*litispendenza*) and dismiss the case before it (*CCP, art 39*);
  first is pending before another court the first court - ex officio or on the application of a party - must lay down a time period with which the second case must be "united" or joined with the first (*CCP, art 40*);
- when there are more proceedings regarding the same case or a connected case pending before the same court or sections of the same court, the second court or section must issue the appropriate orders intended either to join the several actions into single proceedings, or to see that even if they are kept separate they will come before the same tribunal (*CCP, arts 39, 273, 274, 335*).

Suspension of proceedings

Proceedings must be suspended when :

- a pending criminal case may have a bearing on the possible outcome of the civil action;
- a court refers a question as to the constitutionality of a legal norm to the Constitutional Court;
- the decision of the suspending court depends on the decision in another civil and/or administrative case (*CCP, art 295*);
- a party or court submits a question on the assumption of jurisdiction or competence to the *Corte di Cassazione* (the "*regolamento di giurisdizione*" or "*regolamento di competenza*") (*CCP, arts 41 to 50*).

Proceedings may be suspended on the request of all the parties for a period of four months, but this is of theoretical value only considering the length of time ordinary proceedings take and the long delays between one hearing and another.

Class or representative actions

As a rule Italian civil law does not provide for class or representative actions except in very special cases such as labour disputes for alleged infringement of trade union rights by employers ("*condotta antisindacale*"), or for environmental pollution by industrial plants or factories. There are no special procedures provided for in such cases and proceedings follow the normal rules.

Legal aid, called "*gratuito patrocinio*" is guaranteed under *Article*   *Legal aid*
24(3) of the Constitution and is available for all civil and
commercial proceedings in accordance with *Royal Decree No
3282 of 30 December 1923.*

It consists of the right to the assistance of volunteer lawyers who
are on a special list kept by the local Bar Association. Legal fees
are not at present paid for by the state. Special committees are
set up in every civil court to assess applications for legal aid. The
conditions as to when legal aid will be granted are the following :

-     the applicant must be unable to pay the legal
  expenses (poverty), which must be proved by
  producing certificates from the public authorities; and
-     the action must be likely to succeed.

Legal aid may be requested at any time during the proceedings
and may cover all steps in the case save that a party which loses
and wants to appeal must submit a new request. The Public
Prosecutor supervises proceedings covered by legal aid and the
behaviour of lawyers appointed under the legal aid provisions.
During the proceedings legal aid can be revoked if the conditions
under which it was granted cease to apply.

Legal aid gives no exemption from having to pay lawyers' fees,
taxes, technical experts' costs and so forth.

There are special rules on the provision of legal aid in respect of
social security matters (see *Law No 533 of 11 August 1973*).

Italian law distinguishes between "*decadenza*" (time limitation)   *Rules on*
and "*prescrizione*" (prescription). One has a case of *decadenza*   *limitation/*
when a certain specific act is not carried out by a certain date   *prescription*
which cannot be suspended. One has *prescrizione* when the
holder of a right fails to exercise it within the time period laid
down by law (*CCP, art 2934*). The parties may provide for a term of
decadenza in contracts between them provided the term is not so
short as effectively to prevent the other party from acting without
facing very serious difficulties. Parties cannot modify the
applicability of the rules of prescription. The parties may,
however, refuse to take a point on *prescrizione* in the proceedings
and the court cannot of its own motion raise as an issue that
prescrizione has in fact occurred.

Even if a party does not contest a claim on the ground of
prescription, this may be done by his creditors or by any other
party with an interest.

The time limits for prescription can be suspended under the   *Time limits*
conditions defined exhaustively by *Articles 2941-2942 of the Civil
Code,* where there is a relationship between the parties, or under
special objective circumstances such as war.

The running of time for prescription is interrupted by service of a
summons, by recognition of a right asserted by the other party

and, more generally, by any claim, in writing, asking for performance by the other party.

The ordinary term of prescription is ten years from the day on which the right could have been exercised. A twenty year period applies in respect of rights over real property whilst shorter terms apply in respect of other rights such as claims for damages, payment of annuities and interest, and company matters.

A particular rule applies in employment matters so that in certain instances - specifically in the case where salaries remain unpaid - the limitation period cannot start to run while employment continues but only from when employment ends.

A claim is brought before a civil court by issuing a "*citazione*" (summons) or a "*ricorso*" (petition) in accordance with the provisions of *Articles 163, 414, 706 of the Code of Civil Procedure* .

Summons

In ordinary proceedings at first instance and at second instance a party must summon the other to enter an appearance before the court within a certain period. The period will vary depending on the distance from the court.

A summons must indicate :
- the court before which the other party must appear;
- the name and domicile of the party, and the power of attorney given to the *procuratore* (lawyer) for the defence;
- the date of the first hearing;
- the facts and the law supporting the claim;
- the claim made by the plaintiff; and
- the documents produced and the depositions of any witnesses, if so requested.

The summons, after service on the other side, is filed with the clerk to the court ("*cancelleria*") together with all relevant documents.

Ricorso

The *ricorso* is a petition to a court indicating much the same as the *citazione* except that the hearing date is not fixed by the party but will be fixed by a later ruling of the court. The *ricorso* is required for employment proceedings and in such other proceedings where the court can or must examine the matter to see whether an order must/should be issued without even hearing the other side (eg in summary proceedings in respect of very urgent matters).

After the court has fixed the date of the hearing, the petitioner must serve a certified copy of the petition, together with the ruling, on the other party within the time limit fixed by the court.

Initiation of proceedings

To initiate proceedings the papers must be filed with the clerk to the court. Certain fees must be paid when filing the summons and/or the *ricorso* with the clerk to the court.

Service of proceedings as well as service of any other paper or document in the case is effected by the office of the "*ufficiale giudiziario*" (bailiff) on the request of a party or of the Public Prosecutor or of the clerk to the court, by delivering a copy of the document to the interested party and returning the original copy to the party that requested service, with a sworn affidavit attesting that service has been effected. Service is usually by personal service but may also be made by post in cases provided for by law. Initially, service is effected directly on the other party, but after a party has entered an appearance before the court service is on his *procuratore*.

Service of proceedings

Service is effected at the place of domicile, office, factory or shop and/or wherever the other side can be found. If the residence, domicile or the place of abode of the other party is not known, service must be effected in accordance with the following rules : a copy must be delivered to his family or to an employee, or failing that to the door keeper if any. If service cannot be effected because the people mentioned above refuse to accept it, or because they cannot be found, it is effected, care of the Municipality, by leaving a notice at the door of the party and by sending him a registered letter.

Service on a company or on a corporate entity in general has to be effected at its seat or the place where its central management is, and is effected by delivery of a copy to a representative or employee of the company who is authorised to acknowledge service.

Service outside Italy is effected under the provisions of various international Conventions where applicable.

In Italian procedure there is no provision similar to that found in other legal systems for summary judgment, for failure to return an acknowledgment of service or to give notice to defend.

Entering early judgment

However, provided service of proceedings is effected in accordance with the rules for service through the office of the *ufficiale giudiziario*, a judgment can be entered on the merits where the other side does not enter an appearance, or, having entered an appearance, does not appear at the hearing. As a result, the *Code of Civil Procedure* sets out that, at the first hearing, the court must verify that service of the summons was properly effected; if it finds that service was not correctly effected, it must order new service, setting a peremptory time limit for proper service. If that time limit is not respected the proceedings are dismissed. But if service was regular, the court will, on the application of the plaintiff, rule the defendant in default and proceed to hear the case.

The defendant may enter an appearance at any time up to the hearing at which the case is dealt with. The main feature of proceedings in default is that certain documents and orders must be served on the defaulting party which in a normal case would not be so served.

Summary judgment   The notions of summary judgment, leave to defend and conditional leave to defend which are found in the common law system are unknown in Italian procedure. The notion of summary judgment envisaged in the *Italian Code of Civil Procedure* relates to quite different types of special proceedings which have in common the fact that they differ from the ordinary course of proceedings an action may take, but are actually themselves quite different from one another.

Among such summary proceedings are injunctions, interlocutory measures for the seizure of goods, and actions to protect possession of real property.   An example of an injunctive procedure is when, on the request of a creditor who submits written proof of debt, the court makes an order that the defendant pay a liquidated sum without hearing the debtor. Other forms of summary proceedings follow different rules.

Strictly speaking, an order issued in summary proceedings cannot be appealed because the party wishing to oppose it has the right either to file an opposition action before the same court that issued the order, or to contest the order by initiating ordinary proceedings within a fixed time starting from the date of service of the order. The *Code of Civil Procedure* lays down the rules which apply in each particular instance.

Striking out part   A claim may be renounced *in toto* or *pro parte* by a claimant
or all of a party's   provided the other side agrees. Proceedings may simply
pleadings   extinguish themselves when the plaintiff fails to appear after one or more consecutive hearings and the defendant does not ask the judge to proceed. However, a judge has no power to strike out a claim of his own motion.

Notions applied in other systems, such as the application to strike out a claim instead of having to proceed to a full trial when there is no cause of action or there is an abuse of process do not apply in Italian law. Likewise, there is no notion of a special authorisation having to be given by a court to permit a vexatious or habitual litigant to proceed with litigation. Such elements will, of course have a great bearing on any final decision, but there is no prior remedy of striking out provided for before that point.

Security for costs   An order for security for costs is not available under Italian law. In a few special cases a party applying for an order may have to give security (eg in cases of seizure of property, and where a party seeks provisional enforcement of an order to pay a fixed sum of money).

Interlocutory   Italian civil law does not provide a sophisticated system of
relief   interlocutory relief as may be found in other legal systems (but see those measures applicable under *Article 700 of the Code of Civil Procedure*).

Directions as to   The notion of a court hearing at which directions are given as to
the further conduct   the further conduct of proceedings does not really apply in Italy.
of the proceedings

Articles 118 and 120 of the Code of Civil Procedure state that a   *Discovery*
court may, on the application of a party, order the other or a third
party to produce a document or some other thing which it
believes is necessary to the proceedings. Likewise, under *Article
213* the court may ask the Public Administration to supply such
written information as is necessary to the proceedings. In
employment disputes, the court may also ask trade unions to
supply both written and oral information and to submit their
observations (*CCP, art 421*).

Italian proceedings are based on the principle that the task of
suppling evidence (*onus probandi*) rests with the individual
parties, and that neither party can be forced to invert the *onus
probandi*. Consequently, each party is required to disclose solely
those documents which are relevant to its own case and not those
which support an opponent's case. A lawyer is ethically required
to disclose to his client those documents which have been
disclosed to him.

Article 249 of the Code of Civil Procedure states that priests,   *Professional*
lawyers, notaries, doctors, surgeons, obstetricians, civil servants,   *privilege*
and, within certain limits, accountants and journalists can
properly refuse, on the grounds of privilege, to disclose
information acquired in the exercise of their professions. This
professional privilege can be overridden in certain cases where
the information discloses that a criminal offence has occurred.

Without prejudice negotiations and offers of settlement between
lawyers are excluded from the discovery rules outlined above.

The gathering of evidence is a task for the court and is carried out   *Evidence*
by it or under its control either by the single judge where the case
is pending before a single judge court, or by the examining judge
(*giudice istruttore*) when the case is before the *Tribunale*. As a
rule, no party can be forced to disclose evidence before trial, and
all evidence will be produced at the hearing of the case.

No party may challenge the admissibility of any evidence before
trial and hearsay evidence cannot be accepted by the court.

Evidence in the form of witness depositions can be taken abroad   *Evidence abroad*
but only by order of the court on the application of one of the
parties. The grant of such an order is never automatic. Italy is a
party to the *Hague Conventions of 1954 and 1970* on the collection
of evidence abroad in addition to several bilateral Conventions.
The deposition of an Italian citizen residing abroad may also be
taken by the Italian Consul to whom authority to do so is
delegated by an Italian court.

If a person has an interest in a case such that they might be   *Witnesses*
entitled to participate as a party in the proceedings they cannot
be heard as witnesses (*CCP, art 246*). No party can be a witness for
himself; a party may only be forced to make admissions if
questioned by the court at the request of the other party on
specific legal points or facts.

Other limitations on witnesses in the past have been declared unconstitutional by the Constitutional Court in *Decision No 248 of 23 July 1974*. Under *Articles 250 and 255 of the Italian Code of Civil Procedure* witnesses may be compelled to appear.

Witnesses are admitted by the court to give evidence at the request of the party with an interest in having their evidence heard by the court.

Special rules apply in the case of heads of state and/or of government and other high officers of the state.

Persons who lack legal capacity cannot be witnesses, but minors above 14 years of age can be heard without being sworn.

Expert evidence/reports

The court may appoint an expert when an inquiry, a report and/or clarification on technical matters are required. To be appointed by a court, experts must be registered on special lists kept by the clerk of the court. An expert's report is submitted to the court and copies are given to the parties. The expert's report is not considered as evidence in the strict juridical sense, but only as a technical help or support to the court which retains the power to examine the report critically and to assess what bearing it may have on the case. The court may also disregard it provided a proper reason is given for doing so. There are no limitations on the appointment of experts to assist the parties in the proceedings.

Final preparations before trial

The court will give its ruling after the parties have submitted their final written briefs and counter-briefs ("*comparse conclusionali*" and "*repliche*") in which they set out and recapitulate the facts and points of law they consider apply in the case.

Proceedings in court

The parties are represented in court by the *procuratori* who appear on their behalf save where the law requires a party to appear personally. The presentation of argument is in principle, by written pleadings. There may be a short oral hearing but only if specifically requested by a party.

Before the Court of Cassation, in addition to the written pleadings there are always oral arguments.

The order of proceedings is that first the plaintiff must submit his written arguments, either in the summons or the petition. Then the defendant will file his written submissions to counter the plaintiff's arguments and submissions. Final written pleadings must then be filed by the parties within a given time limit which is the same for both the plaintiff and for the defendant. Both parties then have a further equal amount of time to file a counter-brief (*replica*). There is no right to make final submissions.

If witnesses are called, they are questioned by the court following the lists of specific questions submitted by the parties and approved by the court.

The basic principles of Italian procedure are set out in *Articles 99, 112 and 115 of the Code of Civil Procedure*, according to which proceedings are to be conducted by the parties (*impulso di parte*); and except in certain cases specifically provided for by law the court must base its decision only on the evidence submitted by the parties as set out in the claim and supported by the conclusions of the parties (*no extra petita*).

The court may always take into account matters of fact which are within common experience without asking the parties to provide specific proof of those matters. The court may visit the *locus in quo*, as provided for by the *Code of Civil Procedure*, though this is not in practice commonly resorted to.

Judgments are not delivered in open court. Reasons for *Judgment* judgments must always be given. There is no provision for delivering dissenting opinions.

The general principle is that the losing party must pay the costs of *Costs* the other side. The level of such costs is specifically set out by the court and is assessed on the basis of the official scale approved by the Minister of Justice (see Chapter 5). In a typical order for costs, a party will not recover all its costs. The official tariff will indicate which costs will be charged by the court to be paid by the losing party. Costs include lawyers' fees, the general costs of preparing the case, and also court costs which, however, are relatively low when compared with the court costs of other countries.

There is no provision for making a payment into court in satisfaction of a claim.

It is difficult to estimate the average time proceedings take. *Length of* However, one can say that today court proceedings can still take *proceedings* many years, though employment disputes generally take less time. There is great pressure on the government to remedy this present crisis in the Italian courts.

The various stages and levels of appeals are set out in Chapter 4 *Appeals* above.

The average length of time between a judgment at first instance and a subsequent appeal is approximately two years. Decisions from the Court of Cassation will generally take longer.

CHAPTER 7 : CRIMINAL PROCEDURE

Preliminary hearings ("*udienza preliminare*") are initiated when the Public Prosecutor ("*Pubblico Ministero*") deposits with the clerk to the court ("*cancelleria*") responsible for conducting the criminal investigation, a request that proceedings be initiated. The court fixes the date for a preliminary hearing with a ruling which is served on the parties concerned, who must then enter an appearance. The court examines the documents and hears any applications from the Public Prosecutor and the defence, and considers which evidence has been or should be gathered. If the court is satisfied that the accused should be brought to trial, it gives a ruling indicating which charges are to be brought against the defendant. Otherwise, the court orders the case to be dismissed. *Basic structure of court proceedings*

The clerk to the court prepares the file for trial in accordance with the provisions of *Article 431 of the Code of Criminal Procedure*. When the trial date is fixed, the Public Prosecutor or the defendant or both, can ask the court to follow one of the following "Special Proceedings" ("*riti differenziati*") : *Trial*
- a summary hearing ("*giudizio abbreviato*")
- to order a penalty agreed by the parties and at their request ("*applicazione della pena su richiesta delle parti*");
- to give judgment ("*giudizio direttissimo*");
- to give immediate judgment ("*giudizio immediato*");
- to proceed by decree ("*procedimento per decreto*").

The court must ensure that the parties have been properly notified of all relevant matters. The Public Prosecutor will present the facts. Counsel for the accused ("*difensore*") presents the facts the defence intends to prove. The court issues such orders as are needed so that the necessary evidence can be gathered. *Procedure during trial*

The court of its own initiative ("*d'ufficio*") may decide whether to gather new evidence in addition to that requested by the Public Prosecutor and by the accused, and whether part or all the documents on file must be read in open court.

The final representations on behalf of the parties then follow. The Public Prosecutor and counsel for the defence have the right to make one reply only. Once the trial is declared closed, the court will give its decision immediately.

The *Pretore* : (under *Article 7 of the Code of Criminal Procedure*) is competent to deal with all offences punishable with a *Jurisdiction of the courts* maximum penalty of four years' imprisonment or with a fine or both. In addition, he is competent to deal with threats against a public officer, use of force against the latter, offences against a court, the breaking of seals, minor cases of cruelty towards a member of the family or a child, brawling, culpable homicide, burglary, aggravated theft (robbery), aggravated fraud, and receiving stolen goods.

The *Corte d'Assise* : (under *Article 5 of the Code of Criminal Procedure*) is competent to deal with crimes punishable with life imprisonment or with no less than 24 years' imprisonment (other than attempted homicide and crimes against the state provided for under *Article 630 of the Penal Code*), suicide, slavery, homicide of a consenting person, premeditated offences against the person causing death, and crimes against the state punishable with a penalty of more than 10 years.

The *Tribunale* : (under *Article 6 of the Code of Criminal Procedure*) is competent to deal with all offences that do not fall within the competence of the *Pretore* or of the *Corte d'Assise* as set out above.

The prosecution

The Public Prosecutor and the criminal police gather, on their own initiative, the relevant information and will receive all such information as private individuals or companies supply as required by law.

The Public Prosecutor is also obliged to carry out all such acts as are required under the *Code of Criminal Procedure* to instigate, initiate and prosecute criminal proceedings on behalf of the state.

A private party has no right to pursue a private prosecution, and can only bring the circumstances of a possible criminal offence to the attention of the Public Prosecutor and ask him to take action.

Information about an offence

The Public Prosecutor, before carrying out the first judicial act ("*atto qualificato*") at which counsel for the defence has the right to be present, must send by registered mail with a return receipt, a document called the Guaranteed Information ("*Informazione di Garanzia*") to the person subject to investigation. This communication is also sent to the victim. The communication indicates the legal provisions alleged to have been infringed, and the date and place of the alleged infringement. The parties are also invited to appoint counsel to represent them. Special rules apply if the addressee cannot be traced.

At all times during the proceedings the parties and their counsel ("*difensori*") can file written briefs ("*memoria*") and requests; the court is obliged to rule on such requests within a short fixed period of time.

The start of proceedings

Evidence for the prosecution is gathered during the investigation stage by the Public Prosecutor and by the criminal police, who work under the Public Prosecutor's direction. When the court dealing with the preliminary enquiry (*"giudice per l'indagine preliminare"*) has been appointed it may order further evidence to be collected if the Public Prosecutor and/or the parties so request.

The criminal police, on their own initiative, will investigate the facts and must send a written memorandum within 48 hours of an individual being made the subject of preliminary enquiries to the Public Prosecutor who will then give the instructions for an inquiry to be pursued under the direction of the court.

The individual subject to the inquiry has the right to have counsel present at court. If counsel is not present, the results of these investigations cannot normally be used later in the proceedings unless they contain spontaneous declarations.

During the preliminary inquiry (*"indagine preliminare"*) the Public Prosecutor, the person subject to the investigation and the victim can ask the court for a Special Inquiry (*"incidente probatorio"*) to be carried out. Such a Special Inquiry cannot be deferred but will not be valid if not carried out in the presence of counsel for the defence.

The stage of evidence gathering ends when the Public Prosecutor considers he has enough material on which to decide whether to file a request for criminal proceedings to be brought, thus initiating an action before the courts.

There is always a presumption that the accused is not guilty. After *Pleas* the preliminary inquiry (*"udienza preliminare"*) has been carried out by the court dealing with the inquiry, the accused can ask that the case be prosecuted under the Special Proceedings provisions : if so, the defendant will plead guilty. This will usually result from some bargaining between the accused and the Public Prosecutor.

The accused, by agreement with the Public Prosecutor, may ask *Summary* the court to conclude the case at the preliminary inquiry stage. If *judgment* the request is granted, the court will give its judgment on the basis of the existing evidence and the penalty which would otherwise have been imposed is reduced by one third.

The accused and the Public Prosecutor can agree on an *Penalty requested* alternative penalty provided by law, or on a fine diminished by *by the parties* one third, or on a prison term reduced by one third, provided the latter does not exceed two years. The accused may also ask for probation.

The other Special Proceedings (direct judgment, immediate judgment, proceeding by decree) are only available in cases of *flagrante delicto*, clear proof of guilt, and are subject to special provisions which prevent an accused from benefiting from any plea bargaining.

Juries

The jury is chosen only as part of the *Corte d'Assise* at both first and second instance (that is, on appeal). Every *Corte d'Assise* is composed of a judge who acts as Chairman, a second judge *"a latere"* and six jurors, called people's judges (*"giudici popolari"*). To qualify as a juror one must be an Italian citizen and be of good moral behaviour. Jurors must be at least 30 and no more than 65 years old. To sit as a juror at first instance, one must have stayed in education up to at least secondary school level (*"scuola media primaria"*) and to high school level (*"scuola media secondaria"*) to sit as a juror at second instance.

The provisions of the *Code of Criminal Procedure* which apply to disqualification of a judge in a particular case on grounds of incompatibility, abstention or challenge apply also to the case of jurors. The final decision on disqualify rests with the Chairman of the *Corte d'Assise*.

Both the jury and the judges determine the final verdict on the basis of one person, one vote.

Conduct of the trial

An accused has the right to appoint up to two counsel. Where the accused does not appoint defence counsel, the court *ex officio* will appoint counsel (*"difensore d'ufficio"*), chosen from the lists provided by the Bar Council (*"Consiglio dell'Ordine"*).

As indicated above, the Public Prosecutor must identify and prove the facts which constitute the offence and present the necessary proof supporting the charges. Counsel for the defence must submit any relevant evidence and ask for any witness depositions to be taken which will support the accused's case. The judge and the Chairman of the *Corte d'Assise* can indicate the elements they believe need to be proved by the parties and may order, of their own motion, that new evidence be taken.

Hearings are held in public, but, on the request of an interested party to the proceedings, the judge may order that a hearing be held *in camera* in cases involving immorality (*"buon costume"*) or where other matters must be kept secret.

If, during the hearing, an offence emerges which is different from that for which the defendant is then being tried the Public Prosecutor will amend the charge and formally notify the accused.

The verdict

The verdict is given by a majority vote immediately after the hearing has ended. If an accused is found guilty the verdict given covers not only the penalty but also other measures, called "security measures" (*"misure di sicurezza"*), where applicable.

Sentencing

The powers of the judges on sentencing are set out in the *Penal Code*. They include mandatory sentences for certain offences. There are separate rules on sentencing juveniles and persons under 18 years of age.

An accused can always appeal against a conviction. The time *Appeals* limits within which an appeal must be filed are set out in *Article 585 of the Code of Criminal Procedure*. Appeals can be raised on questions of fact as well as of law.

Recourse can be made to the Court of Cassation against a decision of a Court of Appeal, and in other special cases, on specific questions of law only.

There are many international conventions which govern relations *Extradition* between Italy and other countries on this issue.

Where no such convention applies, the *Code of Criminal Procedure* sets out the rules applicable in *Articles 697-746*.

Italian criminal law contains a series of rules dealing with the time *Time limits for* limits within which offences must be prosecuted and particular *prosecuting* procedures followed. *offences*

There are no bail provisions in Italy as understood in common law *Bail* jurisdictions.

Italian legislation is based on the principle that the personal liberty of an individual can only be restricted in the specific instances and within the specific limits provided for by the provisions of the *Code of Criminal Procedure* regarding arrest (*arts 380 to 391*) and custody (*arts 272 to 275, 280, 284, 285, 303*).

CHAPTER 8 : REMEDIES

Damages can be recovered for breach of contract and for a failure to perform an obligation (*"responsabilità contrattuale"*) or in tort (*"responsabilità extracontrattuale"*). A claim for damages is normally made before a civil court but when the claim arises out of circumstances for which the other side is being prosecuted before a criminal court (eg in cases of personal injuries) then the civil claim for damages may be filed before that criminal court under the procedure known as *"costituzione di parte civile"*. *Damages*

Damages for breach of contractual obligations can be recovered when a party has failed to render the exact performance promised, unless it is proved that non-performance or delay was due to an impossibility to perform not attributable to the defendant. *Damages in contract*

Compensation for breach of contractual obligations may be sought before any civil court (or through arbitration, if provided for in the contract) and covers the loss sustained by the plaintiff, including lost profits that are a direct and immediate consequence of the non-performance or delay.

When the obligation in question is the payment of a sum of money, interest at law at the rate of 10% is due from the day of default even if not agreed in advance, and even if the creditor does not prove any damage has been suffered therefrom.

Under *Article 2043 of the Civil Code* a person who commits any fraudulent, malicious or negligent act that causes unjustified damage must pay compensation for that damage. A person who suffers damage is entitled to seek reparation if the damage occurred because of negligence, imprudence, inexperience or a breach of the law, or in circumstances where damage was caused intentionally by a person capable of understanding what they were doing, or when the conduct of the person who caused the damage is not excusable on the grounds of self-defence or necessity (ie necessity in saving himself or others from the threat of serious personal injury). *Damages in tort*

The person injured may seek compensation for actual immediate loss and the loss of any profits.

It is always the task of the judge to award damages. Juries do not sit in civil cases. When a civil claim for damages is made in the context of a criminal case (*"costituzione di parte civile"*), it will usually be the judge who decides whether the defendant should pay damages (*"an debeatur"*), leaving the assessment of any actual sum (*"quantum debeatur"*) to be assessed by a civil court.

The judge will, if necessary, assess damages arising out of a loss of earnings according to the circumstances of the case. Where permanent injury is suffered, the judge may order reparation in the form of a life annuity, in addition to any appropriate interim orders. The judge will also decide if specific redress for the tort is possible or if redress should be simply by payment of damages in cases where specific redress would be excessively burdensome for the defendant.

In personal injury actions the quantum of damages is assessed on the basis of the above rules. There is no fixed award for different types of injury, though the courts follow different tariffs in assessing damages, among which will be a sum to compensate for the total loss or partial loss of function of certain organs as determined by a "legal doctor".

Moral damages are awarded only when loss results from a crime. In principle, damages in tort are awarded by the court on the basis of actual loss suffered and any loss of profits recoverable that the injured party will suffer. When loss cannot be established precisely, damages are awarded by the judge on an equitable basis.

If a person has been slandered he may seek compensation for loss of reputation. The level of damages is determined on the basis of the rules set out above. There is no limit, in principle, to the amount that can be recovered for slander, but the Italian courts take a very cautious line in this area.

Unjust enrichment According to *Article 2041 of the Civil Code*, a person who has enriched himself without cause at the expense of another must make restitution to the other to the extent of the undue enrichment for the financial loss suffered.

If enrichment is of a specific thing, the person who received it is obliged to return it if it still exists. The principle of unjust enrichment also applies in the case of commercial contracts.

Penalty clauses The *Civil Code* provides that parties to a contract may agree on a specific penalty in case of non-performance or delayed performance. A penalty clause has the effect of limiting one's liability for damages. The penalty stipulated must be paid even if there is no evidence of damage. If the party liable does not pay an agreed penalty, the other may bring an action to have it awarded by the courts. Nevertheless, *Article 1384 of the Civil Code* provides that the agreed penalty can be reduced by the court if the principal obligation has been performed in part or if the penalty is manifestly excessive, but in deciding this issue the court must always take into account any interest the plaintiff has in pursuing full performance.

Specific performance Where a party has failed to carry out an obligation to do something, the person entitled thereto can have that performance carried out and paid for by the other in accordance with the formalities set out under the *Code of Civil Procedure*, provided that the performance sought is generic in character.

A contract may be terminated or rescinded (i) for non-performance, (ii) for supervening impossibility, or (iii) for excessive onerousness.

Termination of contracts

When a contract provides for mutual performance, and one party fails to perform his side, the other can choose to demand either performance or that the contract be discharged reserving in any case his claim for compensation for damages.

A contract may be discharged even where an action has already been brought seeking performance; but performance may no longer be demanded after an action to discharge the contract has been brought. A defaulting party may not opt to perform his obligations after an action to discharge the contract has been brought. A contract may not be discharged, however, if non-performance by one of the parties is of slight importance as compared to the interest of the other in maintaining the contract.

In all cases, dissolution must be declared by the court, but only at the express request of the party interested, and with retroactive effect.

Where a contract provides for some eventual counter-performance, a supervening total impossibility to perform will automatically dissolve the contract. The party released may not demand performance by the other, and is bound to restore that which he has already received. When performance is only impossible in part, the other party has a right either to supply a corresponding partial performance due from him, or to withdraw from the contract entirely if he has no interest in partial performance.

According to *Article 1467 of the Civil Code*, courts may discharge a contract at the specific request of one of the parties when performance is to be by periodic instalments or by deferred performance, and extraordinary and unforeseeable events make performance by that party excessively burdensome. A party cannot seek to have a contract discharged if the supervening burden is part of the normal risk that would arise under the contract in any event. This provision does not apply to gambling contracts.

A distinction is drawn between fungible and non-fungible goods in Italian law, the importance of which is relevant in cases of specific enforcement by delivery up or by vacation of real property ("*consegna o rilascio*").

Fungibles/non-fungibles

Article 2930 of the Civil Code states that where an obligation to deliver a specific movable has not been carried out, the person entitled thereto can obtain a court order for delivery of that thing.

Equally where there is an obligation to vacate property this obligation will be enforced by the court. If the goods are generic in nature the court can order the debtor to purchase on the open market goods identical to those he was obliged to deliver (*genus nunquam perit*).

Declarations

Whenever a dispute as to a person's legal entitlement or position arises, that person may seek a declaration as to his own rights. Such proceedings ("*di cognizione*") result in a judgment declaring what the legal position or legal right in dispute is.

Winding-up of a company

Article 2448 of the Civil Code provides that a company can be dissolved in the following circumstances :

- where the time period for which it was created ends;
- where the company's object has been achieved or where a supervening impossibility preventing it from ever being attained has occurred;
- where it has become impossible to operate or where the shareholders refuse to act;
- where capital is reduced below the legal minimum;
- by a resolution of the shareholders in general meetings; and
- in any other circumstances provided for in the Articles of Association.

A company can also be dissolved by governmental decree in circumstances prescribed by law or by a declaration of bankruptcy; in such cases, special laws come into play (see the *Bankruptcy Law Royal Decree No 267 of 16.3.1942*).

The directors of companies cannot undertake any new transactions after an event bringing about the dissolution of the company has taken place The shareholders have the power to appoint liquidators unless otherwise provided for in the Articles of Association. The liquidators take delivery of the company's property and its documents and draw up, together with the managers of the company, an inventory showing the assets and liabilities of the company. After liquidation, the liquidators draw up a final balance sheet, indicating to which portion each shareholder is entitled in the distribution of the assets (*Civil Code, art 2453*).

Actions by and against public bodies

Under the provisions of Italian administrative law, any person with an interest can sue the Public Administration before the courts exercising administrative jurisdiction to obtain a ruling on the validity of an act or order of a public authority. Legal persons (for example, an association) can hold legitimate interests; therefore, they can seek the same remedies as are available to individuals.

The Regional Administrative Tribunals ("*TAR*") and the Council of State ("*Consiglio di Stato*") are competent to decide matters regarding the protection of legitimate interests and civil rights from unlawful action by the executive.

Under present Italian law, it is not possible to obtain an injunction against the public administration nor against a government minister. It is not certain how the Italian courts will react to the recent ECJ decision in Case C-213/89 *Regina v Secretary of State for Transport, ex p Factortame Ltd and Others*[1].

According to *Article 806 of the Code of Civil Procedure*, the parties can agree to submit their disputes to arbitration unless the action concerns employment relationships, the juridical status of persons, or questions relating to the judicial separation of spouses. A prerequisite, however, is that the parties must have the capacity to dispose of the rights which are the subject of that arbitration (*Civil Code, art 1966*). As a result, parties to a contract can agree that disputes arising out of a contract between them should be decided by arbitrators (*Civil Code, art 808*). Such a clause ("*clausola compromissoria*") must be made in writing.

Alternative dispute resolution

In the Italian legal system, there are no special courts in which one submits to arbitration. Special mediation and conciliation procedures are provided for but only in certain cases, such as labour disputes. Parties can always settle their action at any time while it is still pending before the ordinary courts.

1.　　Case C-213/89 *Regina v Secretary of State for Transport, ex p Factortame Ltd and Others* [1990] 3 CMLR 867.

CHAPTER 9 : MATRIMONIAL DISPUTES

A petition for divorce is filed with the court of the place where the   *Jurisdiction of the*
defendant is resident, or if the defendant spouse is not resident in   *courts*
Italy, with the court of the place where the petitioner is resident. If
both spouses reside abroad, the application can be filed with any
Italian court. In the petition, the grounds for divorce and the fact
that there are any children involved must be set out.

The judgment granting divorce will also provide for custody and
for alimony to be paid by the husband to the wife or vice-versa
and/or to the children.

Questions as to the custody of children, if not arising in the   *Custody*
context of a judicial separation or divorce, must be submitted to
the custody judge ("*giudice tutelare*") by petition. In the petition,
the petitioning parent should indicate the question on which
there is a dispute with the other parent. Further, this parent
should propose which action he or she believes is the most
appropriate for the child. The custody judge will then decide the
specific question submitted to him.

Both parents share custody of their children. Ordinary day-to-day
care and control of the child can be carried out by one parent, but
certain extraordinary transactions must be agreed jointly by both
parents. Transactions of "extraordinary management" where
parents disagree as to the best interests of the children must be
authorised by the custody judge.

Custody can continue to be exercised jointly by the parents even
after judicial separation or divorce. Normally, after divorce,
custody will be exercised by one parent only, in accordance with
any conditions laid down by the court. The right to continue to live
in the matrimonial home is normally granted to the spouse to
whom custody of the children has been granted, but the other
parent will usually be granted a right to visit and to have access to
the children. The law also provides for the alternate custody of
the children if this will be useful for the children and beneficial to
them in view of their age.

There has been much debate as to which authority is competent
to deal with questions relating to the custody of and access to
children which arise after a separation or divorce has been
granted by the courts. According to the most recent case law, any
requests for changes in custody or any disputes as to the terms
and conditions of custody of and access to the children set out in
prior divorce or separation proceedings should be submitted to
the same court that dealt with the question originally.

The law expressly provides that measures relating to custody, access and alimony may be changed only on the application of an interested party where there are good reasons for doing so.

The custody judge will only decide that the right to custody of one of the parents should be forfeited where there has been a serious abuse of custody rights or when the actions taken by the parent who has custody are inappropriate (see *Article 333 of the Civil Code*).

Divorce proceedings

There are two forms of divorce proceedings : divorce by mutual consent (which is simpler and shorter), and ordinary divorce proceedings (which take longer). Both proceedings are initiated by petition by one or both spouses. In either case both spouses must appear before the President or the court to attempt a reconciliation.

Divorce by mutual consent ("rito camerale")

A joint petition is lodged with the court ("*camera di consiglio*") by both spouses in which they set out the agreed terms and conditions regulating their economic circumstances and the custody of any children. The court then fixes by decree the date for the first hearing of the proceedings. At the first hearing, both spouses appear and, if the attempt at reconciliation is unsuccessful, the court then issues the divorce decree in the terms agreed to by the parties. If the court does not approve the terms as they affect the children, ordinary proceedings must be initiated.

Ordinary divorce proceeding

In ordinary divorce proceedings, a petition must be filed with the court by one of the spouses, setting out the grounds for divorce, any specific requests regarding any children, and any documentary or witness evidence. The President of the court then fixes by decree the date for the first hearing. The decree of the President of the court must then be served on the other spouse. Both spouses must appear at the first hearing in order to attempt a reconciliation. If he feels it necessary, the President will hear any children involved and will give a ruling, where necessary, as to any urgent and temporary measures affecting the children (custody, alimony, access) and in respect of the other spouse (regarding the matrimonial home, maintenance allowance and so forth).

These measures are temporary and can be revoked by the President or by the court at any time. Very often, however, the final divorce decree does not substantially modify the temporary measures issued by the President. At the end of the hearing, the President will allocate an "investigating judge" ("*giudice istruttore*") to deal with the case. Any documentary evidence must be produced before the *giudice istruttore* by the parties, and witnesses heard. At the end of the investigatory phase, a hearing will be held before the full court ("*udienza collegiale*") to discuss the case. Judgment will be given after this discussion hearing. The average time for divorce proceedings to run their course is not less than two years.

Emergency applications regarding custody, access, or orders *Emergency*
ousting one party from the matrimonial home are normally made *applications*
to the President of the court in the proceedings for separation or
divorce. At the emergency hearing the President will decide any
necessary urgent and temporary measures regarding the
relationship between the spouses. The procedure is the same as
for divorce proceedings. If an emergency application does not
involve separation or divorce, the matter must be submitted to
the custody judge by one of the parents, by a relative, or by the
Public Prosecutor.

Pursuant to *Article 330 of the Civil Code,* "the court can end the
right to exercise custody over a child when the respective parent
violates or neglects the duties inherent in this where there is
serious prejudice to the child. In such an event, and for good
reason, the court may order that the child be taken away from the
family home."

Article 333 of the Civil Code provides that "whenever the conduct
of a parent does not justify forfeiture of the right to exercise
custody, as provided for under *Article 330*, but appears to be in
some way prejudicial to the interests of the child, the court can,
depending on the circumstances, make such provisions as are
appropriate in the interests of the child and can also order that
the child be removed from the family home." These orders can be
revoked at any time by the custody judge.

Divorce was only introduced in Italy in 1970 by *Law No 898*. In *Grounds for*
1987, *Law No 84* reduced the period during which prior separation *divorce*
was required as a ground for divorce from five to three years.

The grounds of divorce pursuant to *Article 3 of Law No 898/1970,*
as amended by Law No 84/1987, are as follows :
1 (a) when the other spouse has been sentenced to life
        imprisonment or to imprisonment for a period of
        more than 15 years (save in the case of political
        crimes);
   (b) when the other spouse has been sentenced to
        imprisonment for any period of time as a result of
        a crime of a sexual nature or one relating to
        profiteering from prostitution;
   (c) when the other spouse has been sentenced to
        imprisonment for any period of time for the
        voluntary homicide of his/her child or for
        attempted homicide of his/her child or of the
        other spouse;
   (d) when the other spouse has been sentenced to
        imprisonment more than once for any period of
        time for serious personal injury against the spouse
        or his/her children.

2 (a) When the other spouse has been found not guilty
        on grounds of mental insanity of any crimes
        referred in 1(b) and (c) above;

(b)   when the husband and wife have been living apart for at least three years following judicial separation, as a result of a separation order, or when the husband and wife have been living apart in fact for at least two years before 18 December 1970[1];

(c)   when the other spouse has carried out actions referred to in 1(b) and (c) above although this has not resulted in a conviction because the proceedings were declared out of time;

(d)   when any criminal proceedings for incest have been closed because there was no public scandal;

(e)   when the spouse is a foreign national and has obtained abroad a divorce decree or annulment of the marriage or has remarried abroad;

(f)   when the marriage has not been consummated; and

(g)   when a judgment certifying the change of sex of one of the spouses has become final.

Grounds for separation

Before the most recent family law reforms, the grounds for separation were specifically contained in the *Civil Code* and included adultery, wilful desertion, excessive behaviour, cruelty, threats of grave injury or, criminal conviction. A great emphasis was put on the question of fault.

Under the present *Civil Code*, judicial separation may be granted for any reasons which make life in common no longer bearable or which is prejudicial to the education of any children. Separation may also be granted where both spouses apply for it ("*separazione consensuale*"). In such cases, the terms and conditions for the separation which have been mutually agreed upon - in particular those relating to custody, maintenance and access - must be ratified ("*omologate*") by the court.

If so requested by one of the parties, the separation order can establish that the grounds for separation is due to the actions of one of the spouses.

Division of matrimonial property

Unless otherwise expressly agreed between the spouses at the time of marriage or by notarial deed after marriage the general rule is that property acquired during the marriage is held under the joint ownership ("*in comunione*") of the spouses. Management of joint property lies with the husband and wife severally, except where measures of extraordinary management are called for and for disposing of property which belongs to the spouses jointly.

Separation and divorce brings the regime of joint ownership to an end. The method of dividing matrimonial property in the event of

---

1.   *De facto* separation is not a ground for divorce in Italy. In 1970, on the introduction of divorce, it was provided that *de facto* separation could be a ground for divorce if this had lasted for more than two years before 1970. It is now a provision of no practical effect.

separation or divorce depends on the legal system (joint ownership or separate property) selected by the spouses to apply during the marriage. The matrimonial home is normally given to the spouse to whom custody of the children is awarded, but the court may decide differently depending on the specific circumstances of the case.

The separation order and divorce decree may provide for a maintenance allowance in favour of one spouse and/or the children. The court sets the amount of the allowance on the basis of the circumstances for which separation was granted and the income of the spouse who is obliged to pay maintenance. A maintenance allowance is granted when one spouse has insufficient income and when separation was not due to the actions of that party.

CHAPTER 10 : PROPERTY TRANSACTIONS

A contract of sale under Italian law is a transaction with real *General* effect, because it results in the immediate transfer of the *principles* ownership of property from the seller to the buyer by the simple consent of the parties.

The transfer of ownership of movable property is governed by the *Movables* basic principle set out in *Article 1153 of the Civil Code* : he to whom movable property is conveyed by one who is not the owner acquires ownership of it through possession, provided that he acted in good faith at the moment of transfer and that there has been an instrument or transaction capable of transferring ownership. As a result, the conveyance of movables is not subject to any particular formal rules, except for movables the transfer of which must be recorded in Public Registers (such as ships, airplanes and autos). In these cases, the rules regulating the transfer of immovables and of securities and negotiable instruments will apply.

Contracts for the transfer of real property must be made in *Immovables* writing, or risk being annulled (*Civil Code, art 1350*), and must be registered (*Civil Code, art 2643*).

Registration, in general, is required so as to make third parties *Registration* aware of what the true situation is in respect of real property. *Article 2644 of the Civil Code* provides that the deeds of transfer of real property will have no effect as against third persons who have in any way acquired rights in the property on the basis of deeds which were registered earlier. Accordingly, a written contract which transfers real property will be valid as between the parties, but in order to be effective as against third parties it must be properly registered. Registration can only be effected on the basis of a public deed (ie a contract drafted by a Notary Public) or of a private deed with the signatures authenticated by a Notary Public (*Civil Code, art 2657*). Hence, in order to be duly registered, all real property transactions must be effected before or with the participation of a Notary Public. The Notary Public who drafts or authenticates a deed of transfer of real property is under a duty to register the deed in the Immovable Property Register within the shortest possible time, and will be liable in damages if there is any delay in doing so (*Civil Code, art 2671*). As a result solicitors do not typically play any part in drafting contracts for the sale of real property.

In cases involving the transfer of ownership of movable property, *Warranties* the principal obligations of the seller are to deliver the property to the buyer, and to warrant to the buyer that there are no defects in title or in the property sold. The first warranty covers cases where the thing sold does not belong to the seller, or belongs to him only partially, or is encumbered with rights of a third party. The contracting parties can extend or reduce the extent of such warranty and can also agree, subject to certain limitations, that the seller does not actually give any such warranties. Even if the parties agree to waive these warranties, the seller will still be liable if the buyer is deprived of his ownership due to the acts of the seller. Any agreement to the contrary will be void under *Article 1487 of the Civil Code*. An agreement excluding or limiting the warranty against defects in the property sold will be without effect if the seller in bad faith omitted to mention such defects to the buyer. Furthermore, *Article 1229 of the Civil Code* sets out a general rule that any agreement which excludes or limits liability of the seller for fraud, malice or gross negligence is void.

A buyer forfeits the protection of the warranties if he fails to notify the seller of defects in the thing within eight days of discovering them, unless a different time limit is agreed to by the parties or is provided for by law. Notification is not necessary if the seller acknowledged that the defect existed or if he himself concealed it. In any event, no action may be brought more than one year from delivery. A buyer who is sued for performance of the contract can always plead the warranty as a defence provided that the defect in the thing was notified within eight days from discovery and within one year from delivery to the seller (*Civil Code, art 1495*).

In addition, the *EEC Directive on product liability* of 25 July 1985[1] has been implemented in Italy by *Presidential decree of 24 May 1988*. Thus, a seller or manufacturer cannot limit liability for defective products in the circumstances set out in the Directive.

In the case of buildings or other immovables intended by their nature to last for a long period of time, if, within ten years from being completed, the work is totally or partially destroyed because of defects in the ground or in construction, or if such work appears to be at risk of destruction or reveals other serious defects, the contractor (ie the builder) will be liable to the customer and his successors in title, provided notice of the said destruction or defects was given within one year of being discovered. The rights of the customer end after one year following the date when notice was given (*Civil Code, art 1669*).

Taxation

The transfer of real property is subject to the payment of certain taxes :
    (a)   by the buyer :
- Registration Tax equal to 8% of the transfer price; and
- Cadastral and mortgage tax equal to 2% of the transfer price;

---

1.   Council Directive (EEC) 85/374 (OJ L210 7.8.85 p29).

(b) by the seller :
- INVIM, a tax on the increase in value of the real property transferred. The tax is determined by calculating the difference between the price of sale and the price of prior purchase, multiplied by the number of years of ownership in order to deduct inflation and proved maintenance expenses paid out during possession.

The law provides tax incentives to first time buyers : the registration tax is reduced to 4 per cent, cadastral and mortgages tax cannot exceed Lit. 200,000, and the INVIM tax is levied at 50% of the ordinary rate.

Under Italian law there are three kinds of charges (*"ipoteca"*) : legal, judicial and by convention. *Article 2817 of the Civil Code* provides that in the case of immovable property, the transferor is entitled to a legal charge over the immovables transferred by him, to ensure payment of the balance of the purchase price due to him.   *Legal charges*

A charge gives the creditor a right to expropriate the property to secure his claim, even against a third party transferee, and a preference as to any proceeds resulting from expropriation of the property.

When the buyer obtains a loan from a bank to purchase immovable property, the loan must be secured by a mortgage on the property.

The main steps of a typical transaction involving immovable property are as follows :   *Steps in a typical transaction*
1. The parties enter into a preliminary agreement in which they agree to execute the deed of sale of the property by a given date. In the preliminary agreement the parties normally set out the agreed price and the main terms of the deed.

2. The buyer requests a bank loan to finance the purchase and agrees with the bank the details of the Loan Agreement. The buyer and/or the bank carries out a survey on the property and asks the Notary Public to inspect the Immovable Property Register to verify that the property is free from any mortgage or other encumbrance.

3. The deed of sale and purchase is executed by the buyer and the seller before a Notary Public and, on the same day, the buyer and the bank enter into the Loan Agreement. The property is then subject to a mortgage in favour of the bank. The loan is made available to the seller as soon as the mortgage is duly registered in the Immovable Property Register. In certain circumstances the mortgage will be registered before the deed of sale is concluded. Where this happens the seller must necessarily consent to such registration.

4. The Notary Public registers the deed of sale and the mortgage. The buyer acquires ownership of the property as from the date of the deed of sale.

5. The fees of the Notary Public are normally paid by the buyer. The taxes payable on transfer are dealt with above.

CHAPTER 11 : RECOGNITION AND ENFORCEMENT OF FOREIGN JUDGMENTS

To enforce a foreign judgment in Italy it is necessary to obtain an exequatur ("*delibazione*") from the competent Italian court. The exequatur thereupon renders the foreign judgment enforceable in Italy as if it were a domestic judgment. When there are no bilateral or multilateral treaties between Italy and the state in which a foreign judgment has been issued, the rules in the *Code of Civil Procedure* will apply. Under these rules, no distinction is made between the recognition and the enforcement of judgments.

Recognition of foreign judgments

Italy is a party to the *1968 Brussels Convention* and incorporated this into domestic law by *Law No 804 of 21 June 1971*. The *Convention* entered into force in Italy on 1 February 1973. Under the *Brussels Convention* the court competent to deal with enforcement proceedings in respect of a foreign judgment is the Court of Appeal for the area where the judgment is to be enforced[1].

Under the *Code of Civil Procedure*, the Court of Appeal will grant the exequatur and declare a judgment enforceable if the following conditions are met :

Procedural rules for registering foreign judgments

- the court of the foreign country in which the judgment was given had jurisdiction over the case under the rules of Italian law governing the assumption of jurisdiction;
- the summons was duly served according to the provisions of the law where the proceedings were held, and that the time limit for appearance by the defendant was sufficient;
- the parties entered an appearance according to the provisions of the foreign law or that any default by the defendant was properly determined according to the rules of the foreign law;
- the foreign judgment has become final under the law of the place where it was handed down;
- the judgment does not conflict with another judgment which has been given by an Italian court;
- there are no proceedings pending before an Italian court relating to the same subject matter and between the same parties;

---

1.   Italy has recently ratified the *Lugano Convention* of 16 September 1988 (by *Law No 198 of 10 February 1992*), with the three Protocols and Final Act, which extends the *1968 Brussels Convention* to several other countries.

- the foreign judgment contains no provisions contrary to Italian public policy or morals.

The following supporting documents must normally be produced with the petition for the exequatur :
- a certified true copy of the foreign judgment;
- evidence that the foreign judgment has become final under the law of the foreign country (that is, is no longer subject to appeal);
- a certificate issued by the competent Italian court verifying that no judgment has been given by an Italian court between the same parties on the same matter and that there is no litigation pending between the parties relating to the same dispute;
- evidence that the summons in the foreign proceedings was duly served in the event that the defendant did not enter an appearance before the foreign court.

In accordance with *Article 798 of the Code of Civil Procedure*, the Court of Appeal, on an application by the defendant, should re-examine the merits of the case when the foreign judgment was issued in default, or where fraud or false evidence by the party enforcing is alleged, where new documentary evidence was found after judgment, where there was an error on the facts or in the event of fraud by the foreign court itself. In such an event, the Court of Appeal will review the merits of the case and, according to its findings, either grant the exequatur or give its own independent judgment.

In such cases, there is no specific requirement as to service of process and the normal rules of civil procedure will apply.

Public policy

Under *Article 797(7) of the Code of Civil Procedure*, one of the grounds for granting the exequatur to a foreign judgment is that the judgment is not contrary to "Italian public policy". According to the Court of Cassation (*No 1680 of 12 March 1984*) the concept of Italian public policy as far as recognition of foreign judgments is concerned corresponds to the "fundamental principles which characterise the social and moral structure of the country which applied during the relevant period and to the mandatory principles of the more important sets of rules". The following principles have therefore been excluded from the ambit of public policy principles : the existence of a subordinate employment relationship and related rights; the duty to produce evidence (*"onus probandi"*, *"onere della prova"*); procedural rules; and rules as to the date from which interest should accrue in favour of a creditor.

In relation to divorce, the concept has been applied by several court decisions as follows :
- when the divorce was granted on grounds substantially similar to those set out in Italian law, the judgment cannot be regarded as contrary to Italian public policy (see *Court of Cassation 1979/1395; 1978/6152; 1978/5919; 1977/3037; 1977/3040*);

- on the other hand, the courts did not grant an exequatur to a divorce order which was based on a unilateral repudiation by one of the spouses (*Tribunale di Genova 27.2.1973*).

Normally, judgments on claims for the payment of monies are not regarded as contrary to public policy, save where contrary to exchange control restrictions (*Court of Cassation 1981/4686*).

The Court of Cassation has said (*1986/4253*) that the mere fact that a foreign law and an Italian law differ does not constitute a breach of the public policy rules preventing recognition of a foreign judgment pursuant to *Article 27 of the Brussels Convention*.

The decision of the Italian Court of Appeal on enforcement of a foreign judgment may be appealed to the Court of Cassation. The time limit for an appeal before the Court of Cassation is 60 days from service of the judgment or, if the judgment is not served by either party, within one year from the date when it was published. The decision at first instance may be enforced immediately even if subject to appeal.

BIBLIOGRAPHY

List of basic texts of general interest

Antolisei, Francesco, *Manuale di diritto penale*, Giuffrè Editore, Milan, 1986-1990 (textbook on criminal law)

Azara, Antonio and Eula, Ernesto, *Nuovissimo Digesto Italiano* (27 vols), UTET, Turin, 1957 - 1975 with an updated appendix 1980-1987 (encyclopaedic digest of Italian legislation)

Brancaccio, Antonio and Lattanzi, Giuseppe, *Esposizione di giurisprudenza sul codice penale*, Giuffrè Editore, Milan (latest edn) (case law on the Penal Code)

Cordero, Franco, *Codice di procedura penale*, UTET, Turin, 1990 (Annotated Code of criminal procedure)

De Martino, Vittorio, *Commentario teorico-pratico al codice civile*, Edizioni PEM, (latest edn) (a commentary on the Civil Code)

De Martino, Vittorio, *Le leggi d'Italia*, Edizioni Giuridiche Istituto De Agostini, Novara (a systematic collection of laws which is periodically updated)

Giannini, Massimo Severo, *Diritto Amministrativo*, Giuffrè Editore, Milan (latest edn) (on administrative law)

Guarino, Giuseppe, *Dizionario Amministrativo*, Giuffrè Editore, Milan (latest edn) (a dictionary of administrative law)

Lavagna, Carlo, *Diritto Pubblico*, UTET, Turin (latest edn) (textbook on constitutional and administrative law)

Mandrioli, Crisanto, *Corso di diritto processuale civile*, Giappichelli Editore, Turin, 1989 (textbook on criminal law)

Martines, Temistocle, *Diritto Costituzionale*, Cedam, Padua (latest edn) (textbook on constitutional law)

Micheli, Gian Antonio, *Corso di diritto tributario*, UTET, Turin (latest edn) (textbook on fiscal law)

Nicolò, Rosario and Richter, Mario Stella *Rassegna di giurisprudenza sul codice civile*, Giuffrè Editore, Milan, 1990 (a survey of case law on the Civil Code)

Rescigno, Pietro, *Trattato di diritto privato*, UTET, Turin, 1987 (a treatise on civil law)

Richter, Mario Stella, *Rassegna di giurisprudenza sul codice di procedura civile*, Giuffrè Editore, Milan, 1986 (a survey of case law on the civil procedure)

Sandulli, Aldo M., *Manuale di diritto amministrativo*, Casa Editrice Jovene, Naples (latest edn) (textbook on administrative law)

Scialoja, Antonio and Branca, Giuseppe *Commentario del Codice Civile*, Zanichelli Editore, Bologna - Il Foro Italiano, Rome, (latest edn) (a commentary on the Civil Code)

Siracusano, Delfino, *Manuale di procedura penale*, Giuffrè Editore, Milan, 1990 (textbook on criminal procedure)

Vigoriti, Vincenzo, *Recenti sviluppi in tema di riconoscimento di sentenze e lodi arbitrali straniere in Italia*, Giustizia

LUXEMBOURG

Bâtonnier Louis Schiltz
Schiltz et Delaporte, Luxembourg

CONTENTS

CHAPTER 1 : SOURCES OF LAW

Luxembourg has a unitary structure of government.

The main sources of law are the *Constitution*, the *Civil Code*, the *Penal Code*, the *Commercial Code*, the *Code of Civil Procedure*, and the *Code of Criminal Procedure*.

Unitary v federal system

Treaties and multilateral international conventions under public international law need to be incorporated into the national legal system by laws passed by Parliament before they can be applied by the courts of the Grand-Duchy of Luxembourg.

Monist v dualist system

The *Treaty establishing the European Coal and Steel Community (ECSC)* was incorporated into national law by law dated 23 June 1952. The two other EC treaties establishing the EEC and Euratom, were incorporated into national law by laws dated 30 November 1957. EC secondary legislation has effect in national law in accordance with the principles of Community law as laid down by the European Court of Justice.

Application of EC law

There has been no reticence on the part of national courts in applying Community law in full.

In essence, national law is applied in the same way to foreigners as to nationals. The same rules apply as regards Community nationals. This position is set out in the following texts:

Application of national laws to foreigners

Principle of territoriality as regards laws on public order and real estate :
Article 3 of the Civil Code :
"Les lois de police et de sûreté obligent tous ceux qui habitent le territoire.

Les immeubles, même ceux possédés par des étrangers, sont régis par la loi luxembourgeoise ..."

Rights granted to foreigners - clause of reciprocity :
Article 11 of the Civil Code :
"L'étranger jouira dans le Luxembourg des mêmes droits civils que ceux qui sont ou seront accordés aux Luxembourgeois par les traités de la nation à laquelle cet étranger appartiendra."

Civil rights - Domicile
Article 13 of the Civil Code :
"L'étranger qui aura été admis par l'autorisation du Grand-Duc à établir son domicile dans le Luxembourg, y jouira de tous les droits civils, tant qu'il continuera d'y résider."

Article 7 of the Treaty of Rome :
"Within the scope of application of this Treaty, and without prejudice to any special provisions contained therein, any discrimination on grounds of nationality shall be prohibited."

Citation of foreign law in national proceedings

There is no presumption that foreign law is the same as national law. However, foreign law is regarded as a question of fact.

Evidence must be adduced either by certificate or in the manner required by the regulations and provisions of the *European Convention on information of foreign law* signed in London on 7 June 1968, and passed in Luxembourg by law on 5 May 1977, setting out the relevant provisions of foreign law and how they have been interpreted in the case law of the Supreme Court of the foreign country.

When a foreign law is in a language other than French or German, the provisions in question need to be translated for the court into French or German.

European Convention on Human Rights

The *European Convention on Human Rights* was incorporated into national law by a law passed on 29 August 1953. National courts can apply directly the provisions of and the case law deriving from the Convention.

Principles of interpretation

There are no written rules on how laws are to be interpreted. Very often courts will refer to the minutes of Parliamentary proceedings regarding the provision in question as an aid to their work of interpretation, but they are not permitted to distort the intention of the legislature where this has been set out clearly.

It is important to note that only the French text of the national law is the authentic text.

Previous decisions on questions of law are regularly used by parties before the courts but strictly speaking have no binding effect, either on lower courts or in respect of the same court which gave that previous decision.

Constitutional texts

The *Constitution* itself and all the other Codes mentioned above, which are normally published under the authority and control of the Minister of Justice, contain annotated texts which reproduce the main case law, or jurisprudence, on the specific provisions of the Codes. All these annotated texts are in French.

CHAPTER 2 : FUNDAMENTAL RIGHTS

Freedom of the individual is guaranteed by the *Constitution*. No one may be prosecuted save in accordance with the law and on the basis of what the law prescribed at the time. In cases of *flagrant delict*, no one may be arrested save on the basis of a reasoned order of a judge which must be authorised at the time of arrest or at the latest within 24 hours.

Constitutional protection of fundamental rights

Everyone shall be judged by the court pre-established to deal with his/her case (save where prior agreement exists to the contrary).

No punishment shall be provided for save in accordance with the law.

There is no Constitutional Court in Luxembourg. The ordinary courts are not competent to rule on the constitutionality of a law. However, all courts shall protect the fundamental rights of the citizen.

Judicial review of the constitutionality of laws

CHAPTER 3 : JURISDICTION OF THE COURTS

Serious crimes, such as crimes of violence, drugs, trafficking and money laundering, come within the jurisdiction of the Criminal Court. *Universal jurisdiction*

There are no restrictions on bringing actions against a state or organs of the state when they act in a purely commercial capacity. *State immunity*

Individuals must normally be sued in the courts within whose territory they are domiciled, save where provided otherwise by law. *Factors determining jurisdiction*

Corporations are to be sued at the place where they have their legal seat. They may also be sued in the courts of a place where they have a branch office.

The assumption of domestic jurisdiction by a court can be challenged on the following grounds: *Forum*
- that the court has no competence to deal with the subject in dispute;
- that the court has no competence to deal with the value of the claim;
- that the court has no competence due to the place where the matters giving rise to the dispute took place; or
- that the case is already pending before another court (*lis alibi pendense*).

CHAPTER 4 : ADMINISTRATION OF JUSTICE

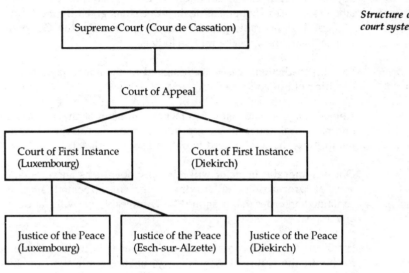

Structure of the court system

A Justice of the Peace (JP) sits as a single judge in civil cases, commercial cases and minor criminal offences and in cases of employment disputes (here the JP is assisted by two lay assessors). *Justices of the Peace*

Appeals against judgments of the Justice of the Peace are dealt with by the Court of First Instance. In the case of employment disputes, however, appeal is direct to the Court of Appeal.

There is no appeal available in cases dealing with claims where the value in dispute is less than 15,000 LUF.

Except for labour law cases, landlord and tenant cases and damage claims arising in criminal proceedings (for all of which there is no upper limit), the Justices of the Peace have no jurisdiction over claims where the value in dispute exceeds 100,000 LUF. This limit may be raised in the near future to 200,000 LUF.

The Courts of First Instance are courts of three judges who have jurisdiction : *Courts of First Instance*
- over civil cases,
- over commercial cases,
- over criminal cases. In criminal cases, this court sits either as a *"tribunal correctionnel"* or as *"chambre criminelle"*, the latter for serious offences,

> \- as an appeal court from judgments given by the Justices of the Peace.

Appeal from the Court of First Instance is normally available in all matters as of right, except where the Court of First Instance sits as an appeal court.

Court of Appeal   The Court of Appeal sitting as a court of three judges hears appeals in civil cases, commercial cases, criminal cases and labour law cases. In appeals against decisions given by the Court of First Instance sitting as a *chambre criminelle*, the Court of Appeal hears the appeal with five judges.

For all jurisdictions, cases are assigned to chambers having that specific field of competence.

Appeals   Appeals may be made either on fact or on points of law, including on procedural issues. If an appeal is permitted as to the value in the dispute, there is no need to obtain leave to appeal.

Once an appeal is made, it will normally operate as an automatic stay of proceedings unless the judgment appealed against contained an order that it should be enforceable notwithstanding any appeal.

Where a judgment contains an order that it is to be enforced forthwith the Court of Appeal may, on the application of the appellant, suspend execution until after the appeal has been heard.

The Court of Cassation   Recourse may be made to the Court of Cassation ("*Cour de Cassation*"), a court of five judges, only on points of law including procedural issues, division of competences and so forth. The Court of Cassation is not permitted to review issues of fact. In addition, recourse to the Court of Cassation is permitted only in respect of judgments against which no other remedy is available.

The remedy of "*cassation*" is possible not only against judgments given by the Courts of Appeal, but also in the following cases :

> \- against judgments from the Justices of the Peace, where no appeal is possible because the value in dispute is too low;
> \- against judgments given by the Courts of First Instance when sitting as an appeal court against judgments of the Justices of the Peace.

Administrative Court   The Administrative Court ("*Comité du Contentieux du Conseil d'Etat*"), which sits in chambers of five judges, is competent to deal with all disputes relating to the acts or omissions of the public administration.

Save where otherwise provided by law, this court has jurisdiction only on points of law, unless the law covering the dispute provides that the *Comité du Contentieux* shall also sit as a Court of Appeal which is competent to review the facts.

There is no appeal against judgments of the *Comité du Contentieux*.

A Social Security Council sits as a first instance tribunal, composed of one professional judge and two lay assessors, able to hear all disputes on social security. *The Social Security Council*

The Social Security Supreme Council ("*Conseil Supérieur des Assurances Sociales*") is competent to hear appeals against judgments given by the Social Security Council. This appeal court is comprised of three professional judges and two lay assessors.

The procedure of these two Councils is governed by the *Arrête grand-ducal of 13 October 1945* (as amended). There is always a right of appeal to the Court of Cassation against judgments given by the Social Security Supreme Council.

Article 177 references can be made from all national courts without special requirements. *References under Article 177 of the EEC Treaty*

For the purposes of *Article 177(3) of the EEC Treaty*, the *Cour de Cassation* and the *Comité du Contentieux du Conseil d'Etat* are regarded in Luxembourg as courts against whose judgments there is no further appeal.

References can be made to the Benelux Court of Justice in respect of matters of law common to the Benelux countries. The procedure follows a similar line to that which applies in respect of *Article 177 of the EEC Treaty*. The relevant articles are to be found, not in the *Benelux Treaty* itself, which goes back to 3 February 1958, but in an additional *Treaty of 31 March 1965 establishing the Benelux Court of Justice*. *References to other courts*

CHAPTER 5 : STRUCTURE OF THE LEGAL PROFESSION

The legal profession is divided into the profession of "*avocats*" and that of notaries.

Structure of the legal profession

The profession of *avocat* is regulated by the *Law of 10 August 1991*. The profession of the *avocat* has a monopoly on drafting legal documents and giving legal advice on a regular basis and for remuneration, save where the law otherwise provides.

Notaries have special public duties particularly concerned with the preparation of formal documents for the transfer of land. They are qualified to certify all original deeds, contracts and documents and to ensure their retention as official documents.

Professional groups other than the *avocat* are not prohibited from providing legal advice, but may do so only insofar as that advice can be said to be part of what that profession is required to do or as an adjunct to their main professional obligations.

These groups are, principally, notaries, chartered accountants, auditors and tax advisers, economic advisers and patent attorneys.

In-house company lawyers may give their employers any legal advice required in the course of their duties and deal with all legal matters necessary to, and directly linked with, the activities of their employer. They are not, however, members of the Bar, and therefore can not appear in court, even for their employer.

Within the Bar, there is no group of lawyers who specialise in appearing before the courts, and all members of the Bar have the right to appear before the courts.

Avocats

All members of the Bar have full rights of audience before all jurisdictions. The right of representation is, however, only open to those members who have completed the three-year training period and successfully passed the final Bar examinations.

Professionals' rights of audience

Representatives of relevant professional organisations and of trade unions may represent or assist their members before the Social Security Council and the Social Security Supreme Council.

Chartered accountants and auditors may represent or assist their clients before the courts where tax matters are directly in issue, for example, before the *Comité du Contentieux du Conseil d'Etat*.

Legal practices

Luxembourg lawyers are allowed to form partnerships with each other, but partnerships with non-lawyers and otherwise multi-disciplinary practices are prohibited.

Partnerships of lawyers can employ foreign lawyers as well as local lawyers and there are no territorial restrictions on partnership practices being formed either within the country or within the European Community.

Branch offices

Within Luxembourg, a lawyer may be a member of only one legal practice. Branch offices are not permitted. Luxembourg law, however, does not restrict the formation of branch offices within other parts of the Community.

Fees

When deciding what level of fees to charge a lawyer should take into account the importance of the case, the difficulty of the case, the result obtained and the financial circumstances of the client.

Clearly, as these criteria may alter as the case develops, the client will know in advance only an approximation of the fees that will have to be paid at the end.

If there is a dispute over fees, the client may appeal to the Bar's professional body : the *"Conseil de l'Ordre"*. This body will review the complaint and the lawyer's file. If it feels that the fees charged are excessive, it will reduce them to a reasonable amount.

Fees may be charged on an hourly rate, and all carry VAT, currently at 6%.

Professional conduct

Professional conduct is regulated by the *"Bâtonnier"* (head of the Bar) and the *Conseil de l'Ordre*.

Where through misbehaviour or misconduct a lawyer has infringed the professional rules of the bar the *"Conseil disciplinaire et administratif"* will be responsible for deciding which penalty should be applied in the case. This *Conseil* is completely separate and independent from the *Conseil de l'Ordre*. However, it is the *Conseil de l'Ordre* or the public prosecutor who have to bring the case before the *Conseil disciplinaire et administratif*.

An appeal can be lodged against the decisions of the *Conseil disciplinaire et administratif* to the *Conseil disciplinaire et administratif d'appel*.

Complaints about legal services provided by lawyers may be filed with the *"Bâtonnier de l'Ordre des Avocats"* in Luxembourg (for members of the Luxembourg Bar) or in Diekirch (for members of the Diekirch Bar). Foreign clients may use the complaints procedures, too.

In general, practising lawyers are covered by professional indemnity insurance, but this is not yet compulsory. The new law regulating *avocats* authorises the *Conseil de l'Ordre* to lay down rules on this subject, and one may assume that there will soon be compulsory professional indemnity insurance.

A distinction is drawn between EC qualified lawyers and non-EC qualified lawyers.

Practice by foreign lawyers

EC lawyers may provide legal services under the *Lawyers' Services' Directive of 22 March 1977*[1], facilitating the effective exercise by lawyers of their freedom to provide services.

They may also join the Luxembourg Bar under the conditions laid down for nationals "by the law of the country where such establishment is effected...", in accordance with *Article 52(2) of the EEC Treaty*.

Finally they may exercise their right of establishment in accordance with the *Diplomas Directive of 21 December 1988*[2] on the mutual recognition of diplomas, after having successfully passed an aptitude test.

Lawyers working for business corporations in Luxembourg cannot become members of the Luxembourg Bar, and may only give legal advice in matters directly linked with the activities of their employer.

Non-EC lawyers are not normally admitted to the Luxembourg Bar. However, the *Conseil de l'Ordre* may accept a non-EC lawyer as a member of the Bar where his/her home country grants reciprocal rights to Luxembourg nationals. In such cases the *Conseil de l'Ordre* has to ask for a non-binding opinion from the Ministry of Justice on the case.

Normally lawyers are instructed directly by clients.

Instructing lawyers

Litigants may represent themselves before the Justices of the Peace in all matters; before the Court of First Instance only in criminal cases, landord and tenant cases and commercial claims; before the Court of Appeal only in criminal cases; before the Social Security Council and the Supreme Social Security Council and before the *Comité du Contentieux du Conseil d'Etat* where tax disputes are directly at issue.

In all other cases, the services of a lawyer are required by law.

There is no directory for legal services, except the general annual roll of lawyers which provides only the names and addresses of all the members of the Bar in order of seniority.

Directory of legal services

---

1.   Council Directive (EEC) 77/249 (OJ L78 26.3.77 p17).
2.   Council Directive (EEC) 89/48 (OJ L19 24.1.89 p16).

The Bar holds lists which indicate which lawyers have stated a "preferential field of activity". These lists can be provided on request.

CHAPTER 6 : CIVIL PROCEDURE

The civil procedural rules are contained principally in the "*Code de procedure civile*" (*Code of Civil Procedure*) published by the Ministry of Justice.   *Basic structure of court proceedings*

Other procedural rules for particular courts apply as follows (see also, *Law of 7 March 1980* on the organisation of Justice (*Lois Speciales v Organisation Judiciaire, p5*)) :   *Division of competences*
-   the *Law of 27 August 1987, arts 21 to 30* dealing with procedure before the Justices of the Peace when landlord and tenant disputes are involved;
-   the *Law of 6 December 1989* on the jurisdiction to deal with employment disputes (heard by a Justice of the Peace with two lay assessors);
-   the *Arrête grand-ducal of 13 October 1945* on the competence and organisation of and procedure before the Social Security Council and the Supreme Social Security Council.

Individuals are able to bring proceedings without restriction before all civil courts. Companies, partnerships, associations of persons, "*collectives*", and interest groups can only be parties before courts when they possess legal personality. Minors and incapable adults must be legally represented.   *Parties to proceedings*

Parties in civil proceedings are identified by their name, address, and in criminal cases, also by their date and place of birth.

Non-physical persons must be identified by name, address of seat and registration.

The public prosecutor ("*procureur*") normally initiates proceedings before the criminal courts. Individuals can do so in some cases, and are always allowed to bring claims for damages in criminal proceedings in respect of criminal actions which have caused them injury.

The public prosecutor can also intervene in civil proceedings. In some civil cases where a question of public interest is involved the public prosecutor must do so. Before the *Cour de Cassation* he must always deliver written pleadings.

No civil action can be brought against a head of state, because of the immunity attached to that office. No action can be brought against a foreign sovereign state or its representatives with   *Heads of state* diplomatic status. However, there are no limits on bringing proceedings against government or state enterprises insofar as they were acting in a commercial capacity.

Joinder of cases   Where two or more cases are pending before the courts of the same jurisdiction, and one or more parties consider they are linked, such parties may request that the court deliver only one judgment which will cover the relevant cases.

Joinder of parties   To join new parties to existing proceedings, the applicant (who
to proceedings   may be either the plaintiff or the defendant) must notify the new parties that it is proposed that they be joined.

Dismissal of   A party may be dismissed from the proceedings if the court
parties from   considers that that party has no interest whatsoever in the
proceedings   outcome of the proceedings, or if the proceedings filed by a party are considered to be void for some procedural reason.

In all civil and commercial cases involving claims for damages for personal injury, the plaintiff must inform the relevant social security authority of the claim by the bailiff, in order to allow the authority to join in the claim for its own expenses. A copy of the claim has to be notified, too.

Class or   Class or representative actions are exceptional, but are possible
representative   though only under certain circumstances in environmental and
actions   consumer protection law.

Otherwise, the old French maxim prevails : *Nul ne plaide par procureur.*

Legal aid   The legislation on legal aid goes back to the Nineteenth Century and is currently under review.

Legal aid in Luxembourg is not a right guaranteed by the Constitution.

Rules on   The normal limitation on time for instituting proceedings
limitation periods   (*"prescription"*) is 30 years; see *Article 2262 of the Civil Code.*

The main exceptions are as follows :
- ten years for claims relating to trade between businesses, merchants and between merchants and non-merchants (*Commercial Code, art 189*);
- ten years for claims against architects and building contractors insofar as the foundations or the solidity of the construction are concerned (*Civil Code, art 2270*; two years, when proceedings are instituted on any other basis);
- three years for claims concerning non-payment of salary (*Civil Code, art 2277*);
- three years for claims based on an insurance contract, instituted by the insured against the insurance company.

The normal period of time may under certain circumstances be interrupted or suspended. A writ of summons, for example, will interrupt the time period running.

Prescription is suspended in favour of minors and persons declared incapable.

The rules of prescription do not apply in proceedings between spouses.

Most actions are started by a writ of summons, called a *"citation"*, when the action is brought before the Justice of the Peace; and *"assignation"* when the action is brought before the Court of First Instance, or before the Court of Appeal. These are served on the defendant by the bailiff by personal service. In proceedings dealt with by the Justice of Peace, service is effected by the bailiff, but by post. *Initiating proceedings*

In all civil matters which come before the Court of First Instance papers must be filed by a lawyer. The same applies to all matters on appeal which are brought before the Court of Appeal and in the case of appeals against judgments given by the Justice of the Peace before the Court of First Instance, except in landord and tenant cases.

In labour law cases (at first instance); landlord and tenant disputes (at first instance); social security cases (at first instance and on appeal) proceedings are not started by a writ of summons served by the bailiff, but by a petition lodged at the court registry. This petition is then served on the defendant by a registered letter from the clerk of the court.

For the purpose of the running of time actions are deemed to have been started on the date when a writ of summons is served by the bailiff on the defendant. Where a petition is lodged at the registry of the court, time runs from the date the petition is lodged.

The fees for the services of a bailiff must be paid by the plaintiff in accordance with a set scale of charges. Where proceedings are initiated by lodging a petition at the court's registry, no fees are payable.

Service of proceedings must be effected in accordance with the following rules : *Service of proceedings*

In cases involving individuals the bailiff should serve proceedings on the person. If this is not possible, the bailiff must serve proceedings at the domicile of the defendant, if known, or alternatively, at the residence of the defendant by delivering a sealed copy of the writ of summons to a person present at that address.

If there is no one present at the defendant's residence, the bailiff must leave a sealed copy at the place of domicile or at the residence as above and the following day send another copy to the defendant by normal post.

Where the defendant is a non-physical person the following rules apply :

-   In the case of service of proceedings on the state : service must be made on the Minister of State who is the President of the Government;
-   In the case of service of proceedings on public institutions : service must be effected on the person qualified to appear on their behalf as their representative before the court;
-   In the case of actions against local government : service must be made on the mayor;
-   In the case of companies, non profit-making associations and institutions of public interest : service must be made on the person or organ qualified to represent them before the court. Service must furthermore be effected at the registered office or on the person in charge of the management of the respective body.

Service out of jurisdiction

The rules relating to service of proceedings on parties out of the jurisdiction are that service is to be effected in accordance with the manner agreed between Luxembourg and the country of domicile or residence of the addressee. If there is no agreed manner for service, the bailiff sends a copy of the writ of summons by registered mail with a delivery note to the place of domicile or residence of the addressee in the foreign country. If the foreign state in question does not allow for service of proceedings by mail, the bailiff must send a copy of the writ of summons by registered mail with a delivery note to the Ministry of Foreign Affairs. The latter serves the proceedings on the addressee through diplomatic channels.

Service is deemed to have been effective on the day the letter is delivered at the Post Office/day of posting at the Post Office or the day on which any other procedure agreed has commenced.

Service of proceedings in foreign countries must be effected by a certain time before the date the defendant is invited to appear before the Luxembourg Court. The time limits are eight days in the case of those who have their domicile in Luxembourg This delay is extended as follows : a further 15 days in the case of Belgium, France, Monaco, the Netherlands, Germany, Switzerland and Liechtenstein; one month in the case of those who live in another European country including Cyprus and Turkey, but not including the Republics of the former Soviet Union; three months in all other cases.

There are no specific national rules governing service of **Brussels** proceedings under the *Brussels Convention on Jurisdiction and* **Convention 1968** *Enforcement of Judgments in Civil and Commercial Matters 1968.*

Where a writ of summons or the equivalent is to have been served on a person domiciled or residing abroad and that person does not appear before the court on the date specified the judge shall suspend the proceedings unless there is evidence (a) that service was effected in the manner prescribed by the law of the home state of the addressee; or (b) that the writ of summons was effectively handed to the defendant; and that, in both cases, service or delivery of the writ of summons has been carried out sufficiently in advance of the date of the hearing to allow the defendant to prepare his defence.

Notwithstanding the aforementioned rules, the court may **Judgment in** determine the case on the merits where the following applies, **default** even if there has been no acknowledgment of service :

(a)   if the writ of summons or equivalent act has been transmitted in accordance with one of the methods agreed in an international convention or with one of the methods allowed for service abroad under Luxembourg law;

(b)   if a sufficient delay, determined at the courts discretion, has passed since the date the writ of summons was sent from Luxembourg;

(c)   if, notwithstanding all enquiries made upon the authorities or competent services of the state of the addressee, it has not been possible to obtain an acknowledgment of service.

In cases of urgency the court may, notwithstanding that the rules of service have not been complied with, grant provisional or preservation measures and order that those measures be provisionally enforceable. In such cases the court has a discretion whether or not to order the party in whose favour the order has been made to lodge security for damages which the other party may suffer from the grant or the provisional or preservation measures.

Where judgment in default has been entered against a defendant domiciled or resident in a foreign country, he may be relieved of the consequences of the expiry of the time limit for filing acknowledgment and intention to defend the proceedings if he proves that, through no fault of his own, he did not have any knowledge of the judgment or that he was unable to act in good time to give notice that he intended to defend the proceedings.

An application to set aside judgment can be ruled inadmissible if it is not filed within a reasonable time after the defendant received notice of the decision, or after any impossibility of acting has come to an end. The court determines what constitutes reasonable delay for these purposes.

An application to set aside judgment filed more than one year after service of the decision will be held inadmissible.

After effecting service the bailiff must draw up a report in which he sets out in detail the enquiries made by him to find the addressee. The same day, or at the latest, the following business day, he shall send to the last known address of the defendant by registered mail with a delivery form, a copy of the act and a copy of the bailiff's report. A second letter must also be posted on the same day by ordinary mail.

Service is then deemed to be effective as of the day of the aforementioned report which must state that the two kinds of letters have been correctly posted.

These formalities also apply to non-physical persons, such as companies or associations which have no known registered office.

If, notwithstanding compliance with all these formalities, the defendant still does not appear before the court, the court may, in addition to and before adjudicating on the merits of the case, order notice of the proceedings to be published in a Luxembourg or foreign newspaper. The court may also order of its own motion that other enquiries be made, but at the same time may grant all provisional preservational measures necessary to protect the rights of the plaintiff.

Entering early judgment

Save in the cases mentioned above where the court can delay a hearing on the merits of a case, the plaintiff can enter judgment in default if :

    (a)   the defendant does not appear before the court on the appointed date, either in person or through a lawyer;

    (b)   the defendant has not instructed a lawyer in due time where the writ of summons has not been served for a fixed date, ie indicating of the date of the hearing.

These rules apply in all civil cases and in all appeal matters, save where expressly stated to the contrary.

The time limit for instructing a lawyer is eight days for residents in Luxembourg, but this is extended in the case of defendants domiciled or residing abroad by the same periods as apply in the case of service of proceedings.

Entering summary judgment

Summary judgment is governed by *Articles 806 to 811(2) of the Code of Civil Procedure*. It is given not by three judges as is usual in civil cases where the value of the claim exceeds 100,000 LUF, but is granted only by the President of the Court of First Instance or a deputy judge sitting as a single judge.

The following cases come within this jurisdiction :

In all urgent matters, the President may grant all emergency orders required in the case when no serious defence or contest is raised.

When there are any difficulties in enforcing a judgment the President will deal with them.

He may also grant all precautionary measures or order any relevant reinstatement to obviate an immediate danger or to terminate an evidently illegal action.

To avoid evidence disappearing he may order that all relevant enquiries and investigations be carried out; the President may also order that evidence be gathered.

When there is no serious dispute in respect of an obligation owed by the defendant, the President may allow part of or even the full amount of the claim to be entered in favour of the plaintiff.

All judgments which come within the summary procedure are immediately enforceable notwithstanding that they may be set aside at a later date.

An application to set aside summary judgment can be lodged before the same court within 8 days from when service of the decision is effected.

An appeal before the Court of Appeal can be lodged within 15 days from service of the decision. These remedies do not operate as a stay of execution, however, and immediate enforcement follows normally without any security having to be given by the plaintiff. There are no procedural rules in Luxembourg law for the grant of "leave to defend" or "conditional leave to defend" on an application for sumary judgment.

Issues of no cause of action, no defence and a failure to prosecute are normally dealt with by the court judge after he has heard the merits of the case. *Striking out part/all of a party's pleadings*

Articles 166 and 167 of the Code of Civil Procedure deal with the issue of security for costs. All foreign parties, whether plaintiffs or interveners, are obliged, on the application of the defendant, to give security for costs and damages. This request must be made before all other pleadings. The actual level of security ordered is within the discretion of the court but will normally be related to the estimated future cost of the litigation. *Security for costs*

No security will be ordered :
- if the defendant has sufficient real estate in Luxembourg;
- in all commercial cases where the defendant is a national of the contracting states to the *International Convention of Civil Procedure signed in the Hague on 1 March 1954.* Practically speaking the maxim *"cautio judicatum solvi"* has fallen into abeyance in Luxembourg.

Interlocutory relief

Save for the following cases, interlocutory relief is not normally available under Luxembourg law.

There is no "Summons for Directions" procedure in Luxembourg, but there is a proposal from the Ministry of Justice now under consideration to introduce what in French civil procedure is called *"le juge de la mise en état"* or *"le juge chargé de suivre la procédure"* who can give instructions and issue directions to the parties as to the conduct of the proceedings.

Discovery

The rules governing the disclosure of documents are set out in *Articles 188 to 192 of the Code of Civil Procedure.* In principle, each party has to disclose all documents which support his case. Initially, documents supporting one's opponent's case need not be disclosed (but see below).

Any documents disclosed must be shown to the parties and to the court. Lawyers are not only allowed but obliged to disclose to their clients documents which have been disclosed to them by lawyers for the other side.

If a party wishes to use a document in the possession of a third party who is not involved in the proceedings, he may file a petition with the court to have that document disclosed. If the court grants the petition it orders disclosure of the relevant document. This decision is provisionally enforceable, but the third party concerned can appeal against the decision.

The same applies if one of the parties requests that a document in the possession of the other side be disclosed.

Legal professional privilege

As documents do not belong to the lawyers but to the clients, there is no legal professional privilege which can be raised to refuse disclosure of documents. However, legal advice given by lawyers to their clients is subject to professional privilege and cannot be disclosed.

Discussions and documents passed between opposing sides assisted by lawyers, as well as "Without Prejudice" or "Confidential" correspondence passing between lawyers cannot be brought to the attention of the court unless a final settlement results from the negotiations. Without prejudice correspondence passing between lawyers must not be shown to the clients without permission of the sender.

Gathering of evidence

Evidence is, in principle, to be gathered by the parties without the benefit of discovery.

Once the system of a *"juge de la mise en état"* is installed, the court will have a supervisory role in the gathering of evidence.

The admissibility of documentary evidence may be challenged on the grounds that the disclosed document is *"res inter alios acta"* or on the ground that the documentation is false, in which case the party seeking to have it excluded has to challenge on the grounds of forgery.

Hearsay evidence is not admitted.

When evidence is to be taken from witnesses living outside Luxembourg, the court may either of its own motion or on the application of one of the parties order that evidence be collected from those witnesses through a rogatory commission. *Taking evidence abroad*

The Hague Convention on the Gathering of Evidence Abroad of 18 March 1970 is part of national law.

In civil cases, if the value of the claim exceeds 100,000 LUF evidence by witnesses is not admissible to prove a legal transaction. *Witnesses*

All physical persons may be called as a witness, save those persons declared incapable to appear as a witness before a court. In divorce cases the descendants of the parties are legally incapable to appear as witnesses.

Immediate relatives and persons related directly by marriage may refuse to appear as a witness. The head of state and children under a certain age within the discretion of the court may not be called.

Apart from these exceptions, witnesses who do not appear before the court when called are to be called again at their own cost. Those who do not appear or when present refuse to testify can be fined up to an amount between 2,000 and 100,000 LUF.

If a court decides that, in order to reach a final judgment, it needs advice on technical issues arising in the case, it may appoint an expert to assist the court. *Expert evidence/reports*

The court may appoint any person of its choice. There is no need for any prior court approval, although there is a list of experts in different fields who have been approved by the courts which can be used as guidance.

Before an expert report can be used in court or before an expert may give evidence in court, his report must be handed over in good time to all parties or their legal advisers.

There are no specific provisions on final preparations before trial under Luxembourg law. *Final preparations before trial*

Before all jurisdictions, the presentation of argument is a mixture of written pleadings and oral argument. The initial writ of summons is regarded as a written pleading. *Proceedings in court*

There is normally no time limit for oral argument, but the court may stop an oral presentation which it regards as excessively lengthy.

The normal order of proceedings is as follows : the plaintiff presents his case first, followed by the defendant, then by any intervener. Each of the parties is given an opportunity to reply. There are no special rules governing summing up.

Witnesses do not give evidence before the whole court if it sits in a chamber of three but do give evidence before the single judge in charge of the legal enquiry. They are questioned only by the judge, but the parties or their representatives may ask questions through the judge.

The decision to call witnesses or to visit the *locus in quo* is to be made by the whole court in an interlocutory decision. The visit to the *locus in quo* is made either by a single judge of the chamber hearing the case or by the whole chamber.

Judgments

Judgments must be given in open court with full reasons. There is no legal time limit within which judgments must be given, save the "reasonable time limit" under *the European Convention of Human Rights*.

No dissenting opinions are given.

Costs

Article 130 of the Code of Civil Procedure states that the losing party must bear the costs of the action in full (its own costs and those of the other party), save where otherwise provided for in the costs order, in accordance with a fixed scale, unless the court decides otherwise by a special and well founded decision. A court may also apportion costs where each party loses some part of its applications.

In respect of interlocutory judgments costs are always reserved and they follow the result of the case as finally determined.

In a typical order for costs, a successful party will recover all its costs. These costs do not include lawyers' fees nor the general costs of preparing for the case, but only the court costs which include all costs charged by bailiffs, and all enforcement costs.

Exceptionally under *Article 131(1) of the Code of Civil Procedure*, if a court feels it is unjust to make a party pay those expenses not normally included in the order of costs (including lawyers' fees), it may order the other party to pay these costs or part of them.

A court may order that certain costs thrown away should be paid by *avoués* or bailiffs, where they did not correctly carry out their duties.

If a party offers to pay a certain amount in satisfaction of a claim and damages awarded later do not exceed the amount previously offered, then the other party must pay the costs from the date of the offer, or even all the costs.

Offers of payment in satisfaction

At present the average length of proceedings is 18 months for civil cases, and 10 to 12 months for commercial cases.

Length of proceedings

The average length of time between completion of the preliminary stage and trial is 12 to18 months in civil cases, and 6 to 9 months in commercial cases.

Appeals are allowed on issues of fact and/or law (see above for the appeal structure).

Appeals

The average time between a judgment given at first instance and a judgment given by the Court of Appeal is between 12 to 24 months.

CHAPTER 7 : CRIMINAL PROCEDURE

There are four levels of criminal courts. The lowest is the "*tribunal de police*" which has jurisdiction to deal with all minor offences called "*contraventions*", such as traffic offences not causing personal injury. There is a *tribunal de police* in Luxembourg, in Esch-sur-Alzette and in Diekirch. *The basic structure of court proceedings*

The second level is the "*tribunal correctionnel*" which has jurisdiction over all other offences not falling within the jurisdiction of the *tribunal de police*; and over crimes. When hearing accusations of crimes, the *tribunal correctionnel* is called the "*chambre criminelle*".

Appeals against judgments of the *tribunal de police* also fall under the jurisdiction of the *tribunal correctionnel*. There is a *tribunal correctionnel* in Luxembourg and another one in Diekirch.

Under the age of 18, juveniles and young persons fall under the jurisdiction of a special court called "*tribunal de la jeunesse*".

Thirdly, the Court of Appeal (Criminal Division), hears appeals against judgments given at first instance by the *tribunal correctionnel*.

Finally, the *Cour de Cassation* will deal with criminal proceedings when points of law are at issue.

Save in the case of the *tribunal de police* (which is a single-judge court) all other courts sit in chambers of three judges; except the Court of Appeal, which, when dealing with appeals against judgments of the *chambre criminelle*, sits in chambers of five judges.

The *Cour de Cassation* sits in chambers of five judges.

The Court of Appeal (Criminal Division) and the *Cour de Cassation* sit in Luxembourg. There is no trial by jury and all courts are composed only of professional magistrates.

The prosecution in criminal courts is carried out by the "*Procureur d'Etat*" or by his deputies called the "*substitut*"; and before the Court of Appeal or the *Cour de Cassation* by the *Procureur General d'Etat* or one of his Advocates-General. *The prosecution*

In nearly all cases where a victim can claim damages, criminal proceedings can be instituted by the victim in parallel proceedings where the claim for damages is linked with the criminal proceedings.

With some kinds of offences, such as calumny and criminal defamation of private persons the prosecution can only be taken at the request of the victim.

A prosecution is started either directly by the *procureur* after he has seen the police report, or on the application of the *procureur* to the examining magistrate, called the *Juge d'Instruction*, to open a preliminary investigation.

If a prosecution appears unlikely to succeed, or appears inopportune, this will be left as an unsolved case. It may result also in a non-suit order before the main hearing starts.

Information about offences

When a prosecution is started directly by the *procureur* the accused will be served with a writ of summons to appear before the relevant court. This writ will contain the information relating to the offence of which he is accused. In such a situation, the defendant cannot challenge the charge other than at the main hearing.

When a preliminary investigation is carried out the accused has the right to challenge the regularity and the way information is gathered during the investigation. Once the investigation has come to an end, he may challenge the order to transfer the case to the competent court or for committal by filing an immediate appeal.

Commencement of proceedings

Where the evidence for the prosecution has been collected by the *procureur* and through police reports and investigations or where there has been an investigation either by the examining magistrate himself or by experts appointed by him, the defendant has the right, and the court has the same right, to ask that the evidence be given at the oral hearing itself.

Pleas

The defendant may plead guilty or not guilty. He may also plead guilty to a lesser offence. A defendant may at any time change his plea.

However, the prosecuting authorities will not normally accept any plea-bargaining on behalf of the defendant.

Juries

There is no trial by jury in Luxembourg.

Conduct of the trial

Only lawyers are admitted to appear as paid counsel in a criminal trial.

The order of the proceedings are as follows :
- The President of the court first calls any witnesses and the experts, if any;

- After having put preliminary questions to the accused as to his identity, the President proceeds with his interrogation on the facts;
- Counsel for the victim, if part of the proceedings, presents the claim for damages;
- The lawyer instructed by the accused and/or the accused himself presents the defence;
- The *procureur* gives a summary of the case and presents his oral submissions to the court ("*réquisitoire*");
- Counsel for the accused has the right of reply. Even in cases where the victim is party to the proceedings his counsel has no right of reply after the public prosecutor.

It is not open to the defence to submit at any stage that the case should be stopped because there is no case to answer. Such an application can only be made with the final pleadings and will be answered in the final judgment.

The court has the broadest powers of investigation and can call on any witnesses it deems necessary to find out the truth.

As a rule, all hearings are open to the public; however, the President may order a case to be heard *in camera* for reasons of public policy or if the hearings concern immoral offences. Even in these cases, though, the oral submissions by counsel are in public.

The verdict need not be unanimous, though dissenting opinions are not published. A defendant may be found guilty of an alternative offence to that with which he has been charged provided the facts remain the same and only the legal characterisation of the offence has changed. *The verdict*

There is no special procedure for sentencing, except that the judges will consult amongst themselves in order to arrive at their decision. *Sentencing*

In criminal trials, an expert may be appointed to assess the defendant's character. This happens before the oral hearing, normally during the preliminary investigation.

The court will consider mitigating factors such as an unhappy childhood, and the degree of interference with public policy caused by the offence. The defendant's previous offences are to be taken into consideration when determining what sentence to pass.

For all offences the range of sentences is a fine, imprisonment, or both, depending on mitigating factors.

For all offences, the *Penal Code* provides for a minimum and a maximum, the court having a discretion as to which sentence to impose. Save that every sentence must be provided for by law there are no guidelines or sentencing manual which sets out the courts' powers. Sentencing powers are provided for in respect of each offence in the relevant provisions of the Penal Code.

Appeals

A defendant may always appeal from the judgment of a criminal court of first instance. He has only to sign an appeal declaration at the registry of the court of first instance.

The length of time between judgment and the appeal hearing does not normally exceed one month.

Extradition

Luxembourg has signed and ratified the *European Convention on Extradition of 13 December 1957,* with the following main reservations :

-   No extradition will be granted in favour of a foreign state if the person involved is a Luxembourg national and no extradition will be granted if in similar cases the applicant state would refuse extradition.
-   The maximum period a person may be detained before appearing before a magistrate (*"Juge d'Instruction"*) and being charged with an offence by him is 24 hours.
-   There is no time limit during which such a person may be detained before trial.
-   After having appeared before the magistrate such a person may only be detained longer under certain conditions provided for by *Article 94 of the Code of Criminal Procedure.*

Bail

An accused who is held in custody is entitled to ask to be released on bail. The application is made to a court called the "*Chambre du Conseil*" which is a three-judge court. This court, or when the case has been transferred to the competent court, the *tribunal correctionnel,* or the Court of Appeal (Criminal Division), will decide whether the accused is to be released on bail and if so will set the level of bail. The main evidence to be heard at this stage will concern any risk that the accused will leave the jurisdiction, interfere with evidence, or relapse into criminal behaviour. The application for bail can be made at any stage in the proceedings. There is no limit on the amount of bail which can be set.

CHAPTER 8 : REMEDIES

Damages can be recovered either before the civil/commercial courts or before the criminal courts where the claimed injury resulted from the commission of a criminal offence. *Damages*

Commercial courts deal with damages sought by a plaintiff in an action where only an insurance company appears as a defendant. When the claim is filed against the party at fault and his insurance company, the civil courts enjoy exclusive jurisdiction.

The awarding of damages is the task of a single judge or of the whole court; damages are never awarded by a jury.

In personal injury actions, the court may either assess the quantum *ex aequo et bono*, or appoint an expert and ask him to deliver a report before deciding what amount to award. There are no fixed awards for particular types of injury. Damages are available for mental distress, when, for example this is the result of a car accident.

Damages are also available for loss of reputation, except in cases of "*dolus*" (serious fault) with no limit to the amount which may be awarded. *Loss of reputation*

A plaintiff may be awarded damages for pure economic loss in cases of a breach of contractual obligations as well as for breaches of tortious obligations. The only difference is that in respect of contractual obligations, pursuant to *Article 1150 of the Civil Code*, the plaintiff can be awarded only those damages which were or could have been foreseen by the parties at the moment they entered into the contract. *Pure economic loss*

An action may be instituted on the basis of "unjust enrichment", pursuant to *Articles 1375 and 1376 of the Civil Code*, only if the following conditions are satisfied : *Unjust enrichment*
- the defendant must have been enriched;
- there must be a loss suffered by the plaintiff; and
- there must have been no other action based on contract, an implied contract or on an offence of any kind, available to the plaintiff.

The third condition shows that the notion is rarely applicable in commercial litigation.

Apart from specific rules applicable to some kinds of contracts, a contract which assigns disproportionate obligations on one of the *Unfair bargains* parties compared with those imposed upon the other, resulting in an unfair bargain (*"lésion"*), is void if that disproportion was in the contract because the other party was abusing a dominant position and exploiting the pecuniary difficulties, the carelessness or, inexperience of the first party. This action, which was introduced by *Article 1118 of the Civil Code* in 1987, must be filed within one year of entering into the contract. In it, the plaintiff may seek either to have his obligations reduced and the contract performed in respect of the remaining obligations, or to have the contract annulled.

Penalty clauses

Article 1152 of the Civil Code allows the parties to include a penalty clause in the contracts between them. If the parties have included a penalty clause and have fixed in advance an agreed sum where one party fails to complete the performance agreed the judge as a rule is not allowed to award more or less than this amount. However, the judge may adjust the sum if it appears that the sum was too high or too low. Equally, the court may also award part of an agreed penalty sum where only part of the contract has been performed and another part remains unperformed.

An obligation to do something or to abstain from doing something, if not respected, entitles the plaintiff only to claim damages *"nemo praecise cogi potest ad factum"*.

Specific performance

As a general rule, an order for specific performance of an obligation cannot be sought unless the obligation consists in paying a certain amount of money. However, notwithstanding this, a plaintiff may seek an order authorising performance of the obligation if this is, in fact, possible. The defendant must pay the costs of such performance.

A contract cannot be rescinded on the grounds of frustration, but delay in performance may be granted under certain circumstances.

Interest

On monetary judgments for debts etc., if the claim contains a specific request for it, the court shall award interest on the awarded sum. Interest will be due from the date of the start of the proceedings. The actual rate is the legal rate, which is currently 8.5%.

When damages are awarded, the court will determine in respect of which date they are to apply and the interest rate which will be applied to them. It may award interest at a higher or lower level than the legal rate.

Action for a declaration

Normally, it is not possible to seek a Declaration as to one's legal rights or legal position. However, this is not to say that the parties may not reach an agreement during the proceedings, in which case they may ask the court to sanction their agreement by way of a judgment.

As a general rule, pursuant to *Article 440 of the Commercial Code*, the Commercial Division of the Court of First Instance will adjudge a company bankrupt if the company has suspended its payments and no more credit facilities are available to the company. In addition, in accordance with *Article 203 of the 1915 Law on commercial companies and associations*, a commercial company may be made the subject of a winding-up order if, on the application of the *"Procureur d'Etat"*, it is shown that a company's activities are prohibited by the *Penal Code*, or seriously in breach of the provisions of the law regulating companies and associations. The court will appoint a liquidator and may declare the bankruptcy law provisions applicable.

Winding-up of a company

Finally, pursuant to the *Law of 27 November 1984* (as amended) on the banking sector, and apart from the provisions concerning controlled management (*"gestion contrôlé"*) and the suspension of payments (which remain applicable to the non-banking sector), a winding-up order may be made against banks which come within these regulations if one of the following conditions is met :
- a previous order suspending payments has not improved the financial situation of the bank;
- the financial situation is such that the bank is unable to meet its obligations towards its creditors and participants;
- the banking licence has been withdrawn by a final decision which has become enforceable.

The request may be filed either by the *Procureur d'Etat* or by the relevant regulatory body - Director of the *Institut Monetaire Luxembourgeois* (IML).

When ordering a winding-up the court will appoint one or more liquidators and may declare the bankruptcy law provisions applicable.

A winding-up order and liquidation are immediately enforceable. This is dealt with broadly under the provisions concerning the jurisdiction of the Administrative Court.

All administrative proceedings, by individuals, for remedies against decisions having an administrative character come within the jurisdiction of the *Comité du Contentieux du Conseil d'Etat*. This applies to all decisions given by an administrative body or authority, including decisions of ministers.

Actions by/against public bodies

Save where otherwise provided by law, this jurisdiction only covers points of law. It is quite common that a decision of a public body is quashed or that an injunction is granted against a public body.

The Administrative Court generally has no jurisdiction to award damages.

Double recovery of damages

To avoid the possibility of double recovery of damages, the law provides that a plaintiff who has brought his claim before a civil or commercial court is not allowed to bring the same claim before a criminal court : "*una via electa non datur recursus ad alteram*".

Alternative dispute resolution

Court proceedings can be set aside on the ground that the dispute in question has already been referred to arbitration. Mediation and conciliation are always available, but are especially encouraged before the Justices of the Peace.

CHAPTER 9 : MATRIMONIAL DISPUTES

The law of proceedings on matrimonial disputes is set out in *Articles 299 to 311 of the Civil Code.*

Questions as to divorce, the custody of children and access to children are heard before a three-judge court of first instance.

A person who wishes to sue for divorce must first present his application to the President of the Court in person. After this stage, both parties must appear before the same magistrate who will try to effect a reconciliation. If this attempt is unsuccessful, leave is given to the plaintiff to bring the case before the court. *Divorce - procedure*

Once the initial petition is filed with the President, the parties may, pursuant to *Article 267 of the Civil Code*, obtain from the President or his deputy judge interlocutory enforceable orders regarding custody, access, the other party's domicile, alimony and so forth. These judgments are regarded as summary judgments. The final judgment handed down at the end of the divorce proceedings will deal with the same questions but in respect of the period after divorce is granted.

The basic grounds for divorce or judicial separation are as follows : mental cruelty, injury or slander (if serious), or repetitious breach of the duties and obligations under the marriage with the result that married life becomes impossible. *- grounds*

Breach of marital duties includes adultery, which, however, is no longer a criminal offence.

Either partner may institute divorce proceedings when separation is continuous and effective for at least three years and if the result is that the marriage has broken down irremediably. One of the partners may start divorce proceedings when they have been separated for at least five years and this is due to the incurable insanity of the other making the breakdown of the marriage irremediable.

There is another form of divorce : divorce by mutual consent. This form of divorce is only available after two years of marriage and only if neither of the partners is less than 23 years old. The proceedings here differ from those for the first three cases and the formalities must be strictly complied with. All details concerning the children, alimony, residence, and any matrimonial property must be resolved and endorsed in a notarial deed before proceedings can be initiated. By law, these proceedings must last one year.

Where the marriage breaks up or the parties separate, in all save the last case, the court shall order the liquidation of the communal or joint estate of the husband and wife, and appoint a notary to deal with the formalities.

CHAPTER 10 : PROPERTY TRANSACTIONS

The courts are not normally involved in real estate property transactions, as long as they are not litigious. All such transactions need to be passed before a notary.

Sometimes an agreement between the seller and the buyer will take the form of a promise to sell and which will then take place on a certain date. This normally provides for a forfeiture clause in favour of the seller where the buyer withdraws from the sale. The sale itself, in order to be final as against third parties, needs to be recorded in an authentic deed prepared by a notary and containing, in particular :
- a full identification of both parties;
- a precise description of the property being sold;
- the origins of ownership, indicating any previous owners during the previous 30 years;
- the price and terms of payment;
- the date of occupancy and the terms for delivery up of the property, the condition of the buildings, any easements, city planning, regulations, etc;
- the involvement of any financial organisation if it is lending any funds for the purchase.

The notarised deed must then be registered, any relevant duties paid to the state, and the deed published at the Mortgage Registry, where there is a file on each property which records all transactions concerning it.

CHAPTER 11 : RECOGNITION AND ENFORCEMENT OF FOREIGN JUDGMENTS

The general rules on the recognition and enforcement of foreign judgments, where the *1968 Brussels Convention* or other Conventions do not apply, are laid down in *Article 2123 of the Civil Code* and the relevant case law. The *1968 Brussels Convention* is applicable under Luxembourg law.

Current case law indicates that the following conditions must be met before an *"exequatur"* judgment rendering the foreign judgment enforceable will be granted : *Conditions for recognition*

-   the original judgment must not be contrary to public policy or to Luxembourg public law;
-   the rights of the judgment debtor must have been respected;
-   the court of origin must have had jurisdiction pursuant to Luxembourg private international law;
-   the court of origin must have given its judgment in accordance with the applicable law; and
-   the original judgment is final and enforceable in the country of origin.

According to case law, no review of the facts or law is possible, save on the basis of the five points stated above (see *Lux 21 November 1956, Pas Lux 17, 180, Lux 5 February 1964, Pas Lux 19, 285 Cour 19 May 1969, Pas Lux 21, 144*).

Save where specific Conventions otherwise provide, the procedure for enforcement of a foreign judgement is initiated by the bailiff issuing a summons on behalf of the judgment creditor to have the foreign judgment declared enforceable against the judgment debtor. The different steps which must be followed before the Court of First Instance will be the same as for a normal civil case.

The documents which must be produced in support of an action to register a foreign judgment include :

-   an authentic copy of the judgment of origin;
-   all relevant documents showing that the rights of the judgment debtor have been respected, (for example, if judgment was gained without a full hearing on the merits);
-   documents showing that the judgment debtor was duly served with the proceedings; and finally,
-   documents showing that the original judgment was duly served on the judgment debtor.

The use of a lawyer is mandatory. Therefore, the address for service of process is the address of the lawyer's firm.

All foreign judgments written in a language other than French or German have to be translated into either or both of these languages.

Public policy

A judgment handed down without reasons may be considered as contrary to public policy. On the other hand, under the *1968 Brussels Convention*, it has been held that the notion of "public policy" does not allow a court to refuse an *exequatur* on the basis that the foreign court had no jurisdiction (see *Court 11 November 1975, Pas Lux 23, 230*). This case concerned *Article 1 of the Protocol annexed to the Convention*, whereby a foreign court should declare itself incompetent when a defendant, who is a Luxembourg national, did not appear before that court.

Appeals

If the normal procedure applies, any appeal must be lodged with the Court of Appeal within 40 days from the date of service of the judgment on the defendant. This time period will be extended by the same extent as applies in the case of service of proceedings.

If the *1968 Brussels Convention* or any other bilateral or multilateral Convention in this area applies, the time period for lodging an appeal is one month, if the appellant is domiciled in the Grand-Duchy of Luxembourg, and two months if domiciled in another country.

BIBLIOGRAPHY

Annuaire officiel d'Administration et de Législation, Ministère d'État, Service Central de Législation, 1992

Diagonales à travers le droit luxembourgeois, Conférence St. Yves, Imprimerie St. Paul, Luxembourg, 1986

Kreiger - Spielmann - Grass, *Bibliographie juridique luxembourgeoise,* Éditions Nemesis, Brussels, 1989

Majerus, Pierre, *L'État Luxembourgeois, Manuel de droit constitutionnel et de droit administratif,* (4th edn completed and updated by Marcel Majerus), Imprimerie St. Paul, Luxembourg, 1977

Mélanges dédiés à Michel Delvaux, Cercle Michel Delvaux, 1990

Thill, Jean, *Documents et textes relatifs aux constitutions et institutions politiques luxembourgeoises* (2nd edn) Centre de Documentation Communale, 1978

THE NETHERLANDS

Professor Willem A. Hoyng
Francine M. Schlingmann
De Brauw Blackstone Westbroek

CONTENTS

CHAPTER 1 : SOURCES OF LAW

The Netherlands has a unitary structure of government. *Unitary v federal system*

However, provinces ("*provincies*") of which there are 12 and municipalities ("*gemeenten*") have certain limited legislative powers pursuant to the *Province Act* ("*Provinciewet*") and *Municipality Act* ("*Gemeentewet*"). These powers are subject to the rule that Acts of Parliament have precedence over local bye-laws.

The principal written documents containing the law of the Netherlands are to be found in : *Principal written constitutional documents*
- the *Constitution,*
- the *Civil Code,*
- the *Penal Code,*
- the *Codes of Procedure.*

In general, the court recognises no difference in the application of law as between nationals and foreigners. *Application of national laws to foreign nationals*

Where a treaty has been approved by Parliament and ratified it can be applied directly by the Dutch courts. If the provisions of such a treaty are considered to have "direct effect" (eg *Articles 85, 86 of the EEC Treaty*) they can be relied upon by individuals before the national courts. *Monist v dualist system*

EC Treaties are incorporated into domestic law after having been approved by Parliament and duly published. *Application of EC Law*

The Dutch courts accept, adopt and implement the principles of Community law unequivocally. There has been no reticence demonstrated by national courts in applying and implementing the provisions of EC law.

Foreign law is treated as a question of fact. It is the court which determines the contents of the foreign law, but usually the court invokes the assistance of the parties to the proceedings by giving (one of) them the task of proving the foreign law. The Netherlands has an International Legal Institute which can give advice on foreign law on request. All means of proof (affidavits, oral evidence etc) are acceptable. Translations are generally not necessary unless the court cannot reasonably be expected to understand the language (the courts are supposed to understand, for instance, English, German and French). *Proof of foreign law in national proceedings*

The European Convention on Human Rights

The *European Convention on Human Rights* is directly applicable and (as any treaty which has direct effect) takes priority over national law.

Principles of interpretation

The main principle of interpretation is the purposive approach. Previous decisions of the courts do play an important role in subsequent cases, but it is possible for the Supreme Court to overrule its previous decisions or simply to interpret them differently. Decisions of higher courts do not have any binding effect on lower courts by virtue of any mandatory provision, but in practice lower courts will follow decisions of the Supreme Court.

Texts of the Constitution

There are no "authorised" annotated texts of the *Constitution*.

CHAPTER 2 : FUNDAMENTAL RIGHTS

The principal articles of the Constitution "guaranteeing justice" are *Articles 1 to 23 in Chapter 1 of the Constitution* entitled "Fundamental rights".   They are generally divided into two groups : "classic rights" and "social rights".

Constitutional protection of fundamental rights

"Classic rights" are rights which guarantee that the governmental authorities "will not interfere". These are the right of equal treatment, the right to political freedom including suffrage (the right to vote and the right to be elected), the right of petition, the right of free expression of one's opinion, the right of free association, meeting and demonstration, freedom of religion, the right to personal freedom, and protection of property rights.

"Classic rights"

"Social rights" are rights which require governmental authorities to "take positive action", such as to guarantee the right to legal aid, to promote employment, social security, health, housing and education.

"Social rights"

The courts cannot review whether a Parliamentary act conforms with the Constitution. Parliamentary acts may be considered by the courts to see the extent to which they comply with treaties. Local bye-laws can be considered to see to what extent they comply with the Constitution and with Parliamentary acts. All the courts can deal with any such questions of compatibility with the Constitution. There is no special court, neither are there any special proceedings for this purpose.

Interpretation by the national courts

CHAPTER 3 : JURISDICTION OF THE COURTS

The assumption of domestic jurisdiction by a Dutch court can be *Forum*
challenged on the grounds that the court does not have absolute
jurisdiction (for instance, employment disputes have to be
brought before the Cantonal Court), and/or on the basis that the
court does not have "relative jurisdiction" (for instance, that the
case should have been brought before the District Court in
Amsterdam and not before the District Court in Rotterdam). As a
general rule - but this is a rule with many exceptions - a civil
matter has to be brought before the court in the region in which
the defendant resides or is established (if the defendant is a
company) and a criminal case has to be brought before the court
in the region in which the offence has been committed. There are
62 Cantonal Courts, 19 District Courts and 5 Courts of Appeal.

There are no limitations on bringing actions against the state or *State immunity*
organs of the state where these are acting in a purely commercial
capacity.

In respect of individuals, their residence, and in respect of *Domicile,*
corporations, the corporate seat or the principal place of business, *residence etc*
will determine whether a court has properly assumed jurisdiction.

CHAPTER 4 : ADMINISTRATION OF JUSTICE

The basic structure of the court system in civil and criminal matters is as follows : *Structure of the court system*

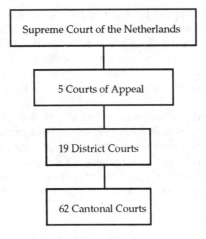

```
┌─────────────────────────────────────┐
│   Supreme Court of the Netherlands   │
└─────────────────────────────────────┘
          ┌─────────────────────┐
          │   5 Courts of Appeal │
          └─────────────────────┘
          ┌─────────────────────┐
          │   19 District Courts │
          └─────────────────────┘
          ┌─────────────────────┐
          │   62 Cantonal Courts │
          └─────────────────────┘
```

The Cantonal Court (a single judge court) deals with : *Jurisdiction : Cantonal Court*
- civil matters : without a right of appeal if the claim does not exceed Dfl. 2,500; and with the right of an appeal to the District Court if the claim does not exceed Dfl. 5,000 and the matter relates to a right in personam, a claim for the payment of rent or a claim for the payment of interest even if the principal amount exceeds Dfl. 5,000 provided that the legal basis of the obligation is not challenged;
- other civil matters without the right of an appeal if the claim does not exceed Dfl. 2,500; and with the right of an appeal to the District Court if the matter (irrespective of the amount of the claim in question) relates to an employment agreement, an agency agreement, a collective bargaining agreement, a hire-purchase agreement, a tenancy agreement, or certain other, less important claims;
- a variety of measures available in family law, and with claims in respect of the alleged nullity of certain decisions made by the management board of a company under the *Works Council Act.*
- criminal matters which relate to criminal trespasses ("*over tredingen*")

The District Court has first instance jurisdiction over all civil matters not specifically submitted to the jurisdiction of other courts. Depending on the nature of the matter and/or its *Jurisdiction : District Court* importance it will be decided by a single judge or by a three-judge court.

Courts of Appeal

The most important task of the five Courts of Appeal is to hear appeals against decisions rendered by District Courts and decisions of the Presidents of the District Courts in interlocutory relief proceedings (see further Chapter 6).

Each Court of Appeal has a special chamber to handle appeals from first instance decisions of tax inspectors in certain tax matters.

The Court of Appeal in Amsterdam has a special Enterprise Chamber ("*Ondernemingskamer*") which hears, as a court of first instance, certain cases relating to violation of the statutory provisions on the annual accounts of enterprises and the *Works Council Act* and actions based on the statutory provisions regarding the right to investigate an enterprise's affairs.

The Court of Appeal in Arnhem has a special chamber handling appeals in matters concerning leases of land (which are at first instance level heard by a court consisting of a cantonal judge and two members who are not members of the judiciary and who may not be lawyers). Also the special chamber of the Arnhem Court of Appeal includes two members who are not members of the judiciary.

Special courts and proceedings

In general, national courts do not hear a case if a specialised court is competent to hear it. Special courts and procedures exist to deal with complaints against decisions by central, provincial, municipal and other non-central government agencies in matters concerning social security, relations between government and public officials, and in respect of certain regulations dealing with industry and business.

Numerous acts (eg dealing with government control and administrative law regarding environment, town and country planning, education, public health etc) provide for administrative procedures. On 1 January 1988 the "*Tijdelijke wet Kroongeschillen*" ("*TWK*") *Provisional Act regarding administrative disputes formerly decided by the Crown* ("*Kroon*") came into force as a result of a decision by the European Court of Human Rights in Strasbourg on 23 October 1985 which held that the Crown is not an independent and impartial tribunal. Pursuant to *Article 1 of the Tijdelijke wet Kroongeschillen (TWK) Provisional Act*, the Department for Administrative Disputes ("*Afdeling voor de geschillen van bestuur*") of the Council of State ("*Raad van State*") will ultimately decide on most administrative disputes. Exceptions apply in respect of local government decisions (eg town and country planning issues), which remain within the jurisdiction of the Crown, after consultation with the Department for Administrative Disputes of the Council of State. Such proceedings deal with issues of policy and administration as well as the legitimacy of decisions. In all other administrative disputes only the issue of the legitimacy of the decision is subject to review.

By virtue of the Act *AROB* (*"Administratieve Rechtspraak Overheids beschikkingen"*), all decrees of central and non-central government agencies against which no appeal is provided for in special acts, are subject to appeal to the Judicial Department (*"Afdeling Rechtspraak"*) of the Council of State. This department may only review the question of a decree's legitimacy, not issues of policy. Most rules of procedure of both Departments of the Council of State are set out in the Act on the Council of State.

Pending the hearing of an appeal before either Department, the President of the Department may be requested to grant provisional measures or to suspend a decree under appeal.

There are no rules as to how to solve conflicts of jurisdiction between the administrative and the national courts. National courts follow decisions of the Judicial Department of the Council of State with respect to its own jurisdiction. All other actions based on a civil law claim belong to the competence of the national courts.

In specific areas of the law, Belgium, the Netherlands and *Benelux Court* Luxembourg, by virtue of the *Benelux Economic Union Treaty of 1958* committed themselves by special treaties to introduce into their national laws uniform provisions or uniform systems of statutory law and uniform regulations based thereon. The uniform interpretation of such laws and regulations is secured by a provision granting exclusive jurisdiction in respect of these matters to a special Benelux Court, provided for by a *Treaty of 31 March 1965*, which became effective on 1 January 1974. The court is composed of nine judges (three from each state) and its sessions are held in Brussels. Questions of interpretation are submitted to the Benelux Court by the national court before which the relevant proceedings are pending. A national court may make a reference to this court upon the application of a party to the proceedings or on its own initiative.

The Benelux Court has, inter alia, jurisdiction over :
- *Benelux Uniform Trademark Act;*
- *Benelux Uniform Act on Designs and Models;*
- penalty sums imposed by a national court on account of civil contempt on a party for the indemnity of another party at whose complaint the President of the District Court has granted a preliminary or final injunction (*Treaty of 24 May 1966*);
- agreements between principals and commercial agents (*Treaty of 26 November 1973*);
- penal clauses in private agreements (*Treaty of 26 November 1973*).

There is an automatic right of appeal or to cassation. *Appeals*

Appeals deal with the merits of a case (including facts - even new facts - and points of law). Whereas, on the other hand, cassation deals with points of law alone.

Appeals operate as an automatic stay of proceedings unless the (civil) judgment appealed from has been rendered "immediately enforceable" (or enforceable by anticipation : *"uitvoerbaar bij voorraad"*). In such a case, the appeal court can only stay the judgment in certain circumstances.

References under Article 177 of the EEC Treaty

If a court deems it appropriate, it may refer questions to the European Court of Justice by way of an interlocutory judgment. The highest courts for the purposes of *Article 177 of the EEC Treaty* are considered to be the courts against whose decisions there is no further appeal - the Supreme Court of the Netherlands; the Central Council of Appeal in, mainly, social security cases in which there is no appeal to the Supreme Court; certain decisions of the Court of Appeal for Business Matters (ie the Enterprise Chamber of the Amsterdam Court of Appeal), the Department for Administrative Disputes and the Judicial Department of the Council of State.

References to other courts

References to the Benelux Court of Justice are made by national judges in respect of points of Benelux law which are not clear. The system works in the same way as the reference procedure under *Article 177 of the EEC Treaty.*

CHAPTER 5 : THE LEGAL PROFESSION

Members of the Bar ("*advocaten*") provide the majority of legal *Structure* services in the Netherlands. There are also bailiffs ("*deurwaarders*") who, apart from serving writs and other official documents (for which they are appointed by the Crown), provide legal assistance in matters before the Cantonal Courts.

Civil law notaries, who are also appointed by the Crown, execute notarial deeds (eg wills, conveyancing, deeds of mortgage, deeds of incorporation of companies, etc) and very often also provide other advisory services.

Other specialist services are provided by patent agents (filing and prosecuting of patent applications); trademark agents (filing and prosecuting trademark applications); and tax advisers.

There is, however, no separate group of lawyers equivalent to the *Advocaten;* "barrister" in the United Kingdom which specialises in appearing *rights of audience* before the courts. In District Courts, the Courts of Appeal and the Supreme Court right of audience is, in general, reserved for *advocaten*.

Legal practices are generally organised as partnerships. *Legal practices*

It should be noted that *advocaten* must comply with the rules and regulations of the Dutch Bar Association ("*Nederlandse Orde van Advocaten*"), for instance on co-operation with other *advocaten* or members of other professions. A partnership may employ local lawyers and foreign lawyers. However, this does not mean that foreign lawyers are automatically allowed to practise as advocaten.

There are no territorial restrictions on partnership practice within the Netherlands and there are also no restrictions imposed on partnership practice within the Community.

There are no restrictions in the Netherlands on the establishment *Branch offices* and/or number of branch offices either within the state or the Community.

In general, fees are charged at an hourly rate. There are *Fees* published guidelines on this from the Dutch Bar Association. Actual fee scales are not published. Clients can ask what the hourly rate will be as the basis of what the advocaat will charge for the services to be rendered. An advocaat cannot take a client to court to demand payment of his bill until the account has been checked by a disciplinary board. Fees carry VAT, in general, at the rate of 18.5% at present.

Professional conduct

The professional conduct of lawyers is controlled by the disciplinary authorities of the local Bar to which all lawyers must belong in addition to being members of the national Bar. *Advocaten* are bound by a code of conduct. If they violate the code, *advocaten* can be given a warning, be suspended or be removed from the Bar. Foreign clients have the right to complain about the conduct of an advocaat. Professional indemnity insurance is compulsory for all lawyers.

Practice by foreign lawyers

If a person wishes to practise as a Dutch advocaat he must comply with the requirements of the *Dutch Advocaten Act.* He must have obtained the degree of master of law from a Dutch university on the basis of exams in Dutch civil, commercial and criminal law and in at least one of the three following subjects : Dutch state, administrative or tax law. As a result of the provisions of the *Lawyers' Services Directive*[1] the *Dutch Advocaten Act* contains several provisions relating to the provision of services in the Netherlands by persons who have been admitted to a Bar in another EC Member State. Such "visiting" EC lawyers (as they are called in the *Advocaten Act*) are subject to the same rules and regulations as lawyers who have been admitted to the Dutch Bar as *advocaten.* If a "visiting" EC lawyer provides services to a client in a matter in which Dutch law requires representation in court by an *advocaat* or *"procureur"* (a special functionary in civil matters), the "visiting" lawyer must co-operate with an *advocaat* admitted to the Dutch Bar.

There are no restrictions on lawyers practising in business corporations (not as *advocaten*).

Instruction of legal services

Any person can instruct an *advocaat* or any other person providing legal services directly.

Directory of legal services

There is no directory of legal services. A client generally finds out which lawyers/law firms have experience in any particular area through the recommendation of the Dutch Bar Association. Most large law firms have specialists practising in various different areas of the law.

---

1.   Council Directive (EEC) 77/249 (OJ L78 26.3.77 p17).

CHAPTER 6 : CIVIL PROCEDURE

In first instance proceedings the normal structure of proceedings **Basic structure of** is : service of a writ of summons (containing the statement of **court proceedings** claim); a written answer; reply and rejoinder and - if the parties so wish (in the Cantonal Court this is not a right) - oral argument. The court will then give a final or interlocutory judgment. An interlocutory judgment may be given if the court feels it is necessary that a party prove a certain fact, eg by hearing expert witnesses. After such a hearing both parties will again have the opportunity to put forward their views in writing and after an optional second round of oral arguments the court will then give its final judgment. Appeals against the judgment can be lodged (normally within three months) by way of service of a writ of appeal. After such a writ has been served the appellant will file written grounds of complaint, followed by a written answer and optional oral arguments. After the decision of the appeal court (again, normally within three months) the party which has lost the case can lodge an appeal to the Supreme Court ("*cassatieberoep*"). The grounds for such an appeal have to be stated in the writ of appeal itself. Both parties will put forward their arguments in writing. It is possible but nowadays very unusual to ask to be allowed to present oral arguments before the Supreme Court.

Many cases in the Netherlands are dealt with in preliminary proceedings before the President of the District Court. Such proceedings start with a writ of summons, followed by oral arguments and a decision of the President, all of which takes a matter of weeks (or, if required, as a matter of urgency, a matter of hours). Appeals are possible, and a party may also choose to start proceedings in the normal way.

The parties which are able to bring civil proceedings are : **Parties to**
- individuals; **proceedings/locus**
- "private" legal entities (companies, associations of **standi** persons with full legal personality, foundations);
- "public" legal entities (the state, provinces, municipalities);
- open partnership firms ("*vennootschappen onder firma*") and limited partnerships ("*commanditaire vennootschappen*") do not have separate legal personality; the law does, however, provide for a special way of serving a writ of summons on a partnership : it is not necessary to state the names of all the partners in the writ of summons, although it is permitted to do so; in practice if the plaintiff wishes to

obtain a judgment enforceable against the "private" assets of each of the partners who are jointly and severally liable, the name of the partnership is stated as well as the names of all the partners and a copy of the writ is served upon each of the partners;

- an ordinary partnership ("*maatschap*") that acts under a particular name may sue and be sued under this name;

- in some cases, proceedings may be brought by interest groups such as consumer organisations (in respect of, for example, cases on misleading advertising);

- in certain specific cases the Public Prosecution Office ("*Openbaar Ministerie*") may bring proceedings (eg certain family law matters; to ask for the dissolution of a legal entity whose objects or activities are contrary to public order or good morals; cases to nullify the registration of a trademark which is contrary to public order).

A minor (person under the age of 18) and a person under legal restraint may be a "material" party to proceedings, but may not be a "formal" party to proceedings; the legal representative of such a party is the formal party to the proceedings and such formal party represents the minor or person under legal restraint who is the "subject" of the legal relationship in respect of which the proceedings were initiated.

Actions against the state

No actions can be brought against the Queen, foreign heads of state or a foreign government save where such government was acting in a commercial capacity. If a question of immunity arises before a Dutch court, the Dutch court should apply the Dutch doctrine of immunity (as to which see the *decision of the Supreme Court of the Netherlands of 22 December 1989*, Dutch Weekly Law Reports ("*Rechtspraak van de Week*") 1990, No 15 and the *decision of the Supreme Court of the Netherlands of 28 September 1990*, Dutch Weekly Law Reports (*Rechtspraak van de Week*) 1990, No 162). Enterprises which have separate legal personality and in which a sovereign state has an interest are not protected by any rules of state immunity simply because the state has such an interest.

In respect of government agencies or other entities or corporations which may be identified with a sovereign state or government, questions of immunity could, theoretically, arise, but generally a claim of State immunity will fail.

The Netherlands follows the doctrine of "restrictive immunity" which distinguishes between acts "iure imperii" and acts "iure gestionis". This practice is in conformity with the *European Convention on State Immunity of 16 May 1972*, which has been ratified by the Netherlands.

Finally, a distinction must be made between immunity from jurisdiction and immunity from execution. In certain circumstances, a state may not be immune from jurisdiction, but nonetheless be protected by immunity from execution, in that certain state assets may not be attached.

A third party may intervene in proceedings in support of the arguments of one of the parties ("*voeging*"), or to put forward his own arguments against the parties ("*tussenkomst*") if the outcome of the proceedings may affect his rights. A third party may also be joined in the proceedings by either of the parties ("*vrijwaring*"). Such joinder will start with a writ of summons or initial incidental statement (depending on which party calls the third party to join) and end with a court decision as to whether or not the third party can be validly joined. There are no rules on informing other parties about proceedings. However, the outcome of any proceedings will only affect the parties to the proceedings. *Joinder to an action*

A party to proceedings pending before one court may request that court to refer the proceedings to another (ordinary) court on the grounds that the first proceedings relate to the same subject matter as that in respect of which proceedings have already been initiated before the other court between the same parties, or that the first proceedings are closely connected to another case already pending before the other court. But "other ordinary court" means another national court determined/referred to in the *Act on the Organisation of the Judiciary* and therefore excludes administrative courts or a foreign court.

It is also possible to request a court to join proceedings/cases which are simultaneously pending before that court between the same parties and on the same subject matter or to join cases which are very closely connected to each other (but not necessarily between the same parties).

In recent years, more and more actions have been brought by groups that look after special interests. Such actions have been based on the groups' interests (that is, the interests of their members) as well as on the public interest. Certain statutory rights to sue are granted to common interest groups, for example in the field of environmental and nature protection, consumer protection and misleading advertising. No special procedure is required to bring the action. *Class or representative actions*

Legal aid is available in civil proceedings. The following regulations apply in particular : *Legal aid*
- the *Act on Legal Aid* ("*Wet rechtsbijstand aan on- en minvermogenden*") of 1957 and the decrees promulgated pursuant to this act;
- the *Decree on Contributions/Payments in respect of Legal Services* ("*Besluit vergoedingen rechtsbijstand*") of 1983;
- certain provisions of the *Act on Fees in Civil Matters* ("*Wet tarieven in burgerlijke zaken*"), of the *Code of Civil Procedure* and of the *Bailiffs Regulations* ("*Deurwaardersreglement*").

An application for legal aid must be made to the Bureau for Legal Aid in the relevant region. Often, this application procedure is carried out by the *advocaat* whose client is (possibly) eligible for legal aid. The client must obtain a statement on his income/financial position from the Social Department of the municipality where he resides. The client or the advocaat submits this statement, together with an application form, to the Bureau for Legal Aid. The request for legal aid is decided with reference to two criteria :

- that the financial position of the applicant is such that he cannot pay the necessary costs (on the basis of given financial limits set out in the relevant rules and regulations pursuant to the *Act on Legal Aid*). Changes in the financial position may lead to the original decision being amended;
- the applicant does not lack legal grounds for his action and the applicant's interest justifies the services to be rendered.

Everyone granted legal aid must pay a contribution himself. The amount of this contribution depends on the level of disposable income (this means income after tax, social security and pension premiums) and may at present vary between a minimum of Dfl. 25.00 (for advice) or Dfl. 50.00 (in the case of proceedings) if the disposable income is Dfl. 1,475 or Dfl. 1,650 and a maximum of Dfl 550.00. A party to proceedings who has been granted legal aid is not exempt from paying a percentage - which is 25% for the lower income groups and 50% for the other groups eligible for legal aid - of the court fees ("*griffierecht*").

In principle, legal aid is available for all civil matters. The Legal Aid Bureaux apply detailed rules, for instance, requiring a new application for legal aid for each new stage in the proceedings, etc. There is no "appeal" from decisions of the Bureaux but the President of the District Court may be asked to intervene. There is no appeal against the President's decisions.

Limitation periods Under the *New Dutch Civil Code* (Books 3, 5 and 6 and several parts of Book 7 came into force on 1 January 1992) the general rule is that, if the law does not provide otherwise, the limitation period is 20 years.

The transitional arrangements which deal with the effect of the *New Dutch Civil Code* came into force on 1 January 1992.

However, for a considerable number of actions which are very important in practice, a shorter term of limitation - of five years - is provided for :

- claims for the performance of an obligation arising from an agreement to give or do something;
- claims for the payment of interest, life annuities, dividends, rentals and all other payments made annually or by a shorter period;
- claims arising from non-payment;

- claims for damages (arising from a wide range of causes, inter alia : breach of contract and tort).

There are further special rules covering the action to dissolve an agreement or actions based on default in performance or for payment of legal or agreed interest.

It is possible to waive the right to invoke the prescriptive form of a limitation period after the limitation period has passed. The parties may also agree to a shorter limitation period.

Certain circumstances will cause the limitation period to be interrupted. According to the *New Dutch Civil Code* the limitation period may be stayed by :
- a written reminder;
- a written statement in which the creditor unequivocally reserves his right to performance (where the plaintiff claims performance of a certain obligation); or
- institution of legal proceedings; acknowledgment of the right of protection on which the claim relates.

Proceedings in the civil courts are started by a writ of summons or by a written request. In general, the date when the writ is issued or the request is received by the court determines when proceedings start. There are no special documents or forms required, except that a writ and a request must meet certain formal requirements. The writ will be served by a bailiff. If proceedings are started by submission of a request, a copy of the request submitted to the court will be sent by the court to the defendant. In most proceedings, representation by a member of the bar (*advocaat*) is required (although this is not necessary - inter alia - in proceedings before the Cantonal Courts). The court fees must be paid. The fees will vary depending on, inter alia, the financial interest at stake. *Commencement of proceedings*

On 30 December 1991 an act came into force which has brought unity in the way proceedings are initiated before a Cantonal Court in all cases other than those which - according to statutory provisions - must be started by a written request. If proceedings are initiated before a Cantonal Court by writ of summons, the plaintiff may choose between two methods :

1. the writ may be served upon the defendant by a bailiff, in accordance with the general rules for such services set out in the relevant provisions of the *Code of Civil Procedure*;

2. the plaintiff may complete a standard form, submit this to the court which sends it to the defendant by registered letter.

The form is generally available at no cost. If the second method is used, the day on which the form is sent to the defendant is deemed to be the date of the writ. The second method cannot be followed if :

- the defendant does not have a place of residence/establishment in the Netherlands; or
- the plaintiff requests the Cantonal Court to shorten the "notice period" between issuing the writ and the date on which the defendant is to appear before the court.

Service of proceedings

If proceedings are initiated by way of a writ of summons, the writ is formally served on the defendant. The law provides that the defendant(s) must receive a copy (copies) of the writ of summons. For the defendant such copy is deemed to be the original writ of summons. The bailiff makes a note on the original and on the copy of the name of the person with whom he has left the copy of the writ of summons. The original is returned to the lawyer acting for the plaintiff. Where the defendant is an individual residing in the Netherlands there are three ways in which service can be effected :

- service on the defendant in person (anywhere within the Netherlands by a bailiff authorised to act in that particular place);
- at the defendant's residence (if the defendant is not at home, the bailiff may give a copy of the writ to a member of the defendant's household);
- if there is no one present with whom the bailiff may leave a copy of the writ, the bailiff may leave it in a closed envelope at the defendant's residence (through the letter box).

In the exceptional circumstance that even the third possible way of service referred to above is not available, the bailiff may post the copy of the writ to the defendant.

If the defendant is a private legal entity, the writ of summons must be served on one of its managing directors (in person or at his residence), or at the statutory seat or place of business of that entity. If the defendant is an open partnership firm or a limited partnership, the writ of summons must be served on one of the managing partners (in person anywhere in the Netherlands or at his residence) or at the place of business of the partnership.

There are special rules for service of writs (and other formal notices) in particular cases such as service on the Queen, the state or any other public legal entity, a trustee/receiver in bankruptcy and on the heirs to the estate of a deceased.

Service of proceedings outside the Netherlands

If the defendant resides or is established outside the Netherlands (at a known address) the writ of summons (or other formal notice) must be served :

- on the official of the Public Prosecution Office (at the court before which the proceedings are to be brought or have been brought)
- at the office of this official.

An official at the Public Prosecution Office sends a copy of the writ or notice to the Ministry of Foreign Affairs which will ensure that the writ (or other formal notice) will be presented to the defendant (or addressee of the notice) through the intermediary of the Dutch diplomatic or consular officials in the relevant country. This procedure is based on the *Hague Conventions on Civil Procedure 1905, 1954* and the Acts in implementation of these conventions. These Conventions have, as between the countries which ratified them, been replaced by the *Hague Convention 1965* on the service abroad of judicial and extrajudicial documents in civil or commercial matters.

Service on persons residing or established in countries which are contracting parties to this Convention takes place in the manner referred to above, but the particular procedure involving the Dutch Ministry of Foreign Affairs is not followed as the Convention provides for its own procedure. The "central authority" in the Netherlands, for the purposes and within the meaning of the Convention, is the Public Prosecutor at the Hague District Court. The Act implementing the Convention provides for additional requirements to which the formal notices are subject. The bailiff immediately sends a second copy to the defendant (or addressee of the notice) by registered mail. The required service is completed once the writ (or other formal notice) has been served on the Public Prosecution Office.

The minimum period of time which has to be observed (ie the period of time between the date of issue of the writ and the date on which the case will be introduced and on which the defendant is summoned to appear in court) where the defendant resides or is established abroad, is one month if the defendant resides or is established in Andorra, Belgium, Germany, Great Britain, Ireland, Italy, Yugoslavia, Liechtenstein, Luxembourg, Monaco, Norway, Austria, Portugal, San Marino, Spain, Iceland, Sweden or Switzerland; two months if the defendant resides or is established elsewhere in Europe; four months in other cases.

Subject to certain conditions, the minimum time periods referred to above for defendants elsewhere in Europe or outside Europe may be shortened.

If the defendant does not file an appearance in court on the day mentioned in the writ of summons, the plaintiff can apply for judgment in default to be entered against the defendant. However, provided judgment has not been given, the defendant can still file an appearance at a later date. *Entering judgment in default*

The concept of summary judgment in English law does not exist in the Netherlands. Nor is there any provision to strike out pleadings before any hearings on the claim. *Summary judgment and striking out pleadings*

If the plaintiff in ordinary civil proceedings before a Dutch court is a foreign national, a (Dutch national) defendant may request the court (in a so-called "incidental" application and before putting forward any defence arguments) to order the foreign plaintiff to provide security for the defendant's costs in the proceedings which the plaintiff may have to pay if unsuccessful. *Security for costs*

Security for costs may also be requested in any appeal or cassation proceedings, provided that the foreign national was a plaintiff at first instance and is also the appellant in the appeal or cassation proceedings. The purpose of the "cautio iudicatum solvi" referred to above is to avoid a defendant against whom proceedings are brought in the Netherlands by a foreign national and whose defence is successful, having to pay his own costs on the grounds that the judgment cannot be executed abroad. However, the *Conventions on Civil Procedure 1905 and 1954* provide that the requirement to give security cannot be imposed upon nationals of the contracting parties to these Conventions who are also domiciled in their own country. This is because the Conventions provide for the judgment to be executed in countries which are contracting parties without costs being payable in the country where such enforcement is to take place.

Interlocutory relief

Such relief can (in general) be sought from the President of the District Court. It can be refused on the ground that it has not been sought speedily enough as the requirement for such relief is "urgency". However, in practice the Presidents are very lenient as far as this requirement is concerned. No relief will be granted without the defendant being heard. Relief can be obtained in a matter of hours and, in exceptional circumstances, a hearing can be conducted in a telephone conference. There is no requirement to give a cross-undertaking for damages, because enforcing a decision from the President of the District Court (or the Court of Appeal) which is overturned on appeal (or on cassation) of proceedings, or where the decision is proved wrong in the course of normal proceedings, may be considered a tort.

Rules of evidence

There are no special rules of evidence in interlocutory relief proceedings, but the President has an absolute discretion in this respect. Generally, evidence will be in writing but the President may decide to hear a witness during the oral arguments. The defendant can obtain relief from an order made by the President of the District Court (or by the Court of Appeal) by succeeding on appeal (or cassation) against the order, or by succeeding in the normal court proceedings which he can start if not started already by the plaintiff.

Directions as to further conduct of proceedings

There are no procedures by which directions may be sought as to the further conduct of the proceedings. However, a party can ask the court to order the other party to file its written answer (reply or rejoinder) by a specific (early) date. The court may also make such an order of its own motion.

Discovery of documents

There is no requirement to disclose documents in legal proceedings. A party discloses only those documents which it wishes to disclose. Documents produced in court must always also be sent to the other party. In general, an *advocaat* will show all the documents disclosed to him, to his client, unless he and his client agree otherwise with the other side. In practice, the court will in certain cases also give directions to that effect.

It is possible to refuse disclosure of documents on the grounds of *Legal privilege* legal professional privilege. It is not possible for such privilege to be overridden by the fact that the documents disclose a criminal offence.

The Bar rules prohibit *advocaten* from disclosing to the court the contents of their correspondence with other advocaten unless the client's interests specifically require disclosure, and then only after prior consultation with the advocaat for the other side. If such consultation does not result in a mutually acceptable solution, the dean of the local Bar must be consulted before disclosure may take place. The bar rules also prohibit disclosure of the contents of any settlement negotiations without the prior approval of the other party's *advocaat*.

In general, evidence will be gathered by the parties themselves. *Gathering of* However, the parties may ask the court, before or during the *evidence* proceedings, to hear potential witnesses. Such a hearing will be conducted by a judge who will question the witness. A court may also oblige a party to disclose/open its books and, in general, may always ask a party to prove certain statements it has made (assuming that the burden of proof rests with that party).

A party may be forced to disclose evidence before trial in *Disclosure of* proceedings for the preliminary hearing of witnesses. At the *evidence* request of an interested party a preliminary hearing of witnesses may be ordered by the court. The court may not order such a hearing of its own motion. Before such an order is granted, the other party is, as a general rule, summoned to be heard on the request. If the request is granted, the other party cannot appeal against this. If the request is refused, an appeal is possible. It is not entirely clear whether it is possible to hear the other side as a witness in a preliminary hearing before such party is summoned as a defendant in actual proceedings. If all the parties were present or represented at the preliminary hearing, the witnesses' evidence given at that hearing has the same force as evidence given at an ordinary hearing.

A party may challenge the admissibility of evidence when that *Admissibility of* evidence is tendered. *evidence*

Hearsay evidence is not admitted. *Hearsay evidence*

If a witness who does not reside in the Netherlands must be *Evidence abroad* heard, that witness can be heard by a judge to whose jurisdiction the witness is subject. A request to that effect is made by the court in the Netherlands handling the case. The Netherlands has ratified the *Hague Convention on the Taking of Evidence Abroad in Civil and Commercial Matters, 1970.* The *Convention* has been in force for the Netherlands since 7 June 1981.

The head of state cannot be called as a witness. The general rule *Witnesses* is that every person who has been called as a witness in compliance with the relevant legal requirements on calling witnesses is obliged to testify (*Code of Civil Procedure, art 191, para 1*). However, certain persons have the right to refuse to appear as witnesses. *Article 191, para 2 of the Code of Civil Procedure* grants this right to :

- the spouse and the former spouse of a party, the blood relatives and relatives by marriage of a party or his spouse up to and including the second remove (except in certain matters of family law);
- those persons who, because of their position as an official or because of their profession, are under an obligation of confidentiality with respect to all that has been confided to them in their professional capacity (in case law, the right to refuse to appear as a witness and thus to testify has been granted to - inter alia - civil law notaries, advocaten, members of the medical profession and clerics.

Article 191, para 4 of the Code of the Civil Procedure further provides that a witness may refuse to answer a particular question if he would thus expose himself or certain blood relatives or relatives by marriage, or his (former) spouse, to a criminal conviction in respect of a felony. A witness is entirely free to decide whether or not to invoke his right not to answer questions as a witness.

If a witness invokes the right to refuse to testify, a procedural "incident" is created on which the Judge-Commissary ("*Rechter-Commissaris*") decides. The witness then becomes a party to the incidental proceedings and may appeal from the decision of the Judge-Commissary. If the Judge-Commissary does not accept that the right to refuse to testify applies, only the witness involved may appeal. However, the party who wishes to have the witness heard may appeal from a decision whereby the witness is allowed to rely on the right to refuse to testify.

There are procedural rules under which one can compel a witness to appear. If a witness who cannot invoke the right to refuse, refuses to testify, he can be held in jail until he is willing to testify.

Expert evidence   The court may ask for advice from experts on particular technical points. If the court considers that it should appoint experts to give advice, the court will, in general, invite the parties to suggest names for such experts. The hearing of (an) expert(s) - if necessary, preceded by an investigation which is carried out by such expert(s) - is ordered by the court by way of an interlocutory judgment. A party always has a right to hand over its own expert reports or offer evidence by experts on its own behalf. The court will decide whether a particular expert has sufficient qualifications.

If a party wishes to submit any expert reports they must always be sent to the other side. An expert witness can always be called by a party, and of course, the other party has the right to put questions to the witness and may also challenge the qualifications of any "expert" tendered.

In the District Courts, Court of Appeal and the Supreme Court the right of audience is reserved for advocaten. In these courts individuals are not permitted to represent themselves. *Proceedings before the courts*

Witnesses are questioned by the court (Judge-Commissary). However, the court will, in general, give the parties the opportunity to put questions to the witness, always given that such questions are relevant to the facts that must be proved.

The court may appoint experts in order to obtain advice on, for instance, a technical point raised by the parties. The judge may - again to clarify a point raised by the parties - visit the "locus in quo", at the request of a party or of his own motion.

Judgment is given in open court and full reasons have to be given. There is no set time limit within which judgment must be given, but if within three months after oral arguments have been heard, no judgment has been given, the parties are entitled to have a new oral hearing. *Judgment*

Preliminary or interlocutory proceedings are independent of the main proceedings. Costs awarded to a winning party are determined on a "points" system in which the various stages in the proceedings (statements, oral pleadings, etc) are given a number of points (0 to 2) and each point is awarded a certain monetary value dependent also on the financial interests at stake in the proceedings. In cases in which the financial interests at stake do not exceed Dfl. 140,000 the number of points that are taken into account to determine the costs of the winning party is limited. In general, this amounts to only a small percentage of the actual costs incurred in any event. *Costs*

Advocaten will, generally, charge clients by way of an hourly rate. They are not allowed to charge on a contingency fee basis.

Costs are taxed by the court. They can be recovered through execution against the assets of the defendant. Such execution involves the services of a bailiff.

In cases of creditor's default, the debtor may offer payment in a formal written notice, prepared by a bailiff or a civil law notary. If the payment is not accepted, the amount may be paid into a special so-called "*consignatiekas*". The creditor may then be summoned to appear in proceedings in which the court validates the offer and the subsequent payment (provided all the requisite requirements have been met). The *New Dutch Civil Code* no longer provides for this stage of validation, and instead provides, in *Article 63 of Book 6* that, within the bounds of reasonableness, the debtor is entitled to compensation for the costs in respect of making an offer of payment and paying into the *consignatiekas* or for costs otherwise incurred in connection with the creditor's default. The *Code* also provides that no interest will be due from the debtor over the amount paid in during the period in which the amount remains in the consignatiekas.

Length of proceedings

Proceedings at first instance will last a year to a year and a half. It depends very much on the speed with which the parties act. If witnesses have to be heard or expert advice is asked for by the court, proceedings may take longer. Appeal and cassation proceedings will, in general, each take at least a year.

Appeals

The law provides for appeals on both fact and law.

Appeals are available from all first instance cases except from Cantonal Court decisions in matters with a monetary interest of less than Dfl. 2,500. In these cases direct appeal in cassation is possible on very limited grounds.

The average length of time between judgment being given at first instance and each subsequent appeal is a year to a year and a half.

CHAPTER 7 : CRIMINAL PROCEDURE

The basic structure of criminal proceedings is as follows : an investigation by police and/or Examining Judge ("*Rechter-Commissaris*"); a decision whether to prosecute taken by the Public Prosecutor; writ of summons/formal charge; a hearing of the Cantonal Court or District Court at first instance; any appeal with appropriate appellate court; any cassation-appeal to the Supreme Court; after annulment of the appeal judgment by the Supreme Court : (again) a decision by the Court of Appeal (with, again, cassation-appeal to the Supreme Court, etc). *Structure of criminal proceedings*

Dutch criminal law distinguishes between two categories of criminal offences : "*overtredingen*" (trespasses), and more serious -"*misdrijven*" (felonies).

In general, trespasses are tried at first instance in the (62) Cantonal Courts ("*Kantongerechten*"), with an appeal to the 19 District Courts ("*Arrondissementsrechtbanken*"). Felonies are tried at first instance by the District Courts with an appeal to the (5) Courts of Appeal ("*Gerechtshoven*").

In the Netherlands, there is no trial by jury. Cases brought before the Cantonal Courts are tried by the Cantonal Judge alone. Cases within the competence of the District Courts are tried either by a Police magistrate alone, or by a full court consisting of three judges.

The District Courts have special judges to try two special categories of criminal offences. The Economic Police Magistrate tries economic offences at first instance. The more serious economic offences are, however, tried at first instance by a full District Court. All offences, committed by juveniles are tried at first instance by the Juvenile Magistrate.

Prosecutions are carried out only by Public Prosecutors on behalf of the state. Although Public Prosecutors are employed by the state, they have complete autonomy in the decision whether or not to prosecute individual offences . *Prosecution*

A prosecution is commenced by either : *Commencement of prosecution*
- an initial writ of summons by the Public Prosecutor; or
- a request by the Public Prosecutor to institute a judicial preliminary investigation by an Examining Judge in the District Court; or
- preventive detention of a suspect by or on behalf of the Public Prosecutor.

Prosecutions do not proceed where the prosecution is either dismissed by the Public Prosecutor or where a settlement is reached between the accused and the Public Prosecutor.

Information relating to the offence

The charge is set out in the writ of summons. If the prosecution was not initiated by a writ of summons, a provisional charge is issued on the request of the Public Prosecutor to the Examining Judge to grant either a judicial preliminary investigation or the further detention of the suspect. The charge has to be a detailed description of the time and place of the offence, as well as of all the legally relevant circumstances whereby it is alleged to have been committed. The accused can oppose the writ of summons by lodging an objection against it with the court competent to try the case.

Commencement of proceedings

Court proceedings are commenced by the summons. The evidence for the Prosecutor is collected through the police investigation and, where carried out, the judicial preliminary investigation. The Prosecutor and the defence may call witnesses to testify in court. There is no formal minimum of evidence required before the writ of summons is issued. A writ of summons brings the case to trial. If a judicial preliminary investigation is carried out, the defence is entitled to request the Examining Judge to collect evidence for the defence. Furthermore, the defence is able to adduce written evidence before the court without restriction.

The defence is also entitled to challenge the request of the Prosecutor to have the accused kept in detention.

Pleas

There is no rule that a guilty plea reduces the level of any penalty that would be imposed. A guilty plea or a not guilty plea brings no formal consequence. Bargaining with the Prosecutor to substitute one charge for another is not prohibited, but does not take place in practice, as Prosecutors are not in favour of this.

Conduct of the trial

In a criminal trial a Dutch lawyer who is admitted to the Bar may appear as counsel. Lawyers from other EC Member States have the same rights in the hearing, the Prosecutor will present the charge to the court orally. The court will then ask the accused questions and, if necessary, hear witnesses and/or experts. Subsequently, the Prosecutor will sum up the prosecution and the defence will make its speech. After replication and rejoinder, the accused will have the last word.

There are no specific rules which entitle the defence to request a case to be stopped on the ground that there is no case to answer. The defence may only achieve something similar by lodging an objection against the writ of summons before any hearing actually takes place. If the case has not been brought to trial by the Prosecutor, the defence may ask the competent court to declare formally that the case has ended.

Expert witnesses

The court is able to call witnesses and appoint experts. They are questioned by the judge. The Prosecutor and the defence can request the judge to ask certain questions. The same applies to witnesses called by the prosecution or the defence. Hence, there is no opportunity to cross-examine in the Netherlands.

If the judge feels that further investigation is required, he can assign the case to the Examining Judge to carry out such further investigation.

Further investigation of the case

The court investigates :
- the validity of the summons (and the charge)
- whether it is competent to hear the charged offence
- whether there is any reason to refuse the Public Prosecutor putting forward the charges
- whether there are reasons to stay the prosecution
- whether the charged facts are proven
- whether the suspect is guilty and may be punished
- the measure of punishment.

The hearings are generally open and public. However, in certain cases the public is not allowed because of forcible reasons.

Hearings

The verdict of the court can be arrived at by majority vote. Whether the verdict is unanimous or by majority vote must remain secret, so any dissenting opinion is not made public. It is important to note that a defendant can only be found guilty of the offence charged.

Verdict

Sentencing takes place by the judge involved in the verdict. The judicial (preliminary) investigation may involve an investigation into the character of the accused by, for example, psychiatric experts. Factors constituting mitigation are the degree of culpability of the suspect, his financial capacity (where a fine may be imposed) and other factors specifically related to the suspect and the circumstances of the case. The judge is free to determine to what extent such factors are to be taken into account.

Sentencing

The maximum penalty for each crime is set out in the *Penal Code*. Apart from the legal maximum, the court has a free hand in sentencing, although there are special rules on the prosecution and sentencing of juveniles.

Sentencing guidelines

There are no mandatory sentences for certain crimes. Possible penalties are : imprisonment, a fine and a range of additional penalties, such as depriving the person found guilty of certain rights, confiscation and publication of the verdict. Penalties can be imposed conditionally or unconditionally, or partly conditionally, partly unconditionally.

In some cases what is known as an alternative sanction can be imposed whereby the accused will not be punished on condition that he will work a specific number of hours as a volunteer on a specific project.

Appeal against judgments of a Cantonal Court are possible to a District Court. Appeals from the judgment at first instance of a

Appeals

District Court is possible to a Court of Appeal. Judgments on appeal can be annulled by the Supreme Court of the Netherlands in a special cassation procedure which is strictly limited to dealing with the legal aspects of the judgment appealed. Ordinary appeals and appeals to the Supreme Court have to be made within 14 days after the judgment in question at the office of the court that gave that judgment. The period of time between the hearing and judgment at first instance and on appeal is 14 days at the maximum. The Supreme Court usually takes longer (approximately between one and four months).

Extradition

Extradition is governed by multilateral and bilateral treaties between the Netherlands and most other states of the world. The Netherlands is a party to the *European Convention on Extradition*.

The Minister of Justice decides whether an individual is to be extradited, but only following a specific decision by the Public Prosecutor. The Public Prosecutor requires the approval of the District Court for such a decision. The defendant is entitled to object against the request for approval, and to appeal from the grant of approval by the District Court to the Supreme Court.

Time limits for detention

The maximum period of time a person may be detained :
- before being charged[1] with an offence is six hours;
- before appearing before a magistrate (the Examining Judge before the District Court) is three days;
- before trial is 105 days (including the time spent before appearing before a magistrate).

Bail

A detainee is not entitled to bail. However, the District Court may suspend the preliminary detention on several conditions, one of which can be the lodging of bail.

---

1. This "charge" is rudimentary and usually only consists in stating the applicable article(s) of the *Penal Code*. A more extensive, but still preliminary charge is issued after three days, when the accused is brought before the Examining Judge.

CHAPTER 8 : REMEDIES

In general, damages may be recovered in cases of tort or breach of contract. Claims of up to Dfl. 5,000 are brought before a Cantonal Court. Claims exceeding Dfl. 5,000 and claims which cannot be assessed in financial terms are brought before a District Court.

Damages

Dutch legal procedures do not involve juries and it is always the task of the judge to award damages.

In personal injury actions, the quantum of damages is assessed by adding the sum for established material damage to, if applicable, any damages for mental distress. As a rule, there are no fixed awards for specific types of injury. However, damages awards for specific types of injury can be limited by Ministerial Order.

Personal injury actions

Damages can only be awarded under specific circumstances provided for by statute (eg intent to cause distress, and personal injury).

Award of damages under special circumstances

In principle, damages are available for loss of reputation. There is no limit to the amount which can be awarded, although judges tend to be restrictive in the amounts awarded.

Loss of reputation

There are no essential differences between damages for breach of contract and in tort. Damages for pure economic loss can be awarded.

Breach of contract, tort and economic loss

If a title of performance is voided or declared void by a court, restitution can be ordered, also in the case of commercial contracts. The same applies to unjust enrichment. The court can alter the content of a contract or declare it void on grounds that it was unreasonable and unfair.

Restitution

It is possible to seek the award of an agreed sum as fixed damages or as a penalty, but not to the extent that such an award would be unreasonable.

In general, an order may be sought for specific performance of an obligation.

Specific performance

A failure of a party to perform one of its obligations under an agreement entitles the other party to rescind that agreement, in whole or in part, unless that failure, given its special nature or its minor importance, does not justify the rescission and its consequences.

Shortcoming

Insofar as the performance of the agreement is not permanently or temporarily impossible, the creditor may only rescind the agreement when the debtor is in default (*"verzuim"*).

Penalty clauses

Even when it is contractually agreed upon that in the event of default of one of the parties involved, the party in default is obliged to pay to the other party a (fixed) penalty, the court upon request of the debtor may, if fairness so requires, moderate the agreed penalty; however, the penalty awarded to the creditor in respect of the default in performance may not be below the amount of damages to which the creditor is entitled by law.

Interest on monetary judgments

Interest is available on monetary judgments at a percentage fixed by royal decree (for 1992 it is 12%) which is due in respect of the period starting on the day it is claimed until the date of payment.

Declarations

A person may seek a declaration as to his legal rights or legal position, if he has sufficient interest.

Moratorium on payment ("surséance")

A debtor who foresees that he will be unable to pay all his debts may request the court to grant a moratorium on payment. The court will grant a temporary moratorium and will appoint one or more administrators. As in bankruptcy, there will also be a supervisory judge. The decision whether there will be a definitive moratorium is made after a court hearing. A definitive moratorium may be refused as the court sees fit. The *Bankruptcy Act* contains specific grounds on which the court must refuse a definitive moratorium. The difference between a bankrupt and a debtor who is granted a moratorium on payment is that the latter does not lose the right to dispose of and administer his property as a result of the judgment. The restriction on a debtor granted a moratorium of payment is that he is not allowed to manage his businesses as far as disposition and administration is concerned without the co-operation, authorisation or assistance of his administrator.

A trustee in bankruptcy replaces the bankrupt but an administrator does not replace a debtor, they have to work together as long as the moratorium on payment continues. The *Bankruptcy Act* provides that a debtor's property is not at risk in cases where contracts have been entered into without the co-operation, authorisation or assistance of the administrator.

Actions against public bodies

In general, all types of remedies are available against administrative bodies. However, the remedies against Acts of Parliament are very restricted and remedies against judgments in final instance are not possible.

Locus standi in administrative proceedings

No person is prevented from seeking legal remedies. To have locus standi in administrative proceedings one must have an interest at stake. Whether one has such an interest is to be determined on the basis of the facts of the case.

Civil remedies in criminal or administrative proceedings are more restricted. Additional remedies can be obtained in civil proceedings. In such civil proceedings damages already awarded in any criminal or administrative proceedings cannot be claimed twice, and any damages already awarded will be deducted from the sum in the civil judgment.

Civil remedies in criminal and administrative proceedings

If the parties had previously agreed to submit any disputes to arbitration, normal court procedures can be set aside. However, a plaintiff proving urgency can institute summary proceedings in court (for preliminary relief) if the agreed arbitration procedure does not provide for such a possibility. Mediation and conciliation do not have a statutory basis, but are possible if the parties agree to adopt these methods. In principle, all remedies otherwise available are possible in such alternative procedures.

Arbitration

CHAPTER 9 : MATRIMONIAL DISPUTES

Three types of matrimonial dispute should be distinguished : *Divorce* divorce, legal separation and dissolution of a marriage after a legal separation.

The District Courts ("*rechtbanken*") are the competent courts to deal with divorce. Within the District Courts a special "chamber" is often made responsible for family matters. Provided that the Dutch courts have jurisdiction pursuant to *Article 814(1) of the Code of Civil Procedure*, the District Court of the place of residence of the defendant is the competent court. If only the claimant resides in the Netherlands, the District Court of the place of residence of the claimant is the competent court. If divorce proceedings are at the "joint request" of the parties, the District Court of the place of residence of either party is competent to hear the case. If neither of the parties resides in the Netherlands (but the Dutch courts nevertheless have jurisdiction), the District Court in The Hague is the competent court.

The following additional claims can be instituted in divorce *Additional* proceedings : *claims (custody, access, etc) and*
- claims for alimony; *provisional*
- claims in respect of the custody of children; *measures*
- claims in respect of maintenance for children; *("voorlopige*
- claims in respect of access to children; *voorzieningen")*
- claims regarding the use of the matrimonial home;
- claims regarding the division of joint property.

The District Court which is competent to hear the divorce case will also decide on such additional matters. In matters concerning the custody of children, the "children's judge" ("*kinderrechter*") will be involved.

The District Court may also impose measures, at the request of either party to the divorce proceedings, which are "provisional" in nature (provisional measures cannot be sought in proceedings to dissolve a marriage following legal separation). They may last for the duration of the proceedings and for some time thereafter. The court can, inter alia, impose the following provisional measures :
- that one spouse has exclusive use of the matrimonial home;
- that the children be entrusted to one spouse (if necessary the court can order the release of the children from the other spouse);
- that an amount of alimony be paid by the other spouse with respect to the education of the children;

- that arrangements are made regarding access to the children by the other spouse;
- that an amount of alimony be payable by one spouse to the other.

The competent District Court is the court which will decide or is already deciding on the divorce.

Institution of divorce proceedings

Divorce proceedings can be instituted by :
- a writ of summons ("*dagvaarding*") served by the claimant upon the defendant;
- a joint request ("*gemeenschappelijk verzoek*") by the parties who are both in agreement on getting divorced.

The proceedings started with a writ of summons are conducted in the way described in Chapter 6. A court hearing with the parties themselves ("*comparitie*") may take place if one party has asked for such a hearing. The "joint request" proceedings start by filing the request with the court. A subsequent hearing of the parties to obtain further information may follow. The court will then give its decision. Until judgment is actually given, either party may withdraw the request.

Additional or ancillary requests

Additional or ancillary requests are usually part of the "main" divorce proceedings. The defendant may also make such additional claims. Where the additional claims concern questions of alimony, the matrimonial home and the division of property, the court will usually decide on these in the same judgment in which the divorce is granted. In the case of the custody of children, the court will usually decide at a later date in a separate ruling. A separate custody hearing will take place. The Council for the Protection of Children ("*Raad voor de Kinderbescherming*") must also be heard and minors who are older than 12 years must be heard. The "children's judge" will participate in the hearing.

Provisional arrangements

The request for provisional arrangements can be filed as separate proceedings or can be made a so-called "incident" in the divorce proceedings. If provisional measures have been granted before the divorce proceedings were instituted, the divorce proceedings must start within a month after the measures were granted. Failing this, the measures will be annulled.

Following the request for provisional measures by one party, the other side may file an answer. There will then always be a hearing of the parties (*comparitie*) before any judgment is given. Provisional measures may also be imposed in preliminary proceedings before the President of the District Court ("*kort geding*", see Chapter 6) if they are required as a matter of urgency.

A party may file a request for provisional measures and may request that such measures be immediately effective notwithstanding any appeal. Some District Courts require that the measures are needed urgently before they will grant them. In very urgent cases, a party may ask for a preliminary injunction from the President of the District Court.

The only ground for divorce and legal separation is "lasting disruption" ("*duurzame ontwrichting*") of the marriage.

Grounds for divorce

Divorce and legal separation cannot take place within one year of the marriage unless there are special circumstances. Any question of "guilt" is relevant only in two respects :
- a claim for divorce will be denied if the claimant is mainly to blame for the lasting disruption and the defendant uses this as a defence;
- if as a result of the divorce, the defendant's pension rights would be considerably reduced or lost, the divorce will not be declared until appropriate arrangements have been made, unless the defendant is mainly to blame for the lasting disruption.

If there is no pre-nuptial contract, the spouses are co-owners of all community property. Upon divorce the community property must be divided into equal parts. The parties may agree to divide the property into unequal parts. The community property consists of all property, rights and obligations of both spouses from the date of marriage, except for :
- gifts and bequests to one spouse if so provided by the person making the gift or bequest;
- assets and liabilities especially connected to one spouse.

Rules relating to matrimonial property on break-up of marriage

CHAPTER 10 : PROPERTY TRANSACTIONS

For the purposes of this chapter, "property" (*"onroerend goed"*) means immovable (corporal) goods, ie land and buildings as well as goods which according to Dutch law belong to the land or buildings and, consequently, are of an immovable nature.

A typical transaction of buying and selling property in the Netherlands would consist of two steps, ie an agreement to sell and purchase the property (the "obligatory agreement"); and the agreement to transfer the property (the "agreement in rem"). As a matter of course, the seller should be entitled to dispose of the property.

Agreement to sell and purchase

The obligatory agreement, which in practice is always in written form (but which may also be oral) provides for the sale and purchase of the property, and for a commitment of the parties to transfer the property at a given date. The agreement will in all cases include a description of the property and the purchase price. The parties may include additional provisions, eg regarding financial arrangements, the maintenance of the property and environmental matters. Often these provisions are included as conditions precedent to the transfer of the property.

The sale and purchase of the property form the two requirements for the transfer of the legal title to the property.

It should be noted, however, that sale and purchase of the property are not the only title to transfer : a transfer may also take place pursuant to a different legal title, such as the terms of a last will.

Agreement to transfer property

The sale and purchase of the property is effected by the agreement to transfer which is governed by mandatory rules of law. According to *Article 3 : 89 of the New Civil Code* (which came into force on 1 January 1992), the transfer of property is effected by execution of a notarial deed of transfer followed by registration of the deed in the relevant public register.

The notarial deed should, in any event, refer to the legal title to transfer and provide the exact description of the property as registered in the public cadastral register. The deed should be signed by the notary and both seller and purchaser.

When the notarial deed is executed it is registered in the public cadastral register. It should be noted that the transfer is only valid once the deed has been registered.

Although registration is a condition for a transfer of property to be valid, registration itself does not, due to the "negative system of publication in registers", provide conclusive evidence of ownership of the property. However, case law has, subject to certain conditions, provided for third parties who rely in good faith on the information contained in the public cadastral register to be protected in such an event. However, the *New Civil Code* provides that a person who has failed properly to check the information appearing from public registers has to bear any negative consequences of such failure. But a person who has properly checked the public registers is protected against certain unexpected events arising from facts which could have been filed in the public registers by the interested parties but have not been thus filed.

CHAPTER 11 : RECOGNITION AND ENFORCEMENT OF FOREIGN JUDGMENTS

As a general rule, a foreign judgment will not be recognised and enforced by the Dutch courts unless there is a treaty between the Netherlands and the foreign state providing for reciprocal recognition and enforcement (or if enforcement is possible pursuant to an act).

The Netherlands has entered into various bilateral treaties with other countries. *The Brussels Convention on Jurisdiction and Enforcement of Judgments in Civil and Commercial Matters 1968* has been in force in the Netherlands since 1973. The Netherlands also signed on 7 February 1989 the *Lugano Convention on Jurisdiction and Enforcement of Judgments* (among EC and EFTA members). Since 1 January 1992 it has been in force as between the Netherlands and France and between the Netherlands and Switzerland.

If a judgment cannot be enforced in the Netherlands, it is possible to bring the case to court for a second time. The Dutch courts will give the foreign judgment binding force unless the foreign judgment contravenes Dutch public policy.

To enforce a foreign judgment in the Netherlands separate leave ("*exequatur*") must be granted by a Dutch court pursuant to *Articles 985 to 994 of the Code of Civil Procedure*. These articles only apply to the extent that a treaty or an act does not give special provisions (see below in respect of the *1968 Brussels Convention*).

The District Courts are competent to rule on requests to grant an *exequatur*.

In addition to the request itself, a certified copy of the foreign judgment must be submitted together with the documents which establish that the foreign judgment is enforceable in the country in which it was given. The District Court can also ask for authentication as valid documents and translations of these documents. The requesting party must chose a "domicile" within the district of the court deciding on the exequatur request. This domicile could, for instance, be the office of the attorney who files the request with the court.

The *1968 Brussels Convention* provides for its own exequatur procedure, which replaces the procedure pursuant to *Articles 985 to 994 of the Code of Civil Proceedure* for cases within the scope of the *Convention*.

Contravention of public policy as a ground for non-recognition of a judgment has been narrowly construed by the Dutch Supreme Court. Violation of the proper course of justice will usually be considered to contravene public order. Obtaining a judgment by deceit or in breach of the law is another example of a violation of public order. In matters regarding the custody of children, violation of the child's interest may be considered to contravene public order.

Appeals against a decision by a District Court to grant an *exequatur* can be instituted within one month of the decision being given. The relevant appeal court is the Court of Appeal ("*Gerechtshof*"). Appeal against the Court of Appeal decision must be lodged with the Dutch Supreme Court within one month.

BIBLIOGRAPHY

Codes and Acts etc

Nederlandse Wetgeving (losbladige editie Kluwer)
    Deel A Staats - en Administratiefrechtelijke Wetten
    Deel B Nederlandse Wetboeken en Aanverwante
           Wetten
    Deel C Fiscale Wetten

(There is also a student edition and an edition of the New Civil Code in this looseleaf publication), Kluwer, Deventer, The Netherlands

Most codes and acts are also available in the extensive series of *Schuurman & Jordens*, published by W.E.J. Tjeenk Willink, Zwolle, The Netherlands

Main Reference Books and Case Law Reports :
General civil law

Asser, C., *Handleiding tot de beoefening van het Nederlands Burgerlijk Recht, Algemeen Deel & delen Personen en Familierecht, Rechtspersoon, Zakenrecht, Verbintenissenrecht en Bijzondere Overeenkomsten* (adaptations by several different authors), W.E.J. Tjeenk Willink, Zwolle, The Netherlands

Pitlo, A., (original author) *Het Nederlands Burgerlijk Wetboek* (adaptations by several different authors), Gouda Quint B.V., Arnhem, The Netherlands

Commercial and bankruptcy law

Dorhout Mees, T.J., (original author) *Nederlands handels - en faillissementsrecht* (adaptations by several different authors), Gouda Quint B.V., Arnhem, The Netherlands

Civil procedure

Hugenholtz, W. (adapted by W.H. Heemskerk) *Hoofdlijnen van Nederlands Burgerlijk Procesrecht*, VUGA, The Hague, The Netherlands

Criminal law and the law of criminal procedure

Van Bemmelen, J.M., *Ons strafrecht*, (series), Samsom H.D. Tjeenk Willink, Alphen aan den Rijn, The Netherlands

Case Law

Nederlandse Jurisprudentie (published weekly by W.E.J. Tjeenk Willink, Zwolle, The Netherlands)

Rechtspraak van de Week, (published weekly by W.E.J. Tjeenk Willink, Zwolle, The Netherlands)

Kort Geding (decisions in preliminary relief proceedings), (published weekly by W.E.J. Tjeenk Willink, Zwolle, The Netherlands)

PORTUGAL

José Manuel Coelho Ribeiro
President of the CCBE
Coelho Ribeiro Associados, Lisbon

CONTENTS

CHAPTER 1 : SOURCES OF LAW

Portugal has a unitary structure of government with some *Unitary v federal* regional legislative competence reserved to the local parliaments *system* of the Autonomous Regions of the Azores and Madeira.

The sources of law in Portugal are found in the *Constitution of the Republic of Portugal,* and in other Laws and Decree-Laws which have been enacted in accordance with the terms of the *Constitution.*

Article 6 of the Constitution provides:
"1. The state is unitary and respects, within its organisation, the principle of the independence of local autarchies and the democratic decentralisation of public administration.
2. The archipelagoes of the Azores and Madeira are autonomous regions endowed with political/administrative statutes and their own Governmental Body."

The legislative power of the Autonomous Regions of the Azores and Madeira is provided for in *Article 229 of the Constitution.* The Autonomous Regions have the power to legislate on matters of specific interest to the Autonomous Regions, provided such matters do not come within the competence of the Sovereign Body, and are compatible with the *Constitution* and the national laws of the Republic.

The principal sources of substantive law are :   *Sources of*
- the *Constitution;*   *substantive law*
- the *Civil Code;*
- the *Penal Code;*
- the *Commercial Code;*
- the *Company Law Code;*
- the *Tax and VAT Codes;* and
- the *Employment Code.*

The principal sources of procedural law are :   *Sources of*
- the *Code of Civil Procedure;*   *procedural law*
- the *Code of Criminal Procedure;*
- the *Code of Tax Procedure;*
- the *Code of Employment Procedure;* and
- the *Administrative Procedure Law.*

(The specific Codes are currently under revision.)

Application of national laws with respect to foreigners

Foreigners and *"apátridas"* (those without any nationality), whether resident or non-resident in Portugal, are subject to and benefit from the same rights as Portuguese citizens. There are exceptions in respect of political rights, access to the civil service (save for predominantly technical positions) and rights and duties reserved exclusively for Portuguese citizens by the *Constitution* and the law.

Citizens of Portuguese-speaking countries may be granted, through international conventions and on the basis of reciprocity, rights which are not otherwise available to foreigners, save for the following : admission to the sovereign and governmental bodies of the autonomous regions; service in the armed forces and membership of the diplomatic service.

Foreigners residing within the national territory may be granted, in accordance with the law and on the basis of reciprocity, electoral rights in the elections of the regional autarchies' governing body (under *Article 15 of the Constitution*).

Monist v dualist system

The rules and principles of international law, whether general or common, are an integral part of Portuguese domestic law.

The principles and rules of international conventions, which have been duly sanctioned or approved, signed and ratified so as to come into force have internal effect after official publication and for as long as they remain internationally binding on the Portuguese State.

The decisions and rules of competent bodies of international organisations of which Portugal is a member have immediate domestic effect, if duly concluded under the provisions of their respective constitutive treaties (*Article 8 of the Constitution*). Where such decisions and rules are in accordance with *Article 8*, the Portuguese courts should directly apply such rules of international law.

Application of EC law

Portugal became a member of the European Communities with effect from 1 January 1986.

Under *Article 2 of the Act on the Accession of the Portuguese Republic*, which is a constituent part of the *Accession Treaty of 12 June 1985*, after accession the provisions of the original treaties and acts adopted by the EC before accession are binding in Portugal in accordance with Community law.

Community legislation after accession which has direct effect is automatically incorporated into Portuguese law.

The above-mentioned act relating to the conditions of accession of the Republic of Portugal and the Spanish Kingdom and to the adjustment of the then existing treaties lays down transitional measures in respect of certain sectors, such as for some agricultural issues, so delaying the full impact of all EC law in Portugal.

According to *Article 8 of the Constitution* and the above-mentioned treaties and the said act, Portuguese courts should accept and adopt Community law in full.

Foreign law is directly applicable by Portuguese courts in accordance with the rules of private international law as provided for in *Articles 16 to 65 of the Civil Code*. Foreign law is treated as a question of law, and must be proved as to its existence and validity by the party wishing to rely on it, in accordance with the provisions of Portuguese procedural law. The same applies to any foreign document which a party wishes to rely on, which must thus be translated into Portuguese.

Citation of foreign law in national proceedings

Portugal has ratified the *European Convention on Human Rights* and it became part of domestic law by virtue of *Law No 65/78 of 13 October 1978*.

Application of the European Convention on Human Rights

Portugal entered no reservations on the application of *Article 53 of the Convention*, therefore the provisions of the *Convention* and case law deriving from it are to be applied directly by the Portuguese courts.

Interpretation is not literal, but should reflect the intentions of the legislature as expressed in the texts, above all, taking into consideration the unity of the legal system, the circumstances in which the law was formulated and the specific conditions of the time when it is being applied. In ascertaining the meaning and scope of the law, one must presume that the legislature expressed its intentions in adequate terms (see *Article 9 of the Civil Code*).

Principles of interpretation

Cases not foreseen by law are decided by applying analogous rules which govern similar cases.

If there is no similar case available, the situation will be resolved in accordance with the rules laid down by the courts as if they were the legislature, always in accordance with the spirit of the legal system (see *Article 10 of the Civil Code*).

Previous decisions are not considered as sources of law, but are regarded simply as jurisprudence. However, there is one situation where the Supreme Court can lay down a source of law. This is provided for in *Article 2 of the Civil Code*. The ruling is called *"Assento"* and applies when, in respect of the same legislation, the Supreme Court of Justice has handed down two judgments which, in dealing with the same fundamental question of law, arrive at contrary solutions. An appeal may be made to the full bench of the court which handed down the last judgment given. Judgments are considered to have been given in respect of the same legislation when from the time of publication of the law no amendments have been made which directly or indirectly affect consideration of the question of law at issue.

Only a previous "transit in rem judicatam" judgment can be invoked as a ground for an appeal.

Texts of the
Constitution
There are no special authorised annotated texts of the Constitution.

CHAPTER 2 : FUNDAMENTAL RIGHTS

The *Constitution of the Portuguese Republic* is considered to be one of the most advanced on the question of protecting fundamental rights.

The general principles (in *Title I*) include the principles of universality and of equality - "all citizens benefit from the rights and are liable to the duties provided for within the *Constitution*. Corporate bodies benefit from rights and are subject to duties compatible with their nature. All citizens have the same social dignity and are equal before the law."

No one can be privileged, gain a benefit, be aggrieved, or deprived of any right or released from any duty for reasons of sex, race, language, country of origin, religion, political or ideological conviction, schooling, economic situation or social condition.

The *Constitution* also sets out basic legal rules governing the position of Portuguese living abroad (*art 14*); of foreigners and *"apátridas"* (*art 15*); access to the law and the courts (*art 20*); the right of residence (*art 21*); the responsibility of public entities (*art 22*); and the powers of the *"Provedor da Justiça"* (the ombudsman) (*art 23*).

Article 16 lays down the extent and meaning of the fundamental rights, declaring that fundamental rights enshrined in the *Constitution* do not exclude the application of other rights which are contained in other laws and the rules of international law.

The constitutional and legal precepts governing fundamental rights should be implemented and integrated in accordance with the *Universal Declaration on Human Rights*.

The *Constitution* provides that the constitutional precepts of the rights, liberties and guarantees are directly applicable and binding on public and private entities. The law can restrict rights, liberties and guarantees only in the circumstances clearly laid down in the *Constitution*, such restrictions being limited to what is necessary in order to protect other rights or interests which are protected under the *Constitution*.

Laws restricting rights, liberties and guarantees must be general and abstract; they cannot have retroactive effect, nor can they diminish the scope or importance of the essential content of the constitutional precepts.

Title II of Part 1 on Fundamental Rights and Duties

Title II of the Constitution (Rights, Liberties and Guarantees) provides for :

- a right to life;
- personal integrity;
- the right to freedom and security;
- special rules on preventive imprisonment;
- the extent of penalties and of security measures;
- "Habeas Corpus";
- extradition, expulsion and asylum rights;
- the inviolability of domicile and correspondence;
- family, marriage and affiliation rights;
- freedom of speech and the media;
- freedom of speech and political representation through the radio and television;
- freedom of conscience, religion and worship;
- freedom of cultural creation;
- displacement and emigration rights;
- the right of assembly and the right to demonstrate one's opinion;
- the freedom of choice of work and access to public offices.

Title II contains two further chapters on political participation and on the rights of the workers.

Title III provides for economic, social and cultural rights and duties, including the basic right to work and rights of workers (*arts 58 and 59*); consumer rights (*art 60*); and of private initiative and private property rights (*arts 61 and 62*).

Chapter II of Title III on social rights and duties, includes rights relating to social security (*art 63*); health (*art 64*); lodging (*art 65*); environment and quality of life (*art 66*); family (*art 67*); paternity and maternity (*art 68*); childhood and adolescence (*arts 69 and 70*); the handicapped (*art 71*); and the elderly (*art 72*).

Judicial review of the constitutionality of government

Legal proceedings to protect fundamental rights are rare in Portugal. Nevertheless, proceedings for such rights are provided for in the *Constitution* itself as well as in other legislation.

The courts cannot apply statutes which violate the *Constitution* or its principles (*Constitution, art 207*). Thus, in principle, all courts are competent to review unconstitutionality as an issue in proceedings before them. However, it is the Constitutional Court which is able specifically to determine issues of a legal/constitutional nature. It is competent to determine whether statutes violate the *Constitution* or the principles laid down therein (*Constitution, arts 207, 225 and 277*).

Law No 28/82 of 15 November 1982, as amended by *Laws Nos 143/85 of 26 November 1985* and *85/89 of 7 September 1989*, laid down the rules of the Constitutional Court and for review of the constitutionality of laws.

All citizens have the right to invoke, and have judged by any court, any issue of the unconstitutionality of laws or breach of fundamental rights under the *Constitution*, with an ultimate appeal to the Constitutional Court - under *Articles 70ff of the law on the Constitutional Court and the review of constitutionality.*

Any lawyer who is a member of the Portuguese Bar Association ("*Ordem dos Advogados Portugueses*") may appear before the Constitutional Court.

Legal representation

CHAPTER 3 : JURISDICTION OF THE COURTS

Portuguese courts may assume jurisdiction on any of the following bases : *Assumption of jurisdiction*

- where the action is initiated in Portugal, in accordance with the rules on territorial competence as provided for under domestic law;
- where the act on which the action is based occurred within a Portuguese territory;
- where the defendant is foreign and the plaintiff is Portuguese, provided that, in the inverse situation, the foreign court would have accepted jurisdiction and the Portuguese person would have had a right to appear and defend the proceedings before the courts of the defendant's state;
- where the action is initiated before the Portuguese courts, for it is the only way to have a certain right recognised, and there is a significant personal or real connection between the action and the Portuguese courts;
- when, under Portuguese domestic law, the courts of the defendant's domicile are competent to hear the action, the Portuguese court can assume jurisdiction provided the defendant has resided in Portugal for more than six months or is accidentally in national territory, provided in the latter case, some liability arose in respect of the Portuguese person;
- where foreign corporate bodies are domiciled in Portugal provided they have there a branch office, agency, sub-office or delegation.

Portuguese courts have exclusive jurisdictional competence over actions concerning real property within Portuguese territory, to determine the bankruptcy or insolvency of corporate bodies whose registered offices are within Portuguese territory, and over actions concerning labour relations.

A breach of these rules on juridical competence renders the court absolutely incompetent to hear the proceedings, and this issue may be raised by either party or by the court of its own motion at any stage of the proceedings.

The court in whose area an offence was committed is competent to deal with it. Where an offence is perpetrated by successive or repeated acts, the court in whose area the last offence took place will be competent.

If an offence has not been completed, the court in whose area the last act took place will have jurisdiction. Where preparatory acts

are punishable, the court in whose area the last preparatory act took place will be competent.

State immunity
The state and all other public entities have civil liabilities concurrent with the incumbent officers of its bodies, employees or agents for acts or omissions effected in the performance of their duties which result in a violation of another's rights, liberties and guarantees, or in damage to another person.

Domicile and other factors determining the courts' jurisdiction
An individual has his domicile at his usual place of residence. If he resides alternately in various places, he is considered as being domiciled in each of them. If there is no usual place of residence, domicile is at the place of occasional residence; or if this cannot be determined, at the place where he is staying at that moment.

The registered office of a corporate body is determined by its Articles of Association or, if none, the place where its central administration normally works. Foreign corporate bodies are domiciled in Portugal provided they have there a branch-office, agency, sub-office or delegation. Business corporations are subject to the law of the state where their registered office is located. A company with registered offices in Portugal cannot, however, be subjected to a law there other than Portuguese domestic law.

CHAPTER 4 : ADMINISTRATION OF JUSTICE

The courts are independent sovereign bodies subject only to the law (*Constitution, arts 205 and 206*).

Structure of the court system

In addition to the Constitutional Court, there are the following categories of courts : the Supreme Court of Justice and the Judicial Courts of first and second instance; the Supreme Administrative Court and the lower Administrative and Tax Courts; the Court of Auditors; and the Courts Martial. There are also Admiralty Courts and Courts of Arbitration. Save for Courts Martial, no court has exclusive competence to judge certain criminal offences.

The hierarchy of the courts is outlined below :

Hierarchy of the courts

The Supreme Court of Justice is the highest body in the judicial courts' hierarchy, without prejudice to the Constitutional Court. The Courts of first instance (trial courts) are, as a rule, County Courts. The courts of second instance are, as a rule, Courts of Appeal. The Supreme Court of Justice operates as an "Instance Court" in the circumstances provided for by law.

The judicial courts hear both civil and criminal matters, and have jurisdiction over all areas not assigned to other judicial bodies. Courts of first instance may have specific competences.

The courts of second instance and the Supreme Court of Justice can operate as specialised chambers.

The Supreme Administrative Court is the highest body in the hierarchy of the Administrative and Tax Courts. The Administrative and Tax Courts deal with proceedings resulting from administrative and fiscal legal disputes.

The Courts Martial are competent to deal essentially with military offences. For any relevant matter the law may include within these courts' jurisdiction offences of fraud analogous to essentially military offences. The law may permit these courts to impose disciplinary measures.

The Court of Auditors is the highest review body dealing with questions of public expenditure and its legality, and the assessing of accounts the law requires to be submitted to it. For example, the Court of Auditors is competent to assess the state's general accounts, including matters of social security; to assess the general accounts of the autonomous regions; to allocate responsibility for finance violations; and to exercise other competences assigned by law. The Court of Auditors can operate through regional chambers. *Law No 38/87 of 23 December 1987,* as amended by *Law No 24/90 of 4 August,* established the judicial courts regulated by *Decree-Law No 214 of 17 June 1987.*

Appeals

Court decisions, with the exception of orders and rulings on the lawful use of a discretionary power, can be challenged on appeal. An appeal may deal with questions as to the purpose or merits of the decision, or with procedural issues.

A normal appeal has two possible stages : from the court of first instance to the court of second instance; and from there to the Supreme Court.

Questions of fact can be re-examined by the court of second instance but never by the Supreme Court of Justice, which, in principle, only rules on questions of law.

Issues as to the erroneous assumption of jurisdiction/ competence may be appealed to the Supreme Court of Justice.

Appeals can be taken by the unsuccessful party and in some cases by the Public Prosecutor in accordance with the law, when notified of an appealable decision or when aware of such a decision.

References under Article 177 of the EEC Treaty

The reference procedure under *Article 177 of the EEC Treaty* is applied in accordance with the terms of the Treaty.

CHAPTER 5 : STRUCTURE OF THE LEGAL PROFESSION

There is one independent legal profession in Portugal. Only *Structure of the* lawyers and probationary lawyers who are members of the Bar *legal profession* Association can carry out acts and practices characteristic of the profession throughout the national territory and before any authority or public/private entity.

"Notaries" are a separate profession, who are holders of public office.

There is a profession called "solicitors" practising law, albeit in a limited manner, under *Decree-Law No 403/76 of 14 July 1976*. However, they are not qualified lawyers as solicitors are in the UK or Ireland. Tax advisers, intellectual property agents and accountants cannot provide legal services.

All advocates who are members of the Portuguese Bar *Advocates and* Association may practise without having to have any kind of *rights of audience* specialisation, and with full rights of audience before all courts.

Advocates can form partnerships as a Civil Lawyers' Society *Law practices* (which is non-commercial), with unlimited personal liability. *Decree-Law No 513-0/79 of 26 December 1979* regulates Civil Lawyers' Societies.

Advocates can have several offices within the national territory *Branch offices* provided these are duly registered with the Bar Association. Portuguese advocates may form branch offices in other EC countries as permitted by the laws of that Member State.

Fees may be charged on an hourly basis. When charging fees, a *Fees* lawyer must set rates which are reasonable according to *Articles 65(1)ff of the Bar Association's rules*. They should be fixed with reference to the duration and difficulty of the case, the importance of the services rendered, the clients' resources, the results and the practice of the particular county. Fees may be agreed before trial provided they do not depend on the result.

Fees can be agreed on the basis of a percentage of the value of the action, provided that, taking all other relevant factors into account, the result is not immediate.

The District Bar's Assembly or, if there is none, the lawyers of a District themselves, can establish a Fee Schedule with average charges.

If there is a dispute or disagreement between a lawyer and client over fees either can request an opinion from the Bar Association. Lawyers can, however, sue for their fees through the courts. It is within the judge's discretion whether to request the Bar's opinion on the matter.

The fee account must be presented to the client in writing and be signed by the lawyer. Fees must be settled in money and in national currency. The account must set out the services rendered, separate fees from expenses and charges, which must all be set out separately and dated. The lawyer may not alter the account presented to the client although he may demand interest as provided for by law (see *Article 4 of the Portuguese Bar Fees Regulation*).

Value Added Tax ("*IVA*") must be paid on lawyers' services, currently at 16%.

Professional conduct

Lawyers are subject to the rules of professional conduct set out in the bye-laws on lawyers (*Articles 76 to 89 of Decree-Law No 84/84 of 16 March 1984*). Breach of these rules may result in disciplinary action by the Bar Association. A lawyer is guaranteed an opportunity to defend himself when any complaints against him are heard. Disciplinary sanctions can be imposed by the Bar subject to an appeal to the competent court. Any client, whether national or foreign, may instigate a complaint before the Bar.

The CCBE Code applies to Portuguese lawyers practising abroad.

Professional indemnity insurance is not yet compulsory.

Practice by foreign lawyers

Foreign lawyers can only practise in Portugal if they are members of the Portuguese Bar Association. There is an exception on the provision of services under the terms of the *Lawyers' Services Directive of 22 March 1977*[1] which has been adopted into Portuguese law.

Instructing lawyers

Lawyers are instructed directly by clients. A lawyer must be instructed if a court appearance is necessary, save in civil proceedings from which there is no appeal, eg in the case of divorce by mutual consent, and before first instance Tax Courts.

Directory of legal services

There is no official directory setting out the specialisations of individual lawyers or of law firms.

---

1.   Council Directive (EEC) 77/249 (OJ L78 26.3.77 p17).

CHAPTER 6 : CIVIL PROCEDURE

The general course of civil proceedings is as follows :

- issue of writ;
- defence contested by the "*Despacho de Especificaçao e Questionario*";
- evidence gathered with witnesses' depositions, documentary and expert evidence;
- trial, followed, where possible, by an appeal to the second instance court and then, if appropriate, to the Supreme Court of Justice.

Basic structure of court proceedings

After transit in rem judicatam, a judgment can be executed by the following process :

- execution petition;
- attachment of assets;
- possible stay of execution;
- citation of preferred creditors;
- court order;
- attachment, sale or award of property to the judgment creditor.

Courts of first instance may assume jurisdiction depending on subject matter, territory, forms of action and structure. They are, depending on the forms of the proceedings, courts of general or specialised competence.

Division of competences

The following courts have specialised competence : Civil Courts, Criminal Courts, Family Courts, Juvenile Courts, Labour Courts and Admiralty Courts.

Tax matters are dealt with by first instance Tax Courts. Provided they are not exclusively assigned by special law to a judicial court or to a compulsory formal arbitration, any legal action not concerning issues of non-transferable rights may be resolved by arbitration agreed between the parties.

The rules governing the attribution of competence are set out under the *Organic Law for Judicial Courts of 23 December 1987*; and the *Law on Voluntary Arbitrations of 29 August 1987*.

All individuals and corporate persons may be parties to legal proceedings. Although not possessing corporate status, heirs and partnerships are also competent to sue and be sued.

Parties to the proceedings/locus standi

The state is represented by the "*Ministério Público*" (Public Prosecutor), which also protects the interests of minors, workers and incompetent persons, and has the right to be heard in almost every law-suit, even if not a defendant or representative of any party.

Immunity

In civil matters, there is no immunity from process for the head of state, the government, public companies or entities with diplomatic status.

Third party intervention

Third parties may intervene in proceedings if they can show a direct interest in the subject matter of the action. Portuguese procedural law is a formal, complex system, but the parties do have the chance to support or challenge the allegations of any third party. Parties may always appeal against the decision of the court to allow a party to intervene.

Joinder of claims

The joinder of claims which are compatible as between each other, and claims in the alternative and supplementary claims are allowed in all forms of action.

A defendant may counterclaim against a plaintiff. Plaintiffs may be joined against one or more defendants, and a plaintiff can sue jointly several defendants in different claims when the cause of action is one and the same or when the actions are mutually dependent.

Brussels Convention

The *Brussels Convention on the Recognition and Enforcement of Judgments in Civil and Commercial Matters 1968* corresponds, in general terms, to the system already in force in Portuguese domestic law. The *Brussels Convention* has been in force in Portugal since July 1992.

"Popular actions"

Everyone has the right either personally or through Defence Associations to institute an *"Acção Popular"*, in the circumstances and on the terms provided for by law, namely the right to prevent, or to instigate prosecution for breaches of public health or of environmental provisions, to promote the protection of the quality of life; to prevent despoliation of historic sites as well as to claim an indemnity where available for any injured person (*Constitution, art 52*).

Legal aid

Article 20 of the Constitution enshrines the principle of access to the law and the courts so that all citizens may defend their rights. It also provides that justice may not be denied because of insufficient economic resources.

Decree-Law No 387/B/87 of 29 December 1987 lays down the system for access to criminal, civil and other proceedings, as well as for access to information and legal advice.

The legal aid system is available in respect of all proceedings before all courts (*Decree-Law No 387/B/87, art 17*). Legal aid can be requested by any interested party, by the *"Ministério Público"* (Public Prosecutor) or by a lawyer representing a client who cannot afford to pay his legal fees. Proof that the petitioner has insufficient resources can be made by any authorised means.

Legal aid is granted by the court dealing with the action and can be objected to by the other side. When granted, legal aid covers all or part of pre-payment costs and the payment of court costs as well as advocates' fees (*Decree-Law No 387/B/87, art 15*).

Official documents are free for legal aid purposes.

If, during the proceedings, evidence comes to light that the petitioner already had or has acquired sufficient economic resources, legal aid will not only be withdrawn but repayment of the amounts spent will be demanded. Criminal proceedings may be brought if any crime was committed in obtaining legal aid.

Limitation/ *prescription* The protection of rights which are not non-transferable or declared exempt from prescription by law must be prosecuted within fixed time limits. Property rights, usufruct, use, habitation and similar rights are not prescribed but can be extinguished for non-exercise where specially provided for by law.

There is a legal situation, similar to prescription, called "*caducidade*". In the *Portuguese Civil Code* the rules on prescription and *caducidade* are governed by *Articles 296 to 333*.

The *Civil Code* does not distinguish *caducidade* from prescription. Whether the latter or the former applies can only be determined by interpreting each legal or, where applicable, contractual provision where time limits within which the rights must be exercised are set. The general limitation periods are laid down in *Articles 309 to 311*. The normal period of prescription is 20 years, although a five year period applies in the case of some legal actions, such as for income and interest.

There are also rules of presumptive prescription which apply to suspend or interrupt the running of time.

There is no time limit for when *caducidade* applies as this must be established on a case-by-case basis by law or by legal act.

Initiating *proceedings* In the summons starting an action, a plaintiff must nominate a court where the action will be dealt with and identify the parties, giving their names, places of residence and, whenever possible, occupation and place of work. The plaintiff must further identify the applicable procedure, set the facts he considers already proved and those he intends to prove and state the law on which the action is based. He must request pleadings and at the end of the declaration, the plaintiff may immediately present witnesses and request further evidence. The declaration will not be accepted if not in accordance with tax law requirements.

The plaintiff must attach a letter of attorney authorising his lawyer to act on his behalf in accordance with the normal requirements.

The declaration must be presented to the court competent to deal with the case. The court's office assigns actions to the judges on Mondays and Tuesdays, save in cases of urgency. When an action is duly assigned, the plaintiff has 7 days to settle pre-payment of the costs amounting to one quarter of the justice tax which will have to be paid in the end by the losing party.

Service of proceedings

The rules for service of proceedings are set out mainly in *Articles 228 to 263 of the Code of Civil Procedure.*

Individuals are personally summoned by the bailiff wherever they are located. Corporate bodies and associations are served by registered mail, or at their registered office by the bailiff on their legal representative, on any employee, or their legal representative wherever located.

When the summons is issued, a duplicate of the writ is delivered to the defendant, indicating the time period within which the claim is to be contested and when any sanctions may be applied.

Portugal has ratified the *Hague Convention of 15 November 1965* on the service of summons and notification of judicial and extra-judicial acts in civil and commercial matters abroad.

Portuguese domestic procedural law permits service of the summons on a defendant residing abroad by registered mail, through a Portuguese Consulate, or by way of Letter Rogatory to the court for the place where the defendant is resident.

The *1968 Brussels Convention* is already part of Portuguese domestic law.

Entering early judgment

If the summons is not properly served on the defendant, the court of its own motion must declare the whole proceedings, save the writ, a nullity.

The defendant may still opt to enforce a decision for non-delivery or irregularity of the writ as from the date when he had notice of the proceedings (*Code of Civil Procedure, arts 194 to 198 and 813*).

Summary judgment

The court cannot generally dispose of a case without the other side being duly called to conduct a defence. It is only in exceptional cases provided for by law that judgment may be given against a person without that person being duly heard. These cases always depend on the action having been properly initiated and proceedings duly served and on the claims in the action having been properly made out.

Typical cases for summary judgment include the provisional restitution of possession (*Code of Civil Procedure, art 393*); denunciation of works wrongfully carried out (*Code of Civil Procedure, arti 412*); and assets rolls (*Code of Civil Procedure, art 421*).

After summary judgment and, in some cases, after the execution of a judgment, a defendant may appeal to the superior courts against these orders. Summary judgment does not create an issue of res judicata.

A writ must be dismissed by the court when the defendant or plaintiff lacks standing or is mentally incapable, when an action is proposed out of time (*"caducidade"* being taken by a court of its own motion), or when for any reason, it is evident that the plaintiff's claim cannot succeed (*Code of Civil Procedure, art 474*). *Striking out part/all of a party's pleadings*

In Portuguese procedural law there is no general system for seeking security for costs. *Security for costs*

The parties are responsible for gathering all documentary evidence required. The gathering of documentary evidence is subject to the general rules of the adversarial system. Documentary evidence in a case must be disclosed within set time limits when all the relevant facts must be alleged by the parties. *Gathering evidence*

The court may of its own motion decide to carry out an examination of personal or real property, or on the application of either party, may request information, technical opinions, plans, photographs, drawings, objects or other documents which may be required to evince the truth. The request may be made to an official organisation, to the parties themselves or to third parties. There is no examining judge in civil proceedings in Portugal.

All documentary evidence relevant to one's case or to the other side must be disclosed within the time periods set out by law and as accords with the correspondent facts alleged. Even if not disclosed within the respective time limits, documentary evidence may still be presented at any time up to the end of the discussion stage in the proceedings at first instance, but the party responsible for non-disclosure will be penalised if it fails to prove that it was unable to disclose them within the set period. *Discovery*

When requesting a document from the other side a party will ask that the other party be ordered by the court to disclose that document within a specified period. The requesting party must identify the document as specifically as possible, and state the facts he claims will be proved by it.

If the party notified does not disclose the document in question, the court will investigate the probative value of the document requested. All relevant documents claimed would be presented to the court for its assessment.

If a document claimed specifically by one of the parties to the action is held by a third party, the latter should be notified to disclose the document within a specified time.

Privilege

Privilege in a document is that of the client, even in the case of documents in the possession of the client's lawyers. Such documents cannot be exhibited; if they are, they will not be considered as evidence in court (*Article 81 of the Portuguese Bar Association's bye-laws*).

Discussions between lawyers are subject to legal professional privilege.

There are no rules governing the non-admissibility of hearsay evidence.

Taking evidence abroad

The *Hague Convention on the Collection of Evidence Abroad* was ratified by Portugal and is part of Portuguese domestic law. The evidence of witnesses residing abroad can be taken by the court of their place of residence.

Witnesses

Any person not ineligible to be a witness by natural incapacity or for moral considerations can be a witness. The court may compel a witness to appear who, without justification, fails to attend court.

Persons incapable by natural incapacity include those of unsound mind, the blind and the deaf when knowledge depends on the senses they lack, and juveniles under seven years old.

Persons incapable for moral considerations include ascendants in cases of their descendants and vice-versa; the father- or mother-in-law in cases of their son- or daughter-in-law and vice-versa; the husband in his wife's case and vice-versa; and those who, because of their status or profession, are bound by professional secrecy in respect of the facts alleged.

Moral incapacity does not apply where the verification of the birth or death of children is concerned.

Expert evidence or reports

Expert evidence is normally sought by the parties. When seeking expert evidence, a party must set out which questions the expert should answer.

When a party has reason to believe that evidence which the experts should investigate may be tampered with, that party may present its questions in a sealed envelope and request that they and the answers be kept secret until the time when the experts carry out their investigations.

If, after examining the questions, the court considers this fear well-founded, it will have them sealed again and, when ordering that the questions be notified to the other side, it will only indicate generally the matters which are required to be investigated by the experts.

During the trial, experts who have been called by the court or the parties are obliged to give any information they have which is useful to the court.

Civil procedure

The court must take into consideration all the evidence which has *Assessment of* been gathered, whether or not disclosed by the party which *evidence* should have disclosed it to the court (without prejudice to the provisions which declare irrelevant the allegation of a fact when not made by the interested party).

The parties may represent themselves or be represented by their *Proceedings in* lawyers before the court. *court*

Before giving evidence, a witness will be asked to identify himself. The judge will ask him if he is a relation, a friend or antagonist of either party and if he has any direct or indirect interest in the case.

Before taking any evidence from a witness, the court will make the witness aware of the moral importance of the oath taken and the duty to be truthful, and will warn the witness of the penalties for giving false evidence. The court will then demand the following oath from the witness : "By my honour, I swear to say the truth, the whole truth and nothing but the truth". A refusal to take the oath will mean that the witness' evidence must be rejected.

The procedure for a witness to give evidence is governed by *Article 638 of the Code of Civil Procedure* :

The witness is questioned on the facts set out in a questionnaire drafted by the party who wishes to have them answered, and must give exact evidence, indicating how he became aware of the matters relevant to the case and any circumstances supporting his knowledge of the facts. This must be as specific as possible.

When giving evidence a plaintiff's witness will be examined by the plaintiff's lawyer, and then cross-examined by the other side's lawyer to complete or to shed further light on any evidence given.

The President of the court must control the proceedings and prevent the lawyers from behaving in an untoward manner towards any witness by posing impertinent, suggestive, insidious or harassing questions or making any untoward insinuations.

The President of the court and the court assistants can also put any questions they consider necessary to attain the truth.

Before answering any questions, a witness may refer to the pleadings and look at any relevant documents and may disclose any further documents which will corroborate his evidence. However, only new documents which could not have been disclosed previously by the respective parties will be accepted and put on the court file.

The court may, as convenient or at the request of the parties (save for matters affecting any individual's or a family's privacy), inspect things or question witnesses in order to clarify any points which may affect its decision.

The court may be assisted by any person competent to elucidate any points the court wants to investigate and understand more fully.

Discussion on points of fact are presented by the lawyers in oral argument after any evidence has been taken. On issues of law, the lawyers may plead orally if they so agree, or in writing. Arguments are presented first by the plaintiff's lawyer and then by the defendant's. Each party may reply once.

Trials take place in open court, save for certain exceptional cases provided for by law (*Code of Civil Procedure, art 656*).

Judgment

Judgment is given on completion of the hearing in open court in less serious cases. But where the matter is more serious, the court will notify the parties of the judgment at a later date.

Dissenting opinions may be given and are often used by the losing party on appeal.

Costs

The general rules on costs are set out in *Article 446 of the Code of Civil Procedure* which states that the judgment shall provide for costs to be paid by the losing party or if there is no losing party whoever "took advantage of the process".

Where there is no difference in the advantage gained between the parties the plaintiff and the defendant will pay costs equally; but if there has been a significant difference in the extent to which they were involved in the action, costs will be awarded in accordance with that degree of participation. Where judgment is given against those under a joint and several liability, this principle applies also to the distribution of any liability for costs.

If a party does not pay costs within a set time, the "*Ministério Público*" (Public Prosecutor) may take action to have the costs paid by that party.

Although in principle it is the parties who must pay the costs, their lawyers may be liable to pay them if they have acted with bad faith in the litigation. The costs to be paid in this case are set out in a fixed table and depend on the value of the matter, varying between 1% and 5%.

The costs that must be paid include the winning party's costs directly related to the action. The costs which the winning party had to pay to the court will be refunded by the court after the losin side has settled the account.

In principle, the client is responsible for paying his lawyer's fees.

There is no provision for payment into court as in the English system.

The length of proceedings depends on the court in which the action is brought.

For example, at the First Instance Court of Lisbon, a contract claim may take from six to nine months.

Normally, appeals are limited to issues of law because the evidence given by witnesses during a trial will have been oral and not written.

The findings of a multi-member court on the issues of fact before it cannot be altered by a second instance court unless all the evidence which was the basis for the decision is included and the evidence produced in the proceedings requires a different conclusion which cannot be supplanted by any other evidence; or if the appellant presents a document which becomes available later which of itself is sufficient to destroy the evidence on which the decision previously given was based.

For actions involving between 250,000 Escudos and two million Escudos there is only one instance of appeal : to the second instance court. For civil matters involving sums of over two million Escudos there are two instances of appeal : to a second instance court; and then to the Supreme Court of Justice.

In general, appeals to second instance courts take about nine months to be heard. Appeals to the Supreme Court of Justice take from nine months to one year.

CHAPTER 7 : CRIMINAL PROCEDURE

Crimes punishable with less than three years' imprisonment and committed to be heard by the criminal authorities or the police are subject to specific ("*sumário*") proceedings. For minor offences punishable with less than six months' imprisonment a different kind of proceedings, without trial, occurs where the defendant can accept a reduction of the charge commuted to a fine or a period of imprisonment (*Code of Criminal Procedure, arts 381 and 392*).

In general, the Public Prosecutor will prosecute all alleged crimes. *Prosecution* However, in some minor cases involving offences against privacy, honour or so-called "private crimes" a private prosecution must first be brought before the Public Prosecutor can be involved.

When the public authorities receive information of any crime they will inform the Public Prosecutor's office which will normally open a case on it. Instead of prosecuting, and for crimes punishable with less than three years' imprisonment, the Public Prosecutor can decide to suspend formal proceedings, provided the defendant agrees to comply with certain rules as to his future conduct and behaviour.

When an accused is questioned he must be informed of the charges against him (in practice no detailed information about the case will be given, but only an indication of what evidence is alleged against him). Later, when formally accused by the Public Prosecutor - or by a private prosecutor - the accused will receive a document which will refer to all the facts alleged. He has the right to read the files at the office of the Public Prosecution Service. There is no specific right to challenge the form of the information.

Court proceedings commence with the laying of the indictment, *Commencement of* after the Public Prosecutor's enquiries have been completed. The *court proceedings* defendant must notify the court, within seven days of being informed of the date fixed for trial, of the list of witnesses and documents he wishes to produce on his behalf.

There is no plea-bargaining system in Portugal. If a defendant admits to the trial court the facts alleged against him, the court can - if the case is punishable with imprisonment of less that three years - consider those facts proved. In the case of minor offences punishable with less than six months' imprisonment, the accused can accept a fine instead of imprisonment.

Trial by jury

Trial by jury is possible on the request of the Public Prosecutor, the private prosecutor or the accused, provided the case involves allegations of serious crimes, that is, ones punishable with more than eight years' imprisonment. Lay jurors are chosen at random from the population who must not be connected in any way with legal institutions. The accused can challenge up to two jurors without cause. Juries are composed of three judges and four lay jurors.

Legal representation

If an accused cannot find a lawyer of his choice, a practising lawyer or even a layman can be assigned by the court to represent him.

Order of proceedings

The prosecution evidence is presented first. The defence cannot submit that there is no case to answer after the prosecution case has been heard. The judge, or the jury, has complete power to interrogate witnesses, to call more witnesses or to refuse a hearing. Hearings are not held in public when it is necessary to safeguard personal dignity and public morals, or to ensure the proper working of the court.

Majority verdict

A simple majority is sufficient for a valid verdict. The judges form part of the jury for this purpose. An accused can be found guilty of an alternative offence to that with which he has been charged provided no substantial amendments to the facts of the charge are required for this.

Sentencing

Special sentencing proceedings are not obligatory. The law permits specific evidence to be presented of any sociological and psychological inquiries. In big cities, the courts require that this be done as a matter of course but, in practice, only evidence of previous and current behaviour is given.

The sentences available are imprisonment, community service and fines. There are no mandatory terms of sentences.

For crimes punishable with more than 3 years' imprisonment the defendant can appeal to the Supreme Court, but only as to questions of law. Any facts which have been proved are not subject to review. Only if the facts set out in the judgment are insufficient to sustain the conviction or if they are self-contradictory can the Supreme Court order a re-trial by another first instance court. It should be remembered that the evidence taken before the court whose decision is appealed will not have been recorded in writing.

Appeals

Appeals in the case of less serious crimes are decided by the Court of Appeal. The evidence of this hearing may be written. From the decision of the trial court one can appeal to the Supreme Court (*Code of Criminal Procedure, arts 427 and 432*).

A person detained must be brought before a judge within 48 hours. After a judicial decision to arrest has been taken a person can be held for :

- six months before an indictment must be laid; and

18 months before a judgment at first instance must be passed.

These time periods can be increased to 12 months and 36 months respectively if the case involves allegations of a serious crime - punishable with more than eight years' imprisonment - where the investigation seems complex and difficult.

Bail is granted, by a decision of the court, if the crime is punishable with imprisonment. There are no financial restrictions on the amount that can be set for bail. *Bail*

Portugal is subject to the *Council of Europe Extradition Convention*. Authorisation is required from the government before the Court of Appeal (the relevant court dealing with questions of extradition) may entertain any such hearings. *Extradition*

CHAPTER 8 : REMEDIES

The basic principle of civil liability is that anyone who violates or infringes another's rights is liable to compensate the injured person for all damage suffered by him (*Portugese Civil Code, art 483*).

Damages - various heads

Damages are available, inter alia, for personal injury, mental distress, and loss of reputation, the awards of which follow the usual principles of civil liability. There are no other specific legal criteria on which any compensation due is assessed. Damages are not assessed by juries in Portugal.

Damages for tort and breach of contractual obligations are assessed on the same principles, and damages can be awarded for pure economic loss.

A person liable to make reparation for any injury caused must put the injured party in the same position as he would have been had the event which gave rise to the injury not occurred.

Reparation is assessed in monetary terms whenever a situation cannot be restored to the previous non-monetary position either at all or in full, or where to do so would be exceedingly onerous on the debtor.

Monetary compensation takes as a benchmark the difference between the injured person's financial situation on the date the claim arose, and what the position would have been on that same date had no damage occurred. Where it is difficult to determine the exact level of damage, the court will determine the amount based on the evidence adduced before it.

Those who, without justification, are enriched at someone else's expense are obliged to make restitution of that enrichment to the person so deprived. The obligation to reimburse unjust enrichment seeks to replace that which is unduly received. This occurs where one has received a benefit in respect of an underlying transaction which no longer exists, or in respect of a transaction which never took place at all.

Unjust enrichment

However, restitution for unjust enrichment is not available as a remedy when other means of compensation or reimbursement are available at law, or where that enrichment is attributable to other causes.

Frustration

If the circumstances on which the parties based their decision to enter into a contract undergo exceptional change, the party then at a disadvantage has the right to dissolve the contract or to counteract those changes in accordance with the rules of equity, as provided for originally in the case law, provided the burden of the obligations he had assumed seriously offends the principles of good faith and is not part of the risks characteristic of such a contract. If a contract becomes impossible to perform due to circumstances attributable to one of the parties, the other party may rescind the contract without having to pay compensation.

Penalty clauses

Where the level of compensation payable is agreed prior to any non-performance by the parties this will constitute a penalty clause. A penalty clause must still comply with the formalities required to establish the principal obligation under the contract, and will be null and void if the principal obligation is itself a nullity.

A creditor cannot call for both performance of the principal obligation and for the sums due under a penalty clause unless the penalty applies where there is non-performance of the principal obligation within an agreed time. Any clause to the contrary will be void.

The extent of a penalty clause may be reduced by the court when it is plainly excessive and inequitable, even where there is some intervening cause. The penalty clause cannot be reduced beyond the extent of the damage effectively caused by non-performance of the obligation in question. Any provision to the contrary will be void (*Portuguese Civil Code, art 812*).

Specific performance

Specific performance of an obligation may be ordered by the courts where the obligation due permits of such an order.

If performance consists in delivering a concrete thing, the creditor has the right to claim specific performance and delivery of that thing even under order of the court. Hence, one to whom a specific thing should have been delivered has the right to have the thing contracted for delivered by another at the debtor's expense.

If a person is obliged not to perform an act but does despite this perform it, a creditor (that is one to whom the obligation not to carry out the said thing was owed) may demand that any works constructed be demolished at the other's expense.

Interest

Interest may be claimed in respect of monetary obligations from the first day of any delay in payment. Interest on debts is charged at the current legal interest rate unless, before the delay in payment, a higher interest rate applied or the parties had agreed on a different interest rate. The non-commercial legal interest on late payment is at present 15% per annum. For commercial interest on late payment a charge, fixed by the Government, applies. Contractual interest cannot be higher than 2% above that legal rate which, at the moment, is 17%.

Anyone may seek a declaration from the court but only in respect of their legal rights. *Declarations*

When a company is wound up extra-judicially, members of the Board of Directors become the receivers from the moment of the company's dissolution, unless the Social Contract provides otherwise (*Portuguese Company Law Code, Chapter XIII*). *Winding-up a company*

When a court orders a company to be wound up, but where there would be a benefit to the partners, receivers are appointed as provided for in the Social Contract but if there is no provision made for such an event that power belongs to the then-existing directors.

In bankruptcy or insolvency cases an administrator is appointed by the court, and has full powers, including censorship and assets petitory powers, including powers to revindicate.

An individual harmed by an administrative act of the state or a public body, including the government, may demand that those acts be annulled by the Administrative Courts. In this case, the court simply renders the act null but will not substitute the decision of the public body with a decision for what it would have done in those circumstances. *Actions by/against public bodies*

An individual can also claim compensation from the state and other public bodies for any damage caused by public administrative acts under *Decree-law No 48.051 of 12 November 1967* which will be ordered by the Administrative Courts.

During criminal proceedings, civil compensation may be claimed in respect of injury suffered due to the commission of that criminal offence. Double recovery of damages is not permitted. The other side may claim res judicata, lis alibi pendens or that the right has been forfeited if that right should have been exercised exclusively in the criminal proceedings. *Civil claims in criminal proceedings*

Any litigation not involving non-transferable rights can be resolved by the parties through an arbitration agreement, provided the subject matter is not exclusively reserved by a special law to a judicial court or to some other obligatory arbitration in any event. *Alternative dispute resolution*

The arbitration agreement can deal with an existing dispute, even if this is currently before a judicial court by way of a compromise and settlement clause, or with disputes which arise in the future during their contractual or non-contractual legal relations (by a compromise clause).

An arbitration award can only be annulled by a judicial court in circumstances provided for by law (*Arbitration Law, art 27*). If, in the face an arbitration agreement, either party starts proceedings before the judicial courts the other side may oppose them, challenging the court's competence to deal with the case.

Arbitrators determine cases before them in accordance with the normal rules of law unless the arbitration agreement or the compromis submitted to them permits judgment to be given in accordance with the rules of equity.

If the parties do not waive their right of appeal to the judicial courts from the arbitration decision, the same right of appeal to the second instance court is available as would be available from a first instance court in an ordinary action. However, if the arbitrators are authorised to give their decision in accordance with the rules of equity, such right of appeal is deemed to have been waived.

CHAPTER 9 : MATRIMONIAL DISPUTES

If there is no specialised Family Court in the county in which the *Jurisdiction of the* action should be inititated in the normal way, the usual court *courts* which has general jurisdiction is competent to deal with matrimonial disputes. In larger counties there are Family Courts specifically competent to deal with questions of divorce, custody and access.

There are two types of divorce : divorce by mutual agreement and contested divorce (*Civil Code, art 1773*).

In divorce by mutual agreement, the parties will present their *Divorce* request to the judge in a joint application, attaching their *proceedings* marriage certificate, evidence of their community property relationship, any custody agreement, any agreement on alimony, and any agreement on how the family home will be dealt with. The court will set a date for an initial meeting where it will ratify the agreements made, provided they are in accordance with the law.

The parties then have a three month period for reflection, at the end of which they may request another meeting before the court. If they still wish to be divorced the court will then make a final divorce order.

Where the divorce is contested after an application has been presented, the court will try to reconcile the parties. If this is not possible, the proceedings continue to trial as if they were normal contested divorce proceedings.

Where divorce is contested, two levels of appeal are always available, up to the Supreme Court of Justice.

Divorce proceedings, judicial separation, agreements regarding *Custody and* property annulment declarations or the annulment of marriage, *access* custody of the children and any alimony may be agreed by the parents, subject to endorsement by the court. Endorsement will be refused if the agreement is not in the best interests of any children who are minors.

If no agreement is reached by the parties, the court will decide what is in the best interests of any minors, and custody may be granted to either parent, to a third person, or to an educational establishment or welfare institution.

Access rights are granted to the parent who is not awarded custody, unless this will not be in the child's best interests.

Procedure

If no agreement is reached, the parties will be notified that they should present their case and any evidence to the court. At the same time, the court will order a social, moral and economic inquiry regarding the parents to be carried out by court-appointed experts.

The court will decide what action should be taken in accordance with the basic rules set out above.

The system for determining the allocation of custody does not lay down any special rules for dealing with urgent applications. On the contrary, it lays down a general rule, flexible enough to deal with any circumstance, which enables the court to decide temporarily, at any stage of the proceedings, on any matters which should be finally determined by it. The court may obtain the services necessary to carry out those interim decisions, establishing a system of temporary custody and access, provided always that this is in the minor's best interests.

Grounds for divorce

Either spouse may request a divorce if the other violates their marital duties, where that violation, due to its seriousness and the fact that it is repeated, compromises their life in common. Marital duties include respect and fidelity, cohabitation, co-operation and assistance.

A spouse cannot obtain a divorce for violation of the marital duties if he/she enticed the other spouse into the conduct complained of as the ground for divorce, or if he/she intentionally created circumstances leading to such conduct; or if it was clear that that matter was not considered an obstacle to their life in common.

Divorce can be based on :
-        complete separation for six consecutive years;
-        absence of a spouse, provided no news of the absentee has come to light for at least four years;
-        degeneration of a spouse's mental faculties for a period of six years which, due to its seriousness, compromises the possibility of their life in common (*Civil Code, art 1781*).

Matrimonial property

There are no specific rules on the division of matrimonial real property, and division follows the general rules for dividing non-divisible assets.

CHAPTER 10 : PROPERTY TRANSACTIONS

Normally, a property transaction is preceded by an Agreement for Sale where the parties agree to enter into a Contract of Sale and settle the essential clauses of the contract, as well as agree a completion date.

In an Agreement for Sale it is usual for the vendor to demand a deposit for the purchase sum.

If concluded in a private document, the Agreement for Sale only has binding force as between the parties. It will have legal effect as against all persons if concluded by public deed and the parties expressly confer that legal effect in the contract. The parties, or the party in charge, must in any event, obtain the documentation necessary to allow the public deed to be drawn up.

In general, the documents essential to conclude a valid deed are :
-     the identification documents of the purchaser and vendor;
-     a certificate from the Property Register identifying the property, and showing that it is registered in the vendor's name;
-     proof that any property tax due to be paid has been paid, which must be paid before the public deed is signed;
-     a certificate from the Department of Finance describing the property and its fiscal value;
-     if the purchaser is a foreigner not resident in Portugal, a previous investment declaration from the *"Instituto de Comercio Externo"* (Portuguese Institute for Foreign Trade) must be obtained.

With these, the party responsible for drawing up the deed will have it settled by a public notary of his choice. The parties must attend or be duly represented by a lawyer with sufficient powers for the purpose and sign the deed.

The property transaction, including the public deed, will be registered at the *"Conservatória do Registo Comercial"* (Conservatory for Commercial Registers).

CHAPTER 11 : RECOGNITION AND ENFORCEMENT OF FOREIGN JUDGMENTS

Without prejudice to any specific rules contained in any relevant treaties or special laws, no decision on private rights given by a foreign court or by arbitrators abroad has any force of law in Portugal, regardless of the parties' nationality, without having been reviewed and confirmed by the Portuguese courts. Review is not necessary when the decision is invoked in proceedings pending before the Portuguese courts as a matter of simple evidence, subject to the discretion of the court on this point.

The court competent to grant an exequatur in respect of a foreign decision in order for it to be "recognised" is the second instance court (Court of Appeal) of the Judicial District in which the person against whom a judgment is to be enforced is domiciled.

The *1968 Brussels Convention* has been ratified by Portugal and has been in force since July 1992.

To have a foreign judgment confirmed and upheld the following conditions are necessary:

- that there should be no doubt about the authenticity of the judgment document, nor about the correctness of the decision;
- that according to the law of the country where it was handed down, it has become res judicata;
- that jurisdiction was properly assumed by the foreign court;
- that the defendant was duly summonsed, unless in respect of an act for which Portuguese law does not require an initial summons; and if the judgment was given on the failure by the defendant to enter a defence, that the summons was in the defendant's own name;
- that the decision is not contrary to Portuguese principles of public order;
- that if the decision had been given against a Portuguese citizen and it would offend Portuguese private rights, then that matter would have been resolved on the same basis according to Portuguese conflicts rules under Portuguese law.

Where the foreign judgment establishes a new legal relationship which should be registered, or where it is condemnatory in nature and should be executed in Portugal, it will always have to be reviewed and endorsed by the Portuguese courts.

The same proceedings apply regardless of the nature of the decisions of the foreign court.

BIBLIOGRAPHY

Albuquerque, Pedro, *Autonomia Da Vontade e Negócio Jurídico em direito da Familia* (1986)

Almeida Costa, *Contrato - Promessa : Uma Sintese do Regime Actual* (1990)

Almeida Costa, Mário Júlio, *Cláusulas Contratuais Gerais* (1987)

Almeida Costa, Mário Julio, *Direito das Obrigações* (1984)

Almeida Costa, Mário Júlio, *Noções de Direito Civil* (1985)

Baptista Machado, João, *Lições de Direito Internacional Privado* (1988)

Brandão Proença, José Carlos, *Do Incumprimento do Contrato-Promessa Bilateral, Dualidade Execução Específica-Resolução* (1987)

Brito Correia, Luis, *Direito Comercial* (3 Vols) (1990)

Caeiro, António - *Código Comercial - Código das Sociedades Comerciais - Legislação complementar* (1988)

Caetano, Marcelo, *Manual De Direito Administrativo - 01* (1984)

Caetano, Marcelo, *Manual De Direito Administrativo - 02* (1986)

Carvalho Fernandes, Luis A., *Teoria Geral do Direito Civil - 01 T.1* (1983)

Carvalho Fernandes, Luis A., *Teoria Geral do Direito Civil - 01 T.2* (1983)

Carvalho Fernandes, Luis A., *Teoria Geral do Direito Civil - 02* (1983)

Castro Mendes, João, *Direito da Família* (1979)

Castro Mendes, João, *Direito Processual Civil* (3 Vols) (1989)

Castro Mendes, João, *Teoria Geral do Direito Civil - 01* (1978)

Castro Mendes, João, *Teoria Geral do Direito Civil - 02* (1979)

Castro, Anibal, *Caducidade Na Doutrina, Na Lei e Na Jurisprudéncia* (1984)

Cavaleiro Ferreira, Manuel, *Direito Penal Portuguès* (2 Vols) (1982)

Conçalves Sampaio, J., *Prova Por Documentos Particulares Na Doutrina, Na Lei E Na Jurisprudéncia* (1987)

Correia, Eduardo - Direito Criminal (2 Vols) (1988)

Costa Gomes, Manuel Januário, *Em Tema de Contrato-Promessa* (1990)

Curado Neves, João, *Comportamento Licito Alternativo e Concurso de Riscos* (1989)

Estatuto Judiciario, *Estatuto da Ordem Dos Advogados* (1985)

Ferrer Coreia, A., *Direito Internacional Privado - Leis e Projectos de Leis, Convenções Internacionais* (1988)

Ferrer Correia, A., *Direito Internacional Privado* (1985)

Ferrer Correia, A., *Lições de Direito Comercial* (3 Vols) (1990)

Figueiredo Dias, Jorge, *Direito Penal* (1988)

Freitas do Amaral, Diogo - *Jurisprudéncia Administrativa - 02* (1990)

Freitas do Amaral, Diogo, *Curso De Direito Administrativo - 01* (1988)

Freitas do Amaral, Diogo, *Jurisprudéncia Administrativa - 01* (1988)

Gomes Canotilho, J.J., *Constituição da República Portuguesa* (anotada) (2 Vols) (1985)

Gonçalves Pereira, André, *Novas Considerações Sobre a Relevância Do Direito Internacional Na Ordem Interna Portuguesa* (1969)

Leite de Campos, Raul, *Revisão e Confirmação de Sentenças Estrangeiras Na Jurisprudéncia Portuguesa* (1986)

Lima, Pires de, *Código Civil Anotado - 01* (1987)

Lima, Pires de, *Código Civil Anotado - 02* (1986)

Lima, Pires de, *Código Civil Anotado - 03* (1987)

Maia Gonçalves, M., *Código Penal Portugués* (anotado, comentado e legislação complementar) (1990)

Marques dos Santos, António, *Breves Considerações Sobre a Adaptação Em Direito Internacional Privado* (1988)

Martins Leitão, Helder, *Lei Orgânica dos Tribunais Judiciais* (1988)

Menezes Cordeiro, António, *Da Alteroção das Circunstáncias* (1987)

Menezes Cordeiro, António, *Direito das Obrigações* - 01 (1988)

Menezes Cordeiro, António, *Direito das Obrigações* - 02 (1988)

Menezes Cordeiro, António, *Direito das Obrigações* - 03- *Contratos em Especial* (1990)

Menezes Cordeiro, António, *Teoria Geral do Direito Civil* - 01 (1988)

Menezes Cordeiro, António, *Teoria Geral do Direito Civil* - *Relatório* (1969)

Miranda, Jorge, *Manual De Direito Constitucional* (4 Vols) (1990)

Mota Campos, João, *Direito Comunitario* (2 Vols) (1988)

Mota Pinto, Carlos Alberto, *Cessão da Posição Contratual* (1982)

Neto, Abilio, *Código De Processo Civil* (Anotado)

Oliveria Ascensão, José, *Direito Comercial* (2 Vols) (1988)

Pais de Vasconcelos, Pedro, *Direito Comercial : Titulos de Crédito* (1990)

Pereira Coelho, F.M., *Curso de Direito Da Familia* (1986)

Pizaro Beleza, Teresa, *Direito Penal* (1985)

Pupo Correia, Miguel J.A., *Direito Comercial* (1988)

Reis, Alberto, *Código de Processo Civil* (anotado) (6 Vols) (1987)

Reis, Alberto, *Processo de Execução* (2 Vols) (1985)

Sousa Brito, José, *Jurisprudéncia Penal* (1981)

Teixeira de Sousa, Miguel, *Competéncia e a Incompeténcia nos Tribunais Comuns* (1989)

Tratado de Adesão de Portugal a Comunidade Económica Europeia-Versão Oficial Portuguesa (1988)

Varela, Antunes and de Matos, João, *Das Obrigações em Geral* - 01 (1989)

Varela, Antunes and de Matos, João, *Das Obrigações em Geral - 02* (1990)

Varela, Antunes, - *Direito da Família* (1987)

Varela, Antunes, *Manual De Processo Civil* (1985)

Varela, Antunes, *Sobre o Contrato-Promessa* (1989)

Ventura, Raul, *Alterações de Contrato de Sociedade : Comentario Ao Código das Sociedades Comerciais* (1988)

Ventura, Raul, *Sociedades Por Quotas* (3 Vols) (1990)

SCOTLAND

Matthew G. Clarke QC

CONTENTS

CHAPTER 1 : SOURCES OF LAW

Scotland has a unitary structure of government. There is one *Unitary v federal*
legislature at national level for the whole of the United Kingdom. *system*
Scotland has its own separate Department of State within the UK
Government. Some statutes apply to the whole of the United
Kingdom but with specific references to Scotland. Other statutes
enacted by Parliament apply to Scotland alone. Scotland does,
however, have a separate legal system except that the House of
Lords is the final appeal court for the United Kingdom.

The principal written documents containing the law of Scotland *Principal written*
are the statutes of the United Kingdom Parliament and reported *documents*
decisions of the courts.

With respect to foreigners the position is the same as in the rest *Application of*
of the United Kingdom in that there is in practice little *national laws*
fundamental difference between nationals and foreigners in the *with respect to*
way national law can be relied on and applied. *foreigners*

Scotland, like the rest of the United Kingdom, is a dualist system *Dualist system*
requiring international treaties to be incorporated into domestic
legislation by Act of Parliament before they can be applied
directly in domestic courts.

The provisions of the EC Treaties and secondary legislation are *Application of*
incorporated into the law applicable in Scotland through statutes *EC law*
of the United Kingdom Parliament and delegated legislation
made thereunder.

The courts in Scotland accept, adopt and implement the
principles of Community law unequivocally. The Scots courts have
demonstrated no reticence in applying and implementing
Community law.

Foreign law is treated as a matter of fact. There is a legal *Citation of*
presumption that it is the same as Scots law save where argued *foreign law in*
that it is different. It is proved by an experienced practitioner *national*
from the foreign legal system speaking to it. It is required to be *proceedings*
translated into English.

As in the rest of the United Kingdom, the *European Convention* *Application of*
on Human Rights is not part of domestic law and domestic courts *the European*
are not empowered to enforce directly the provisions of the *Convention on*
Convention or the case law of the European Court of Human *Human Rights*
Rights unless these have been adopted by the European Court of
Justice as part of applicable European Community law.

Principles of
interpretation

Statute law is interpreted according to various rules of interpretation, the principal rule being the literal rule. Decisions of higher courts bind lower courts (See *R v Registrar General, ex parte Pete Smith* [1]).

Text of the
Constitution

There are no texts on the Constitution as the United Kingdom has no written constitutional document.

---

1.   *R v Registrar General, ex parte Pete Smith* [1991] 2 QB 393.

CHAPTER 2 : FUNDAMENTAL RIGHTS

The position is essentially the same as for England and Wales. However, the *Act of Union 1707* guarantees certain rights regarding the government of Scotland including the preservation of its separate legal system.

CHAPTER 3 : JURISDICTION OF THE COURTS

The domestic jurisdiction of a court in Scotland can be challenged *Forum* on the basis of the doctrine of *forum non conveniens*, that is, that there is a more appropriate forum in which the dispute can be adjudicated upon. The domestic jurisdiction of a court can also be challenged on the basis of *lis alibi pendens* where the same dispute is already before another court in Scotland.

The High Court of Justiciary has universal jurisdiction for all *Universal* crimes unless that jurisdiction is expressly or impliedly excluded *jurisdiction* by statute. It has exclusive jurisdiction to try the most serious crimes, for example, treason, murder and rape.

Generally speaking there are no limitations on bringing actions *State immunity* against the state or organs of the state acting in a purely commercial capacity. There are, however, certain limitations imposed by virtue of the provisions of the *Crown Proceedings Act 1947*. One important limitation is that the state or organs of the state cannot be interdicted from, or ordered to cease, carrying out their function.

Domicile for the purposes of jurisdiction is governed by the *Civil* *Domicile* *Jurisdiction and Judgments Act 1982*, implementing the *Brussels Convention on the Enforcement of Civil and Commercial Judgments 1968*, as amended. A person is domiciled for the purposes of the Act in Scotland only if he resides in Scotland and the nature and circumstances of his residence indicate that he has a substantial connection with Scotland. Three months' residence in Scotland gives rise to a presumption of such a substantial connection. The seat of a corporation or association is treated as its domicile. It may have a seat in more than one place. If a company or an association is incorporated or formed under the law of any part of the United Kingdom and has its registered office or some other official address in Scotland, or its central management and control is exercised in the United Kingdom, it will have a seat in any part or place in the United Kingdom where it has its registered office or some other official address, or where its central management or control is exercised or where it has a place of business.

CHAPTER 4 : ADMINISTRATION OF JUSTICE

The structure of the court system in Scotland is outlined below

Civil courts

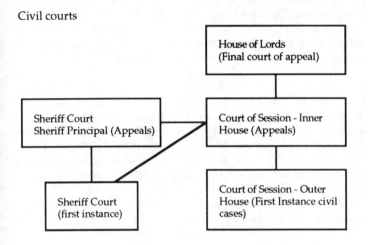

Criminal courts

The Sheriff Court is organised on a territorial basis. For civil cases it exercises a wide jurisdiction which extends to actions for debt or damages regardless of the pecuniary sum involved. There are very few exceptions to its civil jurisdiction. Cases in the Sheriff Court may, however, be remitted to the Court of Session. The Sheriff Court operates as a court of first instance and as a court of appeal in that cases heard first by a Sheriff may be appealed to the Sheriff Principal. From the Sheriff Principal there is an appeal to the Inner House of the Court of Session, and from there to the House of Lords. An appeal can be taken directly from the Sheriff to the Inner House without having to appeal first to the Sheriff Principal.

Civil courts

Court of Session   The Outer House of the Court of Session, like the Sheriff Court, is a court of first instance. It hears the more important cases. The Outer House consists of judges who normally sit singly, but exceptionally with a jury, to determine civil cases at first instance. Its jurisdiction is extensive and covers all kinds of civil claims, unless jurisdiction in a case is expressly excluded by statute.

The Inner House consists of two Divisions, the First and Second Divisions which are of equal authority. Each Division sits with a minimum of three judges and is normally presided over by one of the two most senior Scottish judges, respectively, the Lord President and the Lord Justice Clerk. For some special situations it sits as a court of first instance but it normally sits as a court of appeal reviewing the judgments of the Sheriff Court and the judgments of judges sitting in the Outer House.

House of Lords   Appeals from the Inner House of the Court of Session on both fact and law are taken to the House of Lords. If the case originated in the Sheriff Court the right of appeal is limited to questions of law only. The House of Lords has judges from Scotland, England and Wales and Northern Ireland. These judges normally sit in panels of five and there will normally be at least two Scottish judges hearing appeals from Scotland.

In addition there are in Scotland many tribunals and courts of special jurisdiction dealing with specific technical areas of the law such as landlord and tenant disputes, and employer/employee matters. From some there is an appeal, normally on a point of law only, to the Civil court system just described.

Criminal courts   The District Court is a local court which deals with minor offences and has very limited sentencing powers. An appeal on points of law lies from it to the High Court of Justiciary.

The Sheriff Court can try any crime or offence committed within its district which is not reserved to the High Court of Justiciary. Serious crimes are heard by the Sheriff sitting with a jury. Judges in the Sheriff Court may not impose a sentence of more than three years' imprisonment. Cases will be committed to the High Court of Justiciary where the judge takes the view on reading the papers that upon conviction a court may consider a more severe sentence. An appeal from the Sheriff Court lies to the High Court of Justiciary.

The High Court of Justiciary consists of the same judges who sit in the Court of Session. It has jurisdiction over all of Scotland in respect of all crimes committed within Scotland unless its jurisdiction is expressly or impliedly excluded by the terms of a statute. It operates both as a court of first instance and as a court of appeal. As a court of first instance it comprises a single judge sitting with a jury. As a court of appeal it comprises at least three judges.

Normally an appeal is as of right in criminal matters. In civil *Appeals*
cases, it is only as of right if the lower court has disposed of the
merits of the case, otherwise leave is generally required either of
the court of first instance or the appeal court.

The filing of an appeal within the time limits prescribed by the
Rules of Court normally operates as an automatic stay of
judgment.

References under *Article 177 of the EEC Treaty* are made after an *References under*
application is made to the domestic court or by the court *ex* *Article 177 of the*
proprio motu. In civil matters, the House of Lords is the court *EEC Treaty*
against whose judgment there is no further appeal. In criminal
matters, the court against whose judgment there is no further
appeal is the High Court of Justiciary. In civil cases the Court of
Session has indicated that no *Article 177* reference should
normally be made until the written pleadings, as required by the
court in Scotland, have been put in their final form (see *Prince v*
Secretary of State for Scotland[1]).

---

1.   *Prince v Secretary of State for Scotland* [1985] SLT 74.

CHAPTER 5 : STRUCTURE OF THE LEGAL PROFESSION

The legal profession is divided into two branches, advocates and *Structure* solicitors. Tax advisers, patent agents and other professional persons may give legal advice but cannot provide other legal services.

The Faculty of Advocates is the body of specialised court practitioners in Scotland.

Only advocates and solicitors have rights of audience before the *Rights of* courts. At the moment only advocates can appear in all the courts *audience* and tribunals in the jurisdiction. At present solicitors only have rights of audience in the Sheriff Court and District Court and before tribunals. In the future, from a date yet to be fixed, certain solicitors will have the right to appear in the higher courts.

Solicitors organise themselves in partnerships or operate as sole *Legal practices* practitioners. advocates are prohibited from being in partnership. Advocates all belong to a professional body known as the Faculty of Advocates. They are provided with certain professional services by a company known as Faculty Services Limited of which they are shareholders. They all operate from a library based in the Supreme Court of Scotland, the Court of Session in Edinburgh. Until recently, partnerships of solicitors could not include foreign lawyers but provision is now being made for multi-national partnerships. There are no territorial restrictions on partnership practice.

There is no restriction on solicitors on the establishment and/or *Branch offices* number of branch offices within the United Kingdom or within the European Community.

There are no fixed rules for charging fees. Fees are charged by *Fees* reference to the cost of a day's appearance in court, the complexity of the problem, the time taken in providing advice and the amount at stake. If the advocate is acting for a client who is provided with legal aid, there is a limit fixed by the legal aid authorities as to the fee that may be charged for any particular type of work. The Law Society of Scotland, the governing body for solicitors, gives general guidance on fees which may be charged for various kinds of work by solicitors. Solicitors tend to charge on an hourly rate basis. A client may ask in advance for information about what fees an advocate or solicitor will charge. A dispute over fees may be dealt with by the professional body in the first instance, and secondly by the court.

Lawyer's fees attract VAT at the standard rate of 17.5%.

Professional conduct

The professional body of advocates, the Faculty of Advocates, and the professional body of solicitors, the Law Society of Scotland, both control the professional conduct of the lawyers belonging to these bodies. Both of these bodies have power to censure, fine, suspend or expel from practice members against whom complaints have been brought and proved. Complaints about any legal services should be made to the professional bodies. Foreign clients or foreign lawyers have the right to use the complaints procedures. Professional indemnity insurance is compulsory both for solicitors and for advocates. The Law Society of Scotland also operates a fund from which clients may obtain compensation in the event of their funds being lost through the conduct of solicitors.

Practice by foreign lawyers

In the courts in Scotland the temporary practice of other EC lawyers is governed by the *Lawyers' Services Directive of 1977*[1]. Certain other areas of legal service, for example conveying of property, cannot be carried out by foreign lawyers Otherwise, foreign lawyers may establish offices in Scotland and give legal advice.

Instructing lawyers

There is no restriction on who can instruct a solicitor to provide legal services. Advocates, however, may not be instructed directly by clients unless those clients belong to a recognised body which is authorised to do so, for example, foreign lawyers and chartered accountants, and for appearances in court an advocate must be instructed by a solicitor. Individual litigants may represent themselves in court.

Directories of legal services

There are no directories of specialist services as yet, although this may change shortly. A client can find out which lawyers or law firms have expertise in any particular body by consulting the recognised professional bodies. The Scottish Law Directory which is published annually, is a general directory of legal services.

---

1.   Council Directive (EEC) 77/249 (OJ L78 26.3.77 p17).

CHAPTER 6 : CIVIL PROCEDURE

Civil proceedings in Scotland are commenced either by service of an Initial Writ (for Sheriff Court proceedings) or by service of a Summons (for Court of Session proceedings) or by Petition for certain special types of civil cases, for example, judicial review of administrative action or company law matters. The defender or respondent then lodges with the court Defences or Answers. There then follows a period of adjustment of the written pleadings when the pleadings may be amended. This period of adjustment on average lasts for three months but can be somewhat shorter or longer. After the adjustment of the pleadings is concluded, the parties or any one of them may have a preliminary issue of law determined by the court before the proceedings proceed to a hearing on the evidence. The decision of the court in respect of the issue of law may result in the case being dismissed or the remedy sought being granted. Otherwise, the matter then goes to a full hearing on the evidence followed by submissions on fact and law before the court pronounces judgment.

Basic structure of proceedings

Scotland is divided into six Sheriffdoms based on groupings of local government areas. Each Sheriffdom divides into several Sheriff Court districts centred on a town where the Sheriff Court is held. There are approximately 50 such districts in Scotland. The Sheriff has competence to hear civil cases having a connection with his territory. The civil jurisdiction of the Sheriff Court extends to actions for debt or damages regardless of the pecuniary level involved. Civil jurisdiction extends to most kinds of civil disputes though with a few limited exceptions.

Division of competences

Courts of first instance

Sheriff Court

The Court of Session has universal jurisdiction in all civil cases in Scotland except where the value of the dispute is £1,500 or less. Generally speaking, the more complex and more valuable cases are brought to the Court of Session.

The Court of Session

The Scottish Land Court deals with agricultural matters, in particular, agricultural leases.

Other courts and tribunals

The Restrictive Practices Court exercises jurisdiction under the *Restrictive Practices Act 1956*.

Children's Hearings deal with cases involving children who are thought to be at risk or who have been involved in the commission of offences.

The Lands Valuation Appeal Court is a specialised court which deals with questions of local taxation, and the Lands Tribunal is a specialist tribunal dealing with specific issues of land law including the question of compensation for compulsory acquisition.

Licensing Boards are bodies dealing with the issue of licences for the sale of liquor, and Industrial Tribunals deal with certain employer/employee matters.

Rules of procedure The rules of procedure of both the Court of Session and the Sheriff Court are to be found in the Parliament House Book.

Locus standi The general rule is that any person, natural or artificial, fully possesses the qualification to sue and defend in the Scottish courts. Scots law does not, at present, recognise class or representative actions. Actions by or against the government are normally instituted by or against the Lord Advocate who is the senior law officer for Scotland. The equivalent in England and Wales is the Attorney General. The Secretary of State for Scotland may be a party to legal proceedings in which any department for which he is responsible is involved. In general, any person may conduct his own case. The main exceptions are young children, insane persons, persons voluntarily resident or carrying on business in hostile territory and firms, companies and other artificial entities who must be legally represented.

Actions against heads of state, government, etc The position when the government is being sued or is suing is governed by the *Crown Proceedings Act 1947* which, in some respects, equates the position of the government with that of ordinary litigants. The Crown, that is the government, has, however, a number of privileges both in respect of the substantive law enforceable by or against it and with regard to procedure. The law as to the immunity of foreign states from the jurisdiction of the United Kingdom courts including the courts in Scotland is codified by the *State Immunity Act 1978*. Part I of the Act provides a list of cases in which there is no entitlement to immunity from proceedings. Most of the cases are subject to conditions and exceptions and the general rule is that, in such other cases, a foreign state is immune from the jurisdiction of the courts of the United Kingdom. The *State Immunity Act 1978* broadly assimilates the position of foreign heads of state, their families and private servants to that of the head of a diplomatic mission, his family and servants under the *Diplomatic Privileges Act 1964*. The *1964 Act* divides persons entitled to diplomatic immunity into three classes with varying degrees of immunity.

Joinder of parties In both the Sheriff Court and the Court of Session a third party or third parties may be added to the proceedings by order of the court. In the Sheriff Court the procedure is regulated by *Ordinary Court Rule 50(1)*; in the Court of Session it is regulated by *Rule of Court 85*. Once the order is granted, the person seeking to join or convene a third party, serves a notice on him together with a copy of the existing pleadings in the action. In certain proceedings involving matters of public interest, the court may order that the Lord Advocate as the Minister of the Government who represents the public interest be notified of the proceedings. In addition, any party to proceedings may bring to the attention of the court the existence of some other party who has a direct interest in the proceedings and their outcome and the court may order intimation or service of the proceedings on such a person.

The court itself may, *pars judicis*, take note of the existence of such a person and order intimation or service upon him. *Joinder of actions*

If two or more actions pending before a court involve the same issues they may be conjoined. The question as to whether they should be conjoined is a matter which is left entirely to the discretion of the court. This discretion is normally only exercised when the different actions raise the same issues, the trial of which will settle all the different actions. The parties need not be the same. The courts have a discretion as to whether or not to stay ("*sist*") proceedings to await the outcome of other proceedings pending either in the courts of the United Kingdom or elsewhere. The matter is entirely within the discretion of the court and is subject to no special rules.

Scots Law does not recognise class or representative actions.

Legal aid is available for civil proceedings in Scotland. The basic rules are to be found in the *Legal Aid (Scotland) Act 1986*. Only natural persons are eligible for civil legal aid. Applications for civil legal aid must be made to the Legal Aid Board which determines the application taking into account both the means of the applicant and whether or not, in the opinion of the Board, he can be said to have a probable cause. There is no fixed limit on the amount of legal aid which can be made available in a case, but the client's account is subject to a process known as taxation, where the costs of the case are assessed by an independent tribunal. In addition, the Legal Aid Regulations provide that certain steps in the litigation may not be taken without the sanction of the Board. Civil legal aid is not available for defamation or verbal injury cases, certain simplified divorce cases, certain small claims or before tribunals. The Legal Aid Board has a statutory charge in respect of monies paid out by it over any damages or other property or sums recovered or preserved as a result of the litigation. *Legal aid*

The rules on limitation of time by which proceedings should be raised are codified in the *Prescription and Limitation (Scotland) Act 1973*. The two most important rules are summarised as follows: *Limitation of proceedings*
-   claims for damages in respect of personal injuries must be brought within three years of the date of the event giving rise to the injury. There is provision to relax that period by an application to the court;
-   most other civil claims are extinguished by operation of law after a period of five years from the occurrence of the event giving rise to the claim. In the case of damages claims, the five year period runs from the

occurrence of the event giving rise to the loss and the loss itself. There is no discretion in the courts to extend the five year limit.

Commencement of proceedings

Proceedings in the Court of Session are generally commenced by the serving of a Summons which is a writ running in the name of the Sovereign, setting forth the demands of a party, called the pursuer, against the defender and charging the defender to appear in the Court of Session and to answer the demand contained in the Summons. Authority to convene the defender is conferred by the Royal Signet impressed on the Summons. Summonses are signed by the pursuer's solicitor. The other means of initiating proceedings in the Court of Session is by Petition which is signed by the petitioner's advocate. Proceedings in the Sheriff Court are generally initiated by the service of an Initial Writ signed by a solicitor with a warrant thereon issued by the clerk of the Sheriff Court to serve it. Service of the Summons or Initial Writ is deemed to be the commencement of proceedings for the purposes of the running of any time limits and any limitation periods.

Service of proceedings

Service may be effected by post or personal service or by service at a dwelling place or place of business.

Service of proceedings outside Scotland

For the Court of Session *Rule 74A(1)* sets out the methods for citation and service that may be used in respect of a defender outside Scotland but within the United Kingdom. *Rule 74B* sets out the method of citation and service that may be used in relation to a defender outside the United Kingdom. These methods may be used only if they are permitted under a convention providing for service in the foreign country and if they are permitted by the laws of that country. The relevant conventions are the *Brussels Convention on Jurisdiction and Judgments*, the *Hague Convention on the Service of Writs Abroad*, and a series of bilateral conventions between the United Kingdom and other states. The methods listed in *Rule 74B* include all those permitted under the *Hague Convention*. Apart from personal and postal service, the other methods of service are, at the request of the Foreign Office through the central authorities of the country in which the defender is to be found, or through a British Consular Office there, or at the request of a Messenger-at-Arms, by a Huissier or other judicial or competent officer in the country where the defender is to be found.

Edictal citation

When the place where the defender resides cannot be ascertained, or citation cannot be successfully effected in accordance with a method prescribed under *Rule 74A(1) or 74B(1)* edictal citation can be made. A motion is enrolled when the Summons is presented for signet, craving the court to grant warrant to cite the defender edictally, that is to say to cite the defender by way of advertisement in a newspaper circulating in the area of the defender's last known address or to dispense with advertisement, stating what steps have been taken to trace the defender. Where citation is made edictally it is done at the office of the Extractor of the Court of Session and the defender has six months to appear from the date of service on the Extractor.

The Sheriff Court procedures for service on persons outside Scotland are set out in *Ordinary Court Rule 12* in the Parliament House Book. The appropriate method of service depends on whether there is any international legal agreement regarding the assumption of jurisdiction between the United Kingdom and the country of service.

Service can be effected on any person at a known residence or place of business in another part of the United Kingdom or in any country with which the United Kingdom does not have a convention specifically providing for the service of writs in that country. This can be done either in accordance with the rules for personal service under the domestic law of the place in which service is to be effected or by posting in Scotland a copy of the document in question by registered or recorded delivery letter.

In the Sheriff Court where citation is effected under any of the general rules the defender is obliged to lodge a Notice of Intention to Defend within 21 days after the date of citation (*Ordinary Rule of Court 7(1)*).

In the Court of Session a defender shall have :
- 21 days after the execution of service in the case of citation within Europe to intimate his intention to defend;
- in the case of persons cited under *Rule of Court 74B(1)(d) and/or 74B(1)(e)* outside Europe, 21 days after the date of execution of service; and
- in any other case of citation outside Europe, 42 days after the date of execution of service.

In practice a defender will have a further period after the expiry of the above periods, since the pursuer has first to lodge the Summons for calling in the court and the defender has three days thereafter to enter an appearance (see *Rule of Court 78* and *Rule of Court 81*).

In the Sheriff Court once the period for lodging the Notice of Intention to Defend has expired, the Sheriff Clerk completes and signs a certificate on a form attached to the Initial Writ that no Notice of Intention to Defend has been lodged. On the same form, the pursuer or his solicitor thereafter endorses a Minute craving a decree or such other order as is required by the Rules. In the Court of Session, if the defender fails to enter an appearance or if, having entered an appearance, he fails to lodge Defences, the pursuer may enrol for a decree in absence. The case is enrolled in the Rolls of undefended cases and the judge, on being satisfied that the defender was properly cited, will grant a decree without an appearance being required.

Entering early judgment

Summary judgment   There is no provision for an application for summary judgment in the Sheriff Court. In the Court of Session the matter is regulated by *Rule of Court 89B* which provides that in a civil case to which the Rule applies (which is almost all civil cases) the pursuer may at any time after a defender has lodged Defences apply by motion to the court for a summary decree against the defender on the ground that there is no defence to the action or a part of it disclosed in the Defences. Any appeal against a decision relating to such an application may only be made with leave of the judge in question.

There are no rules requiring leave to defend.

Striking out pleadings   The main means whereby a party may apply to have struck out a claim against him, instead of having to proceed to a full trial on the issues between the parties is to apply to the court to have the claim dismissed or the answer thereto repelled, as the case may be, on the basis that the claim or the response to it is irrelevant, is wholly lacking in specification or is incompetent. This is done after the parties' respective written pleadings are in their final form. In the Court of Session the party wishing to make such an application applies to the court to have the case sent for legal discussion on the Procedure Roll. The court then hears legal submissions, proceeding on the basis that the facts offered to be proved by the parties will be proved. In the Sheriff Court the application is to have the case heard at a hearing which is called a "*Debate*". In both the Sheriff Court and the Court of Session, the parties' failure to comply with the orders of the court, including orders with regard to time limits and their due appearance or representation when the case is called at which their attendance is required, can be met with the sanction of a decree by default.

Vexatious litigants   The right of access to the courts is qualified when the Court of Session has made an order in terms of the *Vexatious Litigants (Scotland) Act 1898* in order to control the oppressive raising of actions. If the Lord Advocate satisfies either division of the Court of Session that a person has habitually and persistently instituted vexatious legal proceedings without any reasonable ground for instituting such proceedings, whether in the Court of Session or in any inferior court, and whether against the same person or against different persons, the court may order that no legal process shall be instituted by that person in the Court of Session or in any other court unless the person obtains the leave of a judge sitting in the Outer House of the Court of Session.

Security for costs   Whether a party to an action should or should not find security ("*caution*") for costs ("*expenses*") which may be awarded against him is a matter entirely within the discretion of the court. The court will not make such an order unless the interests of justice appear to require it. The court may, in its discretion, order either the pursuer or the defender to find caution, but in practice an order is made only in cases where the party against whom it is sought is an undischarged bankrupt or is a nominal pursuer or where there are special circumstances. In addition, the court has statutory powers to order a public limited company to find caution. Where a party to any proceedings is resident outside the United Kingdom the court may order him to "*sist a mandatory*", that is nominate a suitable person resident in the United Kingdom who then becomes responsible to the court for the proper conduct of the case and who may be made personally liable for the expenses of the action. A mandatory may not be required when the party lives in a country where an award of expenses may be readily enforced.

The principal way in which interlocutory relief may be obtained in Scotland is by way of interim interdict against the threat of conduct or the continuance of conduct or the repetition of conduct which amounts to a legal wrong. This remedy is available in both the Court of Session and the Sheriff Court. There are no time limits, as such, within which an application for such a remedy must be made though delay in seeking it may argue against the necessity of granting it at that time. This remedy can be very speedily obtained : there is always a nominated judge available both in the Court of Session and the Sheriff Court to hear such applications at short notice, if necessary at the home of the judge. There does, however, have to be an appearance before the judge, although interim interdict can be granted without notice having been given to the other party. If the interim interdict is granted it is immediately served on the other party, who may then immediately apply for its recall. A person may also lodge in court a document known as a caveat which provides that he must be notified before any application for interim interdict against him is heard. If the interim interdict, once granted, proves to have been sought without good ground the party affected by it may sue for damages for wrongful interdict. There are no special rules governing the production of evidence in such proceedings. The application are almost invariably granted on the basis of *ex parte* statements given by the party's representatives to the court. *Interlocutory relief*

There is no provision in Scottish law for a Summons for Directions to review the preparations for trial after the pleadings have been closed or for automatic directions to govern the final preparations before trial. *Further conduct of the proceedings*

The Court of Session has an inherent power to compel the parties to an action to produce documents which may have a bearing on the issues between them (see *Young v NCB*[1]). In the Sheriff Court, *Rule 80* provides that : "The Sheriff may order production of documents at any stage." *Discovery*

Documents which require to be disclosed are all documents which have a bearing on the issues including those which may be unfavourable to the party disclosing them. They are disclosed both to the court and the parties.

---

1.   *Young v NCB* [1957] SC 99, at p105.

Legal professional privilege

As a general rule, communications passing between a client and his professional legal advisers for professional purposes are non-disclosable on the ground of confidentiality, the privilege of refusing to disclose being that of the client. The general rule is superseded only where fraud or some other illegal act is alleged against the party and where his professional legal adviser has been directly concerned in the carrying out of the transaction which is the subject matter of enquiry. No confidentiality applies where the existence of the relationship of professional legal adviser and client or the extent of the adviser's authority is in issue. A further general rule is that no party can recover from his opponent material which the opponent has made in preparing his own case.

The position with regard to "without prejudice" negotiations is as in England and Wales.

Evidence

Evidence gathering is to be carried out by the parties.

A party may be forced to disclose evidence before trial. An application needs to be made to the court by his opponent for a commission and diligence for the recovery of documents. This procedure involves lodging in a court a "Specification" which lists the documents which it is sought to have recovered and then moving the court to order their recovery. The court has to be satisfied that the documents have a direct bearing on the issues between the parties. By a commission and diligence a party may recover only documents and may do so only after the action has started. By applying under *Section 1(1) of the Administration of Justice (Scotland) Act 1972*, however, a party may obtain a variety of orders relating not only to documents but also to other property, and may do so before and after the action has started.

A party may challenge the admissibility of evidence when an application for the recovery of documents by commission and diligence or an application under *Section 1 of the Administration of Justice (Scotland) Act 1972* is made.

The position on the admissibility of hearsay evidence is now governed by the *Civil Evidence (Scotland) Act 1988. Section 2(1)(a)* of that Act is to the effect that "In any civil proceedings evidence shall not be excluded solely on the ground that it is hearsay". *Section 2(1)(c)* provides that the court, or as the case may be the jury, if satisfied that any fact has been established by evidence in those proceedings shall be entitled to find that fact proved by evidence notwithstanding that the evidence is hearsay.

Evidence abroad

In the Court of Session a party to civil proceedings may apply to the court for a letter of request to a court or tribunal outside Scotland to obtain evidence which is obtainable within the jurisdiction of that court or tribunal. An application may be made to examine witnesses; for the production of documents; for the inspection, photographing, preservation, custody or detention of any property; or for the taking of samples of any property and the carrying out of any experiment on or with any property. The procedure is regulated by *Rule of Court 102* and the *Evidence (Proceedings in other Jurisdictions) Act 1975*. Similar provisions apply in the Sheriff Court. The *Hague Convention* is not part of national law.

A witness is competent unless excluded by rule of law, and is *Witnesses* compellable unless entitled on some legal ground to refuse to give evidence. As a general rule, any person is a competent and compellable witness but some are not competent and some, though competent, are not compellable. Further, a witness may be competent and compellable but his evidence may not be admissible for all purposes or against all parties. A child is admissible as a witness if he is considered to be able to understand what he has seen or heard and to give an account of it and to appreciate the duty to speak the truth. These are matters for the judge to assess. A person suffering from mental incapacity may be a competent witness although again this a matter for the judge to determine. A foreigner, even an enemy alien, is a competent witness. On the question of diplomatic immunity, the position is the same as in the rest of the United Kingdom. There are somewhat complex special rules regarding the competency and compellability of spouses against each other in various situations.

A specially qualified assessor may be appointed by the court to *Expert evidence* assist it at the Proof stage on any technical matter. An application for such an appointment must be made by the joint motion of the parties. It is, in fact, a power rarely used. In addition, the court may nominate a skilled person to report on any particular matter of fact. This remit to a person of skill can be done on joint motion, by motion of one of the parties, or by the court itself. There are no rules as to what qualifications are required of such persons.

There are no general provisions for the exchange or disclosure of expert reports made in preparation for litigation except in certain cases in the Court of Session relating to damages for personal injury or death (see *Rule of Court 188E and 199K*).

There is no provision for pre-trial review so as to ensure the *Final* smooth conduct of the trial. *preparations for trial*

The parties may appear by themselves or have a legal *Conduct of* representative, ie a solicitor or advocate may appear. In the Court *proceedings* of Session, at present, only advocates may appear.

The presentation of argument is by oral argument based on the written pleadings. There is no time limit set on the length of oral argument permitted.

At a Procedure Roll hearing in the Court of Session or at a Debate in the Sheriff Court, the defender, if he is seeking to have the claim dismissed, speaks first. If the pursuer is seeking to have the defender's Defences declared irrelevant or incompetent he speaks first. If both parties are attacking each other's pleadings, the defender begins. In Proofs, the pursuer leads his evidence first with no opening statement. In appeals, the appellant speaks first. There are no rules governing the summing up of arguments.

Witnesses can be examined, cross-examined and re-examined by the parties. The court may ask questions of the witnesses.

The court, on the whole, in Proofs, exercises a passive role leaving it to the parties to adduce all the necessary and relevant evidence. The court has, however, an overriding power to call for evidence and to question witnesses to the extent that this is necessary for the proper deliberation of the issues in the case.

Judgments

Judgment is given in open court. Full reasons must be given if the judgment disposes of the case on the merits. Full reasons must also be given if the parties lodge an appeal against the judgment. There is no fixed time within which judgments must be given. Dissenting judgments arise only on appeals.

Costs

In the ordinary case the court has an inherent discretionary common law power which it may exercise in every case that comes before it, unless that power is expressly taken away or qualified by statute, to determine whether to make an award of expenses and, if it makes an award, to determine by whom, on what basis and to what extent expenses are to be paid. The normal practice is that expenses follow success, that is, the successful party is usually entitled to his full expenses as taxed.

Unless expenses are awarded at a fixed amount, they must be taxed before decree is granted for them.

Taxation is the proceedings by which accounts are submitted to a skilled person in order that he may examine them and allow, disallow, add to or reduce the charges therein. Sums which are disallowed or reduced are said to be "taxed off" and those which are allowable are called "judicial expenses". The skilled person who carries out this exercise of taxing the accounts is known as the Auditor of the Court. A solicitor can claim and be awarded an additional fee if the case has been especially complex and his work in relation thereto has been especially onerous.

A party may make what is known as a "*tender*" which is a judicial offer to pay a part of the sum asked for by his adversary after the action is raised. If the tender is not accepted this has the effect of ensuring that if the sum ultimately awarded by the court is the same or less than that offered in the tender the person who failed to accept the tender will be liable for his expenses from the date of the tender. No money is actually lodged in court.

Length of proceedings

Commercial actions in the Court of Session can be disposed of within six months or sometimes even less. Other civil actions last, on average, 18 months.

The average length of time between completion of the preliminary stage and trial is nine months.

Appeals are generally available on fact and law.   *Appeals*

Appeal lies from the Sheriff Court to the Sheriff Principal to the Court of Session to the House of Lords. An appeal may be taken directly from the Sheriff to the Court of Session. Dissenting judgments are permitted in Civil Appeals.

The average length of time between a judgment at first instance and each subsequent appeal is nine months to a year.

CHAPTER 7 : CRIMINAL PROCEDURE

The salient features of criminal proceedings in Scotland are that *Basic structure* public prosecution is the rule and private prosecution extremely uncommon. Government departments do not prosecute nor do the police conduct prosecutions but the police transmit information and evidence to the Procurator Fiscal with a view to prosecution being taken by the public prosecutors. The important distinction in criminal proceedings is that between solemn procedure (that is indictment before a judge of the High Court of Justiciary and a jury or before a Sheriff and a jury) and summary procedure (trial on complaints before a Sheriff or a Magistrate or one or more Justices of the Peace, in each case sitting without a jury). This distinction depends mainly on the gravity of the particular crime in question. The High Court has exclusive jurisdiction in respect of certain crimes, for example, murder, rape, incest and treason. Other serious crimes can be tried before either the High Court or a Sheriff sitting with a jury.

There is a system of public prosecution. This is directed by the *The prosecution* Lord Advocate who is assisted by the Solicitor General for Scotland and a number of Advocates-Depute. Permanent officials, the Procurator Fiscals, are appointed in each Sheriffdom and are responsible for the investigation and prosecution of crime in the Sheriffdom subject to the overriding control of the Lord Advocate, the Solicitor General and the Advocates-Depute. It is ultimately the responsibility of the Lord Advocate to decide whether to prosecute and in which court to prosecute, whether the prosecution should be on indictment or summary complaint and on what charges. Private prosecution is almost unheard of in modern practice.

The main rules relating to criminal procedure in Scotland are to be found in the *Criminal Procedure (Scotland) Act 1975* and the *Criminal Justice (Scotland) Act 1980*.

The prosecution is commenced in solemn procedure by presenting a Petition to a Sheriff naming the accused, stating the charge and craving warrant to arrest the accused, to search him and his premises, to cite witnesses and, after examination, to permit the accused for further examination or until liberation in ordinary course of law. In less serious crimes, the summary criminal procedure is commenced by the service on the accused of a complaint, and in the case of a statutory offence, a relative notice of the penalties to which the accused is liable on conviction. The complaint runs in the name of the Procurator Fiscal or some other prosecutor and states the substance of the charge.

Information relating to the offence

Information relating to the offence is set out in the indictment or complaint. Prior to pleading the accused may at a preliminary diet in solemn cases object to the competency of the proceedings or to the relevancy or legal sufficiency of the charge.

In summary cases, at the commencement of the trial hearing the accused may raise similar objections. The purpose of the preliminary diet is to clear preliminary matters to be settled prior to the commencement of the trial.

Some matters, if they are to be raised, must be raised (except with the leave of the court, on cause shown) at a preliminary diet. These include, in solemn cases, objections relating to the competency or relevancy of the indictment.

Other matters may be heard by order of the court at a preliminary diet. These include application for separation of charges or trials. The preliminary diet is held before the judge who will conduct the central trial and takes the form of a preliminary Proof or legal debate.

Commencement of proceedings

Solemn proceedings in court are commenced by the pleading diet when the accused can raise objections to the charge and must, in turn, intimate his pleas in bar of trial and any special defences, for example, self-defence. In summary cases, the proceedings are commenced by the fixing of a trial diet. Evidence for the prosecution is gathered by the police and the Procurator Fiscal. There are no fixed rules on providing evidence to the defence. In practice, the prosecution allows the defence representatives to know the evidence that they have against the accused.

Pleas

The plea of the accused is made at the pleading diet in solemn cases and in summary cases at the start of the trial. In summary cases, he may in certain situations plead guilty by letter. He may plead guilty or not guilty. He may plead guilty to a lesser offence. He can change his plea. His representatives may offer to plead to one charge rather than another and this may be accepted.

Juries

Jurors are persons chosen at random by lot from a larger number of qualified persons summoned for the purpose by the appropriate court officials. To qualify as a juror a person must be aged between 18 and 65, be ordinarily resident in the United Kingdom for at least five years and registered as an elector. The jury consists of 15 persons. The prosecution or the accused may challenge five jurors without giving any reasons and any number on showing cause why that person is unsuitable to sit as a juror in that case.

Conduct of the trial

In the High Court, only advocates can appear (although this position is presently under review). In other courts, advocates and solicitors may appear. The prosecutor begins the trial by leading his evidence against the accused. There are no opening speeches. The defence can submit at the end of the presentation of the prosecution evidence that there is no case to answer, a submission which may or may not be accepted by the court. In all cases, the function of the jury is to have regard to the evidence and, subject to the directions on matters of law made by the presiding judge, to return a verdict on one or more questions of fact or of mixed fact and law. The Magistrate or Justice of the Peace or Sheriff acting as a judge assumes the jury's role in assessing matters of fact in summary cases. The judge does not call witnesses. It is the prosecution's duty to present all the relevant evidence to justify the charge. If it fails to do so, the prosecution fails. The judge has no active role in the collection of evidence. Almost all hearings are open and public. The court may on application order evidence to be heard in camera in special circumstances, for example, when the evidence of young children is being given or in certain cases of sexual offences.

In summary cases, the judge must himself determine the *The verdict* credibility and veracity of witnesses and decide whether he finds the charge proved beyond reasonable doubt or not. The judge normally pronounces his findings at once. An accused cannot be found guilty of an alternative offence with which he has not been charged. In solemn cases, after the jury have been addressed by counsel for the prosecution and then by counsel for the defence, the judge instructs them in the relevant law and the points in issue. The jury then retire to consider their verdict. The jury's verdict may be returned by a majority. It may be one of guilty, not guilty or "not proven". The last mentioned verdict, not proven, means that the accused goes free. This verdict is appropriate where the jury simply consider the prosecution has failed to prove its case. The accused cannot be subsequently charged with the same crime. The verdict of the jury is announced in reply to a question from the clerk of court by the foreman of the jury. The verdict is recorded and read over to the jury for their assent to its terms.

Before sentence is passed, the accused, or his counsel or solicitor, *Sentencing* must be given an opportunity to address the judge in mitigation. It is not normal to lead evidence in mitigation and ex parte statements and/or letters or certificates or even medical reports may be received without being proved by witnesses. But where there is any significant dispute about mitigating factors this can be settled only by hearing evidence. The convicted person's character is assessed by reference to what is said in mitigation on his behalf and the reports which the judge can call for from social workers and medical practitioners. The prosecution, when moving the court for sentence, places before the court the accused's previous convictions which are taken into account by the court in fixing sentence.

Sentencing powers are contained in various Acts of Parliament. There is a standard textbook on sentencing powers - *Nicholson, Law and Practice of Sentencing in Scotland*. There are separate sentencing rules which apply in the case of persons between 16 and 18, 18 and 21, and those under the age of 16.

The range of sentences includes imprisonment, monetary fines, community service, probation and compensation orders. A sentence of life imprisonment is mandatory in the case of murder. There are certain mandatory statutory sentences in certain cases of driving offences.

Appeals

A person convicted on indictment in the High Court or Sheriff Court may appeal to the High Court of Justiciary sitting as the Court of Criminal Appeal. Appeal may be taken :

- against conviction on any question of law alone;
- against sentence, unless the sentence is fixed by law; or
- against both conviction and sentence.

The appeal is initiated by completing and lodging within 14 days an intimation of intention to appeal, followed within six weeks by a Note of Appeal stating the grounds of appeal. In summary cases, either party may, on the final determination of a summary prosecution, apply to the court to state a case for the opinion of the High Court of Justiciary.

A stated case may be obtained on very varied grounds so as to cover practically every question likely to be raised on appeal, including objections to jurisdiction, competence, relevance, the admission or rejection of evidence, irregularities in procedure, oppressive conduct by the Sheriff and competence to give that sentence (but not the amount of the sentence). A challenge to a sentence on the basis that it was harsh and oppressive in the circumstances may be raised in a Note of Appeal. Once the Sheriff has stated his case setting out the facts found by him to be established and the legal issues raised, the case is heard by the High Court. Legal argument is presented by both sides.

In criminal appeals the judges of the appeal court regularly give their decision at the end of the hearing. If not, it is given normally within a maximum of a few weeks. There are no dissenting judgments.

Extradition

There are currently two sets of provisions governing extradition from Scotland. The first applies to extradition to foreign countries with which the United Kingdom has an extradition arrangement under the *Extraditions Act 1870*, and the second applies to extradition to United Kingdom colonies or to Commonwealth countries designated by Order in Council and to foreign states (other than Ireland) with whom extradition arrangements have been made under the *Extradition Act 1989*.

Time limits

A person may be detained by a police officer for a maximum of six hours if the police officer has reasonable grounds for suspecting him of an offence (see *Criminal Justice (Scotland) Act 1980, s 2*).

When a person is arrested on a criminal charge he has a right to be brought before a court "as soon as possible", which normally means the first day after being taken into custody.

A jury trial of an accused must be commenced within 12 months of the accused's first appearance on petition. An accused who has been committed for trial in custody may not be detained for a total period of more than 80 days from full committal without having been served with an indictment.

An accused who has been committed for trial in custody must be brought to trial and the trial commenced within 110 days from the date of full committal. If the trial has not begun within that period then the accused must be liberated forthwith and cannot be subsequently recharged with the same offence.

An accused in all cases except treason and murder is entitled to *Bail* be released on bail unless the prosecution objects. If the prosecution objects it is a question for the court's discretion whether to grant or refuse release on bail, having regard primarily to the nature of the crime with which the accused is charged. The grant or refusal of bail may be appealed to the High Court. The application is made and determined on the basis of ex parte statements before the judge including references to previous convictions.

CHAPTER 8 : REMEDIES

Damages can be awarded in both the Court of Session and the *Damages*
Sheriff Court for loss suffered by one person in consequence of a
breach of duty or obligation owed to him by another person. The
most common cases are claims for damages for negligence or
breach of contract, but damages are awarded in a whole variety of
other situations such as for breach of statutory duty, breach of
copyright, etc.

In Scotland, a pursuer suing in respect of personal injuries or *Jury trial*
defamation may, in the Court of Session, but not in the Sheriff
Court, elect to have his case heard by a jury presided over by a
judge. The court may, on an application for jury trial, refuse it or
grant it. A jury trial will only be refused when the issues involved
are complex. When a jury trial is allowed it is the jury which
assesses any damages to be awarded.

In personal injuries actions, the quantum of damages in respect *Personal injury*
of pain and suffering are assessed by reference to previous
awards in similar cases. The injured pursuer is also entitled to
claim for past and future wage losses which are calculated by
reference to his pre-injury wages and income, to which a
multiplier is applied. The position is broadly speaking the same as
in the rest of the United Kingdom. There are no fixed awards for
types of injuries.

Damages for mental distress can be awarded in certain cases of *Mental distress*
personal injury actions, and in certain cases of breach of contract
where, given the nature of the contract itself, it was foreseeable
that breach thereof might result in such suffering.

Damages for loss of reputation are available in defamation cases. *Loss of reputation*
In special and limited cases of breach of contract such an award
might also be made. There is no fixed limit to the amount of any
such awards.

The rules in relation to damages for breach of contractual
obligations and damages for delictual obligation are generally
speaking quite distinct. A pursuer can be awarded damages for
pure economic loss in breach of contract cases, but in delict
claims such a loss is recoverable in a very limited class of cases.

The law of Scotland has a well developed system of quasi- *Quasi-*
contractual remedies based on Roman law principles including *contractual*
the concepts of repetition, recompense and restitution. These *remedies*
principles apply, for example, when a party has no contractual

right to enforce because, for example, the contract has been frustrated. Generally the principles of quasi-contract can be applied where one party has benefited at the expense of another where the other had no intention of bestowing the benefit upon him gratuitously. The concept of restitution can be employed in contractual cases including commercial contract cases. There is no common law general principle of fairness or reasonableness governing contractual terms. The *Unfair Contract Terms Act 1977* gives the courts powers to control certain types of contractual terms, that is, clauses that seek to exempt or limit liability depending on whether or not they can be said to be fair and reasonable in the circumstances.

Penalty clauses

It is possible to seek an award of an agreed sum payable as damages. The court, however, will not enforce such agreed damages provisions, payable on a breach of contract, if they are not considered by the court to be genuine pre-estimates of the damage which would be sustained on breach of contract, but which are considered to be penal in nature.

Specific performance

It is frequently open to a party to a contract to request the court to ordain the other party specifically to implement his contract and to perform what he undertook to do. Scots law favours a claim for specific performance and there is a presumption in Scots law that an obligation is enforceable by a decree of court unless there are equitable grounds to refuse this when damages in lieu thereof will be awarded.

Frustration

The principle of frustration of contract in Scots law can be applied where, after a contract has been made, an unforeseeable turn of events takes place which renders performance impossible, or if possible at all, so delayed or changed that it would not be at all what the parties had contemplated and their bargain would, in fact, be radically different. The effect of the operation of the doctrine of frustration is to discharge both parties from their obligations to perform further under the contract.

Delivery up of goods

An action for delivery up of goods is appropriate and available where the defender is alleged to be in possession of movables possession of which should have been ceded to the pursuer. It may be available in respect of both fungible and non-fungible goods.

Interest on damages

The rules governing interest on judgments are somewhat complex. Generally speaking, interest is available at a fixed standard rate from the date of decree until payment of money awards unless the parties have agreed otherwise prior to the decision of the court. *Section 1(1) of the Interest on Damages (Scotland) Act 1958*, as substituted by *Section 1 of the Interest on Damages (Scotland) Act 1971* provides that where the court pronounces an interlocutor decerning for payment of a sum of money as damages, the interlocutor may include a decree for the payment of interest at such rate or rates as may be specified in the interlocutor on the whole or any part of that sum for the whole or any part of the period between the date when the right of action arose and the date of the interlocutor.

Scots law recognises the remedy of declarator (or a declaration) to **Declaratory** determine any legal right that a pursuer may have an interest to **relief** have declared. The case law of Scotland is full of examples of the enormous variety of rights which pursuers have in different circumstances sought to have declared. The decree of declarator confers no new right on the pursuer but only declares authoritatively that he possesses some status or right previously doubted or denied.

A company may be wound up by either the Court of Session or the **Winding-up a** Sheriff Court on any one or more of the following grounds : **company**
- that the company has, by special resolution resolved that the company be wound up by the court;
- that the company, being a public company, has failed to comply with the statutory requirement for minimum capital and more than a year has expired since it was registered;
- that the company is an old public company;
- that the company has not commenced business within a year from its incorporation or has suspended business for a year;
- that the number of members is reduced to below two;
- that the company is unable to pay its debts;
- that the court is of the opinion that it is just and equitable that the company should be wound up (see *Section 124 of the Insolvency Act 1986*).

The holder of a charge or a debenture created by a Scottish **Receiver** company has the ordinary remedies otherwise available to a creditor. Where a creditor, however, holds a floating charge he may, under the *Insolvency Act 1986, s 51*, apply to the court to appoint a receiver to the company. A receiver may be appointed on the occurrence of any event which is provided for in the instrument creating the floating charge entitling the holder to make the appointment.

The appointment of an administrator may be made in respect of **Administrator** a company which is, or is likely to be, unable to pay its debts. It is available where the court considers that this would be likely to result in the company surviving as a going concern or in a more advantageous realisation of the company's assets than would be achieved in a winding-up.

Administrative law remedies are available against public bodies **Actions by or** or authorities by way of judicial review of the acts or decisions of **against public** those bodies. Judicial review is made by way of petition and is **bodies** available only in the Court of Session. Orders obtainable in such proceedings include the quashing of decisions and orders requiring public bodies to follow certain courses of action. An interdict can be granted against a public body, but is not available against the government or a government minister by virtue of the provisions of the *Crown Proceedings Act 1947*.

The rules relating to legal standing in administrative law cases are the same as in other judicial proceedings - the petitioner must establish his title and interest to sue but the courts have in some cases of administrative law appeared to be less restrictive as to what amounts to title and interest than might otherwise be the case in private law actions.

In criminal cases, a person convicted of a crime may be ordered to pay compensation for any personal injury, loss or damage caused by the acts which constituted the offence.

All the remedies available in civil cases can also be granted in administrative proceedings.

It is a general rule in both breach of contract and delictual cases that the damages which arise from one and the same cause of action must all be assessed and recovered in one action. The pursuer may bring only one action and must recover damages for all the loss past, present and future, certain and contingent, direct and consequent, and either in delict or for a breach of contract.

Alternative dispute resolution   If the parties have agreed that their disputes should be referred to arbitration, the court will "*sist*" (stay) proceedings relating to those disputes pending the outcome of the arbitration, if one or other of the parties brings to the attention of the court the arbitration agreement. Parties are, however, free otherwise, by agreement, to waive their arbitration agreement and instead litigate their dispute. There are no "court related dispute settlement procedures". Mediation and conciliation procedures are not built into the courts' procedures.

CHAPTER 9 : MATRIMONIAL DISPUTES

Both the Court of Session, that is Outer House Judges, and the Sheriff Court, that is Sheriffs, have jurisdiction to hear all questions relating to matrimonial disputes.

In relation to divorce there are two forms of procedure, the first, *Divorce* where the action is defended, follows very closely the form of an ordinary civil action. The second is a simplified procedure where the application is in respect of a marriage which has broken down because of two years' non-cohabitation and the other party consenting to the divorce decree, or on the basis of five years' non-cohabitation. The simplified procedure does not require the parties to appear and generally involves only filling out certain documents with the court.

The court can make orders for custody and access in the course of *Custody and* proceedings for divorce or separation. Apart from that, *access* independent applications in respect of custody and access can be heard both in the Court of Session and the Sheriff Court. Interim custody or interim access will normally be granted on the basis of ex parte statements made to the court. The court often also orders reports to be produced by social workers or other qualified persons as to the position of the child before making such orders. Final custody and access orders are made after hearing oral evidence in court.

Urgent applications can be heard for the custody and access of children when, for example, one parent is threatening to take the child out of the jurisdiction of the Scottish courts or where the child's welfare is being threatened in some way.

Section 4 of the Matrimonial Homes (Family Protection) (Scotland) Act 1981 provides that either spouse may apply to the court for an exclusion order suspending the occupancy rights of the other in the matrimonial home. The court is directed to make an exclusion order if it appears to the court that the making of the order is necessary for the protection of the applicant or any child of the family from any conduct or threatened or reasonably apprehended conduct of the non-applicant spouse which is or would be injurious to the physical or mental health of the applicant or the child.

The sole ground for divorce or judicial separation is irretrievable *Grounds for* breakdown of marriage. Irretrievable breakdown of marriage is *divorce/judicial* established if and only if : *separation*

        the defender is proved to have committed adultery; or

- the behaviour of the defender is of such a kind that the pursuer cannot reasonably be expected to cohabit with him; or
- desertion of the pursuer by the defender has taken place for a period of two years; or
- non-cohabitation has existed for a period of two years with the defender consenting to divorce; or
- non-cohabitation has existed for five years.

The rules in respect of division of matrimonial property are now set out in detail in the *Family Law (Scotland) Act 1985.*

CHAPTER 10 : PROPERTY TRANSACTIONS

For a valid binding contract of sale of land in Scotland, the agreement should be constituted in writing and the writing itself has to comply with certain formal requirements. The normal situation involves making a written offer to buy which is met by an acceptance in writing by the seller. These missives of sale are usually holograph (in the manuscript of the granter or signed by him) or adopted as holograph. The missives themselves create only personal rights and obligations between the parties. Before rights of property in the land in question are transferred it is necessary for the owner of the land to grant a formal deed known as a Disposition of the Property which then has to be registered in the Land Registers. Registration of the Disposition completes the legal title to the land in question. Between the conclusion of the missives and the granting of the Disposition the purchaser, or more commonly his agent, will investigate the validity of the seller's title to sell the land in question. The full purchase price is not payable until a valid Disposition is granted in favour of the purchaser. In movable property cases sale can be effected by either an oral or written agreement. There are no special rules as to the form of such an agreement. A transaction of sale of movable property is regulated by the *Sale of Goods Act 1979*.

CHAPTER 11 : RECOGNITION AND ENFORCEMENT OF FOREIGN JUDGMENTS

It is a general principle of Scots law that a foreign judgment will not be recognised in Scotland unless the issuing court is regarded by Scots law as one which had jurisdiction in the international sense, or had international competence at the time the proceedings were instituted.

Grounds of competence in Scotland in actions in personam

The equitable principles of prorogation, submission and reconvention applied by the Scots courts in assuming jurisdiction are also applied by them in giving effect to agreements by which the parties submit to the jurisdiction of a foreign law.

Prorogation, submission and reconvention

The Scottish common law recognises the assumption of jurisdiction by a foreign court in any action *in personam* when the defender was resident within the territory of the foreign state at the time it commenced

Residence of an individual defender

The Scottish courts, in cases of corporate defenders, would probably follow the English law rule which concedes jurisdiction to a foreign court if the corporation in question carries on business within the territory of that court "at a definite and, to some reasonable extent, permanent place".

Place of business and carrying on business

The Scottish courts assert their exclusive competence to grant decrees in rem in relation to immovable property within Scotland, and conversely concede to foreign courts a similar right in relation to immovables within their territory.

Grounds of jurisdiction recognised in actions in rem

The fact that movables are situated within the territory of a foreign court is deemed to clothe that court with the authority to grant a decree in rem relating to these movables.

Immovable and movable property

The Scottish courts will not enforce decrees of the courts of foreign territories in penal or revenue actions and any recognition given to such decrees is limited to their effect upon property within the country at the time of the action.

A foreign judgment, pre-registered in Scotland under *Section 18* of, and *Schedule 6 and 7 to the Civil Jurisdiction and Judgments Act 1982* may be challenged either on the grounds that the foreign court did not act judicially or on the ground that it was misled by the fraud of one of the parties.

For a foreign decree to be enforced in Scotland it is, at common law, necessary that it is a final decree.

*The Brussels
Convention*

The *Brussels Convention* has been implemented in Scotland by way of the *Civil Jurisdiction and Judgments Act 1982*.

At common law, in Scotland, a foreign judgment was given effect by means of an action in the court of Session for a decree-conform, that is to say an action in which the foreign judgment and not the facts upon which it was based is founded upon as constituting the obligation in question.

Apart from the common law method of obtaining a decree-conform, a foreign judgment can be enforced in Scotland where the applicant complies with various statutory procedures. All of these involve registration in the books of courts in Scotland and thereafter the judgment is enforced as if it were, in fact, a Scottish judgment.

Procedure

The statutory rules normally provide for procedures whereby notice is given to interested parties of the registration of a foreign judgment and on any refusal to register on the ground that the court of origin lacked jurisdiction. The statutory procedures are to be found in various acts - the *Judgments Extension Act 1868*, dealing with judgments obtained in another part of the United Kingdom; the *Inferior Courts Judgments Extension Act 1882*, dealing with the enforcement in Scotland of judgments obtained in inferior courts in other parts of the United Kingdom; the *Administration of Justice Act 1920, Part 2* dealing with the enforcement of certain judgments obtained in the British dominions, the *Foreign Judgments (Reciprocal Enforcement) Act 1933*; dealing with the enforcement in Scotland of other foreign judgments and the *Maintenance Orders Acts of 1950 and 1972* dealing specifically with the enforcement of foreign maintenance orders.

The *European Community (Enforcement of Community Judgments) Order 1972* and the *Rules of the Court of Session 296F and 296K* make provision for the registration and enforcement in Scotland of certain Community judgments and Euratom inspection orders.

As previously noted, the *Civil Jurisdiction and Judgments Act 1982* applies the *1968 Brussels Convention* to Scotland. The Convention supersedes any common law rules which might otherwise apply in matters within the scope of the Convention and it also supersedes various bilateral conventions made by the United Kingdom under the *Foreign Judgments (Reciprocal Enforcement) Act 1933*, but only in relation to matters to which the *1968 Convention* applies.

An application for registration of a foreign judgment under the *1933 Act* is made by way of Petition to the Outer House of the Court of Session. Any application should be supported by an affidavit of the facts :

      (a)   exhibiting a certified copy of the judgment issued by the original court and authenticated by its seal and a translation of the judgment certified by a notary public or authenticated by affidavit;

(b) stating to the best of the information and belief of the deponent :

    (i) that the applicant is entitled to enforce the judgment;

    (ii) as the case may require, either that at the date of the application the judgment has not been satisfied, or if the judgment has been satisfied in part, what the amount is in respect of which it remains unsatisfied;

    (iii) that at the date of the application the judgment can be enforced by execution in the country of the original court;

    (iv) that if the judgment were registered, the registration would not be, or be liable to be, set aside under *Section 4* of the Act;

    (v) that the judgment is not a judgment to which *Section 5 of the Protection of Trading Interests Act 1980* applies.

(c) specifying the amount of the interest, if any, which, under the law of the country of the original court, has become due under the judgment up to the time of registration; and shall be accompanied by such other evidence with respect to the matters referred to in subparagraph (iii) of paragraph (b) above as may be required having regard to the provisions of the Order in Council extending the Act to the country of the original court;

(d) stating where the sum payable under the judgment is expressed in a currency other than the currency of the United Kingdom the amount which that sum represents in the currency of the United Kingdom calculated at the rate of exchange prevailing at the date of the judgment, and

(e) stating also the full name, title, trade or business and the usual or last known place of abode or of business of the judgment creditor and the judgment debtor respectively, so far as known to the deponent.

An application for the registration in Scotland of a judgment under the *Brussels Convention* has to be made to the Court of Session in compliance with *Article 32 of the Convention* and *Form 53 of the Rules of Court*. *Rule 249E of the Rules of the Court of Session* states which documents and affidavits must be produced with the application. The application is made to a judge in the Outer House of the Court of Session but the procedure is administrative in nature, no appearance normally being required.

There is, as yet, no Scots authority on the concept of "contrary to public policy" in the context of the recognition of foreign judgments pursuant to *Article 27 of the Brussels Convention*.

An appeal against a decision to allow registration of a judgment under the *1933 Act* is made by way of Petition to the Outer House of the Court of Session supported by affidavit. The time specified for lodging such an application varies from case to case (see *Rule of Court 249(3)*).

An application opposing the registration of a judgment under the *Civil Jurisdiction and Judgments Act 1982* is made to the Outer House in accordance with *Form 42 of the Rules of Court*. It requires to be taken within one month of intimation of the decree and warrant for registration of the judgment, or within two months of intimation of such decree and warrant where intimation was made on a person domiciled in another contracting state. There is a further appeal on points of law only to the Inner House of the Court of Session (see *Rules of Court 249K and 294L*).

BIBLIOGRAPHY

General Works of Reference

Gloag & Henderson, *Introduction to the Law of Scotland* (9th edn), W. Green & Sons

Greens Encyclopaedia of the Laws of Scotland, W. Green & Sons

Stair Memorial Encyclopaedia of the Laws of Scotland, Law Society of Scotland and Butterworths

Walker, D.M., *Scottish Legal System*, W. Green & Sons

Constitutional Law

Mitchell, *Constitutional Law* (2nd edn), W. Green & Sons

Criminal Law

Gordon, *Criminal Law of Scotland* (2nd edn), W. Green & Sons

Criminal Procedure

Renton & Brown, *Criminal Procedure According to the Law of Scotland*, W. Green & Sons

International Private Law

Anton, *Civil Jurisdiction in Scotland*, W. Green & Sons

Anton, *Private International Law* (2nd edn), W. Green & Sons

Husband and Wife

Clive, E. M., *Husband and Wife* (2nd edn), W. Green & Sons

Law of Obligation

Gloag, W., *Law of Contract* (2nd edn), W. Green & Sons

McBryde, W., *Law of Contract*, W. Green & Sons.

Walker, D.M., *Law of Civil Remedies in Scotland*, W. Green & Sons

Walker, D.M., *Law of Delict* (2nd edn), W. Green & Sons

Land Law

Gordon, W.M., *Scottish Land Law*, W. Green & Sons

Paton & Cameron, *Law of Landlord and Tenant in Scotland*, W. Green & Sons

Rankine, *Law of Land Ownership in Scotland* (4th edn), W. Green & Sons

Movable Property

Gloag & Irvine, *Rights and Security*, W. Green & Sons

Trusts

Wilson and Duncan Trusts, *Trustees & Executors*, W. Green & Sons

Succession

McLaren, *Law of Wills and Succession*, W. Green & Sons

Conveyancing

Halliday, J., *Conveyancing Law and Practice* (4 Vols), W. Green & Sons.

Civil Procedure

Maclaren, *Court of Session Practice*, W. Green & Sons

Macphail, I., *Sheriff Court Practice*, W. Green & Sons.

Maxwell, D., *Court of Session Practice*, Scottish Courts Civil Administration

Parliament House Book, W. Green & Sons

Law of Evidence

Macphail, I., *Law of Evidence*, Law Society of Scotland

Walker, A.G. & Walker, N.M.L., *Law of Evidence in Scotland*, T. & T. Clark

Legal Aid

Stoddart, C. N., *Law and Practice of Legal Aid in Scotland*, W. Green & Sons

N.B. Standard English Textbooks on Commercial Law, Company Law and the Law of Obligations are frequently used in Scotland but care has to be taken with regard to identifying the differences that exist between the two legal systems even in these areas.

Ramon Mullerat
Bufete Mullerat & Roca

CONTENTS

CHAPTER 1 : SOURCES OF LAW

Under the *Constitution*, Spain is a Parliamentary Monarchy with the King as the head of state and its representative in international relations.

Spain is a regionally unified state divided into 17 autonomous regions, ("*comunidades autónomas*"), eg Catalonia, Andalusia, Basque Country, Galicia. Each autonomous region has its own government, with a President and a Council of Ministers and its own Legislative Assembly.

Unitary v federal system

Local governments are made up of municipalities ("*ayuntamientos*") governed by a mayor ("*alcalde*") and councillors ("*concejales*"). Groups of municipalities form provinces ("*provincias*"), which are governed by provincial delegations ("*diputaciones provinciales*"). There are 52 provinces in Spain.

Under *Articles 148 and 149 of the Constitution* certain powers are allocated exclusively to the central government, such as those dealing with matters of national defence, international relations, and the administration of justice, and the Autonomous Parliaments are permitted to legislate on other matters such as economic development, public works, schools, agriculture, hydro-electricity and forestry exploitation, environmental protection, the promotion of culture, health, leisure, and so forth.

According to the *Preliminary Title of the Civil Code*, the sources of Spanish law are the Acts of Parliament (legal provisions published in the Official Gazette); custom (when there is no specific applicable law), provided this is not immoral or contrary to public order; and the general principles of law, such as freedom of contract, good faith, freedom of form, etc. The Spanish legal system is a hierarchical one where statutes ("*leyes*"), which have a different status and legal ranking, prevail over lower-ranked conflicting provisions.

The principal written sources of law are :

Written sources of law

    (a)   The corpus of constitutional law, particularly the *Spanish Constitution of 1978* which is the supreme source of law in Spain. It sets out Spain's economic order as a free market economy based on private enterprise. It creates and sets limits on the extent to and manner in which the powers of the three branches of government : the executive, the legislature and the judiciary may be exercised; and

(b)   The Acts on civil law, which include the *Civil Code* ("*Código Civil*") of 1889, which has undergone several important amendments on filiation, parental authority, the matrimonial property regime, annulment of marriage, separation and divorce, nationality, the protection of minors, arbitration, ownership, etc, the the *Mortgage Act of 8 February 1946* ("*Ley Hipotecaria*"); *Civil Registry Act of 8 June 1957*; the *Horizontal Property Act 49/60 of 21 July 1960*; the *Act on Urban Leases of 24 December 1964*; the *Act on Agricultural Leases No. 83/80 of 31 December 1980* and the *Intellectual Property Act No 22/87 of 11 November 1987*. Examples of the principal legislation in the commercial field are the *Commercial Code of 22 August 1885* ("*Código de Comercio*"); the *Act on the Suspension of Payments of 16 July 1922*; the *Consumers and Users Act 16/84 of 19 July 1984*; the *Patents Act 11/86 of 20 March 1986*; the *Stock Exchange Act 24/88 of 28 July 1988*; the *Trademarks Act 32/88 of 10 November 1988*; the *Advertising Act 34/88 of 11 November 1988* ("*Ley General de Publicidad*"); the *Legislative Royal Decree 1564/89 of 22 December 1989*, approving the *Companies Act* ("*Ley de Sociedades Anonimas*"); the *Commercial Registry Regulations* ("*Reglamento del Registro Mercantil*"), *Royal Decree 1597/89 of 29 December 1989*; the *Protection of Competition Act 16/89 of 17 July 1989*; and so forth.

(c)   In criminal matters there is the *Penal Code* ("*Código Penal*") : *Decree 3096/73 of 14 September 1973*, approving the amended text of the *Penal Code* in accordance with *Act 44/71 of 15 November 1971*. The *Penal Code* was adopted to the *Constitution* by *Act 8/83 of 25 June 1983*. Recently the government has submitted a proposal for a new Code to the Parliament.

(d)   On procedural matters there are the "*Ley de enjuiciamiento civil*" *of 3 February 1881* ("*LEC*") (*Civil Procedure Act*) and the "*Ley enjuiciamiento criminal*" *of 11 February 1881* (*Criminal Procedure Act*) which have been amended several times; and the *Judicial Powers Act 6/85 of 1 July 1985* ("*Ley Orgánica del Poder Judicial*" - "*LOPJ*").

(e)   On employment matters there are the *Workers' Statute* ("*Estatuto de los Trabajadores*"), *Act 8/1980 of 10 March 1980*, and *Act 7/89 of 12 April 1989* which governs procedure in employment matters.

The "*Boletin Oficial del Estado*" ("*BOE*" - Official Gazette) and other official gazettes the of autonomous and local governments publish daily all new legal provisions passed.

Article 96 of the Constitution provides that "Duly concluded *Monist v dualist* international treaties, once officially published in Spain, shall *system* form part of the internal legal system. Their provisions shall only be derogated from, modified or suspended in the form provided for in the treaties themselves or in accordance with the general rules of international law."

Furthermore, *Article 1.5 of the Civil Code* provides that "legal rules in international treaties shall not be applied directly in Spain until they form part of the internal law through their publication in the Official Gazette."

Therefore, once an international treaty has been signed and ratified by Spain, it is automatically part of the Spanish legal system. However, it may not be relied upon as a source of rights and obligations that can be raised before the courts until it has been published in the Official Gazette.

Foreigners have the same individual rights and civil liberties as *Application of* Spaniards on the basis that the rights that protect them are based *national law to* on the human condition. The state is obliged to provide for *foreigners* foreigners treatment amounting to a minimum standard which covers basic rights, ie protection of one's life and interests, protection against unlawful arrest, the chance to be heard, the right not to suffer inhuman treatment, free access to the courts, the right to exercise certain civil rights such as those relating to the paternal-filial relationship and so forth. Foreigners may enjoy other rights by virtue of bilateral and multilateral treaties. The rights and obligations of foreigners are basically regulated in the *Foreigner Act 7/85 of 1 July 1985* ("*Ley de Extranjería*").

On the other hand, there are rights which foreigners are not entitled to exercise, such as the right to vote and the right of access to public office (although, in accordance with the provisions of the *Maastricht Treaty*, the *Constitution* will shortly be amended to allow EC citizens to vote and to be candidates in municipal elections). Certain jobs and the enjoyment of certain social rights such as unemployment benefit and free medical assistance are subject to restrictions in this area.

In civil litigation, nationals and foreigners are treated equally under Spanish law, with limited exceptions in relation to :
- (a) capacity : a foreigner only has capacity to act on his own behalf if deemed to have such capacity under the law of his home country;

- (b) the supply of a bond for court costs if so requested by a Spanish defendant - a foreign plaintiff must pay a bond ("*caución de arraigo enjuicio*" or "*cautio judicati solvi*") into court to guarantee payment of any legal fees and court costs for which he may be liable. However, foreign companies with assets in Spain are not required to pay such a bond, nor is a bond necessary for any appeals or for certain summary proceedings. Moreover, the provisions on supplying a bond do not apply if the treaties or conventions, or reciprocal treaties with the state of the foreigner in question, otherwise apply (eg the *1968 Brussels Convention*); So, in practice, the "*caución de arraigo*" is rarely applicable.

(c)   the preventive seizure of assets : a Spanish court may order seizure of a foreign debtor's assets before trial provided there is a real prima facie liability based on written proof. The courts grant such orders in its own discretion.

Application of EC law

Spain became a member of the European Communities with effect on 1 January 1986 following the *Spanish Accession Treaty of 12 June 1985*. This means that EC law takes precedence over Spanish domestic law, although there is a transitional period in respect of certain specific matters while Spain adapts its laws to the EC legal system. The EC Treaties are considered as the primary source of Community law (including their annexes, protocols, amendments and subordinate legislative acts).

Citation of foreign law

The courts and the government must of their own motion apply the Spanish rules dealing with conflicts of laws. Under certain circumstances, Spanish courts may apply foreign law to civil or commercial matters raised before them (*Civil Code, arts 9 to 12*) but a party requesting that a foreign law be applied must prove its content and force by such means of proof as are admitted and admissable before a Spanish court. However, the judge may order proofs or written evidence and call on the parties to collaborate (*Civil Code, art 12, 6*).

When citing foreign law, the modes of interpretation followed in that foreign legal system to which the law belongs must also be considered by the court. However the Spanish courts will not apply foreign law unless requested to do so by one of the parties. This issue arises most frequently in certain types of cases, such as contractual or non-contractual obligations, real and personal property, trademarks and patents, securities and so forth.

How the conflict of law issue is to be determined is resolved according to Spanish law (*Article 12.1 of the Civil Code* states that "the decision determining the appropriate conflict of law rule to apply must be made in accordance with Spanish law"). Once foreign law is found to be applicable, the court must adopt the rules and concepts governing the case according to such foreign law. *Article 1692 of the LEC* enables the parties to apply to the Supreme Court when the courts have applied foreign law incorrectly.

Evidence from abroad

As far as the use of documents executed abroad and their admissibility in Spain are concerned, the general rule is set out in *Article 601 of the LEC*, which provides that all documents drafted in any foreign language to be submitted to a Spanish court must be accompanied by a translation in Spanish. Any such translation can be done privately, but if one of the parties challenges it, the document must be officially translated. This rule applies both to private and to public documents. A sworn translation ("*traducción jurada*") can be done by official translators appointed by the "*Ministerio de Asuntos Exteriores*" (Ministry of Foreign Affairs), by foreign consuls, or by official translators appointed by Spanish consulates abroad.

The *European Convention on Human Rights* of 4 November 1959 was ratified by Spain in 1979. A right of recourse to the European Court of Human Rights is available if a party's human rights have been violated provided that all remedies available in the Spanish courts have been exhausted.

European Convention on Human Rights

All legal provisions are interpreted in accordance with the *Civil Code*. Three different classifications of interpretation can be made :

Principles of interpretation

- that depending on the person making the interpretation (this is called "authentic", if carried out by the legislator; "doctrinal", if carried out by jurists in legal opinions; and "judicial" if through the judgments and resolutions of the courts);
- that depending on the result - whether an interpretation is "extensive" or "restrictive";
- that depending on the method used. Interpretation can be "literal" or "grammatical", a simple analysis of the words; "teleological", with a view to the purpose or objective aimed at; "historical", looking at the historical background; and "systematic", taking into consideration not only the specific rule to be interpreted but others associated with it.

General rules of interpretation are based on the following principles : good faith, the primacy of the text (direct meaning), the object and purpose (essential to determine the will of the parties) and the scope and content of the text.

There are no authorised annotated texts of the *Constitution* or the Codes. However the *Constitution* and the principal Codes have been annotated and commented on by legal authors with reviews of applicable case law.

Annotated texts of the Constitution

CHAPTER 2 : FUNDAMENTAL RIGHTS

Fundamental rights are protected by the *1978 Constitution (arts 10 to 30)* and although they are directly enforceable it is for the legislature to organise and develop them in detail. These principles must be respected by the legislative, the executive and the judicial branches of the state (a general duty confirmed by the Constitutional Court in *Judgment 185/89, of 14 October 1989*). In addition, the *Judicial Powers Act* and *Act 62/78 of 26 December 1978*, complemented by *Royal Decree 342/79 of 20 February 1979*, provide that fundamental rights are to be protected through the courts.

Constitutional protection of fundamental rights

Article 10.2 of the Constitution provides that the rules on fundamental rights shall be interpreted in accordance with the *Universal Declaration of Human Rights* and relevant treaties ratified by Spain (the *1960 International Resolution on Civil and Political Rights* ratified by Spain on 13 April 1977; the *1966 Resolution on Economic Rights* and, in particular, the *1950 European Convention* ratified by Spain in 1979, etc).

The principal fundamental rights recognised by the *Constitution* are the following : equality before the law (*art 14*); the right to life and physical and moral integrity (*art 15*); freedom of religion (*art 16*); the right to physical freedom and safety (*art 17*); the inviolability of one's home, the right to honour, privacy, and the secrecy of one's communications (*art 18*); free movement and residence within the national territory (*art 19*); freedom of speech (*art 20*); freedom of assembly (*art 21*); freedom of association (*art 22*); the right to participate in public affairs and to have access to public office (*art 23*); the right to justice (*art 24*); legal certainity in criminal proceedings and the non-retroactivity of the criminal law to the prejudice of any defendant (*arts 25 and 26*); the right to education (*art 27*); the freedom to join a union (*art 28*); the right of petition (*art 29*); and the right of conscientious objection (*art 30*).

The *Constitution* provides two levels of fundamental rights :

(a) the direct application of the rights laid down in *Articles 14 to 29 and 30.2* the jurisdictional protection of which is provided for by *Act 62/78 of 26 December 1978* providing for summary proceedings;

(b) the remaining rights which are to be regarded as principles qualifying the law, judicial practice and the activities of the government.

Tribunal Constitucional (Constitutional Court)

The "*Tribunal Constitucional*" (Constitutional Court) is the highest authority on the interpretation of the *Constitution* and guarantees compliance with the *Constitution* throughout the legal system. It defends and protects the *Constitution* and guarantees the fundamental rights and freedoms of the individual. It has jurisdiction over all questions regarding the unconstitutionality of laws through the relevant appeal on the grounds of unconstitutionality. It also resolves jurisdictional conflicts between the state and the autonomous regions or between the latter. If the central government challenges the laws and decisions of the autonomous regions these remain in abeyance until the Constitutional Court determines the issue. Procedural guarantees for the defence of one's rights are ensured by:

Recurso de Inconstitucionali - dad (Appeal on grounds of unconstitution- ality)

(a) "*Recurso de Inconstitucionalidad*" (appeal on the grounds of unconstitutionality) : this is a direct appeal whereby a party may challenge any law or regulation having the force of law in order to determine its legality under the *Constitution*. It is also the means whereby conflicts of jurisdiction between the state and the autonomous regions and among the autonomous regions themselves are resolved.

(b) The ordinary courts can rule on the unconstitutionality of any law enacted before the *Constitution* was adopted and provide for an appeal on the grounds of unconstitutionality before the *Tribunal Constitucional* in respect of any law passed after the *Constitution* was adopted.

Recurso de Amparo

(c) "*Recurso de Amparo*" : (appeal for the enforcement of fundamental rights and public liberties - "protection appeal") the object of the *Recurso de Amparo* is to protect individuals' rights. Only matters contemplated in *Articles 14 to 29 and 30,2 of the Constitution* are amenable to this form of appeal. The *Recurso de Amparo* may be submitted by any person with a legitimate interest, the Ombudsman and the Public Prosecutor ("*ministerio fiscal*"). This appeal is generally subsidiary to protection through the normal courts.

Defensor del Pueblo (Ombudsman)

The office of "*Defensor del Pueblo*" (the Ombudsman), regulated by *Organic Act 3/81 of 6 April 1981* implementing *Article 54 of the Constitution*, was created to protect the rights of individuals laid down in the *Constitution* as against governmental activity, to check abuses and uphold the responsibility of government officials. The *Defensor* may have access to all kinds of government documents and may suggest the appropriate remedies to meet any irregularity. This procedure is open to all individuals with a legitimate interest in the matter complained of.

CHAPTER 3 : JURISDICTION OF THE COURTS

Spanish law distinguishes three bases on which jurisdiction ("*competencia*") is assumed :

(a) "objective jurisdiction", based on the subject matter of the litigation ("*competencia objetiva por razón de la materia*") or on the value of the claim or economic interest at stake in the litigation ("*competencia objetiva por razón de la cuantía*");

(b) "functional jurisdiction", based on the different phases of the proceedings; and

(c) "territorial jurisdiction".

Article 21 Judicial Powers Act ("Ley Orgánica del Poder Judicial" - "LOPJ") provides that :

"Spanish courts and tribunals shall have jurisdiction in respect of all litigation arising on the Spanish territory, between Spaniards, between foreigners and between Spaniards and foreigners in accordance with the provisions of this Act and international treaties and conventions to which Spain is a party. All cases of immunity from jurisdiction or enforcement provided for under the rules of Public International Law are to be exempt from the above rule".

It should be noted here that Spain has ratified the *Brussels Convention on Jurisdiction and Enforcement of Judgments in Civil and Commercial Matters 1968* (see Chapter 11).

In the *Criminal Procedural Act ("LECrim")* the division between objective, functional and territorial jurisdiction as described above also applies. Under objective jurisdiction criminal matters are allocated depending on the nature of the offence ("*delitos graves*", "*delicots menos graves*" or "*faltas*"), and the type of penalties applicable under the *Penal Code* to the offence. Functional jurisdiction divides criminal procedure into two stages : the evidential, instruction stage ("*instrucción*") and the final decision stage ("*plenario*"), which are assigned to different courts. Territorial jurisdiction depends on where the criminal offence was committed.

There is also a distinction between ordinary and military jurisdiction (*Constitution, art 117,5; LOPJ, art 9.3; LECrim, art 10; Military Criminal Code of 13 December 1985* and *Military Jurisdiction Act of 15 July 1987*).

State immunity   There are two main bases for jurisdictional immunity :

1. Immunity derived from international law, ie :
   (a) "absolute immunity", which applies automatically and covers foreign heads of state, ambassadors and diplomats accredited in Spain;

   (b) "relative immunity" (which can only be relied upon under certain conditions and in certain circumstances), which covers ambassadors' families and staff and consular agents (Spain became a signatory to the *Vienna Convention on diplomatic and consular relationships* in 1967), members of foreign armies and navies, delegates and members of the United Nations Missions and European Council Missions (*Statutes of 15 March 1978*), etc.

2. Immunity under domestic law rules which applies to the King (*Constitution, art 56.3*), members of Parliament and the Senate (*Constitution, art 71.1*)unless Parliament's authorisation has been obtained, and the Ombudsman ("*Defensor del Pueblo*"). With the exception of the King, all such exemptions are limited to actions in respect of activities carried out in the exercise of their respective functions.

Domicile and other factors determining the courts' civil jurisdiction   As far as domestic matters are concerned, the first criterion determining territorial jurisdiction is the will of the parties (submission). "Express submission" ("*pactum de foro prorrogando*") arises where there is an extrajudicial agreement prior to the litigation arising whereby the parties agree to accept the decision of the court of a specific place. "Tacit submission" is the legal expression for an implied acceptance of a specific court's jurisdiction which derives from certain acts attributed to the parties (eg when the plaintiff submits his initial claim to a particular court and the defendant acknowledges and answers it without pleading any lack of jurisdiction - *LEC, arts 57 and 58*).

Secondly, there are the criteria listed in *Article 62 of the LEC* which depend on the type of action in question. For proceedings in contract, jurisdiction will be assumed by the court of the place where performance is to be carried out or, failing this, at the plaintiff's option, the court of the defendant's place of residence or of the place of the contract (*LEC, art 62.1*). In respect of actions over property, jurisdiction will be assumed by the court of the place where the movable property or the immovable property is located, or of the defendant's domicile, at the plaintiff's option, (*LEC, art 62.2*) For mixed actions jurisdiction is determined by the place where the properties are located or the defendant's place of residence, at the plaintiff's option (*LEC, art 62.4*).

Labour law   In labour law matters, Spanish courts will have jurisdiction where the services are rendered or the contract is entered into in Spain, the defendant has his domicile, agency, branch or other representative office in Spain, and the employer and the employee are Spanish, even if the contract is executed and/or performed abroad (*Judicial Powers Act, art 25*).

The general rule for civil and contractual matters is that the courts of the defendant's country of residence have jurisdiction. Spanish courts have exclusive jurisdiction in respect of the incorporation, functioning and dissolution of Spanish companies, registration, over Spanish real property rights and the recognition and enforcement in Spain of foreign judgments. Spanish courts have jurisdiction over all contracts entered into in Spain (either between Spaniards, between foreigners or between foreigners and Spaniards) unless otherwise agreed by the parties, as well as over contracts to be performed in Spain and actions in respect of torts committed in Spain.

To determine domicile, the following rules apply :   *Domicile*

(a)   General rule : "domicile" is the place where individuals have their permanent residence ("*residencia habitual*") (*Civil Code, art 40.1*).

(b)   Specific rules :

(i)   that of spouses is determined by mutual agreement or by the courts, taking into consideration the family's interest, in the absence of any such agreement (*Civil Code, art 70*);

(ii)   that of minors is that of the parents unless the minor is emancipated, or else is that of their guardians (*LEC, art 64.4*);

(iii)   that of businessmen ("*comerciantes*") is where they have the centre of their commercial operations;

(iv)   that of employees is their place of employment;

(v)   that of diplomats is the place of the last posting they had in Spain (*Civil Code, art 40.2*); and

(vi)   that of companies is the place referred to in the bye-laws or deeds of incorporation, failing which, the place where they have the centre of their commercial operations (*LEC, art 66* and *1989 Companies Act, art 6*).

CHAPTER 4 : ADMINISTRATION OF JUSTICE

The *Judicial Powers Act 6/1985 of 1 July 1985* ("*Ley Orgánica del Poder Judicial*" - "*LOPJ*") and the *Judicial Organisation Act 38/88 of 2 December 1988* ("*Ley de Demarcación y Planta Judicial*") implementing it lay down the rules on the organisation of the Spanish court system : *Structure of the court system*

    (a)   The Constitutional Court ("*Tribunal Constitucional*" - "*TC*") is the supreme arbiter in respect of matters under the *Constitution* (see chapter 2). Strictly speaking the TC is not part of the administration of justice proper. *Constitutional Court (Tribunal Constitucional)*

    (b)   The Supreme Court ("*Tribunal Supremo*" - "*TS*") is the highest court in Spain in all save constitutional matters. The Supreme Court has five chambers ("*salas*") dealing with civil, criminal, contentious-administrative ("*contencioso-administrativo*"), labour and military matters. It is a final appellate court, although it may serve as a court of first instance in civil or criminal actions against the highest public officials in respect of acts performed in their official capacity, and regarding challenges to decisions of the Council of Ministers. *Supreme Court (Tribunal Supremo)*

    (c)   The National Court ("*Audiencia Nacional*" - "*AN*") is a court of first instance with an exclusive jurisdiction over matters of national interest. The court has three chambers dealing with criminal matters (crimes against the Crown, currency counterfeiting, extradition proceedings, etc), contentious-administrative matters (regarding acts of state bodies) and certain labour disputes (actions regarding national collective bargaining agreements). *National Court (Audiencia Nacional)*

    (d)   The Superior Court of Justice ("*Tribunal Superior de Justicia*" - "*TSJ*") : there is one such court located in every autonomous region (Catalonia, Basque Country, Andalusia, etc). The TSJ also serves as a court of appeal in some matters. It is divided into three chambers dealing with civil/criminal, contentious-administrative and labour matters. It is the highest court for matters expressly reserved to the autonomous regions by the *Constitution* such as trade, industry, agriculture, housing and welfare, roads, and so forth, as well as over matters in respect of the responsibilities of the senior officials of the *Superior Court (Tribunal Superior de Justicia)* autonomous regions and over the control of each region's civil law. In these respects there is no further appeal to the Supreme Court.

Provincial Courts (Audiencias Provinciales)

(e) Provincial Courts (*"Audiencias Provinciales"* - *"AP"*) : there is one provincial court in each of the provincial capitals. It is a first instance court for some criminal matters and an appeal court for some civil matters.

Courts of First Instance and of Instruction

(f) Courts of First Instance and of Instruction (*"Juzgados de Primera Instancia e Instrucción"*) : these are courts of first instance hearing most civil cases; the Courts of Instruction hear only criminal cases.

Justices of the Peace Courts

(g) Justices of the Peace Courts (*"Juzgados de Paz"*) are the lowest courts within the court system. They have non-professional judges and deal with civil and criminal cases of minor importance.

Labour Courts

(h) Labour Courts : Under the *1985 Judicial Powers Act* separate labour courts were maintained but the Central Labour Court disappeared. Appeals are now made to the labour chamber of the Superior Court of Justice (*"Sala de lo Social"*), and, where permitted, to the labour chamber of the Supreme Court.

Administrative Courts

(i) Administrative Courts : these have jurisdiction over the various government bodies. Administrative remedies before these courts must be exhausted before any action through the ordinary courts may be brought. There are also several government bodies which, although not exercising judicial powers, may make decisions (which may in any event be challenged in the courts). Among the more important of these are the Tax Courts, the Court for the Protection of Competition (*"Tribunal de Defensa de la Competencia"*) and the Administrative Claims Courts (*"Tribunales Económico Administrativos"*). The Central Administrative Claims Court (*"Tribunal Económico-administrativo Central"*) is the central administrative appeal court, which also hears at first instance specific matters involving the Ministry of Economy and Finance, the Ministry for Social Security or the autonomous regions.

"international litigation"

In order to determine which jurisdiction applies in any litigation involving parties or subject matter from different countries, several considerations must be borne in mind :

(a) whether a Spanish court has jurisdiction to hear the matter : the subject matter of the claim must be properly identified. In Spain, the courts are divided into four main areas of jurisdiction : civil (including commercial), criminal, administrative and labour;

(b) which court should hear the case at first instance : if the matter is a civil one, this depends on the subject matter and the amount of money involved;

(c)   where the case should be heard : this will depend on the territorial jurisdiction of the court and/or any agreement between the parties. In the absence of any agreement, the provisions of the *Civil Procedure Act* ("*LEC*") will apply;

(d)   which court will deal with any pre-trial or post-trial proceedings, such as the execution of judgments. As a general rule, the court which hears the main action will also deal with any pre-trial and post-trial proceedings.

Appeals are generally a question for the parties. In general, all decisions may be appealed. However, there are usually some basic requirements which must be met (*LEC, arts 377, 386, 1697*), such as:

Appeals

(a)   the appeal must be submitted before the proper judicial body duly having jurisdiction (depending on the type of decision and the proceedings);

(b)   the right of appeal is limited to those who were parties to the initial proceedings;

(c)   the party appealing must have suffered damage;

(d)   the appeal must be submitted within the time limits laid down by law (see Chapter 6). If the time limit has passed, the judgment in question will become final ("*sentencia firme*") and unappealable;

(e)   appeals must be presented in writing (except under *LEC, art 732*). Any one of the parties, on being notified of the judgment, may submit an appeal to the court which made the decision being appealed against.

The various types of appeals and the time limits which apply are as follows :

Types of appeal and time limits

The *recurso de reposición* applies to "*autos*" delivered by judges at first instance. This type of appeal does not apply to "*incidentes*" (incidental matters such as third party motions). The time limit for this type of appeal is three days.

The *recurso de reposición* is also available against "*providencias*" (preliminary rulings on questions of procedure) given by judges at first instance. The time limit is three days.

The *recurso de apelación* is against "*sentencias definitivas*" (final judgments), decisions concerning applications for a stay of proceedings and *incidentes*, and *autos* disposing of appeals at the *recurso de reposición* stage. The time limit is five days.

The *recurso de casación* is against some *sentencias definitivas* and *autos* handed down by the Provincial Courts at second instance. The time limit is 10+30 days. This appeal can only be made on the grounds of an error of law or violation of the essential procedural rules made by the previous court.

The *recurso de súplica* applies to *autos* settling appeals on incidental matters at second instance. The time limit is five days (*LEC, art 402*).

The *recurso de queja* applies to decisions of the *Audiencias* where a *recurso de casación* is refused. The time limit is ten days. It also applies to *autos* and *providencias* of judges at first instance who refuse to allow any *recurso de apelación*. The time limit is 15 days (*LEC, art 398*).

The claim for "*responsabilidad civil*" (civil liability) is a procedure to establish civil liability on the part of judges and magistrates for damage caused by their acting illegally due to negligence or "inexcusable ignorance" in the course of their duties. It can apply to judges in the Provincial Courts and even the Supreme Court. This must be brought within six months.

Competence to hear appeals

Competence to hear an appeal depends on the type of appeal. Competence to hear a "*recurso no devolutivo*" is limited to the court which gave the decision being appealed against ("*recurso de reposición*", LEC, arts 376 to 380; and *recurso de súplica*, LEC, arts 401 to 406).

In the case of a "*recurso devolutivo*", the immediately higher court will have jurisdiction ("*recurso de apelación, recurso de casación, recurso de queja*").

Grounds for appeal

As regards any grounds for appeal being required :

(a)   in ordinary appeals ("*recurso de apelación*", "*recurso de queja*", "*recurso de reposición*" and "*recurso de súplica*") no specific reasons for the appeal are required;

(b)   in extraordinary appeals provisional admissibility depends on alleging some specific ground of appeal which has been laid down by law (*LEC, arts 1692, 1707 and 1710*).

References to the Constitutional Court

Judges may submit an issue of unconstitutionality ("*cuestión de incostitucionalidad*") to the Constitutional Court whenever a rule applicable to the case before them may appear to be unconstitutional (*Constitutional Court Act, art 35*).

References under Article 177 of the EEC Treaty

Any court or judge may generally refer a matter to the European Court of Justice (ECJ) for a preliminary ruling under *Article 177 of the EEC Treaty*.

The reference to the ECJ can be made "ex officio" or at the request of a party. The stage of the proceedings when a matter can be referred to the ECJ lies within the discretion of the court asked to refer. However, in accordance with *Article 177*, a reference to the ECJ is compulsory in the case of courts against whose decisions there is no appeal under domestic law, such as the *"Tribunal Supremo"* and *"Tribunal Constitucional"*.

CHAPTER 5 : STRUCTURE OF THE LEGAL PROFESSION

A law degree in Spain ("*licenciatura en derecho*"), which takes five years, allows one to proceed to qualify as an "*abogado*" (advocate); "*procurador*" (procurator); "*notario*" (notary) or "*registrador*" (registrar). It also opens the way to a career in the "*magistratura*" and the "*Abogados del Estado*" (legal service to the state). The "*magistratura*" is made up of the "*juez*" (judge) and the "*fiscal*" (prosecutor). After gaining the "*licenciatura*", a prospective judge must pass a state exam, and then receive further training at the "*Centro de Estudios Judiciales*" (Centre for Judicial Studies).

Structure of the profession

The legal profession of *abogado* is free and independent. It is regulated by the *General Statute for Spanish Lawyers* ("*Estatuto General de la Abogacía Española*" - "*EGA*"), approved by *Royal Decree 2090/1982 of 24 July 1982* and published in the Official Gazette of 2 September 1982. The *EGA* is currently in the process of being modified. In Spain, parties to legal actions are commonly required to take on two legal professionals, one to co-ordinate their legal position ("*abogado*") and one to represent them at court ("*procurador*"). It is impossible to be an *abogado* and *procurador* at the same time. Only lawyers who are members of the Bar and exercise their calling dedicating themselves to legal defence can use the name of *abogado*. There are 65,000 lawyers in Spain.

Abogado/ Procurador

The *abogados* have two main and exclusive functions : (a) pleading before the court and (b) giving legal advice. All *abogados* can appear before all courts of the territory of their respective "*Colegio*".

The legal profession of the *abogado* is organised on a territorial base in the "*Colegios de Abogados*" of which there are 82. These are corporations under public law with full legal powers and capacity to achieve their aims. Their functions include professional deontology and organising and co-ordinating further legal training to ease access to the profession for new recruits. The autonomous general councils for lawyers and the central "*Consejo General de la Abogacía*" (General Council for Lawyers) co-ordinate and represent the *Colegios*. All *abogados* must be members of a local Bar. This registration does not prevent them from becoming members of other Bars.

Practising as an *abogado* is incompatible with the following positions, pursuant to *Article 27 of the EGA* : Prime Minister, Minister, Secretary of State, Director General and similar positions within the public administration; judge, public prosecutor, secretary of a court and all other judicial personnel.

In addition, an *abogado* may not hold the position of Secretary of the General Council of the judicial authorities or any position within the personnel, inspection or technical secretariat of the General Council.

Procurador

Being a *procurador* is an independent profession that may be practised by those who fulfil the conditions required under the Spanish legislation governing *procuradores* and who apply for and obtain membership of a *Colegio de Procuradores*. It is the equivalent of the French *"avoué"* and the Portuguese *"solicitador"*. Procuradores represent clients in court at trial but they do not argue a client's case before the judge, which is the exclusive task of the *abogado*. The *procuradores* are the functional link between the *abogados* and the courts.

Notary

A notary is a public officer authorised to certify contracts and other extrajudicial acts such as public deeds and wills. Notaries are considered free professionals but they fulfil a state function. As a result, they may not choose their clients.

Registradores

Registrars must pass a competitive state examination. They run their own offices, and receive income from fixed fees. They record and register transactions regarding property (*"registradores de la propiedad"*) and companies (*"registradores mercantiles"*).

Other professionals

There are also other professionals who are involved to some extent in some areas of law; for example, *"graduados sociales"* who represent parties in labour law and social security law matters when a lawyer's intervention is not required, and *"gestores administrativos"* who represent citizens in minor administrative matters such as municipal authorisations, and the obtaining driving licences and passports, etc.

Rights of audience

The *abogado* has the exclusive right to protect the interests of those who require legal representation. He can appear before tribunals or courts only if registered in the *Colegio* of the district of that court. The provision of legal advice is reserved exclusively to *abogados (Judicial Powers Act (LOPJ), art 436)*.

Formal representation (but not defending) of the interests parties in all kinds of proceedings lies with the *procuradores*, except where otherwise provided for by law (*LOPJ, art 438*). The *LEC* provides that parties must be represented in court by a *procurador* duly authorised to act and with sufficient power declared by an *abogado*.

Parties may represent themselves before the courts only in small claims (*"juicios verbales"*) and eviction cases (*"juicios de desatrucio"*) - except in respect of eviction from commercial or industrial premises or plants and rural properties (Procedural Reform Act 10/92 of 30 April 1992), conciliation proceedings (*"actos de conciliación"*), some stages in insolvency proceedings, legal aid proceedings, alimony, or in certain special proceedings such as labour cases.

Abogados are permitted to work in different forms of partnership *Legal practices*
(*despachos colectivos*). Most Spanish lawyers, however, work as
sole practitioners or in small partnerships. Large law firms can be
found in Madrid and in Barcelona. Partnerships are currently
limited to 20 partners, although there is a draft bill proposing to
remove this restriction.

As far as fees are concerned, guidelines are set by the *Colegios de* *Fees*
Abogados for each area of legal practice. As a rule, the level of
fees will depend on various factors, such as time spent on the
case, the complexity of the case, the amount of money involved,
the economic importance of the case to the client and other
considerations. The fees and other rules are in the process of
being amended in a move towards a system of greater
competition.

The actual fees lawyers charge are not published. A client can
arrange with his lawyer in advance what sort of fees the lawyer
may charge before engaging his assistance. Where the client
wishes to challenge the fees charged by a lawyer, the dispute will
go to arbitration before a special commission of the *Colegio de
Abogados*.

The "*Estatuto General de la Abogacía Española*" provides in *Title* *Professional*
III for the application of rules on the conduct of lawyers (their *conduct*
independence, moral integrity, maintenance of professional
confidentiality and so forth). Similar duties are provided for by the
Statutes of each *Colegio de Abogados*. These rules are intended
to guarantee that a lawyer will comply with all the requirements of
the profession. Breach of such rules may entail a disciplinary
sanction. Even though each *Colegio* establishes its own rules for
its members, they follow the same guidelines. When a civil or
criminal complaint is made against a lawyer regarding his
provision of legal services, either in his private capacity or as the
lawyer of a client, the president ("*decano*") of the *Colegio* must be
informed.

All lawyers must have professional indemnity insurance at all *Professional*
times, sufficient to cover the risks they assume in the exercise of *insurance*
their profession.

Each *Colegio de Abogados* publishes annually a directory with a *Directory of legal*
list of all the lawyers who are members of that *Colegio*, including *services*
their professional address and date of joining the *Colegio*.
Advertising is prohibited by *Article 31 of the EGA* (and by *Article
19 of the Statute of the Colegio de Abogados of Barcelona*) which
forbids lawyers to publicise their services either directly or
indirectly, for example, by giving free advice in professional
journals or reviews. Some *Colegios* have authorised limited
publicity.

CHAPTER 6 : CIVIL PROCEDURE

Civil proceedings are mainly written. Oral proceedings are generally limited to dealing with the evidence and to appeals.

The majority of proceedings tend to follow certain basic steps or procedural stages :

1. Making and answering a claim (*"periodo de alegaciones"*) The plaintiff submits his claim by a writ of summons (*"demanda"*) to the competent court, a copy of which is served on the defendant.

The defendant submits a reply or defence to the writ (*"contestación a la demanda"*). The defendant may raise a counterclaim (*"reconvención"*).

Both the *demanda* and the *contestación* must be drafted in a particular form, ie presenting the facts (*"hechos"*), laying down the legal basis for the position adopted (*"fundamentos de derecho"*) and the actual request made to the court (*"suplico"*). All documentary evidence must normally be attached to the written formal pleadings.

In proceedings involving a higher value (*"procedimiento de mayor cuantía"*) the plaintiff can answer/dispute the defendant's reply (*"réplica"*) and the defendant can answer/dispute the plaintiff's *réplica* (*"dúplica"*). The procedure is the same as in proceedings involving a lower value, although the *réplica* and *dúplica* are not possible.

2. Gathering evidence

After the allegations of facts and law are made (*"periodo de alegaciones"*), it is for the parties as part of their procedural duty to obtain the evidence required to support the facts they alleged. This "evidence gathering period" (*"periodo de prueba"*) is generally divided into two parts :

  (a)   laying the ground for the evidence (*"proposición de prueba"*), when each party asks the judge to accept all the evidence sought (documents, witnesses, court examination, etc);

  (b)   the presentation and incorporation of evidence (*"práctica de la prueba"*) when the evidence is actually assembled and incorporated into the court file (*"autos"*).

Concluding period

3. Concluding period

During the concluding period, both parties submit their written conclusions as to what they consider the facts are, along with the evidence used to prove the relevant facts.

The evidence presented in any litigation is exclusively that which the parties have requested following the principle of "requested justice" (*"justicia rogada"*) although the judge has the right to seek complementary evidence in order to arrive at a better judgment (*"diligencias para mejor proveer"*).

The judgment

4. The judgment

When these periods are completed the judge gives his judgment (*"sentencia"*). All judgments can be appealed failing which they become final (*"sentencia firme"*)

Jurisdiction

Jurisdiction is divided into four main types of proceeding : the higher value proceedings (*"juicio de mayor cuantía"*) and lower value proceedings (*"juicio de menor cuantía"*). Proceedings in which the value of the claim or economic interest at stake exceeds 160 million pesetas are classified as higher value proceedings. Proceedings in which the value of the claim or economic interest at stake is between 800,000 pesetas and 160 million are classified as lower value proceedings.

In addition to these two types of proceedings there are :

    (a)   cognitive proceedings (*"juicios de cognición"*) where the value of the claim or economic interest at stake ranges from 80,000 to 800,000 pesetas (*Civil Procedure Act* (*"Ley de enjuiciamiento civil"*- *"LEC"*), *art 486*, and the *Decree of 21 December 1952*);

    (b)   oral proceedings (*"juicio verbal"*) where the value of the claim or economic interest at stake does not exceed 80,000 pesetas (*LEC, arts 486 and 715*).

The Courts of First Instance (*"Juzgados de Primera Instancia"*) are competent to deal with all of the above proceedings, except claims for less than 8,000 pesetas which come within the jurisdiction of the Justices of the Peace Courts (*"Juzgados de Paz"*).

Certain types of proceedings are classified as either "higher value" or "lower value" by virtue of their subject matter, regardless of the amount of money actually involved (if any). Thus :

    (a)   proceedings relating to aristocratic titles are automatically classified as "higher value"; and

    (b)   proceedings concerning filiation, paternity, capacity, civil status, those in which the value of the claim or economic interest at stake cannot be determined, and proceedings for which no other jurisdiction is provided are automatically classified as "lower value".

Functional jurisdiction is assigned to the various courts on the basis of what are called "devolutive remedies" (*"recursos devolutivos"*) : *Functional jurisdiction*

(a)   Appeals remedy (*"recurso de apelación"*) : the Provincial Courts (*"Audiencias Provinciales"*) are competent to hear appeals against judgments given at first instance (*LOPJ, art 82.3*);

(b)   Complaint appeal (*"recurso de queja"*) : this remedy is available when the *recurso de apelación* or the *recurso de casación* are not provisionally admitted. The Provincial Court or the Supreme Court are competent to deal with this.

(c)   The "cassation" appeal (*"recurso de casación"*) is a second appeal from decisions of the Provincial Courts. Competence to hear such appeals lies with the Supreme Court (1st Chamber), or, if the case concerns regional civil law (*"derecho foral"*), the Superior Courts of the Autonomous Regions.

(d)   Revision appeal (*"recurso de revisión"*) : this is an extraordinary remedy against a final judgment and the courts competent are as in (c).

In addition to these legal remedies, the following remedies are also available :

(a)   Challenges (*"recusación"*) to particular judges and magistrates handling a particular case are resolved in accordance with *Articles 224 and 225 of the LOPJ*.

(b)   Questions concerning the correct assumption of jurisdiction (*"cuestiones de competencia"*) are resolved by the court superior to the court the competence of which is challenged if there is no agreement as between the courts claiming jurisdiction (*LEC, arts 60, 73 and 99*; and *LOPJ, arts 82.5 and 85.4*).

(c)   Joinder of proceedings (*"acumulación de autos"*) is decided by the next superior court (*LEC, art 182*) where such joinder is the subject of dispute.

(d)   Incidental matters (*"incidentes"*) are decided by the same court that hears the principal proceedings (*LEC, art 55*).

The general grounds of legal competence (*"fueros legales generales"*) are as follows : *Territorial jurisdiction*

For proceedings in personal actions (*"acciones personales"*), the court competent is that of the place in which the obligation in question has to be performed or failing this, at the plaintiff's election, that of the place where the defendant is resident, or that of the place of the contract (*LEC, art 62.1*).

For proceedings in real actions ("*acciones reales*"), the court competent is that of the place where the particular assets are located or of the place where the defendant is resident, at the plaintiff's option where the action affects chattels ("*bienes muebles*"), or the court for where the property is located if the action concerns real estate ("*bienes inmuebles*").

Proceedings in mixed actions ("*acciones mixtas*") such as actions for the division of property ("*communi dividundo*", "*familiae erciscundae*" and "*finium regundorum*") will be heard by the court of the place where the property is located, or of the defendant's place of residence at the plaintiff's choice.

Special legal jurisdiction ("fueros legales especiales")

Article 63 of the LEC, among others, provides that the rules for territorial jurisdiction will apply in some specific proceedings :

(a) Proceedings concerning fundamental rights, civil status and marriage :

   (i) in matters of fundamental rights, jurisdiction lies with the court of the place where matters have taken place or of the place where the registry where such facts had to be recorded is located (*Act 62/1978 of 26 December 1978, art 11*);

   (ii) in questions concerning issues of civil status and alimony ("*alimentos*"), the court competent is that of the place where the defendant is resident;

   (iii) in questions concerning custody ("*tutela*"), the court competent is that of the place of the guardian's administration or of the minor's place of residence; and

   (iv) marriage proceedings ("*procesos matrimoniales*") will be heard in the court of the place of the spouses' domicile, or if the spouses are living separately, of the place of the defendant's domicile.

(b) Matters regarding rights of obligation ("*derechos de obligación*") are dealt with as follows :

   (i) proceedings for summary judgment ("*juicio ejecutivo*") will be heard by the courts of the place of performance or enforcement of judgments, of the obligation in question or of the place of the defendant's place of residence, or of the place where any immovable assets are located (*LEC, art 1,439*);

   (ii) compulsory repurchase rights ("*retracto*") will be dealt with by the courts of the place where the disputed property is located, or of the defendant's place of residence, at the election of the plaintiff (*LEC, art 63*);

(iii)   questions involving leases (*"arrendamientos"*), will be dealt with in the courts of the place where the leased property is located (*Urban Leases Act, art 121*, and *Rural Leases Act, art 123.1*);

(iv)   Contesting of company resolutions (*"impugna- ción de acuerdos sociales"*) is dealt with by the courts of first instance for the place where the registered office of the company is located (*Companies Act, art 118*).

(c)   Rights in respect of real property are dealt with as follows :

(i)   possessory rights (*"interdictos"*) are dealt with by the courts of the place where the property is located;

(ii)   mortgage proceedings are handled by the courts of the place where the property is located (*Mortgage Regulations, art 137.1*).

(iii)   proceedings under the *Patents Act* come within the competence of the Superior Court of Justice of the autonomous regions where the defendant has his place of residence (*Patents Law, art 125*).

Matters in succession are dealt with by the courts where the deceased person was last resident (*LEC, art 63.5*).

Bankruptcy questions are handled by the courts of the place where the debtor is resident (*LEC, art 63.8*).

Parties to proceedings/locus standi

All individuals (*"personas físicas"*) and companies or legal persons (*"personas jurídicas"*) may bring proceedings and have proceedings brought against them. Any human being born alive, with a human figure and who lives 24 hours separated from his or her mother acquires legal personality (*Civil Code, arts 29 and 30*).

Article 38 of the Civil Code enables legal persons to bring civil or criminal actions provided they have been duly incorporated. Legal persons can be divided into public law bodies (the state, the autonomous regions and municipalities, professional associations, political parties, and so forth); private associations; and private companies (mercantile or civil companies).

Minors (*"menores"*), those absent (*"ausentes"*) or lacking capacity (*"incapaces"*) and spendthrifts (*"pródigos"*) are represented in court through their "necessary" representative : parents, guardians, etc.

The Public Prosecutor (*"ministerio fiscal"*) can act as a party in marriage proceedings when one of the spouses or the children is a minor or suffers from a legal incapacity; in filiation proceedings; in proceedings concerning questions of incapacity; in suspension of payments matters (*"suspensión de pagos"*); insolvency administration and fundamental rights proceedings; or as an adviser to the court on substantive law (eg on the adjudication of bankrupts, or on the question of the enforcement of foreign judgments,) or on procedural law issues (eg on conflicts of jurisdiction, or on the suspension of civil proceedings while a preliminary issue in criminal proceedings is resolved).

Actions against the government

Generally, actions against government bodies (*"órganos de la administración"*) whether national, autonomous or local are initiated through contentious-administrative proceedings (*"jurisdicción contencioso-administrativa"*) before special Contentious-Administrative Courts (*"Tribunales Contencioso-Administrativos"*). However, the government can also be sued in normal civil proceedings (*Law of Contentious-Administrative Jurisdiction (LJCA), art 2*, and *LOPJ, art 9*).

The central government has certain procedural privileges mainly relating to the issue of territorial jurisdiction (being sued only in such courts where there is a Provincial Court); representation and the rights of audience before this court are normally conducted by the "state advocates" (*"abogados del estado"*) and do not require *procuradores* to attend. Before coming to a civil court a person will have had to have initiated an administrative complaint. In addition, no enforcement process can be brought against the government and no government goods can be seized. Some of these privileges operate in favour of the autonomous and local governments as well.

Joinder

The joinder of parties to an action (*"acumulación de acciones"*) is permitted so that several related cases can be dealt with in the same proceedings, thus avoiding the risk of contradictory judgments. The rules governing joinder are found in the *LEC, arts 153 to 187*. Joinder of proceedings can be classified as follows : "objective joinder", where there are various proceedings and the same parties; and "objective-subjective joinder", where there are different proceedings and different parties to each of them. There is a further distinction between joinder of actions (*LEC, arts 153-159*) before the commencement of proceedings and joinder of *autos* (*LEC, arts 160-187*), after initial proceedings have been commenced.

Parties can also be substituted where one disappears from the proceedings (by death, as a consequence of a power of disposal eg bankruptcy or by inter vivos transfer) and a third party then takes his place by way of legal substitution.

"Litisconsorcio" is where several persons (individuals or companies) appear as plaintiff or defendant. This can be either voluntary or required by law.

Third party proceedings

Third party proceedings are not very well developed in Spanish law. However, there are examples where third parties can intervene :

    (a)   Intervention as a principal (*"intervención principal"*), where a third party initiates an action against those already parties to proceedings seeking to protect his interests when these are incompatible with the plaintiff's and the defendant's interests. For example, *Article 1532 of the LEC* allows third parties to intervene on the grounds that they claim ownership of attached assets (*"tercería de dominio"*) or to assert a prior interest (as against the plaintiff) (*"tercería de mejor derecho"*).

(b)   Supporting intervention (*"intervención adhesiva"*), which is where a third party with a direct and legitimate interest intervenes to support the position of one of the parties to the proceedings. For example, the *Act of 26 December 1978* protecting fundamental rights allows any person having a direct interest in the proceedings to intervene as *"coadyuvante"* to the plaintiff or the defendant.

(c)   Provoked or forced intervention (*"intervención provocada o forzosa"*) : as a result of the *"litis denuntiatio"*, that is, where a third person, not actually relevant to the proceedings, is "called" to be a part of the same. Under Spanish law the *"iussu iudicis"* (a direct summons by the judge) is not possible. For example, the *Civil Code* allows a seller to call his own prior seller where a purchaser alleges lack of title.

Class actions are not very well developed in Spanish law. *Class actions* However, some modern laws, such as the *Unfair Competition Act, No 3/91 of 10 January 1991,* do provide for class actions.

Legal aid (*"ayuda legal"*) is governed by : *Article 119 of the* *Legal aid* *Constitution; Article 20 of the LOPJ; Articles 13 to 50, 844 and 845, and 1708 of the LEC; Article 57 of the General Statute for Spanish Lawyers* (*"Estatuto General de la Abogacia Española"* - *"EGA"*), approved by *Royal Decree 2090/82 of 24 July 1982;* the *Legal Aid Regulations,* approved in the General Extraordinary Meeting of the Colegio de Abogados of Barcelona on 5 July 1985; and *Article 40 of the Statute of the Colegio de Abogados of Barcelona,* and similar statutes of the other *Colegios.*

Legal aid is available as part of the right to free justice guaranteed by the *Constitution* commensurate with the principle of equality. All those with insufficient economic resources have free access to the courts and are exempt from having to pay any costs arising during the proceedings. Two main principles underpin the grant of legal aid : the extent of one's economic resources; and the principle that anyone without economic resources has a right to justice.

Legal aid is granted when the following grounds are satisfied :

(a)   that the person comes within the rules on one's economic capacity (fixed at double the national minimum wage);

(b)   that the claim is one that merits going to trial (*LEC, arts 33-41, 844-845 and 1708*);

(c) that the litigation is to protect one's own rights; and

(d) that the benefit sought is some form of declaration. The declaration can be :
  (i) judicial, made by the court on the grounds given above;
  (ii) legal, made by virtue of some statutory provision; and
  (iii) administrative, made by virtue of treaties, international conventions or the principle of reciprocity with a foreign country concerning the declaration of poverty.

Legal aid will cover the lawyers', the procuradores' and any expert assessor's fees, as well as other costs such as publication of official notices in the press or official newspapers. Deposits required for appeals are not included within a grant of legal aid.

Proceedings are before the Court of First Instance and are similar to "verbal" proceedings. They are initiated by way of petition ("*demanda*"), which must include evidence of the economic situation of the applicant. The proceedings end with a judgment with the effect of res judicata, which is only appealable in *apelación*.

Action prior to legal proceedings

Prior to the start of legal proceedings, a conciliation process ("*acto de conciliación*") may take place where the two parties meet before the judge to try and resolve their dispute (*LEC, art 460*). Preliminary inquiries ("*diligencias preliminares*") may be undertaken whereby the plaintiff petitions the judge to obtain information on the defendant to preserve the subject matter of the claim or on other matters which will be material to starting proceedings (*LEC, art 497*).

Starting proceedings

Proceedings are initiated with a statement of claim ("*demanda*") which is a formal written document (*LEC, art 524*) in which the plaintiff sets out the facts on which he bases his petition, the legal grounds on which he relies and the request made to the court (see above).

Documents to be attached to the "demanda"

Under *Articles 503 and 504 of the LEC* the following documents must be attached to the *demanda* or to the reply to the *demanda* (the "*contestación a la demanda*") :

(a) the power of attorney authorising the "*procurador*" to act for that party, which is granted by the parties before a notary public, or a Spanish consul, or before a foreign notary public, in which case the power must be legalised before the consul or bear the Apostille required under the *Hague Convention*;

(b) any documents supporting the plaintiff's role in a case where he represents or acts on behalf of another or when the rights claimed derive from another either by way of succession or by other legal title;

(c)   all documents on which the plaintiff (or defendant) bases his assertions.

After the writ of "*demanda*" or "*contestación*" has been submitted no other documents can be presented (save in limited cases). The reason for this is to avoid procedural fraud.

The *demanda* interrupts prescription, or the running of the limitation period (*Civil Code, art 1973*). The *acto de conciliación* also interrupts prescription time (*LEC, art 479.1*) provided that the *demanda* and the *acto de conciliación* are presented to a court which has due jurisdiction.

In addition to the "ordinary proceedings" ("*juicio ordinario*"), "summary proceedings" ("*juicio ejecutivo*") may be used to quickly enforce certain rights. The action in the *juicio ejecutivo* has to be based on one of the "*titulos ejecution*" listed in the *LEC* : notarial public deed, documents recognised at court, protested bills of exchange or cheques, "confession" at court, commercial documents signed by official brokers, etc. The defendant can raise limited defences (eg fraud, payment, etc) which have to be proved rather than simply raised as triable issues, though this does not preclude the provision of subsequent "ordinary proceedings" (*LEC, arts 1429 to 1481*). *Juicio ejecutivo*

The issue of interlocutory relief is regarded in Spanish procedural law as the right to ensure the effective later enforcement of a future judgment while proceedings are still pending final determination. *Interlocutory relief (medida cautelar)*

No interlocutory relief ("*medida cautelar*") may be granted where there are no principal proceedings in respect of which there will be a judgment which may require that a particular act be done. The *medida cautelar* must be instrumental to and depend on the main proceedings; and any injunction sought must support the objective that the final judgment will not have been given in vain. The injunction sought must therefore be adapted to the nature and object of the claim.

The following requirements must be met before a *medida cautelar* will be granted :

-       There must be a real danger that the delay in obtaining judgment may result in the judgment being for practical purposes ineffective ("*periculum mora*"). Such danger may be determined on the basis of objective circumstances provided for by law, for instance *Article 1400 of the LEC* which establishes the right to the preventive attachment of assets ("*embargo preventivo*") where there is a risk that real property may no longer be available to fulfil an obligation, or where a foreigner may disappear or the assets may be hidden to the prejudice of the creditor. In other cases, the risk is deemed to exist by law, for instance in *Article 1.428 of the LEC* where the need for such security presupposes the existence of the risk without it having to be justified expressly.

- The plaintiff must first establish that he has a strong prima facie case.
- The applicant needs to provide a guarantee to compensate the defendant for any damage caused by the injunction should any final judgment be against the applicant.

Injunctions must be requested by the parties (*"principio de demanda"*) and the court cannot grant *"medidas cautelares"* of its own motion.

Given that the granting of *medidas cautelares* will depend on the facts of each case, it is difficult to lay down any general rules. A distinction is made between *medidas cautelares* for the preventive attachment of assets (*"embargo preventivo"*) and *medidas cautelares* to safeguard judgments or orders to do or not to do a specific thing (*"facere"* or *"non facere"*) (*LEC, art 1428*).

In addition to *medidas cautelares* granted to ensure the effectiveness of any final judgment to do or refrain from doing something, there are other precautionary measures (*"medidas de seguridad"*) which should be noted, such as provisional measures in matrimonial proceedings (*Civil Code, arts 102 and 103*); in filiation proceedings (*Civil Code, art 128*); those relating to proceedings dealing with issues of lack of capacity and prodigality (*Civil Code, arts 211ff*), etc.

Witnesses

Article 1.246 of the Civil Code sets out those who are not capable of giving evidence, ie those afflicted by reason of natural incapacity or madness, those who are blind and/or deaf in such cases where evidence depends on sight or hearing, and minors of fourteen years of age or younger.

Articles 1.247 of the Civil Code and *660 of the LEC* provide for further cases of incapacity for:
(a) those who have a direct or indirect interest in the case;
(b) relatives of the parties within the fourth degree of consanguinity;
(c) those who are in a situation of dependency on any one of the parties;
(d) those who are friendly with or manifestly inimical towards any one of the parties;
(e) those who are obliged to respect professional secrecy;
(f) those who have been convicted of giving false testimony.
Either party may challenge a witness for any one of the causes which if successful means that that person cannot give evidence as a witness (*"tacha de testigos"*) (*LEC, art 661*).

Once witness evidence is to be admitted by the judge the party proposing their evidence must present a list of those witnesses setting out their names, professions and addresses.

Under *Article 638 of the LEC*, when the petition to admit evidence is presented the parties will attach an interrogatory with all the questions on which the witnesses are to be examined. However,

Article 652 of the LEC (as amended in 1984) introduced the right to put to a witness questions not set out in this previous interrogatory list.

The court may refuse any questions which are not clear or precise (*LEC, art 638*) or which are not relevant (*LEC, art 639*). Witnesses must answer the cross-examination questions ("*repreguntas*") prepared by the opposing party on the basis of the interrogatories.

Witnesses are questioned separately, and the court ensures that witnesses do not communicate with one another (*LEC, art 646*). A witness' evidence is recorded in a written minute which is ratified in view of the witness. Evidence is given under oath ("*juramento*") and the court must explain the consequences of giving any false testimony (*Penal Code, art 326*).

Under *Articles 422 to 424 of the LEC* legal costs are made up of : *Costs* *procuradores'* fees governed by *Royal Decree 1030/1985 of 19 June 1985*; experts' fees and lawyers' fees when their assistance is legally necessary (*LEC, arts 11, 2*); compensation to witnesses (*LEC, arts 644 and 645*); other costs, such as for giving notices and for publications and registrations in public registries.

By *Act 25/1986 of 24 December* no court costs ("*tasas judiciales*") need be paid by litigants to the court. Further, all post and telegraphic communications between courts and tribunals in the exercise of their jurisdictional function shall be free.

Parties must pay legal costs in the order in which they arise in the proceedings. In 1984 the *LEC* adopted a new principle, and *Article 523* now lays it down as the general principle, that in all litigation the losing party will pay all the costs of the proceedings. Hence, *Article 523* states that in declaratory proceedings at first instance, costs will be paid by the party whose petitions have been totally refused unless the judge reasonably finds there are circumstances which do not justify this. If the court partially accepts the petitions of each party, the principle is that the costs each party pays are half of all final costs, unless one party has been reckless.

Legal fees, experts' fees and other expenses not subject to official fixed rates may not exceed one-third of the total value of the litigation, unless the court determines that the losing party has conducted the litigation recklessly. In appeals against a matter decided in declaratory proceedings, the general rule is that the appellant may recover all his costs and legal fees if all the points in his favour are confirmed on appeal.

CHAPTER 7 : CRIMINAL PROCEDURE

The following general principles apply in criminal proceedings :   *General*
- the principle of "officiality", or the need to initiate *principles* criminal proceedings whenever there is a potential criminal offence (it is not possible to stop such proceedings on the grounds that there are solely matters of private interest involved);

- the principle of "orality" : "Proceedings shall be principally oral, particularly criminal proceedings" (*Constitution, art 120*);

- the principle of "immediacy", in that evidence must be gathered by the court competent to give a verdict;

- the principle of "publicity" of proceedings and of the verdict (*Constitution, arts 24,2 and 120*); and

- the principle "against undue delay" (*Constitution, art 24,2*).

Criminal proceedings are divided into three basic stages which   *Basic stages* are conducted by different courts : the enquiry or investigation stage ("*fase de instrucción*"), the intermediary stage ("*fase intermedia*") and the trial ("*juicio oral*").

In addition to ordinary proceedings, there are certain special   *Types of* proceedings, more accurately described as ordinary proceedings   *procedures* conducted in accordance with special rules, particularly during the enquiry or investigation stage, such as :
- special proceedings which apply because of the position of the accused : proceedings against Members of Parliament ("*procedimientos contra diputados y senadores*") in *Articles 750 to 756 of the "Ley de Enjuiciamiento Criminal" - "LECrim"* (*Criminal Procedure Act*) and against judges and magistrates ("*procedimientos contra jueces y magistrados*") (*LECrim, arts 757 to 778*);

- special proceedings which apply because of the position of the accused which are regulated outside the *LECrim*. These are proceedings against the President and members of the government (Council of Ministers) ("*procedimientos contra el Presidente y los miembros del Gobierno*") (*Constitution, art 102*); or against members of the security forces (*LOPJ 2/1986 of 13 March*); and

- special proceedings due to the nature of the offence, such as :
    (i) the crimes of *"injurias"* and *"calumnias"* against private individuals (*"delitos de injuria y calumnia contra particulares"*) (*LECrim, arts 804 to 815*). *Injuria* is the criminal offence which in England is treated as libel or slander. *Calumnia* is the criminal offence of falsely alleging that someone has committed a criminal offence;
    (ii) criminal offences committed by printing or engraving or by any other mechanical means of publication (*LECrim, arts 816 to 823*);
    (iii) criminal offences against the fundamental rights of persons (*Act of 28 December 1978* and *Royal Decree 20 February 1979*);
    (iv) crimes falling under military jurisdiction (*Constitution, art 30,2*);
    (v) electoral crimes (*LO 5/1985 of 19 June*);
    (vi) crimes which specially affect public safety;
    (vii) smuggling (*LO 7/1982 of 13 July*);
    (viii) monetary crimes (*Act 40/1939 of 10 December* as amended by *Act 1973 of 16 August*) the number of which has been substantially reduced by *Royal Decree of 20 December 1991*);
    (ix) intellectual property crimes (*Penal Code as amended by Act 6/1987 of 11 November*), etc.

The prosecution   A prosecution may be brought by the following persons :

- The Public Prosecutor (*"ministerio fiscal"*) is under a constitutional duty to promote justice to uphold the law, the rights of citizens and the public interest, either exofficio or ex parte, to monitor the independence of the courts and to promote the public interest (*Constitution, art 124*).

- The popular prosecutor (*"acusador popular"*) : all citizens have the right to take a popular action (*"acción popular"*), ie an action to prosecute a criminal offence even though not the victim (*Constitution, art 125*).

- The personal prosecutor (*"acusador particular"*) : for crimes which can be prosecuted ex officio (public crimes) the victim takes an active part with the Public Prosecutor (*LECrim, art 110*). Foreigners can also bring criminal proceedings for crimes committed against them or their property or against persons or property represented by them (*LECrim, art 270,2*).

- The private prosecutor (*"acusador privado"*) is a necessary accuser in criminal proceedings for crimes which can only be prosecuted ex parte such as *injuria* or *calumnia* (where the Public Prosecutor cannot intervene) (*Penal Code, arts 466 and 467*).

- The civil law plaintiff : civil compensation for damages may be awarded in Spanish criminal proceedings. The parties can waive the civil action or take separate civil proceedings (*LECrim, art 112, 1*).

Criminal proceedings are initiated in the following ways : by a complaint ("*denuncia*"), by a criminal charge ("*querella*") or by the judge "ex officio".

Initiating a criminal prosecution

The *denuncia* is a declaration or notice of facts which may constitute a crime which is notified to the court, the public prosecutor or the police authorities. Any person who is aware that any crime has been committed is obliged to notify this immediately to the court (*LECrim, art 259*). A person who makes a criminal denunciation may be an actual witness (*LECrim, art 259*) or someone who, by virtue of his position, was aware that a crime had been committed (*LECrim, 262, 2*) or who was an indirect witness (*LECrim, art 26*) or the victim (*Constitution, art 24*).

The *querella*, or criminal charge, unlike the complaint, is the act whereby one actually brings a criminal action (*LECrim, arts 100 and 270*), so that the person making the *querella* ("*querellante*") becomes the accuser in the proceedings. In the *querella* the injured party asks the competent court to commence proceedings in which he will be the accusing party.

Under *Articles 270 and 271 of the LECrim* the Public Prosecutor and any Spanish citizen can submit a *querella* regardless of whether they have been injured by the crime ("*accion popular*"). Foreigners can only submit a *querella* if they have been injured by the crime. There are public and private *querellas*. The *querella* initiated by the Public Prosecutor (*LECrim, art 101*) is intended to re-establish the legal order disturbed by commission of the crime. The proceedings cannot be dropped if the accuser objects even if the Public Prosecutor intervenes (*LECrim, art 642*).

The *querella* must be in writing and must set out the court referred to, the identity of the *querellante*, the identity of the person against whom the complaint is made (the "*querellado*"), the facts, the request that the *querella* be admitted and that evidence be gathered, the request that the defendant be detained and imprisoned and that any assets, where appropriate, be attached, (*LECrim, art 277*). The *denuncia* is not subject to any special formalities (*LECrim, arts 267 and 268*).

Under *Title V, Book II of the LECrim* the "*diligencias sumariales*" or investigative acts will be carried out either at the instance of the Public Prosecutor or the other parties provided the judge does not consider this unnecessary or prejudicial. The judge conducts the investigation as the case warrants. The investigation is intended to establish the facts necessary to support the accusation, while the evidence must convince the court that the facts investigated are correct. The investigatory means are : visual inspection ("*inspeccion ocular*"), interrogation of the accused ("*interrogatorio del inculpado*"), confrontation of witnesses ("*careos*"), documentary and other proof, witness statements ("*declaraciones testificales*") and expert reports ("*informes periciales*").

Pleas

There are two kinds of pleas : the *"confesión"* entered at the intermediary stage, and that entered at trial (*"juicio oral"*). In less serious cases, where the accused pleads guilty and admits civil liability for the maximum amount, the court will simply complete the trial and give its verdict unless it is not possible to find the *"corpus delicti"* (*LECrim, art 699*). *Article 406 of the LECrim* provides that where an accused pleads guilty the court should in any case take all other necessary steps to support that guilty plea.

Juries

Citizens may participate in the administration of justice through the institution of the jury (*"jurado"*) in the form and in respect of such criminal proceedings as are provided for by law (*Constitution, art 125*). This constitutional rule has been developed by *Articles 19.2 and 83 of the Judicial Powers Act* ("*Ley Orgánica del Poder Judicial*" - "*LOPJ*") but it has still not been fully implemented by law. Hence, at present, there are no juries in Spain.

Conduct of the Trial

Investigative stage

The stages of criminal proceedings are as follows :

The enquiry or investigative stage (*"instrucción"*) is when the file is put together or the group of preparatory activities (*"sumario"* or *"diligencias previas"*) for the oral or plenary trial (*"juicio oral"* or *"plenario"*) is completed. The *sumario* is an instructive or investigative procedure in which the fact that the crime has taken place and the possible criminal (*"delincuente"*) are investigated.

Traditionally, the investigation procedure is secret. Since *Act No 53/1978 of 4 December 1978* secrecy in the *sumario* does not generally apply to the parties themselves (*LECrim, art 302*) and the right of defence can be exercised from the moment when the accusation of a crime has been communicated to an accused (*LECrim, art 118*).

Once detained, a person has the right to request the presence and assistance of a lawyer during any police and court interrogations (*LECrim, art 520*).

Finally, *LO 7/1988* established a shortened criminal procedure (*"proceso penal abreviado"*) for criminal offences for which the maximum term of imprisonment is six years and one day or less, which thus applies to most criminal offences. Its investigative stage, known as preliminary procedure (*"diligencias previas"*), amounts to the *sumario* stage.

Indictment

As soon as there is a reasonable indication from the *sumario* that a criminal act has been committed by a specific person, the court will declare that person indicted (*"auto de procesamiento"*) (*LECrim, art 384*).

Before the 1967 reforms, all formal indictments by the court would follow this form (*"procesamiento"*), but since these reforms the *procesamiento* only applies to serious crimes, that is, crimes which must be tried by courts different from the investigating court, ie Criminal Courts ("*Juszgados de lo Penal*") or High Courts ("*audiencias*"), either for *sumario* proceedings or a shortened criminal procedure (*LECrim, arts 623 and 789*).

As soon as an accused person has testified before the investigative judge ("*juez de instrucción*") and the judge considers that the facts alleged constitute a criminal offence, the judge will order the proceedings to continue (*LECrim, art 790*). This declaration converts the person in question into a party to the proceedings. From this point (unless he cannot be contacted) the accused has the right to appoint a lawyer so that he can request that the *sumario* be completed, that evidence be produced, or to make any request regarding his particular situation (*LECrim, art 384*).

Once the investigative stage is over, the investigating court ("*juzgado de instrucción*") orders the investigation ("*instrucción*") to be completed and sends the results of the investigation to the court above, which will conduct the oral trial. However, between the end of the *sumario* and the opening of the oral trial there are three alternative ways of proceeding : *The intermediary stage*

(a) The court above, in the light of the evidence requested by the parties, decides whether the *sumario* has been properly completed or whether it must revoke the completion order and remit the investigation below, asking the *juzgado de instrucción* to produce further evidence ("*diligencias*").

(b) The charges may be dropped ("*sobreseimiento*") when it appears from the investigation that no material crime has been committed or that there is no possibility of bringing any charges against any specific person. This *sobreseimiento* can be provisional or final ("*libre*").

(c) If after the investigation any charges against specific persons do appear possible, the oral trial will be ordered to start and the formulation of provisional positions ("*escritos de calificación provisional*") submitted by the accusing and the accused parties will then follow. These must refer to the punishable acts which appear from the *sumario*, the qualification in law of such acts (ie what kind of crime is alleged to have been committed), the various degrees of involvement of the accused persons, and any extenuating or aggravating circumstances, indicating also any persons who may be civilly liable.

In the new summary criminal proceedings introduced by *LO 7/1988* the intermediary phase is completed before the same court (*juzgado de instrucción*) and the formal accusation is addressed to this court.

The oral trial is started by the accuser and the accused setting out their aforementioned provisional positions ("*escritos de calificación provisional*") and ends with the verdict ("*sentencia*"). *The hearing*

The following stages apply inbetween :

There are various acts preparatory to trial which cover the production and admission of evidence, challenging expert evidence, setting down the trial and summarising the witness and expert evidence which will have been produced at the provisional taking of position stage.

First the accused is asked whether he is guilty of the crime alleged and whether he accepts the penalty which has been proposed. If he accepts both his own guilt and the proposed penalty there is said to be *"conformidad"* (*LECrim, art 688*).

Trials in public and in camera

The court must first decide whether the trial will be public or in camera (*LECrim, art 682*). The general rule is that it is held in public, but the trial can be camera if publicity would violate certain fundamental rights such as the right of honour. Once this decision has been made, all the evidence against the accused must be disclosed in court. The President declares the session open (*LECrim, art 688*) and asks the accused about his personal status, whether he has any previous convictions and whether he understands the charge against him (*Constitution, art 24.2*). The President will then ask the accused whether he is guilty of the crime and whether he accepts the penalties sought by the accusing parties.

The parties must intervene in the following order : the Public Prosecutor, any particular accusers, defence counsel and any counsel in respect of any civil claim. All may question the accused, the witnesses and the experts in the same order.

Final conclusions

Once the evidence has been presented all the parties may amend their earlier provisional positions (*LECrim, art 732*) or present them as final in this same order.

Summing up

The representatives of the parties make their submissions to the court (*"informe oral"*) in the following order : the Public Prosecutor, the public and particular accusers, if any, the civil law plaintiff, if any, and the lawyers for the accused and any alleged civilly liable parties (*LECrim, art 734*). Finally, the President asks the accused whether he has anything to say to the court (*LECrim, art 739*).

The verdict

The verdict must be in writing, properly reasoned and must comply with and deal with all the issues raised by the parties, except in the case of summary proceedings (*"procedimentos abreviados"*) where the verdict can be given orally, notwithstanding that it may later be put in writing.

In multi-member courts (*"tribunales colegiados"*) the verdict is suggested by the judge rapporteur (*"magistrado ponente"*) and is decided on after discussion and vote by the judges (*LECrim, art 149*) "behind closed doors" (*"a puerta cerrada"*).

The verdict has three different parts (*LECrim, art 142*):

(a)   that setting out the findings of fact ("*resultando de hechos probados*");

(b)   that setting out the rulings on law ("*fundamentos de derecho*") where the law, as applied to the facts, the participation of the accused and any possible mitigating or aggravating circumstances are set out; and

(c)   the formal verdict ("*fallo*") which can only convict or acquit the accused ("*condenatorio*" or "*absolutorio*").

The verdict can be appealed against to the Provincial Court ("*Audiencia Provincial*") if the verdict at first instance was given by the "*Juzgado de lo Penal*", or to the Supreme Court ("*recurso de casación*") (*LECrim, art 847*) if the verdict at first instance was given by the *Audiencia Provincial*.

Extradition will be granted in compliance with a treaty or a law or on the basis of reciprocity (*Constitution, art 13.3*). There are two types of extradition : "active", where a state requests the surrender of a person accused of a crime, and "passive", where one state is requested to surrender a person accused of a crime under the laws of the requesting state.   *Extradition*

Extradition in Spain is mainly regulated by the *Act on Passive Extradition of 21 March 1985; LECrim, arts 824 to 833*, and the *Royal Decree-Law 1/1977 of 4 January 1977*, creating the "*Audiencie Nacional*" and assigning to it responsibility for dealing with passive extradition; the *European Convention for the Suppression of Terrorism of 27 January 1977*; the *European Convention on Judicial Assistance in Criminal Matters of 20 April 1959*, ratified by Spain in 1982; the *European Convention on Extradition of 13 December 1957* ratified by Spain on 21 April 1982, and several bilateral treaties to which Spain is a party and which are currently in force, which apply preferentially (bearing in mind that extradition is basically regulated by reciprocal extradition treaties between countries).

Under the *Constitution* and the law, extradition is now an administrative-judicial process, which means that it is the government which must authorise the extradition procedure.

Extradition is granted on the grounds not of judging what an accused has done, but whether the defendant can be surrendered in order to be judged. However, extradition will not be granted in the following cases : when the accused is a Spanish national, without prejudice to the obligation to judge the crime in Spain, if the requesting country so requests; when the crime must be heard by a Spanish court; when there is no guarantee that the death penalty or other penalties affecting the defendant's corporal integrity or inhuman or degrading treatments will not be applied; when it relates to people who have obtained political asylum; and in respect of political and military crimes, crimes committed through the media or crimes against minors.

CHAPTER 8 : REMEDIES

Any person may claim damages as compensation, where the rights of that person have been infringed. *Damages*

Damages are generally only awarded by the civil courts ("*jurisdicción civil*") but any damage resulting from the commission of a criminal offence can also be claimed before the criminal courts ("*jurisdicción penal*").

The compensation one may claim as damages depends on whether liability is contractual or extracontractual.

Where a contract is not fully performed by any party then such a party may be liable as provided for by the contract or by law. *Contractual liability*

Article 1101 of the Civil Code provides as follows : "Those who in the fulfilment of their obligations act fraudulently ("*dolus*"), with negligence or with delay or, in any way, are in breach of their obligations shall be liable to pay damages".

An obligee is liable for the extent to which he has not completely fulfilled his obligations :
   (a)   as a general rule, whenever such defective performance is due to his own fraud, malicious intent, negligence or delay;

   (b)   exceptionally, in such other cases and with such other liability as is imposed by law (eg in the case of strict liability in product liability) or as provided for by contract.

One has a case of "dolus" whenever an obligee consciously and willfully breaches his obligations; one has fault ("*culpa*") whenever an obligee is in breach of his obligations negligently, even where there is no deliberate intention to do so. However, an obligee does not entail any liability for a less-than-complete performance of his obligations in the following cases :
   (a)   if non-performance is due to force majeure; or exceptionally

   (b)   when this is allowed for under the contract.

Article 1105 of the Civil Code provides for force majeure and states that "Save where otherwise specifically provided for by law or provided for under contract, no one shall be liable for such events which could not have been foreseen or for those which, though foreseen, were inevitable". Spanish law distinguishes between what is called a "fortuitous case" ("*caso fortuito*") where an event is unforseeable, and "force majeure" ("*fuerza mayor*") where the event may be foreseeable but is inevitable in any event.

Non-contractual (tortious) liability

Article 1902 of the Civil Code provides that "Any person who by his acts or omissions causes damage to another person, through fault or negligence, shall be liable to remedy that damage".

In order to succeed in a claim in tort, one must prove the following : an act or omission, its unlawfulness, fault, damage and the causal link. Strict liability ("*responsabilidad objetiva*") in tort has developed to cover cases where damage was caused by or resulted from inter alia : motor vehicles, air navigation, nuclear energy, hunting, where the government acts as a private person, and product liability (in some cases since the 1985[1] Directive has not yet been implemented).

Tortious liability can arise not only from one's own acts but also from those of third parties such as children, pupils and dependants who are under one's authority or for whom one is made responsible by law (*Civil Code, art 1903*) and from damage caused by animals in one's possession (*Civil Code, art 1905*).

Level of damages

The courts are free to assess the level of damages to be awarded in a particular case. There are no rules fixing the level of damages which should be awarded in civil law claims, and the *Civil Code* is silent on this. According to case law a party should be restored to the position prior to the occurrence of the harmful event (*Supreme Court judgment of 15 December 1981*).

The *Penal Code (art 103)* states that compensation shall be determined depending on the seriousness of any damage suffered as assessed by the court, and taking into account the value of any goods affected, whenever possible, and the sentimental value placed on it by the injured person ("*la reparación se hará valorándose la entidad del daño por regulación del tribunal, atendido el precio de la cosa, siempre que fuere posible, y el de afección del agraviado*"). In practice, however, case law gives some indication of the general amounts which can be recovered for specific injuries such as death or physical injury. The *Ministerial Order of 5 March 1991* approved a system for evaluating personal injuries and the amounts which can be recovered in motor accidents.

Mental distress

Case law has acknowledged that *Article 1,902 of the Civil Code* covers both compensation for material damage and mental distress, provided the plaintiff can prove to have suffered. In assessing the amount to be paid for mental distress several factors must be taken into account : the character of the impairment or harm suffered, the extent of any intention to cause harm by the defendant, and the financial position of the defendant. In some cases redress may include the right to seek

---

1.　　　Council Directive (EEC) 85/374 (OJ L210 7.8.85 p29).

rectification in the press or media or publcation of the conviction judgment of the offender.

The *Act of 5 May 1982* sets out a number of provisions to provide for the "protection of one's right to honour, to personal and family privacy and to one's own image". The said rights, as set out in the preamble of this Act, are fundamental in character and cannot be waived or transferred temporarily or permanently. Protection of these rights can be sought either through ordinary court proceedings or through special judicial proceedings under *Article 53.2 of the Constitution* before the Constitutional Court. Actions for redress of the said acts are subject to a time limitation period of four years as from the time the person entitled to file the said actions could have exercised them.

Rights of one's person

Compensation can be sought for economic loss. *Article 1106 of the Civil Code* distinguishes between the value of the harm suffered (*"damnum emergens"*) and loss of profits (*"lucrum cessans"*) but both elements have to be taken into account so that compensation will put the plaintiff in the position he would have been in had no harm been suffered. This rule applies to contractual as to extracontractual liability.

Economic loss

Unjust enrichment is a general principle of law in the Spanish legal system, as well as a specific action developed through case law. Unjust enrichment also applies to commercial contracts.

Unjust enrichment

The principle of unjust enrichment appears implicitly in several articles of the *Civil Code* : *Article 356* (whoever receives the fruits of any property must pay the expenses of a third party for their production, collection and preservation); *Article 360* (the owner of a plot who works with another's materials is obliged to pay their price to that third party); *Article 361* (the owner of a plot in which someone else builds or plants in good faith has the right to make the work or the crop his own by paying due compensation for work done); *Article 1158* (one who pays another's debt has the right to claim from the debtor the amount paid save where the payment was effected against the debtor's will); *Article 1163* (payment made by one lacking capacity will still be valid insofar as this party has gained a benefit), etc.

An action for unjust enrichment is a personal action to recover a value which has passed from one person to another without due cause. Recourse to this action is available where enrichment by one entailed the impoverishment of another. The impoverishment must have been unjust, unlawful or without due cause. In such a case, the first person is obliged to repair the damage caused to the other by such enrichment either by returning the benefit received, or in monetary terms. In this sense "unfair" or "without due cause" enrichment is a source of obligation.

The time limitation for filing an action for unjust enrichment is 15 years under *Article 1,964 of the Civil Code*, being a personal action to which no specific time limitation is attributed.

Quasi contracts

Chapter I of Title XVI of Book IV of the Civil Code regulates quasi contracts ("*cuasi contratos*"). *Article 1887* defines quasi contracts :

> "Quasi contracts are those licit and purely voluntary acts as a result of which their author incurs an obligation vis-à-vis a third party and, sometimes, a mutual obligation as between any interested parties".

Quasi contracts can also be said to arise where the general principle of unjust enrichment has specifically crystallised.

The *Civil Code* deals specifically with two types of quasi contracts : the management of another's affairs ("*la gestión de negocios ajenos*" or "*negotiorum gestorum*") (*arts 1888 to 1894*); and the collection of what was not due ("*el cobro de lo indebido*" or "*solutio indebite*") (*arts 1895 to 1901*).

Penalty clauses

Penalty clauses are possible under Spanish law. They are regulated by the *Civil Code (arts 1152 to 1155)* and are common in practice.

Article 1152 of the Civil Code provides, in its first paragraph :

> "For obligations incorporating a penalty clause, the penalty shall be substituted for the compensation for damages and the payment of interest in the case of non-performance save where otherwise agreed."

Penalty clauses may operate as a coercive or guarantee mechanism for the exact fulfilment of a principal obligation; or as a punitive mechanism when, in addition to damages ("*daños y perjuicios*"), the obligee is obliged to pay the penalty; and as a liquidation mechanism - when the penalty amounts to a pre-estimate of damages and replaces damages and interest.

When a penalty fulfils the first two functions it is called a "cumulative penalty", when it operates in the third way it is called a "substitutive penalty".

When a substitutive penalty is claimed (and it is presumed to be substitutive unless otherwise agreed) the plaintiff cannot claim performance of the obligation due (*Civil Code, art 1153, second para*). The defendant cannot simply exonerate himself from performing his obligation by just paying the penalty unless otherwise agreed (*Civil Code, art 1153, first para*). If the penalty is cumulative it can be claimed in addition to requiring performance of the obligation or to the damages arising from non or irregular performance of the principal obligation (*Civil Code, art 1153 in fine*). *Article 1154 of the Civil Code* provides that "the judge shall modify the penalty in an equitable manner whenever the principal obligation has been partially or irregularly performed by the obligee" and the courts make good use of this power.

As a general rule, if it is still possible to perform an obligation, one may ask for judgment for complete performance. This is called voluntary specific performance ("*ejecucion procesal voluntaria*"), voluntary, because the debtor still performs voluntarily even in the face of a court judgment. *Article 1096 of the Civil Code* provides "when what has to be delivered is a specific good, the creditor ... can compel the debtor to deliver" or if the obligee refuses to perform despite the court order, the subject matter of the obligation can still be delivered to the plaintiff either: *Specific performance*

- by obtaining it from the patrimony of the debtor and delivering it by court order to the creditor; or

- by having performance completed by a third party at the obligee's cost, taking from his property sufficient assets to pay for the third party performance unless performance is personal, (for example, the painting of a portrait by a reputed artist) (*Civil Code, arts 1096, 1098, 1099*).

These are called compulsory specific performance ("*ejecucion procesal forzosa*"). *Article 1098 of the Civil Code* provides : "if the obligee required to do something does not do it, performance shall be ordered at his cost".

If performance is not possible at all the debtor must pay the damages suffered by the creditor due to non-performance "id quod interest" (*Civil Code, arts 1101, 1135, 1147, 1150, 1185*).

In the case of reciprocal obligations if one of the obligees does not perform his obligation the law allows the creditor to choose between asking for specific performance or the realisation of the obligation with damages and interest in any case (*Civil Code, art 1124*).

A contract may be amended or dissolved where the law or the parties to the contract specifically provide for this. *Change of circumstances*

If not so provided for, it is difficult to determine whether the contract can be amended or dissolved. The courts have held that if the underlying circumstances have fundamentally changed, the contract can be rectified but not dissolved (clause "*rebus sic stantibus*"). In order for a contract to be rectified, the change in circumstances must not be attributable to the plaintiff, and no other procedures to remedy the damage to preserve the contract unrevised available.

A contract is terminated when completed either by performance ("*cumplimiento*"), or by non-performance ("*incumplimiento*") where the obligation which is the subject matter of the contract becomes impossible to perform, or : *Termination of contract*

(a) when the contract even without being completed becomes null and void, by mutual release;

(b) when one of the parties asks for rescission for non-performance; and

(c) when the law provides that this should follow in given circumstances.

Actions by/against public bodies

Decisions of the public administration can be challenged by their addressees either before the administrative body which took the decision or before a special court called the "Contentious-Administrative Court" (*"tribunal contencioso-administrativo"*). This administrative challenge in which one seeks to have the administrative decision in question revoked or amended by the same body which handed down the decision or the superior administrative bodies (*"vía administrativa o gubernativa"*) is a prerequisite to being able to raise a judicial contentious-administrative challenge. These administrative challenges are only a limited guarantee for citizens since the administration is judge and party at the same time. *Article 37 of the Contentious-administrative Jurisdiction Act ("LJCA")* provides that the contentious-administrative challenge is only possible against the decisions and actions of the administration which are not susceptible to any further appeal within the administration.

CHAPTER 9 : MATRIMONIAL DISPUTES

Questions of divorce, custody and access, and all other proceedings concerning the breakup of marriage are heard by the family courts ("*tribunales de familia*") at first instance in the places where such courts exist, or by the general first instance courts elsewhere.

Spanish courts are competent to hear matrimonial disputes (*Judicial Powers Act, art 22 n.3*) when :
- (a) both spouses have Spanish nationality;
- (b) both spouses are resident in Spain;
- (c) the plaintiff is a Spaniard and resident in Spain; or
- (d) the defendant is resident in Spain.

There are three forms of separation :   *Proceedings for*
- (a) agreed and endorsed by the court (judicial *separation*
       proceedings);
- (b) judicial (also judicial proceedings); and
- (c) de facto.

A petition for an agreed separation requested by both spouses or with the consent of the other spouse can be submitted to the court after the first year of marriage. It must be accompanied by a proposed agreement ("*propuesta convenio regulador*") regulating the separation and dealing with the custody of any children, use of the family home, financial arrangements, and by the marriage certificate and the birth certificates of any children. Alimony will be assessed by the court, taking into consideration factors including age, health and professional qualifications, and any personal wealth of the spouses and the length of time the marriage has lasted.

Proceedings for a separation by mutual agreement (or commenced by one spouse with the consent of the other) consist of an endorsement procedure ("*juicio o proceso de homologación*") governed by the 6th Additional Provision of the Act of 7th July 1981. Judicial separation is followed by the "*incidentes*" procedure. A judgment granting separation means the spouses' common life is suspended the other spouse's assets may not be affected by the family's affairs (*Civil Code, arts 83 and 102*).

Article 82 of the Civil Code as amended by *Act 30/81 of 7 July 1981*   *Grounds for* provides the following grounds for separation :   *separation*
- (a) unjustified abandonment of the matrimonial home;
       infidelity within the marriage; injurious conduct or any
       other serious or repeated breach of conjugal duties;

(b)   any serious or repeated breach of the duties towards children common to both spouses or towards any children of either spouse who live in the family home;

(c)   imprisonment for longer than six years;

(d)   alcoholism, drug addiction, mental diseases, provided that the interests of the spouse or of the family require cohabitation to be suspended;

(e)   where marital cohabitation has ceased for a period of six months freely consented to by both spouses;

(f)   where marital cohabitation has ceased for three years;

(g)   any ground for divorce provided for in the *Civil Code, art 86, nos 3, 4 and 5* (see below).

Grounds for divorce

The grounds for divorce are set out in *Article 86 of the Civil Code* :

(a)   where marital cohabitation has actually ceased for at least one year following the presentation of the petition for separation by both spouses or by one spouse with the consent of the other provided that the petition was submitted after at least one year following the marriage;

(b)   where marital cohabitation has actually ceased for at least one year from presentation of the petition for separation and the judgment granting separation has become final;

(c)   where marital cohabitation has actually ceased for at least two years following : (i) the free acceptance by both spouses of their separation in fact, or a final judgment or declaration that either of the spouses has been absent for a requisite period of time; or (ii) when one spouse can prove that the other was actually within one of the grounds for separation when separation in fact started;

(d)   where marital cohabitation has actually ceased for a minimum of five years at the request of one of the spouses; or

(e)   where there has been a final court judgment against one spouse for an attempt on the life of the other, or on any ascendants or descendants.

Matrimonial property

Article 95 of the Civil Code provides that in cases of nullity, separation and divorce, a final judgment ("*sentencia firme*") dissolves the economic relationship between the spouses in respect of all matrimonial property. *Article 96 of the Civil Code* provides that failing a mutual agreement approved by the judge, the use of the family home and the objects contained in it fall to the children and to the spouse the children stay with. Where there are no children, the use of the matrimonial home may be granted to the non-owner spouse provided the circumstances require this. However, the other spouse's consent or, in some circumstances, judicial authorisation, is required.

The *Civil Code* contains a number of articles (*92 to 94*) which ensure that judgments in cases of nullity, separation or divorce cause the least possible damage to children (*"favor filii"*).   *Children*

Article 92 provides that all parental duties owed after nullity, separation or divorce has been granted be replaced. All judicial action on questions concerning the children's care and education will be adopted on their behalf after they have been heard provided they have sufficient understanding and, in any case, if they are over 12 years old. The judgment may decide that parental authority (*"patria potestad"*) over the children be totally or partially exercised by only one of the parents or that both be deprived of this if the children's interest requires this.

Article 93 provides that the judge will decide what contribution each parent should make towards maintenance (*"alimentos"*) of the children and will decide any necessary enforcement measures and will adapt the contributions to the financial circumstances and needs of the children from time to time.

Article 94 regulates the right of the spouse who does not have custody of them to visit the children.

CHAPTER 10 : PROPERTY TRANSACTIONS

The Spanish real property system is based on registration. Real *Land Registry*
property can be duly registered at the Land Registry ("*Registro de
la Propiedad*"). Registration in the Land Registry is not
compulsory nor essential to acquire valid ownership. It is
advisable, however, since a non-registered owner can lose his title
if the registered owner transfers to a bona fide third party who
takes in reliance on the entries in the Registry.

There is one Land Registry in every district. The property details
registered include measurements, the location and description of
the property, the names and title of ownership of the different
owners since the property was first registered and any charges or
encumbrances or rights over the property, such as mortgages,
building restrictions and servitudes. Registration is regulated by
the *Mortgage Act of 8 February 1946 as amended and
Regulations ("Ley y Reglamento Hipotecarios")*.

The transfer of real estate or chattels ("*bienes inmuebles o*   *Transferring*
muebles") in Spain is based on the Roman law system which   *ownership of*
requires "*titulus*" (an agreement on which the transfer is based)   *property*
and "*modus*" (physical or symbolic delivery over of the property).
A purchase made in a "private (non-notarial) agreement" is valid
if followed up by "*traditio*" (delivery). Notarial deeds deem
delivery to have taken place. In order that this may be
enforceable against third parties, acquisition of real property
requires two conditions to be met :
  (a)   that the agreement be executed in a public deed
         ("*escritura publica*") before a notary public; and

  (b)   that the public deed be registered at the relevant Land
         Registry. Private (non-notarised) agreements cannot
         be included in this Registry.

The seller is under no legal obligation to show or deliver his title
documents to the purchaser, since the title documents do not
carry any rights of ownership, and since the purchaser may at any
time check the seller's title to ownership (as well as any charges
affecting the property) by examining the Land Registry records or
by requesting the Land Registry to issue either an information
note or a certificate of charges ("*certificado de cargas*"). However,
the seller would normally do this. A purchaser who buys property
in reliance on the information supplied by the Land Registry is
presumed to be a "bona fides" purchaser, and so enjoys full
protection of that position (*Mortgage Act, art 34*).

Although having the deed executed before a notary public and
then registered is the method most commonly used, a private

agreement is also valid, but only as between the parties. Thus, where a seller who signed a private agreement later sells the same property to another purchaser and if this second purchase is executed before a notary public and registered at the Land Registry prior to the first purchase, then the second purchaser would acquire full ownership rights over the property and the second purchase will prevail over the first unless a fraudulent intent is proved. The (first) private agreement will not be valid as against this second purchaser since it is not enforceable "*erga omnes*", but is only valid "*inter partes*".

Purchase of real estate property by non-residents

Foreign investments in Spain are regulated by the *Act of 1 July 1992* and *Royal Decree of 2 July 1992* and have been liberalised them. In general, the steps to be taken by non-residents in Spain to purchase a property in Spain are :

1. Exchange control verification, if required, (for instance if acquiring business property or where the acquisition exceeds 500 million pesetas or is made from a tax haven); all other acquisitions are unrestricted unless affected by legislation affecting issues of national defence. An application should be lodged with the Directorate General for Foreign Transactions (DGTE) to secure the verification needed for foreign investment in domestic real estate.

2. Should the registered owner or the seller not wish to appear before a notary public, he can grant a power of attorney to a third person before a notary public (see 5 below) (if before a foreign notary public then a power of attorney deed needs to bear the *Hague Convention* Apostille).

3. It is advisable to verify with the Land Registry to ensure that no mortgages or other encumbrance are charged on the property and to verify the municpal zoning plans.

4. Funds should be transferred to a Spanish bank and the relevant bank certificate or cheque secured.

5. A public deed of purchase ("*escritura pública de compraventa*") should be executed before a notary public who verifies the powers of attorney, the verification from the DGTE and the bank certificate or bank cheque evidencing actual payment of the price.

6. Transfer Tax and Municipal Tax on Capital Gains ("*Plusvalia*") must be paid :
    (a) Transfer Tax at a rate of 6% on the price will have to be paid by the purchaser. Should the vendor provide professional services (ie if it is a company) then VAT will apply at the rate of 13%.

    (b) A municipal capital gains tax ("*plusvalia*") is also payable on the transfer of real estate. This tax should be paid by the vendor, although it is frequently agreed that the purchaser should cover this.

(c) The vendor will be subject to tax in Spain on any capital gains arising out of the transfer of the property. In Spain there is no special Capital Gains Tax and the capital gain is treated as normal income subject to Income Tax. As a result a purchaser who acquires real estate from a non-resident will have to withhold 10% of the price as a payment on account of this Personal Income Tax.

7. The purchase deed should be registered at the Land Registry to obtain full legal protection in respect of ownership, as mere possession of the deed will not suffice for this purpose.

8. As a foreign investment the acquisition should be registered with the Foreign Investments Registry.

CHAPTER 11 : RECOGNITION AND ENFORCEMENT OF FOREIGN JUDGMENTS

The *1968 Brussels Convention* was ratified by Spain and entered into force there on 1 February 1991. All foreign judgments within the scope of the *Brussels Convention* will be recognised and/or enforced before the ordinary courts (*"juez de primera instancia"*).

The Brussels Convention

Where the *Brussels Convention* does not apply Spain grants recognition to foreign judgments by the "exequatur" procedure. This is regulated by *Articles 951 to 958 of the Civil Procedure Act* (*"Ley de Enjuiciamiento Civil"* (*"LEC"*)). *Article 951* states that : "Final judgments given in foreign countries shall have in Spain the validity provided for in the relevant Treaties". If there is no applicable treaty, a foreign civil judgment is binding in Spain with the same force and effect as rulings rendered by Spanish courts in this other country only after being deemed to be so by the Supreme Court "exequatur" procedure. In order for a foreign judgment to be enforced in this way the country of origin of the judgment must provide for reciprocal treatment for Spanish judgments. The judgment must be final, with no further right of appeal or for a retrial, and may not conflict with the principles of public order under Spanish law. The judgment must have been given in accordance with the laws of the country of origin and meet all Spanish criteria on the legalisation of documents (*LEC, art 954*).

The exequatur procedure

The procedure starts with a written petition requesting recognition of the foreign judgment and attaching an authenticated copy of the judgment (*LEC, art 600.4*) with an official translation (*LEC, art 956*). The Public Prosecutor and any opponent will be heard (*LEC, art 956*). Without conducting any kind of evidential the Supreme Court examines the petition to determine whether it meets the necessary conditions and issues a ruling (*"auto"*) recognising or refusing recognition to the judgment, which ruling cannot be appealed (*LEC, art 956*). If recognised, the foreign judgment can be referred to the competent ordinary court (*"juez de primera instancia"*) of the place of the defendant's domicile or where the judgment must be enforced for it to then be enforced (*LEC, art 958.2*).

Foreign judgments may have effect in Spain in different ways. Orders issued pursuant to such judgments may be enforced through the Spanish courts, in which case the ruling is said to have executory force (*"fuerza ejecutiva"*). A foreign judgment may also have certain collateral effects. It may bar any future consideration of the matter decided in the foreign judgment as res judicata (*"cosa juzgada"*). A foreign judgment may also be relied upon in other legal proceedings.

Spain has entered into treaties regarding the execution of foreign judgments with Austria, Czechoslovakia, Colombia, Brazil, Mexico, Israel, and Switzerland. Certain multilateral treaties (the *New York Convention on the Recognition and Enforcement of Foreign Arbitral Awards of 1958* and the *European Convention on International Commercial Arbitration (Geneva, 1961)*) allow for arbitration awards to be treated as judgments and executed in the same way as other foreign judgments.

BIBLIOGRAPHY

1. Sources of Law

Alvarez Conde, E., *El Régimen Político español*, Tecnos, 1988

Diez De Velasco, M., *Instituciones de derecho internacional publico* (tomo II), Tecnos, 1983

Entrena Cuesta, *Curso de derecho administrativo*, (Vol I), Tecnos, 1984

La Constitución española y las fuentes del derecho, (Vol I), Direccion General de lo Contencioso del Estado,, Insituto de Estudios Fiscales, 1979.

Miaja de la Muela, A., *Derecho Internacional Privado* (tomo II), Atlas, 1979

2. Fundamental Rights

Cano Mata, Antonio, Estudios jurídicos en honor de José Gabaldán Lopez, *Derechos fundamentales y libertades públicas, protección jurisdiccional en el ordenamiento espagñol vigente*, Trivium, 1990

Fernandez De Casadevante, *La aplicacion del convenio europeo de derechos humanos en España*, Tecnos, 1988

Friginal Fernandez-Villaverde, *La protección de los derechos fundamentales en el ordenamiento español*, Editorial Montecorvo, SA, 1981

Garcia Morillo, Joaquin, *El amparo judicial de los derechos fundamentales*, Ministerio de Justicia. Secretaría General Tecnica. Centro de publicaciones, 1985

Gonzalez Casanova, J.A., *Teoria del Estado y Derecho Constitucional*, Vicens, 1983

Gui Mori, Tomas, *Doctrina constitucional 1981-1988*, Bosch, Barcelona, 1989

Martin-Retortillo, Lorenzo, De Otto y Pardo, Ignacio, *Derechos fundamentales y constitución*, Civitas, 1988

3. Jurisdiction of the Courts

Lopez Ayala, Manuel, *Cuestiones de competencia. Comentarios prácticos a las Reqlas de Competencia en la Ley de Enjuiciamiento Civil (art 56 a 115)*, Editorial Montecarlo, 1979

Pelaez Del Rosal, Manuel, *La competencia territorial en el proceso civil. El acuerdo de sumision expresa*, Ariel, 1974

Ramos Mendez, Francisco, *Derecho Procesal Civil*, Vol I, Bosch, Barcelona, 1986

4. Administration of Justice

Calderon Cuadrado, Maria Pia (edicion preparada por), *Organización judicial*, Civitas, 1989.

De La Oliva, Andres, Vegas, Jaime, Zarzalejos Jesus, Gonzalez Jesus Maria, Aragoneses, Sara, *Nuevos tribunales y nuevo proceso penal*, La Ley, 1989

El poder judicial (Vol I), Direccion General de lo Contencioso del Estado

Gonzalez Casanova, J.A., *Teoría del Estado y Derecho Constitucional*, Vicens, 1983

Monton Redondo, Alberto, *Juzqados y tribunales españoles : orígenes y atribuciones : antes y después de la Ley Orgánica de 1 de julio de 1985*, Tecnos, 1986

5. The Legal Profession

Estatuto General de la Abogacía, approved by Real Decreto (Royal Decree) 2090/1982 of 24 July 1982

Gomez Perez, Rafael, *Deontología jurídica*, Eunsa, Pamplona, 1991

Hernandez Corchero, Dimas, *Manual práctico del aboqado*, Aranzadi, Pamplona, 1977

Lonbay, J., *Training Lawyers in the European Community*, (pp 109-119), (The University of Birmingham, Report on the professional qualifications of the legal professions in the European Community), The Law Society, 1991

Martinez Val, José Maria, *Etica de la Aboqacla*, Bosch, Barcelona, 1987

Rigo Vallbona, José, *El secreto profesional de abogados y procuradores en España*, Bosch, Barcelona, 1988

6. Civil Procedure

Gimeno Sendra, Vicente, *Constitución y proceso*, Tecnos D.L., 1988

Lacruz Berdejo, José Luis, Sancho Rebullida, Francisco, Derjedo Echererría Jesús, Rivero Harnandez, Francisco, *Elementos de Derecho Civil, Derecho de obligaciones*, (II, Vol 1), Bosch, Barcelona 1985

Montero Aroca, Juan, Gomez Colomer, Juan Luis, Ortells Ramos, Manuel, Monton Redondo, Alberto, *Derecho jurisdiccional, Proceso civil* (Vol II, tomo I y II), Bosch, Barcelona, 1989

Montero Aroca, Juan, *Introducción al derecho Procesal*, Tecnos, 1976

Muñoz Sabate, Luis, *Estudios de práctica procesal*, Bosch, Barcelona, 1987

Rich Oliva, M., *Esquemas Procesales, Civiles Laborales* (tomo I), Bosch, Barcelona, 1988

7. Criminal Procedure

Gimeno Sendra, Vicente, Moreno Catena, Victor, Almagro Nosete, José, Cortes Dominguez, Valentin, *Derecho procesal, Proceso penal* (tomo II), Tirant lo blanch derecho, 1990

Montero Aroca, Juan, Gomez Colomer, Juan-Luis, Ortells Ramos, Manuel, Monton Redondo, Alberto, *Derecho jurisdiccional, Proceso penal* (Vol III), Bosch, Barcelona, 1989

Moreno Catena, Victor, *El nuevo proceso penal : Estudios sobre la Ley Orgánica 7/1988*, Tirant lo blanch, 1989

8. Remedies

Garcia De Enterria, Eduardo, *Curso de derecho administrativo* (Vol II), Civitas, 1988

Montero Aroca, Juan, Gomez Colomar, Juan-Luis, Ortells Ramos, Manuel, Monton Redondo, Alberto, *Derecho jurisdiccional, Proceso civil* (Vol II, tomo I y II), Bosch, Barcelona, 1989

9. Matrimonial Disputes

Caballero Gea, J.A., *Procesos matrimoniales : causas, hijos vivienda, pensiones*, Dykinson, 1991

Mascarell Navarro, Maria José, *Nulidad, separación y divorcio*, Editorial Montecorvo, Madrid, 1985

Reina, Victor, *Lecciones de derecho matrimonial* (2 vols) Promociones Publicaciones Universitarias, DL, 1983

10. Property Transactions

Alvarez-Caperochipi, *Derecho Inmobiliario registral*, Civitas, 1986

Castan Tobeñas, José, *Derecho civil español, común y foral* (tomo II), García, Cantero, 1988

Diez Picazo, Luis, *Fundamentos del derecho civil patrimonial*, Tecnos, 1978

Lacruz Berdejo, José Luis, *Elementos de derecho civil* (tomo III), Bosch, Barcelona, 1985

Vila Ribas, Carmen, *El pago de lo indebildo y la transmisión de la propiedad por tradición en el sistema del Codigo Civil español*, Bosch, Barcelona, 1989

11. Recognition and Enforcement of Foreign Judgments

Calvo Caravaca, A.L., *La sentencia extranjera en España y la competencia de juez de origen*, Tecnos, 1986

Miaja De La Muela, A., *Derecho internacional privado*, Atlas, 1979

Remiro Brotons, Antonio, *Ejecución de sentencias arbitrales extranjeras*, Editoriales de derecho reunidas, 1980

GLOSSARY OF TERMS

GLOSSARY OF TERMS

KEY

B - Belgium
D - Denmark
E - England
F - France
G - Germany
GR - Greece
I - Irish Republic
IT - Italy
L - Luxembourg
N - The Netherlands
P - Portugal
SC - Scotland
SP - Spain

Abstrakte Normenkontrollklage	*Abstract Constituitional review*	G
Acção Poppular	*Right to represent oneself*	P
Admiralty	*Branch of the court system dealing with maritime affairs*	E
Advocaat/Advocat/ Rechtsanwalt	*Lawyer*	B
Advocaten	*Members of the Dutch Bar*	N
Advocates	*Lawyers*	SC
Advokat	*Danish lawyer*	D
Advokatfirmaer i Danmark	*Directory of Danish Lawyers*	D
Aerios Pagos	*Court of Cassation*	GR
Afdeling Rechtsprak	*Judicial Department*	N
Afdeling voor de geschillen van bestuur	*Department for Administrative Disputes*	N
Aftaleloven	*Code on Agreements*	D
Aktingesetz	*Stock Corporation Act*	G
Alcalde	*Mayor*	SP
Amtsgericht	*First instance court*	G
An debeatur	*Apportionment of responsibility in a damages action*	IT

Anklageschrift	Writ of indictment	G
Apátridas	Stateless persons	P
Appel/Beroep	An appeal	B
Appellante	Appellent	IT
Appellato	Respondent	IT
Applicazione della pena su richiesta delle parti	Sanctioning of a penalty agreed by the parties and upon their request	IT
Appointment of an exaniner	The equivalent of appointment of an official receiver	I
Apportionment Account	Document sent by Vendor's solicitor to Purchaser's Solicitor towards the end of a property transaction	I
Arbeitsgerichtgesetz	Law Concerning Labour Courts	G
Arrondissementsrechtbanken	District Courts	N
Assento	Decisions of the Supreme Court	P
Assignation	Writ of summons	F
Atto qualificato	The first judicial act in criminal proceedings	IT
Attore	Plaintiff	IT
Audi alteram partem	Right to have a reasonable hearing before any, possibly adverse, decision is made	E
Audience civile	"Civil hearing", after the rendering of sentence, where damages are decided	F
Auditor of the Court	Court official who calculates costs	SC
Auflangen unt Weisungen	Conditions and Orders	G
Ausführungsgesetz	Law implementing the Brussels Convention	G
Ausländergesetz	The Foreigners Act	G
Avocat	Advocate	F
Avocat	Lawyer	L
Avoué	Solicitor	F
Avvocati	The intermediate rank of Italian Advocat	IT
Avvocati cassazionisti	The most senior rank of Italian advocat	IT
Ayuntamientos	Municipalities	SP
Bâtonnier	Head of a Bar	F
Bâtonnier	Head of the Conseil de l'Ordre	L
Berufsrichter	Professional Judges	G
Berufung	General appeal	G

Besluit vergooedingen echtsbijstand	Decree on Contributions/payments in respect of legal servicres 1983	N
Beweisaufnahme	The taking of evidence	G
Boletín del Estado	Official Gazette where legal rules are published	SP
BRAGO	Federal Ordinance on Lawyers' Fees	G
Brief	Plaintiff's writ	F
Bundesgerichtshof	Receives appeals on questions of law	G
Bundesverfassungsgericht	Constitutional appeal Court	G
Bundesverwaltungsgericht	Receives appeals on questions of administative law	G
Buon costume	"Moral matters", one ground for holding proceedings in camera	IT
Bürgerliches Gesetzbuch	German Civil Code	G
by consent	Describes situation where defendant has agreed not to oppose a specified damages award	I
Cadastral	Tax due from buyer of immovable property on transfer	F
Caducidade	Concept similar to precription, but time limits vary from case to case	P
Camera Penale	Loose grouping of penal Lawyers	IT
Cancelleria	Chancery	IT
Cancelleria	Judge's clerk	IT
CARPA-Caisse de Règlements Pécuniaires de la Profession Avocat	Advocates Professional Fund	F
Cassatieberoep	Appeal to the Supreme Court	N
Caución de arraigo	Bond paid into court to guarantee payment of any legal fees and court costs	IT
Cautio Iudicatum Solvi	Method of ensuring that costs can be imposed against a plaintiff who is a foreign national, should the defendant Dutch national be successful	N
Caution	Security	SC
Caveat	Document providing that a defender must be notified before an interim interdict against him is heard	SC
Chambre Criminelle	Court dealing with serious criminal offences	L

Chambre d'Accusation	Criminal division of the Court of Appeal	F
Chambres Correctionelles	Specialised Criminal Courts	F
Chancery	Branch of the court system embracing many different areas of law, none of which are covered elsewhere, eg Probate, trusts, etc	E
Circuit Court	One of the Irish Courts of First Instance	I
Citazione	Summons	IT
Clausola Compromissoria	Contractual clause where parties agree that, in the event of litigation,the dipute is to be settled via arbitration	IT
Code Civile	Civil Code	F
Code de Commerce	Commercial Code	F
Code de l'Urbanisme	City Planning Code	F
Code de Procédure Civile	Code of Civil Procedure	F
Code de Procédure Pénal	Code of Penal Procedure	F
Code du Travail	Labour Code	F
Code Général des Impôts	General Tax Code	F
Code Pénale	Penal Code	F
Código Civil	Civil Code	SP
Código Commercio	Commercial Code	SP
Código das Custas Judiciais	Judicial Costs Code	P
Comité du Contentieux du Conseil d'Etat	The Administrative Court	L
Commercialisti	Accountants	IT
Commissaires-priseurs	Government-appointed officials who carry out official auction sales of furniture and personal objects	F
Commission des Opérations de Bourse	Stock Exchange Transactions Commission	F
Commissione Tributaria Centrale	"Top tier" of Italian fiscal jurisdiction	IT
Commissione Tributaria di primo grado	First instance commission with fiscal jurisdiction	IT
Commissione Tributaria di secondo grado	Second instance commission with fiscal jurisdiction	IT
Commmanditaire vennootschappen	Limited partnership firm	N
Comparitie	Hearing attended by both parties in divorce proceedings	N

Comparse conclusionali	Final written briefs	IT
Compromis de vente/ Verkoopcompromis	Written agreement of sale	B
Comuni	Municipalities	IT
Comunidades Autónomas	Autonimous regions	SP
Comunione	Joint ownership of property by spouses	IT
Concejales	Councillors	SP
Condotto antisindacale	Disputes regarding alleged infringement of trade union right by employers	IT
Connexité	Plea that there is a link between two suits	F
Conseil Constitutionnel	Constitutional Council	F
Conseil de L'Ordre du Barreau	French Bar Council	F
Conseil de l'Ordre	Lawyers' Professional body	L
Conseil de la Concurrence	Competition Board	F
Conseil des Prud'Hommes	Conciliation Board	F
Conseil disciplinaire et administratif	Body which judges alleged misbehaviour or misconduct by lawyers	L
Conseil disciplinaire et administratif d'appel	Appeal body for the decisions of the Conseil disciplinaire et administrative	L
Conservatório do Registo Comercial	Central Commercial Registry	P
Consigli dell'Ordine	The Italian equivalent of the Bar Association	IT
Consiglio di stato	State Council, with appellate jurisdiction over regional administrative tribunals	IT
Consiglio Nazionale Forense	National Professional Bar	IT
Consignatiekas	Fund for the receipt of payments into court which are tendered, but not accepted by the plaintiff	N
Contentieux administratifs	Administrative disputes	F
Control de Calificaci	Verification by the judge of whether or not the alleged events took place	SP
Convenuto	Defendant	IT
Corte d'Appello	Appeal Court with power to reverse decisions of all **Tribunales**	IT
Corte d'Assise	First instance court trying serious crimes	IT

Corte di Cassazione	Supreme Court, deciding questions of law and jurisdiction	IT
Costituzione di parte civile	Procedure for filing a civil claim for damages in front of a criminal judge	IT
Costs in any event	Costs assigned to a particular party, regardless of the final outcome	E
Costs in cause	All costs relating to the proceedings, paid by the ultimate loser	E
County Court	Deals with small-scale civil matters, including some family law matters	E
Cour d'Appel	Court of Appeal	F
Cour d'Appel/HofBeroep	Court of Appeal	B
Cour d'Arbitrage/ Arbitragehof	Court of Arbitration	B
Cour d'Assises/Hofvan Assisen	Court of Assizes	B
Cour d'Assises	Court with sole jurisdiction over felonies	F
Cour de Cassation	Supreme Court	F
Cour de Cassation	Luxembourg's Supreme Court	L
Cour du Travail/ Arbeidshof	Labour Court of Appeal	B
Court of Appeal	Second highest appeal court, split into different divisions, each having a different sphere of competence	E
Curator	Receiver in Bankruptcy	N
D'ufficio	On the judge's own initiative	IT
Dagvaarding	Writ of summons	N
De oficio	Application at the government's initiative on the rules regarding conflict of laws	SP
Debate	Preliminary proceedings where an application for **Striking Out** is held	SC
Decadenza	Time Limitation	IT
Decree by Default	Judgment when parties have not complied with orders of the court eg re. time-limits	SC
Decree in Absence	Early judgment	SC
Defender	Defendant	SC
Défendeur	Defendant	F
Défendeur	Defendant	F

Defensor del Pueblo	The Ombudsman	SP
Delibazione	*Exequatur*	IT
Département	Region of France	F
Deputaciones Provinciales	Provincial delegations	SP
Despacho de Espesificação e Questionario	Procedure where judge specifies those facts which he considers proven and those needing more evidence	P
Deurwaarders	Bailiffs	N
Deurwaardersreglement	Code of Civil Procedure and of the Bailiffs' Regulations	N
Di cognizione	Legal proceedings to obtain a declaration as to legal rights	IT
Difensore	The accused	IT
Difensore d'Ufficio	Counsel appointed ex-officio	IT
Difensori	Counsel	IT
Diritto Tributario	Special branch of law, encompassing procedural and substantive administrative law	IT
Disposition of Property	Formal deed which the owner of the land must grant before transfer of same is possible	SC
District Court	Local courts dealing with minor criminal offences	SC
Divorces subis	Divorces Brought by one party against the other	F
Divorces voulus	Divorces by mutual consent	F
Dossier de plaidoire	Document containing the outline of counsel's case which is submitted prior to hearings before certain courts	F
Dublik	Defendant's rejoinder	D
Duurzame ontwrichting	Lasting disruption to marriage	N
Edictal Citation	Way of serving a summons on a Defender	SC
Erstatningsansvarsloven	Act on Damages	D
Estatuto de los Trabajadores	Workers' Statute	IT
Ex tunc	Way in which decisions of the Court of Arbitration work. (Exact meaning unclear)	B
Exhibits	Pieces of evidence	E/I
Extractor	*Court of Session* Official	SC

Faculty of Advocates	Scotland's equivalent of the Bar Association	SC
Faculty Services Ltd.	Company of which all Scottish advocates are shareholders, and which provides them with certain professional services	SC
Familie og Arveret	Family and Inheritance Law	D
Fase decisioria	Second phase of an Italian court-case, where a decision is made	IT
Fase istruttoria	The first phase of an Italian Court-case	IT
Flagrente delicto	Gross delict	IT
Folketing	Danish Parliament	D
Fonds de commerce/Handelszaak	The sale of a business	B
Formation de Référé	Court of Summary Proceedings	F
Forum non conviens	Term meaning that there is a more appropriate court in front of which a case should be heard	SC/E
Funktionelle Zuständigkeit	Functional jurisdiction	G
Garde à vue	Police Custody	F
gemeenscappelijk verzoek	Joint request for divorce by parties in agreement	N
Gemeenten	Municipalities	N
Gemeentewet	Municipality Act	
Generalia specialibus non derogant	Phrase meaning that general provisions cannot be interpreted as displacing particular statutory enactments	E
Genus nunquam perit	Order to a debtor who owes generic goods to purchase on the market goods identical to those which he promised to supply	IT
Gerechtshoven	Courts of Appeal	N
Geritsverfassungesetz	Law on the Constitution of the Courts	G
Gesamstrafe	The total sentence	G
Gesetz über das Bundesverfassungsgericht	Act on the Federal Constitutional Court	G
Giudice	Judge	IT
Giudice Conciliatore	Civil, small claims judge	IT
Giudice Conciliatore	Judge concerned with conciliation	IT
Giudice istruttore	The investigating judge	IT

Giudice par lindagine preliminare	*Judge for the preliminary hearing*	IT
Giudice tutelare	*Custody judge in matrimonial cases*	IT
Giudici ordinari	*Single judge or court, enforcing Civil Law*	IT
Giudici popolari	*Jurors in the* **Corte d'Assise**	IT
Giudizio Abbreviato	*Shortened judgment*	IT
Giudizio di rinvio	*The principle with which a new decision must conform*	IT
Giudizio direttissimo	*Direct judgment*	IT
Giudizio immediato	*Immediate Judgment*	IT
GmbH-Gesetz	*Limited Liability Corporation Act*	G
Grammatische Auslegung	*Grammatical approach to the interpretation of legislation*	G
Gratuito Patrocinio	*Legal Aid*	IT
Griffierecht	*Court fees*	N
Grundgeset	*The German Constitution*	G
Grundloven	*Danish Constitution*	D
Hauptverfahren	*Main proceeding*	G
Hausratsverordnung	*Regulation on Household Goods*	G
High Court of Justiciary	*Court both of first instance and appeal, with pan-Scottish jurisdiction*	SC
Historische Auslegung	*Historical approach to the interpretation of legislation*	G
Hof van Cassatie/Cour de Cassation	*Supreme Court/Court of Cassation*	B
House of Lords	*Highest Court of Appeal*	SC/E
Huissier	*Judicial officer*	SC
Huissier	*Process server*	F
Højeste Ret	*Supreme Court*	D
Imformazione di Garanzia	*Return receipt sent to the subject of an investigation*	IT
Impulso di parte	*The initiative of the parties*	IT
Incidente Probatorio	*Special Inquiry*	IT
Initial Writ	*Document commencing civil,* **Sheriff Court** *proceedings*	SC
Inner House	*Branch of the* **Court of Session,** *acting as a Court of Appeal*	SC

Institutio de Comércio Externo	Portuguese Institute for Foreign Trade	P
Internationale Zuständigkeit	International jurisdiction	G
Intimation of intention to appeal	Self-explanatory document which must be lodged in order for the appeal process to begin	SC
INVIM	A Capital Gains Tax levyed on the increase in value of the real property transferred	IT
Iterim Interdict	Way of obtaining interlocutory relief	SC
Joinder	Where two cases are merged because they involve identical questions of fact and/or law	E
Juge d'Instruction	Examining Magistrate	F
Juge d'Instruction	Examining Magistrate	F
Juge de l'Expropriation	Judge responsible for deciding the level of indemnity due to an owner deprived of his property	F
Juge de la Mise en état	Judge overseeing cases concerning joinder of issue	F
Juge des Tutelles	Guardianship judge	F
Juge-Rapporteur	Reporting judge	FF
Jugement Réputé Contradictoire	Judgment deemed to have been handed down after hearing both sides	F
Juges aux Affaires Matrimoniales	Judges in the Family Division	F
Jungenderichtsgesetz	Juvenile Courts	G
Jurisprudencia	Previous court decisions	SP
Justice de Paix/Vredergerecht	Justice of the Peace Courts	B
Justice of the Peace	See Magistrate	SC/E
Juvenile Liaison Scheme	An alternative to the prosecution of minors	I
Kammern	Judicial Chamber	G
Kantongerechten	Cantonal Courts	N
Kinderrechter	Judge dealing with matters of custody of children	
Kleine Strafkammer	Small Criminal Chamber	G
Konkersloven	Bankruptcy Code	D
Konkrete Normenkontrollklage	Specific Constitutional Court review of legislation	G
Kort Geding	President of the District Court	N

Kredsbestyrelsen	Danish Bar Association	D
Kroon	Crown	N
Købeloven	Purchase and Sales Code	D
Land Registers	Where **Dispositions of Property** are recorded, thus completing the transfer of ownership	SC
Länder	German regions	G
Landergericht	First instance court	G
Le circuit court	Procedure for deciding uncomplicated cases	F
Leapfrogging Appeal	Occurs when the High Court has certified that there is a point of law to be decided, and the appeal thus goes straight to the **House of Lords**	
Ley de Enjuiciamiento Civil	Civil Procedure Act	SP
Ley de Sociedades Anónimas	Companies Act	SP
Ley enjuiciamento criminal	Criminal Procedure Act	SP
Ley general de Publicidad	Advertising Act	SP
Ley Hipotecaria	Mortgage Law	SP
Leyes	Statutes	SP
Lis alibi pendis	Term meaning that the same dispute is already before another Scottish court	SC
Litigants in person	Persons presenting their own case in court	E
Litis consortio necessario	Pre-emtory term, during which a third party who would be affected by any decision must be summoned	IT
Litis pendenza	Duplication of proceedings	IT
Litispendence	State when case is already proceeding before another court	IT
Lord Advocate	Highest Member of the judiciary in Scotland	SC
Maatschap	Ordinary partnership	N
Magistrate	Lay judge trying minor cases without a jury	SC/E
Master	Judge in **Chancery**	E
Meenger-at-arms	Judicial Officer	SC
Memorie	Written briefs	IT
Ministère Public	**Director of Public Prosecutions**	F
Ministério Público	Public Prosecutor	P

Misdrijven	*Felonies*	N
Mise en état	*Joinder of issue*	F
Missives of Sale	Written offer to buy property, and/or written agreement to sell same.	SC
Misure di sicurezza	Security measures	IT
Moniteur belge	Official Gazette where legislation is published	B
Motion for Directions	Procedure which must be brought in certain actions (eg probate) in order that directions for further conduct of the proceedings can be given.	I
Nebenklage	Public proceedings	G
Nederlandse Orde van Advocaten	Dutch Bar Association	N
Nemo iudex in causam suam	Phrase meaning no man may be a judge in his own cause	E
Next Friend	Guardian	E
No extra petita	Phrase meaning that the judge must base his decision only on the evidence submitted and the requests made by the parties	IT
Notai	Professional group of public officers with exclusive power to authenticate contracts, etc	IT
Notaire	Legal Civil Servant	F
Notaires	Legal functionaries employed by the state	P
Note of Appeal	States grounds for appeal	SC
Notice of Intention to Defend	Self-explanatory Intimation which the **Defender** must make	SC
Notice of Motion	Document, the service of which signifies that proceedings have commenced	I
Notice Party	Party which must be notified of proceedings	I
Oberandergericht	Ordinary Appeal Court	G
Oberverwaltungsgericht	Administrative appeal court	G
Obiter dicta	Statements in a judgment which fall outside the **ratio decidendi**	E
Oet tarieven in burgerlijke zaken	Act on Fees in Civil Matters	N
Oficina de Interpretación de Lenguas	Office for Linguistic Interpretation	SP

Oireactas	Irish Parliament	I
Ondernemingskamer	Enterprise Chamber of Court of Appeal	N
Onere della prova	Duty to Produce evidence	IT
Onroerende zaken	New Civil Code	N
Onroerendgoed	Property	N
Onus Probandi	Burden of proof	IT
Openbaar Ministerie	Public Prosecution Office	N
Opposition/Verxet	Opposition	B
Ordem dos Avogados Portugueses	Portuguese Bar Association	P
Ordinances	Enactments by the B russels-Capital region of Belgium	B
örtliche Zuständigkeit	Local Jurisdiction	G
Outer house	Branch of the Court of Session, dealing with first instance cases	SC
Over tredingen	criminal trespasses	N
Overtradingen	Trespasses	N
Palmario	Lawyer's supplementary fee	IT
Par défaut	By default	F
Parliament House Book	Document containing the rules of procedure for the Court of Session and the Sheriff Court	SC
Parquet	Public assessor	F
Pars judicis	To take judicial notice of the existence of a third party with a direct interest in Proceedings	SC
Partie civile	Plaintiff	F
Payment in	Situation where money is paid to the court in settlement of a Party's claim	E
Penal Clause	Part of the Italian Civil Code which has the effect of limiting the responsibility for damages	IT
Per Incuriam	Describes a decision made by a court when it was in ignorance of a previous desicion made by itself or a higher court	E
Permesso di soggiono	Residence Permit	IT
Petition	Signing this is one way of initiating proceedings at the Court of Session	

Plainte avec constitution de partie civile	Complaint with claim for damages	F
Pleading diet	Commences official criminal proceedings	SC
Pourvoi en Cassation	Appeal to the Court of Cassation	F
Pourvoi en Cassation/ Voorziening in Cassatie	Petition for Cassation	B
Pouvoi en Cassation	Lodging of an Appeal	FD
Preliminary diet	Pre-trial hearing at which the aaccused may object to the competency, relevancy, or legal sufficiency of the charge	SC
Preliminary Examination	Court session where accused is furnished with the exhibits etc to be used against him	I
Prescrizione	Prescription	IT
President/Voorzitter	President	B
Pretore	Single judge with general first instance competence on matters up to 5,000,000 lire	IT
Procedimento per decreto	Procedure by decree	IT
Procédure d'incident de faux	Plea that forgery has taken place	F
Procedure Roll	Standard Procedure	SC
Procurator Fiscal	Scottish Director of Public Prosecutions	SC
Procuratori	The most junior rank of Italian advocate	IT
Procureur	Public Prosecutor	L
Procureur	Special functionary in Civil Matters	N
Proofs	A type of Scottish court case	SC
Proportionality Rule	No authority may take such radical steps to implement its policies that another authority is seriously obstucted in the prosecution of its own policy	B
Providor da Justiça	Ombudsman	P
Province	Provinces	IT
Provincias	Provinces	SP
Provincies	Provinces	N
Provinciewet	Province Act	N
Pubblico Ministero	Public Prosecutor	IT
Pursuer	Plaintiff	SC

Quantum debeatur	The actual amount of damages	IT
Queen's Bench Division	Branch of the Court system dealing with general civil matters	E
Raad van State	Council of State	N
Raad van State/ Conseil d'Etat	Council of State	B
Raad voor de Kinderbescherming	Council for the Protection of Children	N
Ratio decidendi	The underlying legal principle behind a judgment	E
Ratione loci	Phrase meaning competence in terms of locality	B/F
Ratione materiae	Phrase meaning that a court has not got competence to rule in a particular sphere	F
Receiver	Holder of a charge or debenture created by a company	SC/E
Rechtbanken	District Courts	N
Rechter-Commissaris	Judge-Commissary	N
Rechtsanwälte	A German lawyer	G
Rechtsanwältskammer	Local law society	G
Rechtspraak van der Week	Weekly Law Reports	N
Recurso de Amparo	Procedure protecting individuals against violations of their rights	SP
Recurso de Inconstitucioalidad	Unconstitutionality Appeal	SP
Regioni	Regions	IT
Registre de la Commune	Local Authority	B
Registres du Bureau de Conservation des Hypothèques/Register van het kantoor van bewaring der hypotheken	The Mortgage Registry	B
Reglamento del Registro Mercantil	Commercial Registry Regulations	IT
Reglomento di competenza	Question submitted to the **Corte di Cassazione** regarding competence	IT
Reglomento di giurisdizione	Question submitted to the **Corte di Cassazione** regarding jurisdiction	IT
Relator action	When an individual sues in the name of the **Attorney-General** over a matter of public law	E
Relevé cadastral/ Kadastraal uittreksel	Land survey report	B
Repliche	Final counter-brief	IT
Replik	Plaintiff's reply	D

Requete civile/Rekwest Civiel	Request for a decision to be withdrawn	B
Respondent	Title of party being brought to court in certain civil actions	SC/E
Responsabilità excontrattuales	Tort	IT
Resposibilità contrattuale	Obligation	IT
Retsplejeloven	Codes of Procedure	D
Revision	Appeal on questions of law.	G
Richtiger Rechtswig	General term for a branch of jurisdiction	G
Ricoro	Petition to a judge	IT
Riti Differenziai	Special Proceedings	IT
Rito Camerale	Divorce by mutual consent	IT
Rules of the Supreme Court	Official body of rules governing court procedure	E
Sachliche Zuständigkeit	Jurisdiction by subject matter	G
Schöffenwahlausschuß	Lay judge election committee	G
Schwurgericht	Great Criminal Chamber	G
Separazione consensual	Separation by mutual consent	IT
Sheriff	Judge	SC
Sheriff Court	Civil court with wide jurisdiction, organised on a territorial basis. Can be a Court of Appeal.	SC
Sheriffdom	Geographical unit, determining jurisdiction, and based on local government areas	SC
Shöffen	Lay judges	G
Signification/Betekening	Notification by writ	B
Sist	Stay	SC
Skatteloven	Tax Laws	D
Skøde	Deed of conveyance	D
Slutseddel	Bill of sale	D
Sociétés d'Exercise Libéral	Joint ventures, and/or real commercial companies with a purely civil purpose	F
Sospensione	Stay	IT
Specification	List of documents, the discovery of which is sought	SC
Staatsanwaltschaft	Public Prosecutor's Office	G

Stare decisis	Doctrine that courts are bound to follow decisions in earlier cases	E
Statement of claim	Document sent to the defendant giving details of the **Plaintiff's** claim	E
Stating of Cases	Procedure where the opinion of the **High Court** is sought	SC/E
Statsdidende	Danish Legal Gazette	D
Stay	Suspension of proceedings	E
Strafbefehl	Punishment Order	G
Strafbefehlsantrag	Court for the levying of fines	G
Straffeloveen	Penal Code	D
Strafgesetzbuch	Criminal Code	G
Strafprozeeßordnung	Code of Criminal Procedure	G
Strafsenate	Criminal panels	G
Straftatbestände	Individual offences	G
Striking Out	Procedure where a claim can be dismissed before the full trial stage, if it is irrelevant or incompetent	SC
Striking out for Want of Prosecution	Dismissal of a **plaintiff's** claim at a pre-hearing stage, on the grounds that the plaintiff has failed to comply with time-terms.	E
Stævning	Complaint within a writ of summons	D
Subpoeana ad testificandum	Document commanding witness to testify	I
Subpoena	Official document compelling attendance as a witnes s	E
Subpoena duces tecum	Document commanding witness both to testify, and to bring with him certain specified documents.	I
Sumário	Criminal proceedings for crimes punishable with less than three years' imprisonment	P
Summary Summons	Document commencing certain actions (eg debt and land recoveries	I
Summons	Document commencing civil proceedings in the **Court of Session**	SC
Summons	Writ	SC
Supremo Tribunal De Justiça	Supreme Court of Justice	P
Svarskrift	Defendant's witten answer to the plaintiff's writ of summons	D

Systematische Auslegung	Systematic approach to the interpretation of legislation.	G
Sø-og Handelsretten	The Sea and Commmercial Court.	D
Tantum devolutum quantum Appellatum	Points upon which fresh examination of a case is requested	IT
Taoiseach	Cabinet	I
Tariffa Forense	Tariff from which fees are established	IT
Taxed off	Describes sums which are reduced or disallowed when costs are calculated	SC
Technicien	Technical expert appointed by the court as an assessor	
Tender	Judicially-recognised offer to pay part of the sum demanded	SC
The Defences	*Defender's Submissions*	SC
The High Court	Deals with large civil suits	E
The Supreme Court	Highest Irish Court	I
The White Book	Publication containing the main procedural *Rules of the Supreme Court*(see also **The Supreme Court Practice**)	E
Tierce opposition/Derdenverzet	Third party opposition	B
Tijdelijke wet Kroongeschillen	Provisional Act Regarding Administrative Disputes	N
Traducción jurada	Sworn translation of a relevant section of foreign law	SP
Transcription/ Overschrijving	Record of Mortgage Registration	B
Trial Diet	Commmences Summary criminal proceedings	SC
Tribunais Correccionais	Correctional Tribnal	P
Tribunais de Pequeña Causes	Small Claims Court	P
Tribunais de Polícia	Police Tribunal	P
Tribunal Constitutional	The Constitutional Court	SP
Tribunal correctionnel	Court for minor criminal offences	L
Tribunal d'Arrondissement/ Arrondissement-rechtbank	District Court	B
Tribunal de Commerce/Rechtbank van Koophandel	Commercial Court	B
Tribunal de Familía	Family Court	P
Tribunal de Grande Instance	Court of General Jurisdiction	

Tribunal de Menores	Minor Court	P
Tribunal de Police	Police Court	F
Tribunal de Police/Politier-echtbank	Police Courts	B
Tribunal de Relação	Court of Appeal	P
Tribunal de Trabalo	Employment Tribunal	P
Tribunal de Travail/ Arbeidsrechtbank	Labour Court	B
Tribunal des Conflits	Court which rules in disputes regarding the jurisdiction administrative courts	F
Tribunal Marítimo	Maritime Court	P
Tribunal Paritaire des Baux Ruraux	Joint Board of Rural Leases	F
Tribunale	Court of three judges, with general first instance copetence and matters involving more than 5,000,000 lire, and appellate competence regarding praetorian decisions	IT
Tribunale Amministrativo Regionale (TAR)	Court of Administrative first instance	IT
Tribunale per i Minorenni	Juvenile Court	IT
Tribuneís Cíveis	Civil Tribunal	P
Tussenkomst	Argument of a third party which differs from either side's case	N
Udienza Preliminare	Preliminary hearing	IT
Udinza collegiale	The full panel of the court	IT
Ufficiale Giudiziario	Bailiff	IT
Uitvoerbaar bij voorraad	Judgment executable when specified future circumstances arise	N
Underret	Trial Court	D
Vennootschappen onder firma	Open partnership firms	N
Verfassungsbeschwerde	Constitutional Appeal	G
Verwaltungsgericht	Administrative court of first instance	G
Verwaltungsgerichtsordnung	Administrative Procedure Act	G
Voeging	Argument by a third party in support of a main party's case	N
Voorlopige voorzieningen	Provisional measures in divorce proceedings	N
Vorverfahren	Preliminary proceedings	G

Vrijwaring	Joinder	N
Wet rechtsbijstand aan onen Minvermogenden	1957 Act on Legal Aid	N
Writ	Document which commences a civil action	E
Østre Landsret	Court of Appeal	D
Østre og Vestre Landset	Courts of Appeal	D
Zwischenverfahren	Interim Proceedings	G